Cuba Libre

A 500-Year Quest for Independence

Philip Brenner and Peter Eisner

ROWMAN & LITTLEFIELD
Lanham • Boulder • New York • London

Published by Rowman & Littlefield
A wholly owned subsidiary of The Rowman & Littlefield Publishing Group, Inc.
4501 Forbes Boulevard, Suite 200, Lanham, Maryland 20706
www.rowman.com

Unit A, Whitacre Mews, 26-34 Stannary Street, London SE11 4AB, United Kingdom

British Library Cataloguing in Publication Information Available

Library of Congress Cataloging-in-Publication Data
Names: Brenner, Philip, author. | Eisner, Peter, author.
Title: Cuba libre : a 500-year quest for independence / Philip Brenner and Peter Eisner.
Other titles: Cuba libre, a 500-year quest for independence
Description: Lanham, MD : Rowman & Littlefield, [2018] | Includes bibliographical
  references and index.
Identifiers: LCCN 2017023124 (print) | LCCN 2017034717 (ebook) | ISBN
  9780742566712 (electronic) | ISBN 9780742566699 (hardback : alk. paper) | ISBN
  9780742566705 (pbk. : alk. paper)
Subjects: LCSH: Cuba—History—1895– | National liberation movements—Cuba—
  History. | Cuba—History—Autonomy and independence movements.
Classification: LCC F1776 (ebook) | LCC F1776 .B73 2018 (print) | DDC 972.91/05—
  dc23
LC record available at https://lccn.loc.gov/2017023124

Printed in the United States of America

Contents

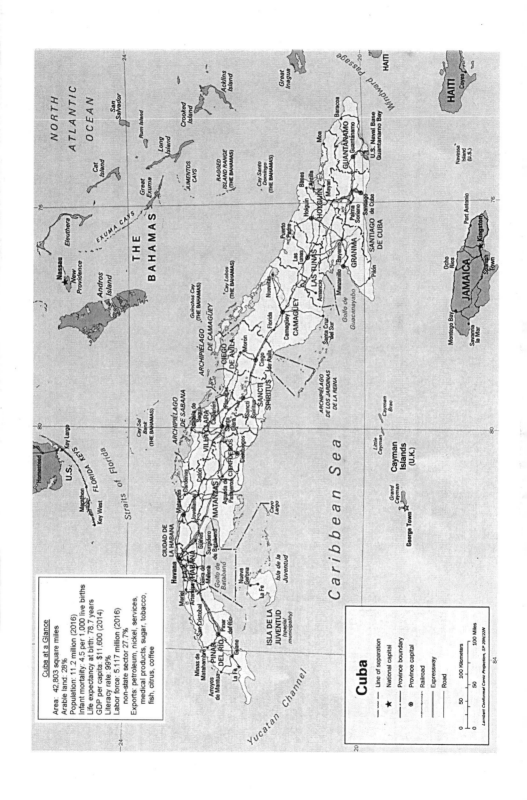

Cuba at a Glance

Area: 42,803 square miles
Arable land: 28%
Population: 11.2 million (2016)
Infant mortality: 4.5 per 1,000 live births
Life expectancy at birth: 78.7 years
GDP per capita: $11,600 (2014)
Literacy rate: 99%
Labor force: 5.117 million (2016)
non-state sector 27.7%
Exports: petroleum, nickel, services, medical products, sugar, tobacco, fish, citrus, coffee

Cuba

-·-·- Line of separation
★ National capital
◉ Province capital
├┼┤ Railroad
═══ Expressway
─── Road

0   50   100 Kilometers
0   50   100 Miles
Lambert Conformal Conic Projection, SP 20N/22N

64

Preface

The *tocororo*, or trogon in English, is Cuba's national bird. Cubans commonly account for the country's selection of this beautiful tropical species by noting that its red, white, and blue feathers are the same colors as Cuba's flag (see photo on back cover). A second explanation is that a tocororo cannot survive in captivity and will die if caged. Thus, the tocororo reflects Cuba's national character, *Cuba libre*, a people who demand to be free.

While their pursuit of freedom has been evident for five hundred years, Cubans began to articulate the goal in terms of nationhood during the nineteenth century. Independence leaders believed that with national sovereignty, Cubans "collectively could do something about the forces that governed their lives," in the words of historian Louis A. Pérez Jr., whose research and sensibilities have informed much of this book. "Nation promised agency and autonomy—for Cubans to be responsible only to themselves."[1]

The vision of a sovereign and independent nationhood animated the revolutionaries who overthrew the dictatorship of Fulgencio Batista on January 1, 1959, and it has been their source of inspiration since then. To be sure, Cuba's decisions in the last sixty years—the period on which this book focuses the most attention—were not always consistent with the vision. Its defense from US attacks and sanctions, and its relationship with the Soviet Union from 1960 to 1991, reduced options available to Cuba's leaders. When the Soviet relationship ended, compromises dictated by the need to find new markets and sources of income seemed to move the country further off a course aimed at the vision. Yet the leaders' determination to maintain as much independence for Cuba as possible often led them to make choices that seemed to defy conventional economic wisdom. Today, too, as the country lurches through a process of "updating" its political and economic organization, independence and sovereignty remain core goals that Cuba's leaders are most concerned about relinquishing.

Importantly, Cuba's leaders are not the only ones to hold this aspiration. When a gravely ill Fidel Castro handed his conductor's baton to Raúl Castro in 2006, there was none of the turmoil or chaos that many US policymakers and Cuban exiles had anticipated. The revolutionary regime did not collapse. While Fidel was the indispensable person without whom the Cuban Revolution would have taken a different course, it also had an organic quality based on an implicit social contract between leaders and followers. The broad mass of Cubans had acquired a personal dignity that they associated with the Revolution's pursuit of national independence.

In emphasizing the importance that Cubans attach to freedom and sovereignty, we do not ignore other explanations for Cuban behavior. These include the roles played by: personality and charisma; institutions and organizational dynamics that can corrupt how well an institution fulfills its intended function; ideology and ideological rigidity; legacies of racism, sexism, and colonialism; and external adversaries, pressures, and alliances. Yet the framework of *Cuba Libre* offers a compelling way to understand Cuba and is one that tends to be denigrated and dismissed in the United States. Cuba libre is so deeply ingrained in Cuba that we needed to begin our chronological narrative with its origins, when Europeans first encountered Cuba a little more than five hundred years ago.

* * *

We have written this book to serve the interests and needs of several audiences. Since December 2014, an increasing number of travelers from the United States—some who devise their own itinerary, some who rely on licensed organizations, and some who are students at US universities—have been going to Cuba on educational trips. This history provides them with the background to appreciate what they have experienced or will encounter. We expect the book will be useful also for a general audience curious about Cuba and for those in courses studying Latin America, third world politics, or Cuba itself. Finally, we hope this book will be instructive for a less obvious group—those with an interest in US foreign policy.

While *Cuba Libre* is not about Cuban-US relations, the connections between Cuba and the United States are so varied and strong that we examine the history of the relationship extensively in several chapters. In doing so, we approach the subject empathetically by placing the reader in each country's shoes, examining how each understood a particular context and sought to navigate a course through the context it perceived in order to achieve its goals. In this regard, note that we refer generally to Cuban leaders Fidel Castro and Raúl Castro by their first names, unlike our references to US presidents or other Cuban officials. This decision is due neither to familiarity nor bias; we name the leaders the way Cubans do.

*   *   *

When our patient, wise, and creative editor at Rowman & Littlefield, Susan McEachern, approached us to write this book many years ago, we imagined the task would be relatively easy and benefit from our complementary strengths. Philip Brenner took the first of his many trips to Cuba in 1974, had studied the country's history, and wrote about and taught courses on Cuban foreign policy and Cuban-US relations. Peter Eisner had reported stories from Cuba on three different occasions, and had lived in Latin America and written about the region as a journalist and editor for the Associated Press, *Newsday*, and the *Washington Post*. But as we probed the subject, we realized how much more we needed to learn. In the process of acquiring this knowledge, we have built up debts to many more people than we name here, but we do want to acknowledge some in particular.

We appreciate the research assistance given to us by Sarah Barnett, Alex D'Agostino, Kathleen Fairchild, Kia Hall, Uri Lerner, Emanuel Saavedra, Colleen Scribner, Althea Skinner, Paul Sparks, and Simone Williams. Our special thanks is reserved for Teresa Garcia Castro, whose knowledge and understanding of Cuban culture and history, and scrupulous dedication to accuracy, strengthened the book in countless ways.

Over the years, many people in Cuba have tried to help us understand the country. We especially appreciate the time and efforts of Ricardo Alarcon, Carlos Alzugaray, José Antonio Arbesú, Miguel Barnet, Hope Bastian, Jorge Bolaños, José Ramón Cabañas, Soraya Castro, Carlos Ciaño, Tomas Díez, Pablo Armando Fernández, Alfonso Fraga, Marc Frank, Fernando Garcia, Jorge Hernández, Rafael Hernández, Warnel Lores, Orlando Marquez, Milagros Martínez, Pedro Monreal, Martha Morales, Marta Nuñez, Jorge Mario Sánchez, Ramón Sánchez-Parodi, Ricardo Torres, Josefina Vidal, and Oscar Zanetti.

Philip Brenner benefited from research support by American University's Center for Latin American and Latino Studies at American University.

In addition to the essential efforts of Susan McEachern, we appreciate the professionalism and efficiency of the production team at Rowman & Littlefield, Rebeccah Shumaker and Janice Braunstein.

We will donate our royalties from this book to a scholarship fund for interns at the Institute for Policy Studies named in honor of Saul Landau, who died in 2013. Saul was a dear friend and colleague who encouraged us to know Cuba from the perspective of Cubans, to write about Cuba honestly, and to work tirelessly as he did to improve US-Cuba relations for the benefit of people in both countries. We hope this book lives up to his demands and carries on his mission.

Our spouses, Betsy Vieth and Musha Salinas, have endured cheerfully more absence and aggravation from us than either of our marriage contracts required, and we have been blessed to have their support.

NOTE

1. Louis A. Pérez, Jr., *The Structure of Cuban History: Meanings and Purpose of the Past* (Chapel Hill: University of North Carolina Press, 2013), 4.

Part I

1492–1958

Chapter 1

Columbus Arrives and Spain Colonizes Cuba, 1492–1550

Those that arriv'd at these Islands from the remotest parts of Spain, and who pride themselves in the Name of Christians, steer'd Two courses principally, in order to the Extirpation, and Exterminating of this People from the face of the Earth. The first whereof was raising an unjust, sanguinolent, cruel War. The other, by putting them to death, who hitherto, thirsted after their Liberty, or design'd (which the most Potent, Strenuous and Magnanimous Spirits intended) to recover their pristin Freedom, and shake off the Shackles of so injurious a Captivity: For they being taken off in War, none but Women and Children were permitted to enjoy the benefit of that Country-Air, in whom they did in succeeding times lay such a heavy Yoak, that the very Brutes were more happy than they: To which Two Species of Tyranny as subalternate things to the Genus, the other innumerable Courses they took to extirpate and make this a desolate People, may be reduced and referr'd.

—Bartolomé de las Casas[1]

COLUMBUS ENCOUNTERS CUBA

"I never saw a lovelier sight. . . . It is the most beautiful island ever seen," Captain Christopher Columbus wrote in his journal when he encountered Cuba.[2] The explorer believed it was Japan, the headlands to Cathay, or perhaps an island that led to the westward passage. The details of Columbus's first voyage to the Americas come from the writings of Bartolomé de las Casas, a Dominican priest whose father sailed on Columbus's second voyage to the Americas in 1493. Las Casas himself traveled to the West Indies with his father in 1502. Still a young man, he recounted the story of Columbus's

2

explorations—including portions and a summary of Columbus's lost journal of the 1492 voyage.

While lying offshore in a rainstorm, before dawn on October 28, 1492, Columbus was welcomed by the indigenous inhabitants, men and women naked and bronzed by the sun. These were the Taino Indians; they had watched and waited as the Spanish ships cautiously approached. The Tainos warmly welcomed these beings on their godlike vessels that floated on the waters.

Columbus and his men found that the native people were "innocently simple," as las Casas wrote, "altogether void of and averse to all manner of Craft, Subtlety and Malice, and most Obedient and Loyal Subjects to their Native Sovereigns; and behave themselves very patiently, submissively and quietly towards the Spaniards, to whom they are subservient and subject."[3]

His three ships had arrived in the Americas on October 12, 1492, touching land in the Bahamas archipelago, most likely on what is now Watling Island. He referred to the people he encountered—the Taino and other indigenous groups—as Indians, assuming he had reached India; and these people told him that further on there was another land they called *Colba*. An alteration of that indigenous name from the Taino language gave Cuba its modern name. Beautiful though it was, the island was protected by shallows and treacherous shoals. Columbus reached Cuba two weeks later, disembarking along the northeastern coast, probably at or near today's port town of Gibara.

The expedition to the "New World" was embroiled in European politics, the drive toward opening trade routes to Asia, and specifically the allure of discovering new sources of wealth. Columbus had set sail from Spain on August 3, 1492, with three ships, the *Niña*, *Pinta*, and *Santa Maria*. His voyage

Map 1.1.   Map of America by Diego Ribero, 1529. Geography and Map Division, Kohl Collection no. 41 (4), Library of Congress, Washington, DC.

represented the culmination of seven years of maneuvering and lobbying with the Spanish court and the kings of Portugal and England. Its official purpose, to establish a western passage to China and India and to find gold and other riches, served Columbus's personal goal of acquiring political power; he later demanded the title of Great Admiral of the Ocean Sea. Ferdinand and Isabella financed the fitting of the three ships and agreed to give the Italian explorer a portion of the wealth he would gather on the journey.

Despite Columbus's shortcomings as a navigator—faulty calculations fed his hope and mistaken notion that a voyage of a month would land him in Asia—the enterprise was equivalent to the most death-defying feat imaginable, as if modern-day astronauts were set free from the tethers of the known world. The prevailing view had been that anyone sailing west would die of thirst and starvation before reaching land. In fact, no ship of his day could have stocked enough food and fresh water for the trip he had envisioned.

According to las Casas's account, Columbus explored Cuba for about five weeks. Finding neither riches nor signs of the Chinese empire, at the beginning of December he set sail eastward toward Hispaniola in search of gold, carrying six Cuban Indians as slaves. He and his crew did in fact discover quantities of gold on Hispaniola's northern coast. As a result, he left behind a troop of thirty-nine men on Hispaniola to search for more; loaded the *Niña* and *Pinta* with gold, spices, and provisions; and embarked on the return voyage to Europe. The *Santa Maria* was abandoned after being disabled off the coast of what is now northwestern Haiti.

Columbus's return to Europe with his spoils and exotic tales provoked competition among the Spanish and Portuguese monarchs for mounting a larger expedition, and Columbus easily was able to outfit sixteen ships.[4] He set out on his second voyage on September 25, 1493, with 1,500 men, many of whom intended to be colonists and a large cadre of whom would serve as soldiers to subdue any indigenes who might stand in their way. They brought munitions, artillery, horses, seeds, and agricultural tools, along with merchandise for trading with the native peoples.[5] When he reached the settlement that he had established on Hispaniola, any hope of peaceful coexistence was discarded. Columbus found that all the members of his first crew had been massacred by the Indians, who had recognized quickly the greedy intent and aggressiveness of the Europeans.

In April 1494, six months after his second arrival in the New World, Columbus sailed back across the Windward Passage to Cuba. This time he explored Cuba's southern coast, moving westward from Guantánamo Bay. He continued to believe that Cuba was a peninsula, part of the Chinese mainland, reasoning that no one previously had encountered an island so large.[6]

Still, without seeing China, he went back to Hispaniola in the late summer. There he launched a series of punishing attacks on the Indians. When he subsequently disembarked in Spain at the end of his second expedition, Columbus displayed five hundred Indians whom he hoped to sell as slaves. He was greeted as a conquering hero, garnered widespread praise for his daring adventures, and finally achieved his personal ambition as the Spanish crown granted Columbus the right to rule over Cuba.

THE INDIGENOUS PEOPLE OF CUBA

The indigenous groups Columbus encountered in Cuba were of the Taino, Ciboney, and Guanahatabey tribes. Some had arrived on the island from Mexico's Yucatan Peninsula and South Florida, and some from what is today Venezuela, between 1000 BCE and 1000 CE. As with the broad range of dates, there are some questions about their exact origins. Recent evidence suggests that historians mistakenly had described two of the groups as one: the Ciboney had been assumed to be related to the Guanahatabey tribe. However, it is now believed that they had separate identities and the Guanahatabey, whose language was never recorded, probably had distinct roots.[7] One piece of evidence for this was that Columbus's interpreter, a Taino from Hispaniola who learned Spanish after the 1492 expedition, could communicate with the Ciboney tribes but was unable to communicate with the Guanahatabey people he met during Columbus's 1494 trip. The Tainos and Ciboney are usually described as Arawak Indians, and the Guanahatabey people as pre-Arawak, having arrived hundreds of years earlier.[8]

The Guanahatabey tended to live along the northern coast and on small keys offshore.[9] They were less populous than the Ciboney, who lived mainly in coastal sections of western Cuba, subsisting on seafood. Their name translates in the Arawak language from the words for "cave" (*siba*) and "man" (*eyeri*).[10] The Ciboney lived in established, stable communities and family groupings, and devised more sophisticated tools than those made by the Guanahatabey, enabling them, among other things, to construct wooden canoes.

The Tainos, originally from northern South America near Venezuela and Guyana, reached the northwestern Caribbean islands about 1,000 years before Columbus's visit; they usurped land held by the other two tribes and pushed them further into western Cuba. The origins of the Taino have been subject to debate. They are usually described as being a branch of the Arawak Nation or having descended from the Arawaks, perhaps the most widespread clan of American aborigines.[11] Scholars now say that they were as distinct as their different languages and cultures, and that the Arawak and Taino emerged from a common ancestor, then developed independently.[12]

While the indigenous groups that Columbus and his men met on Hispaniola were not all Taino, the Europeans used that name for all the people they encountered on Hispaniola, Puerto Rico, Cuba, and Jamaica. The Taino, properly identified, were from the northern Caribbean, and their name means "good" or "noble,"[13] distinguishing themselves from a small clan of aggressive Island-Caribs, who lived on the southern islands.

Taino culture was highly organized and hierarchical, with structured living and farming practices and a class division between nobles and commoners.[14] Villages were characteristically built around a large square that served as a market where residents gathered for social events and recreation. In these common areas, they often used a ball and fashioned a rectangular court to play a game called *batey*.

The local *cacique* or chief had the best house and lived in a prime location fronting the village square; in turn, a cacique had assistants, *behiques*, who also functioned as priests or doctors. The rank of chief was inherited, and both men and women could rise to the post. Even though women generally had lesser standing than men, they did frequently serve as doctors and healers skilled in the use of medicinal herbs.

Class distinction extended beyond the tribe; the Taino looked down on members of the Ciboney tribes as being lower class, and sometimes used them as servants.[15] Taino agricultural practices were technologically more advanced than those of other islanders, and included novel irrigation techniques, as well as mulching and enriching the soil to improve crop cultivation. Cassava root was a staple, and Taino farmers also grew sweet potato, squash, beans, peppers, and peanuts, as well as fruits, tobacco, and cotton. The cotton, in turn, was used to fashion fishing nets, as well as woven to make rope hammocks.

Many words in contemporary Spanish and even English come from the Taino, such as: *aguacate* (avocado), *ají* (garlic), *guayaba* (guava), *guanábano* (custard-apple tree), *güiro* (musical instrument made from a cornstalk), *hamaca* (hammock), and *huracán* (hurricane). The names of several Cuban cities—including Havana, Baracoa, Camagüey, and Bayamo—were derived from their prior Taino designations.

SPAIN ORGANIZES CONTROL SLOWLY

Despite an initial interest in Columbus's conquests, Spain took its time to pursue the riches in these New World territories. It controlled the region via a permanent settlement that had been established on Hispaniola, where colonial rulers focused on the increasingly fierce opposition from local indigenous groups. Very quickly the indigenes had learned that the Spanish explorers were far from godlike.

By the early 1500s, the murder of the indigenous peoples had become widespread. It was evident, Bartolomé de las Casas observed, that the conquistadors sought gold for quick profit and hardly hesitated to cut down Indians who stood in their way. The Spaniards treated the Indians, he wrote, "as the most abject dung and filth of the Earth."

Perhaps the most infamous early act of violence against the Indians was a massacre at Xaraguá in 1503, at the hands of Hispaniola's first colonial leader, Nicolas de Ovando, who killed dozens of tribal chiefs, including a local Taino leader, Queen Anacaona. Las Casas, increasingly outraged by Spanish violence and treachery against the Tainos, reported that dozens of indigenous leaders and others died.

Diego Velázquez de Cuéllar, who had come to the Caribbean with Columbus on the second voyage in 1493, was among the Spaniards who participated in the Xaraguá massacre.[16] A rich Hispaniola landowner by 1509, Velázquez became known as an effective military commander and launched a series of genocidal attacks in response to Indian insurrections on Hispaniola. As Velázquez gained prominence, the Spanish crown sought to recover the concessions it had granted to Columbus, including his claim to control all of the West Indies.[17] This was made easier by Columbus's death in 1506 in Spain, apparently from a heart attack. He was about fifty-five years old, still convinced that his four explorations had been along the east Asian coast.

Spain's King Ferdinand also wanted to establish administrative subdivisions over his newly acquired territories. To do this, he created regional outposts of the crown. Called *audiencias*, each was headed by an appointed royal governor. The king named Christopher Columbus's son, Diego, governor of the first regional outpost at Hispaniola, giving him nominal control over Cuba as well as Hispaniola. To exercise that function and remove Diego's rival from the local center of power, the king directed the younger Columbus to dispatch Velázquez to Cuba with a small army in order to establish a settlement there.

Strategically, Cuba was an excellent departure point for regional conquest.[18] As early as 1513, Pedrarias Dávila sailed from Cuba in order to explore, subjugate, and settle Central America. Hernán Cortés's voyage to Mexico left Cuba in 1519, and Hernando de Soto used Cuba as homeport for his exploration of Florida in 1538.

In all cases, gold fever was central to Spanish exploration. Early voyages led to the development of gold mines on Hispaniola, where Indians worked as slave laborers; the Spaniards assumed they would find just as much gold in Cuba. In fact, the conquistadors did discover gold in the central highlands and the Sierra Maestra shortly after establishing the settlement in Bayamo.[19] But they quickly depleted Cuba's gold reserves. Gold production peaked in 1519, when 112,000 pesos of gold were produced, the equivalent of about $132 million today.[20] By the 1540s, Cuban gold generated only 3,000 pesos annually, far less than could be obtained from Hispaniola.[21] With waning gold extraction, Cuba proved better as a waystation en route to further explorations for gold, and its importance as a colony declined.

Diego Velázquez arrived in January 1511 with 300 Spanish soldiers at what is today Guantánamo Bay. His outpost was at Baracoa, and he set up six more settlements between 1511 and 1515: at Bayamo, Trinidad, Havana, Puerto Príncipe (present day Camagüey), and Santiago de Cuba, staggered along the northern and southern Cuban coastline, and Sancti Spíritus, which was located in the center of the island, about equidistant from the northern and southern shores. All were intended to play key roles in Spain's expansion to Mexico, Central America, and South America.[22]

THE TAINOS RESIST SPANISH DOMINATION

Velázquez's progress was hampered at first by fierce attacks from the Gual-aba Indians, a branch of the Taino.[23] The Gualaba were led by Hatuey, a Taino chief who was thoroughly familiar with Spanish brutality. Hatuey had been present when Velázquez and his soldiers slaughtered Queen Anacaona and other Taino chiefs at Xaraguá eight years earlier. The chief evaded capture in that battle, at first retreating to the mountains in Hispaniola. He later made his way across the Windward Passage to Cuba with 400 Indian fighters.[24]

Hatuey resolved to destroy Velázquez and his colony in Cuba. Bartolomé de la Casas described his stirring speech to his assembled warriors before engaging in battle. He held up a basket of gold and jewels before them, de las Casas wrote, and said: "This is their [the Spaniards'] Lord," he said. "This is what they serve." In order to satisfy this idol, he exclaimed, "they will exact immense treasures from us, and will . . . reduce us to a miserable state of slavery, or else put us to death."[25]

Hatuey's warriors battled so fiercely that Velázquez was forced to call in reinforcements led by Pánfilo de Narváez, whose brutality in dealing with the Indians of Jamaica had already been documented. The battles raged for a year before Velázquez managed to defeat Hatuey's warriors. Chief Hatuey himself was captured and burned at the stake on February 15, 1512.

The defeat of Hatuey—and his warning about the intentions of the Spaniards—presaged the virtual annihilation of the indigenous peoples of Cuba. When Velázquez landed in 1511, there were an estimated 100,000 indigenous people living in Cuba.[26] By all accounts they were decimated—the population was 19,000 in 1519, and by midcentury fewer than 5,000 remained.[27] Hatuey, nevertheless, has become a national hero whom Cubans hold up as a symbol of courageous resistance to foreign domination.

There were multiple reasons for the death of so many people in such a brief period, and some of the explanations are controversial. Clearly, many of the Tainos and others were killed in clashes with the Spaniards, including the yearlong battles with Hatuey and his men. But many more died off the battlefield. Cuban historians Eduardo Torres-Cuevas and Oscar Loyola Vega described the slaughter of two thousand Indians by Pánfilo de Narváez in 1511 as a "true genocide."[28] As many as one-quarter of the Indian population may have committed suicide by hanging themselves, eating dirt, or ingesting poison, rather than live under European subjugation while lamenting the loss of their traditional way of life.[29] In their relentless search for riches, the Spaniards systematically subjugated and enslaved the Indians.[30] Disease also was a factor in indigenous deaths. Smallpox epidemics in 1519 and 1530 killed many. Measles, typhoid, and dysentery wiped out whole villages.[31] As mothers died, infant mortality increased with lack of necessary child care.[32]

Yet the Indian population was not extinguished completely. Some escaped to isolated islands off Cuba's coast.[33] Others fled to the mountains and were known as *cimarrónes*—runaway slaves. So many had died from all causes that by 1515, Velázquez began to import slaves from other Caribbean islands, from Central America, and the Yucatán. Within ten years, slaves outnumbered the indigenous population.[34]

The native culture also persisted, among other reasons, because of miscegenation. Among those women who survived, many married Spaniards and, later, blacks who were brought to Cuba as slaves. A 1514 census recorded that 40 percent of the Spanish men who reported being married had indigenous wives. Their mestizo children generally took the father's Spanish name.[35]

Bartolomé de las Casas was the indigenes' greatest defender, though his sermons were laced with more than a touch of paternalism and romanticism. He referred to the indigenous peoples, for example, as "sheep" and "indolent souls." They were innocents and had greeted the Spaniards with reverence, he said, but eventually "were compelled to take up Arms, provoked thereunto by repeated Injuries, violent Torments, and injust (*sic*) Butcheries."

His criticism provoked clerical and popular condemnation of Spanish colonial cruelty and did win some short-term results. With the death of King Ferdinand in 1516, his grandson Charles I reorganized the Council of the Indies, which oversaw the governance of Cuba and Hispaniola and had been blamed for the harsh Spanish treatment of the indigenous groups.[36] A new set of laws sought to limit the exploitation of the indigenous population in the West Indies and end the *encomienda* system under which groups of indigenous people were granted to Spanish settlers as if they were property. However, in order to discourage Spaniards from leaving Cuba as its fortunes declined, the Spanish crown deferred implementation of the *Leyes Nuevas* on the island.[37]

NOTES

1. Bartolomé de las Casas, *A Brief Account of the Destruction of the Indies* (English version: London, Printed for R. Hewson at the Crown in Cornhil, near the Stocks-Market, 1689; non-paginated Kindle edition).

2. Columbus named the island "Juana," for Don Juan, the son of his patrons, the Spanish regents, King Ferdinand of Aragon and Queen Isabella of Castile; Geoff Simons, *From Conquistador to Castro* (New York: Macmillan, 1996), 70.

3. *A Brief Account of the Destruction of the Indies*, chapter 1.

4. Simons, in *From Conquistador to Castro*, 81, says 18 ships.

5. Eduardo Torres-Cuevas and Oscar Loyola Vega, *Historia de Cuba, 1492–1898*, 3rd ed. (Havana: Editorial Pueblo y Educación, 2006), 43.

6. Simons, *From Conquistador to Castro*, 81.

7. Irving Rouse, *The Tainos: Rise and Decline of the People Who Greeted Columbus* (New Haven, CT: Yale University Press, 1992), 20.

8. Reniel Rodríguez Ramos, "From the Guanahatabey to the Archaic of Puerto Rico: The Nonevident Evidence," *Ethnohistory* 55, no. 3 (2008): 394.

9. Torres-Cuevas and Vega, *Historia de Cuba*, 14–15.

10. Quoted in Richard Gott, *Cuba: A New History* (New Haven, CT: Yale University Press, 2004), 12.

11. Torres-Cuevas and Vega, *Historia de Cuba*, 16.

12. Rouse, *The Tainos*, 5–9.

13. Rouse, *The Tainos*, 5.

14. Simons, *From Conquistador to Castro*, 68–69; Rouse, *The Tainos*, 9, 12, 14, 170.

15. Gott, *Cuba*, 12.

16. Gott, *Cuba*, 15.

17. Herbert S. Klein, *Slavery in the Americas: A Comparative Study of Virginia and Cuba* (Chicago: University of Chicago Press, 1967), 17–18; Simons, *From Conquistador to Castro*, 85–87.

18. Louis A. Pérez, Jr., *Cuba: Between Reform and Revolution*, 5th ed. (Oxford: Oxford University Press, 2014), 23; Klein, *Slavery in the Americas*, 131.

19. Pérez, *Cuba*, 20.

20. Alejandro de la Fuente, *Havana and the Atlantic in the Sixteenth Century* (Chapel Hill: University of North Carolina Press, 2008), 3. A peso, originally a "piece of eight," was a coin that contained 27.47 grams of gold. With the price of gold at about $43 per gram in 2016, a peso would be worth about $1,181.

21. Pérez, *Cuba*, 20; Torres-Cuevas and Vega, *Historia de Cuba*, 157.

22. Estrella Rey Betancourt and César Garcia del Pino, "Conquista y colonización de la isla de Cuba (1492–1553)," in *Historia de Cuba: La Colonia*, ed. Maria del Carmen Barcia, Gloria Garcia, and Eduardo Torres-Cuevas (Havana: Instituto de Historia de Cuba, 1994), 84–85; Gott, *Cuba*, 20.

23. Rouse, *The Tainos*, 156; Torres-Cuevas and Vega, *Historia de Cuba*, 48.

24. Simons, *From Conquistador to Castro*, 86–87; Rouse, *The Tainos*, 56.

25. As quoted in Simons, *From Conquistador to Castro*, 86.

26. Torres-Cuevas and Vega, *Historia de Cuba*, 25.

27. Gott, *Cuba*, 20.

28. Torres-Cuevas and Vega, *Historia de Cuba*, 50.

29. Louis A. Pérez, Jr., *To Die in Cuba: Suicide and Society* (Chapel Hill: University of North Carolina Press, 2005), 3–5.

30. Rouse, *The Tainos*, 157; Torres-Cuevas and Vega, *Historia de Cuba*, 157.

31. Pérez, *Cuba*, 22.

32. Torres-Cuevas and Vega, *Historia de Cuba*, 57–58.

33. Gott, *Cuba*, 22-23.

34. Rouse, *The Tainos*, 158.

35. Rouse, *The Tainos*, 158.

36. Miguel León Portilla and Nicolás Sánchez-Albornoz, *América Latina en la época colonial* (Barcelona: Critica España, 2002), 202–3.

37. De la Fuente, *Havana and the Atlantic*, 3.

Chapter 2

Sugar and Slavery

The true story of my life does not begin until 1809, when destiny began to unleash itself against me with all its fury. For the least childish mischief, I was locked up for twenty-four hours in a coal cellar without floorboards and nothing to cover myself. I was extremely fearful and liked to eat. As one can still see, in order to distinguish an object in my cell during the brightest midday, a good candle was necessary. Here, after the suffering of brutal lashes, I was locked up with orders that anyone who might give me even a drop of water was to be severely punished. Such an order was so feared in that house that no one, absolutely no one, dared give me as much as a crumb even if there were an opportunity. . . . From the age of thirteen to fourteen, the joy and vivacity of my character and the eloquence of my lips, dubbed the "golden beak," all changed completely into a certain kind of melancholy that, with time, became a personal trait of mine. Music enchanted me, but, without knowing why, I would cry. . . . I would cry rather than sob, but I was not faint of heart except during certain states of depression, incurable to this day.

—Excerpt from a slave's diary, 1840[1]

DECLINE AND RESURGENCE OF CUBA'S IMPORTANCE TO SPAIN'S EMPIRE

Half a century after Columbus first visited Cuba, the island's gold reserves were depleted, and Cuba had become less desirable than many other Spanish settlements in the Caribbean. Settlers in Cuba migrated with the Spanish explorers to Mexico and South America where they found significant new supplies of gold.[2] A Cuban census of six cities in 1544 counted 1,749 people; only 112 were Spanish. A 1620 estimate placed Cuba's total population at less than 7,000.[3] For decades the small settlements of Cuba used Indians and African slaves to develop cattle, grow food crops, and cultivate sugar cane, which had been imported to Cuba from the Canary Islands in 1515.[4]

Early on, Cuba exported these supplies to other Caribbean colonies. But as the new colonies became self-sufficient, Cuban exports were no longer required. By the mid-1550s, many Cuban settlements had vanished: "Fields were unattended, mines were deserted, towns were abandoned," historian Louis Pérez recounts.[5] Even the colonial capital, Santiago de Cuba, had been reduced to little more than a hamlet with thirty households.[6]

With labor in short supply, the first African slaves were brought in as early as 1511 to supplement continuing agricultural labor needs. Few European settlers had remained, and the majority of indigenous people had died from new diseases or battles with the conquerors. Less than a few thousand Indians survived, and between 1520 and 1540, Cuba lost 80 percent of its Spanish population.[7] In 1532, there were approximately five hundred African slaves on the island. Three years later, their number had doubled. A 1544 census found the African population was almost as large as the Spanish, 29 and 35 percent, respectively.[8] In a 1606 count, there were twenty thousand Africans.[9]

It took several decades for Cuban commerce and colonial life to rejuvenate itself. Eventually, Cuba emerged as a gateway and a new staging ground for Spanish exploration north, toward Florida and beyond. San Cristobal, on the island's southern coast along the eastern part of the Gulf of Batabanó, was Cuba's first major port. It had become a convenient departure point for the Spanish conquistadors, such as Hernán Cortés, who departed from there on his 1519 foray into Mexico during which he conquered the Aztec capital of Tenochtitlan. As Mexico became a major source of gold and commodities for the Spanish crown, other plunderers recognized San Cristobal's usefulness as a gateway.

Ironically, the exploitation of Mexican wealth led to the rise of Havana. Its location offered an important strategic advantage—it had a natural port that could serve ship commerce and offer protection from attack. In the 1520s, settlers began to migrate north from San Cristobal. Stopping at a site along the Almendares River, close to what is now Havana harbor, they named the new town San Cristobal de la Habana.[10]

The new port emerged as a trade center fairly quickly after its founding. Havana became the key stopover for travelers seeking to restock their supplies or for carousing before and after long, solitary sea voyages. By 1532, it was the most convenient first stop for ships arriving from Europe or last stop for ships heading back across the Atlantic laden with cargo from other colonies. Havana was also the last port from which ships departed without an escort to protect them from pirates and Spain's European antagonists

The Origins of the Name "La Habana"

After his first trip to Cuba, Christopher Columbus wrote to his Spanish backers that "there are in the western part of the island two provinces which I did not visit; one of these is called by the Indians 'Avan,' and its inhabitants are born with tails."* "When Spanish soldier-settlers finally reached and conquered the western part of the island some twenty-five years after Columbus's voyage, they were still calling it 'La Avana' or 'La Abana,' a name which they took from a word often repeated by the inhabitants, a word recorded by the Spaniards as Havaguanex or Habaguanex, which they thought to be the name of a local chief."† Writing shortly afterward about the harbor where the Spanish settlers finally located the city of La Habana, Father Bartolomé de las Casas, the chronicler of the Spanish destruction of native culture in the Caribbean, said, "There are few harbors in Spain, and perhaps not in any other parts of the world, that may equal it."‡

---

* As quoted in Cluster and Hernández, *The History of Havana*, 1.
† Cluster and Hernández, *The History of Havana*, 2.
‡ As quoted in Cluster and Hernández, *The History of Havana*, 2.

during several sixteenth-century wars. The discovery of the Gulf Stream—first described by Juan Ponce de Leon, who was a crew member on Columbus's second voyage to America—added to the advisability of using Havana as a departure point. Mariners realized that by plying the waters off Havana, the northeastern flow of the Atlantic current cut down sailing time for ships heading home to Europe.

As early as 1546, one writer characterized Havana as one of the "most important and famous cities in the world."[11] Its formal crowning as Cuba's center of power came in 1553, when King Charles I of Spain designated the city as the new capital, replacing Santiago de Cuba. Until then, most of Havana's thriving businesses had revolved around transportation and related services—shipyards, slaughterhouses, produce markets—that provisioned ships traveling back and forth to Europe.[12] Taverns that lodged clothing suppliers also developed, accompanied by thriving side pursuits: prostitution, gambling, and the production and consumption of alcohol.

With its new importance, security issues grew. As early as Cortés's exploration of Mexico, Spanish fleets and settlements were subject to periodic attacks by pirates and marauders supported by France, Spain's principal European rival in the early sixteenth century. Havana itself was a frequent target for attack by French marauders, and in 1537 a French fleet occupied the city for nearly a year.[13] After Spain won back control, authorities began to build fortifications to defend settlers from future attacks. The first fortress, the

Castillo de la Real Fuerza, was more a symbolic structure than a meaningful battlement. Poorly located, it had been built too far into the mouth of Havana harbor to serve as an early warning site against attacks.

That became all too evident in 1555 when the French pirate Jacques de Sorés sacked and effectively destroyed the city. Free Indians and African slaves fought the French onslaught alongside Spanish settlers. But they were no match for de Sorés's superior force, which then withdrew before the residents could summon assistance from other Cuban garrisons.

Charles I responded to the devastating raid with a plan that included the construction of more substantial fortifications throughout Cuba. Yet only in 1589, more than thirty years after de Sorés's raid, did the Spanish crown finally authorize the construction of Havana's first significant and defensible fortress—Morro Castle (*Castillo de los Tres Reyes Magos del Morro*)— which was built strategically at the point where the harbor meets the sea.[14] Havana's defense remained far from perfect, though, as the English Royal Navy captured Morro Castle in 1762 and held it until the following year.

Spain built fortresses similar to Morro Castle in Puerto Rico, Hispaniola, and Cartagena. Yet the colonies were not always able to withstand attacks by pirates, notably those supported by Britain, which had been engaged in an undeclared war with Spain even before the attack on the Spanish Armada in 1588. The most famous and feared among the English pirates and privateers of the period was Sir Francis Drake, who plundered Spanish settlements throughout the Caribbean and Spanish commercial ships at sea. Still, the attacks were not enough to weaken Spain's ability to transfer huge stocks of minerals and produce home.[15]

THE EMERGENCE OF THE SUGAR ECONOMY

Cuba Is a Late Bloomer in Producing Sugar

By 1600, Havana was firmly established as Cuba's central city. With a population of 9,000 inhabitants—about 46 percent of the island's total—Havana was the hub for its commerce. Increasingly, the city also had become a regional center for the defense of the empire.[16] Yet Cuba's importance to the Spanish empire would remain principally as a service station for the rest of the colonies. It was not a source of commodities, as the island's vast territory was given more to raising cattle than to agriculture. Only in the eighteenth century would the introduction of sugar plantations transform the island's economy and its political future.

Sugar had been introduced into Cuba from either Jamaica or Hispaniola in the early 1500s, but the processes for growing, harvesting, and milling cane were primitive and yields were small. The Spanish crown provided little investment to develop the island's capacity for sugar production, choosing to focus its resources elsewhere. While Hispaniola had six sugar mills and forty under construction by 1520 and Jamaica had thirty operating sugar mills in 1523, Cuba's first sugar mills were not built until 1576.[17] Until then the small sugar crop was used mainly to make molasses concentrate, most of which was consumed on the island itself.[18]

With the emerging industrial age in the mid-1700s, the Spanish colonial government sought new sources of raw materials and produce.[19] For the first time, Cuba was viewed as a potential source of agricultural products. Slowly, farms were established for growing and exporting cotton as well as coffee, which in particular was well suited to the western mountainous province of Pinar del Rio. This incipient agricultural industry was still limited by primitive methods and small farming operations. But to the degree that export products emerged, cattle production decreased.

British control of Cuba for a little less than one year also contributed to the rise in agricultural exports and a decrease in Spanish mercantile control. In 1762, near the end of the so-called Seven Years' War, a conflict pitting France and Spain against Britain, a British expeditionary fleet laid siege to western Cuba and seized Havana. British entrepreneurs descended on the city, prompting a new drive for sugar production and a surge in slave trading. More than 10,000 slaves arrived in Havana during the ten months of British control. The occupation ended with the 1763 Treaty of Paris, under which British negotiators ceded control of Cuba in return for sovereignty over Florida. Short-lived though it was, the British influence accelerated the transformation of the island's economy and culture. As Louis Pérez aptly concludes, "If the availability of new markets made the expansion of sugar profitable, the availability of new slaves made it possible."[20]

Industrialization of Sugar Production

In this way, two centuries after its introduction on the island, sugar began its expansion until it became king, with the Cuban economy restructured into a monoculture organized around the harvesting and processing of cane on large plantations. The restructuring was accelerated by steadily growing demand in Europe and North America, along with one landmark event: the 1804 Haitian revolution. Culminating a thirteen-year slave rebellion, Haiti's declaration of independence provoked European and North American boycotts of Haitian commerce and products, actions intended to punish the victors and to discourage slave revolts in the Caribbean and the United States. Meanwhile, French refugees from Haiti headed to Cuba, bringing with them expertise in streamlined sugar refining methods. Buyers turned increasingly to Cuba, which accordingly increased sugar production. Between 1792 and 1806 the number of sugar mills around Havana nearly doubled to 416. Large swaths of forest—13,000 acres annually in the 1840s—were destroyed to make way for sugar cultivation.[21] The new emphasis on sugar production highlighted the need to reform agricultural and milling practices, as well as land tenancy laws, to remove obstacles to the creation of large plantations. In this way sugar production became more "rational." As mills were vertically integrated with the production of cane, plantation owners were able to afford the introduction of newer technologies and the entire process became more efficient.[22]

Major sugar planters promoted increased acreage and modern innovation and established a chapter of the *Sociedad Económica de Amigos del País* (the Economic Society for Friends of the Country), a Spanish organization with branches throughout the colonies aimed at promoting economic development. The Cuban branch also focused on its members' desire to continue using slaves for the sugar harvest at a point when slavery was being abolished elsewhere.

The resulting agricultural transformation advanced in stages and changed Cuba in several ways. By the 1860s, sugar provided 80 percent of Cuba's exports. Tobacco was about 10 percent of exports; coffee was 2 percent.[23] Meanwhile, Cuba became less able to provide food and basic necessities for its inhabitants and began to rely on imports that could be purchased with its export income.[24] Farming focused on cash crops rather than the production of food for internal consumption. The conversion to a sugar export economy also moved Cuba toward a "special" and unbalanced relationship it already had been developing with the United States, which offered an expanding market vastly more accessible and convenient than any other trading partner. By the middle of the nineteenth century, 62 percent of Cuba's exports went to the United States and only 3 percent was shipped to Spain. But 30 percent of Cuba's imports came from Spain, with only 20 percent coming from the United States.[25]

A DUAL SLAVERY SYSTEM

As Cuba's plantation economy flourished so did growth in its African slave trade. The custom of using African slave labor in Europe predated Columbus's voyage to America by almost half a century,[26] and Spanish settlers in Cuba did not hesitate to use West African slaves to fulfill their labor needs. Between 1790 and 1820 at least 300,000 slaves were sent to Cuba, triple the total in the previous 280 years.[27] This trafficking in humans reflected a cold calculation of profit and loss, because slave ownership was a significant investment for a landowner.[28] Prior to the rise of sugar, costs often outweighed gains. In 1610, the mean price of a slave was 203 ducats, in purchasing power the equivalent of 185 cattle hides or 140 loads of cassava.

Part of the calculus in buying and maintaining slaves was a brutal reality: it was sometimes less expensive for slave owners to buy a new slave than to keep existing slaves healthy enough to have children who could also be enslaved. As a consequence, Cuban slave owners gave little consideration to the survival of their African laborers. Louis Pérez explains that "Africans consigned to sugar production toiled under execrable circumstances. Tens of thousands of men and women were worked remorselessly: six days a week, eighteen hours a day, often for five and six months at a time. . . . The death of slaves was passed off as a depreciation of capital stock—all in all, an acceptable cost of doing business."[29] Annual slave mortality rates, due to illnesses and inhumane treatment, were as high as 18 percent at some mills. Life expectancy for a slave averaged seven years after arriving in Cuba.[30]

In many other colonies, slave trading was on the decline. Britain abolished the practice throughout the empire in 1807, and the US Constitution forbade the importation of slaves after 1808. Cuban slave shipments continued well into the 1800s and Cuba became a source for illegal slave sales to North America.

The depiction of a relentlessly oppressive system of slavery in Cuba is complicated by the treatment of Africans who were not on sugar plantations.[31] Although slavery was still functioning in the 1800s, the Spanish legal code did not support slavery, and those who had been slaves did not suffer the same stigma experienced by freed men and women in the United States.[32] Historian Herbert Klein notes that "while slavery was accepted as a historic institution . . . it was conceived of as an evil necessity rather than a positive good."[33]

Africans were employed freely in nearly every aspect of production and commerce on the island, partly due to the scarcity of white laborers. In Cuban towns, Africans had jobs and sometimes owned property. A majority of the taverns and lodges in Havana, for example, were owned or managed by African women. Those Africans in the cities who were slaves tended to have considerable independence, in stark contrast to rural slaves. Moreover, slaves had limited legal recognition and the right to own and inherit property apart from what a master might be willing to allow a slave to possess. Slaves could even "rent themselves" out to individual employers, and would then pay a portion of their earnings to their owners. And if they gathered enough money from their employment, urban African slaves in Cuba also could purchase their freedom. Eventually a growing cadre of African freedmen and freedwomen were working alongside slaves in urban areas.

The prevailing attitude toward Africans in Cuba gave them a significant role in Spanish colonial aspirations in the Caribbean. By 1770, blacks and mulattos made up more than one-fourth of Cuba's militia.[34] As Spain and Britain fought for power in Europe, Spain depended on the Cuban militiamen to challenge British holdings in the Western Hemisphere, which gave black Cuban militiamen "some acquaintance with the rhetoric of independence," as historian Jane Landers observes. One battalion even fought under a flag bearing the words, "Victory or Death," similar to Patrick Henry's, "Give me liberty or give me death."[35] Notably, Cuban leaders adopted the same theme in the 1960s: *Patria o Muerte, Venceremos* (Homeland or Death, We Will Be Victorious).

The first major slave revolt erupted on the estate of *Cuatro Compañeros* in 1795. Its timing was significant. News of the uprising in Haiti, which began two years earlier, had crossed the Windward Passage. The ringleader at Cuatro Compañeros was José el Francés, who appeared to have been Haitian. Fear of Haitian influence led Cuban captain-general Jesus de las Casas to prohibit correspondence with foreigners, and in 1796 to ban the importation of French-speaking slaves.[36]

However, word of the successful 1804 Haitian revolution was unstoppable. Tension increased on Cuban plantations as the large numbers of Africans swelled the ranks of slaves after 1808. Talk of rebellion spread quickly from Cuba to other parts of the Caribbean, since the island was a regional and international transportation hub.[37] And then in 1812, as if a growing balloon finally burst, the tension exploded in the Aponte Rebellion.[38]

Named for José Antonio Aponte, a *moreno* (free black) sculptor who had been a captain in the free black militia, the rebellion was a series of separate slave insurrections throughout the island. The first one, in January 1812, took place on plantations surrounding Puerto Príncipe, nearly 400 miles from Havana, and was the result of coordinated planning. In suppressing this plantation revolt, the colonial government decided to set a brutal example to discourage further unrest. Fourteen African rebels were executed in a public square, while 170 slaves and free blacks were whipped and imprisoned.[39]

A month later, a series of revolts were staged around Bayamo, in Cuba's eastern province of Oriente, about sixty miles west of Santiago. Revolts next spread to plantations near Holguín and Havana. As the colonial government fought to suppress the Havana plantation rebellions, they tortured slaves in an attempt to gather information. As several slaves asserted that Aponte was the leader of the rebellions, he became the government's prime target, even though he actually was not a central figure. In fact, the island-wide insurrection was neither orchestrated nor coordinated by one central command. Nevertheless, the colonial government arrested Aponte, convicted him of leading

Figure 2.1.   Plaque on Aponte Street in Havana: "To José A. Aponte and Comrades, 1812–April 9–1948, Association of Ex-Combatants and Anti-Fascist Revolutionaries of Cuba." The bronze plaque disappeared in the 1990s. Photo by Ivor Miller.

the island-wide movement to incite slave insurrections, and hanged him on April 9, 1812. Then it exhibited his decapitated head publicly as a warning against further insurrection.[40] In figure 2.1, we see a now-missing plaque dedicated to Aponte and his fellow insurgents.

Two subsequent movements for the abolition of slavery made Cuban independence an additional goal. They also were named for leading proponents who have come to be known as the intellectual founders of Cuban independence: Félix Varela y Morales, a Roman Catholic priest, and José María Heredia, a poet.[41]

Born in Havana in 1788, Varela was a professor at the prestigious San Carlos Seminary College, where he created a department of constitutional law that produced several of Cuba's leading advocates for abolition and independence. When Varela became a representative to the Spanish *Cortes* (legislature) in 1821, he brought both campaigns—for the abolition of slavery and Cuban independence—to the legislative body. In 1823, the Spanish authorities sentenced Varela to death for his activities and he fled to Philadelphia. There he published an abolitionist paper, *El Habanero*, which was smuggled regularly into Cuba. Varela remained in exile until his death in 1853. His remains were transferred to Cuba in the early twentieth century.

In the same year that Varela departed from Cuba, an independence group named Los Soles y Rayos de Bolívar (Bolívar's Offspring) began operations.

The group's leader, José Francisco Lemus, was a Cuban who had fought with Simón Bolívar, and the organization received support from anti-imperial leaders in Colombia, Ecuador, Peru, and Argentina.[42] One of its prominent members was José María Heredia. Perhaps best known for his stirring poem "Niagara," Heredia began to be recognized as a major poet in the 1820s. Cubans today still recall his 1823 poem, "La Estrella de Cuba" (The Star of Cuba), as a work that was integral to their struggle for independence. It opens with the phrase "¡Libertad! *ya jamás sobre Cuba*" (Liberty! Cuba has never known you), and includes the following stanza:

> Today the people dazed, wounded,
> Deliver us to the insolent tyrant
> Cowardly and stolidly they have not wanted to take up their sword
> All lies dissolved, lost
> So that my exile shall be a noble tomb
> Against terrible, severe fate
> Beyond Cuba and my despair.[43]

Two generations later, the revolutionary leader José Martí spoke of Heredia as his "literary father." Heredia, he wrote, "woke in my soul, as in the soul of all the Cubans, the undying passion for freedom."[44]

NOTES

1. Juan Francisco Manzano, *The Autobiography of a Slave*, trans. Evelyn Picon Garfield (Detroit: Wayne State University Press, 1996), 57, 59, 61.
2. Rouse, *The Tainos*, 158.
3. Simons, *From Conquistador to Castro*, 105.
4. Rouse, *The Tainos*, 157.
5. Pérez, *Cuba*, 25.
6. Pérez, *Cuba*, 25.
7. De la Fuente, *Havana and the Atlantic*, 3–5; Dick Cluster and Rafael Hernández, *The History of Havana* (New York: Palgrave Macmillan, 2006), 5–6; Torres-Cuevas and Vega, *Historia de Cuba*, 52–53, 72; Julio le Riverend, *Economic History of Cuba* (Havana: Ensayo Book Institute, 1967), 62; Ilene Ahoha Wright, *The Early History of Cuba, 1492–1586* (New York: Macmillan, 1916), 224–26.
8. Arturo Sorhegui D'Mares and Alejandro de la Fuente, "El surgimiento de la sociedad criolla de Cuba (1553–1608)," in *Historia de Cuba 1492–1898*, third edition, ed. Eduardo Torres-Cuevas and Oscar Loyola Vega (Havana: Editorial Pueblo y Educación, 2006), 108.
9. Klein, *Slavery in the Americas*, 142.
10. Wright, *The Early History of Cuba*, 74.
11. Quoted in de la Fuente, *Havana and the Atlantic*, 4–5.
12. Klein, *Slavery in the Americas*, 135–36.

13. Gott, *Cuba*, 26–27.

14. Gott, *Cuba*, 29.

15. Gott, *Cuba*, 33.

16. Sorhegui D'Mares and de la Fuente, "El surgimiento de la sociedad criolla de Cuba," 111; Simons, *From Conquistador to Castro*, 132; Pérez, *Cuba*, 27.

17. Simons, *From Conquistador to Castro*, 108; Gott, *Cuba*, 37.

18. Pérez, *Cuba*, 32.

19. Le Riverend, *Economic History of Cuba*, 134–35.

20. Pérez, *Cuba*, 47.

21. Pérez, *Cuba*, 56.

22. Le Riverend, *Economic History of Cuba*, 135–36.

23. Francisco López Segrera, "Cuba: Dependence, Plantation Economy, and Social Classes, 1762–1902," in *Between Slavery and Free Labor: The Spanish-Speaking Caribbean in the Nineteenth Century*, ed. Manuel Moreno Fraginals, Frank Moya Pons, and Stanley L. Engerman (Baltimore: Johns Hopkins University Press, 1985), 84.

24. López Segrera, "Cuba," 83.

25. López Segrera, "Cuba," 83.

26. Klein, *Slavery in the Americas*, 140.

27. Matt D. Childs, *The 1812 Aponte Rebellion in Cuba and the Struggle against Atlantic Slavery* (Chapel Hill: University of North Carolina Press, 2006), 9.

28. De la Fuente, *Havana and the Atlantic*, 150.

29. Pérez, *To Die in Cuba*, 28.

30. Pérez, *To Die in Cuba*, 31.

31. Rebecca J. Scott, *Slave Emancipation in Cuba: The Transition to Free Labor, 1860–1899* (Princeton: Princeton University Press, 1985), 10–18; Klein, *Slavery in the Americas*, 144–46, 162–63.

32. Klein, *Slavery in the Americas*, 59–61.

33. Klein, *Slavery in the Americas*, 60.

34. Jane G. Landers, *Atlantic Creoles in the Age of Revolutions* (Cambridge: Harvard University Press, 2010), 140–42.

35. Landers, *Atlantic Creoles*, 142–43.

36. Childs, *The 1812 Aponte Rebellion*, 38; Manuel Barcia, *Domination and Resistance on Western Cuban Plantations, 1808–1848* (Baton Rouge: Louisiana University Press, 2008), 31.

37. Childs, *The 1812 Aponte Rebellion*, 41–42.

38. Childs, *The 1812 Aponte Rebellion*, 22, 44–45.

39. Childs, *The 1812 Aponte Rebellion*, 122–26.

40. Childs, *The 1812 Aponte Rebellion*, 147–54.

41. Sergio Guerra Vilaboy and Oscar Loyola Vega, *Cuba: A History* (New York: Ocean Press, 2010), 17; Landers, *Atlantic Creoles*, 166, 169.

42. Torres-Cuevas and Vega, *Historia de Cuba*, 141.

43. José María Heredia, "La Estrella de Cuba," in *Poesias de Don José Maria Heredia*, vol. 2 (New York: Roe Lockwood, 1853), 140–41.

44. José Martí, *Obras Completas*, vol. 5 (La Habana: Editorial Nacional de Cuba, 1963–1973), 165.

Chapter 3

Struggle for Independence, 1868–1898

I am in daily danger of giving my life for my country and duty, for I understand that duty and have the courage to carry it out—the duty of preventing the United States from spreading through the Antilles as Cuba gains its independence, and from overpowering with that additional strength our American lands. . . . I have lived in the monster and I know its entrails; my sling is David's.

—José Martí[1]

By 1830, Cuba and Puerto Rico were Spain's last remaining colonies in the Western Hemisphere. Cuba was the more important possession, because it had become the world's largest sugar producer. To punish Haiti for winning independence in 1804—which Europe and the United States viewed in effect as a successful slave revolt—importers of Haitian sugar initiated a boycott of the country's products. In turn, growers shifted production to Cuba, even though it lacked a sufficient number of plantation workers for the increased activity. They solved their labor shortage problem by importing more than 40,000 African slaves from 1802 to 1806. This was almost as many as the number forced into servitude on the island in the previous ten years.[2]

As generally is the case with migrations, the new immigrants to Cuba tended to lack the kind of nationalist consciousness necessary for an independence war. Moreover, there was a decided class difference between blacks already on the island and the newly arrived Africans. Until the plantation economy took hold in the nineteenth century, African slaves had been employed in all aspects of production and commerce. As noted in the previous chapter, urban slaves were allowed to live in their own homes, to earn wages by "renting" themselves to other owners, and even to purchase their freedom. The broad range in the quality of life for Cuban blacks impaired their ability to form a united opposition to the slave system or to find a common bond for an independence struggle with the newer immigrants who worked on the plantations.

The 1842 census revealed that whites were a minority.[3] Moreover they, too, were divided, between the *peninsulares* and the *criollas*. Peninsulares were Spanish-born, remained loyal to the Spanish crown, benefited from Spanish colonial control, and viewed the Spanish military as their protectors. Most lived in Cuba's bureaucratic and commercial centers, essentially acting as agents of Spain, and they tended to dominate Cuba's political and commercial affairs. As a group, they feared that independence would lead to a black-ruled country that could suffer Haiti's fate as an international pariah. Indeed, their stance was encouraged by officials in the United States. Secretary of State Henry Clay warned in 1825 that the "amount and character of [Cuba's] population render it improbable that it could maintain its independence. Such a premature declaration might bring about a renewal of those shocking scenes, of which a neighboring island was the afflicted theatre."[4]

Criollas tended to be the rural elites who owned large farms for cattle, sugar, coffee, and tobacco. Born in Cuba with Spanish ancestry, they would ultimately fund and organize the start of the Cuban War for Independence. Their grievances against Spain arose from the failure of the 1865 reform efforts that would have provided the island's elites with some local autonomy and relief from some Spanish mercantile controls: trade restrictions, high tariffs, and taxes. Lower taxes had been especially demanded because the economy was heading into a depression due to falling sugar prices. When banks suspended payments on obligations in December 1866, this effectively halted all sugar transactions. Then in early 1867, without notice, Spain imposed new taxes. These were particularly harsh for owners of smaller sugar plantations in the eastern half of the island and for cattle barons in Camagüey. In response to the weakening financial conditions, some began to plot rebellion.[5] The conspirators included Carlos Manuel de Céspedes, the owner of a modest sugar plantation in the farthest east province of Oriente.

EL GRITO DE YARA

Ten-Year War

On October 10, 1868, Céspedes called together his slaves. To their astonishment, he announced that they were free and asked them to join him in a war for Cuban independence. His declaration, known as the *Grito de Yara* or Cry of Yara, marked the start of the Ten-Year War. Though Céspedes freed his slaves, the revolutionaries were careful not to include abolition as one of their goals. They hoped to enlist support from western plantation owners for whom slaves made up a significant portion of their wealth. That strategy was successful. Many landowners did support the reformist aims of the rebellion, which called for ending the limitations imposed by Spanish exploitation and mercantilist restrictions.[6]

Still, the Grito echoed noble sentiments reminiscent of those expressed a century earlier in the US and French revolutions and in the more recent wars for independence in South America: "We only want to be free and to see all men with us equally free, as the Creator intended all mankind to be. . . . We constitute an independent nation because we believe that beneath the Spanish roof we shall never enjoy the complete exercise of our rights."[7]

A revolutionary army that began with 147 men grew to 12,000 fighters and by the early 1870s counted as many as 40,000 adherents, reflecting a broad cross-section of the population: men and women, former slaves, free blacks, white workers, and landowners. The revolutionaries called themselves *Mambises*, named for Juan Ethninius Mamby, a black Spanish military officer who joined the successful independence campaign against Spain that had created the Dominican Republic in 1844.[8]

The Mambises made equal rights for women a major goal, one of the earliest such efforts in modern world politics. That aspiration became an aspect of Cuban revolutionary identity, especially after the 1959 revolution.[9] Ana Betancourt, editor of the revolutionaries' newspaper, *El Mambí*, notably called for women's equality at the 1869 First Constitutional Assembly of Cuban Patriots. She declared, "Citizens: The Cuban woman in the dark and peaceful corner of the home waited patiently and resignedly for this beautiful hour, when a revolution would break her yoke and untie her wings."[10]

The Protest of Baraguá

Contemporary Cuban historians focus on four generals as heroes of the Ten-Year War and of Cuba's struggle for independence, with the message that the July 26th Movement of the mid-twentieth century was the inheritor of their earlier campaigns: Máximo Gómez (who was from the Dominican Republic), Calixto Garcia, Ignacio Agramonte, and Antonio Maceo. Maceo was twenty-two when the war began, and he rose rapidly in a succession of promotions that recognized his bravery, determination, and skill. His prominence was especially remarkable because he was young and from a family of free mulattos.[11]

The Mambises scored major successes in the early years of the war, employing asymmetrical guerrilla warfare against the Spanish army's traditional military formations. The rebels defeated superior Spanish forces in several battles, captured some cities, including Bayamo, and established a new government and democratic constitution.

Spain, however, kept the insurgency at bay by using its much larger number of soldiers and unrelenting technical military superiority. After nine years of conflict, rifts developed in the insurgency's political leadership over the extent to which the war should be waged in the west and over which reforms, especially abolition, they should advance.[12] By 1878, the rebels were exhausted and their resources were depleted. An estimated 50,000 soldiers and civilians died in the war.

At that point, Spain sent a new military commander to Cuba, Arsenio Martínez Campos, and offered a compromise to end the conflict. It included some reforms, a guarantee of amnesty, and freedom for any slaves who had fought with the Mambises. In February 1878, rebel leaders signed a pact that freed some slaves and promised future reforms, but left Cuba as a Spanish colony.

General Maceo, however, broke with other Mambises leaders and refused to accept the pact, because it provided neither independence nor the abolition of slavery. In the "Protest of Baraguá," Maceo issued a pledge to continue the war, declaring: "Our policy is to free the slaves, because the era of the whip and of Spanish cynicism has come to an end."[13] He retained a fighting force of about 1,000, but the extension of the conflict ended within six weeks, when the Spanish military captured Maceo and forced him into exile. Nevertheless, the "Protest of Baraguá" has become a contemporary rallying cry, representing Cuba's determination never to surrender.[14]

"Maceo's defiance had two important consequences," historian Patricia Weiss Fagen explains. First, the peace agreement ending the conflict "came to be understood as no more than a truce; second, Maceo's act strengthened the determination of his countrymen to renew the war as soon as possible."[15] But Maceo did not return to Cuba until March 1895.

A new rebellion flared up briefly in August 1879, known as the *Guerra Chiquita* or the Little War. Initiated by General Calixto Garcia, it was poorly organized and lacked resources. The fighting ended after thirteen months.[16] Maceo remained in exile during the Little War, and Garcia prevented him from gaining any leadership role under the pretext that Spain would use the black general's presence to claim the rebellion was a race war.

CUBA SUFFERS AN ECONOMIC DEPRESSION

In addition to the lives lost, the years of war took a toll on Cuba's economy. Dozens of sugar plantations were destroyed. All twenty-four sugar mills in Bayamo, eighteen mills in Manzanillo, and sixty of the sixty-four mills in

Holguín were lost in the years of fighting. The sugar economy also suffered from sugar beet production in France and Germany, which began replacing Cuban cane sugar on the world market.[17] The Cuban share of sugar exports globally dropped from 30 to 11 percent from the mid-1860s to the mid-1880s.

The collapse generated widespread unemployment,[18] which, along with the loss of slaves, significantly reduced planters' wealth. One-third of all cigar workers lost their jobs; the Havana naval yard closed in 1885; government workers were laid off, resulting in problems of sanitation and public works. Five hundred coffee farms halted operation, and coffee production collapsed. The official end of slavery in 1886 compounded the unemployment problem. Former slaves competed for jobs, and the surplus of willing labor contributed to reducing workers' wages. Increased mechanization also resulted in less need for labor. On the other hand, with the end of slavery the issue of abolition no longer was a source of division among *independentistas*. They had more reason to form a cohesive opposition to Spanish domination.

Meanwhile the United States had become Cuba's major trading partner and source of foreign investment. Cuba's trade with the United States was six times greater than with Spain in 1881. By the end of the 1880s, the northern neighbor was essentially the sole purchaser of Cuban sugar—94 percent of Cuba's sugar exports went to the United States. Cuba's increased dependence on the United States meant that problems in the US economy would be magnified on the island. And in the 1880s and early 1890s the problems were enormous, as the United States entered into a prolonged depression.

US economic problems were one reason investors looked to Cuba. At first, they partnered with existing Cuban land and mill owners. But the North Americans quickly began to acquire bankrupted estates outright. By 1895, US investments in Cuba totaled at least $50 million, and only 20 percent of the mills were owned by Cuban families of the former planter class.[19] The new foreign investors combined smaller farms into larger operations, known as *ingenios* and *centrales*, the latter acting as a central agricultural facility that generally produced more than just sugar. As investments spurred increased mechanization, there was less need for labor. So while the increased efficiency helped to restore the macro Cuban economy in the 1890s, the spread of capital-intensive processes produced unemployment and discontent.

A new boost for Cuban sugar production came when the US Congress passed the US Tariff Act of 1890, which removed the duty on raw sugar imports into the United States. Exports jumped from 632,000 tons in 1890 to more than one million tons in 1894. It was a sign that Cuba was becoming more than just dependent on the United States for its economic health; the relationship led to total Cuban integration into the US economy.[20] This state of affairs ran both ways; Cuban economic health depended on US purchasing power. At the same time, political changes in Cuba had a greater impact than ever before on US investors and therefore on US politics.

Class relations in Cuba changed correspondingly as economic ties with the United States tightened. The takeover by foreign investors meant that "Cuba would no longer possess a wealthy class that was independent of US capital," historian Jules Benjamin explains. As a result, no large and self-conscious Cuban class existed to oppose the ownership of land or basic infrastructure by capitalists from the United States and Canada.[21] One sign of Cuban dependency appeared in the early 1890s when another wave of economic depression hit the United States. The US government raised sugar tariffs once more, sending Cuban revenues and the overall economy tumbling as well.

THE INDEPENDENCE WAR

While the Cuban business sector's ardor for independence was tempered by its subservience to foreign investors, the longtime demands for ending colonial rule among other sectors of the population were reaching heights not seen since the Ten-Year War. The unlikely leader who brought together the various factions was a five-foot-tall essayist, journalist, and poet who lived in New York, José Martí. Born in Havana in 1853 to poor Spanish immigrants, Martí began his first attacks on Spanish colonial rule in *La Patria Libre* (*The Free Homeland*), a newspaper he started at the age of sixteen, during the Ten-Year War. Today, Cubans of all political leanings regard him as the father of Cuban independence because of his devotion to the fight for Cuba's sovereignty.

Martí gathered *independentistas* under the banner of the Cuban Revolutionary Party in 1892. With Máximo Gómez, Antonio Maceo, and other veterans of the Ten-Year War, he began to coordinate preparations for what the group hoped would be a final struggle to achieve independence. Their campaign (in Cuba it is often called "The Necessary War") opened on February 24, 1895, in the eastern province of Oriente, the cradle of Cuban insurrections. The Spanish Army had put down a number of other small insurrections since the Little War of 1879–1880. But this time the insurgents were better prepared and organized. By the end of 1895, the struggle for independence had engulfed the entire island. Scattered insurgencies had coalesced into a coherent force of 50,000 fighters organized into twelve divisions and eighty-five regiments.[22]

Six weeks after returning to Cuba via the Dominican Republic with General Gómez, Martí was killed in combat on May 19, 1895. As a martyr, Martí continued to inspire the new Mambises as they rallied around his notions of Cuba libre. These emphasized the unity of the nation, the creation

"Our America" by José Martí*

And in what *patria* can a man take greater pride than in our long-suffering republics of America . . . ? Never before have such advanced and consolidated nations been created from such disparate factors in less historical time. . . . The colony lives on in the republic. . . . Therefore the urgent duty of our America is to show herself as she is, one in soul and intent, rapidly overcoming the crushing weight of her past and stained only by the fertile blood spilled by hands that do battle against ruins and by veins that were punctured by our former masters.

The disdain of the formidable neighbor who does not know her is our America's greatest danger, and it is urgent—for the day of the visit is near—that her neighbor come to know her, and quickly, so that he will not disdain her. Out of ignorance, he may perhaps begin to covet her. But when he knows her, he will remove his hands from her in respect. One must have faith in the best in man and distrust the worst. One must give the best every opportunity, so that the worst will be laid bare and overcome. If not, the worst will prevail. . . . There is no racial hatred, because there are no races. . . . The soul, equal and eternal, emanates from bodies that are diverse in form and color. Anyone who promotes and disseminates opposition or hatred among races is committing a sin against humanity.

*Published in *El Partido Liberal* (Mexico City, March 5, 1892), trans. Jerry A. Sierra; reprinted from HistoryofCuba.com, http://www.historyofcuba.com/history/marti/America.htm.

of a republic that would serve all Cubans equally, and the ability of Cuba to act independently in its own interests. This platform set the stage for an inevitable clash with the United States because the insurgents not only demanded Cuban independence from Spain, they sought to make Cuba sovereign and uncontrolled by any foreigners—"Cuba for Cubans," as Louis Pérez summarized the goal.[23]

The 200,000-soldier Spanish garrison at first seemed sufficient to counter the independentistas. Spain fought back against the revolutionaries with enormous brutality, razing villages and driving Cubans out of their homes. This became the typical Spanish mode of warfare, especially after General Valeriano Weyler arrived in February 1896. Known as "The Butcher," Weyler was the personification of inhumane and ruthless counterinsurgency warfare.[24] Asserting that "I believe that war should be answered with war,"[25] Weyler began with a tactic that he called "reconcentration." He ordered his soldiers to forcibly relocate peasants from the countryside into towns and then to destroy their crops, cattle, and houses so that revolutionaries would not be able to live off the land.

Weyler focused initially on the western province of Pinar del Río where Antonio Maceo, the resolute general of the Ten-Year War, had returned from seventeen years in exile to join the new revolution. At first Weyler's tactics produced some victories, despite widespread criticism of his methods. But public opinion turned decisively against him when his troops killed Maceo in cold blood on December 7, 1896. Weyler denied charges about the manner of Maceo's death, but editorialists in the United States doubted his word. The *New York Times* wrote: "There is a multitude of circumstances confirmatory of the report that Maceo was invited to a parley by the Spaniards and murdered. Such a story would not be believed of the English or the French or the Germans. . . . It is believed of Weyler."[26]

Faced with unrelenting criticism, Spain recalled Weyler at the end of 1897, canceled the reconcentration program, and proclaimed a new policy of home rule with limited autonomy for Cuba. An "Autonomist" colonial government was formed in January 1898, following the lines of the liberal Autonomist Party, which had argued for twenty years that such reforms would prevent bloodshed and insurrection. But the Spanish gesture came too late, especially because Weyler had targeted Autonomists for imprisonment and deportation. In addition, the Spanish army's morale was low and its losses were crippling. Of the 200,000 Spanish troops deployed to the war, 11,000 had been wounded, 4,000 were killed in battle, and 41,000 died from dysentery, malaria, yellow fever, and other diseases.[27] Weyler's repressive tactics also stimulated broad support for the revolutionaries.

The new government gained little support from Spaniards on the island who had given up hope for a Spanish solution. The only viable solution they now envisioned was US intervention. Indeed, assessments of the war by both Madrid and Washington predicted that the rebels would likely win the war by the end of 1898.[28] Business leaders and property owners in Cuba also anticipated an insurgent victory and appealed to the United States either to annex Cuba or "to save us." "The Mother Country cannot protect us," declared a group of business leaders. "If left to the insurgents our property is lost."[29]

NOTES

1. José Martí, "To Manuel Mercado," trans. Eliana Loveluck, in *The Cuba Reader: The Making of a Revolutionary Society*, ed. Philip Brenner et al. (New York: Grove, 1988), 28–29.

2. D. R. Murray, "Statistics of the Slave Trade to Cuba, 1790–1867," *Journal of Latin American Studies* 3, no. 2 (1971): 134, http://latinamericanstudies.org/slavery/Cuba-slave-trade.pdf.

3. The 1842 census counted 1,037,624 inhabitants: 436,495 black slaves, 152,838 free blacks, and 448,291 whites. Philip S. Foner, *Antonio Maceo: The 'Bronze Titan' of Cuba's Struggle for Independence* (New York: Monthly Review Press, 1977), 10–11; Pérez, *Cuba*, 70–73, 80–82.

4. Quoted in Louis A. Pérez, Jr., *Cuba and the United States: Ties of Singular Intimacy* (Athens: University of Georgia Press, 1990), 42.

5. Pérez, *Cuba and the United States*, 50.

6. Pérez, *Cuba*, 94.

7. Quoted in Foner, *Antonio Maceo*, 15.

8. An alternate explanation of the derivation of the name is provided in Teresa Prados-Torreira, *Mambisas: Rebel Women in Nineteenth-Century Cuba* (Gainesville: University Press of Florida, 2005), 1. She attributes *mambisa* to the distortion by Spanish soldiers of a common Yoruba prefix, *mbi*.

9. Prados-Torreira, *Mambisas*, 151; K. Lynn Stoner, "Militant Heroines and the Consecration of the Patriarchal State: The Glorification of Loyalty, Combat, and National Suicide in the Making of Cuban National Identity," *Cuban Studies* 34 (2003): 92.

10. Quoted in Prados-Torreira, *Mambisas*, 84.

11. Patricia Weiss Fagen, "Antonio Maceo: Heroes, History, and Historiography," *Latin American Research Review* 11, no. 3 (1976).

12. Pérez, *Cuba*, 96–97.

13. Quoted in Foner. *Antonio Maceo*, 81.

14. For example, Fidel Castro Ruz, "Discurso En el Acto de Conmemoracion del Centenario de la Protesta de Baraguá, Santiago de Cuba," March 15, 1978, http://www.cuba.cu/gobierno/discursos/1978/esp/f150378e.html. Authors' translation.

15. Fagen, "Antonio Maceo," 71.

16. Foner, *Antonio Maceo*, 94–97.

17. Pérez, *Cuba*, 100, 107.

18. Pérez, *Cuba*, 101–3. There actually was an increase in total exports from $51 million in 1885 to $67 million in 1890, but the one-third increase in the value of exports masked systemic weaknesses in key sectors.

19. Pérez, *Cuba and the United States*, 60–61.

20. Pérez, *Cuba and the United States*, 62–63.

21. Jules Robert Benjamin, *The United States and Cuba: Hegemony and Dependent Development, 1880–1934* (Pittsburgh: University of Pittsburgh Press, 1977), 4.

22. Louis A. Pérez, Jr., *The War of 1898: The United States and Cuba in History and Historiography* (Chapel Hill: University of North Carolina Press, 1998), 7.

23. Pérez, *Cuba and the United States*, 81.

24. John Lawrence Tone, *War and Genocide in Cuba, 1895–1898* (Chapel Hill: University of North Carolina Press, 2006), 156–60, 184.

25. Pérez, *Cuba*, 130.

26. "Weyler's Denials," *New York Times*, December 16, 1896.

27. Tone, *War and Genocide in Cuba*, 9–10.

28. Pérez, *Cuba*, 139–40.

29. Quoted in Pérez, *Cuba*, 89.

Chapter 4

Cuban Independence War and US Occupation

When the revolution in Cuba broke out young [Adolfo] Rodríguez joined the insurgents, leaving his father and mother and two sisters at the farm. He was taken, in December of 1896, by a force of the Guardia Civil, the corps d'élite of the Spanish army, and defended himself when they tried to capture him, wounding three of them with his machete. He was tried by a military court for bearing arms against the government, and sentenced to be shot by a fusillade some morning before sunrise. . . . He made a picture of such pathetic helplessness, but of such courage and dignity, that he reminded me on the instant of that statue of Nathan Hale which stands in the City Hall Park, above the roar of Broadway. The Cuban's arms were bound, as are those of the statue, and he stood firmly, with his weight resting on his heels like a soldier on parade, and with his face held up fearlessly, as is that of the statue. But there was this difference, that Rodríguez, while probably as willing to give six lives for his country as was the American rebel, being only a peasant, did not think to say so, and he will not, in consequence, live in bronze during the lives of many men, but will be remembered only as one of thirty Cubans, one of whom was shot at Santa Clara on each succeeding day at sunrise.

—Richard Harding Davis[1]

US INTERVENTION IN THE CUBAN INDEPENDENCE WAR

Popular US sentiment to intervene in Cuba's independence war grew steadily in 1896. As the violence spread, and as Spain's powerlessness became more evident, US investors feared the economic result of a rebel victory. A fully independent Cuba seemed to be a serious threat to their investments, trade privileges, and dominance in the region. Yet the protection of property owned by US companies was not the only reason the United States was now inclining itself toward intervention.

Multiple Motivations for Intervention

In the 1890s, the United States underwent a series of debilitating shocks.[2] First, the 1890 US census reported the "frontier" no longer existed—settlements now occupied nearly all unclaimed land. The concept of the frontier had contributed to a common narrative that the United States was exceptional, a country of unbounded opportunity where individuals could succeed based on their own merits and self-reliance. The frontier also had served as an escape valve from the oppression of early industrialization, which delayed the formation of meaningful trade unions in the United States. Notably, the American Federation of Labor was founded at this time, in 1886, long after trade unions were active in Europe.

The closing of the frontier, only a generation after the Homestead Act had offered free land to anyone, had a psychologically demoralizing effect on the country. But the widespread foreclosure sales of the farms acquired by homesteaders were even more debilitating. Their outrage fueled the Populist Movement, which arose in this period. In part, the farmers' losses were due to the collusion of large banks, railroad companies, and an emerging agribusiness industry that had provided easy loans for seeds, machinery, and other supplies collateralized by the farms.

Debtors soon began demanding that the government reduce the value of their loans by inflating the US currency, circulating dollars that had no backing ("greenbacks") or that were backed by both silver and gold ("bimetallism"). At the same time, millions of factory workers had no escape valve when they lost their jobs during the economic depression that began in 1893, which was even more severe than the deep recession of the 1880s.[3] The country seemed as if it was on the verge of a revolution as striking workers battled company guards, police forces, and sometimes the national guard.

The collusion and greed of the new captains of industry provided an easy explanation for the economic chaos. A more complex analysis pointed to technological advances that had made US companies so efficient that they were producing more goods than could be consumed by the US market. The culprit of overproduction had validity and appealed to a group of political leaders who believed US greatness could be achieved only by expanding the country's influence globally. Their primary targets were markets in Asia.[4] This objective also seemed to provide a solution to the economic problems at home.

The Route to Asia Lies via Cuba

But US entry into Asia was blocked by the colonized outposts—such as India, Indonesia, and Indo-China—of European imperial powers who also had carved up China with closed deals. Of the remaining countries still available, the Philippines was the most desirable because Spain was having difficulty in suppressing an independence struggle there.[5] Coincidentally, Spain was having the same problem in Cuba.

Cuba itself had long appealed to dreamers of American expansion. Secretary of State John Quincy Adams famously asserted in 1823 that "there are laws of political as well as of physical gravitation; and if an apple severed by the tempest from its native tree cannot choose but fall to the ground, Cuba, forcibly disjoined from its own unnatural connection with Spain, and incapable of self-support, can gravitate only towards the North American Union."[6] Cubans disdainfully call his statement the "ripe fruit theory." Thomas Jefferson wrote to President James Monroe in 1824 that "I candidly confess, that I have ever looked on Cuba as the most interesting addition which could ever be made to our system of States."[7] William Henry Seward, Secretary of State from 1861 to 1869, reasoned that the United States should annex Cuba because "every rock and every grain of sand in that island were drifted and washed out from American soil by the floods of the Mississippi, and the other estuaries of the Gulf of Mexico."[8]

But President William McKinley was reluctant to engage with Spain and sought other ways to fix the lagging US economy. In part, he was concerned that the end of Spanish control over Cuba would create complications others had not foreseen.[9] Annexing Cuba was undesirable, McKinley thought, because the island's population was dominantly of African origin. Instead he supported Spanish rule and urged Spain both to end the insurrection quickly and to protect US property. He also urged the dismissal of General Weyler, an end to the abuses characteristic of Weyler's command, and home rule reforms.

As 1897 morphed into 1898, McKinley realized that Spain was losing the war in Cuba. In an attempt to forestall the inevitable, he dispatched the USS *Maine* to Cuba in January 1898 as a way to bolster flagging Spanish morale and as a warning to the rebels not to harm US citizens or property owned by US companies. The move came too late. Several US political leaders saw in the Cuban independence war an opportunity to demonstrate that the United States had reached the point where it could play a new world role, despite the depression.

The *Maine* Explodes

The *Maine* sailed into Havana harbor on January 25, 1898. In one of the most storied incidents in early US naval history, a blast ripped through the battleship three weeks later. Two hundred sixty-six sailors died. A 1975 US naval inquiry determined that the explosion was probably the result of "heat from a fire in the coal bunker adjacent to the 6-inch magazine," not an external source such as a Spanish mine.[10]

But in 1898, the theories and rumors about what had happened focused on Spain. The yellow journalism of William Randolph Hearst and Joseph Pulitzer's competing newspapers, which claimed that Spanish saboteurs had blown up the ship, fueled a burst of popular passion in the United States. Cries of "Remember the *Maine*" brought demands of US retaliation against Spain. Hearst's *New York Morning Journal* was the first paper in the United States to sell one million copies in one day—the day after the *Maine*'s explosion.[11] Figure 4.1 displays a depiction of Spaniards that would have been commonplace during this time period.

Figure 4.1. The July 9, 1898, issue of *Judge* was typical in the way it portrayed to a US audience the nature of Spain's cruelty in Cuba.

The anti-Spanish narrative followed naturally from depictions of Weyler's brutality and cartoons of Cuba as a damsel in distress who called for help from the United States. Pro-interventionists took up the cry, asserting that US intervention would be a noble and selfless action.[12] For those who also favored expansion into Asia, a war against Spain offered an opportunity to gain a foothold in Asia by taking advantage of Spain's declining fortunes in the Philippine Independence War.

McKinley responded to the *Maine* explosion by beefing up Admiral George Dewey's US Navy fleet in the Pacific and approved an order, issued originally by Assistant Navy Secretary Theodore Roosevelt, that if the United States declared war against Spain, Dewey should attack the Spanish fleet at Manila. After two months of unrelenting reports and editorials by the newspaper barons, and demands from members of Congress responding to the popular calls for retaliation, the president asked Congress for a declaration of war on April 11, 1898.

The resulting congressional debate lasted more than a week and revealed basic disagreements about US war aims. Some favored taking Cuba as a US territory. Notably, McKinley's war message made no reference to Cuban independence. Three groups opposed that position. One did not want a territory predominantly populated by blacks to seek statehood. A second objected to imperial interventions that seemed to mimic European practices. The third group in effect represented the US sugar beet industry, which feared competition from Cuban sugar if the island were annexed.[13] Their leader was Senator Henry M. Teller (D-CO), whose successful amendment to the war declaration prohibited the United States from exercising "sovereignty, jurisdiction, or control over said Island [Cuba] except for the pacification thereof," and asserted the US determination "to leave the government and control of the Island to its people" after pacification was achieved.

THE UNITED STATES DENIES INDEPENDENCE TO CUBA

"A Splendid Little War"

Despite passage of the Teller Amendment, US engagement in the conflict effectively stole Cuban independence from the Cubans. Consider how even the name commonly applied to the conflict in the United States, "Spanish-American War," disregards the role of Cubans and betrays an ignorance about the limited importance of the US contribution in securing victory against Spain. In Cuba, the conflict is called the Spanish–Cuban–North American conflict and is viewed as a continuation of the 1868 Cuban War of Independence.[14] As a parallel, imagine the US reaction if the French, because of their contributions to the victory over Britain in 1783, referred to the US War of Independence as the Franco-British War.

McKinley called for 125,000 volunteers to supplement the 30,000-person regular army. More than one million men answered the call. Ultimately, about 180,000 volunteers were mustered into service and received a scant few days of training. Theodore Roosevelt, one of the ardent advocates of the war, resigned his post at the Navy Department and received a commission as an army officer. Focusing on style along with substance as he gathered a fighting force, Roosevelt immediately placed an order with Brooks Brothers for an "ordinary cavalry lieutenant colonel's uniform in blue Cravenette."[15] Many of his recruits were Native Americans and cowboys from South Dakota, Oklahoma, New Mexico, and Arizona, along with personal friends from New York's high society.

Roosevelt dubbed his 1,060-member unit the "Rough Riders" (officially it was the 1st United States Volunteer Cavalry). "In all the world," he wrote, "there could be no better material for soldiers than that afforded by these grim of the mountains, these wild rough riders of the plains."[16] In fact, like most members of the expeditionary army, the Rough Riders were poorly trained and equipped. Fewer than three-quarters of the original group set off for Cuba, and many arrived without horses, which could not be accommodated on the boats.

While the future president made sure he would receive good press, a balanced look at the record showed that Roosevelt did not wage his battles brilliantly. In the famous charge up "San Juan Hill"—it actually occurred on Kettle Hill in the San Juan Mountains—Roosevelt ignored warnings from a few Cuban fighters with him that Spanish scouts had spotted them. They were lucky to escape alive, thanks to the poor aim of Spanish rifles and the arrival of reinforcements who brought rapid-fire Gatling guns. The Gatlings wreaked havoc against the Spanish forces, discharging 18,000 rounds in less than nine minutes.

The US military involvement did not last long; the Spanish were essentially routed by July 1898. US warships ran Spain's four best battleships aground in Santiago harbor as they tried to flee, and the city fell to US troops two weeks later. Though a ceasefire would not take effect until August 12, US Secretary of State John Hay wrote to Roosevelt from London on July 27, "It has been a splendid little war; begun with the highest motives, carried on with magnificent intelligence and spirit, favored by that Fortune which loves the brave."[17]

In fact, "splendid" was far from an accurate characterization of the conflict. During the three-month campaign, US soldiers suffered 385 battle deaths,

2,061 deaths from other causes (mainly from yellow fever and malaria), and 1,662 wounded. During the three years of fighting from 1895 to 1898, more than 60,000 Spanish soldiers died. Cuban deaths and injuries in the thirty years of independence wars from 1868 to 1898 remain uncertain, though it is likely that several thousand were killed in battle and hundreds of thousands died because of the problems caused by conflict. One-third of the generals in the Cuban Liberation Army died. As an indication of deaths alone, Cuba's population in 1868 was 1.8 million; in 1898, it was 1.5 million. An 1899 count found that one of every two wives in Cuba was a widow.[18]

US Occupation Follows the Treaty of Paris

The war ended with a US-Spanish treaty that Cuba did not sign. The United States and Spain excluded Cuban representatives from the negotiations in Paris and even from the signing ceremony on December 10, 1898. The Treaty of Paris provided for the formal surrender of Spanish sovereignty over Cuba to the United States on January 1, 1899. The US attitude toward the Cubans remained exactly what it had been during the war—contempt toward their national aspirations for Cuba's full independence and sovereignty. The first US military governor of Cuba, General John Brooke, made that explicit. Cubans "cannot *now*, or I believe in the immediate future, be entrusted with their own government."[19] A *New York Times* news story reported that "the Cubans who have made a pretense of fighting with us have proved worthless in the field and unappreciative of modern conditions and humanity and justice in war. It would be a tragedy, a crime, to deliver the island into their hands." The article's headline was, "Cubans Not Fit to Govern."[20]

NOTES

1. Richard Harding Davis, *The Death of Rodriguez, A Year from a Reporter's Note Book* (New York: Harper & Brothers, 1897).

2. Key points in this subsection are drawn from Walter LaFeber, *The New Empire: An Interpretation of American Expansion, 1860–1898* (Ithaca, NY: Cornell University Press, 1963), 63–72, 176–203, 379–406.

3. The national unemployment rate went from 3.7 percent in 1892 to 8.1 percent in 1893 and 12.3 percent in 1894. See Christina Romer, "Spurious Volatility in Historical Unemployment Data," *Journal of Political Economy* 94, no. 1 (February 1986): 31.

4. Richard H. Immerman, *Empire for Liberty: A History of American Imperialism from Benjamin Franklin to Paul Wolfowitz* (Princeton: Princeton University Press, 2010), chapters 3–4.

5. Richard Hofstadter, "Cuba, the Philippines and Manifest Destiny," in *The Paranoid Style in American Politics and Other Essays* (Chicago: University of Chicago Press, 1965), 147–48.

6. John Quincy Adams, "Letter to Hugh Nelson, April 28, 1823," in *Writings of John Quincy Adams*, ed. Worthington Chauncey Ford (New York: Macmillan, 1913), vol. 7, 373.

7. Thomas Jefferson, "Letter to James Monroe, October 24, 1824," in *The Writings of Thomas Jefferson*, ed. Andrew A. Lipscomb (Washington, DC: The Thomas Jefferson Memorial Association, 1904), vol. 15, 479.

8. As quoted in Walter LaFeber, *The American Age: United States Foreign Policy at Home and Abroad Since 1750*, second edition (New York: Norton, 1989), 144.

9. Louis A. Pérez, Jr., *Cuba between Empires, 1878–1902* (Pittsburgh: University of Pittsburgh Press, 1983), 170–74; LaFeber, *The American Age*, 185–90.

10. Hyman George Rickover, *How the Battleship Maine Was Destroyed* (Washington, DC: Department of the Navy, 1976), 128, http://babel.hathitrust.org/cgi/pt?id=m dp.39015004705649;view=1up;seq=7.

11. Lars Schoultz, *That Infernal Little Cuban Republic: The United States and the Cuban Revolution* (Chapel Hill: University of North Carolina Press, 2009), 17.

12. Pérez, *Cuba between Empires*, 138.

13. Carmen Diana Deere, "Here Come the Yankees! The Rise and Decline of United States Colonies in Cuba, 1898–1930," *Hispanic American Historical Review* 78, no. 4 (November 1998): 732.

14. Carlos Alzugaray Treto, "Is Normalization Possible in Cuban-US Relations after 100 Years of History?" Research Report no. 6 (Havana: Instituto Superior de Relaciones Internacionales, 2002), https://www.ecured.cu/Guerra_de_los_Diez_A%C3%B1os.

15. LaFeber, *The American Age*, 194.

16. Theodore Roosevelt, *The Rough Riders* (New York: G. P. Putnam's Sons, 1900), 24.

17. Letter from John Hay to Theodore Roosevelt, July 27, 1898; reprinted in *Scribner's Magazine* 66 (July–December 1919), 533, https://play.google.com/books/reader?id=peU-AQAAMAAJ&printsec=frontcover&output=reader&hl=en&p g=GBS.PA533.

18. Pérez, *To Die in Cuba*, 79.

19. Quoted in Louis A. Pérez, Jr., *Cuba in the American Imagination* (Chapel Hill: University of North Carolina Press, 2008), 114 [emphasis in original].

20. Stanhope Sams, "Cubans Not Fit to Govern; This Is the Opinion of an Observer Who Accompanied Shafter's Army to Santiago," *New York Times*, July 29, 1898, 4.

Chapter 5

From Occupation to "Good Neighbor"

Whereas the Congress of the United States of America, by an Act approved March 2, 1901, provided as follows:

[T]he President is hereby authorized to "leave the government and control of the island of Cuba to its people" so soon as a government shall have been established in said island under a constitution which, either as a part thereof or in an ordinance appended thereto, shall define the future relations of the United States with Cuba, substantially as follows:

That the government of Cuba consents that the United States may exercise the right to intervene for the preservation of Cuban independence, the maintenance of a government adequate for the protection of life, property, and individual liberty, and for discharging the obligations with respect to Cuba imposed by the treaty of Paris on the United States, now to be assumed and undertaken by the government of Cuba.

That to enable the United States to maintain the independence of Cuba, and to protect the people thereof, as well as for its own defense, the government of Cuba will sell or lease to the United States lands necessary for coaling or naval stations at certain specified points to be agreed upon with the President of the United States.

—Platt Amendment (excerpts)

US OCCUPATION

Preparing Cuba for US Economic Domination

With the rationale that the Cubans had to be instructed in the ways of "civilization," US colonial administrators established Cuba's rules of commerce, remarking that "we are dealing with a race that has steadily been going down for a hundred years and into which we have to infuse new life, new principles and new methods of doing things."[1]

The resulting policy was the opposite of independence, wrote one Cuban economist. Rather it was intended to prepare Cuba for US "economic penetration."[2] The US military government ordered the Cuban Liberation Army to disarm and the provisional government and Cuban Revolutionary Party to disband. It mandated that a newly elected assembly could not make laws that contravened US military decisions.

US corporations readily took advantage of the opportunity that the occupation provided, expanding their investments in sugar, tobacco, and land.[3] Approximately 13,000 people from the United States had acquired land titles by 1905. US individuals owned 60 percent of Cuba's rural land; Cubans owned 25 percent. Foreign capital flooded Cuba, and favored US-owned operations, driving Cubans further out of business. Iron mines in Oriente Province were almost all US owned.

Opponents of the US occupation in Congress soon demanded an end to the US presence as specified in the 1898 Teller Amendment, while the Cubans themselves called for US troops to leave. Meanwhile the McKinley administration accepted plans for a new Cuban constitution to be written by an elected assembly, but sought continued control by designating a list of acceptable candidates who could be chosen. In the election to create a constituent assembly in 1900, Cuban voters refused to select the US candidates and instead chose an independent slate to draft the new constitution.

US officials said the election proved their point of view that Cubans were irresponsible and unfit for self-government. General Leonard Wood, the US military governor, said those chosen to write the constitution were among the "worst agitators and political radicals in Cuba."[4] The result was an impasse in which opponents of Cuban annexation continued to pressure for withdrawal, while administration officials in Washington agreed with business leaders that US departure would threaten US property interests and influence.

The Platt Amendment

Secretary of War Elihu Root, a former Wall Street lawyer, crafted a seeming compromise that would adhere to the requirements of the Teller Amendment but vitiate the essence of Cuban independence. Senator Orville Platt (R-CT) added Root's clever loophole as an amendment to an army appropriation bill that Congress passed in 1901.

The Platt Amendment stipulated, among other things, that the United States could intervene in Cuba to restore order whenever it saw fit; that Cuba lease territory to the United States for up to three naval coaling stations; and that

Cuba could not enter into a treaty that offered a military base to any other country. The legislation also required Cuba to include the amendment in its new constitution as a condition for the end of US occupation.

Cubans staged demonstrations in Havana and Santiago to protest the Platt Amendment. The constituent assembly rejected its inclusion in the new Cuban constitution by a 14–2 vote. Members of the assembly, however, changed their minds after they sent a delegation to Washington to meet with US officials. Root, calling the Cubans "ingrates," was adamant that the US occupation would not end unless Cuba acquiesced.[5] Other US officials echoed his position, telling the Cuban delegation that if the Platt Amendment was not included in Cuba's constitution, the United States would not grant freedom to Cuba. Despite such a seemingly firm US stance, the constituent assembly approved including the Platt Amendment in the new Cuban constitution by only one vote.

US cynicism and insincerity outraged Cubans. The amendment mocked terms such as "liberty" and "independence," even though Platt asserted in a 1901 article that with his codicil "the United States set a high and new example to the nations of the world and gave a mighty impetus to the cause of free government."[6] He argued that the United States, in his estimation, became the first conquering nation in history to relinquish territory without giving up responsibility for those whom it had conquered. More candidly—until May 9, 2017—in its official history, the US State Department acknowledged that the real goal of the Platt Amendment was to deny effective independence to Cuba:

> The rationale behind the Platt Amendment was straightforward. The United States Government had intervened in Cuba in order to safeguard its significant commercial interests on the island in the wake of Spain's inability to preserve law and order. . . . By directly incorporating the requirements of the Platt Amendment into the Cuban constitution, the McKinley Administration was able to shape Cuban affairs without violating the Teller Amendment.[7]

Roosevelt's rise to power was one of the most meteoric in US history up to that time, and closely meshed with US plans for Cuba. As assistant secretary of the navy in 1897 and 1898, he had advocated a new role for the United States in the world and promoted war with Spain. Within months of his vaunted charge at the head of the Rough Riders, he was elected governor of New York. He served two years of his term, then won the vice presidency on November 6, 1900, as President McKinley's running mate. When McKinley died from an assassin's gunshot wounds on September 14, 1901, Roosevelt, at the age of forty-two, became the youngest person ever to be president of the United States.

THE PSEUDO-REPUBLIC

A "Special Relationship" with the United States

The US occupation formally ended on May 20, 1902, a date the new Cuban government designated as "independence day" and which is still recognized as such today by some Cuban-Americans and the US government. Yet the departing troops left Cuba with only limited possibilities for self-determination. US military and economic interests would continue to govern the fortunes of the island for the next half century. Generations of Cubans would look to the Platt Amendment as an example of US duplicity that would justify their distrust of the United States a century later. While President McKinley's prediction would prove true—Cuba and the United States would develop a "special relationship" with "ties of singular intimacy"—each country interpreted the significance of his forecast in ways that were polar opposites.

For North Americans, Cuba became a neo-colony, a superficially sovereign country whose politics were controlled by the White House, US Congress, and US ambassador, and whose economic fortunes were controlled by US companies. Within months of Tomás Estrada Palma's inauguration as the first president of Cuba, on May 20, 1902, he signed a reciprocal trade treaty with the United States under which Cuban sugar and tobacco exports to the United States received a 20 percent tariff reduction, and 497 categories of US products exported to Cuba received tariff reductions that ranged from 20 to 40 percent.[8] Thus began "independent" Cuba's "special relationship" with the United States. The preferential tariff for Cuban sugar essentially linked Cuba's main source of export earnings to a single buyer, the United States, and the treaty opened the doors exclusively to US corporations to sell agricultural and manufactured goods to Cuba at such low prices that they were able to stifle the development of Cuban enterprises. The course of events gave life to Martí's admonition that Cuba needed to develop its own infrastructure: "The nation that buys, commands. The nation that sells, serves. . . . Only a nation that wishes to die will sell to a single nation. . . . The excessive influence of one nation on the commerce of another is quickly transformed into political influence."[9]

For Cubans, the "special relationship" led to a transformation of its culture. A new elite emerged, based on its members' connections to North America. They sent their children to US universities and even high schools so that they subsequently could take up management positions with US companies on the island. As the Americanization of Cuba took hold in the twentieth century, baseball became the national pastime, the use of US products conveyed a sense of higher status, and soon anything American was deemed better than anything Cuban.[10]

While some Cubans heralded Estrada Palma's assumption of the presidency as the official end to the four-year US occupation, others protested the legitimacy of his election. Key leaders of the 1895–1898 struggle—notably General Máximo Gómez—refused to be candidates for the presidency on grounds that the ballot had been rigged by the United States. There was evidence for that charge: Governor-General Leonard Wood had appointed a majority of the electoral commission that set the rules for the balloting and then designated Estrada Palma as the preferred candidate.

The new president had been an early independence leader and briefly even the president of the rebel government during the Ten-Year War. He had been living in exile for almost three decades, working as a schoolteacher in New York, though he also was a member of the Cuban Revolutionary Party and helped to obtain guns and ammunition for the fighters.

Unlike Martí, though, Estrada Palma had become a naturalized US citizen. He accepted the Platt Amendment's legitimacy and pledged that US troops would be welcome to return if they were needed to maintain order. Educated at Columbia University, Estrada Palma was a member of the Cuban bicultural elite who traveled freely and easily between the island and the United States.[11] As journalist Richard Gott notes, "American intervention in Cuban affairs was not an insult for such people; they welcomed it, and often requested it."[12]

Such members of the Cuban elite, along with North Americans who had settled in the country and others who obtained semipermanent residency status because of their commercial interests, fully expected that the Roosevelt administration would provide a safe climate for them. US corporations and citizens were coming to the country in increasing numbers, and they saw no way to guarantee their investments without the security umbrella a potential US intervention provided.

A Kleptocracy Emerges

Cuba under Estrada Palma amounted to a kleptocracy. While he was able to assuage the fears of US investors, the new president established a climate of corruption. The public payroll expanded by thousands as senior members of the new government used public funds for patronage as a way to build their own fiefdoms. Estrada Palma knew that staying in office meant maintaining strong, positive ties with the United States, and US companies assumed primary control over banking, land development, and construction. For example, the North American Trust Company of New York, which had been the fiscal agent for the US occupation forces, reorganized itself as Cuba's Central Bank.

In July 1903, Estrada Palma signed a treaty with the United States that paved the way for the construction of the Guantánamo Bay Naval Base in southeastern Cuba. Six months later, on December 10, 1903, he stood with Roosevelt at the ceremony marking the formal transfer of control over the base to the United States.[13] But no other high-ranking Cubans attended.

Cubans close to Estrada Palma, meanwhile, were not the only ones taking advantage of the friendly business climate and largesse of the new government. By 1905, 13,000 North Americans had acquired titles to land in Cuba. Five years later, US companies and individuals owned about 60 percent of all available rural properties on the island.[14]

In 1900, a group of US and Canadian corporate moguls formed the Cuba Company to undertake the largest foreign investment project in Cuban history, a 350-mile rail line between Santa Clara and Santiago. Based in New Jersey because of the state's lax restrictions on corporations, the firm was the brainchild of Sir William Cornelius Van Horne, a Canadian railroad baron who recruited other wealthy investors, including former Secretary of State William R. Day, US railroad tycoon E. H. Harriman, and Levi Morton, a former governor of New York.[15] The Cuba Company acquired thousands of acres of land on the Santa Clara-Santiago route and around railroad stations. By 1915, the Cuba Company was the largest single foreign investor and largest company in the country. Historian Juan Santamarina asserts that by forging informal networks among US and Cuban businessmen and government officials, it established "the framework for US investment in Cuba that fundamentally influenced Cuba's economic, political, and social development."[16]

Spanish émigrés also were active in the rush to Cuba. The population of white Spaniards tripled between 1899 and 1920, from about 100,000 to 300,000. New investments by US companies, particularly in eastern Oriente Province, attracted those from poorer, rural areas of Spain with the hope of jobs and even property ownership. One typical Spaniard who came to Cuba during the period was Ángel Castro, who fought for the Spanish in the Independence War, then returned to his home in Galicia.[17]

When he came back to Cuba around 1904, he first worked as a laborer for the United Fruit Company and then took out a loan to establish a midsized plantation in Oriente. Castro had two children with his first wife, fell in love with a young servant, Lina Ruz Gonzalez, and had seven children with her, including three sons: Ramón, born in 1924; Fidel, in 1926; and Raúl, in 1931.[18]

As foreigners bought land, the remnants of the original Cuban landowning class—the criollas—were overshadowed by the foreigners' presence and tended to fall into line with US economic control. It was the final step in ceding political and economic power and Cuban sovereignty to interests totally enmeshed with the United States.

While Estrada Palma had taken office as a nonpartisan, he soon aligned himself with the more conservative Republican Party and used their control of local politics throughout the country to protect his chances for reelection. Together Estrada Palma and the Republicans proved more adept at voter fraud than their opponents, the National Liberal Party, and the Republicans established a majority in Cuba's first congressional elections, held in February 1904.

Fraud was also widespread in Estrada Palma's successful and unopposed reelection bid in 1905. The Liberals were so outmatched that they withdrew from the balloting. They then organized a 4,000-member army and a Central Revolutionary Committee dedicated to overthrowing the Estrada Palma government.

The Liberals began the revolt in August 1906 with a series of small attacks as they marched toward Havana. The Cuban army of only 3,000 troops was unable to quell the insurrection, and Estrada Palma asked the United States to intervene under the Platt Amendment. President Roosevelt, however, had to contend with opposition at home to what was being called gunboat diplomacy, and he hesitated to intervene.

Instead, the president dispatched Secretary of War William Howard Taft, whom Roosevelt was already promoting as his successor, and instructed him to find a political compromise to end the spreading Liberal revolt. In private, Roosevelt railed: "I am so angry with that infernal little Cuban republic that I would like to wipe its people off the face of the earth. All that we wanted was that they should behave themselves. . . . And now, lo and behold . . . we have no alternative [but] to intervene."[19]

US TROOPS RETURN TO CUBA

Magoon's "Reforms"

By September 21, 1906, Taft had determined that Estrada Palma could not withstand the rebellion, that negotiations were futile, and that military intervention was the only alternative. The Cuban president resigned on September 28, and Roosevelt sent the first 2,000 of an eventual 5,000-member US occupation force that would remain on the island for three years. Today Estrada Palma's tenure in office is reviled in Cuba. A statue that had commemorated his presidency was toppled from its pedestal and carted away after the 1959 Cuban revolution.

Once the reluctant decision had been made, the United States moved to assume full economic and political control of the island. Roosevelt chose Charles Magoon as the new governor general. Magoon was a lawyer and diplomat who had served as the colonial governor of the recently acquired Panama Canal Zone, and Roosevelt viewed him as an adept administrator. With a charge from Roosevelt to clean up Cuba, Magoon ousted both the ministry officials who had benefited most from cronyism under Estrada Palma and the Republican

Party government bureaucracy. Members of the Liberal Party took their place and received key patronage jobs of their own. Magoon, meanwhile, expanded the size of the army, established a professional civil service, and initiated major public works programs, including a road expansion program.

Yet Cubans today characterize Magoon as a master of US treachery and domination. While he carried out Roosevelt's policies without benefiting himself—unlike many other Americans—during his three-year rule there was no semblance of self-determination in Cuba. Under Magoon's direction, the 1908 election led to the victory of Liberals José Miguel Gómez as president and Alfredo Zayas as vice president. The two had withdrawn from the 1905 election after objecting to corruption and violence during the campaign, and their rise to power comforted US officials. Satisfied that he had reformed the government and created a new system friendlier than ever to US interests, President Taft withdrew the occupation forces in 1909.

US corporations fared even better than Liberal Party operatives during the occupation—they won broad concessions for doing business on the island, including subsidies for US-owned Cuban businesses. This changing landscape of Cuba's economy also affected Cuban values. As was often the case under colonial rule, so too under neocolonialism, people in the dependent country shaped their aspirations in accord with the mother country. Cuban tastes also began to reflect those of the United States as US-based companies determined the architecture of new buildings, wealthy Americans defined what passed for high fashion, and even popular foods began to reflect the preferences of North Americans.[20]

Sugar Reinforces Neo-Colonization

Above all other ties, the Cuban sugar industry was the dominant factor in US planning, decision-making, and economic and political influence. The largest sugar producer, the Cuba Cane Sugar Company, was founded in 1915 by US bankers who were eager to profit from the shortages created by World War I. The company's investors came into the business at the right time—the price of sugar increased more than 600 percent in five years, from three cents to twenty cents per pound during World War I.

The Cuba Cane Sugar Company and its competitors were regulated by US-dominated Cuban officials. While the Cuban government formally organized the hiring for the sugar mills, the survival of both the mills and the workers depended on decisions made in Washington. To protect domestic cane and beet sugar owners, the United States had established a quota on imported sugar that determined how much and under what terms foreign sugar could be sold.

Moreover, sugar was produced in *centrales*, essentially company towns that fostered vertical integration, which gave a company total control over the lives of sugar workers. It also gave sugar companies an incentive to seek cooperative arrangements with other major industries. Before long, US bankers and industrialists were running interlocking companies in Cuba, sat on the boards of more than one company, and effectively controlled most aspects of Cuba's economy. Successive Cuban governments, as well as the US occupation authorities, also had granted so much control of iron mining on the island to US firms that they owned nearly all the mines. All of Cuba's railroad companies had a majority US ownership and interlocking directorates with key US financial institutions. A hallmark of Cuba's economy—tobacco—also fell under US domination. The Tobacco Trust, a New Jersey–based corporation, controlled 90 percent of Cuba's cigar and cigarette business after 1902.[21]

With the flood of US investments, there was little chance for the development of a homegrown manufacturing sector in Cuba. North Americans determined what Cuba would produce, and they did not want the island's products competing with those made in the United States. Their decisions insured that the Cuban economy would remain underdeveloped as a monoculture dependent on sugar exports to the United States.

Indeed, the US sugar quota determined the health of Cuba's economy and the survival of workers well beyond the sugar industry, and US politics became a key factor in Cuban development. For example, Cuba had the potential of developing a commercial tomato and catsup business for domestic consumption and even export. But the island was forced to import both the fruit and the manufactured product from the United States in order to placate members of the US Congress representing farming districts.

The system worked well enough to avoid widespread opposition only as long as sugar was in demand at a decent price. That was the situation for a seven-year period starting with World War I, when sugar beets were unavailable. Cane sugar prices rose from 1.9 cents per pound in 1914 to 22.5 cents in 1920, a year dubbed "the dance of the millions." But within months of its zenith, the market plummeted back to old levels, below four cents per pound, which led to the collapse of the Cuban banking system in June 1921.[22]

THE RISE OF THE MACHADO DICTATORSHIP

Depression in the Early 1920s

Alfredo Zayas had been elected president seven months earlier on a platform that opposed US intervention. But his opponent disputed the election's validity, throwing the government into a stalemate. It was precisely the kind of circumstance that previously had led the United States to intervene, and in January 1921 President Woodrow Wilson dispatched General Enoch H. Crowder to Havana aboard the USS *Minnesota*.[23] But Wilson ordered him not to intervene. Instead, Crowder took on the role of mediator to help resolve the election dispute. He then stayed in Cuba another two years as US ambassador and de facto consul general. Crowder effectively ruled over President Zayas, who was powerless in the face of the financial disaster, and even named the key government ministers.

With nearly all of its banks failing, Cuba was forced to seek emergency help from US financial institutions, but they refused. Reluctantly Cuba turned to the US government, which provided a major loan under terms that enabled US banks and investors to gain further control of the island's affairs.

Meanwhile, the economic turmoil caused many Cubans to lose their jobs, and those who still had employment faced rising prices on food and most goods. The loss of revenue brought even more unemployment as government shortfalls forced cuts in patronage jobs. As a result, trade unions gained strength and worker militancy increased in the early 1920s.[24]

In 1922, students at the University of Havana began to engage in political action. Taking inspiration from students at Argentina's University of Córdoba, they demanded autonomy for the university, the removal of corrupt professors, and an end to US intervention. After students took over the university forcibly in 1923, Zayas gave in to most of their demands, and the government gave official recognition to the Federation of University Students (FEU is the Spanish acronym). Julio Antonio Mella, head of the FEU, became a founder of the Cuban Communist Party in 1925. At the same time, calls for suffrage from a nascent women's movement grew more fervent and crystallized in the first meeting of the National Congress of Women in 1923.[25]

Although Zayas had inherited the economic recession and the rampant government corruption, Cubans blamed him for the continuation of hard times. In the 1924 general elections, they turned to Gerardo Machado y Morales, a man of few political accomplishments though a wily self-promoter. He had been a minor general in the Cuban War for Independence, mayor of Santa Clara, and a government minister. But in the preceding quarter century, he also had found ways to become wealthy, owning two newspapers, a bank, a sugar mill, and a construction company. These credentials assuaged concerns US officials might have had about his campaign "platform of regeneration."

Enter the "Tropical Mussolini"

Machado pledged to restore the economy, to build schools and roads, to expand social services, and to replace patronage with a modern civil service. In fact, he did attempt to promote new industries and to diversify agricultural production, and he enacted a tariff law that provided protection that domestic businesses had sought. He also initiated major construction projects that reduced unemployment in between sugar harvests—including a new building in Havana for the seat of government that replicates Paris's Pantheon and bears a resemblance to the US Capitol. Yet the overall economy still depended on sugar, a weak pillar on which to base recovery and growth. Although Cuba attracted an increasing number of Prohibition-era US tourists who could satisfy their thirst with the island's rum, the low price for sugar brought a depression to Cuba even before the 1929 Wall Street stock market crash.[26]

Cuban presidents, like those throughout Latin America at the time, were limited to one term in office. But Machado had dictatorial ambitions and initially sought to extend his term of office by two years without a new election. The Cuban Congress wavered in deciding among several constitutional proposals to change the presidential term, and finally approved a new process that would create a single six-year term for the president and allow Machado to run for the office in 1928.

Given the state of the economy, Machado sought to avoid a meaningful campaign. Under the banner of *cooperativismo*, the "tropical Mussolini"—as student leader Mella called him—relied on ties he created between business and government to maneuver the Liberal and Republican parties to nominate him so that he could be elected by acclamation. At the same time, he gained support from US investors by pushing a law through the Cuban Congress that allowed the foreign entities dominating Cuba's electricity and transportation companies to seize land and property from both the Cuban state and private citizens for the purpose of expanding services.[27]

But then calamity struck. The US economic depression hit Cuba especially hard. Consider that from 1929 to 1932 annual sugar earnings declined from $200 million to $40 million. When demonstrations escalated and turned violent in 1930, Machado responded with waves of attacks on the protesters. Meanwhile, behind the demonstrators, a new generation of leaders organized the University Student Directory (DEU is the Spanish acronym) and plotted to oust Machado along with what they viewed as his illegitimate government.

Original members of the DEU—later nicknamed the "Generation of 1930"—included Carlos Prío Socarrás (Cuban president from 1948 to 1952), Raúl Roa Kouri (foreign minister from 1959 to 1976), and Eduardo Chíbas (founder of the Ortodoxo Party and a mentor to Fidel Castro). As a physiology professor at the University of Havana, Ramón Grau San Martín (Cuban president from 1944 to 1948) was not eligible to join the DEU but served as an adviser.[28]

THE 1933 REVOLUTION

"Good Neighbor" Intervention

Cuba's political turmoil was occurring just as US policy toward Latin America was changing. Shortly after his election in 1928, President-elect Herbert Hoover began a two-month tour of the region. Aimed at recasting the unfavorable image that the United States had acquired during the prior thirty years of intervention, he frequently used the term "good neighbor."[29]

President Franklin Delano Roosevelt picked up the theme in his first inaugural address, pledging to "dedicate this Nation to the policy of the good neighbor—the neighbor who resolutely respects himself and, because he does so, respects the rights of others—the neighbor who respects his obligations and respects the sanctity of his agreements in and with a world of neighbors."[30] The new US policy gave hope to Machado's opponents that Roosevelt was sincere and would not invoke the Platt Amendment to intervene.

But US investors, who watched Cuba's economic collapse and dysfunctional government wreak havoc on their profits, pressured the new American leader through their high-level access. Two members of Roosevelt's informal group of academic advisers, the "Brain Trust," had been president and vice president of the American Molasses Company, which had holdings in Cuba. A third member was on the company's board of directors. Three of the president's cabinet nominees also had various connections to companies with economic interests in Cuba.[31]

Machado's brutality provided an additional impetus for intervention. Roosevelt confidant Sumner Welles reported that it involved daily occurrences of "governmental murder and clandestine assassination."[32] Yet Roosevelt was determined not to send in troops. With a regionwide meeting scheduled for late 1933, Roosevelt wanted to avoid a repeat of the criticism Latin Americans had heaped on the United States at a 1928 conference. Instead he sent Welles as ambassador extraordinary and plenipotentiary to Cuba. Arriving in May 1933, the new envoy sought to calm the waters by offering Machado some "friendly advice"—restore constitutional rule and resign as president.[33] Machado refused to budge.

Welles persisted with his efforts at "mediation," encouraging the established moderate opposition and some minor groups to challenge Machado. The dictator responded by ending press censorship and pushing a general amnesty law through the Cuban Congress. But he refused to resign and widespread protests continued. In July 1933, after police bloodied striking Havana bus drivers, sympathy strikes began to erupt. The next month these escalated into a paralyzing general strike. Welles's patience had run out. He threatened that the United States would cease to recognize the legitimacy of the Cuban government and demanded Machado step down.[34] As a replacement Welles proposed Cuba's recently resigned ambassador to Mexico, Carlos Manuel de Céspedes y Quesada, a man well known in Washington as a reliable ally of US business interests.[35] An apolitical diplomat and son of the 1868 revolutionary Carlos Manuel de Céspedes, Welles's choice was innocuous enough to be palatable to all sides.[36]

With the United States having discarded the pretense of being a neutral mediator, army generals opted to abandon Machado, ousting him in a coup d'etat on August 12. Welles then maneuvered behind the scenes for the military to name Céspedes as secretary of state and then for the Cuban Congress to amend the constitution, making the secretary of state the interim president in case of a vacancy. Céspedes was sworn in as Cuba's new leader on August 13.

The US press hailed him as Cuba's savior and praised Welles for his skillful diplomacy. But Céspedes had little legitimacy inside Cuba. Unaffiliated with a party, he had no political base. He also retained Machado's discredited 1928 constituent assembly and he offered no program for meaningful change. Within a month, a group of unlikely revolutionaries had deposed him from the presidency.

The One-Hundred-Day Government

Late on September 3, sergeants, corporals, and enlistees stationed at Camp Columbia, a base outside Havana, met to finalize a list of grievances against their senior officers—better pay, increased opportunities for promotion, and better living conditions. When the officers in charge dismissed the demands out of hand, members of this "Sergeants' Revolt" grew even angrier. Seizing control of the camp, they arrested their former superiors and by the end of September 4 controlled all of Havana's military garrisons. Their insurrection quickly spread to all the bases throughout the island.

As news of the mutiny leaked out early on September 4, DEU leaders rushed to Camp Columbia, imploring the mutineers to expand their narrow demands into a revolt against the Céspedes government. Faced with the likelihood of severe punishments by the government if they allowed it to stay in power, the soldiers joined forces with the civilians to topple Céspedes, who closed down the provisional government on September 5. Five days later, the coalition established a ruling junta and named Grau San Martín president of the provisional revolutionary government. It was now backed by the military under the direction of Fulgencio Batista, one of the Sergeants' Revolt leaders.[37]

The revolutionary government drew up a new constitution that included many of the political reforms the DEU had advocated in its "Manifesto-

Program to the Cuban People."[38] It also enacted land reforms that limited the size of the farm a family could own, labor reforms that included an eight-hour workday and a minimum wage, and a law that required at least 50 percent of the workers of any company to be Cuban.

Implementing such far-reaching plans was easier said than done. The Grau government lacked internal cohesion because the single cause that united the DEU and the military had been their opposition to Machado. Meanwhile, Washington refused to recognize the government and sent warships off the Cuban coast, stopping just short of intervention. When Roosevelt denied Welles's request for troops, the ambassador began a relentless campaign of subversion. Reinforced by US nonrecognition of the government, he pressured moderates to refuse negotiations with Grau, encouraged former senior military officers to boycott the army, and wooed Batista away from the coalition. Vice President Antonio Guiteras, an ardent anti-imperialist, derided the deserters as "servants" of the United States.[39]

In one of its final acts of defiance, the government nationalized the Cuban Electric Company, which was owned by General Electric through several subsidiaries such as American and Foreign Power, and two mills owned by the Cuban American Sugar Corporation.[40] Then, on January 15, 1934, Grau and the members of his 100-day regime resigned. Batista chose Colonel Carlos Mendieta to be the new president. But the wily sergeant was the principal player the Roosevelt administration trusted and through whom it reasserted US direction over Cuban politics during the next six years. Notably, Roosevelt was not the only North American who found Batista to be a useful ally. In 1933, the former sergeant held his first meeting with Meyer Lansky, the American mobster who viewed Cuba as a future home for his growing nefarious enterprises.

As a gesture of good neighborliness, Roosevelt then abrogated the hated Platt Amendment. But his administration negotiated a new agreement for the 45-square-mile Guantánamo naval base. Under the original accord, the United States could lease the base for 99 years. The 1934 pact provided for a lease that could be held in perpetuity, or until *both* sides agreed to end it.[41] Each year, the United States sends Cuba a check of about $4,000 in payment on the lease. The Cuban government cashed the first check in 1959, but since then it has refused to do so, not wanting to legitimate US occupation of the territory. The funds are held in an escrow account at a New York bank.

NOTES

1. Lars Schoultz, *Beneath the United States: A History of US Policy toward Latin America* (Cambridge: Harvard University Press, 1998), 145.

2. Le Riverend, *Economic History of Cuba*, 206.

3. Pérez, *Cuba*, 156–59; Benjamin, *The United States and Cuba*, 9–10.

4. Pérez, *Cuba*, 145–46.

5. Pérez, *Cuba*, 149.

6. Orville H. Platt, "The Pacification of Cuba," *Independent*, June 27, 1901.

7. Office of the Historian, US State Department, "MILESTONES: 1899–1913: The United States, Cuba, and the Platt Amendment, 1901," accessed December 30, 2016, https://history.state.gov/milestones/1899-1913/platt. On May 9, 2017, the State Department "retired" this account and now makes no reference to the Platt Amendment except to say that the United States abrogated the terms of the amendment in 1934 under the Good Neighbor policy. Accessed May 22, 2017, https://history.state.gov/milestones/1921-1936/good-neighbor.

8. Jorge Ibarra, *Prologue to Revolution: Cuba, 1898–1958* (Boulder, CO: Lynne Rienner, 1998), 17.

9. José Martí, "The Monetary Conference of the American Republics (1891)," in *José Martí: Selected Writings*, ed. and trans. Esther Allen (New York: Penguin, 2002), 307.

10. Louis A. Pérez, Jr., *On Becoming Cuban: Identity, Nationality, and Culture* (Chapel Hill: University of North Carolina Press, 1999), 7, 157.

11. Gott, *Cuba*, 92, 94.

12. Gott, *Cuba*, 114.

13. Stephen Irving Max Schwab, *Guantánamo, USA: The Untold History of America's Cuban Outpost* (Lawrence: University of Kansas Press, 2009), 94.

14. Gott, *Cuba*, 115

15. Juan C. Santamarina, "The Cuba Company and the Expansion of American Business in Cuba, 1898–1915," *Business History Review* 74 (Spring 2000): 41–42.

16. Santamarina, "The Cuba Company," 42.

17. The account here of Ángel Castro's return to Cuba is the one most commonly reported, though there are biographies with conflicting details. Hugh Thomas (*Cuba: The Pursuit of Freedom* [New York: Harper & Row, 1971], 803–4) and Robert E. Quirk (*Fidel Castro* [New York: Norton, 1993], 9) assert that Fidel's father did not return to Spain after the 1898 war.

18. Fidel Castro's official birthdate was August 13, 1926. However, according to journalist Claudia Furiati, he was born in 1927. She asserts that his father changed Fidel's birth certificate making him seem one year older so that he could enroll in *el Colégio Belén*. Claudia Furiati, *Fidel Castro: Uma biografia consentida*, 3a Edição (Rio de Janeiro: Editora Revan, 2001), 53–54.

19. Gott, *Cuba*, 115.

20. Pérez, *On Becoming Cuban*, 7, 157.

21. "Tobacco Trust in Cuba," *New York Times*, May 29, 1902.

22. Pérez, *Cuba*, 176–77.

23. "President Sends Crowder to Cuba to Study Crisis," *New York Times*, January 4, 1921, 1.

24. Le Riverend, *Economic History of Cuba*, 232–33.

25. Oscar Zanetti Leucuna, *Historia Mínima de Cuba* (Mexico City: El Colegio de México, 2013), chapter 7.

26. Luis E. Aguilar, *Cuba 1933: Prologue to Revolution* (New York: Norton, 1972), chapter 5.

27. Aguilar, *Cuba 1933*, 64.

28. Aguilar, *Cuba 1933*, chapter 9; Gott, *Cuba*, 133–34.

29. Schoultz, *Beneath the United States*, 290.

30. Franklin D. Roosevelt, "First Inaugural Address," March 4, 1933, accessed June 8, 2014, http://avalon.law.yale.edu/20th_century/froos1.asp.

31. Robert F. Smith, *The United States and Cuba: Business and Diplomacy, 1917–1960* (New York: Bookman Associates, 1961), 142–43.

32. As quoted in Aguilar, *Cuba 1933*, 129.

33. Aguilar, *Cuba 1933*, 131.

34. Smith, *The United States and Cuba*, 146–47.

35. J. D. Phillips, "Machado 'Leave' Sought by Welles as Cuban Solution: Ambassador Suggests Naming a New State Secretary Who Would Succeed President. Executive Bars Quitting . . . Toll of Rioting Now 30," *New York Times*, August 9, 1933, 1.

36. "Céspedes Served Country as Envoy," *New York Times*, August 13, 1933, 23. Céspedes also served twice as Cuba's ambassador to the United States and France and secretary of state during the first year of Machado's presidency.

37. Pérez, *Cuba*, 208; Aguilar, *Cuba 1933*, 159–62.

38. Aguilar, *Cuba 1933*, 157–59.

39. Antonio Guiteras, "Septembrismo," reprinted in *La Jiribilla: Revista Digital de Cultura Cubana*, no. 290, 25 de noviembre al primero de diciembre, 2006 (translation by the authors), accessed June 29, 2014, http://www.lajiribilla.cu/2006/n290_11/290_07.html.

40. José A. Gómez-Ibáñez, *Regulating Infrastructure: Monopoly, Contracts, and Discretion* (Cambridge: Harvard University Press, 2006), 123–24.

41. Schwab, *Guantánamo, USA*, 134–36.

Chapter 6

Playground of the Western World and the Rise of Batista, 1934–1958

Dirt shacks, no running water—the way those people lived, it's just how life was to me. I was a child. Mother didn't like it, but Daddy reminded her that the company paid them higher wages than any Cuban-owned sugar operation. Mother thought it was just terrible the way the Cuban plantations did business. It broke her heart, the idea of a race of people exploiting their own kind. The cane cutters were all Jamaicans, of course—not a single one of them was Cuban—but I knew what she meant: native people taking advantage of other native people, brown against black, that kind of thing. She was proud of Daddy; proud of the fact that the United Fruit Company upheld a certain standard, paid better wages than they had to, just to be decent. She said she hoped it would influence the Cubans to treat their own kind a bit better.

—Rachel Kushner[1]

THE 1940 REPUBLIC

Batista Wins 1940 Election

Along with a new constitution that had been hammered out in about four months and completed by a constituent assembly in June, the 1940 election gave Colonel Fulgencio Batista's presidency a patina of democratic legitimacy. Batista had resigned from the military to campaign in the election. Conveniently, the constituent assembly exempted him from a provision that required a candidate to have been out of the military for at least one year prior to assuming the presidency.

Not only was Batista the leading candidate; for a time, he also was the only presidential candidate. In order to increase popular acceptance of the outcome,

Batista asked Grau San Martín—who had returned from six years of exile in the United States—to run. Batista garnered more than 40 percent of the vote.

With a kind of New Deal, social democratic program, the new president emphasized economic and agricultural reforms that he had promoted as military leader after the 1933 coup. He also nurtured Cuban ties with the United States, and imports of US products increased from about half to about three-quarters of all of Cuba's imports between 1933 and 1940.[2]

Perhaps more important, Cuban-US economic relations were shaped by two 1934 US laws. Under the Jones-Costigan Act, the US secretary of agriculture set a quota each year for foreign sugar producers. The percentage of the total allotted to each country was based on its average percentage of sugar sales to the United States from 1931 to 1933. This was unfortunate for Cuba, because its exports in those years hit historic lows. In theory, this circumstance might have enabled Cuba to diversify its dependency by trading more with Europe. But the other law, the Reciprocal Trade Agreements Act, enabled the Roosevelt administration to "negotiate" an accord with Cuba that reduced tariffs significantly for US products and thus made European products uncompetitive. Taken together, the two laws ensured that Cuba would remain dependent on the United States and relatively poor.

Notably, the presidential-like residence of the US ambassador in Havana symbolized US-Cuban relations before 1959 (see figures 6.1 and 6.2). Built in 1942, the sixty-five-room estate still sits on 5.25 acres in what had been a wealthy Havana suburb. Its sculpted gardens are punctuated by baroque fountains and sit adjacent to a large swimming pool and tennis courts.[3]

Figure 6.1. Entrance to the sixty-five-room residence of the US ambassador. Photo by Carlos A. Ortega Murias.

Figure 6.2. Dining room in the residence of the US ambassador. Photo by Philip Brenner.

A Reliable US Ally in World War II

As World War II approached, Batista swore "whole-hearted" allegiance to the Allies. He told foreign correspondents before the presidential campaign that "Cuba desires and hopes to maintain her neutrality . . . but the United States can count on us as a factor in its plans for the defense of the Caribbean."[4] Indeed, the Roosevelt administration was certain that the new Cuban president was a solid, dependable ally who would protect US interests.

Even before Batista was inaugurated on October 10, 1940, Cuba played an ignominious role in the lead-up to the war. The Nazi German government allowed a vessel of the Hamburg-Amerika Line, the SS *St. Louis*, to leave Germany bound for Cuba with 938 passengers, virtually all of them escaping Jews. The ship anchored in Havana harbor on May 27, 1939. But Nazi spies and corrupt Cuban officials—combined with ineffective efforts by US diplomats—blocked the passengers from disembarking. It became known as the Voyage of the Damned. The vessel sailed next toward Florida, but President Roosevelt chose not to expand immigration quotas as he contended with isolationists, anti-Semites in Congress, and public opinion hostile to increasing immigration. The *St. Louis* returned to Europe, where US officials quietly tried to arrange for the passengers' safety. Some received asylum in Britain. But those sent to France, Belgium, and the Netherlands soon found themselves again in German hands when the German blitzkrieg overtook those countries in 1940.[5]

Batista's governing alliance, which included support from the Cuban Communist Party, focused on good relations with labor unions in the cities, the creation of local health centers, and a number of political reforms. Two prominent members of the communist party even served for a time in Batista's national unity cabinet. One was Carlos Rafael Rodríguez, who became Cuba's vice president in 1976; the other was Blas Roca, who would become a key strategist in the revolutionary government two decades later.

The war had a positive effect on a few sectors of Cuba's economy but negative effects on most. Between 1940 and 1944, the disparity between the urban working and the rural poor increased. Trade with Europe essentially stopped when maritime commerce collapsed, and the number of tourists overall dropped by 90 percent. Cuba's only safe and reliable trade partner was just north across the Florida Straits. With the resulting dependence on the US market, Cuba's trade deficit with the United States grew and so did US domination of Cuban industry and commerce.[6] Meanwhile, the US Navy used Cuban port facilities for secure transit of military supplies.

As the 1944 election loomed, Batista's only hope of maintaining some power resided with his prime minister, Carlos Saladrigas, because the 1940 constitution did not permit consecutive presidential terms. Although Batista threw his support behind Saladrigas, voters swept Grau San Martín into office in a landslide victory. Grau, the ousted president of the one-hundred-day revolutionary government and candidate of the *Auténtico* Party, was a much different man from the firebrand who left the country in 1934. This time around he was determined to cater to US interests. He reduced taxes on foreign investment and foreign corporations operating in Cuba, and lessened restraints on US businesses operating on the island. He also removed Communist Party members from the government and repressed their labor organizations. (During the war, the Communist Party changed its name to the Popular Socialist Party [PSP].)

A FAÇADE OF PROSPERITY

After World War II, sugar maintained its position as the bedrock of the economy. By 1948, sugar production had risen to a new high of 5.8 million tons and accounted for 90 percent of Cuba's export earnings.[7] In addition, the tourism and cigar industries started to take off as Cuba's economic profile began to evolve.

US businessmen also sought to capitalize on the island's proximity and friendly business climate. Standard Oil of New Jersey (then known as Esso and now ExxonMobil) and Texaco established refineries on the island and shipped the output to the rest of the Caribbean basin. Havana became the regional sales headquarters for the hemispheric operations of several companies and advertising agencies. As the number of visitors began to increase, Cuban officials proudly announced an investment of $5 million to make further improvements in tourist facilities.[8]

Unfortunately, the surface appearance of a thriving economy masked a problematic core. Starting with Grau, presidents padded the government payroll with Auténtico Party patronage seekers who had been previously shut out of public jobs. Corruption grew in the postwar years, making a few Cubans wealthy and helping American businesses gain an even more secure foothold.

Carlos Prío Socarrás, who had been Grau's prime minister, won the 1948 election for president. Known as the "cordial president," he demonstrated little intention or ability to control the increasing US business domination of Cuba's economy, which returned only meager sustenance to it. Moreover, in order to forestall any trouble from Washington, Prío continued Grau's practice of systematically removing PSP members from the Cuban labor movement, which vitiated the energy of some of the unions that were most effective.

This did not stop workers from striking for better wages and conditions. The Ministry of Labor reported 102 strikes and hundreds of disputes involving workers and businesses between January and August 1951. There were also spontaneous demonstrations, some of which turned violent. In rampages that involved looting and even murder, rival "action groups" became as much criminal street gangs as political organizations.

Widespread impunity for such actions had an effect on Cuba's economic climate, which raised concerns among American business leaders. "Despite the country's prosperity and its manifest opportunities for investment, only a few new industries have been established by local capital during the last few years," the *New York Times* reported in January 1952. It added that "the National Association of Industrialists repeatedly has warned the Government that economic development cannot be carried out until relations between capital and labor are stabilized."[9]

Political scientist Jorge Domínguez well describes a pervasive feeling throughout the island by 1951 that the Cuban political "system was somehow not legitimate." The constitution, he explained, "was honored in the breach"; presidents bypassed Congress and the Supreme Court; "corruption was pervasive."[10] Only Senator Eduardo Chibás, the founder of the Ortodoxo Party, had been able to arouse popular hopes. Although Chibás had lost to Prío in the 1948 election, he was untarnished by scandal. With a passionate eloquence, he appeared every Sunday on the radio to rail against President Prío and government corruption.

On August 5, 1951, Chibás opened his live broadcast by denouncing Prío as the most corrupt president in Cuban history, and he finished with an appeal: "Last Sunday . . . I presented to the people irrefutable proof of the immense corruption within Prío's regime. . . . But my wake-up call perhaps was not strong enough. . . . People of Cuba, wake up! This is the final wake-up call!"[11]

He then took out a gun, shot himself in the stomach, and died eleven days later.

BATISTA RETURNS WITH MARTIAL LAW

The dramatic suicide provided Batista with the opportunity he sought when he returned to Cuba from Florida in 1950. But the depth of his unpopularity in the 1952 presidential election was evident from poll data. Batista was in third place despite the lack of enthusiasm the other candidates inspired. Roberto Agramonte y Pichardo, a mild-mannered psychology professor at the University of Havana and conventional Ortodoxo functionary, had replaced Chibás as the party's standard bearer and was running neck and neck with Carlos Hevía, the Auténtico candidate.[12] Counting on the public's disdain for the political system, Batista engaged disaffected junior military officers to stage a coup three months before the scheduled June vote. Declaring martial law, he shut down Congress and canceled the elections. Prío fled to Mexico City and then to Miami, where he spent the rest of his days. One of the Ortodoxo candidates seeking a seat in the House of Representatives was Fidel Castro Ruz, a twenty-four-year-old lawyer who had been favored to win.

Nearly twenty years after his first taste of power, Batista was back in office. But his military takeover was not popular and he governed with an unyielding hand and brutal force. Reports of human rights violations soon became abundant as opposition to the new regime arose quickly. University students and other opponents tried to mobilize popular anger by staging a general strike, and some later plotted with dissident army officers to stage a countercoup. The government discovered the plans, jailed plot leader Professor Rafael Garcia Barcena along with more than one hundred others, and sent several others into exile.[13]

Batista's coup had not fazed Washington, which recognized the new government seventeen days after the former president seized power. But the United States conditioned approval on three demands, which Batista easily satisfied: a clampdown on open activity by communists, the pledge of a favorable climate for US investors, and the promise of elections in the near future. Cleverly, one of Batista's first acts was to break Cuba's diplomatic relations with the Soviet Union.[14] In a November 1954 presidential election, Batista ran unopposed. He won handily.

If there were any concerns in Washington about his iron rule, Batista assuaged them by frequently restating his government's basic anti-communist stance. On the second anniversary of his coup, for example, he emphasized three key themes—anti-communism, stability, and elections. "We remain firm in our aim to preserve order and to solve the political problem of Cuba by electoral means," he declared.[15] As he spoke, soldiers and police surrounded the University of Havana, smashing a student demonstration against the regime.

With stability for foreign investment guaranteed, Batista moved on a number of fronts in an effort to "modernize" Havana. US-managed hotels flourished with attractive rates. Prominent among them were the Nacional (see figure 6.3), the Sevilla Biltmore, and the Presidente. When the Rosita de Hornedo (now called the Sierra Maestra) opened in 1955, it featured exclusive prices for foreign high-rollers. Pan Am and Eastern Airlines established frequent flights between Havana and New York, Chicago, and Miami. The West India Fruit and Steamship Company expanded its passenger operations in the early 1950s, offering passage for thousands of passengers and hundreds of cars across the Florida Straits every day.

The government rushed to complete an international airport at Varadero Beach, about ninety miles east of Havana on the northern Cuban coast. Eventually, the project included a highway that would link the cities, and officials discussed plans to remake the quiet palm-tree retreat in the image of Miami

Figure 6.3.   Hotel Nacional. Photo by Philip Brenner.

Beach. Honeymoon packages were promoted at top Havana hotels, and the government designated special English-speaking tourist police to help Americans get around the city. The goal was to convert Cuba into North America's winter playground.

PLAYGROUND OF THE WESTERN WORLD . . . FOR THE FEW

A Gangster's Paradise

At the same time, Batista encouraged the growth of casino gambling. By the end of 1955, all of the major hotels featured or were in the process of establishing posh gaming operations.[16] The government charged gaming fees and claimed that the greater part was distributed to charities, many of which were managed by Batista's wife, Marta Fernández de Batista. In reality, according to journalist Ann Louise Bardach, "Batista was reported to be pocketing more than $1 million from the gambling casinos *every month* and he maintained Swiss bank accounts with deposits in the hundreds of millions."[17]

From time to time, Batista made a show of policing the casinos' "razzle-dazzle," which is what they called the fleecing of American tourists at the gaming tables. Early in his dictatorial rule, when the appearance of fixing threatened to undermine Cuba's popularity with tourists, Batista pledged reforms and designated one of the fixers as his special "adviser on gambling reform." The choice was Meyer Lansky, a linchpin for syndicates in New York, Chicago, and Las Vegas, who had been operating in Cuba for at least a decade.[18]

In fact, on December 22, 1946, the chiefs of several prominent US organized crime syndicates had convened at Havana's oceanside Hotel Nacional and essentially divided up their opportunities for gambling, money laundering, and related businesses. Among them were Lansky and Charles "Lucky" Luciano, who had been a major Chicago underworld figure until his 1936 conviction for prostitution and racketeering. But in 1946, he was out of jail because of his connections with gangsters who ruled the waterfront at key US ports. The federal government had paroled Luciano from his long prison sentence to assist US counterespionage efforts against German spies by reporting on the departure of troop transport ships during World War II. When Cuba deported him to Italy in 1947, Santo Trafficante, Jr., the mob boss of Tampa, took Luciano's place. (In the 1960s, Trafficante would be involved in US Central Intelligence Agency [CIA] attempts to assassinate Fidel Castro.[19])

The gangsters went on a spending spree after Batista's 1952 coup, opening nightclubs and casinos and building a racetrack and new hotels. In 1957, Trafficante unveiled the fourteen-story Hotel Deauville along Havana's seaside roadway, and Lansky opened the opulent Riviera. Costing $14 million, the Riviera's twenty-one floors housed 440 rooms, a casino, a cabaret, and two restaurants.

However, US organized crime in Cuba stayed away from sex trafficking. As journalist T. J. English notes, "The trade never was as lucrative as narcotics or gambling—businesses that tended to metastasize and create other businesses."[20] Prostitution was left to Cuban entrepreneurs, who made their own contribution to Havana's reputation as a vice capital in the Batista years. In the 1950s, prostitution was the second largest occupation for women, after teaching.

With Batista in charge of the government, organized crime had found what they believed was their paradise. Closer to New York and more pleasant than Las Vegas, and with a friendly government that the crime bosses could control, Cuba provided a haven where the criminals imagined they could center their worldwide operations with impunity. But they had not reckoned with one factor that led to their undoing. Most of the people who lived in Cuba did not benefit from either Batista's rule or the mob's exploitation.

The Other Cuba

Memories of Cuba's wealth in the 1950s and myths about its advanced development die hard. Exiles who left Cuba shortly after the 1959 revolution have described for so long the comfortable lives they led that it has seemed to many US listeners that comfort was the norm. In a 2012 meeting with former US government officials visiting Havana, a recently arrived US diplomat pointed to the former mansions near the US Interests Section (now the US embassy) building and said that these were evidence that the revolution was "not about poverty," because there was "a lot of wealth" in the country.[21]

Superficially, the US diplomat was correct. In the 1950s, Cuba "was far from underdeveloped when compared with much of the rest of the world," as political scientist Richard Fagen observed.[22] Its per capita gross domestic product was eighth in Latin America, ahead of Brazil's. Its literacy rate was 76 percent, fourth best in the region.[23] But Fagen added, "Aggregate statistics do not, of course, tell the whole story. Despite the comforting averages and national comparisons, Cuba was characterized by vast inequalities in the distribution of goods, services, and opportunities."[24]

Consider that while only 26 percent of Cuba's population lived in Havana, the city had 60 percent of the country's doctors and 62 percent of the dentists. Havana had one hospital bed for every 195 inhabitants, but the eastern province of Oriente had one bed per 1,870.[25] The disparities in literacy and the availability of schools between urban and rural areas were even more stark. In 1956, only 50 percent of children between the ages of five and fourteen attended school. The 1953 census revealed that 25 percent of the population over ten years of age had never been to school.[26] Sixty percent of the country's secondary schools were private, which made secondary education unaffordable for most Cubans. Middle- and upper-class Cubans sent their children to private schools or to the United States. In addition, as historian Alejandro de la Fuente reports, "Some of the best schools in the country . . . were American and open only to whites" and the best religious schools were "Spanish and equally discriminatory."[27]

Urban-rural contrasts were evident in housing, where 93 percent of rural homes had no electricity. Agricultural workers also suffered from underemployment. About one-quarter of Cuba's total labor force worked only one hundred days each year. And in the 1950s, as the Cuban economy stagnated apart from the tourist sector, their wages dropped even further. Louis Pérez explains, "A [sugar] worker who earned $5 daily in 1951 was earning $4.35 per day in 1955. . . . Workers in transportation, tobacco, henequen (a tropical plant used to manufacture rope and twine), along with other manufacturing sectors, similarly experienced an approximate 20 percent loss of wages during these years."[28]

Batista's Cuba was in reality two distinct countries. One was distinguished by the high-rolling, vice-ridden lifestyle of North American tourism in Havana, with its circles of Cubans dependent on that dominant industry and US corporations. The other was a country of abject poverty, economic stagnation, and rural underemployment. Batista's government did little to generate meaningful development for the vast majority, and the resulting dissatisfaction and disgust was spread throughout the country.

NOTES

1. Rachel Kushner, *Telex from Cuba: A Novel* (New York: Scribner, 2009), 11.
2. Pérez, *Cuba and the United States*, 205.
3. Rebecca C. Park, "Brief History of the US Residence and Eagle, Havana, Cuba," June 2005 (pamphlet; US Interests Section, Havana, Cuba).
4. "Cuban Aid Pledged to US if War Comes," *New York Times*, May 23, 1940, 4.
5. Richard Breitman and Allan J. Lichtman, *FDR and the Jews* (Cambridge: Belknap Press, 2013), 125–41.
6. Pérez, *Cuba*, 220–21.
7. Pérez, *Cuba*, 223.
8. "Travel to Cuba Rises," *New York Times*, January 3, 1951, 71.
9. "Unsettled Labor Frustrates Cuba," *New York Times*, January 4, 1952, 64.
10. Jorge I. Domínguez, *Cuba: Order and Revolution* (Cambridge: Harvard University Press, 1978), 110.
11. "Eduardo R. Chibás: Last Speech," trans. Walter Lippmann from a transcript prepared by Raúl Chibás, July 31, 1982; original Spanish version available at http://www.partidortodoxo.org/Aldabonazo.htm; English translation available at http://www.walterlippmann.com/docs3896.html.
12. Domínguez, *Cuba*, 113.
13. Marifeli Pérez-Stable, *The Cuban Revolution: Origins, Course, and Legacy*, second edition (New York: Oxford University Press, 1999).
14. Schoultz, *That Infernal Little Cuban Republic*, 49.
15. "Batista Says Cuba Cleaned Out Reds," *New York Times*, March 11, 1954, 5.
16. R. Hart Phillips, "Cuba Is Betting on Her New Gambling Casinos," *New York Times*, November 6, 1955.
17. Ann Louis Bardach, *Cuba Confidential: Love and Vengeance in Miami and Havana* (New York: Vintage Books, 2002), 245. Emphasis in the original.
18. T. J. English, *Havana Nocturne: How the Mob Owned Cuba . . . and Then Lost It to the Revolution* (New York: William Morrow, 2007), 95–96, 132–33.
19. US Central Intelligence Agency, "Inspector General Report on Plots to Assassinate Fidel Castro," May 23, 1967, 25, 35, 104. Available at National Archives and Records Administration, JFK Record Series; Record Number: 104-10213-10101; File Number: JFK64-48 :F52 1998 .06 .23 .11 :39 :07 :420082.
20. English, *Havana Nocturne*, 168, 216. The quotation is taken from 216.
21. Philip Brenner attended the meeting.
22. Richard R. Fagen, *The Transformation of Political Culture in Cuba* (Palo Alto: Stanford University Press, 1969), 22.

23. Luis Bértola and José Antonio Ocampo, *The Economic Development of Latin America since Independence* (Oxford: Oxford University Press, 2012), table A.2; Carmelo Mesa-Lago, "Economic and Social Balance of 50 Years of Cuban Revolution," in *Cuba in Transition: Papers and Proceedings of the Nineteenth Annual Meeting of the Association for the Study of the Cuban Economy (ASCE)* 19 (2009: 377, http://www.ascecuba.org/c/wp-content/uploads/2014/09/v19-mesolago.pdf.

24. Fagen, *The Transformation of Political Culture in Cuba*, 23.

25. Ibarra, *Prologue to Revolution*, 161.

26. Marvin Leiner, "Two Decades of Educational Change in Cuba," *Journal of Reading* 25, no. 3 (December 1981): 202–3; Fagen, *The Transformation of Political Culture in Cuba*, 35.

27. Alejandro de la Fuente, *A Nation for All: Race, Inequality, and Politics in Twentieth-Century Cuba* (Chapel Hill: University of North Carolina Press, 2001), 145.

28. Pérez, *Cuba*, 235.

Chapter 7

The Revolutionary Struggle, 1953–1958

In terms of struggle, when we talk about the people we're talking about the 600,000 Cubans without work, who want to earn their daily bread honestly without having to emigrate from their homeland in search of a livelihood; the 500,000 farm laborers who live in miserable shacks, who work four months of the year and starve the rest . . . the 400,000 industrial workers and laborers whose retirement funds have been embezzled, whose benefits are being taken away, whose homes are wretched hovels, whose salaries pass from the hands of the boss to those of the moneylender . . . the 100,000 small farmers who live and die working land that is not theirs . . . the 30,000 teachers and professors who are so devoted, and so necessary to improve the destiny of future generations and who are so badly treated and paid. . . . To these people whose desperate roads through life have been paved with the bricks of betrayal and false promises, we were not going to say: "We will give you . . . " but rather: "Here it is, now fight for it with everything you have, so that liberty and happiness may be yours!"

—Fidel Castro, October 1, 1953[1]

THE FAILED MONCADA ATTACK

Not long after Batista's 1952 takeover, Fidel Castro began organizing an armed insurgency against the government. An impassioned orator in the mold of Chibás, Fidel had been a radical student leader at the University of Havana. He, too, had begun to speak on a weekly radio program aimed at the Ortodoxo Party's youth wing. During the last half of 1952 and into 1953, he and his younger brother, Raúl Castro Ruz, trained groups of insurgents and planned an assault that they hoped would spark an island-wide rebellion against the Batista dictatorship. Their target was the Moncada Barracks/Armory in Santiago, the second largest barracks in Cuba's second largest city. It seemed more vulnerable than the country's primary military base, Camp Columbia in Havana, and Santiago's location had symbolic importance. Prior insurrections against tyrannical rulers had always started in Oriente, the easternmost province.

July 26, 1953. This was the day when Santiago de Cuba celebrated its carnival, coinciding with the end of the sugar harvest. With a logic similar to George Washington's Christmas Eve attack on Hessian mercenaries during the American Independence War, the Cuban rebels expected to find Batista's 14,000 troops drunk at Santiago's Moncada Barracks. Dressed as sergeants in replicas of regular army uniforms, about 160 of them set out for the twelve-mile trek from their hideout in Siboney. A backup group headed for the Bayamo Barracks, ninety miles farther to the west. They arrived at Moncada just before the sounding of reveille at daybreak. Fidel's group led the charge at the barracks while Raúl's smaller unit attacked the adjacent Palace of Justice.

Even years later, Castro insisted that the foolhardy operation was well planned, but the fighters lacked sufficient experience. "If we'd taken Moncada we'd have toppled Batista, without question," he said. "In Santiago de Cuba, it would have taken them hours to recover from the chaos and confusion that would have been created in their ranks, and that would have given us time for the subsequent steps."[2]

In fact, the rebels were quickly overwhelmed by superior numbers and firepower—and by disorganization. Some of the fighters became lost in Santiago and could not find the Moncada. With eight of his comrades killed and twelve wounded, Fidel ordered a withdrawal. He and Raúl fled with fewer than half the insurgents to the countryside. A few days later, they were captured. Batista ordered that ten prisoners be shot for every soldier killed in the attack (thirteen had died), and the slaughter was halted at seventy only by the intercession of Cardinal Manuel Arteaga y Betancourt, the archbishop of Havana.[3] Two months later, Batista put the remaining July 26th Movement survivors on trial.

"HISTORY WILL ABSOLVE ME"

Fidel served as the defense lawyer in the first of two trials of about 100 defendants, some of whom had not even been connected to the attack. His skilled oratory won leniency for a majority of those charged. A month later, he represented himself as a defendant in the second trial. Speaking extemporaneously (he later reconstructed and published, perhaps with some embellishment, his two-hour defense), the rebel leader declared with a nationalist fervor, "We are Cubans and to be Cuban implies a duty. . . . We were taught . . . to sing every afternoon the verses of our national anthem: 'To live in chains is to live in disgrace and in opprobrium,' and 'to die for one's homeland is to live forever!'" And in conclusion, he told the court, "I do not fear prison, as I do not fear the fury of the miserable tyrant who took the lives of seventy of my compañeros [comrades]. Condemn me, it does not matter. History will absolve me."[4]

The court sentenced Fidel to fifteen years in prison and Raúl to thirteen years. Dispatched to a penitentiary on the Isle of Pines, they were treated as political prisoners, not common criminals, which meant they were able to receive books and even cigars. As biographer Robert Quirk recounts, Fidel saw confinement as an opportunity "to mold his group into an educated and disciplined phalanx of insurrectionists."[5] They requested reading material from friends and relatives, and by the end of the year, their library had over three hundred volumes. Fidel read widely, favoring histories of military battles, masterwork novels of authors such as Fyodor Dostoyevsky, Victor Hugo, and Cirilo Villaverde, and the classic works of Immanuel Kant, Sigmund Freud, and Karl Marx—though he did not dwell on Marxist-Leninist theory.[6] (In a 2001 interview with one of the authors, Castro remarked that his "understanding of socialism did not come from books, like it did for academics, but from personal experiences.")

But school lasted only twenty months. Six months after Batista's 1954 landslide "election" victory, he sought to add further legitimacy to his rule by reinstating some civil liberties, such as a guarantee of free expression, and granting amnesty to all political prisoners, including those involved in the Moncada attack. Yet the veneer of democracy did not produce the intended political effect. Student protests intensified in late 1955, and Batista responded with waves of repression against even moderate opponents.[7]

By then both Fidel and Raúl had left Cuba for Mexico, having decided that the only viable way to effect political change in Cuba would be through armed revolt. Fifty years later, Fidel recalled to Ignacio Ramonet, "I wasn't in any imminent danger, but I couldn't keep agitating in Cuba. . . . In the weeks after we got out of prison, we had engaged in an intense campaign to take our ideas to the people. . . . We had structured our own revolutionary organization—the 26th of July Movement—and we'd shown that it was impossible to carry out the struggle by peaceful, legal means."[8]

By July 1955, when Fidel arrived in Mexico, Raúl already had assembled a contingency of other Cuban exiles. As the group planned for their armed return to Cuba, Raúl introduced Fidel to a twenty-seven-year-old Argentine doctor—Ernesto "Che" Guevara de la Serna—who had fled to Mexico the previous year from Guatemala, where he witnessed the US-sponsored coup against the democratically elected government of Jacobo Arbenz. Castro remembered that "There was nothing surprising about our immediate sympathy with one another: . . . he'd visited Guatemala, he'd witnessed the American intervention there, and he knew we'd attacked a military stronghold, he knew about our struggle in Cuba, he knew how we thought. I arrived, we talked to each other, and right there he joined us."[9]

THE REVOLUTIONARY CONFLICT

Over the next eighteen months, the Castro brothers and Che organized a new plan of attack with the exiles. They trained first at a farm close to Mexico City and then moved farther away after the Mexican government raided the place. In late November 1956, eighty-two of them squeezed aboard a small cabin cruiser, the *Granma*, and set off on a 1,200-mile, treacherous voyage to Oriente Province, the birthplace of Cuban uprisings. Facing rough seas, they made slower progress than anticipated and ran aground on December 2, 1956, two days after their planned arrival, which was intended to coincide with a multipronged set of disruptions in Santiago led by Frank País.

País was a prominent figure among a number of young militants who had been creating an underground network throughout the country—mainly in urban areas—aimed at overthrowing the Batista dictatorship. These included Armando Hart, Faustino Pérez, and Haydee Santamaría in Havana, and Celia Sánchez and Vilma Espín in Santiago.

Within days of the landing, the Cuban military discovered and attacked the *Granma* rebels. Only eighteen—including Fidel, Raúl, and Che—evaded detection by lying under leaves and straw in a sugar cane field. Bone weary and exhausted, they seemed to face certain annihilation as a search plane circled overhead, looking for any signs of movement. "There was never any situation more dramatic," Fidel exclaimed in his autobiography. "When I realized there was no way I could stay awake, that I was sure to fall asleep, I lay down on my side and put the rifle butt between my legs and the end of the barrel under my chin. I didn't want to be captured alive if the enemy should come upon me while I was asleep."[10]

But protected and sustained by sympathetic campesinos, the survivors managed to retreat and regroup in the Sierra Maestra Mountains. Castro said that at one point, they had only seven rifles among them as they sought to rebuild an insurgency once more. Slowly, they made contact with their urban allies, students, and other government opponents. "We are in no hurry," Fidel wrote to País in 1957. "We'll keep fighting as long as is necessary."[11]

As they developed support lines, Fidel chose targets of opportunity whose impact would be more psychological than tactical. The July 26th fighters began attacking lightly defended outposts of the government's rural guard that the local citizenry despised. In January 1957, the rebels ambushed a rural guard column at La Plata, seizing weapons, and in May, successfully attacked another column at El Uvero.[12]

The most powerful impact came from an interview with Fidel Castro, which appeared in the *New York Times* on February 24, 1957. Until that point, there was still uncertainty about whether the military had killed the young firebrand. Journalist Herbert Matthews answered the question dramatically in his lead sentence, "Fidel Castro, the rebel leader of Cuba's youth, is alive and fighting hard and successfully in the rugged, almost impenetrable fastnesses of the *Sierra Maestra*, at the southern tip of the island."[13]

Havana members of the July 26th Movement had arranged for the *Times'* correspondent to make a dangerous and arduous trek to the guerrillas' mountain hideaway. Cleverly, Fidel ordered the small group of fighters there to march continuously around the encampment, changing their clothes, to make it appear that their numbers were far greater than the reality.[14] Matthews reported, "President Fulgencio Batista has the cream of his Army around the area, but the Army men are fighting a thus-far losing battle to destroy the most dangerous enemy General Batista has yet faced in a long and adventurous career as a Cuban leader and dictator."

The journalist then described Fidel Castro in terms that made him inescapably appealing to a US audience:

The personality of the man is overpowering. It was easy to see that his men adored him and also to see why he has caught the imagination of the youth of Cuba all over the island. Here was an educated, dedicated fanatic, a man of ideals, of courage and of remarkable qualities of leadership. . . . He has strong ideas of liberty, democracy, social justice, the need to restore the Constitution, to hold elections. . . . The 26th of July Movement talks of nationalism, anti-colonialism, anti-imperialism. I asked Señor Castro about that. He answered, "You can be sure we have no animosity toward the United States and the American people."[15]

Historian Hugh Thomas has argued that "the significance of the interview was considerable" for the revolutionary struggle. "Matthews created for North Americans the legend of Castro, the hero of the mountains." The story also demoralized the military, he explained, and as word spread throughout Cuba that Castro was alive, it propelled more people to join the movement.[16]

BATISTA IMPOSES A REIGN OF TERROR

Tactics Resemble Weyler's Butchery

In response, Batista ordered his forces to pursue the July 26th Movement vigorously. The army carried out sweeps of the countryside, terrorizing people who might provide logistical support to the rebels. It designated key military zones where peasants and farmers were forced from their homes and taken to relocation camps. The government warned that it would presume stragglers in the militarized zones were guerrilla supporters and thus would be subject to arrest—or worse.[17]

His tactics were remarkably similar to those of General Weyler, the Spanish military tyrant who instituted a "reconcentration campaign" while killing many Cubans during the 1895–1898 Independence War. And they had a similar effect. Castro's fledgling rebel force, which had shrunk to only a dozen men at one point, swelled with new supporters, as had the insurgency against the Spaniards.

Despite Batista's repressive measures, the army failed to quell the rebellion. By early 1958, Raúl Castro had opened a second front in northern Oriente, and Juan Almeida commanded a third front north of Santiago. The insurgency also initiated *Radio Rebelde* from a portable clandestine transmitter in the Sierra Maestra. In bypassing the censured media, the island-wide broadcasts provided encouraging information to supporters, and they were able to organize calls for strikes and demonstrations.

Anti-Batista Forces Composed of Many Factions

But the guerrillas were not the sole threat to Batista's rule, and perhaps were not even the most important. The rebellion was widespread and took many forms, including individual acts of sabotage, spontaneous violent responses to abuses, small strikes against particular employers, and mass mobilizations. Many were not directed by or coordinated with the July 26th Movement because the urban underground (known as the *llano* in contrast to the fighters in the mountains, who were known as the *sierra)* was made up of diverse factions. It included trade unionists, middle-class professionals, students, and even traditional politicians. Raúl Chibás, the brother of Ortodoxo Party founder Eduardo Chibás, led a civic resistance movement. Federation of University Students head José Antonio Echeverria formed a unit to engage in direct action, the Revolutionary Directorate. Ricardo Alarcón de Quesada directed July 26th Movement's National Student Front from Havana.

In July 1957, Frank País organized a meeting between the Sierra Maestra rebels and key Ortodoxo Party members and other civil leaders. The summit culminated in the "Pact of the Sierra," which called for measures aimed at deposing Batista in order to hold a democratic presidential election. The convocation's success set the stage for the unified opposition to Batista that eventually would recognize Fidel Castro as leader of all revolutionary groups.[18]

More than anyone else, País helped to shape Castro's crucial international image in those early months. He met regularly with US officials, including CIA operatives, assuring them that Castro's goals included a pledge of government stability—the perennial concern of US governments dealing with the island, for fear that Cuba under Cuban popular control would become a state similar to Haiti. País assured the Americans that would not be the case. "Indeed the rebels had something of a cheering section back at the analytical section of the CIA, where 'my staff and I were all *fidelistas*,' the lead desk officer for Cuba later noted," as historian Julia Sweig reports.[19]

País was both an "inspirational organizer and political fixer," journalist Richard Gott explains, and had become "the acknowledged leader of the [July 26th] Movement outside the Sierra."[20] He was tireless in uniting the non-sierra factions, and in securing weapons, ammunition, food, and supplies for the fighters. But País's critical contributions to the struggle ended shortly after the July 1957 Sierra Maestra meeting, when the Santiago police gunned him down in an ambush at the end of the month. His assassination provoked a massive funeral and general strikes that spread across the island.

Only after a major misstep nine months later was the insurgency able to pull itself together in a way that could provide a sufficiently broad base to topple the dictatorship. But that achievement, Sweig learned from Cuban archival documents, would not have been possible without "the work of the 26th of July Movement outside of the Sierra Maestra during the first seventeen months of the insurgency, from November 1956 until April 1958." Castro, in effect, confirmed her conclusion in a long account he published in 2010 about the last stages of the revolutionary war. The July 26th Movement, he stated, "never considered developing a military force capable of defeating the Cuban Armed Forces." The strategy was "to create a true revolution," in which the guerrillas were merely "a well-armed vanguard."[21] In fact, Sweig reports, "until the last six to eight months of the two-year insurrection, the lion's share of decisions . . . [was] made by lesser known individuals from the urban underground."[22] The turning point came on April 9, 1958, with a failed general strike.

Fidel Castro had opposed calling the strike, arguing that the necessary preparations for success were not in place—a critical mass of workers and the trade unions were not ready to support it, the July 26th Movement had not coordinated with other organizations, and there were not enough weapons for the urban militia to challenge the inevitable violence against workers by the army and police.[23] But the llano strongly favored it. In part, the disagreement reflected tension within the broader insurrection over who would lead it. Had a successful strike caused Batista's government to fall, as a strike in 1933 had overthrown Machado's dictatorship, leadership of a new government would naturally have fallen to the urban rebels.

REBELS UNITE

Impact of Failed General Strike

The strike was an absolute dud. Faustino Pérez summarized the debacle by highlighting a fatal error: the leaders kept the date of the strike secret and then announced it on the radio "at an hour when only housewives listen to the radio."[24] In Havana, few workers participated; no stores, factories, or offices had to close; sabotage caused blackouts that lasted only for a few hours. In Santiago, many workers went on strike, but were quickly replaced by scabs. The air force attacked guerrillas in control of Sagua la Grande in Las Villas Province, driving them away by April 10. The military and police killed more than two hundred rebels, inflicting a major blow to the insurrection.

Despite his opposition, Castro ultimately supported the strike. But in a letter to Celia Sánchez one week later, he described his disappointment and frustration. The strike, he wrote, "involved a great moral rout for the Movement. . . . I am the supposed leader of this Movement, and in the eyes of history I must take responsibility for the stupidity of others, but I am a shit who can decide nothing at all."[25]

The tactical failure of the general strike gave Batista hope that the rebellion could still be halted. He redoubled his military effort and sent 10,000 soldiers to the Sierra Maestra in a final attempt to root out Castro's rebels.[26] The two-month campaign failed, and the guerrillas' success added stature to the sierra fighters and Castro, who seized the opportunity to plan the final phase of the war. In early May, he had emerged from an intense two-day gathering of July 26th Movement factional leaders as the general secretary of the now unified organization and commander-in-chief of the rebel army.[27]

Pact of Caracas

Two months later, representatives of all of the anti-Batista groups—except the communists—met in Caracas, Venezuela, to hammer out a common program. The breadth of participation in the meeting was unique in Cuban history: trade unionists, students, guerrilla fighters, lawyers from the Civic Resistance and Civic Dialogue, the head of the Catholic Democratic Montecristi Movement, and even Carlos Prío, the discredited president whom Batista had ousted. On July 20, the group endorsed a unity text called the Pact of Caracas, and it named Fidel to be the commander-in-chief of the new united rebel army.[28]

Meanwhile, the Cuban economy was disintegrating. In 1958, more than half a million people—out of 2.7 million in the labor force—were unemployed or underemployed. The proliferation of street crime and the growing presence of beggars garnered support for the insurrection from the middle class. As some major roads had become impassable and railroad tracks were destroyed by insurgents or damaged in battles, there were shortages through-out the island and some sugar mills had to shut down. Business leaders began to turn on Batista, whom they viewed as the main source of instability and impediment to improved economic conditions.[29]

COMMUNIST, SOVIET, AND
US ROLES IN THE REVOLUTION

The Cuban Communist Party (PCC) was founded in August 1925, largely by eastern European émigrés. Political scientist Mervyn Bain notes that its initial proclamations "were written in Yiddish before being translated into Span-ish."[30] It conveyed a sense of being internationalist more than nationalist, and it closely followed whatever party line emanated from Moscow. By the 1940s, however, it also was closely identified with the most militant Cuban trade unions. In keeping with the "popular front" policy of the Third [Com-munist] International, or Comintern, two PCC members even joined Batista's cabinet when he served as the constitutionally elected president during World War II. Recall that the PCC had changed its name during World War II to the Popular Socialist Party (PSP). PSP candidates were able to garner 10 percent of the votes cast in the 1946 congressional elections.[31]

The PSP's electoral success increased Soviet leader Joseph Stalin's interest in Cuba, especially as the Cold War was beginning. But the Soviets were far too weak to confront the United States directly, and sought to avoid provok-ing US intervention. In general, they hoped to gain influence through political means, not armed conflict, which coincided with the aims of the PSP leader-ship. "Cuban communists," political scientist Marifeli Pérez-Stable explained, "espoused militant reform, not revolution. . . . [They] operated in the political mainstream while challenging the predominant logic of corruption."[32]

As a result, the PSP distanced itself from the July 26th Movement's ac-tivities until 1958. The party disparagingly characterized the 1953 Moncada attack as "putschism."[33] PSP sympathizers in the Cuban Labor Confederation discouraged workers from participating in strikes organized by the July 26th Movement, including the April 9, 1958, general strike. It is little wonder that Castro displayed contempt for much of the PSP leadership, and that the July 26th Movement received no assistance from the Soviet Union.

Yet both the Movement and the PSP saw a need to find common ground. If the revolution was going to be inclusive and broad-based—as Fidel, Raúl, and Che intended—it had to involve the communists, who still held considerable influence among trade unionists. From the perspective of the PSP, it feared being left behind as the July 26th Movement gained momentum, and it had nowhere else to turn as Batista increased attacks on the party. In July 1958, after numerous individual meetings between high ranking members of the PSP and the July 26th Movement, a kind of official reconciliation occurred and the PSP joined the unified opposition.[34]

One indication of how little Cuban affairs concerned the Eisenhower administration was its appointment of Earl E. T. Smith as US ambassador in 1957. A Wall Street financier and mayor of Palm Beach, Florida, Smith's major credentials for the post were his chairmanship of the Florida Republican Party's finance committee and his membership on the Republican National Finance Committee.[35] However, by early 1958 top US officials grew worried that Batista's "repressive measures" had "alienated some 80 percent of the Cuban people," which made instability on the island a threat to US interests.[36] And so in March 1958, in an effort to encourage the Cuban dictator to give up power, President Dwight D. Eisenhower suspended new US military assistance to Cuba, which had been receiving the second largest sum in the hemisphere. But he allowed weapons still in the pipeline to flow to Cuba and the US military missions to stay on the island, and he refrained from making a strong public statement against Batista.

While the United States formally maintained a policy of "strict neutrality" in the expanding civil war, some US government agencies sought a "third force" to replace Batista with someone less radical than Fidel Castro.[37] Secretary of State Christian A. Herter made this objective explicit in a memorandum to President Eisenhower on December 23, 1958: "The Department has concluded that any solution in Cuba requires that Batista must relinquish power whether as Chief of State or as the force behind a puppet successor. . . . The Department clearly does not want to see Castro succeed to the leadership of the Government."[38] In accord with this policy, earlier in December the State Department had sent a secret emissary to negotiate with Batista, offering him asylum and monetary incentives to leave. Batista refused.

*   *   *

As the momentum turned toward the rebels in September, Castro came down from the Sierra Maestra and set off on the road to Santiago de Cuba, the country's second largest city. His top commanders fanned out and fought the disintegrating Batista army on all fronts. Finally, before dawn on New Year's Day 1959, the dictator packed up his family and friends, headed to the airstrip at Camp Columbia, and departed into ignominious exile in the Dominican Republic. Twenty-five months after Fidel's exhausted rebel force, armed with only seven guns, began its campaign, the 26th of July Movement had swelled to 50,000 hardened fighters.

NOTES

1. Fidel Castro, "History Will Absolve Me," in *Fidel Castro Reader*, ed. David Deutschmann and Deborah Schnookal (New York: Ocean Press, 2007), 65–66.
2. Fidel Castro and Ignacio Ramonet, *Fidel Castro: My Life, A Spoken Autobiography* (New York: Scribner, 2006), 114–15.
3. Robert E. Quirk, *Fidel Castro* (New York: Norton, 1993), 54–55.
4. Castro, "History Will Absolve Me," 103–5.
5. Quirk, *Fidel Castro*, 61.
6. Quirk, *Fidel Castro*, 62–63.
7. Pérez, *Cuba*, 228.
8. Castro and Ramonet, *Fidel Castro*, 172.
9. Castro and Ramonet, *Fidel Castro*, 173.
10. Castro and Ramonet, *Fidel Castro*, 184.
11. Gott, *Cuba*, 154.
12. Pérez, *Cuba*, 229.
13. Herbert L. Matthews, "Cuban Rebel Is Visited in Hideout," *New York Times*, February 24, 1957, 1.
14. Herbert L. Matthews, *Fidel Castro* (New York: Simon & Schuster, 1969), 108–9.
15. Matthews, "Cuban Rebel Is Visited in Hideout."
16. Hugh Thomas, *Cuba: The Pursuit of Freedom* (New York: Harper & Row, 1971), 919, 920.
17. Pérez, *Cuba*, 229–30.
18. Julia E. Sweig, *Inside the Cuban Revolution: Fidel Castro and the Urban Underground* (Cambridge: Harvard University Press, 2002), 32–36.
19. Sweig, *Inside the Cuban Revolution*, 29.
20. Gott, *Cuba*, 157.
21. Fidel Castro Ruz, *La Victoria Estratégica* (Havana: Oficina de Publicaciones del Consejo de Estado, 2010), 7. [Translation by the authors.]
22. Sweig, *Inside the Cuban Revolution*, 9.
23. Sweig, *Inside the Cuban Revolution*, 131–32.
24. Quoted in Tad Szulc, *Fidel: A Critical Portrait* (New York: William Morrow, 1986), 441.
25. Quoted in Szulc, *Fidel*, 441–42.
26. Castro and Ramonet, *Fidel Castro*, 196
27. Sweig, *Inside the Cuban Revolution*, 150–51.
28. Sweig, *Inside the Cuban Revolution*, chapter 15.
29. Pérez, *Cuba*, 237–32; Morris H. Morley, *Imperial State and Revolution: The United States and Cuba, 1952–1986* (Cambridge: Cambridge University Press, 1987), 58.
30. Mervyn J. Bain, *From Lenin to Castro, 1917–1959* (Lanham, MD: Lexington Books, 2013), 33.
31. Bain, *From Lenin to Castro*, 55.

32. Marifeli Pérez-Stable, *The Cuban Revolution: Origins, Course, and Legacy*, second edition (New York: Oxford University Press, 1999), 49.

33. Bain, *From Lenin to Castro*, 61.

34. Pérez, *Cuba*, 242.

35. Marvine Howe, "Earl Smith, 87, Ambassador to Cuba in the 1950s," *New York Times*, February 17, 1991.

36. Christian A. Herter, "Memorandum from the Acting Secretary of State to the President," December 23, 1958, in US Department of State, Office of the Historian, *Foreign Relations of the United States, 1958–1960*, Volume VI, Cuba, Document 189, 305.

37. Morley, *Imperial State and Revolution*, 62–65.

38. Herter, "Memorandum from the Acting Secretary of State to the President," December 23, 1958, 305.

Part II

1959–1989

Chapter 8

The Quest for Sovereignty

> I believe that this is a decisive moment in our history: tyranny has been overthrown. The joy is immense, but there is much left to be done. Let us not fool ourselves into believing that all that lies ahead will be easy; perhaps all that lies ahead may be more difficult. . . . The destiny of Cuba, our own destiny and the destiny of our people are at stake.

> —Fidel Castro, January 8, 1959[1]

A NATIONALIST REVOLUTION

Fidel set off for Havana on January 2, 1959, leading a truck convoy of guerrilla fighters westward. This "caravan of liberty" crossed the country slowly to greet throngs of cheering Cubans and to swell popular support for the July 26th Movement. He arrived triumphantly in Havana on January 8, 1959.

Cubans embraced the 1959 revolution for many reasons, but the common thread was the broad majority's opposition to the wanton violence and widespread corruption of the Batista regime. The revolution succeeded, Fidel Castro remarked in April 1959, primarily because of the "fear and hatred of Batista's secret police."[2] The Eisenhower administration had been well aware of the cruelty that Batista's forces had inflicted on Cubans. A January 1958 State Department memo recommended that the president suspend arms shipments to Cuba, and urged the White House to warn Batista that "excessive brutalities by certain Cuban officials should be curtailed, some of the more violent and sadistic officials of the army and police be removed."[3]

Cuba's new leaders knew that revolutions can quickly turn ugly and destroy the chance for change to take firm root. They wanted to avoid the kind of Jacobin fury that emerged after the 1789 French Revolution. Yet they also sought an outlet for the seething public desire to avenge the Batista regime's atrocities. By holding public trials in Havana's central sports stadium, the new government provided a kind of cathartic focus for the pent-up emotions. Arguably, the first six months of the revolution might have been even more violent without such trials. Consider that even as one of the Batista's regime's most notorious members—Major Jésus Sosa Blanco—was being tried, vigilantes attempted to lynch two other officers awaiting judgment.[4]

Ultimately, the revolutionary government executed about five hundred Batista officials, military officers, and secret police members, and imprisoned hundreds more. Western governments quickly characterized the trials as kangaroo courts. Indeed, they did lack traditional hallmarks of procedural fairness. Yet the public trials and executions were endorsed even by conservative elements of the anti-Batista coalition, such as Prime Minister José Miró Cardona, who willingly signed numerous execution orders, and President Manuel Urrutia Lleó. While the trials thus cost the new government some international confidence, they helped the July 26th Movement to consolidate power and enhance its legitimacy. The "trials" provided the populace with an outlet for its intense anger about the horrors Batista and his henchmen had inflicted on so many innocent Cubans. In retrospect, the toll of officials and officers executed was modest in comparison to what mob justice might have produced. Moreover, thousands of lower-level military members were dismissed without any penalty.

Leaders of the Movement already had acquired popular support by repeatedly claiming that the revolution was rooted in the ninety years of struggle for independence, which had begun in 1868 with the Ten-Year War. In its Program Manifesto, the July 26th Movement did not focus on the country's growing wealth gap and entrenched poverty of the population's bottom third. It defined the revolution's aims as "national affirmation, human dignity, and democratic order."[5] The leaders charged that earlier revolutionary episodes either had been crushed or stolen by the Spanish or the United States, or had been tainted when inauthentic leaders sold out Cubans' quest for national sovereignty, as in 1933 after the 100-day government of Ramón Grau San Martín failed. Members of the Communist Party, which was called the Popular Socialist Party (PSP), similarly lacked legitimacy. Several PSP leaders had served in Batista's first administration in the 1940s, and the party as a whole had opposed armed struggle against Batista in 1956 and 1957.

The young rebels of the July 26th Movement carried no such baggage. Three of the four revolutionary leaders—Fidel Castro, Che Guevara, and Camilo Cienfuegos—had no ties to communist organizations.[6] (Raúl Castro, the fourth, had once attended a World Youth Congress sponsored by the Soviet Communist Party.) Moreover, they had earned the legitimacy to rule from the testament of battle, a willingness to give up their lives for the struggle. Sacrifice—readiness to die for the cause—became the test of authenticity. The revolutionary leaders held up as exemplars historic figures such as José Martí: "Good Cubans were expected to die for their patria."[7] By 1960, the new leaders had transformed the rebel battle cry—*libertad o muerte*, liberty or death—into a national slogan: *patria o muerte*, homeland or death.[8] In this way authenticity, death, country, and sovereignty became one.

FISSURES ARISE

Competing Interests Emerge

In his in 1796 Farewell Address, President George Washington decried the danger of faction and emphasized the importance of unity for his new, revolutionary country, the United States. He declared, "The Unity of Government which constitutes you one people is also now dear to you. It is justly so; for it is a main Pillar in the Edifice of your real independence, the support of your tranquility at home; your peace abroad; of your safety; of your prosperity; of that very Liberty which you so highly prize."[9] Similarly, José Martí repeatedly called for "social unity," Lillian Guerra explains, which "made him a fiercely seductive symbol whose appropriation became increasingly necessary for competing political sectors in the Republic as they became more divided." Martí, she notes, "emphasized the power of the collective political will and individual self-sacrifice as the means for resolving differences."[10]

Fidel hearkened to Martí as he anticipated that the new revolutionary government would soon confront the challenge of trying to satisfy competing demands from all those who had united in the single goal of overthrowing the Batista dictatorship. Without a common enemy, he feared, fissures in that unity would emerge quickly. On January 8, he asserted,

> The first thing we who created this revolution must ask ourselves is what were our intentions . . . if we created this Revolution thinking that we would overthrow tyranny and then take advantage of perks of power . . . if we thought it was a matter of getting rid of a couple of ministers to replace them with others. . . . Or if each of us acted selflessly, and each of us acted with a true spirit of sacrifice.[11]

Indeed, some moderates had joined the campaign because they were appalled by Batista's violent repression and disregard for human rights; others had focused on his regime's corruption and willingness to give the mafia effective carte blanche over part of Cuba's tourist industry. Some genuinely believed that the enormous gap between the country's rich and poor could be closed significantly through liberal democratic procedures. These moderates charged that Fidel and the July 26th Movement were "betraying" the goals that led them to join the revolution.

Class Warfare

However, some so-called moderates invoked "democracy" merely to protect their property and privilege. Saul Landau astutely observed that they "had little interest in ending the state of dependency with the United States, and absolutely no inclination to channel their wealth to the services of the majority. This was the essence of the class war that confronted Castro and the revolutionaries by the Spring of 1959."[12]

Those who had fought in the mountains and countryside (the sierra fighters) came to believe that the corruption of the old system was so deep that it could not be reformed and should not be restored. Their inclination to take a more radical approach emanated in part from their experiences with the impoverished peasantry. It was reinforced by falling sugar prices, which increased unemployment and exacerbated long-standing problems of inequality between blacks and whites, urban and rural sectors, and western and eastern Cuba. They quickly concluded that foreign domination of Cuba's economy, which prevented the country from shaping its own fate, was the cause of the dire circumstances.

US companies were not the only foreign firms involved, but they owned the largest share of Cuba's basic resources. Ninety percent of Cuba's telephone and electrical services, 50 percent of public service railways, 40 percent of raw sugar production, and 23 percent of non-sugar industries were US-owned. Three-fourths of the value of Cuba's imports originated in the United States; 59 percent of Cuban exports—including 80 percent of its exported sugar—went to the United States.[13]

Earl E. T. Smith, the US ambassador in 1959, acknowledged in congressional testimony that the United States had been "so overwhelmingly influential in Cuba that . . . the American Ambassador was the second most important man in Cuba; sometimes even more important than the President."[14] Sociologist Rafael Hernández sums up what US domination over Cuba meant in 1958: "the United States determined a certain type of Cuban state, an economic and social order, a structure of power, and even a political culture."[15]

AMBIVALENCE ABOUT THE UNITED STATES

In this light, the quest for sovereignty, for an authentic Cuban independence, naturally directed Cuban leaders to transform their country's relationship with

Fidel Castro

After meeting Fidel Castro in April 1959, US vice president Richard Nixon wrote that the Cuban leader "has those indefinable qualities which make him a leader of men."* Robert S. McNamara, former US secretary of defense and World Bank president, told Philip Brenner in 2001 that among the group of more than two hundred world leaders he had met, he would rank Castro as the third most impressive (presumably after John F. Kennedy and Lyndon B. Johnson, presidents under whom McNamara had served). Scores of heads of state attended Castro's funeral in 2016 and lauded his singular contributions to Cuba and the third world. A brief biography cannot capture the essence of what made him a towering historic figure; it provides merely the outline of his life.

Fidel Alejandro Castro Ruz was born in Biran, Holguín, on August 13, 1926. His father, Ángel Castro, had gone to Cuba from Galicia, Spain, in 1895 as a soldier in the Spanish army and went back to Spain in 1898. Impoverished, he returned to Cuba, borrowed funds to buy land, and operated a 25,000-acre plantation, of which he owned only 2,600 acres. His mother, Lina Ruz González, was a servant at the plantation. She was born in western Cuba to Spanish émigrés.

Havana's aristocracy tended to treat Fidel as an unpolished outsider in 1942 when he arrived at the Jesuit-run, prestigious El Colegio de Belén. But his talents and self-confidence enabled him to gain begrudging acceptance among the elites. For some of them, especially those who had known Fidel personally, the ensuing revolution then became a personal as well as a class "betrayal."

Fidel's first wife, Mirta Díaz-Balart, came from a wealthy and politically influential family. Her brother, Rafael, a classmate of Fidel's at the University of Havana, introduced her to the future Cuban leader. Rafael's father, also named Rafael, became minister of communications and transportation during the Fulgencio Batista dictatorship. Batista also named Rafael (the son) as deputy minister of the interior, the dreaded secret police. (Rafael emigrated to the United States in 1959. Two of his four sons were elected to the US House of Representatives where they became virulent opponents of a US-Cuban rapprochement.)

Fidel first began to focus on politics at the University of Havana, where he studied law. Incensed by the corruption of the Ramón Grau San Martín government, he joined the Ortodoxo (Orthodox) Party shortly after Eduardo Chibás founded it in 1947. That same year, he also joined a group committed to the overthrow of Rafael Trujillo, dictator of the Dominican Republic, and another group that advocated the independence of Puerto Rico. He became head of both, as well as a leader of the Federation of University Students.

(continued)

---

* Richard M. Nixon, "Rough Draft of Summary of Conversation between the Vice-President and Fidel Castro," April 25, 1959, reprinted in Jeffrey J. Safford, "The Nixon-Castro Meeting of 19 April 1959," *Diplomatic History* 4, no. 4 (Fall 1980): 431.

Fidel Castro (*continued*)

In April 1948, Fidel traveled to an international student congress in Bogotá, Colombia, which was planned as a protest to the founding meeting of the Organization of American States there at the same time. Caught up in a spontaneous riot (known as the *Bogotazo*) that followed the assassination of popular political leader Jorge Eliécer Gaitán, Fidel claims to have barely escaped from Colombia without arrest. He claimed the experience had "a great influence on me. It reaffirmed some ideas and concepts I already had about the exploited masses, the oppressed, the people seeking justice."*

Fidel was an Ortodoxo candidate for a seat in the Cuban House of Representatives when Batista canceled the 1952 election after the coup. With his younger brother, Raúl, Fidel then organized a group to overthrow the dictatorship and restore the constitutional republic. The July 26, 1953, attack on the Moncada Barracks in Santiago de Cuba led to his arrest. Released in 1955 under a general amnesty, Fidel left for Mexico to organize from exile an armed insurrection. As commander in chief of the rebel army, he directed the military actions of the 26th of July Movement, and following the 1958 Pact of Caracas, Fidel became head of the unified anti-Batista struggle.

In 1959, Fidel was initially the commander in chief of the new Cuban armed forces and quickly took on the responsibility of prime minister. He served as first secretary of the Communist Party of Cuba from its founding in 1965 until 2011. Under the 1976 constitution, he became president of the Council of State and president of the Council of Ministers, positions he temporarily relinquished in 2006 due to illness and formally in 2008. He died on November 25, 2016, in Havana.

---

* Fidel Castro, *My Early Years*, ed. and trans. Deborah Shnookal and Pedro Álvarez Tabío (Melbourne: Ocean Press, 1998), 124.

the United States. That goal did not emerge from an anti-American ideology or from the leaders' visceral hatred of the United States, antipathy to US democracy, or envy of US wealth, as some critics have alleged.[16] The conclusion that Cuba could not be both sovereign and dependent on the United States was based on the accumulation of experiences during the previous sixty-year period, as a result of specific US actions in Cuba, and drew from theoretical currents popular in Latin America known as "dependency theory."[17] Cuban anti-Americanism was akin to what historian Max Paul Friedman described in his seminal study of the phenomenon throughout the world. Especially in Latin America, he observed, anti-Americanism was not a concept or ideology but a response to US intervention and exploitation.[18] Indeed, it was characterized more by distrust than dislike. Louis Pérez aptly observed that there was a "pervasive ambiguity" for Cubans about North Americans, which alternated "between trust and suspicion, between esteem and scorn, between a desire to emulate and a need to repudiate."[19]

Fidel Castro declared in his first public speech on January 1, 1959, "The history of '95 will not repeat itself. This time the *mambises* [revolutionary fighters] will enter Santiago de Cuba!"[20] He was referring to the end of the 1895–1898 Independence War, when US forces prevented General Calixto Garcia from entering Santiago with his troops. The meaning was evident: this time the United States would not be able to seize control from the revolutionaries.

Cuba's relationship with the United States lay at the heart of the divisions among the anti-Batista factions. For the wealthiest 20 percent of the Cuban population, a break with the United States would produce a fundamental identity crisis because it had acculturated itself intimately to North America's social norms and values. Pérez describes how the process of acculturation had shaped the elites' worldview:

> The well-being of many people, specifically as it related to economic development and prosperity, which also implies social peace and political order, was increasingly linked to the United States: entry to its markets, access to its products, use of its capital, application of its technology. . . . These were complex social processes, for they involved the incorporation of a new hierarchy of values into Cuban life. Tens of thousands of Cubans of all classes—children and adults, men and women, black and white—were integrated directly into North American structures at virtually every turn; as customers, clients, coworkers, as employees and business partners, in professional organizations and voluntary associations, at school and in social clubs, in church and on teams.[21]

The Cuban elite had sent its children to US universities so that they subsequently could take up management positions with US companies on the island. They had used US products to convey a sense of higher status, and deemed anything American better than anything Cuban—from the arts to the design of buildings, to business strategies. In the late 1950s, Cubans would proudly point to the new Havana Hilton—now the Habana Libre—as an example of great Cuban architecture (see figure 8.1). In fact, it was a based on a standard template that Hilton used throughout the world.

As wealthy Cubans did in the early twentieth century when radicals seemed poised to change the social order, some once again called on the United States to intervene in Cuban affairs. Washington was receptive. US officials hoped to maintain the "special relationship" that emanated from both the investments US corporations had made in Cuba and the close ties between Cuban property owners and US capital. These were the very bonds the nationalist revolutionaries aimed to cut so that decisions about Cuba's economy could be

Figure 8.1. Poster of the new Habana Hilton from 1957.

made in Havana, not New York or Washington. The United States had almost never allowed a country in its sphere of influence to act so independently.

The revolutionary leadership viewed the 1954 US-engineered coup in Guatemala, which overthrew the democratically elected government of Jacobo Arbenz, as a demonstration of what to expect from the United States. Castro unsuccessfully attempted to blunt the negative US reaction that he expected, making a goodwill trip to the United States in April 1959. Cuba also offered to repay owners of confiscated lands a price that was greater than their assessed values in tax records, and promised to deliver eight million tons of sugar to the United States at a below-market price. But the actions and rhetoric of the revolutionary leaders convinced the US government and most of Cuba's elites that they could not trust the new government.

FAVORING THE "CLASES POPULARES"

Adapting to a New Culture

As New Year's celebrations heralded the coming of 1960, profound changes were evident at all social and economic levels. Many middle-class Cubans already had lost their jobs working for the departing US companies or Cuban bourgeoisie, and those in the former lower ranks saw improvements in their lives. Small farmers gained land, peasants gained education, blacks gained the formal end of racial segregation, urban workers saw reduced rent for housing. "Never before in Cuban history had a government so unabashedly favored the *clases populares*,"[22] political scientist Marifeli Pérez-Stable observes.

Change involved more than a matter of economic losses or gains. The former elite experienced a profound alienation from the new order. Edmundo Desnoes captured the sensation in his 1967 novel, *Inconsolable Memories*. The narrator is a former businessman who survives by living off the wealth he had accumulated. Even though he was unwilling to abandon his homeland—as his wife, family, and friends did—the narrator was unable to accept the revolution's new priorities, which placed a higher value on education and hard work than on consumption and the display of material possessions. "Reality seems to be slipping through my fingers," he observes. "The revolution has introduced a new vocabulary. Words I don't use but hear, as if they were Mexican or Venezuelan expressions, or Argentinisms, my own language but in a foreign country. If I keep on being so isolated from everything that's going on around me, the day will come when I won't understand a thing."[23]

Ending Racial Disparities

Even for those whose lives improved, the disruptions were bewildering as norms and roles changed. The government promoted a new public consciousness that challenged routine daily practices and even the way people talked to each other. In a March 1959 speech, newly appointed prime minister Fidel Castro called for an end to all legal forms of discrimination—in schooling, employment, and public facilities—and said that racism was tantamount to acting as a traitor against the Cuban state. "It should not be necessary to pass a law to establish a right that is earned for the simple reason of being a human being and a member of society," he asserted, adding,

> What should be proclaimed is anathema and public condemnation against those men, full of leftover prejudices, who have so few scruples that they discriminate against a Cuban, mistreat a Cuban, over a matter of lighter or darker skin. . . . We are going to put an end to racial discrimination at work centers by waging

a campaign . . . to end this hateful, repugnant system with a new slogan: work opportunities for every Cuban, without racial or sexual discrimination. In this way we will forge, step by step, the new homeland.[24]

Blacks and mulattos made up a much higher proportion of the population in Cuba than in the United States. The 1953 census recorded 26.9 percent of Cuba as black or mulatto; in the 1981 census it was 33.9 percent.[25] While racial discrimination before 1959 may have been less a result of interpersonal prejudice than in the United States, it was entrenched in the way Cuban institutions functioned. Lourdes Casal, a seminal scholar on the subject of racism in Cuba, pointed out that several factors softened the expression of racism. "[T]he most important leaders of the Cuban independence struggle such as José Martí (white) and Antonio Maceo (black)," she wrote, placed great emphasis on "racial unity and integration."[26]

Still, darker-skinned Cubans attended schools—when they were available—vastly inferior to those for whites. Afro-Cubans had the worst living conditions and held the lowest-paid jobs. There was some social mobility for nonwhite Cubans: Cubans elected Fulgencio Batista, a light-skinned mulatto, as president in 1940. But the white, upper-class Havana Yacht Club denied membership to Batista while he was in office from 1940 to 1944.

Ending Gender Disparities

Gender inequality was perhaps even more entrenched than racism. It also was quickly challenged. Notably, the 1955 "Manifesto Number One" of the July 26th Movement called for the end to "all vestiges of discrimination for reasons of race or sex."[27] Data from the 1953 census reveal some indication of women's inequality in Cuba at the time: only 19 percent of the workforce were women. While the overall literacy rate for men and women was comparable, only two-thirds of ten-year-old girls were attending school; fully two times the number of men versus women over the age of twenty-five had received any university education. The problem was not merely the result of overt discrimination and the lack of opportunity. Cuba, like most of Latin America, had a macho culture whose norms reinforced notions of "men's" and "women's" work. Daily rituals structured different men's and women's roles in the family and in their social relations outside of the home.

While Fidel asserted in 1966 that the "phenomenon of women in the revolution was a revolution within a revolution,"[28] the prominent women revolutionary fighters—such as Celia Sánchez, Haydee Santamaría, and Melba Hernández—focused their energies on ousting Batista, not on fighting for women's equality. Vilma Espín Guillois, Raúl Castro's wife, became the champion for women in the new society (figure 8.2 shows how her contributions garnered her representation on a postage stamp).

Figure 8.2.   A 2008 postage stamp honoring Vilma Espín Guillois.

Espín was the first woman in Cuba to obtain a chemical engineering degree. She fought alongside Raúl in 1957 and 1958, and they married in 1959, three weeks after the triumph of the revolutionary forces. In 1960, she took charge of the newly created Federation of Cuban Women. Her goal was to gain legal equality for women, to make those rights meaningful by providing support that women needed in order to engage fully in society—day care, skills training, education, and cultural awareness—and to advocate for women's advancement in all sectors of society.[29]

Cuban film director Humberto Solás conveyed the impact of the changed status for women in his epic 1968 film, *Lucía*, which consists of three stories about women named Lucía in three different revolutionary periods, 1898, 1933, and the early 1960s. In the first story, Lucía is an idle upper-class Cuban woman who unintentionally betrays her brother, a soldier fighting for independence, as the result of a naïve romance with a Spanish spy. In the 1933 episode, Lucía is a revolutionary, but serves merely as an adjunct to the men. The third Lucía lives in the countryside with her husband, who expects his wife to cater to him in traditional ways. But she wants to be educated and is painfully torn between her love for him and her anger at his attempts to limit and deny her the opportunities for education that the Cuban revolution was offering.

QUEST FOR SOVEREIGNTY

Hovering over all the changes was the quest for sovereignty. The leaders of the 1959 revolution believed that if they failed to secure this goal, their victory would be nearly as hollow as previous revolutionaries. True independence would mean that Cuba, not foreign companies, had control over the country's basic resources and infrastructure. It also meant that Cuba would

Hard Currency

The term "hard currency" refers to money generally accepted for international trade. Economists call such funds convertible currencies. Today only the US dollar, European euro, Japanese yen, and British pound merit the designation.

People who live in countries that create one of the four freely convertible currencies, such as the United States, may find it difficult to appreciate the anxiety most countries of the world suffer because they do not have ready access to hard currency. But consider a simple example that suggests why sellers require buyers to use hard currency for international transactions. Suppose you had traveled to a town in the United States hundreds of miles from home. Short on cash, and without a credit card, you find that all ATM machines are broken when you need to pay your motel bill. Fortunately, you brought a check from Pit Stop Bank in your city. But would the motel owner be likely to accept your check? Would you accept such a check in payment for selling goods or your services? The currencies of most countries are like a check from Pit Stop Bank, which is why those countries need to use a universally acceptable currency.

There are essentially three legal ways in which Cuba obtains hard currency. It can: (1) sell goods or services for hard currency, including sugar, tobacco, pharmaceuticals, beach vacations, and the labor of Cubans; (2) receive "gifts," including foreign assistance grants from governments and remittances from individuals; (3) take out loans from an international financial institution, a bank, a global corporation, or a foreign government, which typically must be repaid in hard currency. "Gifts" have become increasingly less available to poor countries, and loans—in the worst cases—may incur interest payments that could absorb as much as 50 percent of a country's hard currency earnings from the first two sources.

Most countries cannot be self-sufficient and must rely on imports in order to survive. Cuba imports food, oil for heating, electricity, transportation, manufactured goods, and even ordinary items of daily life such as needle and thread. With only a limited reserve of hard currencies earned from selling goods and services, Cuba must evaluate every import in relation to the total amount of hard currency it has available to spend. This situation presses Cuba to search continually for a strategy that will enable it to earn more hard currency in order to develop its economy.

need to expand its trading relations, so it would not depend on only one country, and to diversify how it earned hard currency beyond selling sugar. Relying mainly on sugar exports left the country vulnerable to the variability of the international commodity market, while the cost of finished products that the country needed to import kept rising.

Cuba's reliance on sugar as its main source of hard currency had several harmful consequences. Cane was grown on land that could have produced food for domestic consumption, and as a result, Cuba had to spend scarce hard currency on importing food. Cuba's infrastructure was oriented to sugar production, which made starting other industries expensive. Work in the sugar industry was mostly seasonal, and laborers commonly had no employment or income for eight months of the year. The resulting inequality forced Cuba to depend on foreigners for a range of services that poorly educated Cubans could not provide.

In short, by 1960 Cuba's revolutionary leaders assumed that in order to develop a citizenry that had the dignity to believe in its own self-worth, they had to establish the country's sovereignty, which would require a transformed relationship with the United States. In effect, Cuba's leaders chose sovereignty over dependency and the quest for sovereignty became the Cuban Revolution's guiding objective.

NOTES

1. Fidel Castro Ruz, "Discurso," January 8, 1959, http://www.cuba.cu/gobierno/discursos/1959/esp/f080159e.html.

2. Thomas Bergenschild, "Dr. Castro's Princeton Visit, April 1959," as quoted in Gott, *Cuba*, 166.

3. William A. Wieland, "Memorandum from the Director of the Office of Middle American Affairs (Wieland) to the Assistant Secretary of State for Inter-American Affairs (Rubottom)," *Foreign Relations of the United States, 1958–1960*, Volume VI, Cuba (Washington, DC: US Department of State, Office of the Historian), Document 5, January 17, 1958, 10.

4. R. Hart Phillips, "Batista Major Condemned in Havana Stadium Trial," *New York Times*, January 24, 1959, 1.

5. "Program Manifesto of the 26th of July Movement," November 1956; reprinted in *Cuba in Revolution*, ed. Rolando E. Bonachea and Nelson P. Valdés (Garden City, NY: Anchor Doubleday, 1972), 113.

6. Antoni Kapcia, *Cuba in Revolution: A History Since the 1950s* (London: Reaktion Books, 2008), 28.

7. Pérez, *To Die in Cuba*, 332.

8. Pérez, *To Die in Cuba*, 338.

9. George Washington, "The Farewell Address," Transcript of the Final Manuscript, September 19, 1796; available at the Papers of George Washington, University of Virginia, 5 and 6, http://gwpapers.virginia.edu/documents/farewell/transcript.html.

10. Lillian Guerra, *The Myth of José Martí: Conflicting Nationalisms in Early-Twentieth-Century Cuba* (Chapel Hill: University of North Carolina Press, 2006), 6.

11. Castro, "Discurso," January 8, 1959.

12. Saul Landau, "Asking the Right Questions about Cuba," in *The Cuba Reader: The Making of a Revolutionary Society*, ed. Philip Brenner et al. (New York: Grove, 1988), xxiii.

13. Ibarra, *Prologue to Revolution*, 18–19, 35; Thomas G. Paterson, *Contesting Castro: The United States and the Triumph of the Cuban Revolution* (New York: Oxford University Press, 1994), 35; Robin Blackburn, "Prologue to the Cuban Revolution," *New Left Review*, no. 21 (October 1963): 59–60.

14. Testimony of Earl E. T. Smith in "Communist Threat to the United States Through the Caribbean," Hearings before the Subcommittee to Investigate the Administration of the Internal Security Act and Other Internal Security Laws of the Committee on the Judiciary, US Senate, 86th Cong., 2nd Sess., Part 9, August 30, 1960.

15. Rafael Hernández, "Intimate Enemies: Paradoxes in the Conflict Between the United States and Cuba," in *Debating US-Cuban Relations: Shall We Play Ball?* ed. Jorge I. Domínguez, Rafael Hernández, and Lorena G. Barberia (New York: Routledge, 2011), 20.

16. Brian Latell, *After Fidel: The Inside Story of Castro's Regime and Cuba's Next Leader* (New York: Palgrave Macmillan, 2005); Jaime Suchliki, "Why Cuba Will Still Be Anti-American After Castro," *Atlantic*, March 4, 2013.

17. H. Michael Erisman, *Cuba's Foreign Relations in a Post-Soviet World* (Gainesville: University Press of Florida, 2000), 36–42; Heraldo Muñoz, ed., *From Dependency to Development* (Boulder, CO: Westview, 1981); Fernando Enrique Cardoso and Enzo Faletto, *Dependency and Development in Latin America* (Berkeley: University of California Press, 1979).

18. Max Paul Friedman, *Rethinking Anti-Americanism: The History of an Exceptional Concept in American Foreign Relations* (New York: Cambridge University Press, 2012), chapter 4.

19. Pérez, *Cuba and the United States*, xvi.

20. Antonio Nuñez Jiménez, *En Marcha con Fidel—1959* (Havana: Editoria Letras Cubanas, 1998), 24. Translation by the authors. Original: "¡La historia del 95 no se repetirá! ¡Esta vez los mambises entrarán en Santiago de Cuba!"

21. Pérez, *On Becoming Cuban*, 7, 157.

22. Pérez-Stable, *The Cuban Revolution*, 67.

23. Edmundo Desnoes, *Inconsolable Memories* (New Brunswick: Rutgers University Press, 1990), 140.

24. Fidel Castro Ruz, "Speech," March 23, 1959. University of Texas, "Castro Speech Data Base, http://www1.lanic.utexas.edu/project/castro/db/1959/19590323.html.

25. Alejandro de la Fuente, "Race and Inequality in Cuba, 1899–1981," *Journal of Contemporary History* 30, no. 1 (January 1995): 135.

26. Lourdes Casal, "Race Relations in Contemporary Cuba," in *The Cuba Reader: The Making of a Revolutionary Society*, ed. Philip Brenner et al. (New York: Grove, 1988), 477.

27. Quoted in Sarah Stephens, *Women's Work: Gender Equality in Cuba and the Role of Women in Building Cuba's Future* (Washington, DC: Center for Democracy in the Americas, 2013), 21.

28. Fidel Castro, "Speech at Close of Fifth FMC National Plenum," December 10, 1966, http://lanic.utexas.edu/project/castro/db/1966/19661210.html.

29. Max Azicri, "Women's Development through Revolutionary Mobilization," in *The Cuba Reader: The Making of a Revolutionary Society*, ed. Philip Brenner et al. (New York: Grove, 1988), 457–66; Raisa Pagés, "The Status of Women: From Economically Dependent to Independent," in *A Contemporary Cuba Reader: Reinventing the Revolution*, ed. Philip Brenner et al. (Lanham, MD: Rowman & Littlefield, 2007).

Chapter 9

Consolidating the Revolution

Culture and Politics

The character of "Cuban" had become contested terrain, and the contest itself served as a force of change. Never before had the narrative on nationality so fully engaged the public imagination. Much of this had to do with the affirmation Cuban, of a Cuba for Cubans. . . . The proposition of Cuban resonated across the island. Once more consumption became a way to affirm nationality, but now the products were Cuban-made. Advertisers stressed the virtues of locally produced merchandise. Vitamin supplement Transfusán B-12 was identified as "Cuban and better!" . . . The demand for Cuban spread in all directions. Architects called for a national building style. "Operación discos Cubanos" announced a campaign to organize a national record company. The National Ballet was established in June 1959. A national film company, the Cuban Institute of Cinematographic Art and Industry (ICAIC), was organized in March 1959. Cuban musicians and entertainers began to work the nightclub and cabaret venues. For the first time since its opening in 1957, the Copa Room at the Hotel Riviera staged an all-Cuban production.

—Louis A. Pérez, Jr.[1]

The Revolution exhilarated a broad majority of Cubans, giving them hope that they could right the wrongs of neocolonial exploitation and remedy long-term injustices. (In 1960, a respected public opinion poll found that 86 percent of respondents supported the government and half of those were "fervent" backers.[2]) Yet that spirit alone would hardly suffice to achieve revolutionary goals. The victors faced daunting tasks in four arenas if they were to make the 1959 revolution different than the failed efforts in 1898 and 1933: (1) *Culture*, strengthening Cubans' identity with the country by privileging and even creating a distinctive Cuban culture; (2) *Politics*, changing the relationship between the citizen and the state; (3) *New institutional order*,

96

including new ministries, legal structures, and processes so that the Revolution did not depend only on Fidel's charisma; (4) *Economics*, reconstituting the economy in a way that engendered growth with equity and enabled the government to satisfy everyone's basic human needs. We will explore how they pursued the goals of the first two realms in this chapter, and examine the other two in the next chapter.

CULTURE

Especially in the early years, the possibility that Cubans actually could achieve the revolution of their dreams had to be sustained largely by faith, not results. Revolutionary change would entail sacrifices: the middle and upper classes would lose wealth, privileges, and status; workers and peasants would be deprived of normalcy, some of their values would be challenged, and demands for nonpaid "social labor" would disrupt routines of daily life. Clashes with the United States would involve the loss of life and could cause the economy to suffer. This made Fidel Castro's charismatic leadership essential to the success of the Revolution, infusing it with a messianic energy.

Ever since the 1960s, when American pundits began to misapply the concept of "charisma" to characterize the handsome President John F. Kennedy, the term has been casually used to describe anyone who seems to make a crowd swoon. But true charisma is a rare power that the populace itself grants to a leader, and it is achieved only when followers believe the leader shares their values and goals. "Charisma implies a social relation between leader and followers," sociologist Nelson Valdés explains.[3] In turn, the public accepts and reveres the charismatic leader with a blindness akin to faith. Historian Oscar Zanetti further explains: "In the context of a fluid social situation, with the old political system in crisis and its institutions falling apart, the personality of Fidel Castro was decisive for the consolidation and development of the revolutionary process."[4]

There is no question that Fidel Castro had the captivating public persona, private beguiling charm, and fierce determination that gave him the capacity to be a charismatic leader. Fidel also acquired a godlike imprimatur due to a remarkable coincidence—or perhaps skillful animal training. On January 8, 1959, as he began a two-hour speech at the old military command center in Havana, a dove landed on his shoulder and remained perched there. In the *Santeria* religion—a mixture of Catholic traditions and West African, Yoruba-based rituals widely practiced in Cuba—"a white dove represents the divinity Obatalá," a king among the gods.[5] And thus was Fidel divinely anointed.

The revolutionary leaders understood the importance of symbols as a source of inspiration, legitimacy, and shared experience. They placed seemingly insignificant items, such as the handkerchief that Che Guevara used in the mountains, in a new museum commemorating the Revolution. The date of the failed 1953 Moncada attack became a national holiday and the *Granma*—the boat on which Fidel and company sailed from Mexico to Cuba in 1956—was enshrined prominently on a major artery in Old Havana.

Creating the New Cuban

At its core, the Cuban Revolution sought to put into practice an egalitarian vision, which contributed to its worldwide attractiveness. The vision is based on the Enlightenment assumption that while human beings are "perfectible," their institutions make them imperfect. Socialists, such as Che, who hold this view of human potential assert that people are inclined by their very nature to act with a social conscience for the collective benefit of the whole society. From this perspective, when members of a society act selfishly, greedily, or without concern for the welfare of others, their behavior is unnatural or alien to their true self.

Egalitarians recognize that the human instinct for survival may drive people to be self-seeking in the face of scarcity. But if a society can produce enough for everyone's basic needs yet chooses to create pockets of scarcity through unequal distribution, then the source of the selfishness is the society's institutions and the laws and norms that regulate and protect the institutions. In turn, such laws and norms lead people to focus exclusively on their individual needs—whether these are real or apparent—in order to compete with each other or to use others for their own gain. In this process, people become alienated from their full human potential, which can be realized only within a context of institutions that encourage sharing and a regard for everyone's well-being.

But how could the revolutionaries hope to create a culture oriented to collective welfare with people who had been acculturated to individualistic values of the old society, who believed that selfishness, acquisitiveness, and a dog-eat-dog world were the natural order? Che Guevara responded that they had to recognize that the "flaws of the past are translated into the present in the individual consciousness," and as a result the character of Cubans reflected an "unmade quality." The goal would be to create "a new man."[6] (As was common at the time, Cuban leaders used the gendered term "hombre" or "man" in referring to all people.) Cubans with a new consciousness would eschew "the satisfaction of their personal ambitions," Guevara wrote in 1965, and "become more aware every day of the need to incorporate themselves into society."[7]

Ernesto "Che" Guevara

Ernesto "Che" Guevara de la Serna was born on June 14, 1928, in Argentina, where he trained as a medical doctor. He was in Guatemala in 1954 when US-backed military officers staged a coup against the democratically elected government, and moved to Mexico where he met Fidel and Raúl Castro in July 1955. Accompanying them on the *Granma*, which brought the revolutionary fighters to Cuba in 1956, Guevara became a commander during the ensuing guerrilla war and a leader in the Revolutionary government.

As one of the principal theorists of Cuban revolutionary ideology, Guevara articulated the concept of the *foco*, believing that a small group of dedicated guerrilla fighters could spark a revolution in a country where the conditions were "ripe." In Cuba, he was the leading advocate for the development of the "new Cuban man"—a person who placed the collective welfare ahead of self-interest—in order to bring about a humane and just society.

Guevara left Cuba in 1965 to work with independence and insurgent movements in Africa. He returned briefly in 1966, and then went to fight against the Bolivian government. Bolivian rangers, aided by US intelligence operatives, ambushed him on October 8, 1967, and executed him the next day. In his honor, Fidel proclaimed 1968 as the "Year of the Heroic Guerrilla" and Cuba has designated October 8 as the "Day of the Heroic Guerrilla."

The aspiration to create the new Cuban man effectively served as the cultural guidepost almost from the beginning of the Revolution, even though the leaders did not at first articulate it.[8] The transition process from the old to the new Cuban man, Guevara asserted, required reeducation that should not take place only in schools. Cubans needed to learn the meaning and practice of the new morality repeatedly, through their daily activities and relationships. In Guevara's view, this approach necessitated the use of "moral incentives" to motivate people, not "material incentives," because material incentives would tend to reinforce individualism and self-seeking gain.

A *moral* incentive is one that inspires a person to work harder or to act for the benefit of society—for the communal good—on the basis of a nonmaterial interest, such as patriotism, compassion, or solidarity. A *material* incentive is a tangible reward—such as money or access to scarce goods—provided to those who produce more, take on greater responsibilities or risks, or perform essential tasks for society.

Differences within the leadership over using material or moral incentives to develop the new society became a source of cleavage in the early 1960s. In practice, the use of moral incentives is usually accompanied by inefficiency. Appeals to a common purpose are less likely to engender consistent hard work than differentiated rewards to individuals, especially those who had not

yet developed the mind-set of the "new Cuban man." The reliance on invoca-
tions to solidarity was likely to generate less output. For a poor country like
Cuba, reduced production meant fewer basic necessities would be available,
which could undermine popular support for the revolution itself. The debate
over using moral incentives is one that continues to frame Cuban development decisions even today because the Cuban Revolution has maintained two
goals, which at times have been incompatible: economic growth and equity.[9]

Some scholars have asserted that Che Guevara was unique among the
founding revolutionaries as the main advocate for the use of moral incentives.[10] But Guevara's viewpoint did not lose its potency when he left Cuba in
1965. Fidel Castro continued to be a forceful advocate for moral incentives.
"What is the duty of the revolution other than to strengthen awareness, raising
people's moral values of all kinds?" he asked rhetorically in a 1968 speech.
"Money is still the means of obtaining many things: to go to the movies, to
go here and there . . . as a means of distribution, but it is a bitter transitional
instrument and an instrument that we must abolish."[11]

A New Moral Order

At times the clash between the old and new cultures emerged as a contest
over the meaning of "civilization." Historian Louis Pérez points out that the
revolutionaries sought "to rearrange in usable form the standards by which
to measure civilization and in the process summon a vision of an alternative
moral order."[12] They argued that the level of civilization should be gauged
by the percentage of people who were illiterate and unemployed, and by the
number of children who suffered from parasites, not by the extent to which
Cubans had access to appliances and other conveniences that might enable
them to live comfortably.

Still, at first, officials did not try to bring about the new moral order in a
draconian way, by imposing rigid cultural strictures on writers and artists.
On the contrary, the early years of the revolution unleashed an enormous
outpouring of vibrant cultural expression in search of a distinctive Cuban
culture.[13] Cubans were treated to a lush array of creativity in films, the
plastic arts, theater, dance, television and radio programs, magazines and
books, and music.

Nueva trova, or the new folksong, became a vehicle for expressing a revolutionary spirit, and Cuban folk songs soon became popular internationally
as an expression of political protest. Pablo Milanés and Silvio Rodríguez
sang songs about personal and political liberation. The government promoted
Afro-Cuban rhythms as a way of replacing the cha-cha and big band tunes
that had appealed to American tourists.

The official newspaper of the July 26th Movement, *Revolución*, included a literary supplement every Monday—*Lunes de Revolución*—which quickly gained international acclaim as the most widely read literary supplement in Latin America.[14] *Revolución*'s editor, Carlos Franqui, had aspired to be minister of culture. Instead, Castro gave him license to create a world-class literary magazine. Franqui envisioned the publication would be at the forefront of a Cuban cultural revolution.[15]

Led by acclaimed writer Guillermo Cabrera Infante and his deputy, the poet, playwright, and novelist Pablo Armando Fernández, *Lunes* attracted prominent international contributors: existential philosophers such as Jean-Paul Sartre and Albert Camus, Latin American literary giants such as Pablo Neruda and Jorge Luis Borges, Beat poets such as Allen Ginsberg and Lawrence Ferlinghetti, and feminist advocates such as Virginia Woolf and Simone de Beauvoir. The subject matter in *Lunes* ranged widely as it covered all of the arts. The magazine also established a record company and a publishing house, and produced a weekly television program that featured modern plays, jazz, and experimental films. In effect, *Lunes* became the main forum for debates about Cuban culture and identity.[16]

Pablo Armando Fernández Poem*

En voz baja decir, amor, tu nombre	Quietly, my love, to speak your name
junto a ti, a tus oídos, a tu boca.	next to you, to your ear, to your mouth.
Y ser ese animal	And be that happy animal,
feliz, que junta sus mitades.	which joins its halves.
En voz baja o sin ella, muda	Quietly or silently, the voiceless mouth
la boca revertida a su unidad:	restored its unity:
silencio inaugural que a verbo y carne	inaugural silence which grants new life
otorga nueva vida.	to the word and the flesh.
Los ojos, ciegos, de regreso al todo:	The eyes, blind, returning to the whole:
luz revelando mundos	light revealing worlds
como fueron o son, como serán.	as they were or are, as they shall be.
Vueltos a ser alegria del otro,	Back to being each other's joy,
uno consigo mismo en companía.	be oneself in company.
Una vida otra: la tuya, tan amada.	Another life: yours, so beloved.
Volver a ser origen sin tristeza	Back to being origin without sadness
o dolor, sin miedo, sin nostalgia, o	or pain, without fear, nor nostalgia,
con ellos:	or with them:
tu y yo, nuestros recuerdos y cenizas.	you and I, our memories and ashes.

* From "Suite Para Maruja" in *Learning to Die*, trans. John Brotherton (Havana: Instituto Cubano del Libro, 1995).

The explosion of creativity inevitably ran the risk of challenging the government's determination to maintain unity. The Cuban government's strategy to defend the island from a feared US attack centered on the idea of a "people's war" against the invaders. Toward this end, in the fall of 1959 it created a militia made up of volunteers. Yet the central element of the government's strategy was the assumption that the United States would be deterred from invading if the country appeared unified. Unity thus became a singular goal and officials viewed dissent as a vital threat. In pursuit of unity, the government began to assert that the Revolution and *la patria* were one and the same. This new meaning for Cuban nationalism made criticism of the Revolution nearly equivalent to treason against the nation.[17] Recall, though, that an emphasis on unity was not unique to Fidel and the July 26th Movement. It had been preached by Martí and George Washington for similar strategic reasons.

The rebel leaders also sought unity in order for the government to provide services and goods efficiently, especially to the large part of the population that had been underserved previously. This aim, they reasoned, could not be achieved if there were factional strife and political stalemate.[18] The resulting measures aimed at generating unity left an indelible imprint on the Cuban Revolution.

Repression

By 1961, the leadership began to view independent intellectuals as a threat, because they could undermine both the "faith" of believers and, in turn, the Revolution's fragile unity. In June 1961, Fidel indicated that the government's limits of tolerance had been reached. During the course of a three-day meeting with "intellectuals," he laid down a new principle. "We do not forbid anyone from writing on any subject he chooses," the Cuban leader said, "or in the manner he considers appropriate." The Revolution, he asserted, must give an opportunity to all "honest" writers and artists, even to those who were not animated by a "revolutionary spirit," to express themselves freely and to use their creativity. But this freedom would be available only if their creative work was consistent with the Revolution. Castro tersely summarized the rule by declaring, "within the revolution, everything; against the revolution, nothing."[19]

The phrase left writers and artists confused and apprehensive. The Cuban leader had not specified what was to be considered "within" or "against" the Revolution. Without guidelines, lesser officials enforced Castro's dictum arbitrarily, which had the effect of stifling freedom of expression. In an evocative passage from *The Man Who Loved Dogs*, prize-winning Cuban novelist Leonardo Padura described how Fidel's order impacted one "fictional" writer who had submitted a story to his university's literary magazine. "'How dare you turn this in?'" the magazine's director said "in a rage."

> [T]hat story was inopportune, unpublishable, completely inconceivable, almost counterrevolutionary—and hearing that word, as you can imagine, caused a chill. . . . That day what really happened was that they fucked me for the rest of my life, since . . . I left there deeply convinced that my story should never have been written, which is the worst thing that they can make a writer think.[20]

Stifled expression was the effect that Fidel likely intended, as he sent a clearer message in this regard by closing down *Lunes de Revolución* in November 1961. Carlos Franqui left the country, along with other prominent writers. The government offered a soft exile for Guillermo Cabrera Infante, Pablo Armando Fernández, and poet Héberto Padilla. They became cultural attachés in the Cuban embassies in Brussels, London, and Moscow, respectively.

While some repression was justified at first by the goal of avoiding stalemate, it soon became routine. Spurred on by the seeming demands of national security, the state's repressive apparatus came to eclipse other claims for resources. Fear replaced hope as petty bureaucrats were given license to exaggerate threats or engage in spiteful acts of cruelty.

The height of repression came in the early 1960s. Just prior to the 1961 US-sponsored Bay of Pigs invasion, the Cuban government arrested thousands of people in a roundup intended to prevent the invaders from linking up with internal fighters. While most were released quickly, Fidel acknowledged in 1965 that twenty thousand political prisoners continued to be incarcerated.[21]

Late in that year, the military began to "draft" thousands of people whom the regime designated as "socially deviant": Jehovah's Witnesses and other religious missionaries, homosexuals, and "vagrants." They were placed in prison-like camps euphemistically dubbed "Military Units to Aid Production" (UMAP). Ordered to do nonremunerated labor, the prisoners were ostensibly in the camps to be reeducated. The UMAP program lasted for two years. The government disbanded it in 1967 after the Cuban National Union of Writers and Artists protested the drafting of writers and university professors.[22]

Relations with the Church Sour

Initially the new regime did not perceive the Catholic Church as a threat. Even though Cardinal Manuel Arteaga y Betancourt had close ties to Batista, he "was also on very good official terms with the Revolutionary Government," Fidel Castro remarked in a 1985 interview with a Brazilian priest, Frei Betto.[23] In fact, historian Margaret Crahan has noted, "there had been fairly widespread support on the part of the churches for the overthrow of the Batista dictatorship."[24] Yet the Catholic Church was unprepared for the extent of socioeconomic changes the revolutionaries would undertake, which affected the holdings of foreign entities to which many Church officials were tied. About five of every six priests among the three thousand in Cuba were from Spain. Castro remarked, in this vein, that "The revolutionary laws produced conflicts, without a doubt, because the bourgeois and landed sectors, the rich sectors, changed their attitude toward the Revolution. . . . That's how initial conflicts with the Church began, because those sectors wanted to use the Church as a tool against the Revolution."[25]

Tension came to a head in August 1960, as a majority of bishops approved a pastoral letter declaring that communism and Catholicism were incompatible. The letter reflected increasingly outspoken charges that the government had become infiltrated with communists.[26] At about the same time, Father John Walsh, a US priest, began working with Cuban churches on a CIA-sponsored program that used children as pawns to sow fear and dissent within Cuba in order to undermine the government's legitimacy.

Called "Operation Peter Pan," the project began with a scare campaign. According to Antonio Veciana, a leader in the underground terrorist organization Alpha 66, he and CIA operative David Atlee Phillips spread false rumors that the Cuban government planned to abolish parental rights, remove children from their homes—especially those in religious families—and dispatch them to the Soviet Union where they would be indoctrinated with Marxist-Leninist dogma.[27] Local parishes then offered the frightened families a chance to send their children to the United States where they supposedly would be cared for by well-intentioned US Catholic groups enlisted by the CIA and State Department. More than fourteen thousand children between the ages of six and sixteen traveled unaccompanied by their parents, most without relatives waiting for them in the United States. Some never saw their parents again.[28]

POLITICS

New Government

On January 2, 1959, the day after Batista fled and his government collapsed, the July 26th Movement installed Manuel Urrutia Lleó as provisional president and José Miró Cardona as prime minister. They headed a coalition cabinet that assumed both executive and legislative powers. Urrutia had been a moderate judge whose sympathies lay with the July 26th Movement, but who had not been politically active. His father had been a major in the Independence War against Spain, but he imagined his role essentially as symbolic. He enjoyed rising late, had no taste for political battle, and was fixated on the singular goal of ridding the island of vices such as gambling. Miró Cardona was president of the national bar association (formally, the Cuban College of Lawyers) and had been one of Fidel Castro's law school professors. A civil libertarian, he had refused to accept many of the demands Batista sought to impose on the judiciary, and had attempted to fashion a "Civic Dialogue."[29]

Below them, a range of Batista's opponents took seats in the new cabinet, which moderate reformers dominated. It included only a few members of the July 26th Movement, such as Armando Hart and Enrique Oltuski, or close collaborators, such as Faustino Pérez. Fidel claimed he did not want a government post, but Urrutia named him commander-in-chief of the armed forces.[30]

The coalition did not hold together for long. Barely one month after its formation, Miró Cardona relinquished his position. Arguing that Fidel effectively was running the government, the departing prime minister said that the rebel leader might as well hold the official title. Castro accepted the position, on the condition that he would chair cabinet meetings and that Urrutia could not attend them.[31] In May 1959, the cabinet replaced Urrutia with Osvaldo Dorticós Torrado. An upper-class lawyer, Dorticós already had served the new government as minister of justice.

In October, a cabinet shuffle brought in Raúl Castro as minister of defense, moving Fidel loyalist Augusto Martínez Sánchez to the Ministry of Labor. The next month Faustino Pérez and Manuel Ray resigned their ministerial posts. Pérez had been in charge of cataloging and distributing properties owned by Batista and his cohorts; Ray was in charge of public works. Seventeen months later, Ray was one of the commanders in the Bay of Pigs invasion.

By the beginning of 1960, nearly all of the moderates were gone from the cabinet. With defections seeming to occur daily, the situation provided an opportunity for former PSP adversaries of the July 26th Movement to ingratiate themselves with the new leaders. They had been left out of the coalition initially but had no interest in joining defectors who were headed to exile in the United States. Their steady accumulation of influence in 1960 in turn led to outright opposition by some anti-communist moderates.

Military

Perhaps the most dramatic early rejection came from Húber Matos, a former rice grower who had risen to the rank of comandante (major) in the rebel army and was serving as the military governor of Camagüey Province. Matos felt especially aggrieved by the new government's agrarian reforms, which he viewed as evidence that communists had seized control of the Revolution. On October 19, 1959, he resigned his post and several of his lieutenants left with him.

To Fidel and Raúl, the resignations were an ominous threat to the country's stability in its heartland, in part because of Camagüey's economic importance as a source of cattle for the country.[32] The day after Matos resigned, Fidel sent Camilo Cienfuegos, the army chief of staff, to arrest the dissident major in his home. Speaking to a rally of half a million people, the prime minister asserted that Matos was a "traitor" who intended "to use soldiers against the Revolution, against the rights of the Cuban people."[33] A court convicted Matos of treason and he served twenty years in prison.

Matos's departure highlighted a challenge the revolutionary government faced in constituting a new national army. It certainly was not going to use senior officers in the hated Batista military, which numbered 18,500 troops when his government fell.[34] But the victorious rebel army was less than half that size at the time of the Revolution. Nevertheless, it became the cornerstone of Cuba's new military, the Fuerzas Armadas de la Revolucion (FAR) or the Revolutionary Armed Forces. In addition, in the wake of Matos's arrest, Fidel announced on October 26 the creation of the National Revolutionary Militia, a people's army.

Raúl Castro took the central role of transforming the rebel forces into a professional institution within three years, expanding it to about 300,000 members at its largest.[35] While some have attributed the makeover to the organizational help of the Soviet Union, it actually happened before the Soviet Union came on the scene in a major way. By 1962, the militia numbered nearly 150,000 members.

The most difficult campaign that the new army faced was the seven-year war against counterrevolutionaries, most of whom operated out of the Escambray Mountains in west central Cuba.[36] From 1959 to 1966, various groups of "bandidos"—as Fidel dismissively labeled them[37]—engaged in a variety of attacks that today most Americans would describe as terrorism. They not only killed Cuban soldiers and militia, but also volunteer teachers; they detonated bombs in factories and stores, burned crops, and destroyed aqueducts and electric transmission lines.[38]

General Fabián Escalante Font, a former head of Cuban counterintelligence, asserts that during the seven-year period, these groups committed 5,780 acts of terror, of which 716 were acts of sabotage against industrial sites.[39] While former Batista officers and officials did make up the initial counterrevolutionary units, some wealthy Cubans who had opposed the Batista dictatorship began to take up arms against the new regime as it nationalized more property and increased the distribution of wealth. Veteran journalist Richard Gott identifies an additional factor leading to counterrevolution: "The old elite . . . was also alarmed by the way in which the Revolution had allowed the black population, hitherto largely invisible, to

Destruction of *La Coubre*

On March 4, 1960, an explosion in Havana harbor destroyed the French freighter *La Coubre*, killing more than eighty people and wounding more than three hundred. Dockworkers had been unloading from the ship tons of Belgian-made munitions the Cuban government had purchased. Fidel Castro blamed the CIA. The United States denied the charges of CIA involvement, and the cause of the blast has never been determined definitively.* The following day, Castro declared a national day of mourning. At the funeral, he declared for the first time a refrain that became a national slogan, *¡Patria o Muerte, venceremos!* (Homeland or Death, we will be victorious!).

* R. Hart Phillips, "Castro Links U.S. to Ship 'Sabotage'; Denial Is Swift," *New York Times*, March 6, 1960, 1; Carlos Alzugaray and Anthony C. E. Quainton, "Cuban-U.S. Relations: The Terrorism Dimension," *Pensamiento Propio*, no. 34 (July–December 2011): 72.

emerge onto the stage."[40] During a 1996 conference about the Bay of Pigs, exiled militants estimated that there may have been as many as ten thousand armed fighters among the various resistance groups, and one hundred thousand supporters of the counterrevolution.[41]

Two of the most important groups were backed by the Catholic Church: the Movement to Recover the Revolution (Movimiento de Recuperación Revolucionaria, or MRR) and the Christian Democratic Movement (Movimiento Demócrata Cristiano, or MDC), both of which began to receive covert funding in 1960 from the CIA. The MRR emerged in December 1959 from the Comandos Rurales, or Rural Commandos, an organization of Catholic activists with an avowed mission to teach literacy to the counterrevolutionaries. Its founder was Manuel Artime Buesa—a lieutenant in the Rural Commandos who previously had been designated to be a provincial agrarian reform manager. But he feared the agrarian reform process would go too far, and hoped to use the MRR as the base to fight for his own vision of a Cuban revolution.[42]

By mid-1960, most of the groups were coordinating plans under the umbrella of the Democratic Revolutionary Front (Frente Revolucionario Democrático, or FRD), and the new organization selected Artime, the MRR leader, as its national coordinator. But once the CIA became involved, the autonomy of the Cuban counterrevolutionaries essentially ended. Lino Fernández, a medical doctor and the military commander of the MRR, commented in 1996 that "the idea of calling the internal resistance and giving us control of the Cuban fight was inconceivable to the CIA. The CIA tried to do everything themselves. . . . It was almost—again I speak as a psychiatrist—pathological."[43]

By 1962, Raúl's organizational success had produced an efficient force that was versatile enough to perform important nonmilitary functions: building roads and infrastructure, helping to distribute goods, and providing for health care, especially important because so many Cuban doctors already had emigrated to the United States. As Hal Klepak explains, Fidel Castro turned to the military for a large number of tasks because he wanted "people he could trust in positions of importance, especially those such as agrarian reform where US and local opposition was soon strong and always vocal." But given the small size of the FAR, his choices were limited. Klepak notes that as a result, young soldiers "took over portfolios for which they often had little or no training. Loyalty to the comandante and to his revolutionary program counted for more than efficiency in these trying but heady days."[44]

NOTES

1. Pérez, *On Becoming Cuban*, 482–83.
2. Domínguez, *Cuba*, 198.
3. Nelson P. Valdés, "The Revolutionary and Political Content of Fidel Castro's Charismatic Authority," in *A Contemporary Cuba Reader: Reinventing the Revolution*, ed. Philip Brenner et al. (Lanham, MD: Rowman & Littlefield, 2007), 28.
4. Zanetti, *Historia Mínima de Cuba*, chapter 9. [Authors' translation.]
5. Ivor L. Miller, "Religious Symbolism in Cuban Political Performance," *TDR: The Drama Review* 44, no. 2 (Summer 2000): 30.
6. Ernesto Che Guevara, "Man and Socialism in Cuba," in *Man and Socialism in Cuba: The Great Debate*, ed. Bertram Silverman (New York: Atheneum, 1973), 341–43.
7. Guevara, "Man and Socialism in Cuba," 343–44.
8. Fagen, *The Transformation of Political Culture in Cuba*, 13.
9. María del Carmen Zabala Argüelles, "Poverty and Vulnerability in Cuba Today," in *A Contemporary Cuba Reader: The Revolution under Raúl Castro*, ed. Philip Brenner et al. (Lanham, MD: Rowman & Littlefield, 2014), 191–93.
10. See, for example, Jorge Castañeda, *Compañero: The Life and Death of Che Guevara* (New York: Vintage, 1998); Carmelo Mesa-Lago, *The Economy of Socialist Cuba: A Two Decade Appraisal* (Albuquerque: University of New Mexico Press, 1981), 23–32.
11. Fidel Castro Ruz, "Speech Commemorating the 11th Anniversary of the March 13, 1957, Action Held at the Steps of the University of Havana," March 13, 1968 [authors' translation], http://www.cuba.cu/gobierno/discursos/1968/esp/f130368e.html. Also see Julie Marie Buncke, *Fidel Castro and the Quest for a Revolutionary Culture in Cuba* (University Park: Pennsylvania State University Press, 1994).
12. Pérez, *On Becoming Cuban*, 482. Also see Bertram Silverman, "Introduction: The Great Debate in Retrospect: Economic Rationality and the Ethics of Revolution," in Bertram Silverman, ed., *Man and Socialism in Cuba* (New York: Atheneum, 1973), 15.

13. Ana Serra, *The "New Man" in Cuba: Culture and Identity in the Revolution* (Gainesville: University Press of Florida, 2007), 2–3.

14. Quirk, *Fidel Castro*, 384.

15. Interview with Pablo Armando Fernández, January 8, 1992, Havana, Cuba.

16. William Luis, "Exhuming *Lunes de Revolución*," *CR: The New Centennial Review* 2, no. 2 (Summer 2002).

17. Valdés, "The Revolutionary and Political Content of Fidel Castro's Charismatic Authority," 30, 32, 34.

18. Jesús Arboleya, *The Cuban Counterrevolution*, trans. Rafael Betancourt (Columbus: Ohio University Press, 2000), 46, 50; Fidel Castro Ruz, "Discurso para Respaldar las Nuevas Tarifas Telefonicas y la Intervencion, Efectuada en el Teatro de la CTC," March 6, 1959, http://www.cuba.cu/gobierno/discursos/1959/esp/f060359e.html.

19. Fidel Castro Ruz, "Discurso como Conclusion de las Reuniones con los Intelectuales Cubanos," June 16, 23, and 30, 1961." Translation by the authors. http://www.cuba.cu/gobierno/discursos/1961/esp/f300661e.html.

20. Leonardo Padura, *The Man Who Loved Dogs*, trans. Anna Kushner (New York: Farrar, Straus and Giroux, 2014), 70–71.

21. Domínguez, *Cuba*, 253.

22. Larry Oberg, "The Status of Gays in Cuba: Myth and Reality," in *A Contemporary Cuba Reader: Reinventing the Revolution*, ed. Philip Brenner et al. (Lanham, MD: Rowman & Littlefield, 2007); Domínguez, *Cuba*, 356–57.

23. Betto, *Fidel and Religion* (Havana: Publications Office of the Council of State, 1987), 194.

24. Margaret E. Crahan, "Freedom of Worship in Revolutionary Cuba," in *The Cuba Reader: The Making of a Revolutionary Society*, ed. Philip Brenner et al. (New York: Grove, 1988), 212.

25. Betto, *Fidel and Religion*, 195.

26. Joseph Holbrook, "The Catholic Church in Cuba, 1959–1962: The Clash of Ideologies," *International Journal of Cuban Studies* 2, no. 3/4 (Autumn/Winter 2010): 270–71.

27. Saul Landau, "The Confessions of Antonio Veciana," *Counterpunch*, March 12, 2010.

28. María de los Angeles Torres, *The Lost Apple: Operation Pedro Pan, Cuban Children in the US, and the Promise of a Better Future* (Boston: Beacon Press, 2003), 8.

29. Thomas, *Cuba*, 1065–66.

30. Zanetti, *Historia Mínima de Cuba*, chapter 9.

31. Thomas, *Cuba*, 1197.

32. Herbert L. Matthews, *Revolution in Cuba: An Essay in Understanding* (New York: Scribner, 1975), 138–40.

33. Fidel Castro Ruz, "Discurso," October 26, 1959, http://www.cuba.cu/gobierno/discursos/1959/esp/f261059e.html; Antonio Nuñez Jiménez, *En Marcha Con Fidel—1959* (Havana: Fundacion de la Naturaleza y el Hombre, 1998), 323–40.

34. Domínguez, *Cuba*, 347.

35. Hal Klepak, *Raúl Castro and Cuba: A Military Story* (New York: Palgrave Macmillan, 2012), 23–26.

36. Norberto Fuentes, *Nos Impusieron la Violencia* (Havana: Editorial Letras Cubanas, 1986).

37. Antonio Nuñez Jiménez, *En Marcha Con Fidel—1961* (Havana: Fundacion de la Naturaleza y el Hombre, 1998), 33.

38. Nuñez Jiménez, *En Marcha Con Fidel—1961*, 34.

39. Fabían Escalante Font, *The Secret War: CIA Covert Operations against Cuba, 1959–1962*, trans. Maxine Shaw (Melbourne: Ocean Press, 1995), 152.

40. Gott, *Cuba*, 172.

41. James G. Blight and Peter Kornbluh, eds., *Politics of Illusion: The Bay of Pigs Invasion Reexamined* (Boulder, CO: Lynne Rienner, 1998), 19–21.

42. Blight and Kornbluh, *Politics of Illusion*, 174–75; US Congress, House Select Committee on Assassination, 1979. "Investigation of the Assassination of President John F. Kennedy," vol. X: Appendix to Hearings, March, 7.

43. Blight and Kornbluh, *Politics of Illusion*, 13.

44. Hal Klepak, "The Revolutionary Armed Forces: Loyalty and Efficiency in the Face of Old and New Challenges," in *A Contemporary Cuba Reader: The Revolution under Raúl Castro*, ed. Philip Brenner et al. (Lanham, MD: Rowman & Littlefield, 2014), 74.

Chapter 10

Consolidating the Revolution

Economic Reforms, New Institutions, and Basic Needs

NO ROAD MAP TO GUIDE PLANS
FOR DEVELOPMENT WITH EQUITY

US vice president Richard M. Nixon was prepared to encounter anti-US demonstrations when he traveled to eight South American countries on a goodwill tour in April and May 1958. After all, the purpose of the trip was to assuage some of the hostility toward the United States that had been growing in the region.[1] But he was not expecting the depth of antagonism he experienced in Venezuela on May 13, when four thousand people attacked his motorcade with rocks, eggs, tomatoes, and spit. With only twelve Secret Service agents to protect him, demonstrators nearly succeeded in turning over his car.

A shocked President Eisenhower then sent his brother, Milton Eisenhower, to the region to discern the root cause of such vehement anti-Americanism. In a report released on December 27, 1958—four days before Batista fled Cuba—Dr. Eisenhower provided a stark picture of despair and turbulence, much of which could have described Cuba as well:

> Latin America is a continental area in ferment. While its productivity is increasing, so is its population, at an unprecedented rate. A high degree of illiteracy, poverty, and dependence on one-commodity economies with consequent wide fluctuations in income still characterize most of this vast area. But the people generally, including the most humble of them, now know that low standards of living are neither universal nor inevitable, and they are therefore impatiently insistent that remedial actions be taken.[2]

In terms of standard indicators such as per capita income, literacy, infant mortality, and life expectancy, Cuba actually ranked among the top five countries in Latin America.[3] But it was hardly thriving. Most Cubans suffered from declining real wages as the cost of basic goods increased faster than wages, which contributed to a growing and unsustainable income gap between rich and poor. More than 40 percent of Cuban workers in 1958 were either underemployed or unemployed (the official unemployment rate in 1958 was 16 percent).[4]

Recall from chapter 6 that sugar cane workers made up approximately 25 percent of the national labor force, and averaged less than four months of work each year. Cuba's literacy rate was only 75 percent while thousands of teachers were unemployed. Advanced medical services were concentrated in Havana and unavailable to most Cubans. Inequities between the rich and poor were reflected not only in housing, education, health care, and other basic services, but more generally in the aspirations of urban and rural Cubans.

There was no map to guide the revolutionaries, no example of a poor country that had been able to achieve both sustained economic growth and an end to inequality in a short time. One possibility was a strategy called "import-substitution industrialization" (ISI) to which several Latin American countries had been attracted. It was based on the premise that third world countries remained poor because advanced capitalist nations took advantage of them in their trade relationships: the richer countries purchased commodities (coffee, sugar, copper, wood, rubber, and the like) at low and declining prices, and in turn sold finished products using these commodities back to the poorer countries at increasingly higher prices. One solution to this structural disadvantage seemed to be for the poor countries to produce industrial products themselves. In fact, ISI was the strategy the United States followed in its early days in order to overcome its dependency on Great Britain, which purchased the largest share of US agricultural exports such as cotton and had been the main source of finished goods imported by the United States.

While no Latin American country had been successful in using the ISI strategy, it was the most attractive model to the new Cuban leaders. They believed that the fundamental obstacle to the country's economic growth was its reliance on sugar for export earnings and its dependent relationship with the United States. In addition, they were not enamored of the rigid Soviet model of state planning and centralized control, or the Chinese model of extreme collectivization. Those models seemed inapplicable to Cuba. Both of these large countries had populations vastly greater than Cuba's, and possessed natural resources—especially sources of energy—that enabled them to rely less on imports than Cuba did.

Yet the revolutionary government chose to institute other changes before diversifying what Cuba produced and reducing what it needed to import.

Look at Me

Figure 10.1. **Campesino husband, wife, two daughters, and their friends, Matanzas Province, 1974. Photo by Philip Brenner.**

On a trip through rural Matanzas Province in 1974, Philip Brenner stopped unannounced late one afternoon at the home of a farm worker. His house had a thatched roof with sides and floors made of wooden boards. In front, there was a small garden featuring a banana and a lemon tree. A tall, thin man with a broad, toothless grin opened the door. Inside, his two young children played with friends in the eight-by-ten-foot entrance hallway that served as the living room. His wife was in the kitchen at the back of the living room. After some chitchat, Brenner began his questioning in the manner of a probing investigative reporter. Did the man support the Cuban revolution? Brenner asked. A blank stare. The thin man blinked his eyes. He could not fathom the stupidity of the question. "Look at me," he began calmly. He was thirty-five but looked a haggard sixty-year-old. "Look at my healthy children," he exclaimed. "Look at this house—it has solid walls and a floor." The government provided the wood, nails, and tools; he and his neighbors built the house in a weekend. He and his wife had their own bedroom. There is a paved road in front of their house, a school to which their children can walk in five minutes, and a medical clinic nearby that obviously did not exist when the man was growing up in this area. "Yes, I support the Cuban revolution." He smiled.

These reforms created a dynamic that ultimately limited the options Cuba could choose in attempting to advance growth with equity.

MAJOR ECONOMIC AND SOCIAL CHANGES

Agrarian Reform Law

Land reform had been a high priority for the July 26th Movement because of the high concentration of land ownership in Cuba. Only twenty-two *latifundio* (plantations) controlled more than 70 percent of the land used for producing sugar.[5] But the aim of redistributing property was hardly a novel or even radical objective. Cuba's Ortodoxo Party had long advocated land reform. In the early 1960s, the Alliance for Progress, a hemisphere-wide development program that the United States spearheaded, sought to break up large plantations in Latin America and distribute land to individual farmers. Defending the Alliance's goals on its first anniversary in 1962, President John F. Kennedy declared, "Those who make peaceful revolution impossible will make violent revolution inevitable."[6]

In May 1959, the revolutionary government announced an Agrarian Reform Law that limited the maximum landholding size to one thousand acres.[7] The government parceled out land in excess of that acreage to farm workers. About 100,000 rural farm workers each received sixty-six acres free under this "land-to-the-tiller" program.[8] At the same time, the government took control of 40 percent of Cuba's rural property, creating large state farms. Workers on state farms received a salary throughout the year, which significantly raised their standard of living.

Instituting land reform also involved the creation of new towns in the countryside. From 1959 to 1962, the government built eighty-three towns, each with three hundred to five hundred residents. The settlements offered basic services, such as schools and health care, that previously only had been found in urban areas. Indeed, the goal of agrarian reform was not merely redistribution of land. "Fidel and his comrades," according to Antonio Nuñez Jiménez, the first head of the National Institute for Agrarian Reform (INRA) and a Fidel Castro confidant, were concerned about "the precarious health of the peasants," which they reasoned was a consequence of a lack of adequate sanitation, electricity, and communications in the countryside.[9] Sociologist Susan Eckstein notes that in 1958 "less than ten percent of rural homes had electricity, and less than three percent had indoor plumbing." In all of Cuba's rural areas, there were only three general hospitals.[10]

At the same time, rents for most urban dwellers were cut by 50 percent as the government limited what a landlord could charge for an apartment. It also required Cubans owning more than two properties to hand over the excess to the government, which then classified them as social property. Large houses, for example, were transformed into day care centers. In October 1960, under the Urban Reform Law, the government took over all rental property and established that rent would be no more than 10 percent of a tenant's income.

By the end of 1960, the wealthiest 10 percent of the population had lost nearly all of their property, privileges, and political power. They were forced to pay new luxury taxes; their private schools and clubs were closed; private beaches were opened to the public; private clinics were forced to treat indigent patients. In turn, the lower classes—especially urban Afro-Cubans and all those in rural areas—received immediate benefits because historically they had suffered the greatest unemployment and had received the fewest public services.

Making Lemonade from a Lemon

The 1959 Agrarian Reform Law proved to be a turning point for the Cuban elite. A few began to organize themselves to wage a counterrevolutionary war against the new government. Many others voted with their feet, leaving Cuba. The emigration of skilled Cubans affected the Revolution in both negative and positive ways. On the one hand, the loss of doctors, teachers, and technicians deprived the country of essential expertise needed for development. With novices replacing experienced government planners and administrators, key services became unavailable or were provided poorly. Militants who were barely into their twenties and accustomed to guerrilla informality quickly found themselves overwhelmed by bureaucratic rules

Death of a Bureaucrat

In his 1966 film, *Death of a Bureaucrat*, acclaimed Cuban director Tomás Gutiérrez Alea mocked bureaucratic logjams Cubans were experiencing. When an exemplary worker dies, his family honors his dedication by burying him with his worker identification card. Problems arise when they need the ID in order to obtain a new ration card to purchase food. The sons opt to exhume their father's body to obtain the card. But before they can return the cadaver to its grave, a policeman wanders by, and so they run off with it to their home. When they try formally to return the body, an official tells them that it cannot be reburied because there was no record of the dead man being exhumed. In one evocative scene, an uncle attempts to locate a supervisor in a large office building to solve the problem. Arriving at midday, he encounters empty offices, rows of file cabinets, and a lone man with a broom, fruitlessly sweeping a hallway strewn with papers flying all around.

and impossible goals. As output dropped, the resulting serious shortage of foreign exchange prevented the government from importing goods that could provide for basic needs.

On the other hand, emigration gave the revolutionaries opportunities to make lemonade from this lemon, to turn the loss into a positive for the Revolution. Migration removed opponents who might have challenged the revolutionary government had they stayed on the island, and it created a safety valve that released pressure, which might have animated potential opponents to organize themselves if the possibility of leaving did not exist.[11]

With this class of Cubans gone, the government could more easily forge ahead with programs that would benefit a large majority of Cubans. As a result, enthusiasm was partly able to substitute for expertise. Cubans of all ages willingly put in extra hours doing voluntary work as they shared in a common national experience to develop the country together. Everyone became a teacher, sharing personal knowledge with someone less knowledgeable. Sixth graders taught third graders and retired doctors taught medical students who, in turn, trained new nurses. The most well known example of this phenomenon was the National Literacy Campaign.

Educational Change

Fidel Castro announced the literacy campaign in a UN address on September 26, 1960, setting a goal "of teaching every single inhabitant of the country to read and write in one year." This followed on what already had been a determined effort to direct resources toward educating children. Elementary school enrollment jumped between 1958 and 1960 from 625,000 to more than one million. The number of schoolteachers in the country increased by nearly 50 percent to 24,400; in rural areas, the number doubled to more than 10,000. At the same time, the government built as many new rural classrooms as prior governments had created in total during the prior fifty years.[12]

The ambitious effort to educate illiterate Cubans—to enable everyone to read minimally at a first-grade level—mobilized nearly 250,000 people, including 100,000 students mostly between the ages of ten and seventeen, inspired by what Jonathan Kozol described as "a kind of 'ethical exhilaration.'"[13] Young *brigadistas* were trained for a few weeks and then sent off throughout the country, typically living with a family where there was an illiterate person.[14] This mode of teaching served many purposes.

There was a pedagogical rationale for the approach. Abel Prieto, who later became minister of culture, explained in 1981 that "an illiterate is usually embarrassed when another person thinks that he or she is ignorant. So it is better to put the literacy worker into the house of the illiterate," that is, into

Literacy Campaign

The teachers' manual, *Alfabeticemos* (*Let Us Teach Literacy*), included guidelines (*orientaciones*) for helping the brigadistas work effectively with rural Cubans. "Remember," it cautions, "that many students have vision and hearing defects that can make learning difficult."* It also included brief lessons about the goals of the Revolution and problems Cuba faced (see cover and table of contents in figures 10.2 and 10.3), as well as a glossary of political terms. The curriculum in the students' workbook, ¡Venceremos! (*We Shall Overcome!*), included some revolutionary sloganeering ("The fishermen's cooperative helps the fisherman. The fisherman is no longer exploited."). Exercises involved writing, using words in simple sentences, and repeating key words to teach pronunciation.

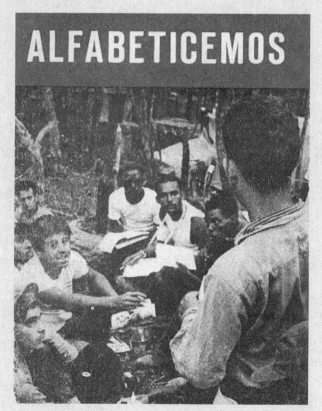

Figure 10.2.   Cover

(continued)

---

* *Alfabeticemos: Manual para el Alfabetizador*, Comisión Nacional de Alfabetización, Ministerio de Educacion, Cuba, 1961 (copy in possession of the authors).

Literacy Campaign (*continued*)

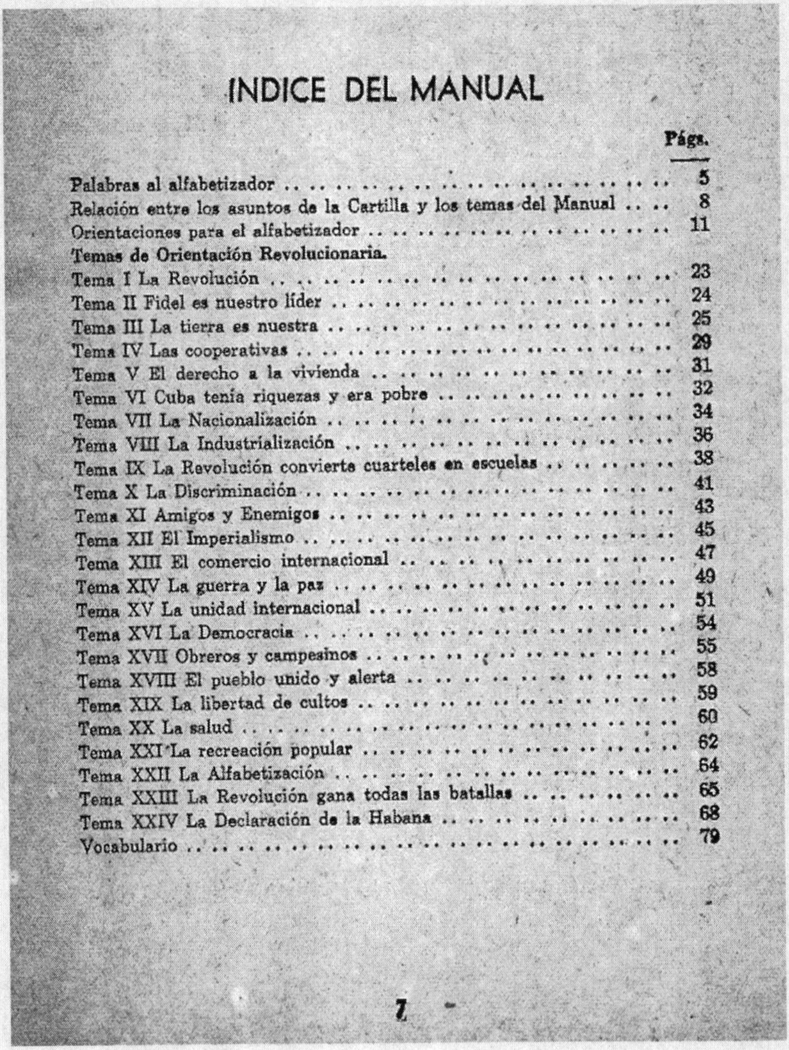

INDICE DEL MANUAL

7

Figure 10.3. Table of contents

a comfortable environment rather than a traditional classroom.[15] Indeed, a brigade's first task was to determine who lacked literacy in an area because embarrassment kept people from identifying themselves as such. The campaign ultimately determined there were 980,000 illiterate adults out of the approximately four million adults in the country. When the National Literacy Campaign ended after one year, Cuba's literacy rate had skyrocketed to 96.1 percent, the highest in Latin America. Many Cubans were grateful for the campaign's efforts, as shown in the letter presented in figure 10.4.

The literacy campaign also served political objectives. By involving so many people—the people who acquired literacy and their families, the teachers and their families, and communities—it provided an example of a collective effort that proved successful. The curriculum offered a way of

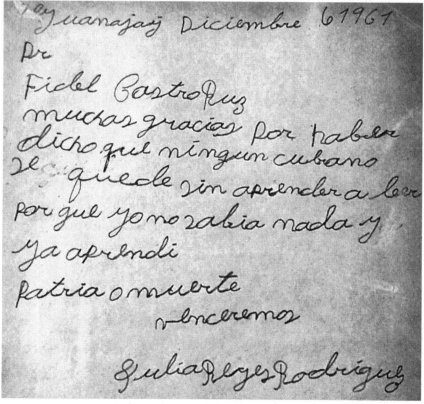

Figure 10.4. Letter from Julia Reyes Rodríguez to Prime Minister Fidel Castro Ruz, written at the end of the 1961 Literacy Campaign; archived in the Museum of the Literacy Campaign, Havana, Cuba. Photo by Sonya Grier. Translation by the authors: *Guanajay December 6, 1961, Dr Fidel Castro Ruz, Thank you very much for having said that no Cuban should be left without learning to read because I knew nothing and now I learned. Homeland or death we shall be victorious. Julia Reyes Rodríguez*

spreading the Revolution's ideas to the countryside, and it helped the teachers
to develop a revolutionary consciousness. It also gave the urban brigadistas
an understanding about rural poverty that the Revolution was committed to
eradicating, as well as a meaningful experience with rural workers, which
helped to break down negative stereotypes.

Improving Health Care

Cuba has been acclaimed as a model for providing excellent health care
for all its citizens.[16] While the revolutionary government deserves credit
for extending comprehensive care beyond the larger cities, such as Havana,
Santiago de Cuba, and Camagüey, the country's health indicators in 1958 already were above average for Latin America. Previous governments also had
established a national public health service and a few mutual aid cooperatives
that functioned like health maintenance organizations.

This structure provided a basis for the revolutionary government to launch
an effort in 1962 to eradicate polio. Within one year, "Cuba became the first
country in the Americas and the second country in the world to effectively
eliminate" the disease, Marguerite Rose Jiménez reports.[17] Notably, though,
the existing health system alone would not have enabled the country to
achieve this feat. Jiménez explains that the Cuban model, which the rest
of Latin America adopted in some version, also required central coordination, community mobilization, an extensive public education campaign, and
outreach to the entire population. Cuba's achievement in eradicating polio
was made all the more remarkable by the fact that almost two-thirds of the
medical professionals—including more than 2,000 of the 6,300 doctors on the
island—left the country in the first few years of the Revolution.[18]

Providing Adequate Nutrition

Food was a thornier problem. As noted earlier, Cuba's colonial relationship
with Spain and neocolonial relationship with the United States distorted its
agricultural production in favor of a single export crop—sugar—along with
tobacco. Small farmers did grow crops for their own subsistence. But even
if they had harvested more fruits and vegetables than they consumed, the
country lacked distribution networks to get the produce from farms to cities,
where the majority of Cubans lived.

Consider the Cuban diet today. Cubans tend not to favor fish—which is
plentiful in the sea around the island—because fish was not traditionally part
of a Cuban's diet. There was no commercial fishing industry before the Revolution, which would have been necessary for deliveries of sufficient quantities
in urban areas. As a consequence of its sugar monoculture, Cuba had to use

scarce hard currency resources to import food. In the early 1960s, as exports declined so did food imports. Hunger became a serious concern, except for those who could afford to buy imported food.

The revolutionary government's partial solution was food rationing. To be sure, other countries have relied on various types of rationing. During World War II, US consumers could buy only limited amounts of items such as sugar, butter, and gasoline, because of the need to divert supplies to the war effort. Starting in 1962, Cuba used rationing to provide everyone with enough food for a basic diet. The ration book, called a *libreta*, covered a large number of items and was distributed to every household.[19] But a family's libreta was usable only at a designated store, and many times stores did not have the food supposedly "guaranteed" by the program.

Shortages were acceptable, though, because they affected everyone, not only the poor. Cuban officials demonstrably suffered too. Fidel, Raúl, and Che were vigilant about avoiding the kind of corruption that delegitimated reform and revolutionary governments elsewhere. Ultimately the system of food rationing functioned well enough so that malnutrition disappeared in Cuba until the 1990s.

ADDING ORDER TO REVOLUTIONARY FERVOR

Intent on bringing about change quickly, the revolutionary leaders made decisions on the fly, continually experimenting as they simultaneously tried to solve immediate problems and fashion a coherent plan for the country's development. In one case, the government hastily constructed a housing complex at the edge of Havana for squatters from the countryside. The new residents brought their farm animals with them—chickens, pigs, and even cows—and within a year the complex became uninhabitable. Problems arose as turf battles between ministries created duplication, waste, and inefficiency.[20] The leadership soon recognized that slogans, good intentions, and trenchant critiques were not enough to transform the economy. They needed new organizations to move the Revolution forward, and a set of rules to coordinate the work of the new structures. The process of rationalization, adding order to revolutionary fervor, began with the creation of several new ministries, each empowered to control a critical aspect of the economy.

New Ministries

INRA, the agrarian reform institute, was foremost among the new ministries, and it spawned several others: the Ministry of Industries (headed by Che Guevara), the Ministry of Fishing, and the Ministry of Mining.[21] By the end of

1960, two-thirds of the economy was state controlled and the Central Planning Board (JUCEPLAN) became the coordinating body for the whole economy. It was backed up by the Ministry of Internal Trade, which was responsible for wholesale and retail distribution, and the Ministry of Foreign Trade, which controlled international commerce.

Carlos Rafael Rodríguez replaced Nuñez Jiménez in 1962 as INRA's chief. Rodríguez was one of the few who did have governmental experience and a background in planning. A member of the PSP, the old Cuban Communist Party, he had been a minister in Batista's unity government during World War II. Older than Raúl and Fidel, Rodríguez gained their trust in part because of his strategic acumen, and in part because he had defied Moscow in supporting the July 26th Movement.

In the late 1950s, the Soviet Union pursued a policy of promoting "peaceful coexistence" with the United States. To Nikita Khrushchev, the Soviet premier and Communist Party general secretary, this meant that the Soviet Union would not interfere with US interests in the Western Hemisphere and the United States would not meddle in Eastern European affairs. In line with this policy, Moscow ordered Communist parties in Latin America neither to support nor engage in armed struggle and violent revolution. The order was especially relevant to Cuba's PSP, which watched as the Revolution unfolded under their noses.

Moscow did not vilify Rodríguez for his insubordination and relied on him as a link to the revolutionary government. Still, Rodríguez played a quiet role at first, mainly as an adviser to Raúl Castro. The revolutionaries sought to obscure any ties to Communists, in part to avoid arousing US concerns that Cuba would become a Soviet outpost. Rodríguez was well known as a theoretically sophisticated Marxist-Leninist and Stalinist.

However, by March 1960 former PSP officials were openly serving in government posts and Havana had established diplomatic relations with Moscow. Castro began to include Rodríguez in the small group that determined government policy, and so his appointment to head INRA was not a surprise. In 1976, he was elevated to the post of second vice president after Raúl Castro.

New Political Organizations

Fidel and those close to him believed the Revolution could succeed only if Cubans discarded a subservient mentality the Spanish had fostered during the colonial period and the United States reinforced from 1898 to 1958.[22] They wanted Cubans to embrace the Revolution as their own achievement. In this light, Castro's initial weeklong trek—from Santiago to Havana starting on January 2, 1959—had both cultural and political importance. "The salt of the earth, the *guajiros*, were bringing political freedom to the metropolis," sociologist Valdés explains. "The *guerrilleros* repeated their message at each stop: the revolutionary cause had triumphed; it was not the victory for a particular organization but a 'people's victory.'"[23]

The revolutionaries placed a great emphasis on full participation, because they believed that Cubans would develop a selfless, communitarian consciousness by actively behaving that way, not merely by reciting slogans.[24] The institutions they created for engagement were mass organizations. These were intended to link one or more significant aspects of a Cuban's daily life to the larger society. While the mass organizations were outside the governing political party, they functioned to engender loyalty and adhesion to the system.[25] They also served as a means to protect the Revolution, monitoring potential threats festering below the surface.

By the mid-1960s there were five mass organizations: Confederation of Cuban Workers (CTC in the Spanish acronym), National Association of Small Farmers (ANAP), Federation of Cuban Women (FMC), Committees for the Defense of the Revolution (CDR), and the Federation of University Students (FEU). While each organization featured voting for local representatives, they were not intended to be involved with elections for political offices. Also, in contrast to the US model of interest-group democracy—in which theoretically individuals express and promote their interests through groups such as labor unions or trade associations that then pressure the government—the Cuban model assumed that seemingly disparate interests could be made compatible once class differences were demolished. For example, where the CTC once fought for workers' interests vis-à-vis managers of private companies, the revolutionary model assumed that the old CTC role would no longer be necessary. The state had become the new management and would supposedly serve, not exploit, workers. The new role for the CTC would be to stimulate workers to be more productive, with the benefits of increased output shared universally.[26]

CDRs were created in September 1960 as a response to increased attacks by counterrevolutionaries. Organized on nearly every city block, these neighborhood watch committees became an expanded form of the people's militias formed in 1959. Their symbol was a large eye and a stylized figure raising a sword over the Cuban flag. In part, they also functioned as a means of socialization, engaging everyone in the process of providing security. By the end of the 1960s—after the government had successfully routed organized counterrevolutionary activity and the United States had ended most of its support for anti-Castro terrorists—CDRs took on a different role as a civic organization and an adjunct to social service agencies (see figures 10.5 and 10.6 for the logo and propaganda of a CDR).

Polyclinics relied on CDRs to monitor and assist released patients with their recovery. They helped to reintegrate ex-convicts into society, foster school attendance by checking on absentees, and enlist volunteers for public

Figure 10.5.   Contemporary CDR logo

Figure 10.6.   Bulletin board outside a CDR in 1974. Photo by Philip Brenner.

events and campaigns.[27] As a center of civic life, CDRs organized local sports activities and block parties.

In December 1974, one of the authors, Philip Brenner, participated in voluntary work that a CDR had organized on a Sunday morning in Varadero, in preparation for a New Year's Eve fiesta. The "workers" consisted of Brenner, who swept fallen leaves from the street, and two children, aged nine and eleven, who climbed telephone poles in order to hang streamers. Most of the neighbors were out on the street, mainly gossiping and occasionally offering advice to the three workers. No one seemed to fear being labeled counter-revolutionary for their lack of effort.

University students had long been organized through a national grassroots organization, the FEU, which had produced several national leaders prior to the Revolution and had wielded some political influence. Wary of its potential influence, the new government tried to shape the FEU's agenda. While it successfully co-opted the leadership, discontent bubbled up among the members when the government imposed constraints on universities, in terms of curriculum and students' freedom of expression. Late in 1967, the government forced the FEU to disband, claiming that it duplicated efforts because the youth movement of the Cuban Communist Party, the Young Communists (UJC), had the same members as the FEU. In reality, only the FEU leadership overlapped with the UJC. When the FEU was reconstituted in 1971, its first proclamation avowed loyalty to the Revolution.[28]

Communists (PSP)

Until mid-1961, there was no organization or party that coordinated the several mass organizations and linked them to the purposes of the government. At that point, Fidel created a new entity to serve this purpose, the Integrated Revolutionary Organizations (ORI). It was made up of members from the July 26th Movement, the Revolutionary Directorate, and the PSP. Fidel reluctantly brought PSP members into the process of rationalizing the Revolution, because he believed there was a need to include a cadre of disciplined people who could teach others about socialist principles. Aníbal Escalante, former editor of the PSP newspaper, *Hoy*, and a slavish follower of Moscow's dictums, became the ORI's organizational secretary. This proved to be a source of disruption, as Escalante used his position to place former PSP buddies in key ORI posts, providing himself with a base from which he could control the ORI.

Fidel cut Escalante's plans short in March 1962, denouncing him for "sectarianism," charging that he was "blinded by personal ambition," and exiling him to Czechoslovakia.[29] He also purged several other former PSP members from the ORI leadership, and replaced Escalante with Emilio Aragonés, who was national coordinator of the July 26th Movement. Notably, the move came at an especially sensitive moment in Cuban-Soviet relations, when Cuba was looking for military support in what it anticipated would be a new US invasion. In removing those who advocated that Cuba should adhere closely to advice from Moscow, Castro made clear that even under these dire circumstances, he would not allow the Soviets to dictate Cuba's internal affairs.

The Cuban leader contrasted his vision of the party he was proposing to what were unmistakable references about the Soviet Communist Party. The Cuban party, he declared, would have an integral link with the masses; it would not stand above them, dominating, dispensing favors as a means of control. The new ORI leaders reorganized the party at the end of 1962 and gave the new entity the name that Fidel wanted: the United Party of the Socialist Revolution (PURS). The PURS lasted until 1965, when the reestablished Cuban Communist Party (PCC) replaced it.

Thus, a communist party did not exist in Cuba in 1959. Cuba did not even renew diplomatic relations with the Soviet Union until the following year. US hostility toward the revolutionary regime during its first year emanated less from a concern about communism than about the loss of US domination over Latin America and control over a country with which the United States believed it had "ties of singular intimacy."

NOTES

1. "Letter from the Secretary of State to the Vice President," *Foreign Relations of the United States, 1958–1960*, volume V, American Republics, Document 42, Washington, DC, March 6, 1958, https://history.state.gov/historicaldocuments/frus1958-60v05/d42.

2. Milton S. Eisenhower, "United States–Latin American Relations, 1953–1958: Report to the President," December 27, 1958; reprinted in *Department of State Bulletin* 40, no. 1021 (January 19, 1959): 90.

3. Claes Brundenius, *Revolutionary Cuba: The Challenge of Economic Growth with Equity* (Boulder, CO : Westview, 1984), 5.

4. Brundenius, *Revolutionary Cuba*, 12–13.

5. Brundenius, *Revolutionary Cuba*, 43.

6. John F. Kennedy, "Address on the First Anniversary of the Alliance for Progress," March 13, 1962; American Presidency Project, University of California, Santa Barbara, http://www.presidency.ucsb.edu/ws/?pid=9100.

7. The limit was 30 *caballerías*, or 995 acres. Farms used for range land, or that were fifty percent more productive than the national average, could be as large as 100 caballerías, or 3,316 acres.

8. Domínguez, *Cuba*, 438.

9. Nuñez Jiménez, *En Marcha Con Fidel—1959*, 148. Also see Minor Sinclair and Martha Thompson, *Cuba, Going Against the Grain: Agricultural Crisis and Transformation* (Boston: Oxfam, 2001), 13.

10. Susan Eva Eckstein, *Back from the Future: Cuba Under Castro*, second edition (New York: Routledge, 2003), 18.

11. Silvia Pedraza, *Political Disaffection in Cuba's Revolution and Exodus* (New York: Cambridge University Press, 2007), 122, 268.

12. Abel Prieto, "Cuba's National Literacy Campaign," *Journal of Reading* 25, no. 3 (December 1981): 216. Also see Fagen, *The Transformation of Political Culture in Cuba*, chapter 3.

13. Jonathan Kozol, *Children of the Revolution: A Yankee Teacher in the Cuban Schools* (New York: Delacorte Press, 1978), 5.

14. Catherine Murphy's film about the literacy campaign, *Maestra*, captures the feelings that four *brigadistas* express fifty years later. Available at http://www.mae strathefilm.org.

15. Prieto, "Cuba's National Literacy Campaign," 218.

16. Julie M. Feinsilver, *Healing the Masses: Cuban Health Politics at Home and Abroad* (Berkeley: University of California Press, 1993); Conner Gorry and C. William Keck, "The Cuban Health System: In Search of Quality, Efficiency, and Sustainability," in *A Contemporary Cuba Reader: The Revolution under Raúl Castro*, ed. Philip Brenner et al. (Lanham, MD: Rowman & Littlefield, 2014).

17. Marguerite Rose Jiménez, "Polio and the Politics of Policy Diffusion in Latin America," PhD diss. (American University, Washington, DC, 2013), 424.

18. Felipe Eduardo Sixto, "An Evaluation of Four Decades of Cuban Healthcare," in *Cuba in Transition*, vol. 12 (McLean, VA: Association for the Study of the Cuban Economy, 2002), 326.

19. Media Benjamin, Joseph Collins, and Michael Scott, *No Free Lunch: Food and Revolution in Cuba Today* (San Francisco: Institute for Food and Development Policy, 1984), chapter 3.

20. Domínguez, *Cuba*, 233–35.

21. Edward Boorstein, *The Economic Transformation of Cuba* (New York: Monthly Review Press, 1968), chapter 3.

22. Albert Memmi, *The Colonizer and the Colonized*, trans. Howard Greenfeld (Boston: Beacon Press, 1991).

23. Valdés, "The Revolutionary and Political Content of Fidel Castro's Charismatic Authority," 33.

24. Fagen, *The Transformation of Political Culture in Cuba*, 7.

25. William LeoGrande, "Mass Political Participation," in *The Cuba Reader: The Making of a Revolutionary Society*, ed. Philip Brenner et al. (New York: Grove, 1988).

26. Maurice Zeitlin, *Revolutionary Politics and the Cuban Working Class* (New York: Harper & Row, 1970).

27. Fagen, *The Transformation of Political Culture in Cuba*, chapter 4 (especially 80–96).

28. Domínguez, *Cuba*, 279–80.

29. "Fidel Castro Denounces Sectarianism" (Speech of March 26, 1962), Ministry of Foreign Relations, Republic of Cuba, Political Documents: 2, 12, 17, 23–25; available at http://collections.mun.ca/cdm/compoundobject/collection/radical/id/40999/show/40921.

Chapter 11

Bay of Pigs/Playa Girón[1]

[José Ramón] Suco, the head of the squad from Battalion 339 that had been guarding the radio at Larga Beach, recalled: "One of the literacy teachers had his head on my shoulder, when a mercenary [Bay of Pigs invader] walked up to him and asked, 'What kind of uniform is that?' 'A literacy teacher's uniform.' 'Are you a Communist?' 'I support Fidel,' the boy, who wasn't even fifteen yet, answered. And the mercenary replied, 'You know that everyone who supports Fidel is a Communist.' 'Well, then, I'm a Communist.'

"If Castro's planes had been destroyed, if the U.S. Government hadn't left the exiles to their fate, if they had had greater participation in the planning, if the attack had been made at Trinidad, if the underground had been alerted, if a diversionary landing had been made at Baracoa, if air cover had been provided, if the Brigade had been better equipped, if there had been direct intervention. . . . The exiles thought that, if any of those things had happened, it would have ensured their success. They refused to accept the real reason for their defeat . . . the Cuban people were at the peak of their patriotism and revolutionary fervor, and their support for the Revolution."

—Juan Carlos Rodríguez[2]

CUBA BECOMES A THREAT

US Response to Revolution

At first, Washington did not know what to make of the Cuban Revolution. US officials were well aware of Batista's atrocities, and formally had suspended new military aid to Cuba in 1958. But the Eisenhower administration did not want to signal its support for armed conflict against established governments, and so at first it took a "wait and see" approach.

On January 7, 1959, the United States gave diplomatic recognition to the new government. One week later, the State Department replaced the US ambassador, Earl E. T. Smith. He had been a Batista booster and large benefactor of the Republican Party, which landed him the appointment to what seemed at the time like a posh, nonproblematic post. The new envoy, Philip Bonsal, was a Spanish-speaking career diplomat known for his sympathy to reformers in Colombia and Bolivia. Concerned about the US reputation for intervention in Latin America, he hoped to find a way that the United States could live with the new regime.[3]

Beneath this seemingly benign approach, though, lingered an attitude of superiority that we saw in chapters 4 and 5 when the United States occupied Cuba after the Cuban War of Independence. Historian Louis Pérez observes that US officials imagined Cubans as if they were young children: immature, ignorant, and untutored in the ways of civilized people. And as a parent, the United States had "the duty to protect and nurture Cuba," which justified US domination of Cuba as a selfless fulfillment of parental duty.[4]

Embedded in the parent-child metaphor, linguist George Lakoff explains, is the expectation that the parent has the responsibility to teach the child right from wrong. And so when children are disobedient, they must be punished in order to instill them with discipline.[5] To spare the rod was to spoil the child. In turn, an offspring had the responsibility to be appropriately grateful and deferential to the parent.

But to the victorious leaders of the 1959 Revolution, playing their "proper" role as children would have been snatching defeat from the jaws of victory. They refused to be either compliant or appreciative. In response, US officials, editorial writers, and cartoonists soon began to depict the new Cuban government, and Fidel Castro, as a screaming, ranting, temperamental child—the kind of nuisance President Theodore Roosevelt had castigated in 1906, when he called the country "that infernal little Cuban republic."[6]

From Irritant to Menace

During the first months after the victory over Batista, the US concern over Cuba was not about the Soviet Union, with which Cuba had neither diplomatic nor trade relations. Officials worried about Fidel Castro's charisma and his penchant to have Cuba chart an independent course. This concern was evident in a confidential memo Vice President Richard Nixon wrote after meeting with Fidel in April 1959. The Cuban leader, Nixon judged, has those indefinable qualities which make him a leader of men. Whatever we may think of him he is going to be a great factor in the development of Cuba and very possibly in Latin American affairs generally. He seems to be sincere. He is either incredibly naive about Communism or under Communist discipline—my guess is the former. . . . But because he has the power to lead to which I have referred we have no choice but at least to try to orient him in the right direction.[7]

Nixon met Fidel while the new prime minister was in the United States on a public relations gambit to improve his image prior to rolling out the Agrarian Reform Law. Staying at a Harlem hotel, he toured the city, spoke to thirty thousand people in Central Park, visited Yankee Stadium, and appeared on *Meet the Press*. When Castro arrived in Washington, President Eisenhower pointedly departed for a golfing date in Georgia, leaving Nixon to meet with the bearded revolutionary. The two engaged in a wide-ranging conversation for several hours, with Fidel graciously speaking in broken English.

The Cuban leader not only rejected US "orientation." He did not request any US foreign assistance, which troubled US officials, because they hoped that US aid would be a mechanism for binding Cuba to the United States. In addition, there was inconclusive evidence that Cuba was sending missions to support insurgent activity against dictatorships in the Dominican Republic, Panama, and Nicaragua.[8] These alleged expeditions implicitly challenged US dominance in the region and the US conception of itself as protector of the hemisphere, an idea nurtured since the Monroe Doctrine in 1823.

By October 1959, the US image of Cuba as a wayward child seemed too benign. The revolutionary government had transformed Cuba into a juvenile delinquent, a menace more than an irritant. Incapable of being disciplined, and unwilling to acknowledge that it owed gratitude to the United States for the "blessings of liberty" bestowed on the island since 1898, Cuba had betrayed its parent's heritage and upbringing. Wayne S. Smith was a junior foreign service officer in the embassy at the time, and later became chief US diplomat in Cuba from 1979 to 1982. He recalls that "by October 1959 most of us in Havana" had decided Castro was turning toward the Soviet Union.[9] In an October 1959 policy paper later endorsed by the secretary of state, Assistant Secretary R. Roy Rubottom Jr. concluded:

> That the policies and programs of the Castro Government which are inconsistent with the minimal requirements of good Cuban-US relations and with US objectives for Cuba and Latin America will not be satisfactorily altered except as a result of Cuban opposition to Castro's present course and/or a change in the Cuban regime.[10]

Secretary of State Christian Herter summarized for President Eisenhower why Cuba's resistance to US discipline posed a threat to the United States. In a November 1959 memo, he observed that Castro "has veered towards a 'neutralist' anti-American foreign policy for Cuba which, if emulated by other Latin American countries, would have serious adverse effects on Free World support of our leadership."[11] By the end of November 1959 even Ambassador Bonsal had become critical of Cuba's "independent position in world affairs."[12] Before the new year began, the Central Intelligence Agency (CIA) was developing plans to overthrow the Cuban government.[13]

Enter the Soviet Union

The Soviets knew little about Fidel Castro and the July 26th Movement, and at first they tended to operate from the assumption that Cuba was still within the US sphere of interest. They also were not eager to support rebels who neither would take orders from Moscow nor were likely to survive US antagonism. Moscow waited a year before proposing that a Soviet trade delegation go to Havana.

The group that came in February 1960 was a prominent one, headed by First Deputy Premier Anastas Mikoyan. Shortly afterward, the two countries reestablished diplomatic relations, which Batista had broken in 1952 after he seized power. Mikoyan concluded the trade mission by announcing $100 million of commercial credit for the Cuban government, including oil shipments, and pledging to buy five million tons of Cuban sugar annually for five years. It was a signal of a major change after decades of Cuban economic dependence on US trade, and it spurred President Eisenhower to approve plans for a covert operation on March 17, 1960, to overthrow the Cuban government—plans that became the Bay of Pigs invasion.[14]

The operation was to be based on the CIA's 1954 intervention in Guatemala, when the agency helped to overthrow the democratically elected government headed by Jacobo Árbenz Guzmán. Its plan called for the creation of opposition and propaganda units among exiles in Miami, an acceleration of intelligence operations on the island, and support for counterrevolutionaries, along with the training of five hundred exiles who would invade the island. Their arrival was supposed to spark an island-wide revolt that would oust the revolutionary government. The CIA turned to the now friendly Guatemala dictatorship to provide facilities for preparing the invaders.

Tensions Increase

In June 1960, President Eisenhower ordered Esso and Texaco not to refine Soviet petroleum at the companies' Cuban facilities. In a speech vehemently denouncing imperialism, Prime Minister Castro responded by announcing the nationalization of the refineries. One month later, the United States reduced Cuba's sugar quota to zero, effectively imposing a ban on Cuban sugar.

Given the centrality of sugar to the Cuban economy, the zero-quota decision is often cited as the start of the US economic embargo. But Eisenhower's advisers viewed the action as nothing more than "a good solid slap," that is, a restrained response to Cuba's expropriation of the refineries, short of deadly options that the United States might have chosen.[15]

The United States followed up in August by pressuring the Organization of American States (OAS) to condemn Cuba for permitting Soviet "extra-continental intervention" in the hemisphere that "endangers American solidarity and security."[16] Castro reacted to the OAS condemnation with the "First Declaration of Havana" on September 2, 1960. Throwing down a gauntlet to the United States, he proclaimed Cuba would be committed to ending what Herter had called US "leadership" and Castro characterized as "domination": "[T]he People of Cuba strongly condemn US imperialism for its gross and criminal domination . . . of all the peoples of Latin America . . . affirm their faith that Latin America, united and victorious will soon be free of the bonds that now make its economies rich spoils for US imperialism."[17]

From the US perspective, the speech was an aggressive assault. And then Cuba added fuel to the simmering fire. Late in 1960, it received a few shipments of antiquated arms from Soviet bloc countries, which confirmed US government fears that Cuba might become a beachhead for Soviet influence in the Western Hemisphere.[18]

Charges that Castro had betrayed the Cuban revolution swirled around Washington, and the US press turned sharply against the revolutionaries. Accordingly, plans to overthrow the Cuban government took on the air of a noble enterprise. Dazzled by the mistaken assumption that Cubans yearned for the prerevolutionary relationship, US officials convinced themselves that the Cuban people would rise up spontaneously against the Cuban government and invite the United States to restore order in the country.[19] On January 3, 1961, in the final days of his administration, President Eisenhower contributed to the seemingly unstoppable momentum for an invasion. Citing "harassments" by the Cuban government—Cuba had demanded two days earlier that the US embassy reduce its staff to eleven people—the US president broke diplomatic relations with Cuba.[20]

THE PLAN CHANGES

As Secret as Christmas Day

Richard Bissell was an ambitious CIA deputy director for plans who had voted for John Fitzgerald Kennedy in the November 1960 election. An Ivy Leaguer, he felt a rapport with the president-elect and hoped that Kennedy would choose him to succeed Allen Dulles as CIA director. But when he briefed Kennedy about the covert operation ten days after the presidential election, Bissell neglected to inform the president-elect that the plan had changed. The CIA had decided that the initial plan—to slowly infiltrate five hundred paramilitaries into Cuba to reinforce counterrevolutionaries already in place—was no longer feasible.

The new plan called for a force three times as large that would seize and hold a piece of territory, declaring itself to be the new legitimate government of Cuba. The invasion was expected to "precipitate a general uprising throughout Cuba and cause the revolt of large segments of the Cuban Army and Militia," as Jack Hawkins, the US field commander for the Bay of Pigs operation, wrote in a January 1961 memo.[21]

Bissell also neglected to inform Kennedy about two other essential elements of the operation: an ongoing CIA program to assassinate the Cuban leadership and his expectation that the president ultimately would need to use US military forces to support the invaders. US attempts to assassinate Fidel Castro have been acknowledged officially since the 1975 US Senate hearings chaired by Frank Church (D-ID). But only in the mid-1990s did it become certain that murdering the Cuban leadership was an essential component of the Bay of Pigs attack.

As historian Michael Warner wrote in a now declassified study, Dulles and Bissell were unconcerned about the logistical shortcomings of the exiles' attack because they believed "Castro would either be assassinated or President Kennedy would send in the Marines to rescue the Brigade."[22] Jacob Esterline, the operational director for the invasion in the CIA's Directorate for Plans, quickly understood the implication of the assassination strategy when he saw documents about it for the first time at a 1996 conference. As tears welled in his eyes, he said, "I'll tell you what really bothers me about this. This stupid cockamamie idea may well have compromised serious support and backing of the brigade operation that was the main event, or should have been. . . . Maybe [Bissell] didn't even care much about whether my people made it or not."[23]

While the Soviet bloc had not yet provided Cuba with significant military equipment, Cuba compensated for its lack of military strength with a capable intelligence operation. It infiltrated several agents into the Guatemala training camps, which turned out to be relatively easy. When the CIA increased the number of the invaders from five hundred to fifteen hundred, it desperately sought recruits with advertisements in Miami. Journalist Peter Wyden quoted one disgruntled CIA official saying that the covert operation had become "as secret as Christmas Day."[24] Cuban leaders were aware, therefore, that the United States was preparing for an exile invasion. But they did not know precisely when and where the assault would occur.

Cuban military planners evaluated several likely invasion sites. One obvious entry point was the US Naval Station at Guantánamo Bay. The United States could secretly bring exiles to the base and launch the attack from there. But the site was so obvious that the Cubans came to discount its importance. However, they did worry that an exile force might masquerade as regular Cuban soldiers, attack the US base, and thus create a pretext for a US invasion. The Guantánamo Bay naval station was in Oriente Province, which had historical significance as the location where earlier Cuban revolts had started. The second possibility was given so much credence that Raúl Castro took personal command of Cuban defense forces in Oriente.

Meanwhile, Cuban militia members were deployed in small numbers along the northern and southern coasts as lookouts. Internal security was tightened—any report of suspicious activity led to arrests, which did result in abuses. In April 1961 alone, thousands were imprisoned.

Kennedy Wants a "Quiet" Landing

Prior to his inauguration, the newly elected president raised few objections about the planned invasion. But once in office, he began to worry that an incursion could worsen the already negative US image in Latin America. This concern led him to tell the CIA on March 11 to move the planned landing site from the city of Trinidad—on Cuba's southern coast—to a place that would "provide for a 'quiet' landing," according to the CIA's inspector general's postmortem report. It added that the president wanted to avoid "the appearance of a World War II type of amphibious assault" that would expose the hand of the United States.[25]

The CIA came back four days later with a new location, the Bay of Pigs, which had an existing airfield capable of handling "tactical air operations" and where there could be "An Unspectacular Landing."[26] In fact, the location was less than ideal. Only three roads led to the beaches, easily enabling the Cuban military to establish roadblocks. Had the exiles landed at Trinidad, they would have been able to flee to the adjacent Escambray Mountains where counterrevolutionaries were based. The Bay of Pigs is seventy miles west of the Escambray. Survivors would have had to traverse the crocodile-infested Zapata swamp to reach the mountains.

Despite its logistical shortcomings, subordinates sensed that President Kennedy was reluctant to cancel the operation. No one wanted to be marked as a naysayer early in an administration that was trying to create a can-do image. In part, the young president himself had undermined the possibility of calling off the invasion, by attacking Nixon during the election campaign for failing to come to the aid of counterrevolutionaries, whom he called "fighters for freedom."[27] Now that he was in a position to help them, critics were certain to harp on his apparent hypocrisy if he had not acted. And the window for action was closing quickly. On February 17, the CIA had concluded that "the Castro regime is steadily consolidating its control over Cuba—there was no significant likelihood that the Castro regime will fall of its own weight."[28]

TWO PERSPECTIVES ON THE DEFEAT OF BRIGADE 2506

Each member of the invading party received a number, starting at 2,501. The numbering was intended to make the Cubans think the group was larger than the 1,500 actually involved. In the aftermath, the survivors named themselves Brigade 2506, after the number of the first invader who was killed.

At 1:15 a.m. on April 17, 1961, the first landing party arrived at Playa Girón, the beach at the mouth of the eighteen-mile-long Bay of Pigs, on the southern coast of Cuba. Three days later, 114 members of Brigade 2506 lay dead, 1,189 had been captured, and the fighting was over. The narrative of the invasion has been told many times, most often from the US perspective, which contrasts with the Cuban view.

US Perspective: "A Perfect Failure" or Betrayal

There are two popular US perspectives. The most common focuses on the constellation of logistical errors that led to the outcome, which journalist Theodore Draper dubbed as "a perfect failure."[29] The other US narrative, often heard from Brigade 2506 survivors, emphasizes President Kennedy's unwillingness to provide more military support, which they have characterized as a betrayal.[30]

A map of the Bay of Pigs area (see map 11.1 on next page) indicates the swamps to the east and northeast of the landing site, which made escape to the Escambray Mountains nearly impossible. Cubans name the invasion after one of the beaches, Playa Girón, around which significant fighting occurred. There was also a landing at Playa Larga, at the northern end of the bay.

Two days before the invasion, the CIA attempted to destroy the small Cuban air force and make airfields inoperable. Eight crews made up of Alabama National Guard members and Cuban exiles flew B-26 bombers camouflaged to look as if they were Cuban military planes. In anticipation of the attack, Fidel had ordered mock planes made of balsa wood to be placed outside hangars and the actual planes to be hidden. The air raid left Cuba with almost its entire air force undamaged—two B-26 bombers, three British World War II Sea Fury fighter planes, and three T-33 jet trainers. All of the airstrips

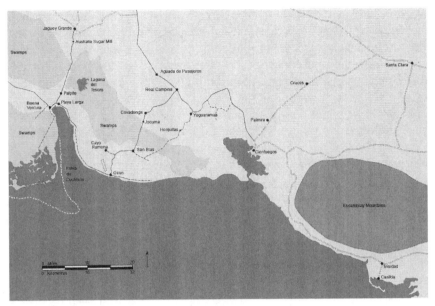

Map 11.1. Bay of Pigs Area. Map by Peter WD.

remained operable. The CIA then requested authorization for a second bombing run. Kennedy refused, still seeking to keep the US role hidden.

Thus, one explanation for the Bay of Pigs failure was that the tiny and bat-
tered Cuban air force was able to sink the invaders' resupply ship, dooming
the operation, because Kennedy refused to order an air strike on the morning of the invasion. But the report by the CIA inspector general (IG) on the
operation concluded that additional air strikes would have made little difference because of many other organizational problems.[31] For example, a 160-
man diversionary unit, which was supposed to land about thirty miles east
of Guantánamo on April 15, decided to avoid capture and stayed safely on
its boat. The Taylor Committee—created by President Kennedy and headed
by General Maxwell D. Taylor—judged that "This failure may have had a
considerable affect [*sic*] on the main landing as the diversion was intended to
draw Castro's forces to the east and confuse his command."[32]

The CIA training program had problems from the outset. Most of the
project officers did not speak Spanish. They prepared the brigadistas mainly
for an assault, not for guerrilla warfare, and for a daylight invasion, although
the plan called for night landings. Food in the Guatemala camp was terrible
and the living conditions were harsh. Morale was so low that some of early
recruits abandoned the operation.

This problem was not only a logistical issue. It reflected, as the IG starkly
concluded, the "contempt" CIA officials felt toward the Cubans and the

"high-handed attitude" with which they were treated.[33] Such contempt was the ultimate betrayal of Brigade 2506. The CIA did not believe the Cuban exiles could run their own program. Project officers described the brigadistas as "yellow-bellied," and the Cuban Revolutionary Council—the supposedly future political leaders of Cuba whom the CIA had hand-picked—as "idiots," according to the IG.[34]

Just before the invasion began, the Cuban Revolutionary Council members were locked in a "safe house" at Opa Locka airfield outside Miami, despite their protestations, while the CIA wrote and issued public statements in the name of the brigade's political leaders. Kennedy ordered Arthur Schlesinger, Jr., and Adolf A. Berle, a longtime Latin American adviser to Democratic presidents, to rush to the base to calm down the Cubans. One of them reportedly was threatening to commit suicide.[35]

Cuban Perspective: "First Defeat of Imperialism in the Americas"

While the April 15 bombardment of airfields did little damage to Cuba's so-called air force, it did kill a number of workers. The next day, thousands of Cubans attended a rally outside the Colón Cemetery in Havana, where Castro and other officials condemned the attacks and mourned the dead. In his speech, the Cuban leader for the first time described the "character" of the Cuban Revolution as socialist.

Several lightly armed members of Cuba's People's Militia detected the landing of the first brigade on April 17 within fifteen minutes of its arrival and sent a radio warning. A similar signal came soon after from a militia unit at Playa Larga, the beach at the head of the bay, eighteen miles away. A Cuban army battalion stationed at a sugar mill about 45 miles from the Bay of Pigs mobilized before dawn and engaged the attackers, but lacking armored vehicles, it quickly retreated.

Fidel Castro quickly took charge, shouting orders into telephones in a frenzy, mobilizing the air force and battalions throughout the country. José Ramón Fernández, a professional military officer who was director of Cuba's military schools that were training new cadets for the armed forces, became commander of the main unit at the Bay of Pigs. At about 2:00 a.m. on April 17, Castro woke him with a call, ordering to him to go to the battle front. A few minutes later Castro called again, demanding to know what Fernández was doing. He was still getting dressed. Ten minutes passed and Castro called again: "Why are you still there?"[36]

Cuban air force planes arrived at daybreak and began bombing. Fidel had ordered that their priority should be the supply ships. They hit two, destroying one and damaging another. By midday, the Cuban leader was there himself, fighting alongside the militia and regular soldiers. In figure 11.1, we see a photo

Figure 11.1.   Fidel Castro (in glasses) during the battle at the Bay of Pigs. Photo courtesy of *Granma*.

of Castro on this historic day. When the 72-hour conflict ended, eighty-seven Cuban defenders had been killed, and more than two hundred were wounded.

Fidel was triumphant. He declared the victory as "the First Defeat of Imperialism in the Americas." News of the outcome resounded throughout the third world, inflating further the symbol of the Cuban David challenging the US Goliath. Soviet leader Nikita Khrushchev reevaluated his earlier judgment, decided that the Cuban revolution had a good chance to survive, and authorized increased shipments of military equipment and subsidized trade with Cuba.[37] (However, by December 1961 the Soviets had not shipped any of the promised MIG-15 fighters, MI-4 helicopters, torpedo boats, advanced communication equipment, or military specialists.)

THE FATAL FLAW

The story of the Bay of Pigs invasion commonly told in the United States tends to echo the official histories. By emphasizing logistical failures, it reproduces the lack of respect for Cubans that the CIA showed for the Cuban exiles. Indeed, the low regard most US officials showed for all of the Cubans involved was the fatal flaw of the mission.

US planners seemed unable to appreciate the genuine, widespread support the Cuban Revolution had earned in its first two years. Ordinary Cubans who lived in the Bay of Pigs vicinity fought tenaciously against the invaders because they had something to protect. Consider that "a contingent of volunteer teachers was assigned to work throughout the swamp" in January 1961, and for the first time "thousands of children who lived on the Zapata Peninsula began to go to elementary school."[38] Similarly, the area had been without a hospital until the government built one in 1959, and farmers there had felt isolated because there were no roads until 1960.

The US-sponsored Bay of Pigs invasion was bound to fail because US officials denied that Cubans could be agents of their own history. The flawed assumption that the invasion would spark a mass insurrection—not its logistics—was the Achilles' heel of the project. It was fueled by a political misjudgment about what a large majority of Cubans wanted. They wanted neither the form of democracy the United States had supported in Cuba from 1940 to 1952—characterized by corruption and politicians who did the bidding of the US government and corporations—nor the brutal Batista dictatorship, which the United States tolerated and which gave a free reign to organized crime. Cubans wanted independence and sovereignty. The 1959 Cuban revolution was a nationalist uprising. Most Cubans believed that the many errors committed by the revolutionary government were made in good faith, for the benefit of ordinary Cubans. They also were beginning to believe that Cubans themselves could solve their problems.

NOTES

1. Several excellent studies have been published about the planning for and execution of the US invasion at Playa Girón, as Cubans refer to the events, or the Bay of Pigs, as the invasion generally is called in the United States. These include James G. Blight and Peter Kornbluh, eds., *Politics of Illusion: The Bay of Pigs Invasion Reexamined* (Boulder, CO: Lynne Rienner, 1998); Howard Jones, *The Bay of Pigs* (New York: Oxford University Press, 2008); Peter Kornbluh, ed., *Bay of Pigs Declassified: The Secret CIA Report on the Invasion of Cuba* (New York: New Press, 1998); Jim Rasenberger, *The Brilliant Disaster: JFK, Castro, and America's Doomed Invasion of Cuba's Bay of Pigs* (New York: Scribner, 2011); Juan Carlos Rodríguez, *The Bay of Pigs and the CIA*, trans. Mary Todd (Melbourne: Ocean Press, 1999). Unless otherwise noted, the narrative of this chapter is based on these secondary sources. A large number of primary documents are available from the National Security Archive, http://nsarchive.gwu.edu. In particular, see document sets "The Cuban Missile Crisis, 1962," "The Cuban Missile Crisis: 50th Anniversary Update," and "The Cuban Missile Crisis Revisited: An International Collection, From Bay of Pigs to Nuclear Brink." Also see *Foreign Relations of the United States, 1961–1963*, volume X, Cuba,

January 1961–September 1962, ed. Louis J. Smith (Washington, DC: Government Printing Office, 1997), cited as *FRUS, 1961–1963, volume X*; *Foreign Relations of the United States, 1961–1963, volume XI, Cuban Missile Crisis and Aftermath*, eds. Edward C. Keefer, Charles S. Sampson, and Louis J. Smith (Washington, DC: Government Printing Office, 1996), cited as *FRUS, 1961–1963, volume XI*.

2. Rodríguez, *The Bay of Pigs and the CIA*, 142, 176.

3. Wayne S. Smith, *The Closest of Enemies: A Personal and Diplomatic Account of US-Cuban Relations since 1957* (New York: Norton, 1987), 47. Also see Philip W. Bonsal, *Cuba, Castro, and the United States* (Pittsburgh: University of Pittsburgh Press, 1971), 25–28, 39–42.

4. Louis A. Pérez Jr., *Cuba in the American Imagination* (Chapel Hill: University of North Carolina Press, 2008), 113.

5. George Lakoff, *Thinking Points: Communicating Our American Values and Vision* (New York: Farrar, Straus and Giroux, 2006), 57–58.

6. Schoultz, *That Infernal Little Cuban Republic*, 25.

7. Richard M. Nixon, "Rough draft of summary of conversation between the vice-president and Fidel Castro," April 25, 1959, reprinted in Jeffrey J. Safford, "The Nixon-Castro Meeting of 19 April 1959," *Diplomatic History* 4, no. 4 (Fall 1980): 431.

8. *FRUS, 1958–1960*, volume VI, Document No. 325, June 25, 1959. Cuba has acknowledged its active support only for a raid against the Dominican Republic's Rafael Trujillo.

9. Smith, *The Closest of Enemies*, 52.

10. *FRUS, 1958–1960*, volume VI, Document No. 376, October 23, 1959.

11. *FRUS, 1958–1960*, volume VI, Document No. 387, November 5, 1959.

12. Morley, *Imperial State and Revolution*, 85.

13. Thomas G. Paterson, *Contesting Castro: The United States and the Triumph of the Cuban Revolution* (New York: Oxford University Press, 1994), 242, 258.

14. *FRUS, 1958–1960*, volume VI, Document No. 486, March 17, 1960.

15. Morley, *Imperial State and Revolution*, 109.

16. "Text of O.A.S. Declaration of San Jose," *New York Times*, August 29, 1960, 3.

17. "First Declaration of Havana," September 2, 1960, in *Cuban Revolution Reader: A Documentary History of 40 Key Moments of the Cuban Revolution*, ed. Julio García Luis (Melbourne: Ocean Press, 2001), 45–51.

18. Sergio del Valle Jiménez, ed., *Peligros y Principios: La Crisis de Octubre desde Cuba* (Havana: Editora Verde Olivo, 1992), 48.

19. US Central Intelligence Agency, "Inspector General's Survey of the Cuban Operation," October 1961, p. 48, available at the National Security Archive, Washington, DC, Accession No. CU00223; reprinted in Peter Kornbluh, ed., *Bay of Pigs Declassified: The Secret CIA Report on the Invasion of Cuba* (New York: New Press, 1998), 48.

20. E. W. Kenworthy, "Regime Is Scored; People Suffer Under 'Yoke of Dictator,' President Says," *New York Times*, January 4, 1961, 1.

21. *FRUS, 1961–1963*, volume X, Document 9, January 4, 1961.

22. Michael Warner, "Lessons Unlearned: The CIA's Internal Probe of the Bay of Pigs Affair," *Studies in Intelligence*, Winter 1998/99, https://www.cia.gov/library/center-for-the-study-of-intelligence/csi-publications/csi-studies/studies/winter98_99/art08.html.

23. Blight and Kornbluh, *Politics of Illusion*, 85.

24. Peter Wyden, *Bay of Pigs: The Untold Story* (New York: Simon & Schuster, 1979), 119.

25. US Central Intelligence Agency, "Taylor Commission Report on Cuban Operations," Memorandum No. 1, June 13, 1961, 10; available at the National Security Archive, Washington, DC, Accession No. CU00181 [hereafter cited as Taylor Commission, Memorandum No. 1].

26. *FRUS, 1961–1963*, volume X, Document 61, March 15, 1961.

27. "Text of Statement by Kennedy on Dealing with Castro Regime," *New York Times*, October 21, 1960, 18.

28. *FRUS, 1961–1963*, volume X, Document 46, February 17, 1961.

29. Theodore Draper, *Castro's Revolution: Myths and Realities* (New York: Praeger, 1962), 59.

30. Blight and Kornbluh, *Politics of Illusion*, prologue and chapter 1; Haynes Johnson with Manuel Artime, *The Bay of Pigs: The Leaders' Story of Brigade 2506* (New York: Norton, 1964).

31. Kornbluh, *Bay of Pigs Declassified*, 41.

32. Taylor Commission, Memorandum No. 1, 14–15.

33. Kornbluh, *Bay of Pigs Declassified*, 73.

34. Kornbluh, *Bay of Pigs Declassified*, 74.

35. Rasenberger, *The Brilliant Disaster*, 286.

36. Fidel Castro and José Ramón Fernández, *Playa Girón* (New York: Pathfinder Press, 2001), 107.

37. Carlos Lechuga, *In the Eye of the Storm: Castro, Khrushchev, Kennedy and the Missile Crisis*, trans. Mary Todd (Melbourne: Ocean Press, 1995), 18; Aleksandr Fursenko and Timothy Naftali, *One Hell of a Gamble: Khrushchev, Castro, and Kennedy, 1958–1964* (New York: Norton, 1997), 139–40, 146.

38. Rodríguez, *The Bay of Pigs and the CIA*, 118–121.

Chapter 12

The Missile Crisis

We're already a modern country, we have twentieth-century weapons, atomic bombs, we're no longer an insignificant colony, we've already rushed into history, we have the same weapons that the Russians and the Americans rattle at each other. Our power of destruction makes us an equal for a moment to the two great world powers. Still, I'm sure they'll never accept us on equal terms, they'll take our weapons away, ignore us, crush this island.

—Narrator of *Inconsolable Memories*[1]

Writing to Fidel Castro in 1965, Che Guevara recalled the October 1962 missile crisis in the following way: "I have lived magnificent days and I felt at your side the pride of belonging to our people in the luminous and sad days of the Caribbean crisis."[2]

Luminous and sad? You would be hard pressed to find any American or Russian who recalled those days as luminous and sad. "Harrowing," "exhausting," "stressful," "frightening," and "horrifying." These were the words used by those who experienced the crisis. Did Guevara and his Cuban comrades experience the same crisis as the Americans and Soviets?

In fact, the significance of the 1962 trilateral confrontation over ballistic missiles in Cuba was different for Cubans than for others. The crisis had a lasting impact on Cuba's foreign relations, though the Cuban perspective about the crisis is not widely known in the United States.

While the 1962 missile crisis brought the world closer to a nuclear war than any other crisis, it also seemed to end well. The United States and the Soviet Union did not go to war; the Soviets removed the missiles; the United States promised not to invade Cuba. Only one US soldier died in combat, Major Rudolph Anderson, who was piloting the U-2 surveillance plane the Soviets downed with a surface-to-air missile (SAM) on October 27.

142

Most Americans understand the Cuban Missile Crisis as teachers and commentators repeatedly have summarized it: The Soviet Union placed ballistic missiles in Cuba to threaten the United States. These missiles could hit major US cities and ports in less than ten minutes. The crisis lasted for thirteen days, from October 16, when President Kennedy learned about the missiles, until October 28, when Soviet premier Nikita Khrushchev agreed to remove the missiles in exchange for a US promise not to invade Cuba. The outcome was a great success for the United States, and perhaps Kennedy's "finest hour." In early 2001, one of the authors took his fourteen-year-old

Map 12.1. Map used by CIA briefers for President John F. Kennedy on October 16, 1962, indicates the estimated range of the Soviet ballistic missiles. Central Intelligence Agency, "Probable Soviet MRBM Sites in Cuba," October 16, 1962.

daughter to see *Thirteen Days*, a film that tells the missile crisis story from the traditional US perspective. As they exited the theater, he asked her why the Soviets had placed the missiles in Cuba. On the basis of the film, she said, "Because they were bad people."

A Cuban's view of the crisis provides a stark contrast to an American one. Cubans even give it a different name, the "October Crisis." The name embodies several elements, according to Cuban political scientist Carlos Alzugaray Treto. Cubans, he explained, at first used "Caribbean Crisis"—the Soviet name for the confrontation—and "October Crisis" interchangeably. But over time, he said, they "began to settle for "crisis de octubre," because "there were so many crises with the US that what defined each crisis was the month in which it happened and not the place."[3] A second explanation for the Cuban appellation is that Cubans have used it to indicate that their understanding of the crisis differs from the Soviet interpretation. The name thus highlights Cuba's ongoing tension with the United States, which Cubans argued led to the crisis over the missiles, and Cuba's claim of betrayal by the Soviet Union. From Cuba's perspective, Soviet and US interests defined the terms by which they avoided a nuclear war. The two superpowers neither addressed nor resolved the underlying causes of the crisis, the US war against Cuba.[4]

THREE PERSPECTIVES

"Eyeball to Eyeball": The Traditional US Narrative

Harvard political scientist Graham Allison articulated a view in 1971 that summarizes nearly all early analyses of the crisis: "For thirteen days in October 1962, the United States and the Soviet Union stood 'eyeball to eyeball,' each with the power of mutual annihilation in hand. . . . During the crisis, the United States was firm but forbearing. The Soviet Union looked hard, blinked twice, and then withdrew."[5] From this perspective, the crisis involved only the two superpowers and lasted less than two weeks.

In fact, prior to October 16, 1962, US officials had become concerned about the increasing Soviet military buildup in Cuba. The Central Intelligence Agency judged in late August that the Soviets were delivering large quantities of defensive equipment to Cuba, but not ballistic missiles. Still, the president directed the Defense Department to examine ways of removing the Soviet military presence in Cuba.[6]

Meanwhile, several US senators repeatedly charged that the Soviet deliveries included offensive weapons, perhaps even ballistic missiles. Kennedy responded to the charges on September 4 by asserting there was no evidence of "ground-to-ground" missiles in Cuba. He then warned, "Were it otherwise the gravest issues would arise." Congress followed up with a joint resolution on October 3, approving the use of force against Cuba. The same day—nearly two weeks before the United States discovered the ballistic missiles—the commander in chief of Atlantic forces ordered that US warships be in place by October 20 in preparation for a blockade of Cuba.[7]

By establishing a limit of zero ballistic missiles in Cuba, Kennedy unwittingly created the circumstances in which he ultimately found himself engulfed. Once he learned about the missiles, he believed he could accept nothing less than their complete removal. As a result of the kind of Maginot Line that Kennedy drew in early September, he and his advisers—a group he dubbed the "Executive Committee of the National Security Council" or "ExComm"—then perceived Khrushchev's action as a provocative test of US determination to resist Soviet pressure. Once they framed the Soviet action this way, it became a major national security threat because the credibility of US resolve was central to the strategy of deterrence. The ExComm erroneously surmised that Khrushchev believed Kennedy was timid and unsure of himself.[8] They concluded that Kennedy's seeming weakness had led Khrushchev to take the risk of sending missiles to Cuba, in order to give himself a "bargaining chip," something he could later give up in negotiations with the United States over Berlin.[9]

Caribbean Crisis: The Soviet Perspective

Like US officials, the Soviets viewed the crisis principally as a clash between the two superpowers. But they preferred to call it the "Caribbean Crisis." While Cuba's security figured into their reasons for bringing the missiles there, the actual confrontation for them occurred on the high seas, in the Caribbean.[10] But unlike the US narrative, the Soviet story of the missile crisis begins well before October 1962.

In his memoirs, Khrushchev suggests it dated from April 1961, when the United States failed to overthrow the Cuban government with the Bay of Pigs invasion. This is consistent with his claim that the primary reason for placing missiles in Cuba was to protect the revolutionary government from a US invasion.[11] Khrushchev's second motivation for deploying missiles to Cuba was to redress the significant imbalance in nuclear forces that favored the United States.[12] In 1962, the United States had 5,000 strategic nuclear warheads; the Soviet Union had 300. It may have had as few as ten intercontinental ballistic missiles (ICBMs); the United States had more than 150 ICBMs, in addition to intermediate-range missiles in Europe that could reach the Soviet Union. In effect, the Soviets believed they could not credibly deter a US attack because they did not have the means to retaliate against US territory with nuclear bombs if the United States launched a first strike against the Soviet Union.

With thirty-six ballistic missiles based in Cuba that had a 1,400-mile range, and another twenty-four missiles each with a 2,800-mile range on the way, the Soviet Union would be able to compensate for its deficit of long-range missiles and have a credible deterrent. At the same time, it would provide a powerful disincentive for the United States to use military force to overthrow the Cuban government.

Soviet generals were more concerned than Khrushchev about the US-USSR nuclear disparity. But the Soviet premier was compelled to respond to their demands for a faster ICBM buildup than he wanted when they pointed to Kennedy administration plans to spend billions more on strategic forces, and to statements by US officials about the desirability of the "first use" of nuclear weapons.[13]

From the Soviet perspective, Khrushchev ended the crisis on October 28 because he feared that the two superpowers were moving precipitously close to the brink of nuclear war, not because he feared that the Soviet Union would suffer conventional defeat in a war.[14] The incident that most provoked Khrushchev's anxiety was the destruction of a U-2 reconnaissance plane over the eastern part of Cuba by a Soviet SAM.

The United States had been sending two to four U-2s daily to take photos of the missile sites since October 16, and there had been no Soviet attempt to fire on the planes.[15] But in the face of an expected US attack, Lt. Gen. Stepan Grechko, commander of the Soviet air defense in Cuba, requested permission from the Kremlin on October 26 to use "all available antiaircraft means" against US forces. He had not received approval on the morning of October 27 when Fidel Castro gave a rousing speech over the radio and ordered Cuban anti-aircraft to open fire on any US planes. In the exhilaration of the moment Grechko ordered three SAMs to be launched at a U-2.[16]

After he learned of the U-2's downing, Khrushchev sensed he could no longer control events with verbal orders from Moscow. The one-megaton warheads for the ballistic missiles—each of which had a force more than sixty times greater than the US atomic bomb that destroyed Hiroshima—already had arrived in Cuba. In addition, the Soviets had shipped smaller nuclear warheads for more than 100 tactical nuclear and cruise missiles they had sent to Cuba. Unbeknownst to the United States, several of these cruise missiles were aimed at the US Guantánamo Naval Base.[17]

Moscow had ordered that the nuclear warheads not be mated to the missiles without direct authorization. Still, Khrushchev feared that in the event of an invasion, a local commander could overrule the order because Soviet ballistic missiles did not have permissive action links, essentially two "keys." Moreover, the nearly 200,000 invading US forces would likely suffer enormous casualties if an errant general launched a tactical nuclear missile at them. The firewall that had prevented a nuclear war until then might be breached.

In a private letter on October 26, Khrushchev had offered to remove the missiles from Cuba in exchange for a US promise not to invade Cuba. Then he followed with a public message on October 27, which was more like an ultimatum. The Soviet Union would withdraw the ballistic missiles if the United States removed its comparable missiles from Turkey, a NATO ally. When Attorney General Robert Kennedy informed Soviet ambassador Anatoly Dobrynin on October 27 that "time is of the essence"—because after the downing of the U-2 "there are many unreasonable heads among the generals, and not only among the generals, who are 'itching for a fight'"—Khrushchev perceived that the world was at the brink of an unthinkable nuclear war.[18] This compelled him to accept President Kennedy's proposed compromise. The US president offered to accept the terms of Khrushchev's first letter with a secret promise to extract the US missiles in Turkey within four months.

The Soviet leader also was concerned that Fidel might do something to increase the likelihood of a nuclear conflagration. The Cuban leader had sent a letter to Khrushchev early on October 27 (the message was dated October 26) warning that a US air strike or an invasion was likely in the next 24 to 72 hours. Castro estimated that an invasion was "less probable although possible." He then advised ominously that if there were a US invasion, the Soviet Union should launch a nuclear first strike against the United States.

In Khrushchev's mind, the Cuban leader had "lost his bearings."[19] (It is possible that Khrushchev had not actually read Castro's letter, but was frightened by a cable from Soviet ambassador Alexander Alexseev that summarized the letter before it was completed.) The Soviet premier advised Castro on October 28 "not to be carried away by sentiment . . . by provocations, because the Pentagon's unbridled militarists . . . are trying to frustrate the agreement and provoke you into actions that could be used against you." In a letter two days later, he told Castro that "you proposed that we be the first to launch a nuclear strike against the territory of the enemy. . . . Rather than a simple strike, it would have been the start of a thermonuclear war."[20]

Conflict Averted but Crisis Endures: The Cuban Perspective

Cuban historians tend to locate the start of the missile crisis in 1961. Government leaders anticipated that Kennedy would retaliate against Cuba after the failed Bay of Pigs invasion. Castro remarked in 1992 that "Girón, the Bay of Pigs, was undoubtedly the prelude to the October crisis, because, for Kennedy, this was a severe political blow."[21] Their expectations were on the mark. A covert assassination plan was already under way.[22]

In August 1961, after the OAS meeting in Punta del Este, Uruguay, White House aide Richard Goodwin met with Che Guevara. They sat on the floor, lotus-position style, each smoking a Cuban cigar. Goodwin reported to Ken-

Fidel Castro's Letter to Nikita Khrushchev, October 26, 1962*

Dear Comrade Khrushchev:

Given the analysis of the situation and the reports which have reached us, I consider that the aggression is almost imminent within the next 24 to 72 hours.

There are two possible variants: the first and likeliest one is an air attack against certain targets with the limited objective of destroying them; the second, less probable although possible, is invasion. I understand that this variant would call for a large number of forces and it is, in addition, the most repulsive form of aggression, which might inhibit them.

You can be assured that we will firmly and resolutely resist attack, whatever it may be.

The morale of the Cuban people is extremely high and the aggressor will be confronted heroically.

At this time I want to convey to you briefly my personal opinion.

If the second variant is implemented and the imperialists invade Cuba with the aim of occupying it, the danger that that aggressive policy poses for humanity is so great that following that event the Soviet Union must never allow the circumstances in which the imperialists could launch the first nuclear strike against it.

I tell you this because I believe that the imperialists' aggressiveness is extremely dangerous and that if they actually carry out the brutal act of invading Cuba in violation of international law and morality, that would be the moment to eliminate such danger forever through an act of clear legitimate defense, however harsh and terrible the solution would be, for there is no other.

It has influenced my opinion to see how this aggressive policy is developing, how the imperialists, disregarding world public opinion and ignoring principles and the law, are blockading the seas, violating our airspace and preparing an invasion, while at the same time frustrating every possibility for talks, even though they are aware of the seriousness of the problem.

You have been and continue to be a tireless defender of peace and I realize how bitter these moments must be, when the outcome of your superhuman efforts is so seriously threatened. However, up to the last moment we will maintain the hope that peace will be safeguarded and we are willing to contribute to this as much as we can. But at the same time, we are ready to calmly confront a situation which we view as quite real and quite close.

Once more I convey to you the infinite gratitude and recognition of our people to the Soviet people who have been so generous and fraternal with us, as well as our profound gratitude and admiration to you, and wish you success in the huge task and serious responsibilities ahead of you.

Fraternally,
Fidel Castro

---

* National Security Archive, Accession No. CU00754; official translation by Cuban Council of Ministers.

nedy that Guevara had proposed Cuba and the United States find a "modus vivendi"—a way of living together. Toward that end, Guevara also declared that Cuba "could agree not to make any political alliance with the East."[23]

The young Kennedy aide reasoned that Guevara's outreach was due to Cuba's failing economy and Soviet unwillingness or inability to help Cuba sufficiently. Given these circumstances, he judged Cuba was vulnerable, and therefore the opportunity was ripe for the United States to mount a concerted attack to overthrow the revolutionary government, using "economic pressure," "military pressure," increased covert activities, and "propaganda."[24] Kennedy followed up in November 1961 by authorizing Operation Mongoose, the largest CIA covert operation until that time. Forty-one years later, Philip Brenner asked Goodwin if he was embarrassed or chagrined by the advice he gave President Kennedy. Without a shred of remorse, Goodwin shrugged and said, "It was the Cold War. That's how we thought then. We all did."

Mongoose involved a multifaceted operation explicitly intended to overthrow the Cuban government. Major General Edward Lansdale, a famed

Operation Mongoose

Authorized on November 30, 1961, by President Kennedy, Operation Mongoose was a plan explicitly intended to "overthrow the Communist regime and institute a new government with which the United States can live in peace."* It included:

- *Terrorism*: The CIA organized Cuban exiles to deliver supplies and weapons to counterrevolutionary forces inside Cuba for the purpose of bombing stores, blowing up infrastructure such as electric lines and power plants, sabotaging factory machinery, burning fields, contaminating exports, and attacking literacy brigade teachers.
- *Isolating Cuba Politically*: Beginning with a January 1962 vote in the OAS, which suspended Cuba's membership, the United States attempted to make Cuba a pariah in Latin America.
- *Economic Warfare*: In February 1962, President Kennedy invoked the authority granted to him by Congress to establish an embargo on all transactions between Cuba and the United States, including food and medicine. The United States also pressured European allies to cease trading with Cuba.
- *Military Intimidation*: The US military was directed to develop contingency plans for intervention in Cuba, in case a civil war erupted. This led to more extensive than usual navy exercises in the Caribbean, including one against a fictitious island named ORTSAC, that is, CASTRO spelled backward.

* *FRUS, 1961–1963*, volume X, Document 291, January 18, 1962. Also see US Senate Select Committee. *Alleged Assassination Plots Involving Foreign Leaders* (Washington, DC: US Government Printing Office. 1975), 139–69; Jacinto Valdés-Dapena, Operación Mangosta: Preludio de la invasión directa a Cuba (Habana: Editorial Capitán San Luis, 2002).

guerrilla fighter, became the operational director. In a meticulously detailed plan, he estimated that the operation "aims for a revolt which can take place in Cuba by October 1962." He also noted that it probably would require the use of US military forces.[25]

Largely because of his expectation of a US invasion, Fidel sought a military treaty with the Soviet Union under which "an attack on Cuba would be the equivalent to an aggression against the USSR." But Khrushchev refused to bring Cuba into the Warsaw Pact, the Soviet-led military alliance of Eastern European communist countries. Instead, in May 1962 he offered to send ballistic missiles to Cuba. Cuba had not asked for such weapons, which Fidel said were "not indispensable . . . here to defend Cuba."[26]

In fact, Cuban officials took a calculated risk in accepting the emplacement of ballistic missiles on the island. The decision made Cuba a US strategic target in the event of a major war. In addition, there was the potential that Cuba would be perceived in Latin America as nothing more than an outpost of the Soviet Union.

But the benefits of the decision seemed to outweigh the costs. The ballistic missiles and associated Soviet military personnel would surely deter a US invasion, Cuban officials reasoned. Cuba's close collaboration with the Soviets also would serve as an endorsement of Cuba's call for a hemisphere-wide revolution, which Fidel had voiced in the February 1962 Second Declaration of Havana.[27]

While Castro wanted to make the missile agreement public, Khrushchev refused to do so. In June, he told Castro's emissaries, Che Guevara and Emilio Aragonés, that revealing the plan in advance would lead the United States to intervene in Cuba. The Soviet leader wanted to confront his adversary with a fait accompli in November 1962, on the 45th anniversary of the Bolshevik Revolution.[28]

Ultimately Khrushchev's position became a source of Cuban anger and distrust. In 1968, Castro said, "we believe that the whole problem should have been dealt with in a different manner: Cuba is a sovereign, independent country, and has a right to own the weapons that it deems necessary. . . . From the very outset it was a capitulation, an erosion of our sovereignty and our right to respond to that campaign." However, he acquiesced in the secrecy, explaining that in 1962 he believed the Soviets "had a much better grasp of the overall situation than we did and therefore we left the decision to them."[29]

Once the United States discovered the missiles, Castro was far less accepting of supposedly superior Soviet tactical prowess. Anticipating that Kennedy's October 22 address would be about Cuba, Castro ordered a rapid mobilization of the island's forces before the speech was delivered. "The Nation on a War Footing," was the headline emblazoned across the next day's

Revolucion, the official government newspaper. As nearly 400,000 Cuban soldiers and militia members prepared for a US invasion over the next few days, Castro counseled Soviet generals about the placement of SAMs and about the need for anti-aircraft weapons to defend them.[30]

Castro's intended message in his October 26 letter to Khrushchev was quite different than the Soviet leader's interpretation. He explained to Khrushchev on October 31, 1962, that he was offering the Kremlin the same sort of tactical advice he was giving Soviet generals in Cuba. "I did not suggest to you," he wrote, "that in the midst of the crisis the USSR attack, but rather that in the aftermath of an imperialist attack, the USSR act without vacillation and certainly not commit the error of allowing the enemy's chance to discharge against her a nuclear first strike."[31]

Castro assumed, incorrectly but understandably, that the United States knew the Soviet nuclear warheads for both the ballistic and tactical nuclear missiles had reached the island. He reasoned that if the United States launched an invasion—not only air attacks on the missile sites—it would be expecting the Soviet military to respond with nuclear weapons. Given those conditions, he calculated that the United States would use nuclear weapons as an adjunct to the invasion, perhaps even attacking the Soviet Union first.

Imagine Castro's surprise to hear on October 28—by way of a radio broadcast, without the courtesy of a prior telephone call from Khrushchev or the Soviet ambassador—that the Soviets had agreed to remove the missiles. He did not find the Soviet explanation for the oversight credible—that Khrushchev did not consult him because there was a lack of time given the urgency of the situation. In fact, Khrushchev made the decision to remove the missiles three days earlier, which gave him sufficient time to inform Castro about the change in the Soviets' position and to consult with the Cubans about strategy.

The Soviet fear of nuclear war was real, but lack of time was not the reason for failing to consult with the Cubans. The Soviet leaders thought that if they involved Castro in negotiations, a peaceful resolution of the crisis would have been more difficult. They believed the Cuban leader was not ready to compromise. In his memoirs, Khrushchev scornfully remarked, "In those days, you know, Fidel was very fiery . . . he hadn't even thought about the obvious consequences of his proposal, which placed the world on the brink of destruction."[32]

On October 28, Cuba notified Acting Secretary-General U Thant that Cuba wanted five demands satisfied before it would permit international verification that the ballistic missiles had been removed. They were: (1) Cease the US economic embargo and US pressure on other countries to cut commercial links to Cuba; (2) end US subversive activities against Cuba; (3) stop US supported "piratical attacks" from bases in the United States and Puerto Rico;

(4) discontinue US violations of Cuban airspace; and (5) US withdrawal from Guantánamo Naval Base.[33]

Soviet leaders judged that if they included any of Cuba's demands, their negotiations with the United States would have been even more complicated. Yet if the Soviet leaders had been less dismissive of their Cuban allies, they might have found Kennedy willing to accept at least one of Cuba's requirements, that the United States meet with Cuba face-to-face to discuss Cuba's complaints about US aggression.[34] A Soviet demand for direct negotiations between Cuba and the United States also would have acknowledged that Cuba's conflict with the United States was the source of the crisis, and that Cuba had the sovereign right to negotiate its own fate.

Yet the leader of a superpower has difficulty in thinking this way. Khrushchev and Kennedy were able to empathize with each other more easily than either could with Castro. In accepting Kennedy's stipulation that international inspectors confirm the missiles' removal, Khrushchev cavalierly ignored Cuban sovereignty. Neither the United States nor the Soviet Union had asked Cuba for permission to make inspections on Cuban territory, and Fidel refused to allow inspectors to enter the country.

Meanwhile, the United States continued surveillance flights in Cuban airspace. Indeed, the crisis did not actually end on October 28, because the United States maintained its strategic forces at Defense Condition 2 (DEFCON-2), the highest state of alert short of nuclear war. Its full might remained at a hair trigger, where the slightest error might have set off Armageddon.

THE NOVEMBER CRISIS

Such were the circumstances when Soviet deputy premier Mikoyan arrived in Cuba on November 2. Khrushchev had sent him halfway around the world to gain Cuban acquiescence in some form of international inspection, because that issue had become an obstacle to concluding the crisis. Mikoyan also hoped to assuage the anger of Cuba's leaders.[35]

But Castro was unyielding. He told Mikoyan on November 4, "We cannot take that step. If we agree to an inspection, then it is as if we permit the United States of America to determine what we can or cannot do in foreign policy. That hurts our sovereignty."[36]

Adding injury to insult, Khrushchev had volunteered to remove all Soviet troops from the island. Recalling this decision in 1968, Castro noted scornfully that Kennedy's demands "did not include those divisions, which were not offensive or strategic weapons." This decision, Castro said, "was a freely granted concession to top off the concession of the withdrawal of the strategic missiles."[37] Moreover, Khrushchev acquiesced to Kennedy's demands to take back both obsolete IL-28 bombers and Komar patrol boats, which had been delivered to Cuba to ward off attacks from Operation Mongoose operatives.

The Soviet retreat on the IL-28s and Komars, despite a firm promise to Cuba that they would not be removed, was the final confirmation of Soviet treachery from Castro's viewpoint. Five years later he explained that Cuba found itself in "the special circumstance of . . . an aggressive and emboldened enemy, an ally on the retreat and . . . our resolve to prevent relations with that ally from deteriorating to the point of rupture."[38] Thus for Cuba, the crisis was never fully resolved. "An international conflict was avoided," Castro observed in 1992, "but peace had not been achieved. For our country, there was no peace."[39]

Mikoyan could not understand this point of view. Like other Soviet officials, he was unable to comprehend the anger that Cuba's leaders expressed about the outcome of the confrontation. He said to Fidel and Raúl Castro, Che Guevara, Carlos Rafael Rodríguez, and Osvaldo Dorticós in November 1962, "Let our enemies die. We must live and live. . . . Sometimes, in order to take two steps forward," Mikoyan advised, "it is necessary to take a step back."[40] But this was not a choice the Cubans felt they had. The Soviet Union was a large country. It could absorb defeats. For Cuba, a small country, a defeat by the other superpower essentially would mean annihilation.

The crisis formally ended on January 7, 1963, with two letters to UN Acting Secretary-General U Thant. One was a joint letter from the United States and the Soviet Union. The other was from Cuba alone.[41] The occasion was reminiscent of the treaty signing in 1898 that ended Spain's colonial domination of Cuba. Cuba had been excluded, and only the United States and Spain ratified the treaty.

CUBA'S LESSONS

Cuba's dilemma was daunting at the end of the missile crisis. As the location of the nuclear confrontation that US leaders understood came harrowingly close to a devastating war, Cuba had become a mortal enemy of the United States in the very heart of the traditional US sphere of domination. The Cubans surmised that any appearance of weakness would stimulate a US impulse to rid itself of this threat in the Caribbean. While Cuba had strengthened its military after the Bay of Pigs invasion, it still lacked a meaningful air force, navy, and anti-aircraft weaponry, and it had even lost the obsolete

IL-28 bombers. Meanwhile, the Soviets demonstrated to the Cuban leaders that they cared more about maintaining a positive relationship with their superpower adversary than they did about their small socialist ally. "We realized," Castro told the Cuban Communist Party Central Committee in 1968, "how alone we would be in the event of a war."[42]

Cuban leaders viewed the US no-invasion guarantee and Soviet promises of protection as hollow. Both countries had ignored Cuba's interests during the crisis and its immediate aftermath. Terrorist attacks resumed even while US forces were at DEFCON-2 in November 1962.[43] Castro's suspicion that the Soviets were treating Cuba as a bargaining chip were confirmed in 1963 during a trip to the Soviet Union, when he learned inadvertently that Kennedy had agreed secretly to remove US missiles in Turkey in exchange for Soviet ones in Cuba.[44]

Trusting neither superpower, Cuba attempted to codify the Kennedy-Khrushchev agreement in a UN Security Council protocol that also would have addressed Cuba's desire to end the US economic embargo and engage the United States in negotiations over the Guantánamo Naval Base.[45] But the United States refused to consider negotiating the proposed protocol and the Soviets did not insist on it.

Cuban fear of the United States and distrust of the Soviet Union provided the motivation for a new international approach around which the revolutionary government organized its foreign policy for the remainder of the 1960s. This is the topic we take up in the next chapter.

NOTES

1. Edmundo Desnoes, *Inconsolable Memories* (New Brunswick: Rutgers University Press, 1990), 171–72.

2. Ernesto Che Guevara, "Letter to Fidel," 1965; read by Fidel Castro Ruz in a speech delivered to the Central Committee of the Cuban Communist Party on October 3, 1965, http://www.cuba.cu/gobierno/discursos/1965/esp/f031065e.html. [Translation by the authors.]

3. James G. Blight and Philip Brenner, *Sad and Luminous Days: Cuba's Struggle with the Superpowers after the Missile Crisis* (Lanham, MD: Rowman & Littlefield, 2002), 256n81.

4. Castro and Ramonet, *Fidel Castro*, 271. Also see Tomás Diez Acosta, *October 1962: The 'Missile' Crisis as Seen from Cuba* (New York: Pathfinder Press, 2002); James G. Blight, Bruce J. Allyn, and David Welch, *Cuba on the Brink: Castro, the Missile Crisis, and the Soviet Collapse* (Lanham, MD: Rowman & Littlefield, 2002, enlarged paperback edition); Ramón Sánchez-Parodi, *Cuba-USA: Diez tiempos de una relación* (La Habana: Editorial de Ciencias Sociales, 2012), 152–55.

5. This summary of the US understanding of the crisis is repeated in the revised edition: Graham Allison and Philip Zelikow, *Essence of Decision: Explaining the Cuban Missile Crisis*, second edition (New York: Longman, 1999), 77.

6. *FRUS, 1961–1963*, volume X, Document 383, August 22, 1962, and *FRUS, 1961–1963*, volume X, Document 386, August 23, 1962.

7. United States, Atlantic Command. 1963. *CINCLANT Historical Account of Cuban Crisis*. Serial: 000119/J09H, April 29; National Security Archive, Accession No. CC03087, 39–40.

8. William Taubman, *Khrushchev: The Man and His Era* (New York: Norton, 2003), 493–500; Michael R. Beschloss, *The Crisis Years: Kennedy and Khrushchev, 1960–1963* (New York: HarperCollins, 1991), 224–28.

9. Michael Dobbs, *One Minute to Midnight: Kennedy, Khrushchev, and Castro on the Brink of Nuclear War* (New York: Alfred A. Knopf, 2008), 216–17; Sheldon M. Stern, *Averting 'The Final Failure': John F. Kennedy and the Secret Cuban Missile Crisis Meetings* (Palo Alto: Stanford University Press, 2003).

10. Bruce J. Allyn, James G. Blight, and David A. Welch, eds., *Back to the Brink: Proceedings of the Moscow Conference on the Cuban Missile Crisis, January 27–28, 1989*, CSIA Occasional Paper No. 9 (Lanham, MD: University Press of America, 1992), 36.

11. Nikita Khrushchev, *Memoirs of Nikita Khrushchev*, ed. Sergei Khrushchev, trans. George Shriver (University Park: Pennsylvania State University Press, 2007), 321.

12. Anatoli I. Gribkov and William Y. Smith, *Operation ANADYR: US and Soviet Generals Recount the Cuban Missile Crisis* (Chicago: edition q, 1994), 13; Aleksandr Fursenko and Timothy Naftali, *One Hell of a Gamble: Khrushchev, Castro, and Kennedy, 1958–1964* (New York: Norton, 1997), 170–71.

13. Gribkov and Smith, *Operation ANADYR*, 10–11.

14. Sergo Mikoyan and Svetlana Savranskaya, *The Soviet Cuban Missile Crisis: Castro, Mikoyan, Kennedy, Khrushchev, and the Missiles of November* (Palo Alto: Stanford University Press, 2012), 186–89; James G. Blight, *The Shattered Crystal Ball: Fear and Learning in the Cuban Missile Crisis* (Savage, MD: Rowman & Littlefield, 1990), chapters 7 and 8.

15. Dino A. Brugioni, *Eyeball to Eyeball: The Inside Story of the Cuban Missile Crisis* (New York: Random House, 1991), 461.

16. Gribkov and Smith, *Operation ANADYR*, 66–67.

17. Dobbs, *One Minute to Midnight*, 248–49.

18. "Dobrynin's Cable to the Soviet Foreign Ministry, 27 October 1962," *Cold War International History Project Bulletin* 5 (Spring 1995): 79–80.

19. Khrushchev, *Memoirs of Nikita Khrushchev*, 348.

20. Blight et al., *Cuba on the Brink*, 510–11, 514.

21. Blight et al., *Cuba on the Brink*, 196.

22. National Archives and Records Administration, JFK Assassination System, Record Series: JFK; Record Number: 104-10213-10101; Agency File Number: 80TO1357A; released June 23, 1998.

23. *FRUS, 1961–1963*, volume X, Document 257, August 22, 1961.

24. *FRUS, 1961–1963*, volume X, Document 258, August 22, 1961.

25. *FRUS, 1961–1963*, volume X, Document 304, February 20, 1962.

26. Blight et al., *Cuba on the Brink*, 206.

27. "Manifesto for the Liberation of the Americas: 'The Second Declaration of Havana,'" in *Fidel Castro Reader*, ed. David Deutschmann and Deborah Shnookal (Melbourne: Ocean Press, 2007).

28. Khrushchev, *Memoirs of Nikita Khrushchev*, 331; Blight et al., *Cuba on the Brink*, 83–84, 349–351.

29. Fidel Castro Ruz, "Speech to the Central Committee of the Cuban Communist Party," January 25–26, 1968, in *Sad and Luminous Days: Cuba's Struggle with the Superpowers after the Missile Crisis*, James G. Blight and Philip Brenner (Lanham, MD: Rowman & Littlefield, 2002), 41–42.

30. Blight et al., *Cuba on the Brink*, 211.

31. Castro, "Speech to the Central Committee," 55.

32. Khrushchev, *Memoirs of Nikita Khrushchev*, 348.

33. "Fija Fidel Las Cinco Garantias Contra La Agresion a Cuba," *Revolucion*, October 29, 1962.

34. Castro and Ramonet, *Fidel Castro*, 278.

35. Mikoyan and Savranskaya, *The Soviet Cuban Missile Crisis*, 195–207.

36. "Mikoyan's Mission to Havana: Cuban-Soviet Negotiations, November 1962," *Cold War International History Project Bulletin*, no. 5 (Spring 1995): 95.

37. Castro, "Speech to the Central Committee," 57–58.

38. Castro, "Speech to the Central Committee," 61.

39. Blight et al., *Cuba on the Brink*, 297.

40. "Mikoyan's Mission to Havana," 108, 159.

41. Carlos Lechuga, *In the Eye of the Storm: Castro, Khrushchev, Kennedy and the Missile Crisis*, trans. Mary Todd (Melbourne: Ocean Press, 1995), 176–81.

42. Castro, "Speech to the Central Committee," 60.

43. Desmond Fitzgerald, "Memorandum for the Record," *FRUS, 1961–1963*, vol. XI, Document no. 348, June 19, 1963, 837–38.

44. Blight et al., *Cuba on the Brink*, 224–25.

45. Lechuga, *In the Eye of the Storm*, 139–44.

Chapter 13

Foreign Policy in the 1960s

Exporting Revolution, Chinese Flirtations, Soviet Tensions

First of all I raised the question of policy with regard to Latin America. Fidel said: you don't accept our policy toward the countries of Latin America. I responded: yes, we don't accept. And the controversy began. I said to Fidel: conducting revolution in the countries of Latin America through expediting there a few people is adventurous. Fidel responded: "So was the Cuban revolution too?" He added that Che Guevara is fighting in Bolivia and has successes. Most of the communist parties in Latin America are not parties—said Fidel—but Marxist clubs. He was particularly angry at Venezuela. He called them traitors, saying that communist parties have become bureaucratized, lost their revolutionary character and interest in leading their nations to a revolution. We believe, he said, in a military coup and in the formation of popular-revolutionary parties, which in Bolivia are created by Che Guevara. I responded: I have not heard that he had been invited by the Bolivians. Fidel said he had been invited. I expressed my opinion on the communist parties in those countries. Fidel disagreed with me. But all the time (we chatted the whole night) he was repeatedly raising this subject. Then he took up our letter and said: you have said here that if we continue taking such position and conduct such activity in other countries, there will be conflicts and you will not take responsibility on yourselves. Thus, you learned that we were under threat and you sent out to us such letter to wash your hands of this matter. He was saying all of this in a quite abrasive tone.

—Soviet Premier Alexei Kosygin, "Report on Trip to Cuba," July 1967[1]

OUTREACH TO THE UNITED STATES FAILS

Only a few weeks after the missile crisis, Cuba resumed negotiations with the United States over the release of the 1,113 surviving Bay of Pigs invaders, and quickly lowered its demands. Cuba accepted $53 million worth of food, medicine, and medical equipment in exchange for the prisoners' release. On December 29, 1962, President Kennedy promised a joyful crowd of 40,000 at Miami's Orange Bowl that he would return Brigade 2506's flag to these fighters "in a free Havana."

In 1963, US intelligence analysts noted that Castro had toned down his anti-American rhetoric after the missile crisis, and had indicated "through various channels, public as well as private, that he is interested in an accommodation with the United States."[2] In fact, the Cuban leader used a January 1963 trip by James Donovan, a New York attorney who had negotiated the release of the Bay of Pigs prisoners, to float a proposal for Cuba and the United States to normalize relations.[3]

As Donovan prepared to return to Cuba in March, the CIA and State Department recommended three nonnegotiable guidelines for the lawyer to convey to the Cuban prime minister: (1) that "Castro . . . must get the Russians out of Cuba lock, stock and barrel"; (2) that he "must agree to stop all Communist subversion efforts directed at Latin America"; (3) that he should "throw the Communists out of his government."[4] But Kennedy wanted to be more conciliatory. He overruled the recommendation, saying that Donovan's instructions should not include "the breaking of Sino/Soviet ties." McGeorge Bundy, the national security adviser, wrote that the president declared, "We should start thinking along more flexible lines."[5]

The January proposal was the first of several possible openings between the two countries that year. Others involved Lisa Howard of ABC News, the first woman to anchor a major network news program, Ambassador William Attwood, a former editor of *Look* magazine, and Jean Daniel, a French journalist. Daniel was meeting with Castro on November 22, 1963, when the two men learned of Kennedy's assassination, which essentially shut off US receptivity to normalization feelers.[6]

Despite these efforts by both countries to develop a rapprochement, the Kennedy administration reactivated its assassination program aimed at the top Cuban leaders and in June 1963 renewed its support for anti-Castro terrorists.[7] President Lyndon Johnson stopped supporting them in 1964, worried that the so-called autonomous groups had become too independent after one attacked a Spanish freighter, the *Sierra Aranzazu*, believing it was a Cuban vessel.[8] Confronted by what seemed to be an ongoing US threat and a worthless Soviet defense commitment, Cuba's leaders in 1963 modified the country's foreign policy and aimed it at three goals: to acquire economic and military security; to transform the third world through revolutions that would change the world's balance of power in favor of the poor; and to establish Cuba's independence from foreign domination.

DEPLOYING A NEW FOREIGN POLICY

Repairing Relations with the Soviet Union

The Cuban leaders' angry reaction to the Soviet withdrawal of missiles, bombers, and patrol boats generated so much tension that it actually threatened the Cuban-Soviet relationship. Attempting to prevent a break in January 1963, Khrushchev wrote a 27-page personal letter to Castro, inviting the Cuban prime minister to visit the Soviet Union. Castro recalled in 1968 that "It was a bucolic letter, poetic in many ways."[9] Khrushchev recommended that Castro travel when the weather would be warmer, and the Cuban leader arrived on April 27.

During a five-week grand tour, Fidel was treated repeatedly to red-carpet welcomes and large enthusiastic crowds. He returned to Havana with an agreement for military hardware, including anti-aircraft guns and eighty World War II–vintage tanks, construction equipment, development loans, oil shipments, and a Soviet guarantee to defend Cuba from aggression, even if that required the use of nuclear weapons. Khrushchev also agreed to leave a three-thousand-person brigade in Cuba to act as a kind of trip wire against a US invasion.[10]

In turn, Castro promised that Cuba would abandon economic plans for import substitution and increase sugar production with guaranteed deliveries to the Soviet bloc. Most important from Khrushchev's perspective, the Cuban leader agreed to moderate his stance on armed struggle by conceding that the path to socialism should be determined by the people in each country according to their circumstances, in order to achieve "the Leninist policy of peaceful coexistence."[11]

The trip provided Cuba with the economic and military security it sought. Castro's success on the trip was partly due to a card in his hand, which he played deftly—the China card. Sino-Soviet hostility had intensified by 1963 as both countries claimed to be the natural leader of the third world. Cuba was one of the twenty-five founding members of the recently created Non-Aligned Movement, which had become the principal forum for the world's poor countries. Were Cuba to break with the Soviet Union and favor China, it could have been a significant blow to the legitimacy of Soviet aspirations for leadership, especially in Latin America.

In reality, Castro would have gained little from actually playing the card, because China had far less than the Soviet Union did to offer Cuba. Indeed, when we asked him in a 2002 interview why Cuba had opted for close relations with the Soviet Union instead of China in the Sino-Soviet split, President Castro told us succinctly, "The Soviet Union had oil." By late 1964, it was clear to the Chinese leaders which side Cuba had chosen. They even rebuffed Che Guevara, seemingly the member of Cuba's leadership most favorably inclined to China, when he went to Beijing in January 1965 seeking to assuage Chinese anger toward Cuba.[12] Still, in May 1963 Khrushchev could not be certain about the decision Cuba would make.

Exporting Revolution

The risky and unconventional second part of Cuba's strategy was the support of revolutions throughout the third world. The full extent of Cuba's contributions to antigovernment guerrilla groups and independence movements in the 1960s still remains uncertain. We do know that Cuba put more effort into such support after the missile crisis.

Cuban leaders reasoned in 1963 that they could not base the country's long-term development on hopes of the US embargo ending, or on the goodwill of an untrustworthy Soviet Union that had its own economic problems. Cuba needed trading partners that could potentially remove themselves from either superpower's sphere, such as resource-rich third world states that were still colonies or were in neocolonial relationships with the advanced industrial countries. If these states gained their independence and shared Cuba's revolutionary ideology, then they might provide an alternative to dependence on the United States or the Soviet Union.[13]

In addition, all the world's poor could benefit from this plan, which enhanced its attractiveness to Cuba's leaders. Indeed, from the start they had asserted the Revolution was committed to "proletarian internationalism," a loosely defined concept that conveyed the idea of a historic mission grander than the liberation of only one country. Castro proclaimed a version of this vision in the 1962 Second Declaration of Havana when he declared, "The duty of every revolutionary is to make the revolution. It is true that the revolution will triumph in the Americas and throughout the world, but it is not for revolutionaries to sit in the doorways of their houses waiting for the corpse of imperialism to pass by."[14]

The policy of exporting revolution would seem to have contradicted Cuba's security goal—the centerpiece was reducing the US threat—because supporting third world revolutions was likely to antagonize the United States. But Castro remarked in a 1992 conference that he believed US hostility had little to do with Cuba's actual behavior. "The United States is always inventing something new in connection with Cuba," he said. "You never know what the next reason is going to be."[15]

Applying what could be called a "strategy of the weak," Castro hoped that by fanning the flames of revolution in a wide variety of locations, Cuba would force the United States to "overextend" itself as it attempted to suppress insurrections everywhere, and at the same time its attention would be distracted away from Cuba.[16] Che Guevara famously alluded to this idea in his 1967 message "from somewhere in the world" to the Organization of the Solidarity of the People of Africa, Asia, and Latin America (OSPAAAL). He wrote, "How close and bright would the future appear if two, three, many Vietnams flowered on the face of the globe."[17]

Avoiding Foreign Domination

After the missile crisis, Cuba and the Soviet Union locked horns on several issues, as Fidel tried to demonstrate that Cuba would not allow itself to be controlled by the Soviet Union. Despite Soviet requests, Cuba refused to sign both the 1963 Limited Test Ban Treaty and the 1967 Tlatelolco Treaty, which declared Latin America a nuclear-free zone. When the Soviet Union and its Eastern Europe allies broke diplomatic relations with Israel during the June 1967 Six-Day War, Cuba maintained its diplomatic relations with the Jewish state. Che Guevara, speaking on behalf of the Cuban government at a 1965 conference in Algeria, castigated the Soviets for their regressive ideological views and for their immorality in not adequately supporting liberation movements.[18]

In January 1966, Cuba frontally challenged the Soviet Union's claim to be the natural leader of the third world. It brought more than five hundred delegates to Havana from Africa, Asia, and Latin America to the Tricontinental Conference. The purpose: to initiate an organization dedicated to promoting and supporting armed liberation struggles on the three continents.[19] Soviet leaders nominally endorsed the Tricontinental Conference, which they hoped would undermine China's influence with revolutionary movements. But they repeatedly admonished Castro—before and after the conference—to back away from supporting armed struggle.[20]

Soviet officials thus were startled by the conference's open call for global violent revolution. (They also may have been affronted by the barely veiled criticisms during the meeting of alleged weak Soviet support for North Vietnam.) Castro received prolonged applause when he declared in his closing speech that "the world is big, and the imperialists are everywhere, and for the Cuban revolutionaries the field of battle against imperialism spans the whole world."[21] Even worse, from the Soviet viewpoint, the Tricontinental Conference established OSPAAAL, headquartered in Havana, to spearhead the global struggle. Subsequently, Cuba invited mostly noncommunist revolutionary movements to the first meeting of the Organization for Latin American Solidarity, an OSPAAAL offshoot.[22]

Meanwhile, with Cuba's support, Guevara had gone to Africa in 1965 to work with insurgents in the Congo and Guinea-Bissau. He returned briefly to

Cuba in 1966, and then headed to Bolivia with a small group of revolutionaries to begin a guerrilla struggle there against the government.

In June 1967, Soviet premier Alexei Kosygin pointedly told Castro that he should have informed the Soviets in advance about Guevara's expedition, and that such activities in Latin America only harmed the communist cause. Unbowed, Castro responded critically that the Soviet leaders had abandoned their own revolutionary tradition.[23]

From Fidel's perspective, the Soviet reaction to his criticism was a nearly unforgiveable act. In October 1967, Bolivian rangers supported by a US Special Forces team captured and killed Guevara. It was a terrible blow to Castro. He blamed his comrade's death on the Bolivian Communist Party and, by implication, on their Soviet masters.[24] Shortly afterward, both Fidel and Raúl Castro were conspicuously absent at the fiftieth anniversary celebration in Moscow of the "Great October Revolution," and they chose to absent Cuba from a Soviet-organized preparatory meeting of world communist parties in Budapest.[25]

The fault line in the Cuban-Soviet bond was widening. Support for national liberation movements had exactly the opposite strategic value for the Soviet Union and Cuba. The Soviets believed that their own security depended on easing tensions with the United States, a policy they called "peaceful coexistence." To Cuba, peaceful coexistence meant accepting US domination of Latin America. It also seemed to imply an acquiescence to informal deals between the two superpowers at the expense of small, poor countries such as Cuba.[26]

A FATEFUL 1968: "WE WILL FOLLOW OUR OWN ROAD"

Cuba was now at a crossroads. Castro could not allow the Cuban-Soviet relationship to reach a breaking point. He had no other option but to reduce the tension and cease his open challenges to Soviet leadership. This was underscored by a Soviet decision to reduce Cuba's anticipated oil shipments for 1968. On January 2, 1968, Castro publicly reported the troublesome news about oil deliveries, warning Cubans that the shortfall would require new limits on gasoline purchases, greater conservation efforts, and a reliance on alternative sources of fuel to run sugar mills. He held out the hope that the hardships would be temporary, lasting at most for three years.[27] By achieving a goal of harvesting ten million tons of sugar in 1970, the Cuban leader promised, Cuba would earn enough hard currency to be self-reliant.

While Fidel would tone down his public criticism of Soviet foreign policy, he would not have Cuba play the role of supine lapdog. He was determined to make the Soviet Union give Cuba respect befitting an equal, or at least a fully sovereign country. Cuba's effort to traverse a narrow strait—between the rocks of a total break with the Soviet Union and the shoals of total capitulation to its superpower patron—made 1968 a fateful transition year.

Purge of the "Micro-Faction"

The journey began on January 23, at a meeting of the entire Cuban Communist Party (PCC) Central Committee, the first such conclave since the new Communist Party's founding in October 1965. The main purpose was to conduct a "trial" of thirty-seven party members, labeled the "micro-faction." Most prominent among them was Aníbal Escalante, a leader of the PSP before 1959 and an ardent pro-Soviet critic of Castro. Raúl Castro, supposedly the brother who was most sympathetic to the Soviet Union, chaired the sessions, which found the Escalante contingent guilty of "treasonable and counterrevolutionary activities." They had conspired with Soviet embassy officials, according to Raúl's report, and provided the Soviets with false and viciously anti-Castro information. What made this behavior treasonable was the unproven claim that the conspiracy's ultimate objective was a Soviet-backed coup, a transfer of power to a group of Moscow-aligned communists led by Escalante.[28]

While official denunciations of the micro-faction avoided blaming the Soviet Union directly, Castro's message to Soviet leaders was evident: if you want to work with Cuba, you will need to work with Cuba's revolutionary government. Moscow seemed to have understood the message.[29]

Questioning Soviet Commitments: "Feeble-Minded Bureaucrats"

The micro-faction trial was reported in Cuban newspapers and was open to Communist Party officials from other countries. But a closed session ensued after the trial during which Fidel Castro castigated the Soviet leaders for their lack of both loyalty to Cuba and commitment to revolutionary goals. The text of the speech was secret, and remained so for more than thirty years. In it, Castro recounted the history of the 1962 October Crisis from the Cuban perspective.[30]

Castro was unable to ascertain Escalante's popularity among the members of the Central Committee because the new group was so new. The Cuban leader apparently believed he needed to justify the micro-faction purge in terms that went beyond the formal charges, and he used the missile crisis as an object lesson about Soviet incompetence and unreliability. In effect, he argued that the purge was necessary to protect Cuban sovereignty, because the micro-faction allegedly wanted to turn Cuba into a Soviet pawn, which would have placed Cuba's fate in the hands of "feeble-minded bureaucrats."[31] Despite the speech's secrecy, the Soviet leaders apparently learned what Fidel had said and responded by suspending shipments of military supplies to Cuba and curtailing their technical assistance and training.[32]

Undaunted, in March 1968, Fidel proclaimed the beginning of a "revolutionary offensive," which further unnerved those in Moscow who wondered about the wisdom of continuing the current relationship with Cuba. In a passionate speech on March 13, he announced the government would nationalize 56,000 small businesses—restaurants and bars, barbers, taxis and street vendors, and consumer services such as shoe and car repair shops—and shutter nightclubs such as the famed Tropicana. The order in effect closed all of the remaining private enterprises in the country other than small farms. "Gentlemen," the Cuban leader thundered, "a Revolution was not made here in order to establish the right to do business."[33]

Thus seemingly focused on the domestic economy and against a culture of materialism, the "offensive" was closely linked to Cuba's evolving foreign policy. Fidel made this point clear in the same speech, declaring: "We will follow our own road, we will build our Revolution and we will do it fundamentally by our effort. . . . Let us fight bravely, among other reasons, to minimize our dependence on all that is foreign."

Soviet Invasion of Czechoslovakia: "Not the Slightest Trace of Legality Exists"

Castro had made clear his position about Cuban sovereignty. It was time to let the Soviets know that he would not push them to the breaking point. That opportunity arose on August 21, 1968. Armored divisions of Soviet and other Warsaw Pact forces moved across Czechoslovakia's borders, crushing the "Prague Spring," an attempt to construct what its leader Alexander Dubček called "socialism with a human face." Western European socialist and communist parties uniformly condemned the Soviet intervention and declared sympathy for the Czech reformers. Even Cuban media coverage of developments in the months preceding August had a striking pro-reform bias. Cubans saw the reformers as brave pioneers, trying to construct their own approach to socialism independent of the Soviet Union.

Apart from their sympathy for the goals of the Prague Spring movement, Cuban leaders were wary of Soviet Communist Party Chairman Leonid Brezhnev's justification for the invasion. In what became known as the Brezhnev Doctrine, he said that a great power had the right to intervene to control an errant smaller power within its sphere of influence. If Cuba accepted that justification, it would have endorsed a rationale the United States had used repeatedly to intervene in Latin America.

These considerations were tempered by charges that the United States and its allies had taken advantage of Czechoslovakia's new openness to manipulate the movement's leaders and Czech public opinion, in the very way Cuban leaders imagined the United States would try to penetrate an "open" Cuban society and encourage antirevolutionary behavior and values.[34] This was one reason Castro emphasized in his March "revolutionary offensive" speech that a true revolutionary is someone motivated by moral incentives, not materialism. He was targeting US counterculture attitudes that had become increasingly popular among Cubans under thirty, which Cuban leaders viewed as individualistic. The fear of the counterculture as a leading edge of US cultural imperialism was so great that Cuban officials banished the music of the Beatles from the island.[35]

Fidel waited for nearly three days after the Soviet invasion to give Cuba's response. His silence during that period was resounding. By 1968, Cuba had become the reference point for anti-imperialism globally. Protesters at Columbia University who seized campus buildings, students in Mexico City who were beaten (and later killed) by police, and reformers in Prague who threw rocks at Soviet tanks wore T-shirts emblazoned with Che Guevara's image. Hopeful idealists throughout the world wanted to know Fidel Castro's reaction. Would he be willing to risk a break with the Soviet Union by denouncing the invasion?

The decision weighed on him heavily. When he was ready to speak, on August 23, he chose an austere setting—alone at a desk, on a television set, with only a Che Guevara portrait and the Cuban flag behind him. Castro somberly opened his address to the nation uncharacteristically, almost with an apology: "Some of the things that we are going to state here will be, in some cases, in contradiction with the emotions of many; in other cases, in contradiction with our own interests."[36] Saul Landau, a US filmmaker and historian, was in the television studio at the time, working on his prize-winning documentary, *Fidel*. He recalls that "Fidel was obviously uncomfortable. He read his speech—he usually spoke without notes—and then he just rushed out."[37]

Castro's presentation was a carefully worded lawyer's brief, which argued that the Prague Spring reforms were leading in the direction of splintering the socialist bloc and undermining international socialism. "And our point of view," he stated, "is that the socialist camp has the right to prevent this one way or another. . . . We acknowledge the bitter necessity that called for the sending of those forces into Czechoslovakia; we do not condemn the socialist countries that made that decision."[38]

This was the statement on which many analyses of Cuban-Soviet relations have dwelled, suggesting that August 1968 was the point when Cuba caved in and accepted Soviet domination. But Castro was far from done, and what he declared later in the address informs us about the terms under which he was willing to accept Soviet leadership. He argued, now with passion, that the Soviet intervention "unquestionably entailed a violation of legal principles and international norms. . . . Because what cannot be denied here is that the sovereignty of the Czechoslovak State was violated." He could justify the invasion only in political terms, to maintain the unity of the "socialist camp" so that it could advance international socialism. "In our opinion," he said, "the decision made concerning Czechoslovakia can only be explained from a political point of view, not from a legal point of view. Not the slightest trace of legality exists."

Now, if the only justification is political, he reasoned, then the socialist camp must be consistent. It would be obliged also to engage itself to a greater degree in "Vietnam if the Yankee imperialists step up their aggression against that country . . . the Democratic People's Republic of Korea if the Yankee imperialists attack that country . . . Cuba if the Yankee imperialists attack our country."[39]

Less an endorsement than a noncondemnation of the Soviet invasion, Castro thus threw a gauntlet in front of the Soviets, conditioning Cuban acquiescence in the illegal invasion on the Soviets' willingness to support revolutionary struggles. As with his pointed admonitions earlier in 1968—that the Soviets should not interfere in Cuban domestic politics or try to dictate the character of Cuba's economy—Castro now asserted that Cuba's relations with the Soviet Union had to be based on mutual respect and a shared commitment to a worldwide socialist revolution.[40]

In practice, the lofty rhetoric gave way to the reality of Cuba's vulnerabilities. The Soviets acknowledged their appreciation of Cuba's noncondemnation with symbolic initiatives such as exchanging visits by the Soviet and Cuban defense ministers. But a meaningful change in the relationship did not occur immediately. Only after Cuba failed to achieve the ambitious goal of harvesting ten million tons of sugar in 1970 did it readily welcome Soviet economic and military assistance.

NOTES

1. "Kosygin's Report on Trip to Cuba to Meeting of Communist Party First Secretaries, Budapest, Hungary, 12 July 1967," Cold War International History Project (CWIHP), Washington, DC. KC PZPRXIA/13, AAN, Warsaw. Obtained by James

Hershberg. Translated by Jan Chowaniec. http://digitalarchive.wilsoncenter.org/docu
ment/115803.

2. *FRUS 1961–1963*, vol. XI, Document no. 349, June 20, 1963.

3. *FRUS 1961–1963*, vol. XI, Document no. 275, January 26, 1963.

4. As quoted in LeoGrande and Kornbluh, *Back Channel to Cuba*, 63.

5. LeoGrande and Kornbluh, *Back Channel to Cuba*, 64.

6. Lechuga, *In the Eye of the Storm*, 197–208; LeoGrande and Kornbluh, *Back Channel to Cuba*, 67–78.

7. Don Bohning, *The Castro Obsession: US Covert Operations Against Cuba, 1959–1965* (Washington, DC: Potomac Books, 2005), chapters 7 and 9; *FRUS 1961–1963*, vol. XI, Document nos. 346, 348, 388, June 8, 1963, June 19, 1963, December 19, 1963.

8. Bohning, *The Castro Obsession*, 217–18.

9. Castro, "Speech to the Central Committee of the Cuban Communist Party," January 25–26, 61–63. The full text of the letter is available at: "Letter from Khrushchev to Fidel Castro," January 31, 1963, History and Public Policy Program Digital Archive, Archive of Foreign Policy, Russian Federation (AVPRF), http://digitalarchive.wilsoncenter.org/document/114507.

10. Jacques Lévesque, *The USSR and the Cuban Revolution: Soviet Ideological and Strategical Perspectives, 1959–77*, trans. Deanna Drendel Leboeuf (New York: Praeger, 1978), 91–96; Fursenko and Naftali, *One Hell of a Gamble*, 329–34.

11. "Text of Joint Statement, Tass in Russian to Europe 2255 GMT 24 May 1963," in "Material on Castro Visit in Soviet Union," *Foreign Broadcast Information Service (FBIS)*, USSR International Affairs, May 27, 1963, BB13; Jorge I. Domínguez, *To Make the World Safe for Democracy: Cuba's Foreign Policy* (Cambridge: Harvard University Press, 1989), 64–66.

12. US Central Intelligence Agency, Intelligence Report, "The Sino-Soviet Struggle in the World Communist Movement Since Khrushchev's Fall," Part 1, September 1967, http://www.foia.cia.gov/document/intelligence-report-sino-soviet-struggle-world-communist-movement-kruschevs-fall-part-1, 113.

13. H. Michael Erisman, *Cuba's International Relations: The Anatomy of a Nationalistic Foreign Policy* (Boulder, CO: Westview, 1985), 27–28.

14. "The Second Declaration of Havana," 264.

15. Blight et al., *Cuba on the Brink*, 298, 300.

16. "*Playboy* Interview: Fidel Castro," *Playboy*, January 1967, 70; Blight and Brenner, *Sad and Luminous Days*, 86–88.

17. Ernesto (Che) Guevara, "Vietnam and the World Struggle for Freedom," in *Che Guevara Speaks*, ed. George Lavan (New York: Pathfinder, 1967), 159.

18. Ernesto (Che) Guevara, "Speech in Algiers to the Second Seminar of the Organization of Afro-Asian Solidarity, February 25, 1965," in *Che Guevara Speaks*, ed. George Lavan (New York: Pathfinder, 1967), 107–8.

19. US Congress, Senate Committee on the Judiciary, "The Tricontinental Conference of African, Asian and Latin American Peoples, A Staff Study," 89th Cong., 2nd Sess., June 7, 1966.

20. Lévesque, *The USSR and the Cuban Revolution*, 102–4.

21. Fidel Castro Ruz, "Discurso en el Acto Clausura en la Primera Conferencia de Solidaridad de los Pueblos de Asia, Africa y America Latina," el 15 de enero de 1966," http://www.cuba.cu/gobierno/discursos/1966/esp/f150166e.html.

22. Domínguez, *To Make a World Safe for Revolution*, 270–71; W. Raymond Duncan, *The Soviet Union and Cuba: Interests and Influence* (New York: Praeger, 1985), 66–72.

23. "Kosygin's Report on Trip to Cuba to Meeting of Communist Party First Secretaries, Budapest, Hungary, 12 July 1967," History and Public Policy Program Digital Archive, Woodrow Wilson International Center for Scholars, Washington, DC, http://digitalarchive.wilsoncenter.org/document/115803. Also see: CIA Intelligence Information Cable, IN-73140, October 17, 1967; Subjects: "Background of Soviet Premier Aleksey Kosygin's Visit to Havana; Content of Discussions Between Kosygin and Cuban Premier Fidel Castro," 2–3; available through Declassified Documents Reference System (DDRS), Gale Cengage Learning.

24. Saul Landau, "Filming Fidel: A Cuban Diary, 1968," *Monthly Review* 59, no. 3 (July–August 2007).

25. Lévesque, *The USSR and the Cuban Revolution*, 130–31.

26. Blight and Brenner, *Sad and Luminous Days*, 96–97.

27. Fidel Castro Ruz, "Discurso Pronunciado al Conmemorarse el IX Aniversario del Triunfo de la Revolucion," January 2, 1968, http://www.cuba.cu/gobierno/discursos/1968/esp/f020168e.html.

28. *Granma*, International Edition (English), February 4 and 11, 1968; Blight and Brenner, *Sad and Luminous Days*, 133–37. Castro used the Escalante case as evidence of the Soviet character in 1977 when he reportedly warned Angolan president Antonio Aghostino Neto about the possibility of a Soviet-sponsored coup. See Piero Gleijeses, *Visions of Freedom: Havana, Washington, Pretoria, and the Struggle for Southern Africa, 1976–1991* (Chapel Hill: University of North Carolina Press, 2013), 73–77.

29. SED CC Department of International Relations, "Information on the Third Plenum of the Central Committee of the Cuban Communist Party and on the Attacks of the Cuban Communist Party against the Socialist Unity Party of Germany," January 31, 1968, History and Public Policy Program Digital Archive, Woodrow Wilson International Center for Scholars, Washington, DC, http://digitalarchive.wilsoncenter.org/document/115812.

30. Castro, "Speech to the Central Committee," 35–71.

31. Castro, "Speech to the Central Committee," 36.

32. Domínguez, *To Make a World Safe for Revolution*, 75; Yuri Pavlov, *Soviet–Cuban Alliance: 1959–1961* (New Brunswick: Transaction, 1994), 89.

33. Fidel Castro Ruz, "Speech Commemorating the 11th Anniversary of the March 13, 1957, Action Held at the Steps of the University of Havana," March 13, 1968. The Spanish is "¡Señores, no se hizo una revolución aquí para establecer el derecho al comercio!" http://www.cuba.cu/gobierno/discursos/1968/esp/f130368e.html.

34. Mark Kramer, "Ukraine and the Soviet-Czechoslovak Crisis of 1968 (Part 1): New Evidence from the Diary of Petro Shelest," *Cold War International History*

Project Bulletin, issue 10 (March 1998); Mark Kramer, "The Prague Spring and the Soviet Invasion of Czechoslovakia: New Interpretations (second of two parts)," *Cold War International History Project Bulletin*, issue 3 (Fall 1993).

35. Nelson P. Valdés, "What Was Forbidden Then Is Promoted Now: Cuba, the Beatles and Historical Context," *Counterpunch*, March 29/30, 2008.

36. Fidel Castro Ruz, "Speech Analyzing Events in Czechoslovakia," August 23, 1968, in Blight and Brenner, *Sad and Luminous Days*, 215.

37. Telephone interview with the authors, May 30, 2011.

38. Castro, "Speech Analyzing Events in Czechoslovakia," 221.

39. Castro, "Speech Analyzing Events in Czechoslovakia," 221.

40. Pavlov, *Soviet–Cuban Alliance*, 91–92.

Chapter 14

Internal Adjustments and Advancing Equality, 1963–1975

In the House of the Americas I met Ramón, who is the "expert" on my poetry, as they told me. To find an expert on my poetry was another of my surprises in Cuba. Ramón was a young boy with an honest look and a constant smile who worked for gangsters before the Revolution. He told me, smiling, that he worked in the Sans Souci, one of the most corrupt casinos. His job was to play cards with the customers: to play "for the house." He also worked in the Kennel Club, the dog-racing club, for other gangsters. His job was to inject morphine into the dog that was not supposed to win, or else to keep him thirsty and, just before the race, give him lots of water to drink. . . . When he was sixteen the Revolution triumphed. Ramón stopped working for the gangsters, left the casinos, and began to study literature. He said: "Because that was what really interested me."

Once when we were going to the Varadero beach resort . . . we went by the former Biltmore, which had been the district of the most elegant mansions in Cuba and which is now called Siboney and is the district of the scholarship students—where some fifty thousand farm boys live in the mansions of the rich. Ramón, smiling, pointed out a huge building in the distance and said: "That is the Kennel Club, where I used to inject the dogs." The Kennel Club, I was told, is now the stadium of the country scholarship students. It was very moving to see the children of farmers and laborers in the houses of millionaires. . . .

Farther along, where the Havana slums had been: beautiful pine groves and ten-story apartment buildings behind those pine groves. Ramón told me: "These are the families that used to live in the slums. Those ghettos that used to exist around the cities no longer exist. The dirty water drains used to go right through the middle of the houses. The houses were made of cardboard and tin cans. People lived in the midst of filth. One of the first tasks of the Revolution was to get rid of all that. It was done very soon; the first houses built were for those people."

—Ernesto Cardenal, *In Cuba*

By 1963, the average rural worker's diet had improved significantly in comparison to pre-Revolution days. All Cuban families with children younger than seven could purchase one liter of milk per day for each child at a subsidized price. Higher wages for most workers, decreased rents, and free public transportation gave many people more disposable income, enabling them to buy products previously available only to the middle and upper classes. But increased demand quickly reduced the reserve stocks of these products, and soon even ordinary items like toothpaste and soap were missing from store shelves.

The economy was suffering from two shocks. As the Cuban revolutionaries implemented their plans, disaffected Cubans voted with their feet and left Cuba. The first wave of émigrés, from 1959 to 1962, consisted largely of landowners, wealthy businesspeople, officials in the Batista government and army, employees of US corporations, small proprietors, and professionals—doctors and nurses, skilled managers, architects, pharmacists, and engineers.[1]

Meanwhile, Cuba lost its principal market and supplier, the United States. Once President Kennedy formally invoked the US embargo in 1962, its draconian impact was felt by every Cuban. In contrast to trade sanctions the United States had imposed on other countries until then, and unlike any sanctions since, the embargo against Cuba even included all food and medicines. Unable to buy machinery, chemicals, or spare parts from the United States, Cuba was forced to let buses lie idle, electrical generators break down, and many plans for development gather dust. Even the small chores of daily life—washing clothes, repairing a tire, or preparing meals—became exhausting, time-consuming tasks. Trade with the Soviet Union provided some relief, but it was far from sufficient to enable Cuba to remake its whole economy.

Economist Claes Brundenius explains that this "was the atmosphere when the so-called great debate started in Cuba."[2] It lasted from 1963 to 1965, as positions on material versus moral incentives, centralization versus decentralization, and the use of market mechanisms to determine the price of basic necessities were hashed out in newspapers, magazines, and meetings of mass organizations. By the end, a tentative consensus emerged that Cuba could not move to industrialization as quickly as leaders had envisioned initially, and that for the time being the country's development had to rest on agricultural production. In part, this outcome was spurred on by a brief rise in the world price of sugar in 1964, which held out the promise that increased sugar output could provide for the economic diversification the leaders wanted.

A PREFERENTIAL TREATMENT FOR RURAL AREAS

Despite economic problems, the government proceeded with several major reforms, many of which were rooted in a preferential treatment for rural areas. In practice, this meant nonpreferential treatment for Havana, the country's dominant urban center. Castro summarized the policy in 1966 by saying that "we must promote a minimum of urbanization and a maximum of ruralism."[3] This commitment, which the July 26th Movement consistently had articulated, served both idealistic and practical objectives. The highest levels of poverty and inequality in Cuba occurred in rural areas. Both could be attacked by improving the lives of rural workers. Rural areas along with what was then the eastern province of Oriente also had a larger percentage of black Cubans than Havana. As the government improved basic human services and infrastructure, and created opportunities for meaningful work in rural areas, it gave life to the promise of ending racism in law and practice. At the same time, the government was able to reduce internal migration because rural towns were becoming as attractive as the major cities had been.

The preferential policy resulted in the Cuban population being dispersed in a way that departed significantly from the pattern common in Latin America, where urban migration had begun to create megacities such as São Paulo, which today are ringed by shantytowns with millions of people.[4] Metropolitan Mexico City today has a population of more than twenty-one million, five times that of Guadalajara, Mexico's second largest city. In contrast, from 1960 to 1980 Havana's population increased only slightly, from about 1.6 million to 1.9 million, though the country overall grew from 7 million to almost 10 million people. The city's population today is about 2.1 million people.[5]

Holguín's growth provides an example of the deliberate nature of the government's policy. Holguín had been a minor city in Oriente, thirty-five miles from Cuba's northeastern coast. As a result of the preferential policy, it doubled in size to 187,000 people between 1960 and 1980, and today has a population of nearly 300,000. The city became a provincial capital and a manufacturing hub in accord with the plan to locate new factories closer to natural resources and in parts of the country that had been previously underdeveloped (see a Holguín factory in figure 14.1).[6] Similarly, the government developed provincial ports in order to reduce the country's reliance on Havana for international trade. Holguín became one of the first cities in Cuba to build a new university—the University of Holguín—which was founded in 1973 and today has 4,400 students.[7]

Attraction, not coercion, was the principal means the government used to shape Cuba's human geography. While the policy did include some legal

Cuba Doubles the Number of Provinces

In 1976, Cuba reorganized its administrative jurisdictions, dividing its six provinces into fourteen provinces and 169 municipalities. The fabled Oriente Province became five new provinces: Las Tunas, Holguín, Granma, Santiago de Cuba, and Guantánamo. The Island of Youth (Isla de la Juventud) became a "special" municipality. In 2010, the government made further adjustments, reducing the number of municipalities to 167 and creating an additional province. Starting in the west, the fifteen provinces are: Pinar del Río, Artemisa, La Habana, Mayabeque, Matanzas, Villa Clara, Cienfuegos, Sancti Spíritus, Ciego de Ávila, Camagüey, Las Tunas, Granma, Holguín, Santiago de Cuba, and Guantánamo.

An elected provincial assembly governs each province and elects a provincial committee, the president of which is the provincial governor. An elected municipal assembly governs each municipality and chooses the mayor.

Map 14.1.   Cuba's Administrative Divisions

restrictions on a person's free movement—through the use of work and residency permits—its essential character was humane. Many decisions would not have passed muster if they were based solely on a cost-benefit analysis.

In addition to guaranteeing year-round employment to farmers, some of the unemployment rampant in rural areas was absorbed by new construction—roads, electric lines, and sewage disposal—and new social services. Stipends provided to encourage people to attend school also removed some people from the workforce. There were also agricultural experiments that officials hoped would contribute to rural development.

For example, Fidel gave his elder brother, Ramón Castro Ruz, the task of developing dairy cows that could survive in the tropics. While Cebú cattle were best suited to the Cuban climate, a Cebú produces no more than six liters of milk a day. Holsteins, in contrast, produce more than thirty liters daily. Crossbreeding led to the development of an "H4 cow," a hybrid that could thrive in the tropical climate and produce twice as much milk as a Cebú.

Figure 14.1. Toilet factory in Holguín that opened in 1979. Cuban officials in the 1970s regarded their ability to produce light industry goods, which previously were imported, as an important developmental advance. Photo by Philip Brenner.

ADJUSTING TO THE SOVIET SYSTEM

Ten-Million-Ton Sugar Harvest Fails

Between 1967 and 1970 the dream of true Cuban independence died two deaths. First came the assassination of Che Guevara in Bolivia. Che had inspired Cubans to believe that his magnetic persona and *foco* theory (the idea that a small group could spark revolution in a country where the population is downtrodden) could bring the third world into an alliance with Cuba. The second came in 1970 with the failure of the ten-million-ton sugar harvest, which sent an unmistakable message that Cuba would need to defer achieving economic independence. Cuba's leaders perceived that the Revolution's only chance of survival rested with the Soviet trading bloc.

Recall from the previous chapter that Fidel had promised in January 1968 that Cuba would be free from foreign dictates if it harvested ten million tons of sugar in 1970. Journalist Richard Gott aptly characterized the plan as a quixotic effort "to defeat the laws of nature and economics."[8] Neither Cuba nor any other country had ever produced so much sugar in one year. The 1968 harvest had been only 3.7 million tons. Still, the "battle for sugar" captured the public's imagination and engaged a large portion of the population in a chaotic, almost festive endeavor. Vacations were curtailed, land intended for other crops was given over to sugar, factories reduced output as workers took to the fields, and schools closed early. This meant that even if the ten-million-ton goal had been reached, it would have been a pyrrhic victory. In the process of trying to produce ten million tons of sugar, the country compromised much of what it needed for future development. And Cuba harvested only 8.5 million metric tons of sugar in 1970.

On July 26, in front of hundreds of thousands of assembled Cubans, Castro acknowledged the fault was his. "We are going to begin," he declared, "by pointing out the responsibility that all of us, and I in particular, have for these problems."[9] Then, dramatically, he offered to resign his post as prime minister (he also served as commander in chief of the armed forces and general secretary of the PCC). "No," a few hundred people shouted, in a rejoinder that was not quite an affirmation of his leadership. "The people can replace us any time they wish," he said plaintively. The chants grew louder and louder: "Fidel, Fidel, Fidel." He then consented to the crowd's wishes and stayed on.[10]

Cuba Joins the Soviet Trading Bloc

Cuba expected no help from the United States or China. With only one option left, Cuba accepted an offer to join the Council of Mutual Economic Assistance (CMEA), a planned common market made up of the Soviet Union and Eastern bloc countries. CMEA members had assigned responsibilities for the production of particular commodities and industrialized products that would be exchanged in an almost barter-like fashion with all the others. Cuba's role was predictably agricultural. It was designated as producer of sugar and citrus for the trading group, with the tobacco crop as an auxiliary product.

The task of retooling the Cuban economy, so that it could use CMEA products, was vast. Consider the matter of spare parts for existing machinery, including the famous 1940s and 1950s American automobiles of Havana. Spare parts now had to come from Eastern Europe; screws, bolts, nails, and all implements would be sized with metric calibrations. And the automobiles were no longer Chevrolets and Fords, but Polish and Russian Fiats that were built under the brand name Lada. For Cubans, the brand name became a common joke, because Lada sounds much like the Spanish word *lata*, which means tin.

Indeed, Ladas were tinny and of low quality. Similarly, refrigerators and washers produced in Eastern Europe were inferior to US products. Cubans did not only feel they were receiving lower-quality goods. The upheaval was cumbersome, time-consuming, and expensive. They also realized that

A Brief Respite

As Cuba's integration into the CMEA was getting under way, sugar prices began to rise dramatically. In 1974, the world market price of sugar rose to $0.65 per pound. It had been about $0.04 per pound only four years earlier.[*] Though Cuba was the world's largest sugar producer, it had fixed price contracts with the Soviet-bloc trading system that prevented it from selling most of its output at the higher price. Still, the sixteen-fold jump in prices enabled Cuba to buy higher-quality products from Western Europe, such as milking machines, and to rev up one of its prize projects—a world-class pharmaceutical industry—by purchasing medical equipment from Nordic countries, mostly Sweden. Cuba also was able to use the bounty of hard currency to buy food and medicines from US corporations based in Latin America, because in 1975 the Ford administration relaxed the embargo on sales to Cuba from US subsidiaries in other countries. Cuba also bought US air conditioners from Canada and Dodge and Ford taxis from Argentina. But the period of high sugar revenues was short-lived. The price of sugar collapsed to less than ten cents per pound within two years.

---

[*] Carmelo Mesa-Lago, *Cuba in the 1970s: Pragmatism and Institutionalization*, revised edition (Albuquerque: University of New Mexico Press, 1978), 57.

refitting from a Western to a Soviet system meant that crossing back to a higher standard in the future would be equally difficult, and would make establishing economic independence from those countries less likely.

Did Dependency on the Soviet Union Replace Cuba's Dependency on the United States?

Cuba's economy had been so closely tied to the United States before 1959 that the island lacked meaningful independence or sovereignty. The resulting dependency had four components:

1. Trade: Cuba relied on the United States to purchase 75 percent of the island's exports and about the same percent of its imports came from its northern neighbor.
2. Terms of trade: The income Cuba received for the commodities it sold to the United States (mainly sugar) often did not cover the cost of the finished products and basic necessities it purchased from the United States, which meant there was little available for development.
3. Loans: Without sufficient hard currency to import basic necessities, Cuba relied on loans from the United States and Canada that had to be

repaid in hard currency. This further tied it to North America in a sub-servient position.

4. Ownership: US companies owned or controlled a majority of Cuba's basic industries, railroads, communications, and banks. Using a variety of loop-holes that they designed, they tended to pay far less in taxes than required by law, which also made funds for development scarce.

This pattern of dependency was common between third world countries and their former colonial rulers. Jamaican prime minister Michael Manley described the dilemma his country faced in the early 1970s with respect to sugar, its primary export. The sugar prices rarely went up, he wrote, but the price of manufactured goods generally rose. As a result, he explained, "it took more and more sugar to buy a tractor, a turbine or a motor car. How-ever, the limits imposed by geography . . . make it impossible to produce more and more sugar."[11]

As a member of the CMEA, Cuba largely escaped the declining terms of trade other poor countries suffered, because the cost of imports from the Soviet bloc were based on long-term commitments, not market prices, which also reflected a subsidy from the Soviet Union. In fact, the subsidies gave Cuba a favorable balance of trade with the Soviet Union, which contrasted with the unfavorable balance it had maintained with the United States.[12] Moreover, the Soviets provided long-term loans to Cuba, many of which were "forgiven" when Cuba could not repay them, and the Soviet Union did not own any part of Cuba's productive facilities.

In short, while Cuba's trade with the Soviet bloc did limit its independence, the dependent relationship with the Soviet bloc was less extensive and ex-ploitative than its relationship with the United States had been. Membership in the CMEA actually provided the revolutionary government with enough resources to resume the pursuit of equity.

ADVANCING EQUALITY

Income and Benefits

On October 18, 1967, at a massive memorial service for Che Guevara, Fidel Castro called on Cubans to emulate the fallen hero. To be a revolutionary, he intoned, "we must say without any hesitation, 'Be like Che'" (*¡Que sean como el Che!*).[13] The slogan became a standard that few, if any, Cubans could emulate, but it conveyed a commitment to fight selflessly for equity and in-dependence. In practice, Communist Party and government officials did live in modest houses, sent their children to the same schools as ordinary workers, and relied on common doctors and hospitals available to anyone at no cost. Echoing the slogan, the Cuban government in the 1960s and 1970s dedicated itself to providing social services for everyone in the country, including a livable old-age pension and guaranteed health care. The extreme poverty evident during the Batista years disappeared.

Yet starting in the 1970s, a small degree of inequality was allowed with the introduction of modest material incentives. Work centers received a limited number of refrigerators, televisions, washing machines, or Ladas. On the basis of everyone's job performance, which the workers themselves evaluated, the best workers were permitted to purchase one of the items with a long-term no-interest loan. New apartments were made available in the same manner.

Housing distribution, though, involved an additional element—"voluntary" labor, called "microbrigades," made up of about thirty people each from a work center. Those in a microbrigade took leave from their regular employment to participate in construction full-time, and the work center received 40 percent of the units that its microbrigade built. In a sense, everyone in a workplace participated, because the remaining employees made up for lost productivity by putting in overtime. The construction workers were not necessarily rewarded with an apartment.

New housing units were allotted by a democratic vote of all the workers. In 1972 and 1973, the efforts of microbrigades generated 65 percent of all new housing units produced in the country. Microbrigades were a way to compensate for the shortage of skilled construction workers, and they used prefabricated concrete slabs to build lifeless Soviet-designed units often more appropriate for Moscow winters than the tropics.[14]

Alamar was the largest housing project constructed by microbrigades (see photo in figure 14.2). Intended to house 120,000 residents, the project included day care centers, sports facilities, polyclinics, and boarding schools. Facing the sea just to the east of Havana, Alamar is located on land that had been designated before 1959 for wealthy investors. Today, it houses about 60,000 people.

Education

After the National Literacy Campaign, the government set a new goal beyond universal basic literacy—everyone should have at least a sixth-grade education. Classrooms were created in factories so that laborers could advance their education at lunch or after work. The government built new universities so that there was at least one in every province on the island. In the 1970s, it initiated an ambitious but controversial project based on a utopian socialist vision of breaking down barriers between manual and

Figure 14.2. Children outside their school with Alamar apartment buildings in the background. Photo by Philip Brenner.

intellectual labor—the secondary school in the countryside, *la Escuela Secundaria Básica en el Campo* (ESBEC).[15]

ESBECs were boarding schools at which students would devote part of their day to agricultural labor, learning how to cultivate, plant, and harvest crops. They spent the other part of the day learning traditional secondary school subjects. The program was intended to address several issues. One was the long-standing urban denigration of campesinos and rural life. A second was the shortage of agricultural workers. The government turned over much of Cuba's citrus production in the 1970s to these schools. Third, the schools provided relief to families who were experiencing food shortages or tight housing arrangements, and as a consequence, the schools also could improve the health of Cuba's next generation by giving students proper nutrition. In addition, the schools attempted to give Cuban youth a sense of ownership in the Revolution—that they and their families felt they were contributing to society in a personal way.

A skeptic might view the ESBECs as an attempt to indoctrinate a new generation of loyal communists and to undermine the centrality of families in Cuban culture. But the Cuban government did not take young children forcibly from their parents, as Operation Peter Pan claimed the revolutionaries

Figure 14.3. Students at an ESBEC boarding school prepare to go home for the week-end. Photo by Philip Brenner.

would do. Rather, a family's decision to send an adolescent to an ESBEC was voluntary; the schools began at grade seven, a point when children already would have been imbued with family values, and students were provided with free transportation to go home for the weekend (see ESBEC students getting ready to travel home in figure 14.3).

Today, most of the boarding schools have been closed down as fewer students have enrolled. Those still functioning are specialty schools in each Cuban province—schools for aspiring athletes and others for gifted students—called "vocational schools," such as the prestigious Lenin School for Exact Sciences in Havana's suburbs, which requires a difficult entrance exam and admits only the very top scorers.

In some ways, the ESBEC project mimicked the kind of education well-to-do Cubans provided for their children before the Revolution by sending them to boarding schools. Fidel and Raúl Castro's father, for example, enrolled them in the prestigious Belén Jesuit Preparatory School in Havana, hundreds of miles from their home. However, given the ESBECs' emphasis on manual labor, a closer analogy is the education provided in early Israeli kibbutzim, where children lived apart from the parents during the week. The ESBECs and kibbutzim also shared a philosophical approach to education espoused by John Dewey, an American educator who championed "experiential education" as a basis for fully developing human potential.

Cuba's advances in education from 1959 to 1980 are evident from several indicators. The percentage of children 13–16 years of age enrolled in school increased from about 6 to 82 percent. Per pupil spending in this period grew from twelve pesos per student to one hundred thirty-seven pesos.[16] In 1959, there were only three universities in the country, all in provincial capitals. By 1980, there were thirty-nine. Day care centers for children as young as two months old became available for a large proportion of the population. Today, every Cuban family has access to free day care.

Health Care

Fidel Castro long displayed an idiosyncratic bias in favor of medical doctors. Many of his confidants and top aides—such as Che Guevara—had been formally trained as physicians. Even though training nurse practitioners and physician's assistants would have enabled Cuba to expand its capacity to provide health care more quickly, the Cuban leader placed an emphasis on educating doctors. Medical education was free, but students had to agree to work in underserved, mainly rural, areas for the first three years after their training. By 1974, the number of doctors per capita had returned roughly to prerevolutionary levels, and they were distributed evenly throughout Cuba. (By 2000, Cuba was ranked first in Latin America for doctors, nurses, and hospital beds per capita.)[17]

The departure of so many medical professionals at the start of the Revolution might have produced a health care disaster. Thus, the improvement in Cubans' health during the first two decades after 1959 is all the more remarkable. In emphasizing preventive medical practices, and charging Cubans nothing for medical services or pharmaceuticals, the government raised the level of health in the country by the end of the 1970s to that of an advanced industrial country. At the same time, it built full-service polyclinics in rural areas, increased the number of hospitals, and targeted several diseases for immunization campaigns in addition to polio, mentioned in chapter 10. Rural-urban disparities in health indicators were virtually eliminated. As a way to encourage communities to engage in their own health improvement, polyclinics had a democratic aspect similar to community health centers in the United States. Each polyclinic was required to include community representatives on its advisory board. Sociologist Julie Feinsilver explains that such participation creates "greater social cohesion and allows non-administrators and non-health workers a voice in polyclinic operations."[18]

ADVISORY DEMOCRACY

Popular Power

Community polyclinics were not the only institutions to embody a kind of advisory democracy that Cuba championed in the 1970s. The ten-million-ton sugar fiasco convinced the leaders that a fundamental reorganization was needed, which they promised would transfer power from the center to localities. The transfer involved three major political changes: the enlargement of the Cuban Communist Party (PCC) so that its membership reflected the whole population, the creation of a new constitution framed by a Cuban conception of socialist justice, and the establishment of a system of governance that—at least on paper—decentralized political power and brought individual Cubans into the decision-making process through elections.

A high-level commission of the PCC began work on the new constitution in 1974. A draft was debated nationwide, in meetings of mass organizations and in work centers. The debates resulted in some minor modifications, but their real purpose was to give Cubans a sense of ownership over the document.[19] The PCC then held its first congress in 1975, ten years after the party was formally created. It had grown from about 50,000 members in the late 1960s to 202,000, and there were many new faces at the congress, people in their twenties and thirties who essentially had grown up under the revolutionary government. The PCC Congress placed its imprimatur on the new constitution, which was approved by a national vote in February 1976.

The new constitution proclaimed that Cuba was a "socialist state." First, this meant that the major means of production were owned socially. Second, it meant that Cuban law and institutions were to be guided by the goal of egalitarianism. As legal scholar Debra Evenson explains, "Since egalitarian values are at the core of Cuban socialism, the constitution also establishes both equality of rights and duties for all citizens and prohibits discrimination based on race, color, sex, or national origin."[20] In a bow to Soviet demands, the constitution declared that the PCC is the "leading force" that "organizes and guides the common effort toward . . . the construction of socialism." But the Communist Party had no legislative authority. That was granted to a new National Assembly and its executive committee, the Council of State, which sat at the pinnacle of the system of governance, dubbed Poder Popular or People's Power, that functioned from 1976 to 1992.

Castro began in 1970 to articulate a commitment to grassroots democracy that entailed giving "the masses decision making power" over the "scores of problems . . . in the cities and countryside." This would mean substituting "democratic methods for the administrative methods that run the risk of becoming bureaucratic methods."[21] Local affairs were better handled at the ground level, not by dictates from Havana, he said, and local councils could lead people "to take an interest in the problems of production, absenteeism, amount and quality of the product."[22] But as political scientist Carollee Bengelsdorf observes, the goals of participatory democracy and decentralization contradicted the aim of "ending the wasteful aspects of the social and political chaos of the 1960s." To infuse programs with greater rationality, the leaders believed, would require "control from the center."[23]

Poder Popular attempted to resolve the contradiction between decentralized participation and centralized control by creating a system of indirect democracy. But a 1992 law gave citizens greater direct voice in choosing their representatives at all three levels of government.[24] At the first level, called *circunscripciones*, Cubans elect representatives to municipal councils. Each *circunscripción* has about two thousand residents. Nominations come from neighborhood meetings organized by the CDRs, not from a PCC-determined slate, and are open to anyone, whether or not a person is a member of the PCC. Municipal council members maintain their normal full-time jobs, serving as citizen-legislators. Citizens can vote starting at the age of sixteen.

The members of provincial assemblies and the National Assembly are also chosen by direct election, though an official Nominations Commission creates the slate of candidates. The commissions at each level are made up of representatives from mass organizations at that level. For example, the members of the provincial nominations commission for Pinar del Rio are representatives from the provincial councils of the Center of Cuban Workers (CTC), Committees for the Defense of the Revolution (CDR), Federation of Cuban Women (FMC), Association of Small Farmers (ANAP), Federation of University Students (FEU), and the Federation of Middle School Students (FEEM).

Until now, only members of the PCC or Communist Youth (UJC) have been chosen to serve in the National Assembly, which has 614 members and is mandated to have one deputy for every twenty thousand citizens in a district. It meets twice a year for a few days each time. When it is not in session, the Council of State—which the Assembly elects—exercises legislative power. The National Assembly also elects the country's president, who serves as head of both the Council of State and Council of Ministers, the executive branch's coordinating body.

In practice, Poder Popular failed to reconcile the prerogatives of decentralized power with the need to increase efficiency in the production and distribution of goods. Local councils were granted the right to make decisions about only a few issues, and they had limited resources at their command to institute significant innovations. Moreover, the PCC essentially determined who could be elected to the National Assembly. Remarkably, local elections were actively contested for many years, and neighborhood meetings did engage the citizenry. While it seemed Cubans tended to view popular power as a useless exercise by the 1990s, the greater freedom of expression and debate for twenty years produced a new kind of interest expressed in voters leaving ballots partially blank.[25]

Family Code

While the Cuban Revolution aspired to make the nuclear family "the basic unit" of society, Debra Evenson observes, it added a twist that reflected egalitarian goals.[26] These were embodied in the 1975 Family Code, a visionary law whose enactment was spearheaded by Vilma Espín and the Federation of Cuban Women. Under the Family Code, spouses had "absolute equality"—both partners were given equal property rights, and both had the same obligations to care for the home and children. One partner, for example, was permitted to initiate divorce proceedings if the other did not participate equally in cleaning the house. This orientation was a marked contrast to Cuba's pre-revolutionary Civil Code, which decreed that a married woman was obligated to obey her husband, who was the partner solely in control of marital property.[27]

Another provision eliminated discrimination that had existed in earlier laws against some children. Under the Family Code, all children were considered to have the same rights, whether they were born to married or unmarried parents or were adopted. One notable provision of the Family Code, which many countries even today have not yet adopted, recognized informal marriages as having the same rights and obligations as formal marriages established by a legal authority. The Code defined informal marriages as a "union between a man and a woman who are legally fit to establish it and which is in keeping with the standards of stability and singularity."[28] The basic tenet was a carryover from the 1940 constitution, but Cuban courts generally had applied it only with respect to inheritance.[29]

The Family Code did not recognize unions between same-sex partners, and Cuban law today still does not provide for gay marriages. Moreover, changes in Cuba's patriarchal culture cannot be attributed exclusively to the Family Code. Though women did gain greater equality in the workplace, most continued to bear the brunt of housework and child care when they arrived home. But the Code set an aspirational norm for society. As the Center for Democracy in the Americas observed in a 2013 report, the Family Code created a "foundation for policies that . . . brought Cuban girls into the classroom, tripled the number of Cuban women at work and provide[d] Cuban women with rights and opportunities that are rare in the developing world."[30]

The 1976 constitution included the rights that the Family Code had established. Laws immediately flowing from the constitution included guarantees of equal rights for women to health care and social security and job protections such as maternal leave. The government also significantly increased the availability of free children's day care, which provided women with an essential service that enabled them to work. By 1985, the number of day care centers had doubled in comparison to 1976 and was six times greater than in the mid-1960s.[31]

A DARK DECADE

Despite Cuba's significant educational achievements in the first decade after the Revolution, there were troubling signs of problems. Dropout rates were high, many schools lacked up-to-date textbooks, and teacher training seemed inadequate. In April 1971, the government held the First National Congress of Education and Culture, ostensibly as a response to the problems. Indeed, the delegates put forth more than two thousand proposals for educational reform. But Fidel signaled that the conclave was about more than failing schools. His speech took aim at "bourgeois liberals" who are "at war with us," who show no understanding of the underdevelopment Cuba was trying to overcome as a result of the "centuries of plunder" the patrons of these "agents of cultural imperialism" brought to bear on countries like Cuba.[32] The congress then declared that all trends "based on apparent ideas of freedom as a disguise . . . for works that conspire against the revolutionary ideology" are "damnable."[33] This "ushered in a period of profound dogma"—a dark decade of artistic repression known as the "gray years"—that pushed many artists and writers into exile.[34]

It remains unclear why the government tightened its grip on writers and artists in 1971. But recall that the 1968 Revolutionary Offensive coincided with official criticism of the global counterculture because it supposedly encouraged hedonism and individualism. The 1971 crackdown may have emerged from this root. Possibly the leaders feared dissent, because the economic difficulties were beginning to challenge Cubans' faith in the viability of the Revolution. Leaders sought unity as a way to prevent the further erosion of hope.

The circumstance that sparked Fidel's denunciations was the response by major writers around the globe—including Jean-Paul Sartre, Simone de Beauvoir, Octavio Paz, Gabriel García Márquez, and Carlos Fuentes—to the incarceration of Héberto Padilla in March 1971.[35] Padilla was an internationally respected avant-garde poet whom the government had sent abroad when it shut down *Lunes*. After he returned in 1967, his writing became increasingly hostile to the Revolution. In his 1968 prize-winning collection of poems, *Outside the Game* (*Fuera del Fuego*), he emphatically proclaimed that artists had to be nonconformists, independent of politics.

During Padilla's five-week detention in the basement of a former Catholic boys' school, more than twenty writers signed a letter to *Le Monde* that denounced the Cuban government's action and called for his release. When Padilla was released on April 27, he did not go quietly. In a "confessional" speech, which he fashioned to seem as if he had written it under duress, Padilla thanked his Ministry of Interior jailors for being "more intelligent" than he was, and for helping him appreciate how he had sinned by publishing his self-centered poetry.

Padilla had a well-known penchant for sarcasm and satire. But government officials missed the joke, believed he was sincere, and took him at his word, which included damning condemnations of his fiancée, Belkis Cuza Malé, and his closest friend, Pablo Armando Fernández. Almost instantaneously, they were placed on a blacklist that prevented them from publishing their writing. Pablo Armando described to us his humiliation when writers crossed the street to avoid making contact with him. He had become a pariah. Padilla and Cuza Malé left Cuba before the end of the decade. Pablo Armando stayed, and ultimately was honored as "poet laureate."

NOTES

1. Silvia Pedraza, *Political Disaffection in Cuba's Revolution and Exodus* (New York: Cambridge University Press, 2007), 78–79.

2. Claes Brundenius, *Revolutionary Cuba: The Challenge of Economic Growth with Equity* (Boulder, CO: Westview, 1984), 51.

3. Fidel Castro Ruz, "Discurso al Encontrarse con los Integrantes de la Marcha al Segundo Frente 'Frank Pais,'" Septiembre 26, 1966, http://www.cuba.cu/gobierno/discursos/1966/esp/f260966e.html.

4. Eckstein, *Back from the Future*, 151–53.

5. Oficina Nacional de Estadística e Informació, *Anuario Estadístico de Cuba 2013*, Edición 2014, POBLACIÓN/POPULATION, tables 3.1 and 3.10, http://www.one.cu/aec2013/esp/03_tabla_cuadro.htm.

6. Eckstein, *Back from the Future*, 154.

7. "¿Quiénes Somos?" Universidad de Holguín, http://www.uho.edu.cu/?page_id=526.

8. Gott, *Cuba*, 240.

9. Fidel Castro Ruz, "Speech," July 26, 1970, http://www.cuba.cu/gobierno/discursos/1970/esp/f260770e.html.

10. Quirk, *Fidel Castro*, 644.

11. Michael Manley, *The Politics of Change: A Jamaican Testament* (London: André Deutsch, 1974), 79.

12. Carmelo Mesa-Lago, *The Economy of Socialist Cuba: A Two Decade Appraisal* (Albuquerque: University of New Mexico Press, 1981), 184.

13. Fidel Castro Ruz, "Discurso Pronunciado en Memoria del Comandante Ernesto Che Guevara, en la Plaza de la Revolucion," October 18, 1967; translation by the authors, http://www.cuba.cu/gobierno/discursos/1967/esp/f181067e.html.

14. Gary Fields, "Economic Development and Housing Policy in Cuba," *Berkeley Planning Journal* 2, no. 1 (1985): 73; Eckstein, *Back to the Future*, 158–59.

15. Leiner, "Two Decades of Educational Change in Cuba," 208–9.

16. Leiner, "Two Decades of Educational Change in Cuba," 205.

17. Eckstein, *Back from the Future*, table 5.1, 250.

18. Feinsilver, *Healing the Masses*, 81.

19. Debra Evenson, *Revolution in the Balance: Law and Society in Contemporary Cuba* (Boulder, CO: Westview, 1994), 21.

20. Evenson, *Revolution in the Balance*, 22.

21. Fidel Castro Ruz, "Speech at the Tenth Anniversary of the Founding of the Federation of Cuban Women," August 23, 1970, http://www.cuba.cu/gobierno/dis cursos/1970/esp/f230870e.html.

22. Fidel Castro Ruz, "Speech Commemorating the Tenth Anniversary of the Founding of the Committees for the Defense of the Revolution," September 5, 1970, http://www.cuba.cu/gobierno/discursos/1970/esp/f280970e.html.

23. Carollee Bengelsdorf, *The Problem of Democracy in Cuba: Between Vision and Reality* (New York: Oxford University Press, 1994), 107.

24. Asamblea Nacional del Poder Popular de Cuba, Ley No. 72, "Ley Electoral," *La Gaceta Oficial Extraordinaria*, no. 9, November 2, 1992, 52, 57–59, https://www .gacetaoficial.gob.cu/codbuscar.php.

25. Bengelsdorf, *The Problem of Democracy in Cuba*, 113–18; Jorge I. Domín-guez, "Re-Imagining Cuba's National Assembly," *Cuban Counterpoints*, July 27, 2015, http://cubacounterpoints.com/archives/1697.

26. Evenson, *Revolution in the Balance*, 123.

27. Evenson, *Revolution in the Balance*, 125.

28. Executive Branch of Council of Ministers, "Cuban Family Code" (New York: Center for Cuban Studies, 1975), 6.

29. Max Azicri, "The Cuban Family Code: Some Observations on Its Innovations and Continuities," *Review of Socialist Law* 6 (1980): 186.

30. Sarah Stephens, "Women's Work: Gender Equality in Cuba and the Role of Women in Building Cuba's Future" (Washington, DC: Center for Democracy in the Americas, 2013), 32.

31. Eckstein, *Back from the Future*, 43.

32. Fidel Castro Ruz, "Discurso en la Clausura del Primer Congreso Nacional de educacion y Cultura," April 30, 1971, http://www.cuba.cu/gobierno/discursos/1971/ esp/f300471e.html.

33. As quoted in Domínguez, *Cuba*, 393–94.

34. Leonardo Padura Fuentes, "Living and Creating in Cuba: Risks and Chal-lenges," in *A Contemporary Cuba Reader: Reinventing the Revolution*, ed. Philip Brenner et al. (Lanham, MD: Rowman & Littlefield, 2008), 348.

35. Lillian Guerra, *Visions of Power in Cuba: Revolution, Redemption, and Resis-tance, 1959–1971* (Chapel Hill: University of North Carolina Press, 2012), 353–57; Gott, *Cuba*, 246–48.

Chapter 15

Becoming a Third World Leader, 1970s

On 5 November [1975], at a large and calm meeting, the leadership of the Communist Party of Cuba reached its decision without wavering. Contrary to numerous assertions, it was a sovereign and independent act by Cuba; the Soviet Union was informed not before, but after the decision had been made. On another such 5 November, in 1843, a slave called Black Carlota, working on the Triunvirato plantation in the Matanzas region, had taken up her machete at the head of a slave rebellion in which she lost her life. It was in homage to her that the solidarity action in Angola bore her name: Operation Carlota. Operation Carlota began with the dispatch over a period of thirteen days of a 650-man battalion, strengthened by special troops. They were transported to Luanda airport itself, then still occupied by the Portuguese. ... But there can be no doubt that the immense majority left for Angola filled with the conviction that they were performing an act of political solidarity, and with the same consciousness and bravery that marked the rout of the Bay of Pigs landing fifteen years earlier. That is why Operation Carlota was not a simple expedition by professional soldiers, but a genuine people's war.

—Gabriel García Márquez, "Operation Carlotta"[1]

Cuban leaders viewed the world differently at the beginning of the 1970s than they had just five years earlier. Détente between the Soviet Union and the United States reduced Cold War tensions, which provided space for Cuba to pursue an opening with the United States. In the Western Hemisphere, new possibilities emerged for constructive state-to-state relations in Chile, Peru, Jamaica, and Guyana. The growth of the Non-Aligned Movement (NAM) enhanced the organization's viability as an agency that could empower poorer countries. Yet these changes in the global environment coincided with Cuba's new Soviet bloc relationship, which constrained the impulse of Cuba's leaders to support third world insurgencies.

OPENING TO THE UNITED STATES

Even though President Richard Nixon signed a strategic arms control treaty with the Soviet Union and opened talks with Communist China, he resolutely rejected proposals to reduce tension with Cuba at the start of his first term. But necessity intervened to overcome dogmatism as US officials sought to end a wave of airline hijackings, many of which landed in Cuba.

Cuba also had an interest in discouraging air piracy. In September 1969, the government announced that it would prosecute or extradite hijackers, but that extradition would occur only to countries with which it had an anti-hijacking agreement. Cuba's policy led to negotiations with the United States in November 1972, facilitated by Swiss diplomats in Havana. In February 1973, the two governments signed a reciprocal "memorandum of understanding" against hijacking that included boats.[2] Secretary of State William P. Rogers, though, emphasized that the accord did not "foreshadow a change of policies" toward Cuba overall.[3]

Rogers's statement did not deter some House members and senators from pursuing a policy change. The moderate Republican Wednesday Group in the House had just issued a report that called for an end to the US embargo against Cuba.[4] (The report's author was Bill Richardson, a young staffer who went on to become a Democratic representative from New Mexico, governor of New Mexico, US ambassador to the UN, and secretary of energy.) In the Senate, the chair of a Foreign Relations subcommittee—Senator Gale Mc-Gee (D-WY), an outspoken anti-communist and hawk on Vietnam—began a set of hearings on US-Cuba relations in March 1973 with a clear warning to the executive branch: "Judging from statements that any number of my colleagues have been making in the *Congressional Record* lately," he said, "perhaps the time is ripe, maybe a little late, for a reexamination of what our Cuba policy both is and perhaps should be."[5] Indeed, in September 1973, when Henry Kissinger became secretary of state and was forced to take Congress into consideration in ways he had not while he was national security adviser, he worried that the legislature might preempt the executive in trying to change US policy.[6]

In June 1974, as President Nixon was beginning to lose his grip on power due to the Watergate investigation, Kissinger appointed William D. Rogers as assistant secretary of state for Latin America. A prominent lawyer and Democrat, Rogers was a member of the Commission on United States-Latin American Relations (commonly known as the Linowitz Commission, after its chair, former US ambassador to the OAS Sol M. Linowitz). The commission's 1974 report urged "that the United States act now to end the trade embargo" in order to achieve "a normal relationship with Cuba."[7] In July 1974, Kissinger initiated secret talks with Cuba, and six months later sent two emissaries (Lawrence Eagleburger and Frank Mankiewicz) to meetings with two Cuban representatives (Ramón Sánchez-Parodi and Néstor García) in a coffee shop at New York's LaGuardia Airport. The talks were a closely held secret; even President Gerald Ford was given only limited details.[8]

Meanwhile, Congress continued to move on Cuba policy. In September 1974, two senior senators—Republican Jacob Javits of New York and Democrat Claiborne Pell of Rhode Island—met with Fidel Castro in Havana. The first elected US officials to go to Cuba since 1960, the two senators reported that the Cuban leader appeared open to negotiations and concluded that "the time is ripe for beginning the process of normalization."[9] In 1975, Republican Representative Charles Whalen (OH) traveled to Cuba, as did Democratic Senators George McGovern and James Abourezk (SD). At the same time, a House subcommittee on trade held televised hearings on ending the embargo, as a way to foster a more favorable public attitude toward a new policy.[10]

As a signal of its intention to move the process forward, the United States supported an OAS resolution in the summer of 1975, declaring that all countries in the hemisphere had the right to conduct relations with Cuba in any "form that each State deems desirable."[11] The measure was tantamount to ending the 1964 hemisphere-wide embargo. President Ford then significantly relaxed the US embargo so that subsidiaries of US corporations in third countries could trade with Cuba. The measure had two goals: to place the United States in compliance with the OAS resolution and to satisfy US companies that wanted to sell to Cuba via their foreign subsidiaries. In particular, Ford and Chrysler wanted to sell their Argentine-made cars to Cuba and were pressuring the administration for authorization.

But at almost the very moment that the United States eased the embargo, Cuba introduced a resolution in the UN Committee on Colonialism calling for the independence of Puerto Rico, even though US officials had warned Cuban emissaries with whom they had been meeting that the Cuban resolution could dismantle the nascent rapprochement.[12] Three months later, in November 1975, Cuba sent troops to Angola to support the People's Movement for the Liberation of Angola (MPLA) government there. Kissinger saw the Cuban move as a direct assault on US-Soviet détente and a slap in the face after his moves to end the embargo. In December 1975, Ford announced that Cuba's Angola operation "destroys any opportunity for improvement of relations with the United States."[13]

Despite the hostile US public posture toward Cuba, secret talks did continue early in 1976.[14] But these were soon overwhelmed, in an election year, by right-wing pressure on President Ford to harden his stance against Cuba.

Kissinger's Two Views about Cuba in Angola

Former secretary of state Henry A. Kissinger was perplexed. Why would Castro send troops to Angola in November 1975, he asked, when he was making progress on normalizing relations with the United States? Three months earlier, he noted, the United States had essentially lifted the embargo by allowing US subsidiaries in third countries to trade with Cuba.

Kissinger was talking to a small group of scholars—including Philip Brenner—at the palatial Rockefeller estate in Pocantico Hills, New York, in 1993.* The academics offered several possible explanations for Castro's behavior, and one in particular struck Kissinger as the most likely. Castro must have assessed, Kissinger agreed, that he could get no more concessions from the Ford administration than those he had obtained already. Further, Castro may have assumed that the war in Angola would be over by the beginning of 1977, and that he could resume the dialogue with a new presidential administration.

Yet in his 1999 memoir, Kissinger argued that Castro sent troops to Angola "because he considered a normal relationship with the United States incompatible with his self-appointed role as leader of the revolutionary struggle." He added that "Castro needed the United States as an enemy to justify his totalitarian grip on the country and to maintain military support from the Soviet Union."†

---

* A report of the meeting is provided in Peter Kornbluh and James G. Blight, "Dialogue with Castro: A Hidden History," *New York Review of Books*, October 6, 1994.

† Henry Kissinger, *Years of Renewal* (New York: Simon & Schuster, 1999), 785, 786.

Then, in October 1976, terrorists linked to the United States blew up Cubana Airlines flight 455 off the coast of Barbados.[15] The explosion killed all 73 people aboard the Cuban civilian airliner, including the two dozen members of Cuba's Olympic fencing team. Cubans reacted with an outpouring of grief at a mass funeral, at which Castro announced he was suspending the 1973 hijacking accord and charged that the CIA was ultimately responsible for the terrorist bombing.

In fact, the US intelligence community had learned of a possible terrorist attack against a Cuban airliner and did not notify Cuban officials. Luis Posada Carriles, one of the bomb plotters, worked for the US Central Intelligence Agency in the 1960s as a demolitions trainer, and remained in contact with operatives in Latin America. A Venezuelan prosecutor had indicted Posada Carriles for planning the Cubana bombing, but he "escaped" in 1985 from prison (led out the front door by the warden) and turned up in El Salvador. There he served as chief of the contra supply operation, transporting weapons for the US covert war against Nicaragua.[16]

CUBA IN AFRICA

While Kissinger, and much of Washington's elite, believed that Cuba "was operating as a Soviet surrogate" in Angola, Cuba actually was acting contrary to Soviet wishes.[17] Soviet leaders worried that a Cuban military intervention in Africa would undermine their efforts to reduce tension and increase trade with the United States. Indeed, Soviet premier Leonid Brezhnev "flatly refused to transport the Cuban troops or to send Soviet officers to serve with the Cubans in Angola."[18] And so the Cubans did not inform the Soviets when they sent the first combat soldiers to Angola in November 1975, even though some were transported in Soviet planes (figure 15.1 shows Cuban troops en route to battle in Angola).[19]

Cuba had begun its involvement in Africa more than a decade earlier, when it provided medical assistance to Algerian rebels in January 1962, as historian Piero Gleijeses details in the first of his masterful two-volume study of Cuba's Africa policy, *Conflicting Missions*. Cuba's commitment to African anti-colonial struggles then continued in 1964 and 1965, when it sent troops to Zaire and began supporting independence fighters against the Portuguese in Guinea-Bissau, Mozambique, and Angola.[20]

It was no surprise, then, that the MPLA sought Cuba's help in the civil war that broke out in Angola after a new Portuguese government announced in 1974 that it would be granting independence to its African colonies. Two other groups challenged the MPLA's claim to rule the country. The National

Figure 15.1.   Cuban troops and weapons supported the MPLA in 1975. Photo by Arnaldo Santos, courtesy of *Granma*.

Front for the Liberation of Angola (FNLA) was supported largely by the United States, and the National Union for the Total Independence of Angola (UNITA) received support from the United States, the People's Republic of China, and later from South Africa. The MPLA's call to Cuba became urgent in mid-1975, when South African troops entered Angola essentially to help UNITA.

US policymakers and black African leaders viewed the battle for Angola in a strikingly similar way. They understood that the outcome could destabilize the South African apartheid regime. The South African government feared that an MPLA-ruled Angola would likely become a safe haven for fighters of the South West African Peoples Organization (SWAPO), who were struggling for the independence of Namibia, which was then called Southwest Africa. South Africa had been defying a UN demand to give up control over Namibia, believing that once independent, it would become a safe haven for African National Congress (ANC) insurgents who sought to overthrow South Africa's white minority-ruled government. In effect, there was a shared view that the result of the Angolan conflict could have a domino effect, leading to the end of the apartheid regime.

Though many US officials may have preferred a more virtuous ally than South Africa, the regime had the singular "virtue" of being decidedly anti-Soviet. On the other hand, some of the ANC and SWAPO leaders seemed to be sympathetic toward the Soviet Union. From the US perspective, Cuba had entered a major battle on the "wrong" side in a region that the United States perceived was a vital location in its Cold War rivalry with the Soviet Union.

By mid-1976, there were more than 30,000 Cuban troops in Angola. Meanwhile, Castro also had been cultivating positive working relationships with the leaders of other newly independent African states, such as Julius Nyerere, president of Tanzania, and Ahmed Sékou Touré of the Republic of Guinea. Cuban support for anti-colonial movements and newly independent governments raised its international standing significantly. In particular, its armed support against South Africa led the NAM to select Cuba as the site for its 1979 summit.

Cuban troops had enabled the MPLA to secure control of much of the country, and in early 1977, Havana announced it would be withdrawing its forces from the region. This provided newly inaugurated President Jimmy Carter with the opportunity to follow his inclinations and endorse the recommendations of the Linowitz Commission regarding Cuba.[21] On March 15, 1977, Carter signed Presidential Directive/NSC-6, which stipulated that the United States "should attempt to achieve normalization of our relations with Cuba."[22] This followed on the heels of a State Department announcement that the president would not renew the ban on travel to Cuba by US citizens.

Notably, Carter's principal Latin America specialist on the NSC staff, Robert Pastor, had been executive director of the Linowitz Commission, and he may have been influential in shaping Carter's initial views about Cuba. For example, in a memo to National Security Adviser Zbigniew Brzezinski, Pastor urged "that we try to use a different term to refer to the Cubans other than 'Soviet puppet.'" He argued that "puppet" suggests that the Soviet Union was controlling what Cuba did, which, he explained, "is not the case."[23] Dismissing the threat Cuba posed to US interests in southern Africa, another prominent Carter adviser, UN ambassador-designate Andrew Young, asserted that Cuban troops brought "a certain stability and order."[24]

These decisions altered the rationale for the US embargo, which had been premised on the alleged threat that Cuba posed to the United States. Instead, the sanctions were justified as a bargaining chip in an attempt to improve human rights in Cuba, to discourage Cuba's foreign intervention, and to gain compensation for expropriated property.

For his part, Fidel sent positive signals about engaging diplomatically with the Carter administration. In January 1977, Cuba proposed negotiations with the United States over fishing boundaries. On February 8, in an interview broadcast on CBS, the Cuban leader said "he believes President Carter is a man with a 'sense of morals' who may bring an end to 16 years of hostility between the United States and Cuba."[25]

Carter also approved negotiations with Cuba over maritime boundaries and fishing rights and an agreement was finalized in April 1977. In September, the two countries expanded the opportunities for diplomatic engagement by reopening their old embassy buildings as "interests sections" and staffing the offices with Cuban and US diplomats, respectively. (When two countries do not have diplomatic relations, a third country typically handles the interests of the other two in its own embassy. Such interests, for example, might be helping a traveler to recover a lost passport. From 1961 to 1977, Czechoslovakia had an office for Cuban interests in Washington, and Switzerland had one for US interests in Havana.)

However, Brzezinski did not think US-Cuban relations should be isolated from the US-Soviet rivalry, and he relentlessly urged the president to interpret Cuban behavior in that context. Carter later acknowledged the influence Brzezinski had on his thinking. "I was an eager student," he wrote, "and took full advantage of what Brzezinski had to offer. As a college professor and author, he was able to express complicated ideas simply."[26]

The national security adviser also used the media to press his point of view. For example, State Department officials were surprised in November 1977 to find the *New York Times* featuring a major front-page story that suggested Cuban troops had been deployed throughout Africa as a stalking horse for Soviet advancement on the continent.[27] Insiders immediately guessed, correctly, that the leak of this top-secret analysis came from Brzezinski. And a close look at the map revealed that in several instances the Cuban deployment was merely a handful of security advisers, technicians, or medical personnel.

As Brzezinski and the State Department waged their internal struggle to shape Carter's worldview, Cuba's decision to send troops to Ethiopia tilted the balance in the national security adviser's favor. The United States had supported the Ethiopian government under the long rule of Emperor Haile Selassie, who was deposed in a September 1974 coup. When General Mengistu Haile Mariam, the leader of the military junta that took over, consolidated his power in 1977, he declared Ethiopia to be a socialist state and asked the United States to leave. At the time, Ethiopia was engaged in two wars, one with neighboring Somalia over disputed territory in the Ogaden Desert, and the other with Eritrean secessionists trying to separate their province from Ethiopia. Cuba had provided some support for the Eritreans when they were fighting against Selassie and the Soviet Union had been backing Somalia.

In response to Mengistu's moves, the Soviet Union shifted its support from Somalia to Ethiopia and asked Cuba to divert 20,000 troops from Angola to Ethiopia. Castro initially attempted to mediate a ceasefire between the two countries. But when that effort failed, he complied with the Soviet request.

The Ethiopia case seems quite different from Angola, and scholars have not yet been able to explain adequately Cuba's motives for sending troops to the Horn of Africa. Mengistu already had become a brutal, corrupt dictator who was doing little to improve the lives of Ethiopians and was not widely respected in Africa. The conflict with Somalia did not threaten the regime's viability and focused on a section of desert land that held no mineral wealth. While Cuba refused to support Ethiopian military actions against Eritrean separatists, they in effect provided indirect support by freeing up several Ethiopian divisions. Cuba's decision, thus, seems based on a response to Soviet pressure, because the action did not clearly serve Cuban interests and was inconsistent with Cuba's general practice.

In his memoir, Brzezinski expressed no doubt that the Soviet Union was using Cuba as a "military proxy" in Ethiopia.[28] As the president adopted Brzezinski's worldview, he repeatedly painted himself into rhetorical corners. He responded to each new Cuban "challenge" with a tough stance, even when the reality turned out to contradict the allegations.[29] Wayne Smith, who was in charge of the State Department's Cuba desk at the time, recalled Cuba made sincere efforts to be cooperative in 1978 and 1979. But the White House rebuffed those efforts. When Smith tried to provide the president with a "balanced assessment" of Cuba's role in Africa, noting that Cuba had "contributed to peaceful solutions and had been helpful to us," a National Security

Council aide informed him that the NSC was interested only in emphasizing how "the Soviets and the Cubans are the aggressors."[30]

CUBA'S NEW LEADERSHIP ROLE

Cuba's shifting role in international relations also was evident in the Western Hemisphere. A 1975 Defense Intelligence Agency report stated that "Cuba is virtually inactive in subversive support in Latin America at this time."[31] After Che Guevara's death, Cuba had reduced its support for insurgencies there and sought cooperative state-to-state relationships with governments less inclined to follow a pro-US line. Salvador Allende, the president of Chile from 1970 until his death during a right-wing coup in 1973, provided the first major opening for Cuba when he restored diplomatic relations on his first day in office. Cuba had already established friendly contacts with the leftist military government of Peru. In 1974, when Argentina's populist leader Juan Domingo Perón returned to Buenos Aires from exile in Spain, Cuba created ties there.

As the hemisphere turned left in the 1970s, Cuba offered technical and development assistance to established governments, especially in the Caribbean basin. Large contingents of Cuban teachers and doctors went to Jamaica starting in 1974. After Maurice Bishop's New Jewel Movement overthrew the government of Grenada in 1979, Cuban engineers helped to construct a modern airport to stimulate the island's tourist trade. (Though President Ronald Reagan charged that the airport was intended as a refueling station for Soviet bombers, it had been designed by the US Agency for International Development prior to the coup.) In Nicaragua, Cuba provided some training to the Sandinista rebels, but did not send arms until they ousted the country's dictator, Anastasio Somoza, in 1979. Cuba then contributed significant development and military aid, including weapons and training, to the new Sandinista government. But Castro also advised the Sandinistas to take a measured approach in consolidating their revolution in order to avoid angering the United States. While the Reagan administration charged that Cuba was arming El Salvador's Farabundo Martí National Liberation Front, State Department officials had convincing evidence that the vast majority of rebel arms in El Salvador came from seized government weapons caches or were obtained via the black market within El Salvador.

Meanwhile, Castro developed a working relationship with General Omar Torrijos, the military leader of Panama, and his intelligence chief, Colonel Manuel Antonio Noriega. Panama had allowed Cuba to set up several front companies that were used to circumvent the US embargo. But the relationship became complex because Torrijos and Noriega had close relations with US officials. Noriega, for example, served as an intermediary between Fidel Castro and the Reagan administration to defuse tensions in the aftermath of the 1983 US invasion of Grenada.[32]

Cuba, all the while, was establishing its role as a leader of the Non-Aligned Movement. In 1973, the NAM first called for the creation of a "New World Economic Order" in which developing countries would use their "commodity power" (control of oil and strategic minerals) and market potential to obtain more favorable terms of trade. Castro envisioned Arab oil-producing countries as a key component in the plan to develop a South-South trading alliance that could challenge Northern domination and make commodity power meaningful. In part for this reason, Cuba broke diplomatic relations with Israel in 1973 and sent military advisers to Syria during the Arab-Israeli War that year. In 1974, Castro invited to Havana Yasser Arafat, the Palestinian Liberation Organization's leader, and the next year Cuba supported a majority of the UN General Assembly in declaring that Zionism was a form of racism.

Ninety-six nations sent their heads of state to the September 1979 NAM summit in Havana (see a photo of the summit in figure 15.2). Along with their foreign ministers and other members of their delegations, they convened in a spanking new, modern convention center with telecommunications facilities for the 1,200 journalists covering the conference. But attendees were jarred just prior to the opening by US charges that the Soviet Union had secretly dispatched a "combat brigade" to Cuba. In fact, the "discovery" turned out to be misinterpreted intelligence—the 3,000-soldier unit had been

Figure 15.2.   The sixth summit of the Non-Aligned Movement met in Havana in 1979. Photo by Philip Brenner.

in place, with US acquiescence, since the 1962 missile crisis. But Carter insisted it had to be removed because it could be used for military intervention in the Western Hemisphere. In October 1979, he created the Caribbean Contingency Joint Task Force in Key West in order to protect the region from the threat posed by the brigade. He also signed Presidential Directive 52, which declared that US policy was "to contain Cuba as a source of violent revolutionary change," and he ordered national security agencies to devise strategies for "isolating" Cuba.[33]

The summit gave Cuba a mandate to develop a long-range agenda for South-South relations. Yet Cuba's leadership role was significantly compromised less than four months later when the Soviet Union invaded Afghanistan. Afghanistan was a member of the NAM and the inviolability of each member's sovereignty was a core NAM principle. The Soviet leaders had not even informed Fidel in advance about the intervention. But he felt constrained to support the Soviet action by not condemning it, which was a position exactly opposite to the one that NAM countries expected their chair to take.

As in 1968, when the Soviet Union invaded Czechoslovakia, Cuba's "benefactor" had placed the revolutionary government in a no-win situation. With advance notice, Fidel might have been able to find an acceptable compromise. But faced with the fait accompli of the invasion, he chose the option of not siding with the NAM and vitiating Cuba's potential to strengthen the organization and its members' bargaining power because it seemed less costly. In hindsight, the cost proved to be greater than in 1968, and it contributed to tension between Cuba and the Soviet Union that lasted until the Soviet empire collapsed.

This is not where Cuban leaders earlier in the decade imagined that they would be standing—once again caught in the middle of US-Soviet Cold War tensions. Their hopes for a new world order were quickly evaporating. They had lost key allies in the hemisphere as the result of right-wing coups and the 1980 electoral defeat of Jamaica's Michael Manley. Tensions with the United States had increased to their highest levels in fifteen years, signified by President Carter's order to resume aircraft reconnaissance flights over Cuba. And on the island, there was growing unrest as 1980 began because the economy was sputtering.

NOTES

1. Gabriel García Márquez, "Operation Carlota," trans., Patrick Camiller, *New Left Review*, nos. 101–102 (January–April 1977), 126, 128, 137.

2. Schoultz, *That Infernal Little Cuban Republic*, 257–59; LeoGrande and Kornbluh, *Back Channel to Cuba*, 123–26.

3. Bernard Gwertzman, "Rogers Says US Is Firm on Cuba," *New York Times*, February 16, 1973, 77.

4. Charles W. Whalen et al., "A Détente with Cuba," *Congressional Record*, January 29, 1973, H-2507-9.

5. US Senate, 93rd Cong., 1st Sess., "US Policy Toward Cuba," Hearings before the Subcommittee on Western Hemisphere Affairs, March 26 and April 18, 1973, 1.

6. LeoGrande and Kornbluh, *Back Channel to Cuba*, 126.

7. Commission on United States–Latin American Relations, *The Americas in a Changing World* (New York: Quadrangle Books, 1974), 29.

8. LeoGrande and Kornbluh, *Back Channel to Cuba*, 128–33.

9. As quoted in Schoultz, *That Infernal Little Cuban Republic*, 267.

10. US House, 94th Cong., 1st Sess., "US Trade Embargo of Cuba," Hearings before the Subcommittees on International Trade and Commerce and International Organizations, Committee on International Relations, on H.R. 6382, May 8 to September 23, 1975.

11. Schoultz, *That Infernal Little Cuban Republic*, 271.

12. Henry Kissinger, *Years of Renewal* (New York: Simon & Schuster, 1999), 782; Leslie H. Gelb, "US Relaxes Ban against Trading with the Cubans," *New York Times*, August 21, 1975, 1.

13. *New York Times*, December 21, 1975, 3; Piero Gleijeses, *Conflicting Missions: Havana, Washington, and Africa, 1959–1976* (Chapel Hill: University of North Carolina Press, 2002), 255–72; 285–93, 329–38; Kissinger, *Years of Renewal*, 782–84.

14. LeoGrande and Kornbluh, *Back Channel to Cuba*, 146–47.

15. US Central Intelligence Agency, Directorate of Operations, "Activities of Cuban Exile Leader Orlando Bosch during His Stay in Venezuela," Digital National Security Archive, Accession number: CL01549; Document number: IN 069101; ProQuest document ID: 1679043549, October 14, 1976.

16. Saul Landau, "The Cuban Five and the US War against Terror," in *A Contemporary Cuba Reader: Reinventing the Revolution*, ed. Philip Brenner et al. (Lanham, MD: Rowman & Littlefield, 2014), 273; Peter Kornbluh, "A Safe Harbor for Luis Posada Carriles," *NACLA Report on the Americas* 39, no. 4 (January/February 2006): 17.

17. Kissinger, *Years of Renewal*, 816.

18. Odd Arne Westad, "Moscow and the Angolan Crisis, 1974–1976: A New Pattern of Intervention," *Cold War International History Project Bulletin*, Issue 8–9 (Winter 1996/1997): 25–26.

19. Gleijeses, *Conflicting Missions*, 306–7.

20. Gleijeses, *Conflicting Missions*, 7–9, and chapters 2–6.

21. David Binder, "Carter Says Cubans May Leave Angola, Is Receptive on Ties," *New York Times*, February 17, 1977.

22. Jimmy Carter, Presidential Directive/NSC-6, "Cuba" (Washington, DC: The White House,. March 15, 1977), http://www.jimmycarterlibrary.gov/documents/pd directives/pd06.pdf.

23. Quoted in Schoultz, *That Infernal Little Cuban Republic*, 295.

24. Kathleen Teltsch, "Young, Taking Over U.N. Duties, Prepares to Leave for Africa Today," *New York Times*, February 1, 1977, 2.

25. Associated Press, "Castro, Praising Carter, Sees a Prospect of Ties," *New York Times*, February 10, 1977.

26. Jimmy Carter, *Keeping Faith: Memoirs of a President* (New York: Bantam Books, 1982), 51.

27. Hedrick Smith, "US Says Castro Has Transferred 60's Policy of Intervention to Africa," *New York Times*, November 17, 1977, 1.

28. Zbigniew Brzezinski, *Power and Principle: Memoirs of the National Security Adviser, 1977–1981*, revised edition (New York: Farrar, Straus, and Giroux, 1985), 180–90; quotation is on 180–81.

29. Smith, *The Closest of Enemies*, 128–40.

30. Smith, *The Closest of Enemies*, 141–42.

31. Quoted in Schoultz, *That Infernal Little Cuban Republic*, 271.

32. Manuel Antonio Noriega and Peter Eisner, *America's Prisoner: The Memoirs of Manuel Noriega* (New York: Random House, 1994), 93–95.

33. PD-52 (October 29, 1979) is available at http://www.jimmycarterlibrary.gov/documents/pddirectives/pd52.pdf. Also see David D. Newsom, *The Soviet Brigade in Cuba* (Bloomington: Indiana University Press, 1987); Gloria Duffy, "Crisis Mangling and the Cuban Brigade," *International Security* 8, no. 1 (Summer 1983).

Chapter 16

Mariel Exodus—
A Warning Signal, 1980

Pablo Armando Fernández had been a leader of Cuba's avant-garde artistic community in the early days of the revolution. As the deputy editor of *Lunes de Revolución*, he used the publication to link many of the world's most creative masters to Cuba's writers, artists, dancers, and film directors. His first novel won a coveted award from Casa de las Americas in 1968.[1] But by 1971, he had ruffled too many feathers. The government banned publication of his writing.

In the 1970s, several of Cuba's great writers went into exile. Fernández stayed, working as a copy editor for a Cuban publisher and maintaining his faith that the revolutionary government would rectify its error in isolating him. That moment came in April 1980, when he was allowed to accept invitations to speak at three US universities. The poet went to the US Interests Section for a visa dressed in his finest suit. His large mane of blondish white hair added to the image a distinguished man of letters who deserves the highest respect.

Figure 16.1. Pablo Armando Fernández in 2009. Photo by Philip Brenner.

But as he approached the entrance, angry onlookers waiting in a line that stretched around the building began to shout at him: "Get back in line, you bum. Who do you think you are that you can jump ahead?" They were among hundreds of Cubans who had begun to queue outside of the US diplomatic mission each day, hoping to secure a visa in order to emigrate.

"Tears came to my eyes," Pablo remarked, "because this was so beautiful. Twenty years earlier, such working-class people would have shuffled out of the way to make a path for a well-dressed person like me who had an appointment. But the Revolution had given these people something they did not even know they had, even as they turned their backs to it. These ordinary Cubans had acquired dignity."

—Interview with Pablo Armando Fernández[2]

Events during the second half of the 1970s were like the winds that create a perfect storm. The flood that followed was the emigration of more than 125,000 Cubans in the span of nine months—from April to December 1980—many of whom left from the small port town of Mariel, twenty miles west of Havana. The Mariel exodus was a startling wake-up call for the Cuban leadership, because the *marielitos* were the very people whose lives the Cuban Revolution was supposed to improve.

The United States was the natural destination for Cuban emigrants. It was the richest country in the world and a short boat ride away. Prior to 1959, there was a modest but steady flow of Cuban emigration to the United States. Pablo Armando Fernández's family moved to New York City in 1945, and he returned to Cuba only after the 1959 revolution. The United States received 65,000 Cuban immigrants between 1950 and 1958. Almost 100,000 Cubans emigrated to the United States in the first two years after the revolutionaries overthrew the Batista dictatorship. In the next two years, an additional 125,000 arrived, and by the end of 1979, nearly 700,000 Cubans had moved north.[3]

PRELUDE TO THE MARIEL EXODUS: RISING DISCONTENT

The Cuban economy was coming out of the doldrums by 1973. In the first half of the 1970s it grew at a remarkable annual rate of about 7.5 percent.[4] Thanks to rising sugar prices, Cuba increased trade with Western countries. At the same time, a critical mass of newly trained professionals enabled the government to increase productivity, provide for increased personal consumption, and complete major projects. But the boom was short-lived. In the latter part of the 1970s, the price of sugar fell. Annual growth was only 5 percent in 1978 and 1.6 percent in 1979.[5] While Cubans' daily life worsened only slightly, government leaders had led them to believe their lives would be getting even better. Their comparison to the "good times" just a few years earlier engendered widespread discontent.

Projects were placed on hold and half-finished buildings began to deteriorate. Young Cubans were now better educated and more workers had advanced training, but with the economy slowing down, many could not find jobs commensurate to their skills. Moreover, the babies born in the boom immediately after the Revolution were now entering the labor force. Underemployment was growing even as the official rate of unemployment dropped in the late 1970s to 1.3 percent. Factory and construction workers were laid off temporarily due to shortages in raw materials.[6]

Meanwhile, Cuba's larger role on the world stage entailed personal sacrifices for young Cubans, especially those with African ancestry. More than 35,000 Cuban troops were deployed to Angola starting in late 1975. Another 15,000 went to Ethiopia in 1977. By 1980, more than 100,000 had served in combat missions. The conditions in both countries were harsh, and there were times when the troops were ill-equipped or short of supplies. Between 1975 and 1979, the Cuban military may have suffered as many as 10,000 combat deaths and many more casualties. These losses, along with the long tours of duty, reportedly led to significant discontent among Cuban families with soldiers in Africa.

In 1979, a potent ingredient was added to the concoction of discontent brewing on the island: an opening to Cuban-American visitors from the United States. Until then, few exiles had been allowed to return to Cuba for family visits. The process that set in motion this breakthrough began early in the Carter administration's second year, when there was a brief moment of reprieve in Cuba's long conflict with the United States. After Bernardo Benes, a Cuban-American banker who favored improved relations and gave large sums to the Democratic Party, had several meetings with high-level Cuban officials, he informed National Security Adviser Zbigniew Brzezinski in March 1978 that Cuba wanted to discuss the possibility of releasing all political prisoners. This report quickly led to direct, secret negotiations between the two governments, and Fidel offered to release all political prisoners by the end of 1979.[7] According to Wayne Smith, who was at the time the principal US State Department expert on Cuba, the United States would have to accept all of the Cuban prisoners who wanted to emigrate. This stipulation, among others, generated disagreements between the State and Justice Departments, and the National Security Council staff, which in turn stalemated the process.[8]

Frustrated by the official US nonreaction, Fidel brought a new group into the fray, the Committee of 75, a courageous assemblage of Cuban-Americans who hoped to improve US-Cuba relations through a "dialogue." At a press conference in September 1978, he publicly invited the group to Cuba and proposed discussing with them family visits by Cuban-Americans.[9] In part, the Cuban leader sought to divide the exile community by elevating those who wanted a rapprochement with Cuba.

Despite death threats from paramilitary organizations in Miami, and the assassination of one of the group's members, the committee traveled to Havana in November 1978 to escort the first of 3,600 released political prisoners to the United States, and to bring back the news that Cuban-Americans would be allowed to visit their homeland. The first horde of visitors arrived in Cuba in time for Christmas. By the end of 1979, more than 100,000 Cuban-Americans had traveled to the island, spending more than $100 million.[10] On some days, as many as six charter flights arrived at José Martí Airport from Miami.

Philip Brenner was leading a group of twenty Americans on an educational tour of the island in February 1980 when he came upon a Cuban electrician at a hotel bar in Camagüey—a city in the middle of the island. José, as we will call him, was in Camagüey as part of a crew from Havana to repair electrical power lines. He and Brenner began to chat in Spanish, but José asserted that he preferred to practice his English. "Oh?" Brenner responded skeptically. "Yes," he said. "I like to talk to Americans." As they started on a third beer, José asked almost rhetorically, "Perhaps you know my brother. He has the best pizza restaurant in Miami." "No," Brenner replied, "I don't know your brother or the pizzeria. But perhaps I could take a photo of you and send it to your brother when I return to the States, so that he can see how you are doing?" "No need for that," José chuckled. "He was here last month, and my sister is coming next month."

The best pizza restaurant in Miami! That was quite a claim, and no doubt José was shocked to see the reality when he arrived in Miami, after the journey we confidently assume he took from Mariel a few months later. How was he to know that his siblings, like many of those who visited in 1979, exaggerated their success in the United States? While Cubans who migrated before 1980 tended to be wealthier than other immigrants from Latin America, the differences were not large.[11] Yet it was understandable that the émigrés sought to justify their decision to leave by suggesting that the Miami streets were paved with gold. Exile is rarely an easy choice and invariably leaves an emotional scar.

Cuban authorities did not anticipate the huge quantity of material goods the visitors would bring—cargo loads of small stoves and refrigerators, air conditioners, and other appliances that were difficult to obtain in Cuba. Within months, though, they restricted what visiting exiles could bring into the country, and at the same time permitted them to purchase overpriced Soviet-bloc appliances for their families. The goods were sold at the former Sears department store in Old Havana, which had been shuttered for twenty years, and only Cuban-Americans were permitted to buy them.

Until then, a Cuban earned the right to purchase durable goods by being an exemplary worker. Refrigerators and the like were apportioned to work centers, which in turn allocated them to the best workers, though political factors also were taken into account. All of a sudden, the system for obtaining scarce goods changed. All that one needed was a visiting relative who would buy it for you, or a friend who had a visiting relative. Cuban-Americans often bought three or four refrigerators for their families, who sold the excess on the black market. This change began to unravel the former incentive system controlled by the state, which relied on bonuses such as refrigerators to reward meritorious work, and it contributed to a further decline in productivity.

Darker-skinned Cubans, though, did not share equally in the new largesse. Their families disproportionately had stayed in Cuba during the previous twenty years because they tended to benefit from the Revolution. And so there were fewer black relatives bearing gifts from Miami in 1979. The resulting distribution of luxuries along racial lines added to a growing sense of unfairness that some Afro-Cubans perceived. They had borne a greater cost in the African conflicts, sacrificing for the Revolution, and were rewarded with the short end of the bargain.

THE EXODUS

For months, there had been small incidents at several foreign missions in Havana. People seeking to leave Cuba were illegally entering embassy grounds in search of asylum. The growing discontent was combustible and needed only a spark for it to explode. On April 1, 1980, a Cuban policeman was killed trying to stop six Cubans from crashing through the gate at the Peruvian embassy. Cuba asserted the six had no justifiable claim for diplomatic protection and demanded they be tried for the policeman's murder. When Peru refused, Castro withdrew guards from the embassy. In less than three days, 10,800 people crowded onto the Peruvian embassy grounds seeking asylum.[12]

A few months earlier, the Cuban leader had denounced the warm receptions given to boat hijackers who arrived in Miami as tantamount to an endorsement of such behavior. On April 21, he announced that Cubans would be free to emigrate if they were picked up at Mariel harbor—about twenty miles west of Havana—by boats arriving from Florida. A front-page editorial in *Granma* declared, "We have ended our protection of the peninsula of Florida . . . now they will begin to harvest the fruit of their policy of encouraging illegal departures from Cuba, including the hijacking of boats."[13] The next day, a flotilla of small boats from Florida lined up outside the port.[14]

Anti-Castro exiles charged that Castro added to the wave of émigrés by emptying his jails and psychiatric hospitals. In reality, the United States determined in 1984 that only 2,746 out of the more than 125,000 who left Cuba in the Mariel exodus were excludable from the United States for reasons of criminal behavior or mental incapacity.[15]

Still, the marielitos were different than previous waves of Cuban immigrants. They included more dark-skinned and younger Cubans. Nearly half had held semiskilled or unskilled jobs, whereas only 8 percent of the 1959–1962 cohort were semiskilled or unskilled workers.[16] They had experienced advancements the Revolution had produced: improved health care for everyone and the eradication of epidemic diseases; the end of illiteracy and universal access to a quality education. They had watched Cuba's global stature soar, and they had begun to acquire a new pride in what it meant to be Cuban. Yet they were no longer willing to sacrifice for a future that seemed to recede farther away, no longer able to suspend belief that life was not better in the United States, and no longer motivated by revolutionary ideals to work selflessly for a greater good.

NOTES

1. Pablo Armando Fernández, *Los niños se despiden* (Havana: Casa de las Americas, 1968).

2. Personal interview with Pablo Armando Fernández by Philip Brenner in Washington, DC, April 18, 1980.

3. Felix Roberto Masud-Piloto, *From Welcomed Exiles to Illegal Immigrants: Cuban Migration to the US, 1959–1995* (Lanham, MD: Rowman & Littlefield, 1996), xxiv.

4. Andrew Zimbalist and Susan Eckstein, "Patterns of Cuban Development: The First Twenty-Five Years," in *Cuba's Socialist Economy: Toward the 1990s*, ed. Andrew Zimbalist (Boulder, CO: Lynne Rienner, 1987), 12–13.

5. Brundenius, *Revolutionary Cuba*, 40.

6. Mesa-Lago, *The Economy of Socialist Cuba*, 129–31.

7. Schoultz, *That Infernal Little Cuban Republic*, 320–322; Peter Kornbluh and William M. LeoGrande, "Talking with Castro," *Cigar Aficionado*, January 2009, 8.

8. Smith, *The Closest of Enemies*, 148–59. Also see Robert M. Levine, *Secret Missions to Cuba: Fidel Castro, Bernardo Benes, and Cuban Miami* (New York: Palgrave, 2001).

9. Schoultz, *That Infernal Little Cuban Republic*, 327–28; Smith, *The Closest of Enemies*, 160–63; Masud-Piloto, *From Welcomed Exiles to Illegal Immigrants*, 74–78.

10. Barry Sklar, "Cuban Exodus 1980: The Context," in *The Cuba Reader: The Making of a Revolutionary Society*, ed. Philip Brenner et al. (New York: Grove, 1988), 344.

11. Lisandro Pérez, "Immigrant Economic Adjustment and Family Organization: The Cuban Success Story Reexamined," *International Migration Review* 20, no. 1 (Spring 1986): 4–20.

12. Sklar, "Cuban Exodus 1980," 340–41; Jo Thomas, "Crowd at Havana Embassy Grows," *New York Times*, April 7, 1980, A1.

13. As quoted in Schoultz, *That Infernal Little Cuban Republic*, 355.

14. Smith, *The Closest of Enemies*, 210–12.

15. Masud-Piloto, *From Welcomed Exiles to Illegal Immigrants*, 93–95, 100–102.

16. Susan Eva Eckstein, *The Immigrant Divide: How Cuban Americans Changed the US and Their Homeland* (New York: Routledge, 2009), 16, 19.

Chapter 17

Change and Rectification at Home and Abroad, 1980s

"Hey, what do you think we are, bourgeois?" shouts a short, thin man in work clothes. "I make 138 pesos a month. You think I can afford to buy onions at two pesos a pound? Three lousy onions for two pesos. ¡Que va!" [No way!] All heads turn toward him, some voicing their agreement, others just nodding. The vendor remains imperturbable. "You don't have to buy them, you know. It's a free choice." The worker looks up at him in disgust. "You're all just a bunch of bandidos [bandits]," he snorts. "And just look at those hands. You've never even been near the soil!"

—*No Free Lunch*[1]

A NEW ECONOMIC PLAN

For most countries in Latin America, the 1980s were a "lost decade." Western banks, which were flush with deposits from oil-rich countries that had benefited from the tenfold rise in petroleum prices during the previous decade, needed new places to invest. They turned to South America, where the region's dictatorships were only too happy to use the easy loans to buy weapons, monumental projects, and personal luxuries. They spent little of the money on development and could not repay the loans when they came due. Some governments, such as Peru, had to make interest payments that were as much as 50 percent of the hard currency they earned from exports. Mexico depleted its hard currency reserves in 1982 and nearly defaulted on billions of dollars in loans. Cuba's economic problems were not as severe, but the 1980 Mariel exodus had exposed decay eating away at the Revolution's foundation.

208

Economic Problems

In the mid-1970s, Cuba had introduced reforms modeled on the Soviet system as a way of integrating into the Council of Mutual Economic Assistance (CMEA), the Soviet-led trade group. For example, the government created its first five-year plan, which was accompanied by a program called the "New System of Economic Management and Planning" (SDPE in the Spanish acronym). JUCEPLAN, the Central Planning Board, was transformed from a mere coordinating body to the main unit that directed all central planning.

There should have been little surprise that the new system would produce exactly the opposite of the intended results, namely, increased productivity and a greater number of products produced domestically. Productivity went down, diversification lagged, and the country had to rely even more on imports from the CMEA. Centralized rules, bureaucratic inflexibility, and prices unrelated to costs led to widespread popular criticism, with even top leaders themselves expressing frustration.

The SDPE was supposed to decentralize economic activities, and it did achieve this goal with respect to farming. Until the mid-1970s, farmers were allowed to sell their produce only to the state, and the government pressured small farmers to work on state farms. Under the reforms, the government reduced the pressure to work for the state and provided incentives for private farmers to create cooperatives. The number of cooperatives increased from forty-four in 1977 to nearly 1,500 in 1983.[2]

In 1980, in a seeming response to the Mariel exodus, the government permitted farmers to sell their surplus output—their production beyond the quota of products they had to sell to the state at fixed prices—to the public at "farmers' markets." The prices in these markets were unregulated and were generally much higher than at state stores. Still, the farmers' markets were popular because they provided items, such as garlic, that were often difficult to find in stores. For pensioners on fixed incomes and less well-off Cubans, the ration book (libreta) continued to provide a safety net of basic commodities in state stores at a subsidized price.

New regulations stipulated that the sellers at the farmers' markets had to be the actual producers. They also had to provide their own transportation to the market. But the rule was honored in the breach, because farmers found that both selling and cultivating their crops was too time consuming and transporting produce to urban centers was too expensive. Instead, they turned to entrepreneurial private distributors who were willing to serve as illegal distributors and vendors.

The farmers' markets did increase the variety of food available to Cubans in urban areas, and perhaps even the total supply available. One report observed that farmers reduced waste because they could sell items that otherwise they would have discarded.[3] But the markets also created undesired consequences. Some farmers illegally withheld some items from sale to the state in order to reap higher prices from the private markets. Some stole state property—seeds, pesticides, and fertilizer that they could not buy anywhere—in order to increase production of commodities for the farmers' markets.

A Plague of Intermediaries

Because the state could sell farm equipment only to cooperatives, individual farmers were unable to plow their profits into capital investments—even items as mundane as a hose for irrigation. Instead, they and the newly wealthy middlemen engaged in conspicuous consumption. They bought expensive items intended for export, such as high-quality rum, and paid exorbitant prices for cars that only exemplary workers had been able to purchase.[4] As the anecdote at the opening of this chapter highlights, the growing wealth of the vendors soon began to generate resentment among workers who were angry about the high prices and the fact that most sellers were not farmers themselves.[5] In effect, the farmers' markets and the legalization of some private services such as repairing cars were generating class divisions and income inequality that was anathema to the founding revolutionaries.

Fidel made his displeasure known publicly as early as 1982. In a speech to the Young Communists, he described the middlemen as "a plague of intermediaries . . . who produced nothing and bought and hoarded products that in many cases the farmers should have sold to storehouses for normal distribution."[6] He acknowledged that farmers would want to earn more for their produce, just as consumers would want lower prices. But they all had to consider what was good for the country as a whole. The excesses caused by privatization, like the desire of Marielitos to leave the country, he believed, was evidence that there needed to be a greater emphasis on ideological development.

By 1986, Cuba's leaders were fed up with the markets. They had tried to control them by increasing taxes, monitoring sellers, and regulating what could be sold. But the tactics expanded the black market and middlemen continued to thrive. Finally, in April, Castro terminated the experiment. He shut down private farmers' markets and denounced the distributors of agricultural produce who earned sums far greater than ordinary workers. "There are people who unfortunately confuse income earned from working," he declared, "and from speculation and scams bordering on theft or that actually are theft." At the same time, he criticized managers of state enterprises for applying capitalist principles—favoring the production of higher priced goods, which earned more money for their firms, over the production of goods needed for social projects.

"These practices have to be rectified," Castro asserted, by returning to the fundamental principles of the Cuban Revolution. "There are some," he said,

> who think that socialism can be created without political work . . . I believe that the problems must be resolved on the basis of morals, honor and principles. . . . In the face of external enemies and danger that lurks from the outside . . . the Revolution will not only know how to overcome its weaknesses, its own weaknesses, it will know how to defend itself from external enemies; that this country will never return to capitalism, that this country will never revert to being imperialist property.[7]

Rectification Campaign

At a deferred session of the Third Party Congress in December 1986, the PCC set into motion the "process of the rectification of errors and combating negative tendencies." It involved doing away with the material incentives introduced by the SDPE reforms, ending the privatization of some services along with the farmers' markets, and recentralizing economic decision-making. It also returned the Revolution to its 1960s roots in renewing Che Guevara's emphasis on "moral incentives."[8]

Party leaders blamed the stagnation of Cuba's economy in the late 1970s and early 1980s on their own blind adherence to Soviet practices.[9] Cuba would now march in step to its own drummer. In setting Cuba on this course, Castro and the PCC pointedly rejected perestroika, the new economic model Soviet premier Mikhail Gorbachev had just introduced. Perestroika was a set of proposals for economic restructuring through which the new Soviet leader hoped to reduce the state's role in the economy and place greater reliance on market mechanisms.

Though Castro pointed to commitments he shared with Gorbachev—for peace, ending world hunger and poverty, and fighting imperialism—in a February 1986 speech in Moscow, relations between the two leaders already were becoming cool. Whether disagreements about economic policy contributed to the tension between them is uncertain. Yet over the next five years, Cuba grew ever more distant from the Soviet Union.[10]

FOREIGN AFFAIRS

Recall from chapter 15 that the 1979 Soviet invasion of Afghanistan was a major blow to Castro's ambitions for the Non-Aligned Movement. He also had hoped that Jamaican prime minister Michael Manley would succeed in convincing OPEC members of the NAM to invest their newfound wealth— as a result of oil price hikes—in third world countries instead of New York banks. But this dream of South-South development evaporated as Manley's demarche failed.

Meanwhile, Cuba had to contend with increased hostility from the United States. By the end of the Carter administration, relations had returned to the depths of the early 1960s. Thus, when President Ronald Reagan took office he could rely on existing US hostility to provide firm ground from which to launch a more threatening policy toward Cuba.

Cuban-US Relations in the Reagan Years

Several Reagan officials had advocated harsh measures against Cuba long before they assumed office. In 1981, Cuba quickly became the focal point of their anti-communist crusade, as they pursued a "get tough" policy. Secretary of State Alexander Haig set the tone in February 1981, declaring that the United States must "deal with the immediate source of the problem [in El Salvador]—and that is Cuba."[11] Arguing that Cuba had been fomenting strife throughout Central America and was the source and principal support of civil unrest and revolution in Nicaragua and El Salvador, he reportedly recommended that the United States turn "that fucking island into a parking lot." Senior Reagan officials were appalled by the suggestion and rejected it out of hand.[12]

Still, the 1983 US invasion of Grenada was the kind of action Cuban officials could not dismiss lightly. Under the pretext of saving US medical students on the island, the United States sent more than twenty thousand marines to gain control of this small country of 100,000 people. The invasion was triggered by dissension within the ruling party that led to the assassination of Prime Minister Maurice Bishop. President Reagan had charged earlier that Grenada was a threat to US security because eight hundred Cuban construction workers were building an airport on the island. Using top secret surveillance photos that mimicked those taken in 1962 of Soviet missiles in Cuba, the president claimed that the airport was intended as a layover port for Soviet bombers. In fact, the airport construction itself was a tourist attraction not hidden from public view and the Cubans used architectural plans created by USAID for the previous government. Grenada lacked an airport at which standard Boeing 737 planes could land, which hobbled its potential for tourists. Otherwise, its only source of income was sugar and nutmeg, a "strategic" spice used in making pumpkin pies for Thanksgiving celebrations.

In many ways, the Reagan administration's policy was a carryover from previous administrations. Its goal was to isolate Cuba from the international community and undermine the Cuban government's legitimacy domestically. In practice, the policy involved: threats to confiscate imported goods that contained Cuban nickel; pressure on European allies not to renegotiate Cuba's outstanding loans; and reinstatement of the ban on US citizens traveling to Cuba that President Carter had chosen not to invoke.[13] In addition, the US Navy demonstrated a show of force in the Caribbean reminiscent of military exercises just prior to the 1962 missile crisis. Called "Ocean Venture 82," the three-week set of maneuvers involved forty-five thousand troops, 350 airplanes, and sixty ships, and included an exercise to evacuate noncombatants from the Guantánamo Naval Base. Cuba responded by placing the country on full military alert.

Prior to 1981, Cuban-Americans had not relied much on traditional lobbying to achieve their aims. President-elect Ronald Reagan's foreign policy adviser, Richard Allen, sought to fill this vacuum with a group to which the administration could claim it was responding as it shaped a hardline policy against Cuba. Allen sent a team to Miami immediately after the 1980 election to meet with Jorge Mas Canosa and other former Bay of Pigs veterans to discuss creating the new lobby. Thus was born the Cuban American National Foundation (CANF).[14]

It was no surprise, then, that Mas Canosa found a ready welcome at the White House in 1981, as Allen had become President Reagan's first national security adviser. The Reagan administration's encouragement of the CANF was more than mere lip service. It funneled construction contracts, federal grants, and program funding to CANF board members who plowed money back into the organization, as well as congressional campaigns. At Allen's urging, CANF staff members reportedly received coaching from the American Israel Public Affairs Committee, one of the most influential lobbying organizations in Washington.[15]

When Mas Canosa called for a radio propaganda station aimed at Cuba, he was pushing on an open door. The idea had been proposed in a 1980 advocacy paper by the archconservative Committee on Santa Fe. One of its authors was Roger Fontaine, the first Latin America director of Reagan's National Security Council.[16] The station was supposed to function in the way Radio Swan did twenty years earlier, when the CIA created the propaganda outlet as a way to support the 1961 Bay of Pigs invasion. But Congress forced the administration to place the operation, named Radio Martí, under the Voice of America's nominal supervision.

Still, Radio Martí was headquartered in Miami and Mas Canosa served as its first advisory board chair. The station began broadcasting its twenty-four-hour mix of music, soap operas, slanted news, and anti-communist propaganda in 1985. Though Cuba tried to jam the station's short- and medium-wave broadcasts, its soap operas were popular on the island (though in 1994 the station changed its format to all "news"). Cuba has been more successful in blocking the signal from TV Martí, which was launched five years later. The US General Accountability Office reported in 2009 that less than 2 percent of the Cuban population ever listened to Radio Martí and less than 1 percent to TV Martí.[17]

Cuba attempted to find ways to engage the Reagan administration positively. One time it even prevented an assassination attempt against Reagan that Cuban intelligence agents uncovered. But the responses from the United States were repeatedly negative. Wayne Smith, who served as chief of the US Interests Section in Havana from 1979 to 1982 and courageously resigned in protest, observed that "the administration cared not a whit about the facts or the objective evidence." Its policies in Central America and toward Cuba, he said, were based on "ideological preconceptions and would not be budged from that policy no matter what the Cubans and Nicaraguans might do."[18] Though Smith was generally recognized as perhaps the most knowledgeable Cuba expert in the government, the Reagan administration did not even inform him about a planned meeting between Haig and Cuban vice president Carlos Rafael Rodríguez in November 1981.

A Dialogue of the Hearing Impaired

The Haig-Rodríguez meeting was the first of four times Cuba and the United States engaged in negotiations during the two Reagan administrations. Arranged by Mexican president José López Portillo, the first encounter was more like a dialogue of the hearing impaired than a negotiation. After issuing barely veiled threats of possible US actions against Cuba during the meeting, Haig asserted that the United States was most concerned that Cuba was acting as a stalking horse for the Soviet Union to create unrest in Central America and harm US "vital interests" by sending troops to Nicaragua and El Salvador. Rodríguez responded at length. He denied that there were any Cuban soldiers in Central America and affirmed that while Cuba's foreign policy at times may have coincided with Soviet policy, Cuba was a sovereign country that acted independently on the global stage.[19]

Analyst Peter Kornbluh notes that the two men came away from the meeting with contradictory assessments. Haig, he wrote, "appears to have interpreted the meeting as evidence that US pressure on Castro was working." Rodríguez viewed Haig as more level-headed than he had believed before, and "reasonably intelligent." He was impressed that "Haig was willing to send [Lt. Gen. Vernon] Walters . . . as an envoy to continue the talks."[20]

Walters had served as deputy director of the CIA in the Nixon administration and became US ambassador to the UN in 1985. A close confidant of President Reagan, he was a "roving ambassador" in March 1982 when he went to Cuba. But Walters arrived "with a preconceived conviction that Castro's ideological commitment to communism foreclosed any prospect of compromise. . . . Even Cuba's suspension of aid to the Sandinistas [Nicaragua's governing party] and the Salvadoran guerrillas was discounted as ephemeral."[21] Thus, the second instance of negotiations came to naught.

As we discussed in the previous chapter, the third engagement came in 1984 over migration. The United States agreed to accept up to twenty thousand Cuban émigrés annually. Cuba agreed to accept the return of some 2,700 exiles whom US authorities deemed excludable. But the success of these talks did little to mitigate the Reagan administration's antagonism toward Cuba or Cuba's fear of a US attack.

The focus of Reagan's animus toward Cuba was Central America. In 1982, the United States included Cuba on its list of state sponsors of terrorism, largely because of Cuba's relationship "with the Sandinista Revolution in Nicaragua, and with the on-going guerrilla movement led by the FMLN in El Salvador."[22]

State Department Propaganda Report on Central America

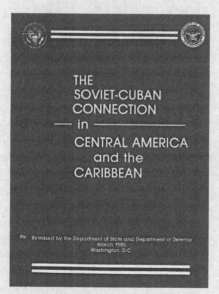

THE
SOVIET-CUBAN
CONNECTION
— in —
CENTRAL AMERICA
and the
CARIBBEAN

Re Released by the Department of State and Department of Defense
March 1985
Washington, D.C.

The Soviet Union sees in the region [Caribbean basin] an excellent and low-cost opportunity to preoccupy the United States—the "main adversary" of Soviet strategy—thus gaining greater global freedom of action for the USSR. . . . The Soviet Union and Cuba have worked effectively toward the objective of establishing additional Marxist-Leninist regimes in Central America and the Caribbean. Although Castro has become more calculating in his export of violence and exploitation of poverty, his aims remain as they were in the 1960s. . . . For its part, the Soviet Union has intensified its efforts to create chaos or conflict near the United States to divert US attention and resources from Soviet challenges in other critical areas of the world.*

---

* US Departments of State and Defense, "The Soviet-Cuban Connection in Central America and the Caribbean (Washington, DC: March 1985), 2, 10.

Repeatedly, the president charged the civil wars in the region were due to a "Soviet-Cuban connection" that manipulated the populace's anger over their poverty. A 1984 presidential commission on Central America—commonly known as the Kissinger Commission after its chair, former secretary of state Henry Kissinger—even devoted a section of its report to the "Cuban-Soviet Connection."[23] In 1985, the State and Defense Departments issued a propaganda pamphlet entitled, "The Soviet-Cuban Connection in Central America and the Caribbean." It was produced by the Office of Public Diplomacy (OPD), an agency with a benign-sounding name housed in the State Department's Latin America bureau. Later, OPD was caught up in the Iran-contra scandal because of its illegal diversion of US government funds to election campaigns against members of Congress who opposed the US-backed contra war.[24]

By 1987, US-Cuban relations were at their lowest ebb since the 1962 missile crisis. In March, the United States forcefully pursued passage of a resolution in the UN Human Rights Commission accusing Cuba of persecuting political dissenters. (It failed when Latin American members of the commission supported Cuba.) In July 1987, Cuba countered with a television documentary that detailed espionage activities by personnel in the US Interests Section.[25]

Yet in January 1988, representatives of the two countries met for the first time to discuss the conflicts in Angola and Namibia. Until then, the United States had refused to attend any meeting about Angola with Cubans present. One factor that moved the United States was the victory of Cuban military forces at Cuito Cuanavale, Angola.

Cuito Cuanavale is a small town in southeastern Angola. The departure point for a failed July 1987 attack by Angola against South African forces, it was the location at which South Africa hoped to achieve "the total destruction of the enemy forces north of the Lomba [River]," in effect securing its control over Namibia.[26] The South African Defense Force (SADF) assembled the largest set of ground and air forces for a single operation since World War II. It combined with units from UNITA, one of the two guerrilla groups fighting against the Angolan government. Angola's military was supported by 1,500 Cuban troops and some Soviet advisers, as well as Cuban engineers and construction workers who built airstrips south of the conflict zone from which MIG-23s could threaten important dams. Fighting lasted four months and ended on March 23, 1988.

The four-party (Angola, South Africa, Cuba, and the United States) negotiating sessions occupied the better part of a year and led to a historic accord: Cuba agreed to withdraw troops from Angola and South Africa agreed to withdraw from Namibia and allow free elections there. Namibia gained its independence in 1990, and all South Africans were able to vote in April 1994 elections held under the rules of a new non-apartheid constitution.

Cuba's cooperation and initiatives turned out to be essential for success. The chief US negotiator later remarked, "We might still be at the table today were it not for the Cuban factor."[27] Cuban officials hoped their positive contributions would moderate US policy in the new administration of George H. W. Bush. But from the new president's perspective, Cuba had ceased to be a country of significant interest. The Cold War was winding down and the United States had achieved its particular objectives vis-à-vis Cuba when Cuban troops withdrew from southern Africa, Nicaraguan 1990 elections removed Cuba's Sandinista allies from power, and negotiations ended the civil war in El Salvador. So Bush turned Cuba policy over to Congress, where CANF-backed anti-Castro members took charge, and Cuba policy moved from the foreign to the domestic realm.

Cuban-Soviet Relations

Good relations between the Soviet Union and Cuba progressively deteriorated in the 1980s. The falling out began with a trip to Moscow by Raúl Castro in September 1981. In reaction to "the Reagan Administration's aggressiveness toward Cuba," he told an interviewer in 1993, he was seeking Soviet reassurance of military support in the event of a US attack.[28]

The Soviet response embittered and chastened Cuba's leadership. Leonid Brezhnev, the Soviet premier, reportedly told the Cuban vice president, "In case of US aggression against Cuba, we can't fight in Cuba. . . . We'd only get a thrashing." The message was clear. Cuba was utterly alone—"alone, as we had always waged our wars of independence," Raúl remarked in the interview. His attitude echoed Fidel Castro's 1968 comment to the first full meeting of the PCC's Central Committee, when he described his perception of Soviet abandonment at the end of the missile crisis. "We realized," he explained, "how alone we would be in the event of a war."[29]

Cuban leaders called the Soviet position "the Pandora case," and sought to keep knowledge of it as secret as possible. They feared that if the United States learned about Soviet unwillingness to protect Cuba, the Reagan administration would be emboldened to commit aggression. In order "to disinform the enemy," Raúl Castro said, Cuba's public posture toward the Soviet Union remained cordial and even improved. At the same time, Cuba's leaders requested more modern military equipment from the Soviet Union, built tunnels beneath Havana where people could go in case of an American attack, and expanded its recently created Territorial Troop Militias (MTT).

The MTT was intended to provide Cuba with the capability of countering a US invasion with protracted warfare by citizen-guerrillas, which Cuba calls a "War of All the People." Fidel described the change to editors of the *Washington Post* in 1985. "Every citizen in this country knows what to do" if there were an invasion, he said. "It would be very costly for us. . . . But it would be very costly for the aggressors."[30] In 1981, half a million Cubans were enrolled in the MTT. Once the rapid build-up began, its size grew quickly. By 1984, it had 1.2 million members, more than one-tenth of the country's population.[31]

Cuba and the Soviet Union also disagreed over support for El Salvador's insurgent organization, the Farabundo Martí National Liberation Front (FMLN), and Nicaragua's Sandinista government. Despite Reagan administration charges that Cuba and the Soviet Union were supplying weapons to the Salvadoran guerrillas, the communists within the FMLN coalition actually lost some influence when Moscow turned down their appeal for assistance. The Soviet Union also tried to keep its distance from Nicaragua. Fidel did not attend the 1985 funeral of Soviet president Konstantin Chernenko as a way of showing his displeasure with the Soviet Union's low level of aid to Nicaragua.[32]

Cuban Internationalism in Central America and Africa

Cuba continued to support the Sandinista government in the 1980s by sending some of its own materiel, especially once the contra war heated up in 1982. It also deployed military advisers to Nicaragua. Yet Castro advised Nicaragua's leaders to avoid some of the errors he believed the Cuban Revolution had made in its early years, especially antagonizing the United States needlessly. In 1984, he urged them to work with other countries in the region trying to end the US-sponsored internal conflict by supporting the *Contadora* proposals.[33]

Political scientist Jorge Domínguez wrote in 1978 that "Cuba is a small country, but it has a big country's foreign policy."[34] In one sense, the assessment accurately captured a distinguishing feature of Cuba's international behavior. Unlike great powers, small countries tend to focus narrowly, on their immediate neighborhoods and not on the globe. Great powers with large military forces can act with a greater sense of freedom than small countries, because they perceive that only another great power can truly threaten them. Despite its size, Cuba focused globally.

Cuban leaders shared with Fidel Castro a vision that their country should lead a revolution on behalf of poor people everywhere. Party-controlled newspapers such as *Granma* and state-run radio and television stations covered world events extensively. Generally, these outlets are no more informative than in-house corporate public relations newsletters. But their depth of information about international topics—which is not commonly found in most US media—has enabled ordinary Cubans to identify with the struggles of people in other third world countries, as well as to understand global affairs better than most Americans.

Even though Domínguez reformulated his summary description in 1985, many observers of Cuba's foreign policy—especially critics—stayed with the early version. It includes a subtle denigration of Cuba's behavior as being inappropriate for the country's size—as if Cuba were a child trying to wear an adult's shoes. Yet the old formulation overlooks a key difference between Cuba's international orientation and those of most great powers. Cuba has not sought to dominate and control other countries, nor has it exploited the resources of another country for Cuba's exclusive benefit. There is an altruistic quality to Cuba's internationalism, even as it may have served Cuba's interests.

Cuba's commitments to the Popular Movement for the Liberation of Angola (MPLA) and Namibia's South West Africa People's Organization (SWAPO) were not based on expedient short-term calculations or spontaneous bursts of revolutionary zeal. They developed deliberately and patiently, starting in the 1960s, and were deeply rooted in the Cuban revolutionaries' belief that internationalism ultimately served Cuba's long-term goals and interests.[35] Cuba's military contributions to liberation struggles, technical assistance to newly independent states, and education and health care to people from the third world generated goodwill and allies. It also strengthened Cuba by enhancing its "soft power"—the attractiveness of its ideas and culture in other countries and the legitimacy of its approach to global politics.[36]

Cuban leaders hoped that as more countries shared Cuba's views, its internationalism would have helped to build South-South coalitions.[37] Internationalism also brought ordinary Cubans into contact with the deep poverty many third world people suffer so that new generations of Cubans who had no memory of the 1950s would gain an appreciation for the achievements of the Revolution. By the mid-1980s, approximately fifteen thousand Cubans—one out of every 625—were working in civilian foreign aid missions in more than thirty countries. At the same time, 24,000 students from 82 countries were enrolled in Cuban high schools and universities. In 1984, three-fourths of them were studying at "internationalist schools" on the Isle of Youth.[38]

The Isle of Youth was the location of the infamous prison where Fidel and Raúl Castro served time after the failed 1953 Moncada attack, when the island was named the Isle of Pines. The government changed the name in 1978 when it established a novel education program for third world students, who paid nothing for their schooling, room, board, and transportation. Selected by their governments—in the case of Namibia, by SWAPO—they attended schools designated for their country, taught mostly by instructors from their home country, whom the government also supported. Cuban teachers taught math, science, and Spanish language courses.[39]

CORRUPTION

A distinguishing characteristic of the Cuban Revolution had been the lack of corruption among senior officials. Most ministers and high party officials lived in modest homes, drove rusting Ladas, and did not wear the kind of expensive watches and jewelry that are conspicuous signs of inequality. At times, when either of us wanted to show special appreciation to an official who had provided assistance during one of our trips to Cuba, we would buy a $25 bottle of Scotch whisky. The hearty thanks we received made clear that this was a treat not regularly imbibed.

The military, on the other hand, seemed to be more privileged. In 1987, Philip Brenner met Norberto Fuentes in his apartment, in a building reserved for officers. A journalist, Fuentes had written favorably about the military in a book and several articles, and had become a confidant of several senior officers. He claimed to have access to a secret report that Fidel Castro had written about the missile crisis that Brenner and Scott Armstrong, executive director of the National Security Archive, hoped to obtain. The apartment was filled with high-end consumer electronics, including three different kinds of videotape machines for watching films. In offering Brenner a drink, Fuentes opened a closet filled from top to bottom with imported whiskies. "How can you afford all of this?" Brenner asked. Fuentes avowed that he earned substantial fees for his lectures about Ernest Hemingway. Two years later, he was arrested for serving as a kind of "bag" man for military and intelligence officers engaged in illicit activities. Fidel Castro revealed that $200,000 was found in Fuentes's apartment.[40]

Fuentes was particularly friendly with General Arnaldo Ochoa and Tony de la Guardia. Ochoa had been decorated as a "Hero of the Republic," led the team of military advisers in Nicaragua, and was a leader of Cuba's force in Angola in 1987 and 1988. De la Guardia had been a trusted though somewhat irregular official in the Ministry of Interior (MININT), which houses Cuba's intelligence service and national police. He headed the security team protecting Fidel Castro during his trip to Chile in 1971, and in 1980 took charge of a unit within MININT responsible for importing and exporting goods blocked by the US embargo.

When Cuban troops in Africa were short on necessities, including weapons, Ochoa smuggled items such as diamonds for supplies through de la Guardia's networks. But Ochoa became too cavalier, and at one point approved one of his aides to work with de la Guardia to help transship drugs through Cuba.[41] The aide met with Pablo Escobar's drug cartel in Colombia.

Fidel was furious about the contact. "That was a matter of enormous seriousness," he told Ignacio Ramonet. "It put the country in the position of being accused of being involved in drug trafficking."[42] Indeed, in December 1989 the United States invaded Panama, ostensibly to oust Manuel Noriega because of his alleged involvement in facilitating drug shipments.

A nationally televised trial in June 1989 exposed Ochoa's and de la Guardia's corrupt practices, and a subsequent military tribunal sentenced them and two others to death by firing squad. Another two—including de la Guardia's brother, Patricio—received thirty-year sentences. Interior Minister General José Abrantes was arrested shortly afterward and received a thirty-year prison term.

As journalist Richard Gott aptly observed, "Not just the individuals involved but the Revolution itself was on trial."[43] While some US commentators have argued that the real purpose of the executions was to clamp down on an incipient move in the military to oust Fidel Castro and replace him with the supposedly popular Ochoa, only hearsay evidence from some defectors has materialized in nearly thirty years to support those allegations. In fact, Castro attacked the intelligence service, not the military, replacing several interior ministry officials with military officers. Our interviews at the time indicated that the revelations of corruption actually shocked and angered Cuban leaders because they believed that the corrosive petty criminality that was beginning to proliferate, due to economic problems, could not be halted unless the leadership remained uncorrupted.

NOTES

1. Medea Benjamin, Joseph Collins, and Michael Scott, *No Free Lunch: Food and Revolution in Cuba Today* (San Francisco: Institute for Food and Development Policy, 1984), 61.

2. Benjamin et al., *No Free Lunch*, 167.

3. Benjamin et al., *No Free Lunch*, 69.

4. Eckstein, *Back to the Future*, 54.

5. Benjamin et al., *No Free Lunch*, 72–73.

6. Fidel Castro Ruz, "Speech at the Closing of the Fourth Congress of the UJC," April 4, 1982, http://www.cuba.cu/gobierno/discursos/1982/esp/f040482e.html.

7. Fidel Castro Ruz, "Speech Delivered on the 25th Anniversary of the Girón Victory," April 19, 1986, http://www.cuba.cu/gobierno/discursos/1986/esp/f190486e.html.

8. Fidel Castro Ruz, "Discurso en la Clausura de la Sesion Diferida del Tercer Congreso del Partido Comunista de Cuba," December 2, 1986, http://www.cuba.cu/gobierno/discursos/1986/esp/f021286e.html; Partido Comunista de Cuba, *Informe Central Tercer Congreso*, 1986, http://congresopcc.cip.cu/wp-content/uploads/2011/01/Informe-Central.pdf.

9. Max Azicri, *Cuba Today and Tomorrow: Reinventing Socialism* (Gainesville: University Press of Florida, 2000), 24–26, 55–59.

10. Mervyn J. Bain, "Cuba-Soviet Relations in the Gorbachev Era," *Journal of Latin American Studies* 37 (2005): 773–77.

11. Alexander M. Haig, "Excerpts from Haig's Briefing about El Salvador," *New York Times*, February 21, 1981.

12. William M. LeoGrande, *Our Own Backyard: The United States in Central America, 1977–1992* (Chapel Hill: University of North Carolina Press, 1998), 82–83.

13. John M. Goshko, "US Acts to Tighten Cuban Embargo," *Washington Post*, April 20, 1982.

14. Patrick J. Haney and Walt Vanderbush, "The Role of Ethnic Interest Groups in US Foreign Policy: The Case of the Cuban American National Foundation," *International Studies Quarterly* 43 (June 1999): 346–50; Elizabeth A. Palmer, "Exiles Talk of PACs and Power, Not Another Bay of Pigs," *CQ Weekly*, June 23, 1990, 1929–33.

15. Philip Brenner and Saul Landau, "Passive Aggressive," *NACLA Report on the Americas* 24, no. 3 (November 1990): 18.

16. Lewis Tambs, ed., "A New Inter-American Policy for the Eighties" (Washington, DC: Council for Inter-American Security, 1980), 46.

17. US Government Accountability Office, "Broadcasting to Cuba: Actions Are Needed to Improve Strategy and Operations," Report #GAO-09-127, January 2009, 22.

18. Smith, *Closest of Enemies*, 249–56; quotation is on p. 256.

19. James G. Hershberg, ed., "Conference of Deputy Chairman of the State Council of the Republic of Cuba Carlos Rafael Rodriguez with US Secretary of State Alexander Haig, in Mexico, 23 November 1981," *Cold War International History Project Bulletin*, Issue 8–9 (Winter 1996–1997): 207–15.

20. Peter Kornbluh, "A 'Moment of Rapprochement': The Haig-Rodriguez Secret Talks," in *Cold War International History Project Bulletin*, Issue 8–9 (Winter 1996–1997): 219.

21. LeoGrande and Kornbluh, *Back Channel to Cuba*, 233.

22. Carlos Alzugaray and Anthony C. E. Quainton, "Cuban-US Relations: The Terrorism Dimension," *Pensamiento Propio*, no. 34 (July–December 2011): 75.

23. US Department of State, "Report of the National Bipartisan Commission on Central America" (Washington, DC: January 1984), 88–91.

24. Thomas Blanton, ed., "Public Diplomacy and Covert Propaganda: The Declassified Record of Ambassador Otto Juan Reich," National Security Archive Electronic Briefing Book no. 40, March 2, 2001, http://nsarchive.gwu.edu/NSAEBB/NSAEBB40.

25. Lewis H. Diuguid, "Spy Charges Strain US-Cuban Ties," *Washington Post*, July 25, 1987, A17.

26. Piero Gleijeses, *Visions of Freedom: Havana, Washington, Pretoria, and the Struggle for Southern Africa, 1976–1991* (Chapel Hill: University of North Carolina Press, 2013), 398–99.

27. As quoted in LeoGrande and Kornbluh, *Back Channel to Cuba*, 257.

28. Mario Vázquez Raña, "Interview with Raúl Castro," *El Sol de Mexico*, April 21, 1993, excerpted in García Luis, *Cuban Revolution Reader: A Documentary History of 40 Key Moments of the Cuban Revolution* (Melbourne: Ocean Press, 2001), 226–33.

29. Blight and Brenner, *Sad and Luminous Days*, 60.

30. Leonard Downie Jr. and Karen DeYoung, "Cuban Leader Sees Positive Signs for Ties in Second Reagan Term," *Washington Post*, February 3, 1985.

31. Phyllis Greene Walker, "National Security," in *Cuba: A Country Study*, ed. James Rudolph (Washington, DC: US Government Printing Office, 1985), 267.

32. William M. LeoGrande, "Cuba," in *Confronting Revolution: Security through Diplomacy in Central America*, ed. Morris Blachman, William M. LeoGrande, and Kenneth Sharpe (New York: Pantheon, 1986), 253.

33. Center for Cuban Studies, "Fidel Castro on Central America," *Cuba Update* 4, no. 4 (August 1983).

34. Jorge I. Domínguez, "Cuban Foreign Policy," *Foreign Affairs* 57, no. 1 (Fall 1978): 83.

35. Gleijeses, *Conflicting Missions*, 93–99.

36. Carlos Alzugaray Treto, "Cuban Foreign Policy during the 'Special Period,'" in *Redefining Cuban Foreign Policy: The Impact of the "Special Period,"* ed. H. Michael Erisman and John M. Kirk (Gainesville: University Press of Florida, 2006), 62–63.

37. H. Michael Erisman, *Cuba's Foreign Relations in a Post-Soviet World* (Gainesville: University Press of Florida, 2000), 42–45.

38. Domínguez, *To Make a World Safe for Revolution*, 171.

39. Donna Rich, "Cuban Internationalism: A Humanitarian Foreign Policy," in *The Cuba Reader: The Making of a Revolutionary Society*, ed. Philip Brenner et al. (New York: Grove, 1988), 607; Anne Hickling-Hudson, Jorge Corona Gonzalez, and Rosemary Preston, eds., *The Capacity to Share: A Study of Cuba's International Cooperation in Educational Development* (New York: Palgrave Macmillan, 2012), chapters 2, 5, 7, 12.

40. Castro and Ramonet, *Fidel Castro*, 372.

41. Julia Preston, "The Trial That Shook Cuba," *New York Review of Books*, December 7, 1989.

42. Castro and Ramonet, *Fidel Castro*, 371.

43. Gott, *Cuba*, 281.

Part III

1990–2016

Chapter 18

The "Special Period" in a Time of Peace, 1990–2000

I met the joyful young Cuban boy with bilateral retinoblastoma on a ward round at the National Institute of Oncology and Radiology in Havana. Although he had already lost his sight in one eye, he was a candidate for an implant of radioactive iodine to treat the other eye. The medical skills were available in Cuba, but the U.S. government had denied the pediatric oncologist a license to import the iodine because "the radioactive medication was a threat to U.S. security."

—Robin C. Williams[1]

RESOLVER

Imagine your reaction if you had to substitute sugar water for food every third day for a year, and as a result you lost your eyesight because of a vitamin deficiency (as happened to 50,000 Cubans temporarily), and 20–25 pounds (the average for Cubans in 1993–1994). Imagine oil imports dropping by 70 percent over a four-year period (1989–1993) so that you could not drive your car and buses ran infrequently because of gasoline shortages. Picture yourself undergoing an operation at a formerly reliable hospital, where now several doctors and nurses were absent because of transportation problems, and there were hardly any anesthetics, medicines, or bandages. In 1990, few Cubans imagined they would ever live this kind of life, even when Cuban president Fidel Castro announced that the country was entering a "Special Period in a Time of Peace," which he said meant that "our country has to face an extremely difficult situation in supplying basic necessities."[2]

By 1990, Cuba had developed to the point where infectious diseases had been eradicated and its rate of infant mortality was comparable to that of advanced industrial nations; where there were more doctors per capita than in any other country in the world and free universal health care was available throughout the island; where universities had been established in every province, education through graduate school was free, and racial and gender disparities were disappearing because of educational opportunities. Though Cuba was still a poor country by standard measures of GDP, it was an egalitarian society where most people considered themselves to be middle class and could reasonably hope that their children's lives would be better than their own.

Cuban planners had long nurtured an ambition to transform the economy into a vibrant engine of self-sufficiency that would enable the country to reduce its reliance on imports.[3] That dream had been stymied by Cuba's ties to the Soviet Union and the Soviet trading group, the Council for Mutual Economic Assistance (CMEA), which designated Cuba as a supplier of sugar, citrus, and tobacco in return for oil, steel, and manufactured goods. As a result, Cuba focused much of its internal investment on producing goods for the Eastern bloc instead of on diversifying its economy.

Still, the government did manage to develop some new industries— pharmaceuticals and genetic engineering—based on its increasingly well-educated population. It also was able to expand dairy production and create light industries that produced items for domestic use, such as toilets. However, Cuba's ability to diversify even to this minimal extent depended on Soviet subsidies.

As the Soviet Union hurtled toward its ultimate demise, its economy could no longer sustain losses on the products that it sold to Cuba at subsidized prices. The overthrow of communist party–ruled regimes in Eastern Europe and the collapse of the CMEA also forced the island to find new trading partners. Eighty-five percent of Cuba's international commerce had been conducted with CMEA countries on the basis of long-term barter-like contracts. The terms of trade in these exchanges, especially with the Soviet Union, tended to favor Cuba and function like subsidies.

The CIA estimated that in 1989 Cuba received $4.5 billion in trade subsidies and $1.4 billion in other development aid.[4] It also had accumulated low interest rate loans from CMEA countries worth $10 billion.[5] The actual subsidies were less than the CIA estimates because it valued CMEA products such as tractors as if their prices on the world market were the same as seemingly equivalent US products. But CMEA tractors, refrigerators, and so on were inferior and attracted little demand beyond the socialist countries themselves. Economists Andrew Zimbalist and Howard J. Sherman note that the CIA calculations also did not take into account the millions of pesos Cuba wasted on Soviet "mechanical cane harvesters, which didn't work."[6]

Despite these limitations, the subsidies did enable Cuba to ride out economic problems in the 1980s, and to use its scant hard currency earnings to buy food and medicines that were distributed in an egalitarian way. Recall that President Gerald Ford relaxed the US embargo in 1975 by permitting US subsidiaries in third countries to sell products to Cuba. In 1990, food and medicine made up 90 percent of Cuba's purchases from these subsidiaries.[7] Without the Soviet subsidies and CMEA barter arrangements, Cuba's hard currency earnings had to be apportioned among other necessities besides food and medicine, such as oil. And Cuba had limited ways to obtain international convertible currency. The global market prices for its commodities in the early 1990s were falling—sugar had dropped to ten cents per pound, which barely covered the cost of production.

As its international trade plummeted between 1990 and 1993, Cuba's gross domestic product (GDP) declined by 30 percent.[8] Cubans experienced the decline in the first instance by suffering hunger and then shortages of everything, especially health care. By 1993, average daily caloric intake had fallen below the basic level established by the World Health Organization. The insufficiency of vitamins and minerals in the daily diet led to outbreaks of medical disorders that had long vanished from Cuba. Even high Communist Party officials experienced neuropathy—nerve damage—which can produce sharp pains in fingers and feet, loss of a sense of touch, inability to control muscle movement, and even temporary blindness.[9] While the government did establish a special food program to protect the health of the elderly, children, and women who were pregnant or lactating, and maintained subsidies for some basic items, most Cubans found the rations insufficient.

One project that Cuba abandoned because of Special Period hardships was the schools-in-the-countryside (ESBEC) program. In practice, the students turned out to be mediocre farmers. The citrus crop for which they were responsible languished, and in 1994, Cuba turned to Israel to help revive its citrus industry. In addition, families increasingly opted out of the program, even though the schools continued to provide food, lodging, and clothing for the students. Most of the boarding schools that still operate today are specialty schools in each Cuban province—for aspiring athletes and gifted students—such as the prestigious Lenin School near Havana.

Resolver—to find ways of overcoming hardship—became the catchword term everyone used to signify both frustration and determination. "How are things going?" a visitor would ask. *"No es fácil"*—nothing's easy—would be the reply. People waited in long lines for food or buses that seemed never to show up. They rode bicycles instead of cars as Cuba imported more than one million bikes from China. They cheered Cuban Olympic teams that previously had amazed the world by attaining as high as fourth place in total medals, though in 1996 Cuba dropped to ninth place. At the 1993 Central American and Caribbean Games in Puerto Rico, nearly 50 of the 450 Cuban athletes sought asylum and chose not to return to Cuba.[10]

Philip Brenner was in front of a Havana hotel in 1994 when a rail-thin man on a bicycle wheeled up to him with a hearty, "Hi, Phil." Brenner searched his memory but could not recognize the stranger. "It's me, Carlos," former Cuban ambassador Carlos Alzugaray blurted out. "It seems you have been doing a lot of bike riding," Brenner responded. Alzugaray, who is more than six feet tall, usually had weighed at least two hundred healthy pounds. Yes, he acknowledged, "but mostly I have lost weight from eating only three or four dinners each week. We have teenagers, and the food goes first to them." On the other days, he explained, he and his wife relied on sugar water to satiate their hunger.

An Oxfam report described Cuba's food dilemma by pointing to the disaster Cuban farmers faced:

Imported inputs vanished—no chemical fertilizers, animal feed, tools, seeds, wire, or animal vaccines. Fuel for tractors and irrigation systems was practically unobtainable, as were tires or batteries or spare parts. Cuban-produced goods such as feed, pipes, tools, fertilizers, and pesticides dried up because of the same litany of problems: no raw materials, no electricity to run the factories, no functioning trucks, and no petroleum. . . . Tractors stood useless in the fields, electric pumps went dry and crops wilted . . . and animals died or were slaughtered for food as their feed disappeared.[11]

Cubans' poor diet contributed to an increase in health problems just when the end of Soviet subsidies made importing medicine and medical supplies more difficult. Polyclinics, hospitals, and pharmacies had shortages of everything, from aspirin and antibiotics to spare parts for ventilators and monitoring equipment. In 1995, a delegation of physicians from the American Association for World Health found that the US trade embargo made Cuba's health situation even worse. "Patient charts," one of the doctors noted, "consisted of microscopic handwritten entries jammed on every square inch of mismatched and reused paper. . . . Water supply and treatment is a serious problem. Cuba is not able to produce enough chlorine to disinfect the water," he wrote.[12]

In the first years of the Special Period, Cuba's oil imports declined from 13 million to 1.8 million barrels annually. Electricity blackouts became so commonplace that Cubans joked about having the occasional *alumbrones* (periods when lights were available) rather than *apagones* (blackouts). The energy crisis included insufficient gasoline and diesel for delivery trucks, buses, and private cars. It contributed to the government's decision to downsize the military from almost 300,000 full-time members to fewer than 100,000.

Its budget was cut by nearly 40 percent from 1990 to 1993.[13] The Cuban Air Force eliminated 80 percent of its flight training and practice missions because it lacked fuel and spare parts.

DUAL-CURRENCY ECONOMY EMERGES

As Cuba's economic catastrophe endured, many of the more than one million Cuban-Americans in the United States sought to help their families. But Cubans were not permitted to spend US dollars on the island. When a family sent money via a courier, a Cuban could use it only on the black market. In order to undermine this rapidly growing informal economy, and to capture hard currency that could be used for national purposes, the government legalized the spending of US dollars in 1993 and opened Shops for the Recovery of Hard Currency, or "dollar stores" as they were known generally, which sold scarce commodities.[14] In 1994, remittances rose to $262.8 million, and the next year, they totaled $582.6 million. Nearly one-fifth of Cuba's hard currency earnings in 1995 came from these monetary gifts from families.[15] Thus, the dual-currency economy began: Cubans were able to buy some goods (and later services) only by using hard currency, a currency such as the US dollar that was freely convertible in the international market. For everything else, they used Cuba's national currency, the peso (CUP).

Those who had access to hard currency generally fell into one of two groups: (1) Cubans with relatives sending remittances from abroad and (2) Cubans with jobs in the newly emerging tourist sector that enabled them to earn hard currency from gratuities. Hard currency recipients in either category unquestionably had an easier life than other Cubans. Even a monthly remittance of fifty dollars from a relative in Miami could mean the difference between suffering and comfort.

The uneven distribution of hard currency undermined the Cuban Revolution's proud achievement of broad economic, social, and racial equality.[16] Before the 1990s, the highest paid Cubans—such as doctors and engineers—earned four to five times more than the lowest paid workers. The difference between managers and workers was even less. That system of reward contributed to the egalitarian character of the society, a reduced emphasis on individualism, and incentives that enabled Cuba to develop a society notable for its educated and healthy population. But the dual-currency economy engendered new levels of inequality. If you wanted cheese, it was an import that you had to purchase in a dollar store. Adhesive tape, needles and thread, and even the most basic items associated with Cuban culture—coffee, rum, and fine cigars—were available only in dollar stores.

Cuban scholars characterize the new inequality as an "inverted pyramid." Sociologist Mirén Uriarte explains that the term describes "a phenomenon that reflects the devalued return on education and professional preparation in the new economy."[17] A doctor might have earned 1,200 CUP in one month, but a taxi driver could earn that much in one week from tourists' tips because one US dollar was the equivalent of about 27 CUP in the 1990s. Suddenly the incentive to study many extra years in order to be a professional and contribute to the common good was overwhelmed by the need to earn money in order to *resolver*, or even to survive. During the two-year period from 1993 to 1994, 8 percent of Cuba's teachers took jobs that required only a minimal education in the tourist sector.[18]

Families soon invented novel ways to earn extra income to make up for low salaries, which was facilitated by a 1993 law that made self-employment legal for 117 occupations—the most significant turn back to private enterprise since the start of the Revolution. Individuals were now allowed to engage in small businesses of their own, such as family restaurants known as *paladares* (derived from the Portuguese word *paladar*, which means palate), bed and breakfast accommodations in their homes, and craft stands. A 1998 study reported that nearly half of the self-employed Cubans, or *cuentapropistas*, were involved in "services and repair," though accurate data on the number of self-employed Cubans at the end of the 1990s is not available.[19] While 209,000 individuals were licensed to conduct their own business in the peak year of 1996, there were reports that the true number of self-employed businesses might have been twice as great as the official count.[20]

Most paladares operated illegally. These began as food carryouts from homes and then expanded into eat-in restaurants. Legal paladares could accommodate no more than twelve guests at a time, and only immediate family members were permitted to work in a paladar. But the most popular ones featured items such as lobster that one could obtain only on the black market and were illegal to sell in a paladar. Indeed, hard times engendered corruption. Many daring entrepreneurs drove unlicensed taxis or rented rooms for travelers without registering in order to avoid high taxes. Despite stiff penalties for those caught, others sold scarce goods—tires, car batteries, copper wire, cement, tools, and the like—on the expanding black market.

Some black-market products were provided by fishermen, farmers, or skilled craftsmen who withheld a portion of their output from the official distribution network. But many of the available items were stolen from government supplies, which led to further breakdowns in service. In 1995, Fidel called for a crackdown on corruption, which was taking a significant toll on Cuba's recovery and undermining a culture of shared sacrifice for a common national purpose. He charged that foreign investment was the root cause of corruption.[21] Yet the more likely source was scarcity and the growing inequality fostered by the dual-currency economy. A few months before Castro's speech, for example, a Cuban friend of ours described how he was able to afford paying for the gasoline he used in his unregistered taxi business. He knew a service station attendant who short-changed each customer by a hardly noticeable 0.1 liter of gasoline. At the end of the day, the attendant had enough "surplus" fuel to sell gasoline cheaply to his family and trusted friends.

RENEWING THE TOURIST INDUSTRY

The 1993 law that created the legal space for some small businesses was motivated in part by the need for tourist facilities. Yet the decisions to seek salvation via remittances and tourism were not made lightly. In a speech on July 26, 1993, a chastened Fidel Castro suggested that they were taken because Cuba was at a point where "we are willing to do whatever is necessary to save the homeland, the Revolution and the achievements of socialism." He hoped the solution would be temporary so that one day hard currency that came to Cuba "by way of remittances from abroad . . . tips, tourism, etc." could be used for the common good instead of enriching the few.[22]

Another concern about tourism on which top Cuban officials collectively agreed was that it would lead to the acceptance of behavior the Revolution had tried to devalue: conspicuous consumption, prostitution, and the glamorization of non-Cuban culture. Indeed, prostitution returned to the island between 1992 and 1996. The government had suppressed and effectively shut it down in the early years of the Revolution. But during the first years of the Special Period, it turned a blind eye to sex tourism. It only began a crackdown in 1996.[23] Today, prostitution remains only a minor albeit visible element of Cuba's attractiveness to some tourists.

An additional problem associated with tourism, as Marguerite Rose Jiménez explains, is "that local artists tend to skew their own social reality so that it conforms to tourists' expectations."[24] For example, while visiting foreigners often want to hear the "authentic" songs of the *Buena Vista Social Club*, Cubans themselves no longer embrace this pre-revolutionary style of music. Much more popular, especially among young Cubans, is a distinctive form of hip-hop that Cuban artists developed in the early 1990s. Musicians initially mimicked rap songs they heard from Miami, but their music evolved into a variant based on Afro-Cuban rhythms and Cuban instruments, and became a vehicle for popular criticism of problems in Cuba.

Despite the leaders' well-founded misgivings about tourism, it seemed to provide the only short-term means of earning the hard currency that the country needed to recover from its deep depression. Yet two technical problems confronted the government in trying to use tourism as the leading sector for recovery. First, net earnings in hard currency tend to be low in the first years of developing a tourist industry because so many of the comforts that international tourists expect—new taxis, functioning air conditioners, hot water showers—require products that must be bought abroad. As much as eighty-eight cents out of every tourist dollar that Cuba initially received was spent on the purchase of foreign goods.[25]

Second, Cuba's hotel capacity could not accommodate the large increase in the number of tourists the government suddenly sought, and many facilities were not up to international tourism standards. Prior to 1959, Cuba had been a popular destination for US vacationers. But, recall from chapter 6, its popularity was fostered partly by gambling and prostitution, which were controlled by organized crime. In 1957, about 275,000 tourists had gone to Cuba. In 1972, while other Caribbean islands drew five million visitors, fewer than 100,000 went to Cuba.[26]

In order to increase the stock of hotel rooms, Cuba needed a quick infusion of foreign investment. Under a 1982 constitutional amendment, modified by a 1992 law, foreign entities had been allowed to own only 49 percent of an enterprise. In September 1995, the Cuban government approved a new law that allowed foreigners to own 100 percent of a business. Cubanacán, a semi-autonomous state agency, was set up to facilitate foreign investment in tourism, mainly hotel construction, as well as to lure international companies to manage hotels, which had been notorious for their poor service. It promised investors that they could expect a full return on their principal within five years.[27]

The reforms produced the desired result, an increase in the number of available hotel rooms from 12,900 in 1990 to 37,200 in 2001. Foreign participation in running the hotels jumped from 10 percent to nearly 50 percent in the same period. Even by the mid-1990s, gross revenues from tourism already had surpassed those from sugar.[28] In 2000, Cuba hosted 1.78 million tourists, and more than 2 million in 2003. (The total reached four million in 2016.) The largest number came from Canada, followed by Germany, Italy, and Spain.

THE UNITED STATES TRIES TO "WREAK HAVOC" ON THE ISLAND

As the Soviet Union began its months-long descent into oblivion in 1991, Cuban leaders felt increasingly vulnerable. In September, Soviet leader Mikhail

Gorbachev announced the withdrawal of all Soviet military forces from the island. Pointedly, he did so without consulting Cuba in advance and after meeting with US secretary of state James Baker.[29] The Soviet Union seemed more willing to placate the other superpower, Cuba's avowed enemy, than to give even the mere courtesy of prior notification to Cuba. Gorbachev's announcement reminded Cubans of the 1962 missile crisis when Nikita Khrushchev publicly declared on October 28—prior to informing Castro—that the Soviets were withdrawing the missiles from Cuba.

The Soviet abandonment of Cuba encouraged the most determined anti-Castro hardliners in the United States to strike what they imagined would be the final blows that could overthrow the regime. This assumption was reflected in the House Foreign Affairs Committee's report on the 1992 Cuban Democracy Act (CDA), which asserted:

> The committee believes that the demise of Cuba's patrons in the former Soviet Union and Eastern Europe has intensified and brought to a head the inevitable crisis of Cuban communism, and that the United States now has a unique opportunity to influence the course of change in Cuba in a democratic direction. The bill sets forth a series of measures, consisting of both carrots and sticks, designed to hasten a democratic transition in Cuba by increasing the isolation of the regime while creating openings to democratic opposition groups that will shape Cuba's future.[30]

The CDA tightened the embargo by prohibiting foreign subsidiaries of US firms from trading with Cuba, which had been authorized by the Ford administration in 1975. It also denied foreign ships entry to US ports within six months of having docked in Cuba. The latter provision was intended to raise transportation costs for Cuba. International cargo vessels typically could not fill their capacity with goods destined for Cuba because of its small market, and would need to convey a portion of their hold to the United States for the trip to be economical. Robert Torricelli (D-NJ), the principal House sponsor of the CDA, almost gleefully told an academic audience in 1993 that his intention was to "wreak havoc" on the Cuban economy.[31]

The legislation became law because of presidential electoral politics. Arkansas governor Bill Clinton's campaign funds were drying up after allegations surfaced in January 1992 about his relationship with Gennifer Flowers, an actress and model. While he sought to control the damage by appearing on the CBS News program *60 Minutes* with his wife, Hillary Rodham Clinton, his campaign contributions did not increase sufficiently. Desperate for funds, he came out in support of the CDA at a fund raiser that garnered $275,000 for his campaign from Cuban-Americans.[32] Even though

President George H. W. Bush had opposed an earlier version of the CDA on grounds that portions were inconsistent with US treaty obligations, he felt political pressure to accept the legislation once Clinton endorsed it. It became law two weeks before the election.

RAFTER EXODUS

While the CDA did not topple the regime, it did contribute to the misery Cubans were suffering. By the summer of 1994 daily life—the lack of food, money, and hope of improvement—had become intolerable for many Cubans, especially in the cities. Despite the danger they faced in crossing the perilous Florida Straits, an increasing number of people (known as *balseros*, or rafters) attempted to leave the country in fragile rafts made of inner tubes, wood slats, or anything that might float (see one such raft in figure 18.1). In all of 1993, the US Coast Guard rescued 3,600 balseros. Nearly that many balseros were rescued in the single month of July 1994. In August, nearly one thousand departed Cuba each day.[33]

Figure 18.1.   Cubans attempt to leave the island on makeshift rafts in 1994. Photo by Willy Castellanos: "La Regata" (The Regatta); from The Series "North Bound, beyond The Blue Wall," 1994.

The situation already was getting beyond control in July 1994 when two Cuban Coast Guard tugboats rammed a hijacked tugboat in Havana harbor, drowning thirty-two balseros. On August 4, forty-one died after the Coast Guard used high-pressure hoses to stop a ferry that the rafters had commandeered. In response, on August 5, more than one thousand people joined a series of spontaneous street demonstrations not seen in Havana since the end of 1958.

An incensed Fidel Castro blamed the exodus on US encouragement of the rafters, and he warned that Cuba would stop preventing émigrés from departing illegally if the United States continued to welcome them and facilitate their movement. Indeed, Radio Martí, the US propaganda radio station beamed at Cuba, regularly broadcast bulletins about the suitability for travel by small boats in the Florida Straits. In addition, as Cuban sociologist Ernesto Rodríguez Chávez observed, the United States had welcomed "those arriving in July and August, 1994, after stealing boats, using violence, endangering the lives of people who did not wish to emigrate, and even committing murder."[34]

Until that point, it had been US policy to rescue rafters in the Florida Straits and bring them safely to shore. Émigrés would then claim political asylum, and after one year under the terms of the 1966 Cuban Adjustment Act were able to secure permanent resident status. However, the Clinton administration feared that in light of Cuba's economic turmoil, the existing policy could lead to a massive influx of refugees, perhaps even greater than the 1980 Mariel exodus.

On August 19, 1994, the US president announced a new policy under which Cubans picked up at sea would be transported to Guantánamo Naval Base where the US Coast Guard already had sent more than twenty thousand recent Cuban rafters who were living in makeshift housing and eating C-rations for their meals. In September, the United States and Cuba signed a new immigration accord, permitting at least twenty thousand Cubans to obtain visas through a lottery system or family reunification regulations, though the Guantánamo balseros could not apply for visas.

In 1994, about 39,000 Cubans successfully entered the United States by using rafts. But twice as many may have died in the attempt, swamped by waves or swept away in the ocean. The new exiles were strikingly different from the first group who left Cuba immediately after the Revolution. While only 15 percent of the 1959–1962 group of émigrés had held semiskilled, unskilled, or service jobs in Cuba, 58 percent of those arriving in the mid-1990s held positions in those categories. It was an indicator that the poorest in Cuba suffered the most during the early days of the Special Period.

REORGANIZING THE CUBAN ECONOMY

The rafter exodus and popular demonstrations shocked Cuba's leaders. The 1993 economic reforms were not producing change fast enough. Cuba needed foreign investment beyond the tourism industry. It also needed to find a way to import less food and produce more of it on the island.

Foreign Investment

Cuba's record of expropriations and failure to repay foreign loans in a timely manner contributed to the reluctance many European companies shared about investing in Cuba. Yet the International Monetary Fund (IMF) was an even greater obstacle. Private international financing often depended on a country first receiving the IMF's seal of approval. As the fund's largest shareholder, the United States most often determined decisions, and it opposed any dealing with Cuba. In turn, Cuba refused to be a member of the IMF.

While sugar had been Cuba's main export for two centuries, the more meaningful potential for development rested with its nickel reserves. The worldwide demand for nickel was growing in the 1990s because it is essential for producing corrosion-resistant alloys such as stainless steel and was used as a component in many batteries. Cuba has the world's fifth largest reserves, with deposits thirty-four times greater than those in the United States.[35] It also has petroleum deposits that could have reduced its import needs. But its antiquated equipment hampered the extraction of both nickel and oil.

Until 1991, Cuba exported all of its nickel and cobalt to the Soviet Union for refining. But after successfully wooing Canada's Sherritt International to modernize operations at the decrepit Moa nickel mine facility, Cuba began to earn money from nickel exports. By 2001, it was the world's sixth largest producer of nickel and accounted for 10 percent of the world's cobalt, a byproduct in the nickel extraction process.[36]

Meanwhile, with the end of subsidized oil shipments from the Soviet Union, Cuba began serious exploration for crude oil and gas. Between 1994 and 2000, production doubled to nearly 50,000 barrels of crude oil per day, about 25 percent of its daily consumption.[37] Cuba also signed agreements with several foreign companies—Brazil's Petrobras, Venezuela's PDVSA, China's Sinopec, India's OVL/ONGC, Spain's Repsol-YPF, and Canada's Sherritt—to begin deep-water oil and gas exploration off Cuba's northern coast.

While the efforts to attract foreign capital led to accumulated investments of just over $2 billion by 2001, the GDP at that point was still 18 percent lower than it had been in 1990, at the start of the Special Period, and annual totals fluctuated widely.[38] However, the government's determination to capture hard currency did result in a notable success. By 2002, Cuba was keeping sixty-eight cents from every dollar that tourists spent.[39]

Food Production

In late 1993, the Cuban government issued a broad decree that would fundamentally change the basis of agricultural production, breaking up more than two-thirds of state farm enterprises into smaller units that would be given to individuals or run by cooperatives. By 2003, the measure had created 36,000 such cooperatives, named Basic Units of Cooperative Production (UBPC) (Unidades Básicas de Producción Cooperativa). Within a decade, the UBPCs operated 55 percent of Cuba's arable land and employed 300,000 people.[40]

Under the new regulations, the government permitted both individual farmers and UBPCs to sell whatever they produced beyond the amount they had agreed to deliver to the state. This meant that private farmers could offer their produce at *mercados agropecuarios*—farmers' markets—established by the government in late 1994. This incentive-based farming did much more than provide domestically grown food for tourists; it increased the amount of food available for Cubans and undercut the prices they had been paying on the black market.

At about the same time, Cuban officials opted to turn their shortages into an advantage—"going against the grain" as an Oxfam America report characterized the decision—to promote urban organic farms. Along with its development of cooperatives and farmers' markets, urban farming constituted an agrarian reform as significant as the nationalization and land distributions that took place from 1959 to 1963.[41] The earlier reforms had created large state farms that produced sugar, cattle, citrus, and rice. Even before the Special Period, they had proved to be inefficient, in part because each farm focused on a single commodity, which damaged the soil and caused environmental damage.[42]

Urban farms began as a spontaneous response to the problem of food shortages and survival (see an urban farm in figure 18.2). By 2001, such farms generated half of Havana's fresh produce. Initially, "farms" were small plots located on vacant lots or even in alleys between buildings. Without access to petroleum-based fertilizers and other chemicals, the farmers relied on organic methods because there was no alternative. They used compost to create raised beds, flowers for defense against insects, and fecal matter and decay from worms to fertilize the soil. Because the lack of fuel prevented crops from being transported long distances, growers needed to be close to the point of sale. A environmental movement—"buy local"—that is now becoming popular in the United States emerged in Cuba twenty years ago out of necessity.

Figure 18.2.   An urban farm in Havana. Photo by Doyle L. Niemann.

A 1997 law granted urban dwellers the right to cultivate up to 15 percent of a hectare (about one-third of an acre) in plots on the periphery of cities. Within two years the government had distributed such land to nearly 200,000 people.[43] Environmentalist Bill McKibben judged in 2005 that the resulting agricultural system "may be the world's largest working model of a semi-sustainable agriculture, one that doesn't rely nearly as heavily as the rest of the world does on oil, on chemicals, on shipping vast quantities of food back and forth."[44] Indeed, Cuba has become a world leader in the field of agroecology, the "attempt to minimize the use of fossil fuels, including petroleum, and their derivatives, such as chemical pesticides and fertilizers, in production and transportation," economist Sinan Koont reports. He adds, it "is holistic and pays full attention to environmental concerns and to the human participants in their political, economic, social, and cultural settings."[45]

NOTES

1. Robin C. Williams, "In the Shadow of Plenty, Cuba Copes with a Crippled Health Care System," in *A Contemporary Cuba Reader: Reinventing the Revolution*, ed. Philip Brenner et al. (Lanham, MD: Rowman & Littlefield, 2007), 281.

2. Fidel Castro Ruz, "Speech at the Sixteenth Congress of the CTC," XVI Congreso de la CTC, January 28, 1990, http://www.cuba.cu/gobierno/discursos/1990/esp/f280190e.html.

3. Pedro Monreal, "Development as an Unfinished Affair: Cuba After the 'Great Adjustment' of the 1990s," in *A Contemporary Cuba Reader: Reinventing the Revolution*, ed. Philip Brenner et al. (Lanham, MD: Rowman & Littlefield, 2007), 117–19.

4. Eliana A. Cardoso and Ann Helwege, *Cuba After Communism* (Cambridge: MIT Press, 1992), 31.

5. Domínguez, *To Make the World Safe for Revolution*, 90.

6. Andrew Zimbalist and Howard J. Sherman, *Comparing Economic Systems: A Political-Economic Approach* (Orlando: Academic Press, 1984), 386.

7. Donna Rich Kaplowitz and Michael Kaplowitz, *New Opportunities for US-Cuban Trade* (Washington, DC: Johns Hopkins University, 1992), 11–13.

8. Jorge I. Domínguez, "Cuba's Economic Transition: Successes, Deficiencies, and Challenges," in *The Cuban Economy at the Start of the Twenty-First Century*, ed. Jorge I. Domínguez, Omar Everleny Pérez Villanueva, and Lorena Barberia (Cambridge: Harvard University Press, 2004), 19.

9. Katherine Tucker and Thomas R. Hedges, "Food Shortages and an Epidemic of Optic and Peripheral Neuropathy in Cuba," *Nutrition Reviews* 51, no. 12 (1993): 349–57.

10. Paula Pettavino and Philip Brenner, "More Than Just a Game: The Dual Developmental Aspects of Cuban Sports," *Peace Review* 11 no. 4 (December 1999): 527.

11. Minor Sinclair and Martha Thompson, "Going Against the Grain: Agricultural Crisis and Transformation," in *A Contemporary Cuba Reader: Reinventing the Revolution*, ed. Philip Brenner et al. (Lanham, MD: Rowman & Littlefield, 2007), 157.

12. As quoted in Williams, "In the Shadow of Plenty," 282–83.

13. Hal Klepak, "Cuba's Revolutionary Armed Forces: Last Bulwark of the State! Last Bulwark of the Revolution?" in *A Contemporary Cuba Reader: Reinventing the Revolution*, ed. Philip Brenner et al. (Lanham, MD: Rowman & Littlefield, 2007); Klepak, *Raúl Castro and Cuba*, 57–68

14. Eckstein, *The Immigrant Divide*, 214–15.

15. Lorena Barberia, "Remittances to Cuba: An Evaluation of Cuban and US Government Policy Measures," in *The Cuban Economy at the Start of the Twenty-First Century*, ed. Jorge I. Domínguez et al. (Cambridge: Harvard University Press, 2004), 368.

16. Mayra Paula Espina Prieto, "Social Effects of Economic Adjustment: Equality, Inequality and Trends toward Greater Complexity in Cuban Society," in *The Cuban Economy at the Start of the Twenty-First Century*, ed. Jorge I. Domínguez et al. (Cambridge: Harvard University Press, 2004), 219–25.

17. Mirén Uriarte, "Social Impact of the Economic Measures," in *A Contemporary Cuba Reader: Reinventing the Revolution*, ed. Philip Brenner et al. (Lanham, MD: Rowman & Littlefield, 2007), 286.

18. Uriarte, "Social Impact of the Economic Measures," 286.

19. Philip Peters and Joseph L. Scarpaci, "Cuba's New Entrepreneurs: Five Years of Small-Scale Capitalism" (Arlington, VA: Alexis de Tocqueville Institution, August 1998), 7.

20. William M. LeoGrande and Julie M. Thomas, "Cuba's Quest for Economic Independence," *Journal of Latin American Studies* 34, part 2 (May 2002): 354; Ted Henken, "Vale Todo: In Cuba's Paladares, Everything Is Prohibited but Anything Goes," in *A Contemporary Cuba Reader: Reinventing the Revolution*, ed. Philip Brenner et al. (Lanham, MD: Rowman & Littlefield, 2007), 171–73.

21. Fidel Castro Ruz, "Discurso," Plaza de la Revolucion, Havana, July 26, 1995, http://www.cuba.cu/gobierno/discursos/1995/esp/f260795e.html.

22. Fidel Castro Ruz, "Discurso," Santiago de Cuba, July 26, 1993, http://www.cuba.cu/gobierno/discursos/1993/esp/f260793e.html.

23. Elisa Facio, "Jineterismo during the Special Period," in *Cuban Transitions at the Millennium*, ed. Eloise Linger and John W. Cotman (Largo, MD: International Development Options, 2000).

24. Marguerite Rose Jiménez, "The Political Economy of Leisure," in *A Contemporary Cuba Reader: The Revolution under Raúl Castro*, ed. Philip Brenner et al. (Lanham, MD: Rowman & Littlefield, 2014), 177.

25. Philip Peters, "International Tourism: The New Engine of the Cuban Economy," (Arlington, VA: Lexington Institute, 2002), 7.

26. Rosalie Schwartz, *Pleasure Island: Tourism and Temptation in Cuba* (Lincoln: University of Nebraska Press, 1997), 205.

27. Eckstein, *Back to the Future*, 69, 104.

28. Schwartz, *Pleasure Island*, 206.

29. Thomas L. Friedman, "Soviet Turmoil; Gorbachev Says He's Ready to Pull Troops Out of Cuba and End Castro's Subsidies," *New York Times*, September 12, 1991, A1.

30. US Congress, House of Representatives, "Cuban Democracy Act of 1992," Report from the Committee on Foreign Affairs on H.R. 5253, 102nd Cong., 2nd Sess., House Report 102615, Part 1, June 25, 1992, 1.

31. Comments to the Cuba Study Group, Georgetown University, Washington, DC, May 13, 1993.

32. Tom Fiedler, "Clinton Backs Torricelli Bill: 'I Like It,' He Tells Cuban Exiles," *Miami Herald*, April 24, 1992, A1.

33. Masud-Piloto, *From Welcomed Exiles to Illegal Immigrants*, 137–41.

34. Ernesto Rodríguez Chávez, "La crisis migratoria . . ." as quoted in Masud-Piloto, *From Welcomed Exiles to Illegal Immigrants: Cuban Migration to the US, 1959–1995* (Lanham, MD: Rowman & Littlefield, 1996), 138.

35. US Department of the Interior, US Geological Survey, "Mineral Commodity Summaries 2015," January 2015, 109.

36. Omar Everleny Pérez Villanueva, "The Role of Foreign Direct Investment in Economic Development: The Cuban Experience," in *The Cuban Economy at the Start of the Twenty-First Century*, ed. Jorge I. Domínguez et al. (Cambridge: Harvard University Press, 2004), 180–81.

37. A. Alhajji and Terry L. Maris, "The Future of Cuba's Energy Sector," in *Cuba Today: Continuity and Change since the "Periodo Expecial*," ed. Mauricio A. Font (New York: Bildner Center, CUNY, 2004).

38. Jorge I. Domínguez, "Cuba's Economic Transition: Successes, Deficiencies, and Challenges," in *The Cuban Economy at the Start of the Twenty-First Century*, ed. Jorge I. Domínguez et al. (Cambridge: Harvard University Press, 2004), 19–20; Paolo Spadoni, *Failed Sanctions: Why the US Embargo Against Cuba Could Never Work* (Gainesville: University Press of Florida, 2010), 67–68.

39. Peters, "International Tourism," 7.

40. Frederick S. Royce, "Agricultural Production Cooperatives: The Future of Cuban Agriculture," *Transnational Law and Contemporary Problems* 14, no. 1 (Spring 2004): 20.

41. Minor Sinclair and Martha Thompson, *Cuba, Going Against the Grain: Agricultural Crisis and Transformation* (Boston: Oxfam America, 2001), 19.

42. Sinan Koont, "Cuba's Recent Embrace of Agroecology: Urban and Suburban Agriculture," in *A Contemporary Cuba Reader: The Revolution under Raúl Castro*, ed. Philip Brenner et al. (Lanham, MD: Rowman & Littlefield, 2014), 399.

43. Sinclair and Thompson, *Cuba, Going Against the Grain*, 23.

44. Bill McKibben, "The Cuba Diet: What Will You Be Eating When the Revolution Comes?" *Harper's Magazine* 310, issue 1859 (April 2005): 62.

45. Koont, "Cuba's Recent Embrace of Agroecology," 399–400.

Chapter 19

The Cuban Diaspora and Racial Inequality

My father's family came to Cuba from Spain in the 1800s and settled in Bayamo, Oriente, where the family had rice plantations. I was born in Havana, went to Bayamo at the age of six months and stayed there until the age of five, when I started attending Havana's most elite academy, the Sacred Heart School run by French nuns.

My mother's family arrived in Cuba from Spain in the 1700s, settling in Matanzas. The family was very wealthy; my grandfather's grandfather established the first sugar refinery on the Island. My grandfather was born in Cárdenas but was educated in the United States. His aunt and uncle—Emilia and Miguel Teurbe Tolón—created the Cuban flag. They were very nationalistic and against Spain because of the colonial system's abuses. Sugar gave them close ties to the United States, and they aligned themselves with the United States. Emilia was the first woman to have been expelled from Cuba for political reasons. The Spaniards had expelled Miguel before her and she joined him in New York.

It was there in 1849 that Narciso López, a Spanish general, asked Miguel to design the flag and Emilia to sew it. Gen. López had sought recruits and financing in the United States in order to invade Cuba, with the goal of freeing the country from Spain.

When the Revolution triumphed, my family had enormous expectations. They disliked Batista enormously. We were not in politics or politically inclined, but we definitely supported the Revolution. My grandfather even hosted some of the rebels at the Havana Yacht Club. There was a feeling that this was a great new beginning for the country.

But when [Soviet Deputy Premier Anastas] Mikoyan arrived [in 1960] my parents got nervous. The conversation became one of good and evil: good United States, evil Russia. End of the discussion. There was no compromise there. So that's when my grandfather decided to send me and my cousin to the United States with Operation Peter Pan, for what they considered would be a short period of time. It was January 1961 and I was 14 years old. Everybody and their brother knew the invasion was coming. And they wanted me out of the country. And then when the invasion backed by the US won, we could come back to Cuba and resume our lives.

By 1962 all of my immediate family had moved to Miami. They always thought they were going back to Cuba, especially in the first ten years, when they were in a holding pattern, making the best of it. And it was rough. My grandfather must have been in his late sixties, and he was parking cars as a valet in Miami Beach. He was also a night clerk at a hotel in Coral Gables because we had to eat. They brought nothing with them, maybe $50 or $100 dollars. We were not allowed to take more, not even jewelry. There were Cubans that did come out with a lot of money, millions that they stole, people tied to the Batista government. But the vast majority of Cubans who came in the sixties, came with nothing. It was five of us in two bedrooms and one bath. But I never felt poor, because we had the United States and my family had enormous dignity.

I wasn't politically active. I was trying to be an American, trying to make ends meet economically. I got married, had children. I was trying to survive in a very Cuban environment. In my workplace I only socialized with Americans. But my life was of a Cuban-American. There were so many of us here. All my friends that left were here. It was like transplanting Havana to Miami.

—Silvia Wilhelm, July 2016[1]

DIASPORA

The Cuban diaspora has long been an essential part of Cuba's story. In 1824, the poet José Maria Heredia referenced his exile in the stirring poem "Niágara," a metaphor for Cuban independence, and the next year he wrote "Himno del Desterrado" (Hymn of the Exile).[2] José Martí, Cuba's independence leader, wrote from exile in New York in the 1880s. The literature about the Cubans' sense of identity highlights exile as a primary element, especially in the way Cubans relate to the United States. "The experience of exile," historian Louis Pérez informs us, "was decisive to the ways Cubans arrived at nationality and identity."[3] In Spanish, the infinitive form of the word "to exile" (desterrar), also means "to remove earth from." It suggests, Pérez explains, "adaptation as a means of survival. . . . The deployment of migratory energies propelled vast numbers across boundaries to chart new territories and explore new possibilities. . . . Exile was an occasion to discard the old and adopt the new."[4]

About 5.5 million people lived in Cuba in 1959. That year, fifty thousand (about 1 percent of the population) left as quickly as possible. By the end of

1979, another 550,000 had departed. These émigrés were largely conservative Catholics and light-skinned—natural opponents of the Revolution, which "represented a rejection of all that they stood for," sociologist Susan Eckstein points out.[5] In leaving Cuba rather than opposing revolutionary changes from within, the exiles enabled the Revolution to develop without the kind of blood bath or wrenching civil war that other countries with similar upheavals have endured. Instead, some exiles sought to use the United States to achieve their aim of changing the regime. But the stereotype of a "typical" anti-Castro Cuban American misses the way the community has changed since 1959.

Not all emigrants went to the United States. Some favored Spanish-speaking countries, and Spain became especially attractive in 2002 when the Madrid government allowed foreign-born children and grandchildren of Spaniards who had emigrated to claim Spanish citizenship. Still, Cuba's diaspora community largely lives in the United States. Between 1959 and 2004, 89 percent of Cuba's émigrés went to the mainland and Puerto Rico. A 2013 Pew study found that nearly "two million Hispanics of Cuban origin reside in the United States" (nearly 4 percent of the US Hispanic population), of whom 850,000 are US-born.[6]

Waves of Cubans Go to the United States

Cubans moved to the United States in five distinct waves after 1958. From 1959 to 1962 approximately 225,000 departed in the first wave. They comprised the wealthiest Cubans, those tied to US corporations or associated with the Batista regime, as well as professionals, engineers, and 80 percent of the country's physicians—people whose expertise was essential for the country's stability and the regime's survival. Eckstein and Lorena Barberia aptly characterize this first wave as a "class exodus."[7]

This brain drain placed an immediate stress on the country and stymied plans for development. While many left because they opposed the economic and political direction in which the Revolution was heading, the United States also encouraged such people to leave, in order to undermine the revolutionary government's viability. In addition, as we described in chapter 9, the CIA and the Catholic Church airlifted about 14,000 Cuban children to the United States in Operation Peter Pan after disseminating false information about alleged Cuban government plans to deny parents any rights over their children.

Regardless of the reasons why Cubans left the country, they all tended to justify their exile in political terms, as anti-communist, even though the Cuban leadership had its own disagreements with members of the old communist party.[8] The United States quickly classified all Cuban émigrés as political refugees, declaring that Cubans "fleeing from Communist oppression" were entitled to political asylum.

Incensed by the US politicization of emigration, and seeking a way to defuse growing domestic discontent, Fidel announced in September 1965 that any Cuban with a relative in the United States could depart freely from the port of Camarioca, sixty-five miles east of Havana on Cuba's northern coast.[9] This began the second wave. Nearly seven thousand took advantage of the opening, with flotillas of small boats arriving from South Florida to retrieve them. In December 1965, Cuba and the United States signed a memorandum of understanding with the Swiss government, which provided for an orderly departure of refugees via Pan American Airways. There were 45,000 in 1966 alone, and by 1973, when the program ended, the Swiss had arranged for some 260,000 Cubans to migrate to the United States. The United States dubbed the program "freedom flights."[10]

Congress responded to the influx by passing the 1966 Cuban Adjustment Act (CAA), which allowed exiles to obtain permanent resident status—and ultimately citizenship—after being in the United States for one year and a day.[11] In practice, that meant nearly all Cuban exiles could obtain citizenship because the review of an asylum case typically took more than one year. In effect, the review became moot once a Cuban was on US territory for more than one year.

The CAA remains in effect today and continues to serve as a magnet for Cubans. However, in the waning days of his administration, on January 12, 2017, President Barack Obama did end the policy of presuming that any Cuban who arrives on US territory, with or without a visa, is a political refugee.

Apart from the CAA, the US government provided more than $1 billion in assistance to Cuban exiles through the Cuban Refugee Program, which operated from 1961 to 1974.[12] New arrivals received generous adjustment payments for food and clothing, housing, relocation assistance, and education, as well as health care and ready access to Small Business Administration loans. Historian Felix Masud-Piloto observes that the program was "the largest . . . and most expensive aid program for refugees from Latin America ever undertaken by the United States."[13]

Still, Cubans who applied for visas often did so at great personal cost. In some cases, they lost their jobs. Local Committees for the Defense of the Revolution marked them as "anti-social," and their children were taunted at school. Cuban government officials stigmatized them as *gusanos*, or worms.

In chapter 16, we described the third wave of emigration, the 1980 Mariel exodus, during which more than 125,000 people left Cuba. Both islanders and exiles referred to them as Marielitos. In part as a reaction to this wave, the Reverend Jesse Jackson traveled to Cuba in 1984, seeking to spur Cuban-US negotiations on migration. Jackson all but dragged President Castro to a church service with him one Sunday and then encouraged the Cuban leader to engage with the United States in talks. As a result, Cuba agreed to allow the return of 2,746 Marielitos whom the United States had considered "excludable" from receiving permanent US resident status, and the United States agreed to allow the orderly entry of up to 20,000 Cubans annually. But the modifier "up to" became a source of dispute between the two countries. Cubans expected the United States would grant 20,000 immigrant visas annually. The actual numbers were far lower. In 1990, the United States issued only five thousand immigrant visas to Cubans, and the total went as low as two thousand in some years.

The fourth wave of émigrés came in the 1990s, during the rafter episode that we discussed in the last chapter. Nearly forty thousand Cubans arrived in the United States in 1994 and 1995, and at least that number probably drowned as they challenged the terrifying Florida Straits. A fifth phase of emigration began in the aftermath of the 1995 accord, which eliminated the imprecision in the previous quota agreement. The words "up to" were removed—the number was to be 20,000 entry visas every year. The quota was reached by various means, including a lottery system in some years and by spousal entry. Between 1996 and 2015, there was a fairly regular legal exodus of at least 20,000 Cubans to the United States every year.

After the December 2014 Cuban-US announcement of diplomatic relations, the number of Cubans trying to enter US territory without visas swelled. A Pew Research Center study found that at least 43,159 Cubans entered the United States without visas in the 2015 fiscal year (October 2014 to September 2015); that number was reached in just the first nine months of the 2016 fiscal year. The 2015 mark was a 78 percent increase over the previous year.[14] The major reason for the sudden increase was that Cubans feared diplomatic relations would lead the United States to repeal the Cuban Adjustment Act.[15]

In 2013, the Cuban government abolished the need for an "exit" permit to travel abroad and permitted most Cubans to obtain a passport. In addition, a Cuban could leave the country for up to two years without losing citizenship or property rights. This was a long-awaited and popular decision. Whether or not a Cuban used the new freedom, the creation of the opportunity was cathartic. Cuba is a large island, but many Cubans had felt island-bound or trapped, which is common to inhabitants of any island after a while.

Some Cubans used their new passports to travel to countries—especially Ecuador—that would permit entry without a visa. From there, they attempted to go to the United States. The surge led Ecuador to close its doors to Cubans in 2015 and other countries, such as Nicaragua, to deny thousands of migrants the right to cross their borders, leaving the Cuban émigrés in limbo.

A Changing Cuban-American Community

At first, many in the US exile community did not learn English or try to assimilate. They believed—or hoped—their stay in the United States would be temporary.[16] Even after fifteen years, some had not even purchased property or applied for US citizenship because of their expectation that they would be returning to Cuba. As a result, they were unable to vote in US elections. In part, this explains why Cuban-Americans had not developed a traditional lobbying group to represent their interests until 1981, when the Reagan administration encouraged Jorge Mas Canosa to form the CANF.

But the Cuban exile community did not have only one set of interests because it was not monolithic. A stereotypical passionate animus against the Revolution and communism is far less evident among those who arrived more recently. The newer émigrés also tended to come from different classes than the earlier ones. For example, only 8 percent of the group that migrated between 1959 and 1962 held jobs in Cuba that were classified as semi- or unskilled. In the 1994–1995 cohort, 41 percent were in that category. A remarkable 97 percent of the exiles who arrived in the 1960s identified themselves as "white" in the 1970 US Census.[17]

Newer arrivals also have been much more clearly driven by economic rather than political motives. Exiles of the 1980s and 1990s tended to be people who fled the island because they lacked economic opportunity or suffered harsh conditions during the Special Period. These economic migrants had grown up with and were educated by the Revolution. They have been more likely to favor rapprochement between the United States and Cuba because most still had close family members in Cuba with whom they wanted to stay in contact. One consequence of this demographic change is that the newer arrivals have been more comfortable voting for Democratic candidates who espouse a liberal agenda and favor engagement with Cuba than Republicans who tout traditional conservative values and favor maintaining sanctions. In the 2012 election, President Obama won nearly 50 percent of Florida's Cuban-American vote.[18]

By the 1980s, the early arrivals had become firmly planted in the United States. Most had settled in South Florida. (Today 68 percent of Cuban-Americans live in Florida.[19]) Their families included mature children and grandchildren who were US-born English speakers, well integrated into American society. A sizable proportion of the first wave had worked for US companies before the Revolution and were comfortable with US corporate practices and

norms. Cuban exiles became among the first Latinos rising to national prominence. Carlos Gutierrez, for example, was the chief executive of the Kellogg
cereal company and later secretary of commerce. Roberto C. Goizueta was
chairman of the board and CEO of Coca-Cola.

Yet the depiction of all Cuban-Americans as wealthy is belied by the fact
that 20 percent live in poverty. The poverty rate for all Americans is 16 percent.[20] With less desirable skill sets, later waves of émigrés tended to be less
prosperous than the first wave. Their lack of advancement, no doubt, has been
due also to discrimination they encountered from white America, as well as
from lighter-skinned exiles who came before them. Eckstein reports that "earlier émigrés spoke to me disparagingly about *Marielito* language, dress, and
demeanor, and their 'weird slang.'"[21] In fact, Miami was a cauldron boiling
with racial hostility in the 1970s, as blacks watched white Cuban-Americans
gain positions of power and wealth while job opportunities for blacks declined and their neighborhood schools deteriorated. In May 1980, the tension
erupted during three days of violence in black communities that left eighteen
people dead and property damage of more than $100 million.[22]

RACIAL INEQUALITY

After the Revolution and prior to the Special Period, historian Alejandro de
la Fuente asserts, "Cuban society had made remarkable progress in the reduction of racial inequality in a number of crucial areas, including education,
indicators of health care, and the occupational structure." Racial disparities
still existed, he notes, "but the trend was unequivocally towards equality."[23]
Then the Special Period intervened. The changes in Cuba's economy undermined the advances, many of which had depended on government spending
that declined after 1990.

Darker-skinned Cubans also found fewer opportunities as market reforms
took hold. Foreign hotel owners and Cuban managers seemed to assume
that international tourists would prefer lighter-skinned service providers
such as waiters, which gave these Cubans greater access to hard-currency
tips.[24] Moreover, darker-skinned Cubans received much less hard currency
from remittances. Black Cuban exiles tended to have less disposable income to send to their relatives, and whites constituted the largest portion of
Cuban émigrés—68 percent of US Cuban Americans identified themselves
as "white" in 2004.[25]

Racial differences in income also resulted from historic disparities in educational attainment. To its credit, the revolutionary government had eliminated the disparity between whites and blacks/mulattos in terms of university

graduation rates. In fact, a smaller percentage of whites graduated from college in 1981 than blacks and mulattos. (In contrast, the US percentage of white twenty-five-year-olds who had graduated from college was twice as great as the black percentage in 1987.)[26]

However, the exclusion of darker-skinned Cubans continued to exist at the best schools. For example, black and mulatto students make up only 3 percent of the total at Havana's Lenin School, Cuba's most prestigious high school to which adolescents are admitted after achieving the highest scores on a nationwide competitive exam. In a 1977 interview with then minister of education José Ramón Fernández, Philip Brenner remarked that the admissions process was likely to function against black youths. Their parents would have been less well educated than whites before the Revolution, and so they would tend not to have a home environment as oriented to professional achievement as whites. Fernández dismissed the concern, arguing that his ministry was overcoming the problem by setting aside 10 percent of the places in highly competitive schools for darker-skinned applicants. But by the 1990s, the effect of such institutional racism was evident from the skin color of the best trained doctors and skilled professionals who were able to supplement their regular incomes with hard currency because the government had sent them on missions abroad.

While "Cubans today are more than ever equal before the law," social scientist Esteban Morales observed in 2011, "we continue to be unequal in racial terms, to grasp the opportunities that social policy itself puts at our disposal."[27] In effect, those able to *resolver* successfully during the Special Period tended to be lighter-skinned Cubans.

Even Fidel pointed to the widening gap between whites and blacks in a September 2000 speech in New York City, and remorsefully said,

We believed at the beginning that when we established the fullest equality before the law and complete intolerance for any demonstration of sexual discrimination in the case of women, or racial discrimination in the case of ethnic minorities, these phenomena would vanish from our society. It was some time before we discovered that marginality and racial discrimination with it are not something that one gets rid of with a law or even with ten laws.[28]

The speech was remarkable because Cuban officials had treated the open discussion of race—or any issue that divided Cubans into socially constructed categories—almost as if it were counterrevolutionary.

The "official silence" about racial inequality, de la Fuente argues, actually "contributed to the survival, reproduction, and even creation of racist ideologies. . . . [Racist] discourse found fertile breeding ground in private spaces, where race continued to influence social relations among friends, neighbors, co-workers, and family members."[29] However, Cuban leaders have countered the taboo in the twenty-first century, as Fidel Castro's 2000 speech suggests. Notably, Raúl Castro acknowledged the persistence of racism during his opening speech to the Seventh Congress of the Cuban Communist Party in April 2016. "The fight against any trace of racism that impedes or halts the rise to leadership roles of Black and mixed race Cubans," he declared,

> must continue without respite. To consolidate the results in this important and just policy of the Revolution, we must work systematically, with foresight and intentionality. A matter of this importance cannot be at the mercy of spontaneity or improvisation.[30]

Yet scholars are still unable to determine the extent of racial disparities because the government does not collect the necessary data. For this reason, Morales argues, a key step in overcoming racism in Cuba is to require that official statistics "be gathered by color." Even though all Cubans benefit from an "extraordinarily humanitarian social policy," he writes in a blog widely read in Cuba, "we have historically different starting points, the experiences from which are transmitted generation to generation, carrying with them a colonial and neocolonial history of five hundred years." He concludes that "the only way to obliterate this complex reality is to base social policy on inequalities that actually exist."[31]

DIALOGUE

The absence of discussion in Cuba about institutional racism, and the "silence" about the way darker-skinned Cubans suffer more than lighter-skinned Cubans from the growing inequality on the island are akin to the lack of meaningful dialogue between Cubans on the island and those in the diaspora. Greater openness and dialogue about both issues would likely benefit everyone.

As Morales recommends, a first step with regard to racism would be for the government to gather the necessary data for analysis. It also should encourage open debate of the subject and follow up with serious efforts at ameliora-tion. Speaking from the audience in May 2009 at a conference sponsored by Queen's University in Kingston, Ontario, Mariela Castro Espín criticized use of the term "Afro-Cuban." She argued that it embodies a redundancy, because every Cuban has some African blood, every Cuban is of a mixed race. But, she acknowledged, discrimination against Cubans with darker skins exists in Cuba, which is a problem that needs solving without dividing people into tribal-like categories. Her comments echoed those of Fidel Castro in 1959, which we noted in chapter 8, when he emphasized the unity of all Cubans and condemned discrimination "against a Cuban . . . over a matter of lighter or darker skin." The problem of racism in Cuba will not disappear if the government tries to sweep it under the rug. It is more likely to emerge with violence and anger if such a discussion is suppressed, which would not benefit any Cuban.

Jorge Domínguez suggests that both Cuba and its diaspora would also benefit from increased dialogue that would enable the country to involve émigrés in its development. He argues that such a dialogue would need to occur within the diaspora. In fact, the likelihood that diaspora Cubans will play a greater role in Cuba's future has been increased as a result of more family travel, "thanks to the measures taken by the US government in 2009 and accepted by the Cuban government," Domínguez notes. This "has already generated multiple dialogues within many Cuban families. These valuable dialogues represent a breakthrough in communications."[32]

NOTES

1. Recorded telephone interview with the authors, July 22, 2016.

2. José María Heredia, "Niágara" and "Himno del Desterrado," in *Poesias de Don José Maria Heredia*, 98–103, 156–60.

3. Pérez, *On Becoming Cuban*, 37.

4. Pérez, *On Becoming Cuban*, 37–38.

5. Eckstein, *The Immigrant Divide*, 15.

6. Gustavo N. López, "Hispanics of Cuban Origin in the United States, 2013" (Washington, DC: Pew Research Center, September 2015), 1, http://www.pewhispanic.org/2015/09/15/hispanics-of-cuban-origin-in-the-united-states-2013.

7. Susan Eckstein and Lorena Barberia, "Cuban Americans and Their Transnational Ties," in *A Contemporary Cuba Reader: Reinventing the Revolution*, ed. Philip Brenner et al. (Lanham, MD: Rowman & Littlefield, 2007), 267.

8. Nelson Amaro and Alejandro Portes, "Una Sociologia del Exilio: Situación de los Grupos Cubanos en Estados Unidos," *Aportes*, no. 23 (January 1972): 13.

9. Associated Press, "Castro Tells Rally Cubans Are Free to Leave Country," *New York Times*, September 30, 1965, 1, 2.

10. Masud-Piloto, *From Welcomed Exiles to Illegal Immigrants*, 61–68.

11. The Cuban Adjustment Act, Public Law No. 89-732, November 2, 1966.

12. Eckstein and Barberia, "Cuban Americans and Their Transnational Ties," 267.

13. Masud-Piloto, *From Welcomed Exiles to Illegal Immigrants*, 54.

14. Jens Manuel Krogstad, "Surge in Cuban Immigration to US Continues into 2016," *FacTank*, Pew Research Center, August 5, 2016, http://www.pewresearch.org/fact-tank/2016/08/05/cuban-immigration-to-u-s-surges-as-relations-warm.

15. Fulton Armstrong, "US-Cuba: Migration Policy Growing Tortuous, Dangerous," *AULA Blog*, Center for Latin American and Latino Studies, February 4, 2016, https://aulablog.net/2016/02/04/u-s-cuba-migration-policy-growing-tortuous-dangerous.

16. Roberto González Echevarria, "Exiled by Ike, Saved by America," *New York Times*, January 7, 2011, A23.

17. Ecsktein, *The Immigrant Divide*, 16, 19.

18. Jens Manuel Krogstad, "After Decades of GOP Support, Cubans Shifting toward the Democratic Party," *FacTank*, Pew Research Center, June 24, 2014, http://www.pewresearch.org/fact-tank/2014/06/24/after-decades-of-gop-support-cubans-shifting-toward-the-democratic-party.

19. López, "Hispanics of Cuban Origin in the United States," 2.

20. López, "Hispanics of Cuban Origin in the United States," 2.

21. Eckstein, *The Immigrant Divide*, 27.

22. Steven A. Holmes, "Miami Melting Pot Proves Explosive," *New York Times*, December 9, 1990, E4.

23. Alejandro de la Fuente, "Recreating Racism: Race and Discrimination in Cuba's Special Period," *Socialism and Democracy* 15, no. 1 (Spring 2001): 68.

24. De la Fuente, "Recreating Racism," 77–79.

25. Pew Hispanic Center, "Cubans in the United States," *Fact Sheet*, August 25, 2006, http://www.pewhispanic.org/2006/08/25/cubans-in-the-united-states.

26. De la Fuente, "Recreating Racism," 69.

27. Esteban Morales, "Notas Sobre el Tema Racial en la Realidad Cubana de Hoy," *Esteban Morales Domínguez Blog*, September 2011 (authors' translation), http://estebanmoralesdominguez.blogspot.ca/2011/09/notas-sobre-el-tema-racial-en-la.html.

28. Fidel Castro Ruz, "Speech at the Cuban Solidarity Rally," New York, September 8, 2000, http://www.cuba.cu/gobierno/discursos/2000/ing/f080900i.html.

29. De la Fuente, "Recreating Racism," 81.

30. Raúl Castro Ruz, "The development of the national economy, along with the struggle for peace, and our ideological resolve, constitute the Party's principal missions," April 18, 2016 (*Granma International* translation), http://en.granma.cu/cuba/2016-04-18/the-development-of-the-national-economy-along-with-the-struggle-for-peace-and-our-ideological-resolve-constitute-the-partys-principal-missions.

31. Morales, "Notas Sobre el Tema Racial en la Realidad Cubana de Hoy."

32. Jorge I. Domínguez, "Dialogues within and between Cuba and Its Diaspora," in *A Contemporary Cuba Reader: The Revolution under Raúl Castro*, ed. Philip Brenner et al. (Lanham, MD: Rowman & Littlefield, 2014).

Chapter 20

Helms-Burton, US-Cuban Relations, and Terrorism, 1995–1998

Although US policies on Cuba mean relatively little in Washington, the implications of even the most trivial policy have enormous impact on the island. In Cuba, every nuance and component of US policy carries potentially profound consequence. Indeed, for Cuba, US politics constitutes a major determinant in the creation and implementation of both foreign and domestic policy.

—Soraya M. Castro Mariño, Cuban political scientist[1]

HELMS-BURTON

At mid-decade, Cuba's leaders finally were able to take a deep breath. With two successive years of growth in the gross domestic product, the worst of the early 1990s was over.[2] US efforts to wreak havoc on the island had immiserated many, but the regime had survived. The revival emerged largely in the service sector, as a result of increased tourism, and from more than two hundred joint venture agreements with Western companies by 1995.

Cuba's staying power frustrated anti-Castro hardliners in the United States. They also feared that President Clinton's advisers were pushing him to reduce tensions with Cuba.[3] National Security Council staffers Morton Halperin and Richard Feinberg, in fact, had been advocates of improved relations with Cuba before entering the Clinton administration. At the State Department, Undersecretary for Political Affairs Peter Tarnoff had negotiated the 1994 migration accord that ended the "rafter" exodus by sending 25,000 Cubans to Guantánamo Naval Base. Meanwhile, the Cuban government made it easier for the United States to have further negotiations by releasing several prominent political prisoners. In June 1995, Eloy Gutiérrez Menoyo made his peace with the Revolution. A founder of the counterrevolutionary terrorist organization Alpha 66, Gutiérrez Menoyo had spent twenty-two years in Cuban jails.

However, the fortunes of the anti-Castroites also turned favorable at the start of 1995. Republicans in Congress had gained House and Senate majorities in the 1994 midterm elections, which made Jesse Helms (R-NC) the new chair of the Senate Foreign Relations Committee. Dan Burton, a right-wing Republican from Indiana, became chair of the House International Relations Committee's Western Hemisphere subcommittee. Cuban-Americans had donated generously to both of their campaigns, and Burton's first hearing as subcommittee chair focused on Cuba. The star witness was Jorge Mas Canosa, leader of the CANF, who proclaimed that "the Cuban-American community could not have expected a dearer friend . . . to assume the chairmanship."[4]

Helms recognized that the Cuban economy had begun to rise from its nadir because of foreign investment, which then became the focus of his energies. In February 1995, he and Burton sponsored bills in the Senate and House titled "The Cuban Liberty and Solidarity (LIBERTAD) Act," aimed at discouraging investment in Cuba and further limiting trade.

In presenting his version on the Senate floor, Helms made clear its intent— the overthrow of the Cuban government. Yet he noted that he would allow Cubans to decide "whether Castro leaves Cuba in a vertical or horizontal position." Otherwise, he gave them no choice, saying, "but he must and will leave Cuba."[5] The lengthy and detailed measure, which became commonly known as the Helms-Burton Act, read as if it were a formal indictment of the Cuban government. The bill mandated that US sanctions could be lifted only after Cubans elect a new government "democratically" and that it "does not include Fidel Castro or Raúl Castro."

Cuban political scientist Soraya Castro likened Helms-Burton to the 1901 Platt Amendment, writing that it would "bring Cuba back to the status it had early in the twentieth century, when the United States dictated the destiny of the Cuban nation."[6] Similarly, Harvard scholar Jorge Domínguez asserted that the law "is quite faithful to the theme of the Monroe Doctrine and the Roosevelt Corollary. It claims for the United States the unilateral right to decide a wide array of domestic policies and arrangements in a nominally sovereign post Castro Cuba."[7]

The House and Senate versions of Helms-Burton were not identical, and neither commanded an immediate majority in its respective chamber. Helms and Burton were willing to bide their time, a Senate staffer told us in an interview, hoping to pressure Democrats into supporting an amalgam of the legislation during the 1996 presidential election year. They had little idea how Cuban-American militants would enable the legislators to pass a law they only dreamed might be possible.

CUBAN-AMERICAN MILITANTS TAKE CHARGE

New Immigration Policy Provokes Anti-Castro Hardliners

At the start of 1995, conditions at the Guantánamo Naval Base were bleak. The Cuban detainees had few recreation facilities and their main food staple was C-rations. Some had begun to mutilate themselves, "injecting diesel fuel in their veins," hoping to be sent to the United States for treatment.[8] In April 1995, General John Sheehan, commander of the US Atlantic Command, warned the White House that some Cubans were likely to stage riots on the base during the summer months, when the temperature would rise past 120 degrees Fahrenheit, endangering both US soldiers and the refugees themselves.[9] His warning propelled the administration into new talks with Cuba. The Clinton administration needed a way out of a dilemma its September rafters agreement had created. If the US government did nothing, it would have to deal with a restive group of exiles who saw no end to their quasi-imprisonment. Yet if Clinton permitted the Guantánamo Cubans to emigrate to the United States, he would be encouraging a new wave of rafters who believed they could reach their desired destination after suffering the naval base conditions for only nine months.

So Clinton sent Tarnoff back to negotiate with Cuban National Assembly President Ricardo Alarcón, first in New York and then in Toronto. The talks were so secret that officials on the State Department's Cuba desk were not informed for fear they would try to scuttle the mission. The result was a policy known as *wet foot–dry foot*. The Clinton administration announced that it would admit most of the 25,000 Cubans housed at the naval base. But to discourage future rafters, the US Coast Guard would thereafter return to Cuba any migrants it intercepted at sea. (Those who managed to touch dry US territory would continue to be classified as political refugees and given parole status.) In turn, the Cuban government pledged it would take no punitive actions against those whom the United States returned, and it would permit US diplomats to make periodic visits anywhere in the country to ensure that returning rafters were not punished.

Anti-Castro Cuban exiles and their allies in Congress responded to the announcement with outrage. But José Basulto, a Bay of Pigs veteran who had engaged in violent actions against Cuba in the 1960s, also was fed up with the so-called Cuba Lobby in Washington. Traditional lobbying for new laws was too slow and unreliable for him. Basulto had founded Brothers to the Rescue, an organization that flew small planes over the Florida Straits in search of Cuban rafters who needed assistance. While US media generally described Brothers as "humanitarian," Basulto's goal was to destabilize Cuba. In frequent broadcasts on Radio Martí and Miami radio stations, he encouraged Cubans to leave the island, promising to find them and notify the US Coast Guard to bring them to the United States. But that promise was no longer viable after the September 1994 agreement required the Coast Guard to send rafters to Guantánamo—and following the May 1995 agreement, back to Cuba.

Brothers to the Rescue Repeatedly Violates Cuban Airspace

In July 1995, Basulto found a new raison d'être for his organization: provoking the Cuban government in the hope of derailing rapprochement. With a Miami television cameraman on board, he flew low over the Malecon, Havana's waterfront roadway, dropping religious medals and bumper stickers along the route.[10] The Malecon is lined with tourist hotels, apartment houses, office buildings, and Cuba's Ministry of Foreign Relations. That evening, Miami's NBC affiliate station aired film of the mission. On subsequent flights, he dropped leaflets advocating that Cubans rise up against their government. Cuban officials assert that Basulto's planes made more than twenty-five such flights, a claim the US State Department partially validated.[11]

Given Basulto's background, Cuban security officials viewed the flights as a serious threat. He had come to his "humanitarian" project late in life, claiming he had converted to nonviolence after engaging in militant actions for many years. After the Bay of Pigs invasion, he worked with the Central Intelligence Agency on Operation Mongoose, but left the terrorist program allegedly because he was frustrated by its slow pace. He then orchestrated a spectacular raid on a Havana tourist hotel where he believed Fidel spent his leisure time, firing scores of rounds at the building from small cannons.[12] "We were pretty [lousy] terrorists," he told the *Washington Post* in 1997, "because somebody else would have got explosive ammunition." He devoted the remainder of the 1960s to anti-Castro activities with violent groups in South Florida, believing "that the only hope for the Cuban people lay in the physical elimination of Fidel Castro."[13] In the 1980s, he again worked with the CIA, training and helping the contras to launch terrorist attacks against Nicaragua.[14]

The Cuban government protested Basulto's flights officially to US authorities on at least four occasions. It did so informally as well, once to Rep. Bill Richardson (D-NM) and on another occasion to a group of former high-ranking US military officers visiting Cuba. The group then reported to the National Security Council staff that Cuba was likely to shoot at future flights that violated Cuban airspace.[15] From Cuba's perspective, Basulto's flights were akin to Al Qaeda pilots flying over Washington and dropping innocuous leaflets. The risk was too great that on a future flight Basulto might switch from leaflets to bombs. Cuban exiles had done that before. Yet US officials made minimal efforts to stop the flights. When asked by a radio interviewer what pressure the US government had placed on him, Basulto joked that the authorities had been "on vacation."[16]

Cubans Shoot Down Two Planes

On February 24, 1996, he set out again, along with two other Brothers to the Rescue Cessnas. The details about what happened during the flight are still open to question. Basulto claims that none of the planes entered Cuban airspace that afternoon. Cuba maintains that all three planes entered Cuban airspace and were over its territorial waters when pilots flying Cuban MIGs shot down two of them. US air traffic control tracking data indicates that the two planes were over international waters at the time of the shootdown, and that Basulto's plane may have crossed into Cuban space. Four men were killed. Basulto headed for clouds to evade the Cuban fighters and returned safely to Florida.[17] Cuba's political leaders did not make the decision to shoot down the planes lightly. They had allowed the incursions to go on for several months, during which time they issued numerous warnings. But senior Cuban military officers were pressing Fidel for some retaliatory action.

The Clinton administration reacted harshly, placing all of the blame on Cuba. At the instigation of the United States, both the UN Security Council and the Council of the International Civil Aviation Organization deplored Cuba's action. Clinton condemned it "in the strongest possible terms" and two days after the event announced retaliatory measures that tightened the embargo, including the cancellation of direct charter flights between Miami and Havana and new restrictions on the movements of Cuban diplomats within the United States.

In the US Congress, the dynamics of the ongoing debate over versions of the Helms-Burton bill took a dramatic turn. In the new atmosphere of increased hostility toward Cuba, House-Senate conferees opted for the House version's more radical approach, which constrained the president's prerogatives to modify the embargo. Prior to the shootdown, the legislation had stalled in the Senate and the Clinton administration had not proposed an alternative. Now the president was confronted with three options in a year when he hoped to win Florida's electoral votes: (1) do nothing; (2) conduct a military strike against Cuba; (3) sign the unsavory bill.[18] Attorney General Janet Reno urged Clinton to veto Helms-Burton, arguing that the law would place undesirable limits on the president's constitutional powers as commander in chief.[19] But Clinton viewed signing the bill as the least worst option, and Helms-Burton became law on March 12, 1996.

The Least Worst Option

The measure codified existing executive orders that made up the US economic embargo against Cuba. This seemed to mean that embargo modifications presidents previously could make at their sole discretion now would require new congressional action. Helms-Burton also granted to US citizens who had been Cuban citizens when the Cuban government nationalized their property the right to have the US government advocate for their claims. In addition, any claimant could sue a foreign company in a US court for allegedly "trafficking" in stolen property. It was a significant departure from accepted international law because it involves a US court in an extraterritorial dispute, which some referred to as the "Bacardí provision." Bacardí, Ltd. lobbied for the measure, claiming its former distilleries in Cuba were being used to manufacture Havana Club rum. Though the company is headquartered in Bermuda, the family owners moved to Puerto Rico in 1960 and most members became US citizens. They hoped to sue Pernod, the French distributor of Havana Club, which has assets in the United States. However, the law also permits a president to waive the Bacardí provision, and Presidents Clinton, George W. Bush, and Barack Obama invoked that loophole consistently after 1996.

That autumn, the international community condemned the Helms-Burton Act in a UN General Assembly vote of 138 to 3, with 24 abstentions. (In 2016, the General Assembly unanimously condemned the US embargo, with the United States and Israel abstaining for the first time.) International businesses then voted with their money to defy Helms-Burton, increasing foreign direct investment in Cuba by 22 percent from 1996 to 1997.[20] The growth of investment came in part as a result of new laws in 1995 by which Cuba allowed foreign companies to own 100 percent of an investment, with guaranteed protection against nationalization.

Congressional passage of the Helms-Burton Act was emblematic of the decline in fortune and clout of CANF. The bill's coauthor, Daniel Fisk, at the time a Senate staffer who worked for Helms, reportedly did not even talk to CANF officials before drafting the legislation.[21] Helms sponsored the bill for ideological reasons, but the CANF took credit in any case.

TERRORIST CAMPAIGN AGAINST CUBA

With Helms-Burton failing to deter new investors, a violent sector in the anti-Castro exile community turned to terrorist strikes to scare off tourists. The *New York Times* identified Luis Posada Carriles as the organizer of a series of 1997 bombings at major hotels in Havana and one popular restaurant,

Bodeguita del Medio, in which several people were injured and one Italian tourist was killed.[22]

In 1998, Cuba invited FBI investigators to examine information that demonstrated the attacks originated with anti-Castro groups in southern Florida. The FBI found that the evidence also indicated CANF had supported some of the terrorists.[23] Yet the FBI did not arrest any of those involved in the bombing attacks. Instead, it used the information to identify and arrest fourteen Cuban agents whom Cuba had sent to monitor the terrorist groups. Some were deported; others confessed to minor crimes and were given short prison terms. Five of the Cubans declared their innocence. As a result, Miami prosecutors charged them with conspiracy to commit espionage and asked for sentences ranging from fifteen years to two life sentences. Notably, the evidence prosecutors offered against them validated the defendants' claims that they had conducted surveillance only on anti-Castro groups planning attacks against Cuba. They became known as the "Cuban Five."[24]

Posada had been linked to years of terrorist actions against Cuba, including the 1976 bombing of Cubana Airlines flight 455. In 2000, he planned to assassinate Fidel Castro in Panama by blowing up a car laden with dozens of pounds of C-4 explosive. It was parked adjacent to a university auditorium packed with students where the Cuban leader was speaking, when police nabbed Posada and three accomplices. Convicted of "disturbing the peace," the four terrorists were pardoned by outgoing Panamanian president Mireya Moscoso in 2004.

While the United States barred Posada from the entering the country because of his terrorist activities, he illegally found his way to Texas. After federal marshals captured him, prosecutors put him on trial merely for lying on an immigration form. The jury members, seemingly intimidated by militant Cuban-Americans in the audience who glowered at them throughout the trial, decided that Posada was not guilty. He then moved to Miami, where local politicians and anti-Castro Cuban-Americans feted him as a hero.[25]

Both Venezuela and Cuba have requested that the United States extradite Posada to their countries. The requests have been denied. Yet Posada was not the only anti-Cuban terrorist the United States has harbored. His alleged co-planner of the Cubana bombing, Orlando Bosch, also had been barred from the United States because, in the State Department's judgment, he had a "criminal history and involvement in terrorism." Indeed, a House of Representatives committee characterized Bosch as "the most aggressive and volatile of the anti-Castro leaders," and reported that he had organized more than eleven bombing raids over Cuba in 1963 alone.[26] After he entered the United States illegally, President George H. W. Bush paroled him in 1990, against the Justice Department's recommendation. Once out of jail, Bosch publicly hailed the

destruction of the Cuban airliner, saying, "It was a legitimate war action.
. . .We are at war, aren't we?" Bosch, too, became a hero in Miami.[27]

Other Miami-based terrorists carried out attacks on Cuban targets throughout the world. For example, two Cuban diplomats, Adriana Corcho and Efren Monteagudo, were killed by a bomb in Lisbon in 1976. Omega 7, one of the major anti-Castro groups, claimed responsibility for the assassination of Félix García Rodríguez on September 11, 1980. A member of Cuba's mission to the United Nations, he was the first UN diplomat to be assassinated in New York City.[28]

The Cuban government has tended to link most terrorist acts to some US government agency, whether or not there was evidence of direct US involvement. For example, former general Fabián Escalante asserted in 2006 that there had been more than six hundred attempts to assassinate Fidel Castro sponsored by the United States.[29] The United States has acknowledged only eight attempts, and has not revealed any that may have occurred after 1966.[30]

It was in this context of terrorism that the Cuban government prevented dissidents from holding a conference in February 1996, and sentenced several of them to fourteen-month prison terms. The Clinton administration had been disbursing modest payments to hundreds of Cubans who identified themselves as dissidents and had formed a coalition of 130 loosely organized groups throughout the country. The groups had planned to meet in Havana on February 22, 1996, under an umbrella organization named Concilio Cubano. The United States also had urged the European Union (EU) to condition aid to Cuba on its willingness to allow the coalition to be placed under the EU's protection.[31]

Cuban officials were troubled by Concilio's conference precisely because of the US connection. The meeting's timing further heightened their suspicions. Brothers to the Rescue had issued a press release announcing that its next flights over Havana would coincide with the gathering, and Cuban security specialists viewed the Brothers' prior missions as preparation for a terrorist attack. With the experiences of US-sponsored terrorism inflating their calculation of a threat, they imagined a worst-case scenario that linked the meeting to the announced flights in a conflagration designed to pressure President Clinton into taking aggressive action during an election year.

Instead of making Cuba more secure, though, the preventive measures reinforced the country's international image as a human rights offender. The European Union held up aid to Cuba, the UN General Assembly condemned the shootdown of the Brothers to the Rescue planes, and President Clinton felt compelled to sign a toughened Helms-Burton bill into law.

NOTES

1. Soraya M. Castro Mariño, "Cuba-US Relations, 1989–2002: A View from Havana," in *Redefining Cuban Foreign Policy: The Impact of the "Special Period,"* ed. H. Michael Erisman and John M. Kirk (Gainesville: University Press of Florida, 2006), 305.

2. Oficina Nacional de Estadísticas (ONE), "Panorama Económica y Social, Cuba 1996" (Havana: 1997)

3. Walt Vanderbush and Patrick J. Haney, "Policy toward Cuba in the Clinton Administration," *Political Science Quarterly* 114, no. 3 (Fall 1999).

4. Jorge Mas Canosa, "Statement," in US Congress, House, 104th Cong., 1st Sess., "Cuba and US Policy," Hearing Before the Subcommittee on the Western Hemisphere, Committee on International Relations, February 23, 1995, 14.

5. Jesse Helms, "Remarks," *Congressional Record*, February 9, 1995, S2411; 141 Cong. Rec. S 2399.

6. Soraya M. Castro Mariño, "US-Cuban Relations During the Clinton Administration," *Latin American Perspectives* 29, no. 4 (July 2002): 62.

7. Jorge I. Domínguez, "US-Cuban Relations: From the Cold War to the Colder War," *Journal of Interamerican Studies and World Affairs* 39, no. 3 (1997): 58.

8. Pentagon official quoted in Schoultz, *That Infernal Little Cuban Republic*, 472.

9. Philip Brenner and Peter Kornbluh, "Clinton's Cuba Calculus," *NACLA Report on the Americas*, September/October 1995.

10. Carl Nagin, "Backfire," *New Yorker*, January 26, 1998, 32.

11. John M. Goshko, "Cuban Aide Defends Air Attack; Supporting Evidence Not Presented to U.N.," *Washington Post*, February 29, 1996, A16; Bradley Graham, "US Tried to Restrain Group's Flights," *Washington Post*, February 27, 1996, A5.

12. Felix I. Rodriguez and John Weisman, *Shadow Warrior* (New York: Simon & Schuster, 1989), 109–11.

13. Jefferson Morley, "Shootdown," *Washington Post Magazine*, May 25, 1997.

14. Mireya Navarro, "Nonviolence of Castro's Foes Still Wears a Very Tough Face," *New York Times*, February 28, 1996, A1.

15. Nagin, "Backfire," 32–33.

16. Schoultz, *That Infernal Little Cuban Republic*, 482; Wayne S. Smith, "The US-Cuba Imbroglio: Anatomy of a Crisis," *International Policy Report*, May 1996 (Washington, DC: Center for International Policy); Thomas W. Lippman and Guy Gugliotta, "US Data Forced Cuba to Retreat on Shooting; Basulto Bragged of Buzzing Havana Previously," *Washington Post*, March 16, 1996, A19.

17. Morley, "Shootdown."

18. Daniel W. Fisk, "Cuba in US Policy: An American Congressional Perspective," in *Canada, the US and Cuba: Helms-Burton and Its Aftermath*, ed. Heather Nicol (Kingston, Ontario: Centre for International Relations, Queen's University, 1999), 34.

19. Vanderbush and Haney, "Policy toward Cuba in the Clinton Administration."

20. Paolo Spadoni, *Failed Sanctions: Why the US Embargo against Cuba Could Never Work* (Gainesville: University Press of Florida, 2010), 63–64.

21. Patrick J. Haney and Walt Vanderbush, "The Role of Ethnic Interest Groups in US Foreign Policy: The Case of the Cuban American National Foundation." *International Studies Quarterly* 43 (June 1999).

22. Ann Louise Bardach and Larry Rohter, "Life in the Shadows, Trying to Bring Down Castro," *New York Times*, July 13, 1998; Juan Tamayo, "Exiles Directed Blasts That Rocked Island's Tourism, Investigation Reveals," *Miami Herald*, November 17, 1997.

23. Sánchez-Parodi, *CUBA-USA*, 209–10.

24. Landau, "The Cuban Five and the US War against Terror," 274–76.

25. Landau, "The Cuban Five and the US War against Terror," 273; Glenn Garvin, "Panama: Exile Says Aim Was Castro Hit," *Miami Herald*, January 13, 2001; Ann Louise Bardach, "Twilight of the Assassins," *Atlantic*, November 2006.

26. US Congress, House Select Committee on Assassination, "Investigation of the Assassination of President John F. Kennedy," 90–91.

27. Quoted in Andres Oppenheimer, *Castro's Final Hour: The Secret Story behind the Coming Downfall of Communist Cuba* (New York: Simon & Schuster, 1992), 325–26; US Department of Justice, Office of the Associate Attorney General, "Exclusion Proceeding for Orlando Bosch Avila," File: A28 851 622, A11 861 810, January 23, 1989.

28. Robert D. McFadden, "Cuban Attaché at U.N. Is Slain from Ambush on Queens Road," *New York Times*, September 12, 1980, A1.

29. Fabián Escalante Font, *Executive Action: 634 Ways to Kill Fidel Castro* (Melbourne: Ocean Press, 2006).

30. US Central Intelligence Agency, "Inspector General Report on Plots to Assassinate Fidel Castro," May 23, 1967.

31. Morris H. Morley and Chris McGillion, *Unfinished Business: America and Cuba After the Cold War, 1989–2001* (New York: Cambridge University Press, 2002), 96.

Chapter 21

The Pope Goes to Cuba; Elián Goes to Miami, 1998–2000

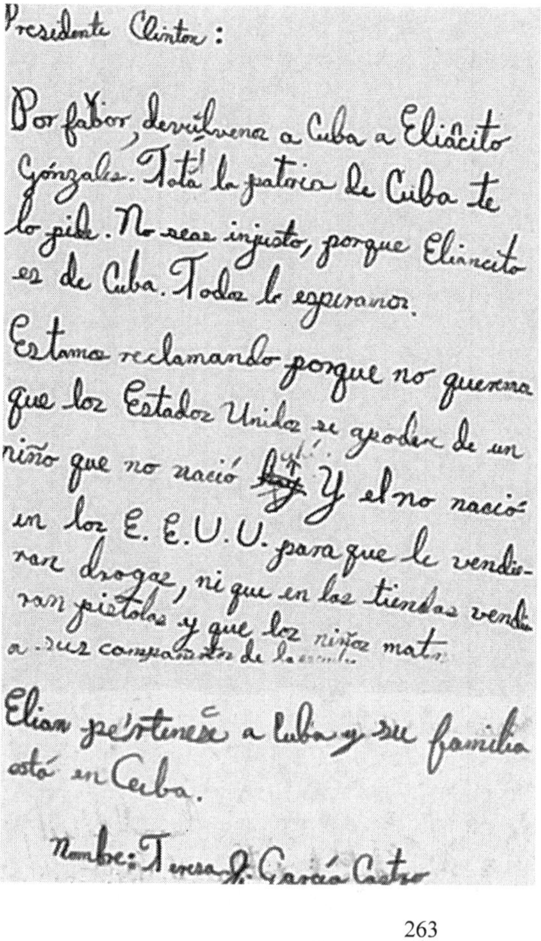

Presidente Clinton:

Por fabor, devuélvena a Cuba a Eliancito Góngales. Toda la patria de Cuba te lo pide. No seas injusto, porque Eliancito es de Cuba. Todo lo esperan.

Estamos reclamando porque no queremos que los Estados Unidos se queden de un niño que no nació allí. Y el no nació en los E.E.U.U. para que le vendieran drogas, ni que en las tiendas vendieran pistolas y que los niños matan a sus compañeros de la escuela.

Elian pertenece a Cuba y su familia está en Cuba.

Nombre: Teresa J. García Castro

Figure 21.1. In the spring of 2000, Cuban children were asked to write letters to President Clinton asking him to return Elián González to Cuba. Eight-year-old Teresa García wrote this letter. Translation: *President Clinton: Please, return little Elián Gónzales* [sic] *to Cuba. The whole country of Cuba asks you to do this. Do not be unjust, because Elián is from Cuba. Everyone is waiting for him. We are making this demand because we do not want the United States to hold onto a child who was not born there. And he was not born in the US where drugs are sold, even guns are sold in stores, and children kill their classmates in school. Elián belongs to Cuba and his family is in Cuba. Name: Teresa J. García Castro*

POPE JOHN PAUL II VISITS CUBA

In the mid-1980s, Fidel Castro began trying to improve the government's quarter-century-long hostile relationship with the Catholic Church, which had turned against the Revolution in 1959. The move was partly defensive, prompted by the role Pope John Paul II was playing in strengthening anti-communist movements in Eastern Europe. It also was a way to improve relations with countries in Latin America. Ultimately, it was an acknowledgment that the Cuban Catholic Church could play a positive role in the future development of the country.

The first major opening took the form of a twenty-three-hour interview in May 1985 with Frei Betto, a Brazilian Dominican friar who was deeply committed to liberation theology and had been working with "base communities." Near the end of the interview, the friar broached the subject of whether Marxism—which he characterized as class hatred—was incompatible with religious belief. The Cuban leader answered: "We who are revolutionaries, socialists and Marxist-Leninists don't preach hatred as a philosophy. . . . What we are preaching is the repudiation, rejection and hatred of the [capitalist] system—hatred of injustice. . . . I don't think there is any contradiction with Christian teachings, because, if somebody says 'I hate crime' or 'I hate injustice, abuses and exploitation,' I don't think that would be against Christian teachings."[1]

Soon afterward, the government established an Office of Religious Affairs to serve as a direct liaison to all religious organizations in the country. In 1990, the government permitted the Church to broadcast Easter and Christmas services on the radio, and in 1991, the Cuban Communist Party allowed religious adherents to become party members. This led to a 1992 revision of the Cuban constitution, which declared that the nature of the state, which had been until then atheist, was now secular.

Fidel's 1988 invitation to Pope John Paul II to visit the country had gone unanswered. But after the Cuban leader delivered it in person at the Vatican in 1996, and Cuba reinstated Christmas as a national holiday, the Pope decided to make the journey in January 1998. Castro welcomed him at the airport, along with the members of the powerful Political Bureau of the PCC (see Fidel welcoming him in figure 21.2). On the street, crowds greeted the pontiff with unvarnished enthusiasm. Signs in windows of homes declared, *No tengo miedo*—"I am not afraid."

More than one million people attended a public mass that John Paul II led in Havana's Revolution Square on January 25, 1998, his first stop of the five-day visit. His message to those assembled offered a kind of vindication for Cuba's leaders: "For many of the political and economic systems

Figure 21.2.   Fidel Castro greets Pope John Paul II in Havana, January 25, 1998. Photo by Ahmed Velázquez, courtesy of *Granma*.

operative today, the greatest challenge is still that of combining freedom and social justice."[2]

He continued with this theme in a series of masses across the island, during which the leader of the Roman Catholic Church found common ground with Cuba's leader by sharply rebuking global capitalism's "blind market forces." He also pointedly called for an end to the US embargo, which he characterized as "oppressive economic measures imposed from outside the country."[3] Cuba reacted to the Pope's plea for greater freedom by releasing more than three hundred political prisoners, relaxing travel restrictions on priests, and permitting more Church radio broadcasts.

US OPPONENTS OF RAPPROCHEMENT LOSE STRENGTH

Clinton Relaxes the Embargo

The Pope's visit also reverberated in the United States, where the Clinton administration found itself under increasing international pressure to diminish US hostility toward Cuba. Several South American countries had signed trade pacts with Cuba, and Caribbean countries gave Castro a hero's welcome at a summit in which the region's leaders signed a free-trade agreement.[4]

Publicity generated by the pontiff's trip and the Cuban government's responses added to the pressure.

Clinton responded with modest changes that did little more than reverse some earlier moves tightening the embargo. Direct charter flights between the United States and Cuba were restored, and Cuban-Americans again were allowed to send remittances up to $300 every three months to their families.

Yet a new dynamic between opponents and advocates of a changed relationship began to emerge in 1998. The death in November 1997 of Jorge Mas Canosa, the politically sophisticated head of the vaunted CANF, led to fissures and cracks in the seemingly invincible influence of the hardline anti-Castro lobby. Its legitimacy in Washington was also eroded by detailed reports in the *New York Times* and Knight Ridder news service about CANF's links to terrorist attacks in Havana and assassination attempts against Fidel Castro.[5]

At the same time, the Cuban exile community was going through generational changes and shifts in leadership. Mas Canosa's power base had been with the Republican Party, but now wealthy Cuban-American Democrats had gained greater favor with Clinton's political advisers inside the White House.[6] In addition, younger Cuban-Americans, especially those born in the United States, did not share the hope for revenge many of their parents harbored. An increasing number favored a dialogue with Cuba, and, along with business, church, and academic groups, they became more vocal in 1998.

In October 1998, a bipartisan call for change in policy came from an unlikely group of former US officials that included Republican Secretaries of State Henry Kissinger, George P. Shultz, and Lawrence Eagleburger. They asked President Clinton to establish a commission to provide a broad review of US relations with Cuba. But that was a step too far for the president. Anti-Castro Cuban-Americans warned Vice President Al Gore that his 2000 presidential bid would suffer from a Cuba policy review, especially among voters in the key swing state of Florida. Then Representative Robert Menendez (D-NJ) reportedly told Gore that if the policy review went forward, it would be known as the "Gore Commission."[7]

In rejecting the proposed bipartisan commission, Clinton also sought to mollify its advocates in January 1999 by announcing a series of new regulations that seemed to undercut the Helms-Burton law. The regulations themselves were small but nonetheless significant for two reasons. First, Clinton made the changes unilaterally, without any demand that the Cuban government meet conditions or reciprocate, and he thus abandoned the prior approach, called "calibrated response."[8] He would justify US actions toward Cuba on the basis of US interests, not Cuban behavior.

Second, the new regulations went beyond what analysts said would be possible under the Helms-Burton Act, which seemed to limit presidential discretion in implementing the embargo. When asked whether the changes were consistent with the law, a senior National Security Council official asserted publicly that "Helms-Burton codified the embargo and at the same time, it codified the President's licensing power. That is, it codified a process by which there was an embargo to which exceptions could be granted on a case-by-case basis by the President."[9] That interpretation opened the door virtually to any license for trade with Cuba that a president would wish to make.

The new rules expanded who could send remittances to Cuba. For the first time, any US citizen would be allowed to send up to $300 every quarter to a Cuban family. Nongovernmental organizations, such as educational foundations, would be allowed to send larger sums to "independent" organizations in Cuba. At the same time, the Treasury Department's Office of Foreign Assets Control (OFAC) was ordered to further streamline licensing procedures for US and Cuban citizens traveling between the two countries and allow group licenses for the purpose of educational, cultural, humanitarian, religious, journalistic, and athletic exchanges, or what were called "people-to-people" exchanges.

Baseball Diplomacy

Baseball truly is an American pastime—in Cuba and in the United States. This provided the inspiration for Scott Armstrong and Saul Landau to propose an intriguing opportunity to Peter Angelos, owner of the Baltimore Orioles, to play a major role in a baseball diplomacy initiative with Cuba. The idea had been batted around for twenty years, ever since South Dakota Democratic Senators George McGovern and James Abourezk suggested it after traveling to Cuba in 1977 with the University of South Dakota basketball team. But Armstrong and Landau faced insurmountable obstacles in their new effort until Clinton announced the January 1999 changes.

While the president authorized OFAC to issue a license to the Orioles to travel to Cuba as a result of Armstrong and Landau's behind-the-scenes urging, Secretary of State Madeleine Albright added a troubling proviso to Clinton's announcement of the decision. Any profits from the games, she said, would need to be distributed to the Cuban people through Caritas, the Cuban Catholic charitable organization. She did not want to signal that the games would lead to a warming of relations between the two countries, as so-called Ping-Pong diplomacy led to improved ties between China and the United States. Cuba viewed the secretary's remarks to mean that the baseball games had

become part of the US "people-to-people" campaign, which they well remembered Congressman Torricelli devising in 1992 as a subversive tactic
to sow seeds of discontent in the country. Her demand almost scuttled the
initiative. After two months of negotiations, and a last-minute 3:00 a.m. call
to National Security Adviser Sandy Berger, negotiators resolved the problem
when they realized that the two exhibition games were unlikely to generate
any profits.[10] The Orioles flew to Havana for the first game on March 28,
1999, and Cuba's All-Star team played in Baltimore on May 3.

ELIÁN AND THE FUTURE OF CUBA

On Thanksgiving Day 1999, a fisherman found five-year-old Elián González
clinging to an inner tube in the ocean near Fort Lauderdale, Florida. His
mother, Elizabet González, her boyfriend, and eight others had died when
their makeshift raft overturned during their ill-fated trip across the Florida
Straits. Rushed to a hospital, the young boy had survived in remarkably good
condition. But soon Elián was nearly torn apart as he became a symbol of
who would control Cuba's future: Florida's anti-Castro Cuban-American
community or Cubans on the island.

By all accounts, Elián's first five years were relatively comfortable.
Though his parents had divorced, they shared custody and responsibility for
Elián, who was also close to his four grandparents. Juan Miguel González,
Elián's father, had remarried, and his mother lived nearby with her boyfriend.
Both parents worked in the tourist industry in Varadero, a resort area close to
their small town of Cárdenas, about ninety miles east of Havana.

When Elián was released from the hospital, the US Immigration and Natu-
ralization Service turned him over to his father's uncle, Lázaro, a frequently
unemployed laborer whose children had a history of trouble with the police.
Though Lázaro and his family had not maintained contact with Elián's father,
they quickly claimed custody of the boy and demanded the US government
grant him parole as a political refugee. CANF then led a campaign to shower
the family with money, to buy presents for Elián, to pay for a dazzling birthday trip to Disney World in early December, and to demand that the boy not
be repatriated to Cuba. Meanwhile, at the request of Juan Miguel, the Cuban
government on November 29 demanded that the United States return Elián
to his father.

International covenants favored the claims of the father, but the Clinton
administration moved slowly to recover the boy from the custody of his
Miami relatives. On the island, his case became a cause célèbre. Regular
demonstrations were held across Cuba, billboards demanded that the United

States "send Elián home," and schoolchildren wrote heartfelt letters appealing to President Clinton, such as the one that opens this chapter.

In March 2000, a federal judge ruled that Elián should live with his father, who had come to the United States to retrieve him while they waited for a court to decide whether the boy should be repatriated to Cuba. But the Miami relatives refused to give him up, until federal agents—in a dramatic break-in at Lázaro's home in April—seized Elián at gunpoint (see Elián reunited with his father in figure 21.3). Even then, court battles and delays kept the boy from returning to Cuba with his father until June 28, 2000.

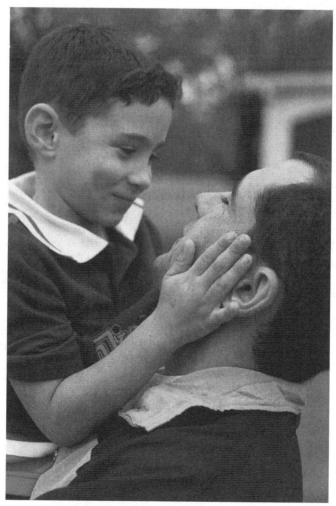

Figure 21.3. Elián González is reunited with his father, April 22, 2000. Photo by David Burnett.

Puentes Cubanos

Founded in 1999 by Silvia Wilhelm, Puentes Cubanos (Cuban Bridges) is a nongovernmental organization that has been dedicated to promoting normal relations between Cuba and the United States by breaking down barriers—political, cultural, linguistic, economic, and psychological—between Cubans on the island and in the United States. It was a major voice that opposed the severe restrictions President George W. Bush placed on Cuban-American travel in 2004.

Figure 21.4. Silvia Wilhelm

The case put a human face on the abstract debates about US policy toward Cuba. US public sentiment overwhelmingly viewed the boy's father sympathetically, believed Elián should be reunited with his family in Cuba, and opposed the Miami zealots. As a result, the saga further discredited the anti-Castro lobby and made legislators even less wary about voting to ease sanctions against Cuba.[11] And they were being given several opportunities to do so.

Missouri's archconservative Republican senator, John Ashcroft, was facing a tough reelection fight. In a move to support his state's agriculture industry, he sponsored a farm bill amendment that would have lifted sanctions on the sale of food and medicine to Cuba. The Ashcroft amendment also blocked future presidential decisions from imposing unilateral agricultural or medical sanctions against any foreign country. But despite considerable support from other Republican senators, the measure failed in a House-Senate conference committee.

This led Representative George R. Nethercutt (R-WA) to offer a less ambitious version of the Ashcroft amendment in the House Appropriations Committee, which approved it in the spring of 2000. Nethercutt, who represented a farm district, expressed the rationale of other Republicans in supporting the legislation: "I need to stand up for the farmers in my district," he declared.[12] With US policy toward Cuba reframed to focus on trade instead of national security or ethnic politics, legislators had found a noncontroversial way to chip away at the embargo that Helms-Burton had codified.

The final version of the Nethercutt amendment required Cuba to pay for any products in advance and in cash, and it prohibited US entities from extending credit to Cuba for the sale of food and medicine. But it did permit food exporters to travel to Cuba under a general license. The measure was approved as part of the 2000 Trade Sanctions Reform and Export Enhancement Act (TSRA).

Thus as the new millennium began, Congress appeared to have liberated itself from the hardline anti-Castro lobby. It seemed that US-Cuban relations might finally be headed toward a modus vivendi that would end forty years of hostile relations between the two neighbors.

NOTES

1. Betto, *Fidel and Religion*, 317–18.

2. Larry Rohter, "Pope Asks Cubans to Seek New Path toward Freedom," *New York Times*, January 26, 1998.

3. S. Fainaru, "In Cuba, Awe and Exhilaration," *Boston Globe*, January 26, 1998, A1.

4. Philip Brenner, Patrick J. Haney, and Walt Vanderbush, "The Confluence of Domestic and International Interests: US Policy Toward Cuba, 1998–2001," *International Studies Perspectives*, no. 3 (2002): 202.

5. Ann Louise Bardach and Larry Rohter, "A Plot on Castro Spotlights a Powerful Group of Exiles," *New York Times*, May 5, 1998; Tamayo, "Exiles Directed Blasts That Rocked Island's Tourism, Investigation Reveals"; Ann Louise Bardach and Larry Rohter, "A Bomber's Tale: A Cuban Exile Details the 'Horrendous Matter' of a Bombing Campaign," *New York Times*, July 12, 1998.

6. Schoultz, *That Infernal Little Cuban Republic*, 498–500.

7. R. Ferreira and R. Fabricio, "Graham y Gore Convencieron al Presidente," *El Nuevo Herald*, January 10, 1999.

8. Philip Brenner, "Washington Loosens the Knot (a Little Bit)," *NACLA Report on the Americas*, March/April 1999.

9. James Dobbins, Special Assistant to the President and Senior Director for Inter-American Affairs, NSC, "On-the-record briefing on Cuba," Released by the Office of the Spokesman, US Department of State, January 5, 1999.

10. Paula Pettavino and Philip Brenner, "More Than Just a Game: The Dual Developmental Aspects of Cuban Sports," *Peace Review* 11, no. 4 (December 1999).

11. Karen DeYoung, "Can Elián Case Alter US-Cuban Dynamic? Custody Fight Renews Debate on Relations," *Washington Post*, May 2, 2000, A4.

12. Quoted in Karen DeYoung and Eric Pianin, "Congressional Mood Shifts on Cuba Trade Ban," *Washington Post*, May 23, 2000, A1.

Chapter 22

The Search for a
Viable Strategy, 2001–2006

The loss of values is something very common today in the world, not only in Cuba, and I didn't want my film to be a story of degradation of marginal characters. They are two college students who love each other, had a house, a workplace and were not in discrepancy with the law. Supposedly, they had it all, but they were living in a place where that was not enough, and were compelled to become the most wanted, as Bonnie and Clyde, but without actually killing anyone, or steal big things. That is, to have a full life, they must find some solutions not entirely positive. My main intention was to say that in this place, to survive, to be an exemplary family they had to lie and do certain prosecutable things because the sugar mill, what gave them a spiritual and material life, had been stopped.

—Carlos Lechuga, discussing *Melaza*, a 2012 film he directed[1]

HOPES AND REALITIES IN THE NEW MILLENNIUM

Hope Rests on Weak Pillars

As the new millennium opened, Cuban leaders were more hopeful about the future than they had been for some time. They had weathered the collapse of the Soviet Union and its socialist trading bloc, which had accounted for more than 85 percent of Cuba's foreign commerce in the 1980s. Economic reforms had enabled the country's gross domestic output to register steady growth, though it was not yet back to its 1989 level. Relations with the United States had improved, despite Helms-Burton, and the US Congress had passed legislation in 2000 that could allow more trade. A new generation of leaders, who took inspiration from the Cuban revolution, was emerging in Latin America.

But the reality was not nearly as bright as their hopes. Food production and distribution remained a serious concern. From 2001 to 2005, a series of hurricanes menaced the island. Food crops and poultry production were hit especially hard by Hurricane Dennis in July 2005. But the real problem, as economist Jorge Mario Sánchez emphasizes, was that a country with 40 percent of its arable land left idle was importing an unsustainable $1.5 billion worth of food annually, due to a "lack of incentives" and "bureaucratic restraints."[2]

The economic turnaround in the 1990s had rested on three problematic pillars: tourism, remittances, and two export commodities, nickel and sugar.[3] Leading Cuban economists had been advocating, instead, that the country needed to focus its resources on the Revolution's two major achievements, health care and education. They urged Cuba's leaders to make the country more hospitable to foreign investment, especially in knowledge-based sectors such as pharmaceuticals and computer software, which would enable Cuba to build lucrative niches in the global economy, generate surplus capital, and diversify itself for sustainable growth.[4] In 2003, services made up two-thirds of the country's GDP, which meant that Cuba increasingly depended on imports for many goods.

Recall from chapter 18 that tourism was a weak pillar, because it did not generate enough net hard currency and depended on the whims of consumers in wealthy countries. Perhaps even worse, the tourist industry reduced the incentive for young Cubans to advance their education. A taxi driver with no more than a high school education could earn a monthly salary that was roughly five times greater than a university-trained chemist. Remittances from families abroad—mostly those living in the United States—came with two problems. First, they were vulnerable to US policy changes—President Clinton had stopped their flow in 1994. Second, they already were generating inequalities, as we observed in chapter 19.

Thanks in part to investments made by Canada's Sherritt International conglomerate, Cuba was the world's sixth largest producer of nickel in 2003.[5] But the United States had set back Sherritt's plans by applying Helms-Burton Act restrictions against it. Other investors shied away because they expected the price of nickel not to rise sufficiently to warrant their investment. While China did invest $1 billion to modernize Cuba's nickel operations, it drove a tough bargain. China required that it recoup the full cost of capital investment in the mining industry before Cuba could begin sharing 50 percent of production income.

Meanwhile, sugar production had become so unprofitable that the cost to cultivate, harvest, mill, and ship the sweetener was greater than earnings from its sales. In 2002, Cuba did the unthinkable. The country that had been Sugar King announced it would close down more than half of its sugar mills and switch cane fields to other agricultural purposes. The decision came after more than a decade of declining sugar production and had been delayed largely to avoid the displacement of rural families and communities. But the state could no longer afford what had in effect become a large subsidy. Between 1989 and 2002, sugar production fell by 56 percent, Cuba's rank among sugar-producing countries declined from third to tenth place, and the world price for sugar dropped from thirteen cents to six cents per pound. Fidel said that just the first year's savings from downsizing would be $200 million.[6]

The Urgency for Reform

Cuba's fundamental economic problems were no match for the modest market reforms introduced in the 1990s that had led to the creation of paladares and other self-employed businesses. While cuentapropistas cushioned some discontent and provided wealth for a few enterprising entrepreneurs, the high taxes and elaborate licensing procedures discouraged many potential small business owners. For example, the license for a private home to operate as a guest house required the owner to pay a tax rate of 70 percent on estimated revenues, not actual income. If such a casa particular had a bad month, the owner might pay more tax than the business actually earned. Such confiscatory taxation reduced the incentive to create small businesses, or it encouraged illegal behavior in the form of not registering for a license.

In addition, cuentapropistas could employ only family members, which reduced the ability of small private businesses to generate jobs. They employed only half a million people by 2003. In addition, the government began to discourage their growth once the worst of the Special Period ended. By December 2003, the number of active licenses was down to 151,000, and ten months later, the Ministry of Labor and Social Security cut the number of self-employment categories from 158 to 118.[7]

The urgency for reform was evident beyond the economic spreadsheets. We detected a palpable discontent—a lack of hope about the future—among Cuba's youth. In part this was due to increased unemployment and underemployment, to the fatigue of listening to long speeches laden with promises that would go unfulfilled, and to a focus on individual gratification that had not been socially acceptable before the Special Period.

During a trip to Cuba by Philip Brenner at about this time, a twenty-year-old woman engaged him in a conversation as he walked along the Malecon on a windy winter day. She was dressed in a worn bomber-style leather jacket, a sweatshirt, and loose fitting jeans—not the style of a typical prostitute. In fact, what she was offering was conversation in return for some coffee and ice cream at a café for tourists. After high school, he learned, she had studied for a job in the hospitality industry and was working as a waitress, where she could earn a modest amount of hard currency. At one point Brenner asked her what she would say to President Castro if the Cuban leader gave her the chance for one wish. Without hesitation she answered, "I'd ask him for a passport to leave the country."

Corruption

Consequences of the widespread discontent were an increase in petty theft, a disregard for rules, and the appropriation of public goods for private purposes. In short, corruption became a part of daily life throughout the country.[8]

Battle of Ideas

Beginning in 2000, Fidel Castro sought to counter the population's alienation with a multifaceted effort aimed at reinvigorating revolutionary enthusiasm. Called the Battle of Ideas, the effort grew out of weekly patriotic rallies throughout the island in support of Elián González's return. Each of the "Saturday speak-outs," journalist Marc Frank reports, "was televised to the nation . . . the crowds waving little Cuban flags on sticks as they were entertained by local talent." It soon became a movement, headquartered in an office adjacent to the Cuban president's, aimed at Cuba's disaffected youth. As at the start of the Revolution, young Cubans were sent out with an idealistic mission, "to become teachers, health care providers, and social workers." Castro intended the young recruits to serve as "battering rams against creeping corruption."[*]

In 2003, an additional forum made its debut. *Mesa Redonda* ("Roundtable"), a two-hour weekly television program, often served as a propaganda platform. But it also aired open debates about controversial subjects and became a venue for serious discussions of proposed reforms. *Mesa Redonda* continues today under the banner of a state-sponsored media outlet, *CubaDebate*.

Castro viewed the Battle of Ideas as essential for Cuba's security. In 2003, he declared:

The decadent imperialist capitalist system in its phase of neoliberal globalization can no longer offer any solutions for the huge problems facing humanity. . . . That system has no future. It is destroying nature and expanding hunger. . . . In the face of political threats and aggression from abroad . . . we are profoundly studying and increasingly perfecting our concepts of the war of all the people, for we know that no technology, no matter how sophisticated, can ever defeat man. The battle of ideas, our most powerful political weapon, will not let up for a minute.[†]

---

* Marc Frank, *Havana Revelations: Between the Scenes in Havana* (Gainesville: University Press of Florida, 2013), 37, 39.

† Fidel Castro Ruz, "Speech on the Current World Crisis," Havana, March 6, 2003, http://www.cuba.cu/gobierno/discursos/2003/ing/f060303i.html.

An "informal economy" or black market—the sale or exchange of goods and services without a government license or the government's knowledge—is common in most third world countries. But it had not been common in Cuba until the Special Period. By 2000, as nearly every Cuban participated in the black market for some household necessity, the petty illegalities corroded the sense of community the Revolution had developed. Cubans looked out for their own families and immediate friends, even if that meant undermining the common good, which many believed no longer existed as they watched inequality escalate.

Privatization added to the problem. Opening a private restaurant or guest-house meant acquiring capital to renovate rooms and purchase goods. Some Cubans obtained the money from relatives abroad. Others stole resources from the government—construction materials, flour, tools, spare tires—and sold the booty on the black market. Theft became so integral to the way of life for some that it shaped how they made decisions about where to work. A study by Hope Bastion Martinez found that access to hard currency in a job was less important for some workers than the ability to pilfer goods they could sell or barter.[9]

Protest Music

In the 1990s, Cuban hip-hop music became the outlet for youth protest (see one such hip-hop group in figure 22.1). "Young, mostly black Cuban men adopted the genre," Margot Olavarria explains, "first by imitating it and eventually infusing it with their own roots and reality, transforming it into a space for self-expression." She notes that "while not all rap is politically charged," the government still censored it initially. But its widespread popularity forced official acceptance, and Cuban hip-hop artists now travel internationally and are regular participants at public music festivals. As Cuban hip-hop evolved independently of US influence, its lyrics and themes became a distinctive contrast to the American genre. Instead of promoting sexual exploitation and consumption, Cuban artists focused on the problems of daily life. The music provided a way for the generation of the 1980s and 1990s "to speak out about racism, prostitution, police harassment, growing class differences, the difficulty of daily survival, and other social problems of contemporary Cuba."[10]

Americans may know the stirring folk songs of Silvio Rodríguez and Pablo Milanés, who were leading artists in the *nueva trova* (new folk music) movement of the 1960s. Cubans in the new millennium favored more critical singers such as Carlos Varela. Many of his songs went right to the edge of what censors would allow and became wildly popular. Consider "William Tell," which recounts the famous story from the perspective of the archer's son.

Figure 22.1. Cuban hip-hop group Anónimos Consejos (Anonymous Advice), in a makeshift studio, works on an album that protests increasing racism. Photo from video, *Changing Cuba*, produced and reported by Peter Eisner for World Focus, https://www .youtube.com/watch?v=IDvENDarA3c.

Tired of holding the apple on his head, the boy runs away. William Tell cannot understand why his son would abandon him, so the singer explains: "William Tell, your son has grown up / And now he wants to shoot the arrow himself."

In short, despite the superficial appearance of a successful rebound, at the start of the millennium there was a broad consensus on the island that Cuba needed a new economic strategy, one that would engender development and enable it to maintain the Revolution's commitment to equity. But there was no successful model on which to base the desired strategy.

"William Tell" by Carlos Varela

William Tell didn't understand his son
Who one day got tired of having the apple placed on his head,
And started to run away.
His father cursed him—
How could he now prove his skill?
William Tell, your son has grown up,
And now he wants to shoot the arrow himself.
It's his turn now to show his valor with your crossbow.
Yet William Tell did not understand the challenge:
Who would ever risk having the arrow shot at them?
He became afraid when his son addressed him,
Telling William that it was now his turn
To place the apple on his own head.
William Tell, your son has grown up,
And now he wants to shoot the arrow himself.
It's his turn now to show his valor with your crossbow.
William Tell was angry at the new idea,
And refused to place the apple on his own head.
It was not that he didn't trust his son—
But what would happen if he missed?
William Tell, your son has grown up,
And now he wants to shoot the arrow himself.
It's his turn now to show his valor with your crossbow.
William Tell failed to understand his son—
Who one day got tired of having the apple placed on his head.

The model that Western advanced industrial nations advocated—the so-called Washington Consensus—had lost its credibility. Argentina, which accepted the strictures of the Washington Consensus in the early 1990s and had become its poster child, was experiencing an economic collapse at the start of the new century. Even the scholar who coined the term for the export-led privatizing model acknowledged it was a prescription only for macroeconomic growth, not equity.[11]

Other Latin American countries had reduced their poverty rates, yet the region's total number of poor people was climbing and the gaps between rich and poor were still the world's largest. China had made enormous leaps in its overall growth rate, but it had large areas where people remained ill-fed and its gains came partly from exploitative sweatshops with horrific working conditions. Vietnam's seemingly miraculous recovery had similar problems.

UNITED STATES AND EUROPE PRESSURE CUBA

Changes in Washington

Adding to Cuba's problems, it faced a Republican administration in Washington that owed its electoral victory to hardline Cuban-Americans. On November 22, 2000, the Miami-Dade County Canvassing Board stopped its hand count of 10,750 votes that machines had not recorded because a group of Cuban-Americans menacingly demonstrated outside the building where the board was meeting. A full tally likely would have provided Vice President Al Gore with a sufficient majority to win Florida's electoral votes and the presidency. The moblike rally added to other favors, such as campaign contributions, that George W. Bush needed to repay to the anti-Castro Cuban-American community.[12]

Surprisingly, the Bush administration's Cuba policy in its first year was distinguished more by continuity than change. The president continued the practice of waiving implementation of Title III of the Helms-Burton Act, which otherwise would allow US citizens to sue in US federal courts persons who "traffic in property confiscated in Cuba." In November 2001, in the wake of Hurricane Michelle's devastation of the island's crops, President Bush also relaxed some cumbersome provisions of the Trade Sanctions Reform and Export Enhancement Act of 2000 (TSRA) to facilitate the sale of food and medical supplies to Cuba.

But the president also laid the groundwork for a harsher policy by appointing longtime opponents of rapprochement throughout the executive branch.[13] For example, he named Otto Reich as assistant secretary of state for Western Hemisphere affairs, Lino Gutierrez and Daniel Fisk as Reich's deputy assistant secretaries, Roger Noriega as ambassador to the Organization of American States, Adolfo Franco as director of the Latin American bureau in the US Agency for International Development (USAID), and Emilio González as the National Security Council staffer handling Caribbean affairs, including Cuba. Members of this group had worked together for many years, always championing the most extreme policies against Cuba.

A decidedly hostile tone soon emerged in US policy pronouncements. Notably, the United States criticized Cuba over its reaction to the 9/11 terrorist attacks, ignoring the Cuban government's condemnation of the terrorism on the afternoon of September 11, 2001, and its offer of medical assistance and the use of Cuban airspace for US aircraft.[14] The Cuban government did refuse to give carte blanche to the US campaign against terrorism, arguing that the United Nations, not the United States, should direct this global effort. By October 2001 Cuba had ratified twelve UN resolutions against terrorism stemming from the September 11 attacks. It also chose to avoid a confrontation over US use of the Guantánamo Bay Naval Base as a prison camp, although US occupation of this Cuban territory had long been a source of anger for Cuba. Raúl Castro, at the time Cuba's defense minister, even offered to provide medical assistance to the detainees.

As most US foreign policymakers concentrated on Afghanistan and the Middle East after 9/11, the anti-Castro hardliners maintained their focus on Havana. In May 2002, for example, Undersecretary of State John R. Bolton attempted to undermine former president Jimmy Carter's planned visit to Cuba by falsely charging that "Cuba has at least a limited offensive biological warfare" capability and had "provided dual-use biotechnology to other rogue states."[15] When a National Intelligence Council officer challenged Bolton's claims, the undersecretary demanded he be fired. Yet the allegations were never substantiated and were not included in the State Department's annual report on global terrorism.[16]

Carter broached the issue of human rights during his visit to Cuba. In a lecture at the University of Havana—broadcast twice over Cuban radio and television and reprinted in the next day's *Granma*—he called for political reforms and praised a petition drive spearheaded by Oswaldo Payá Sardiñas, founder of the Christian Liberation Movement, to change the constitution. Called the Varela Project, the constitutional initiative demanded that the National Assembly consider amendments to permit freedom of association, expand private enterprise, and establish a new electoral system.[17]

The Varela Project collected more than 11,000 signatures between 1998 and 2002. But the National Assembly rejected the petition's demands. Instead, it accepted a counterpetition that one million Cubans signed in a drive the government organized. It called for a constitutional revision declaring Cuba's political system could not be changed merely by new laws, and that "Cuba will never return to capitalism."

Carter received a warm reception from the Cuban government despite his call for reform. A Cuban official explained at the time that the government reacted positively because Carter had made his proposals with respect, acknowledging that it was Cuba's prerogative to organize its society without external pressure or influence. In contrast, the chief US diplomat on the island, James Cason, seemed determined to antagonize the Cuban government. In 2002, he increased the number of shortwave radios the US Interests Section gave away to Cubans, saying the project would enable Cubans to gain access to information, including Radio Martí, whose shortwave broadcasts Cuba did not jam. The radios also were capable of receiving coded messages sent by covert operatives. While acknowledging that diplomats typically do not engage in subversion, Cason told *USA Today* that Cuba "is a different place."[18]

Meanwhile, USAID increased funding for "independent" journalists and libraries to produce and distribute anti-regime information. A 2001 study by the American Library Association reported that the "independent libraries" were essentially private collections held by political dissidents.[19] In March 2003, President Bush signed executive orders designed to limit official and nongovernment contacts between the countries, and he canceled semi-annual migration talks between the two countries. These involved the review of how the 1995 migration accord—under which the United States returned to Cuba exiles picked up at sea—was being implemented. At about the same time, US officials began to issue fewer visas to Cuban scholars for travel to the United States.

Commission for Assistance to a Free Cuba

The renewed hostility directed at Cuba was not sufficiently harsh to satisfy hardliners, who pressured President Bush to do more.[20] On October 10, 2003—the 135th anniversary of the start of Cuba's 1868 ten-year Independence War against Spain—he announced the creation of a Commission for Assistance to a Free Cuba (CAFC), headed by Secretary of State Colin Powell and Secretary of Housing and Urban Development Mel Martinez, a Cuban-American.

Assistant Secretary of State for Western Hemisphere Affairs Roger Noriega, the deeply ideological coauthor of the Helms-Burton bill, coordinated the commission's activities. Dan Fisk, who also had been a staffer for Senator Jesse Helms, led the working group that drew up plans aimed at "hastening Cuba's transition." Bush's charge to the commission was "to plan for the happy day when Castro's regime is no more."[21]

The CAFC's May 2004 report included delusional plans for a US occupation, from reorganizing the economy and the educational system to the holding of multiparty elections. Its essential strategy for accelerating regime change was to deny Cuba money from US visitors and to limit all forms of contact between Americans and Cubans. President Bush used the report's recommendations to tighten the embargo. His action proved particularly onerous for Cuban-Americans who had been able to travel to Cuba on grounds of family medical emergencies.

Under the new rules, "An individual can decide when they want to travel once every three years," Fisk callously told Reuters. "So if they have a dying relative they have to figure out when they want to travel."[22] In addition, only parents, grandparents, siblings, and one's own children qualified as "family"; previously, uncles and aunts had been included. The new regulations also curtailed three hundred college and university study abroad programs and educational travel sponsored by organizations such as the Smithsonian Institution and National Geographic. In 2003, an estimated 30,000 Americans had gone to Cuba on educational programs licensed under relaxed Clinton administration rules.

In 2005, after winning a second term, President Bush appointed Caleb Mc-Carry to be Cuban Transition Coordinator, in effect centralizing the effort to overthrow the Cuban government. McCarry was given an $80 million budget, though the money was largely spent inside the United States as a form of patronage to anti-Castro Cubans who created organizations with names fancifully larded with terms like "freedom" and "democracy." The Government Accountability Office harshly criticized McCarry's project, finding there was "misuse of funds" and "weaknesses in program oversight that increased the risk of grantees' improperly using grant funds and failing to comply with US laws."[23] Cuban foreign minister Felipe Pérez Roque described McCarry as the "Paul Bremer for Cuba," referring to the US consul who disastrously ruled Iraq after the 2003 invasion; activist Oswaldo Payá criticized the plan by saying, "Any transition in Cuba is for Cubans to define, lead, organize and co-ordinate."[24]

Trouble with Europe

The Bush administration's tougher sanctions and bombastic rhetoric in 2003 set off alarm bells in Havana. US officials had used similar language prior to the March invasion of Iraq, which was undertaken on the basis of manufactured evidence.[25] Cuban leaders imagined hardliners could convince President Bush that widespread criticism on the island was evidence that Cubans would be waiting for American liberators with roses and jubilation.[26]

As a result of a military that had been downsized during the Special Period, Cuban security was based on a "people's war" strategy that depended on the solidarity of the Cuban citizenry and everyone's willingness to fight. Cuba's generals worried that even a small crack in the façade of unity might invite US intervention, which made the harsh suppression of dissent necessary. This mind-set in part explains why the Cuban government arrested seventy-five prominent anti-regime critics in March 2003 and gave them unusually long prison terms—from six to twenty-eight years. Their arrests were a sharp warning aimed at discouraging further dissent.[27]

Nearly twenty of the "dissidents" turned out to be state agents who had infiltrated groups opposing the regime and obtained evidence that those charged were receiving money directly from US agencies or indirectly through organizations such as the National Endowment for Democracy. Notably, the government did not arrest Payá, who had refused to compromise his project by accepting such funds.

About a month after the arrest of the group of seventy-five, several European countries individually declared they would reevaluate their trade, economic assistance, and diplomatic contacts with Cuba as a response to the arrests and the summary execution of three ferry hijackers.[28] Two weeks later, the European Union (EU) announced it was freezing "the procedure to consider the admission of Cuba into the Africa-Pacific-Caribbean (ACP) Cotonou Agreement."[29] The EU presidency (held by Greece) followed up in June, denouncing Cuba's "deplorable actions" and demanding that Cuba release all political prisoners. These moves were a serious matter for the economy: more than 50 percent of direct foreign investment had come from EU states, 25 percent from Spain alone.

Yet Cuban leaders were willing to risk a break with Europe, because they perceived that suppressing internal dissent was more important than cultivating favorable international opinion. On June 12, 2003, Fidel led hundreds of thousands of people in a protest march past European embassies in Havana. The *New York Times* reported that "marchers carried . . . signs ridiculing Prime Minister José María Aznar of Spain and Prime Minister Silvio Berlusconi of Italy as fascists."[30] In his July 26th speech, on the fiftieth anniversary of the failed Moncada attack, the Cuban president dismissed the importance of Europe's decisions. "Cuba does not need the aid of the European Union to survive," he asserted bluntly, noting that the EU had donated only an average of about $4 million annually over the prior three years. "What does this amount really mean for a country that suffered the impact of three hurricanes between November of 2001 and October of 2002, resulting in 2.5 billion dollars in damages for our country?" He added that the loss of trade with Europe also would not be significant because in the previous five years Cuba had imported on average $1.5 billion of goods annually from Europe while exporting less than half that value in Cuban products.[31]

Ironically, the decrease in commerce with Europe was offset by increasing imports from the United States. Cuba was able to step up purchases of food and medicine produced by US companies—made legal under the 2000 TSRA—after US officials reduced the red tape involved in these transactions because of the damage caused by Hurricane Michelle in November 2001. In 2002, Cuba bought $146 million in goods from the United States, an amount that more than doubled to $340 million by 2006.[32] US food imports also came with lower shipping costs than European food. Some Cuban officials even imagined that the renewed trade might spur agrobusiness lobbyists and some members of Congress from farm districts to pressure the Bush administration to relax or end the embargo. The TSRA still required that the US Treasury Department license each sale, which had to be made without credit. Sellers also had to verify that none of the products were available to the Cuban military.

CUBA TURNS TO LATIN AMERICA AND CHINA

Despite Cuba's increased trade with the United States, 2003 marked a turning point in its foreign-policy orientation. Cuba once again concentrated its attention on third world countries to which it could relate with mutual respect, not asymmetric requirements. Cuba had built a deep well of appreciation in the third world because of its assistance programs and sustained military commitment in Angola against the apartheid South African regime. Nelson Mandela highlighted this respect during a 1991 trip to Cuba, the year after he was released from prison (see box on next page). In a speech on July 26, with Fidel Castro at his side, Mandela declared: "The Cuban people hold a special place in the hearts of the people of Africa. The Cuban internationalists have made a contribution to African independence, freedom, and justice, unparalleled for its principled and selfless character."

Third world countries acknowledged Cuba as a global leader in February 2003 by naming it as the host of the 2006 Summit of the Non-Aligned Movement (NAM), and consequently the organization's chair for the three years that followed. Havana had been the venue of a summit once before, in 1979. Only Yugoslavia, one of the four core founders of NAM, had been previously honored this way.

Two months later, Latin American countries elected Cuba to hold one of the region's six seats on the United Nations Human Rights Commission, despite Cuba's harsh sentencing of seventy-five people in March. (The General Assembly voted by region in choosing the fifty-three members of the commission, which was replaced by the UN Human Rights Council in 2006.) The vote was a clear rebuke to the United States, which had lobbied against Cuba's selection, and it left White House spokesperson Ari Fleischer spitting mad. "Having Cuba serve again on the Human Rights Commission is like putting Al Capone in charge of bank security," he said.[33]

A leftward turn in Latin American politics was one reason for Cuba's increased confidence. Hugo Chávez's election in 1998 as Venezuela's president was followed by the victories of Brazil's Luiz Inácio Lula da Silva in 2002, Argentina's Néstor Kirchner in 2003, Uruguay's Tabaré Ramón Vázquez in 2004, Ecuador's Rafael Correa in 2005, and Chile's Michelle Bachelet and Bolivia's Evo Morales in 2006.

Venezuela

Political scientist Max Azicri explains that the Cuban-Venezuelan association was held together by three interconnected ties: the personal relationship between Fidel and Chávez, the shared political goals for the hemisphere of

Nelson Mandela in Cuba, 1991

We have come here today recognizing our great debt to the Cuban people. What other country has such a history of selfless behavior as Cuba has shown for the people of Africa? How many countries benefit from Cuban health care professionals and educators? . . . How many countries threatened by imperialism or fighting for their freedom have been able to count on the support of Cuba?

I was still in prison when I first heard of the massive help which the Cuban international forces were giving to the people of Angola. The help was of such a scale that it was difficult for us to believe it, when the Angolans were under attack by the combined forces of South Africa, the FALA [Armed Forces for the Liberation of Angola] who were financed by the CIA, mercenaries, UNITA [National Union for the Total Independence of Angola], and Zaire in 1975. . . . We also acknowledge that the action was carried out by the masses in Cuba and that those who fought and died in Angola are only a small portion of those who volunteered to go. To the Cuban people internationalism is not only a word but something which they have put into practice for the benefit of large sectors of mankind. . . . The defeat of the racist army made it possible for the people of Namibia to achieve their independence. The decisive defeat of the aggressive apartheid forces destroyed the myth of the invincibility of the white oppressor. . . . Without the defeat of Cuito Cuanavale our organizations would not have been legalized. The defeat of the racist army in Cuito Cuanavale made it possible for me to be here with you today.*

Figure 22.2. During his visit to Cuba in 1991, Nelson Mandela delivers an address in Matanzas at the annual July 26 commemoration. Photo by Liborio Noval, courtesy of *Granma*.

---

* Nelson Mandela, "Speech at the Rally in Cuba," July 26, 1991, in Nelson Mandela and Fidel Castro, *How Far We Slaves Have Come!* (Atlanta: Pathfinder Press, 1991). Copyright © Pathfinder Press (1991). Reprinted by permission.

the two leaders, and the mutually beneficial exchange of goods and services between the two countries.[34] Chávez looked to Fidel Castro as his spiritual mentor and once in office turned to the Cuba leader for advice. He told Larry King in 2009 that the Cuban leader is "like a father to me, like a father, a political father."[35] Their relationship was cemented even more firmly in 2002, when Castro's advice and actions may have saved Chávez's life and presidency during an attempted coup against the Venezuelan president. The Cuban president reportedly counseled the Venezuelan by phone and then arranged for his daughter, María Gabriela Chávez, to speak via telephone on Cuban radio. She announced that her father had not resigned, contrary to reports the Venezuelan media had conveyed. International broadcasts of her message then spurred Chávez supporters to mount large demonstrations against the coup leaders.[36]

In October 2000, Venezuela began to sell oil to some South American countries and Cuba at a price that was one-third lower than the world market price. The purchases could be made with credit; the interest rate was 2 percent and the loan would be due in fifteen years. By 2001, Cuba was importing more oil from Venezuela than it had imported from the Soviet Union in 1990. Under a 2005 agreement, Venezuela sold 53,000 barrels of oil daily to Cuba at a subsidized rate of $27 per barrel. Cuba paid for the oil, in part, by sending sports trainers, teachers, and doctors to Venezuela.

More than three million Venezuelans benefited from the *Barrio Adentro Deportivo* (Sports in the Neighborhood) program, and Cuban coaches trained 68 of the 109 Venezuelan athletes at the 2008 Beijing Olympics.[37] Teachers in Cuba's Misión Robinson program contributed to the reduction of illiteracy in Venezuela, and the doctors helped Venezuela establish a medical program for the poor, Barrio Adentro (Inside the Neighborhood). Cuba sent 30,000 medical personnel to Venezuela, trained 40,000 doctors, and provided eye operations to more than 100,000 Venezuelans though *Operación Milagro* (Operation Miracle). Milagro later expanded to other countries in Latin America and by 2013 had restored the eyesight of more than two million people.[38] Cuban doctors in Venezuela also provided basic health care to impoverished populations in the Venezuelan countryside, which in turn brought praise and support for Chávez among the poorest sectors of the country.

At the start of the millennium, Cuba and Venezuela also began to implement an ambitious project, as Castro described it in October 2000, "to unite the Latin American and Caribbean nations and to struggle for a world economic order that brings more justice to all peoples."[39] What started with the sale of oil and free medical care emerged in 2004 as ALBA, the Spanish acronym for Bolivarian Alternative for the Peoples of Our America. (The name was changed in 2009 to the Bolivarian Alliance for the Peoples of Our

America.) Aimed at competing with the US-proposed Free Trade Area of the Americas, ALBA sought to economically integrate Latin American and Caribbean countries. It also created a development bank and served as a co-ordinating mechanism for development projects. Following the January 2006 inauguration of Evo Morales, Bolivia became the third country in ALBA.

China

Despite China's size, wealth, military power, and potential for domination, Cuban leaders have tended to view China differently than powerful countries that once dominated Cuba. In part, their attitude reflects the belief of Cuba's leaders that China's Latin American policy is based sincerely "on the Five Principles of Peaceful Coexistence," which mandates that "China and Latin America and the Caribbean will treat each other as equals and respect each other."[40] China scholar Adrian Hearn notes that analysts "detect genuine traces of traditional values in Chinese policymaking," particularly a Confucian "emphasis on consensual 'harmonious' development, their pursuit of 'holistic' outcomes, and their implicit advocacy of state stewardship over national and international affairs."[41]

Cuba was the first Latin American country to have diplomatic relations with the People's Republic. But China had little capacity to provide much support to Cuba until the late 1980s, just at the time when the Soviet Union and CMEA were falling apart. In the 1990s, as China searched for raw materials to fuel its fast-growing industrial complex, it began to invest in Latin America.

The Asian giant did not place Cuba very high on its initial target list. It did ship half a million bicycles to Cuba in 1992 and 1993 on credit, and in 1997, it funded and provided technical assistance for the start of a small Cuban bicycle industry. But it was not until 2001 that China provided nearly $400 million in long-term loans and credits to upgrade Cuba's telecommunication infrastructure and to enable Cuba to purchase Chinese televisions, washing machines, and air conditioners. As noted earlier, it also made a $1 billion investment in modernizing Cuba's nickel mining and production facilities. Notably, Chinese trade with Caribbean Basin and South American countries jumped from $12.6 billion in 2000 to $102.6 billion in 2007.[42]

Once the economic relationship began to grow, China sought to influence Cuba's business practices by encouraging greater reliance on privatization. Sensitive to the Cuban leadership's concern about growing inequality and the loss of control over the direction of the economy, China's advisers proposed simply a greater standardization of routine accounting procedures and the slow introduction of enterprise-to-enterprise contact so that not all interactions would occur at the state level.

But while Fidel remained in charge, the advice tended to fall on deaf ears. He generally viewed privatization and market mechanisms as fundamental threats to the Revolution's values. In a November 2005 speech to students at the University of Havana, he sarcastically referred to the reforms in the 1990s as "the 'progressive advances' of the special period," arguing that in fact they were "robbery" that engendered inequality and theft.

Pointing to the collapse of the Soviet Union, he suggested that it was caused by reforms that produced inequality, and he feared the same was happening in Cuba. "Were you aware of all these inequalities that I have been talking about?" he asked.

Did you know that there are people who earn forty or fifty times the amount one of those doctors over there in the mountains of Guatemala, part of the "Henry Reeve" Contingent [Cuban international medical brigade], earns in one month? . . . saving lives and earning five percent or ten percent of what one of those dirty little crooks earns, selling gasoline to the new rich, diverting resources from the ports . . . stealing in a five-star hotel by exchanging a bottle of rum for another of lesser quality and pocketing the dollars for which he sells the drinks.[43]

SETTING CUBA ON A NEW COURSE

On July 31, 2006, news spread quickly throughout Havana that President Castro had been rushed to the hospital. At 9:15 p.m. that evening, his chief aide, Carlos Valenciaga, reported that Fidel had undergone surgery for major intestinal bleeding and an intestinal blockage. (This would be the first in a series of emergency abdominal procedures, during which the Cuban leader reportedly almost died three times on the operating table.) As a consequence, he temporarily ceded his three positions—head of state, first secretary of Cuba's Communist Party, and commander in chief of the Revolutionary Armed Forces—to Raúl Castro. Fidel was twenty-six days shy of his eightieth birthday. His younger brother was seventy-five.

Some people cheered and danced in the streets of Miami's Little Havana. It was the moment about which many US policymakers and Cuban exiles had been dreaming. But for President George W. Bush, it was a nightmare. Anticipating chaos and a massive exodus, he warned Cubans "against leaving the island."[44]

In fact, there was no turmoil, no rush for the exit. Reality confounded critics who believed the country was held together only by Fidel's charisma or iron fist. On Havana's streets, people expressed sadness and continued on their way. Daily life in Cuba was undisturbed. The transition occurred almost seamlessly. Historian Julia Sweig noted that "Fidel's almost five decades in power came to a close last summer not with the expected bang, or even really a whimper, but in slow motion, with Fidel himself orchestrating the transition." She aptly characterized the handover as the Cuban leader's "final victory."[45] A new era had begun.

For a government to remain legitimate after the passing of its charismatic leader, it needs to substitute another form of legitimacy, that is, another basis on which the leaders can justify their right to rule. Consider that the United States had the same problem in its early years. The five presidents who followed the charismatic George Washington gained their legitimacy by their connection to the American Revolution, though that legitimacy was thinning when the son of a revolutionary leader, John Quincy Adams, became president. Political struggles over the next thirty years, and ultimately a civil war, settled the legitimacy of the national government.

In a similar way, establishing the government's legitimacy without Fidel was a primary task that confronted Raúl Castro as he accepted the reins of power. Of course, as one of the Cuban Revolution's leaders, he was able to rely on his personal bona fides as a revolutionary—as early US presidents did. In addition, he surrounded himself with officials who also participated in the Revolution. But the members of the "historical" generation that overthrew Fulgencio Batista in 1959 (los historicos) were roughly all the same age.

High on Raúl's agenda, then, was strengthening a more rational, legal, and institutional basis for authority that would be necessary to sustain the Cuban Revolution in the future.[46] At the same time, he had to institute change, to develop a model appropriate for the twenty-first century that would enable Cuba to develop its economy, maintain its commitment to providing basic needs for all Cubans equitably, sustain Cuba's high standing in Latin America and the third world, and remain independent and sovereign over its own affairs.

NOTES

1. Lázaro J. González González, "Melaza (Molasses) That Tastes Like a Movie," *On Cuba*, January 18, 2013, http://oncubamagazine.com/culture/melaza-molasses-tastes-movie.

2. Jorge Mario Sánchez-Egozcue, "Challenges of Economic Restructuring in Cuba," in *A Contemporary Cuba Reader: The Revolution under Raúl Castro*, ed. Philip Brenner et al. (Lanham, MD: Rowman & Littlefield, 2014), 134.

3. Archibald R. M. Ritter, "Cuba's Economic Reorientation," in *Cuba: In Transition? Pathways to Renewal, Long-Term Development and Global Reintegration*, ed. Mauricio Font (New York: Bildner Center, CUNY, 2006).

Chapter 22

4. Pedro Monreal, "Development as an Unfinished Affair: Cuba after the 'Great Adjustment' of the 1990s," in *A Contemporary Cuba Reader: Reinventing the Revolution*, ed. Philip Brenner et al. (Lanham, MD: Rowman & Littlefield, 2007).

5. Peter H. Kuck, "Nickel," in US Department of the Interior, US Geological Survey, *Minerals Yearbook—2003*, 52.21, http://minerals.usgs.gov/minerals/pubs/commodity/nickel/nickemyb03.pdf.

6. Philip Peters, "Cutting Losses: Cuba Downsizes Its Sugar Industry," in *A Contemporary Cuba Reader: Reinventing the Revolution*, ed. Philip Brenner et al. (Lanham, MD: Rowman & Littlefield, 2007), 135–37.

7. Philip Peters, "Cuba's Small Entrepreneurs: Down but Not Out" (Arlington, VA: Lexington Institute, September 2006), 6, 7.

8. Hope Bastion Martinez, "'Adjusting to the Adjustment': Difference, Stratification and Social Mobility in Contemporary Havana, Cuba," PhD diss. (Washington, DC: American University, 2016), 134–40.

9. Martinez, "'Adjusting to the Adjustment,'" 131–32.

10. Margot Olavarria, "Rap and Revolution: Hip-Hop Comes to Cuba," in *A Contemporary Cuba Reader: Reinventing the Revolution*, ed. Philip Brenner et al. (Lanham, MD: Rowman & Littlefield, 2007), 367.

11. John Williamson, "What Should the World Bank Think about the Washington Consensus?" *World Bank Research Observer* 15, no. 2 (2000): 251–64.

12. Dexter Filkins and Dana Canedy, "Counting the Vote: Miami-Dade County; Protest Influenced Miami-Dade's Decision to Stop Recount," *New York Times*, November 24, 2000, A41; Evan Thomas and Mark Hosenball, "Cubans at the Wheel," *Newsweek*, December 11, 2000, 40.

13. Schoultz, *That Infernal Little Cuban Republic*, 516–17; Morley and McGillion, *Unfinished Business*, 187.

14. Soraya M. Castro Mariño, "Like Sisyphus's Stone: US-Cuban Relations in the Aftermath of September 11, 2001," in *A Contemporary Cuba Reader: Reinventing the Revolution*, ed. Philip Brenner et al. (Lanham, MD: Rowman & Littlefield, 2007), 220–21.

15. David Gonzalez, "Carter and Powell Cast Doubt on Bioarms in Cuba," *New York Times*, May 14, 2002.

16. Wayne S. Smith and Anya K. Landau, "Cuba and Bioweapons: Groundless Allegations Squander US Credibility on Terrorism," *CIP Special Report*, July 12, 2002 (Washington, DC: Center for International Policy, 2002).

17. Tim Padgett, "Cuba's Catholic Dissident: The Saga of Oswaldo Payá," in *A Contemporary Cuba Reader: Reinventing the Revolution*, ed. Philip Brenner et al. (Lanham, MD: Rowman & Littlefield, 2007).

18. Bill Sternberg, "US Works for Regime Change in Cuba, Too," *USA Today*, October 23, 2002, 10A.

19. American Library Association, "Report of Visit to ACURIL XXXI and Its Host Country, Cuba, May 23–May 30, 2001," July 13, 2001, http://www.ala.org/offices/iro/iroactivities/alacubanlibrariesreport.

20. Patrick J. Haney and Walt Vanderbush, *The Cuban Embargo: The Domestic Politics of an American Foreign Policy* (Pittsburgh: University of Pittsburgh Press, 2005), 132–34, 150.

21. "President Bush Discusses Cuba Policy in Rose Garden Speech," October 10, 2003 (Washington, DC: Office of the Press Secretary, the White House).

22. Quoted in Silvia Wilhelm, "New Cuba Policy Is Cruel, Ineffective," *Progressive*, June 23, 2004.

23. US Government Accountability Office, "Foreign Assistance: US Democracy Assistance for Cuba Needs Better Management and Oversight," GAO-07-147, November 2006, http://www.gao.gov/assets/260/253560.pdf.

24. As quoted in Daniel P. Erikson, *The Cuba Wars: Fidel Castro, the United States, and the Next Revolution* (New York: Bloomsbury, 2010), 23.

25. Peter Eisner and Knut Royce, *The Italian Letter: The Forgery That Started the Iraq War* (Amazon Digital Services: Kindle Edition, 2014).

26. Wayne S. Smith, "Provocation, War Spawned Cuba Crackdown," *Baltimore Sun*, April 15, 2003.

27. Edward B. Atkeson, "Why Cuba Fired," *Washington Post*, March 13, 1996.

28. Patrick Michael Rucker, "European Nations May Downgrade Cuba Ties after Castro Crackdown," *Financial Times*, April 22, 2003.

29. Joaquín Roy, "The European Union's Perception of Cuba: From Frustration to Irritation," in *A Contemporary Cuba Reader: Reinventing the Revolution*, ed. Philip Brenner et al. (Lanham, MD: Rowman & Littlefield, 2007), 254.

30. "Huge March in Havana Protests European Criticism of Castro," *New York Times*, June 13, 2003.

31. Fidel Castro Ruz, "Speech at the Ceremony Commemorating the 50th Anniversary of the Attack on the Moncada," Santiago de Cuba, July 26, 2003, http://www.cuba.cu/Gobierno/Discursos/2003/Ing/F260703i.html.

32. US Department of Commerce, Census Bureau, "Foreign Trade: Trade in Goods with Cuba," May 16, 2016, https://www.census.gov/foreign-trade/balance/c2390.html.

33. Ari Fleischer, "Press Briefing," Office of the Press Secretary, the White House, April 29, 2003, https://georgewbush-whitehouse.archives.gov/news/releases/2003/04/20030429-3.html#2.

34. Max Azicri, "The Castro-Chávez Alliance," *Latin American Perspectives* 36, no. 1 (January 2009): 108.

35. Hugo Chávez, "Interview," *CNN Larry King Live*, September 24, 2009, http://transcripts.cnn.com/TRANSCRIPTS/0909/24/lkl.01.html.

36. Castro and Ramonet, *Fidel Castro*, 526–28.

37. Carlos A. Romero, "South-South Cooperation between Venezuela and Cuba," *Special Report on South-South Cooperation: A Challenge to the Aid System?* (Reality of Aid Network, 2010), 108, 110; http://www.realityofaid.org/wp-content/uploads/2013/02/ROA-SSDC-Special-ReportEnglish.pdf.

38. John M. Kirk, "Cuban Medical Internationalism Under Raúl Castro," in *A Contemporary Cuba Reader: Reinventing the Revolution*, ed. Philip Brenner et al. (Lanham, MD: Rowman & Littlefield, 2014), 258.

39. Fidel Castro Ruz, "Key Address to a Solemn Session of the National Assembly," Caracas, Venezuela, October 27, 2000, http://www.cuba.cu/gobierno/discursos/2000/ing/f271000i.html.

40. "China's Policy Paper on Latin America and the Caribbean," Xinhua, November 5, 2008, http://news.xinhuanet.com/english/2008-11/05/content_10308117.htm.

41. Adrian H. Hearn, "China and the Future of Cuba," in *A Contemporary Cuba Reader*, ed. Philip Brenner et al. (Lanham, MD: Rowman & Littlefield, 2014), 233.

42. David Shambaugh, "China's New Foray into Latin America," *YaleGlobal Online Magazine*, November 17, 2008, 1, http://yaleglobal.yale.edu/content/china%E2%80%99s-new-foray-latin-america.

43. Fidel Castro Ruz, "Speech Delivered at the Commemoration of the 60th Anniversary of His Admission to University of Havana," November 17, 2005, http://www.cuba.cu/gobierno/discursos/2005/ing/f171105i.html.

44. Pablo Bachelet, "US Policy Gives the Bush Administration Few Options in Cuba, Critics Say," *McClatchy Newspapers*, August 2, 2006.

45. Julia E. Sweig, "Fidel's Final Victory," *Foreign Affairs* (January/February 2007).

46. Carlos Alzugaray Treto, "Continuity and Change in Cuba at 50: The Revolution at a Crossroads," in *A Contemporary Cuba Reader*, ed. Philip Brenner et al. (Lanham, MD: Rowman & Littlefield, 2014), 42–43.

Chapter 23

The Transition from Fidel to Raúl Castro, 2006–2009

[S]ince March, an experiment has been underway in six municipalities . . . where twenty thousand liters of milk have been directly and consistently delivered by the producer to 230 rationed stores and for social consumption in these localities every day. In this fashion, we have eliminated absurd procedures through which this valuable food product traveled hundreds of miles before reaching a consumer who, quite often, lived a few hundred meters away from the livestock farm, and, with this, the product losses and fuel expenses involved. I will give you one example. . . . Currently, in Mantua, one of the western most municipalities in Pinar del Rio, 2,492 liters of milk, which meet established consumption needs, are being distributed directly to the municipality's forty rationed stores and two thousand liters of fuel are being saved every month. What was the situation until four months ago? The closest pasteurizer is located in the Sandino municipality, forty kilometers away from Mantua, the most important town in the area. Thus, in order to deliver the milk to that plant, a truck had to travel a minimum of eighty kilometers. . . . The milk that children and other consumers in Mantua receive on a regulated basis, once pasteurized at the Sandino plant, returned, shortly afterwards, on a vehicle which, as it is logical to assume, had to return to its base of operations after delivering the product. In total, it traveled 160 kilometers, a journey which, as I explained, was in fact longer.

—Raúl Castro, July 26, 2007[1]

PROFOUND DEBATE

As Raúl Castro took over the reins of leadership, Cuba was at a high point in its relations with countries in Latin America, Africa, and Asia, and at a nadir in its relations with the United States and Europe. The Cuban government had weathered a Special Period that might have destabilized most other countries, but it was clear that political and economic reforms were necessary if the Cuban Revolution was going to be sustainable. The Cuban people had demonstrated a remarkable resilience and ability to adapt, but in 2006, the new leader could not be certain how much longer they would be patient.

No One Can Afford to Spend More Than What They Have

More than 70 percent of Cuba's population—all those born after the Revolution—had known no leader other than Fidel Castro when he passed the reins of power to his brother. This presented an enormous challenge to Raúl Castro, even though he was first vice president and minister of the Revolutionary Armed Forces (FAR), had been a revolutionary commander, and served at Fidel's side for the previous forty-seven years. He was still merely the interim president, supposedly in the position only until the elder Castro recovered his health. Recognizing that his authority was tenuous, the new leader proceeded cautiously. He announced few changes and made no dramatic moves during his first eighteen months in office. Yet he began to prepare the country for what he hoped would be a reinvented Cuban revolution.

A three-part investigative report on corruption in *Juventud Rebelde*, the official newspaper of the Communist Party's youth wing, was an early signal of changes to come. Published in October 2006, the series could not have appeared without Raúl's approval. It revealed what most people already suspected. State-owned stores routinely sold products that weighed less than the amount customers had paid for; food at state restaurants had less meat or cheese than regulations required. Headlined "The Big Old Swindle" (*La vieja gran estafa*), the two reporters found in their three-month investigation that 52 percent of the centers they visited had price violations or alterations in the standard quality of products.[2] A subsequent story in February 2007 reported that the sale of counterfeit products was widespread, especially in the production of "alcoholic drinks, cigarettes and cigars, soap, perfume, deodorant, coffee, ice-cream, and bottled water." At one store in Havana, bags labeled as export-quality Cubita coffee—requiring buyers to pay with Cuban convertible currency, the CUC—were filled with old coffee and ground peas.[3]

In December 2006, the acting president encouraged university students to engage in the kind of open debate about Cuba's future that his older brother had eschewed. Drawing on his own experience, the younger Castro said, "The first principle in constructing any armed forces is the sole command. But that doesn't mean that we cannot discuss . . . that way we reach decisions, and I'm talking about big decisions."[4] He followed this admonition in July 2007, offering a frank assessment of Cuba's economic circumstances in the annual address commemorating the 1953 Moncada attack.[5]

Significantly, Raúl did not pin all of Cuba's problems on the United States. He did observe that the US embargo "has a direct influence both on the major economic decisions as well as on each Cuban's most basic needs." But he emphasized that it was one of several external factors Cuba had to take into account in "ensuring the socialist principle that each should contribute according to their capacity and receive according to their work." The main issue, he declared, was that

> No one, no individual or country, can afford to spend more than what they have. It seems elementary, but we do not always think and act in accordance with this inescapable reality. To have more, we have to begin by producing more, with a sense of rationality and efficiency, so that we may reduce imports, especially of food products—that may be grown here—whose domestic production is still a long way away from meeting the needs of the population.

Then he warned that to achieve this goal "structural and conceptual changes will have to be introduced."

Challenging the Bureaucracy

It would have been difficult to find a Cuban who did not despise the labyrinthine system of bureaucratic rules and procedures that the interim president pinpointed as a source of inefficiency and economic stagnation. As we quoted him at the beginning of this chapter, he highlighted the problem on July 26, 2007, by describing the waste entailed in shipping fresh milk forty kilometers to be pasteurized. Pasteurization, he noted, "makes sense" in "large urban centers—even though it is customary in Cuba to boil all milk at home, whether the milk is pasteurized or not." But, he added, pasteurization "does not prove viable" for a few liters in a rural area.

Members of the Communist Party and Young Communists studied that speech in detail over the next months, not as commandments to be repeated by rote, but almost as Delphic pronouncements that needed to be debated and interpreted. Journalist Marc Frank obtained the guide prepared for discussion leaders and reports that it admonished them to foster a "profound debate." This should occur, Frank quotes it saying, "in an atmosphere of complete freedom and sincerity around the central themes of the [July 26th] speech." The main topics suggested for discussion included food production, import substitution, and increasing production and efficiency.[6] But as discussions moved beyond the party into work centers, community meetings, and even some publications, a new set of issues replaced the recommended topics.

Cubans vented their anger over the dual-currency system, the resulting inequality, and their declining ability to purchase necessities with the state salaries they were earning. They also complained about longer wait times to see
a medical professional, or the lack of a family doctor's availability because
so many were serving in other countries. A large percentage of complaints
focused on onerous rules and bureaucratic red tape, which made bribes an
increasingly necessary cost in order to obtain a state service or license or to
avoid trouble from inspectors or the police.

There were still many achievements for which Cubans could be proud.
The UN's 2009 *Human Development Report* ranked Cuba at 51 out of 194
countries, just behind Argentina (49) and Uruguay (50), and ahead of Mexico
(53), Costa Rica (54), and Brazil (75).[7] In the 2004 Summer Olympics, Cuba
came in eleventh with twenty-seven medals. But the Special Period clearly
had taken an enormous toll. Increasing inequality, decreasing access to health
care and a good education, and above all a growing individualism and a
declining sense of communal solidarity had eroded distinctive aspects of the
Cuban Revolution. The wellspring of hope that nurtured Cubans' belief in
the future, which had given them the energy and strength to defy the odds in
building a new society, seemed depleted.

No wonder, then, that the founding leaders worried about the Revolution's
survival. In a 2005 speech, Fidel publicly vented his own foreboding about
the consequences of corruption. He declared, "This country can self-destruct;
this Revolution can destroy itself, but they [the United States] can never
destroy us; we can destroy ourselves, and it would be our fault."[8] For this
reason, Raúl sought to overcome the public's ennui by renewing a flame of
idealism in his July 26, 2007, speech: "We must always remember—and not
to repeat it from memory like a dogma, but rather to apply it creatively in our
work every day—what comrade Fidel affirmed on May 1, 2000. . . . Revolution is unity, it is independence, it is fighting for our dreams for justice for
Cuba and for the world, it is the foundation of our patriotism, our socialism
and our internationalism."

PRESIDENT RAÚL CASTRO

A Shared Vision of Sovereignty

Andrés Oppenheimer, a Pulitzer Prize–winning journalist for the *Miami Herald,* captured the conventional wisdom in Washington and Miami when he
wrote in 1992 that "Cuba's socialist experiment" would soon be over. Fidel
Castro, he predicted, "would be able to muddle through and stretch his final

hour for a few months, perhaps even a few years, but his socialist dream was doomed."[9] Yet Fidel managed to confound knowledgeable journalists, pundits, politicians, government analysts, and scholars who predicted his and the regime's demise.

They mistakenly assumed the Cuban Revolution was akin either to East European regimes, which fell quickly when the threat of Soviet intervention evaporated, or South American military dictatorships led by caudillos, which collapsed when the leader died or was removed. The Cuban Revolution was different. It was a genuinely popular revolution, a revolution whose aims the broad mass of Cubans supported.

Historian Antoni Kapcia discerningly summarizes the Revolution's essence as an "emphasis on the 'nation' and sovereignty, a belief in community (and especially in solidarity and social conscience) and a reawakened sense of Cuba's 'Latin American-ness.'"[10] While Cubans throughout the island believed that Raúl fully embraced these goals, they also wanted a government that helped them secure basic needs and fulfill their dreams.

The Cuban Communist Party (PCC), according to the country's constitution, "is the highest leading force [la fuerza dirigente superior] of the society and State."[11] Yet by 2008, it was languishing. Led by old men and increasingly disconnected from the travails most Cubans felt at the grassroots, it had not even managed to hold a Party Congress since 1997, though one was supposed to be held every five years. In part, its decline resulted from Fidel's efforts to energize Cubans through participation in new mass organizations disconnected from the PCC. These included the Association of Veterans of the Cuban Revolution and the revitalized Federation of University Students.

In seeking to instill revolutionary fervor among younger Cubans, as the 1961 Literacy Campaign did, and in building off the popular emotional campaigns in support of Elián González's return to Cuba, Fidel also inaugurated several projects outside of regular institutional boundaries in 2000 and 2001. The government sent tens of thousands of university students identified as "disaffected" to new schools of social work, where they were trained in a one-year course and then deployed to communities to work with the elderly, young prisoners, and the physically challenged. High school students from eastern provinces were brought to Havana to teach in elementary schools abandoned by seasoned instructors who sought to earn hard currency in tourism or abroad. As an accompaniment to new projects, the government began to air university-level classes on television—*Universidad Para Todos* (University for Everyone)—to train the "emergency teachers" and to provide new skills for laid-off workers in the downsized sugar industry.[12]

Raúl Castro

Known for his discipline, extraordinary organizational ability, and pragmatism, Raúl Castro's essential role in shaping Cuban history was long overshadowed by his larger-than-life older brother, Fidel. Born in Biran, Holguín, on June 3, 1931, Raúl Modesto Castro Ruz also was the son of Ángel Castro and Lina Ruz. Raúl attended Colegio Dolores in Santiago de Cuba and Belén Jesuit Preparatory School in Havana, and studied social sciences at the University of Havana. In 1953, he joined Socialist Youth, a wing of the Popular Socialist Party, and represented the group at a Soviet-sponsored International Conference in Vienna.

With his older brother, Fidel, Raúl then planned and engaged in the July 26, 1953, attack on the Moncada Barracks in Santiago de Cuba, for which he was sent to prison. Released in 1955, when Cuban dictator Fulgencio Batista issued a general amnesty, Raúl went to Mexico to work on plans for the guerrilla war in Cuba. He was the leader who recruited Che Guevara into the effort. In 1958, Raúl became commander of the second front in Oriente (Cuba's eastern-most province), which entailed aggregating and coordinating several disparate guerrilla groups and establishing a quasi-government that even had its own medical clinics, hospitals, and schools.

Possessing little equipment and starting only with young fighters from the July 26th Movement, Raúl built a professional military force during the first years of the revolutionary government's operation. Initially named as second commander, he became minister of the Revolutionary Armed Forces in late 1959 and held that position until 2008. Under his leadership, the Cuban military not only had an international reputation for combat effectiveness; it took on many roles, from developing the country's infrastructure to organizing a one-million-person militia. In the early 1990s, in the face of Special Period shortages, Raúl successfully managed to downsize the military by 60 percent without significant reaction. He advocated economic reforms such as the legalization of the US dollar as a currency, and developed semi–state enterprises that employed former military personnel and were largely controlled by the military.

Raúl also served as the first vice president of the Councils of State and Ministers and second secretary of the PCC from the time of its founding in 1965 until 2011, when he was elected first secretary. In 2006, he became the temporary president when Fidel took ill; the National Assembly elected him president on February 24, 2008. Reelected in 2013, he announced that he would not stand for election again when his term ends in 2018. The Seventh Congress of the PCC reelected him as first secretary in 2016 for a five-year term.

In 1959, Raúl married Vilma Espín Guillois, a July 26th Movement revolutionary who also fought in the 1956–1958 conflict. She founded and served as president of the Cuban Federation of Women until her death in 2007. They had four children.

Raúl's Preference for Organizational Order

Most of these ad hoc efforts ended after the National Assembly formally elected Raúl as the new president in February 2008. In his inauguration speech, he emphasized the importance of institutionalization and reestablishing the PCC in the role the constitution gave it, as the highest leading force of the society and state. "Fidel is Fidel, we all know it well. Fidel is irreplaceable," he declared, in effect acknowledging that this was the moment to transfer the basis of the Revolution's legitimacy from charisma to legal-rational structures. "Only the Communist Party, the certain guarantor of the Cuban nation's unity," he proclaimed, "can be the worthy heir to the confidence the people endow in their leader." In addition, he said, "Today's circumstances require a more compact and functional structure, with fewer centralized State administrative agencies and a better distribution of the functions they fulfill. This will . . . allow us to aggregate some decisive economic activities that are presently dispersed among several agencies."[13]

Perhaps because he had been so successful in building a well-functioning military organization and then succeeded in adapting it to the Special Period circumstances, or perhaps because he had worked in that organization for nearly fifty years, or maybe because his personality was so different from his brother's, Raúl honored well-defined lines of authority and sought to establish accountability for achievements and errors.

Under Fidel's leadership, the administration of policy tended to lack coherence because three power centers had overlapping authority: governmental ministries, the PCC, and the so-called *Grupo de Apoyo* (Support Group)—Fidel Castro's tight-knit, little-publicized kitchen cabinet of confidants who were in their twenties and early thirties. This not only led to duplication of efforts and poor coordination. It allowed the people in each group to avoid taking responsibility for failures—passing the blame onto those in another group. Young and inexperienced though they were, members of the Grupo de Apoyo wielded the greatest influence because of their proximity to Fidel and their personal connections when he appointed them to high posts in the PCC or ministries.

With Fidel at the hub of the three-pronged power structure, stagnation tended to accompany any policy initiative. No one felt secure in making decisions; it seemed as if every action had to wait for the comandante's approval. Even his closest allies acknowledged that Fidel could only make so many decisions that were based on well-reasoned analysis. Raúl would not run a system that he perceived was so chaotic.

Slow but Deliberate Change

Raúl's election came with widespread anticipation that he would bring about significant changes in Cuba's economy and even its politics. There was thus a nearly ear-shattering sigh of disappointment when he chose seventy-eight-year-old José Ramón Machado Ventura to be first vice president of the Council of State. A mere eight months younger than the president, Machado Ventura commanded broad respect from older and still powerful members of the PCC, many of whom opposed the introduction of market mechanisms. He shared their skepticism about Cuba's salvation via the market and his selection served to reassure party members that Raúl would take their views into account. While Raúl had the military solidly behind him, he could not assume unconditional support from the PCC. Moreover, even though the National Assembly had elected him as president, he was still only the interim head of the PCC. Fidel continued to retain the title of first secretary. (See table 23.1

Cuba's Power Structure

Formally, Cuba has a tripartite governmental structure like the United States, with executive, legislative, and judicial branches. Laid over this structure is the Cuban Communist Party (PCC), which in effect acts as a coordinating mechanism. High officials in the executive and legislative branches are also leaders in the PCC.

The National Assembly of People's Power is composed of 614 delegates elected directly from districts of roughly equal population throughout the country. It elects the president of the country, whose formal title is president of the Council of State, which is the executive committee of the Assembly. All the Council's members are elected deputies in the National Assembly, which meets twice each year. When it is not in session, the Council of State issues decrees on its behalf. There is also a president of the National Assembly.

The executive branch is headed by the Council of Ministers, which is similar to the president's cabinet in the United States, though it meets more frequently and makes formal decisions. There are twenty-two members of the Council. An additional nine members, which include President Raúl Castro, the first vice president (currently Miguel Díaz-Canel), and four other vice presidents, serve as the Executive Committee.

The PCC is nominally governed by the Party Congress, which is supposed to meet once in five years. Its most recent meeting occurred in April 2016, when nearly 1,200 delegates participated. The Party Congress elects the Central Committee (currently it has 120 members) and the first secretary of the PCC. Like his brother, Raúl Castro serves both as PCC first secretary and as president of the Councils of State and Ministers. While he announced in 2011 that he would not seek reelection as president in 2018, he was reelected as the PCC first secretary in 2016, and so will still hold some power until 2021.

Table 23.1. Cuban Government Organizational Structure

Legislative Bodies	Executive Bodies	Judicial Bodies
National Assembly 614 delegates elected directly from equally proportioned districts Assembly formally approves all laws Headed by the president of the National Assembly	**Council of Ministers** Highest administrative and executive body, which, in effect, constitutes the government of the republic Coordinates and directs execution of political, economic, cultural, scientific, social, and defense policies Members include: chief of state, vice presidents, and heads of government ministries; may include others designated by law; currently, the Council of Ministers has 33 members	**People's Supreme Court** Nominally independent Elected by and accountable to the National Assembly
Council of State 31 members Serves as executive committee of National Assembly Acts in place of the National Assembly when it is out of session Headed by president of Cuba who is the chief of state		
Provincial Assemblies Each province has its own assembly Delegates elected directly by districts Responsible for overseeing provincial administration	**Provincial Administration** Carries out provincial-level administrative functions Responsible to provincial assembly	**Appeals Courts** Seven regional courts National Assembly elects judges
Municipal Assemblies First level of political authority Oversee functioning of municipal administration One delegate elected from each district	**Municipal Administration** Carries out administrative functions at the local level Responsible to municipal assembly Expected to be given more authority in future as national government attempts to decentralize decision-making	**People's Courts** Municipal assemblies elect judges Implement decisions from Supreme Court
Popular Councils Support the municipal assembly in the exercise of its powers and facilitate better understanding and addressing the needs and interests of the inhabitants of its area of action		**District Courts** Adjudicate civil and criminal cases

Source: Chart produced by Philip Brenner and Teresa Garcia from Cuban government sources.

for an overview of how the Cuban government is organized at the national, provincial, and local levels.)

The new president waited one year to institute any major reform. Then, in a quick stroke on March 2, 2009, he dismissed Carlos Lage Dávila, secretary of the Council of Ministers and the vice president in charge of the Cuban economy, Fernando Remírez de Estenoz, head of the international committee of the Communist Party's Central Committee who had been a vice minister of foreign relations, ambassador to the United Nations, and head of Cuban Interests Section in Washington, and eight ministers, including Foreign Minister Felipe Pérez Roque.

Lage, Remírez, and Pérez Roque had been members of Fidel's Grupo de Apoyo and were generally viewed as likely leaders among the generation that would take over when the historicos retired. The three had been caught on surveillance tapes sharing information with Conrado Hernández, a man who allegedly worked for Spain's intelligence service and whom Cuban authorities had arrested in February 2009.[14] But none of the three went to prison. Remírez, for example, was relegated to working as a doctor in a local neighborhood clinic (he had been trained as a physician).

The purge was less an attempt by President Castro to put his own loyalists in place than it was to break down the competing lines of authority and establish the orderly administrative process he promised in his inaugural address. Fidel made clear he understood this rationale by justifying the dismissals in an article published in *Granma*. He wrote that the lure of power had "awakened ambitions that led them to disgrace."[15]

At the same time that Raúl removed officials, he combined four existing ministries into two: the Ministries of Foreign Trade and Investment and Food. He also promoted some younger PCC leaders whom he viewed as exemplary managers into key governmental positions. Miguel Díaz-Canel Bermúdez, who had been party chief in Holguín Province, became the new minister of higher education, though he was a civil engineer with no experience in education administration. Earlier, Raúl had returned some former party leaders who were governmental ministers to party leadership roles so that they wore two leadership hats. Ramiro Valdés Menéndez, minister of communication, for example, became a member of the Political Bureau. The president's ultimate vision was to have the party function more as a board of directors than an operational branch.

However, changes in the political structure were accompanied by only minor economic reforms. Economist Jorge Mario Sánchez aptly judged that they "pointed in the right direction but were insufficient to deal with the roots of dysfunctionality."[16] In 2007, the government began to issue licenses that allowed drivers to use private cars as taxis. In 2008, it lifted the ban on selling computers, DVD players, and cell phones and permitted Cubans to pay for services—such as hotel rooms, food in tourist hotels, or rental cars—with Cuban convertible currency. It also doled out land to individual farmers and raised the prices it paid to farmers for produce. But Cuba still had not found a way to generate enough hard currency to develop a sustainable and equitable economy. While its gross domestic product had reached $100 billion, hard currency earnings amounted to only 4 percent of the total. The country continued to spend too much on importing food that could have been grown domestically.[17]

A CHANGING INTERNATIONAL LANDSCAPE

Cuba bought a record $711 million worth of food, agricultural equipment, and medicine from the United States in 2008. Despite the embargo, the hovering giant was the island's fifth largest trading partner.[18] The hopes of some Cuban officials—that the purchases would encourage major US companies to lobby for a changed US policy—were reinforced when Americans elected Barack Obama as president in November 2008.

During the campaign, Sen. Obama said he would be willing to meet with President Castro and he promised to end the Bush administration's restrictions on travel to Cuba by Cuban Americans. The new US president also took office with little obligation to Cuban-American hardliners. His margin of victory in Florida—204,600 votes—was large enough that he virtually did not need any Cuban-American votes to win the state, though approximately 35 percent of their ballots were cast for him.[19] He also had political cover created by a flurry of proposals from several ad hoc groups made up of former US government officials and members of Congress, leading scholars, and prominent public intellectuals, several of whom had previously supported harsh measures against Cuba. They shared a view that the existing policy undermined US interests in the Western Hemisphere and that the stable succession in Cuba has "challenged the effectiveness of a half century of US economic sanctions," as a Council on Foreign Relations task force report declared.[20]

By 2009, all of the countries in the Western Hemisphere except the United States had established diplomatic relations with Cuba. In November 2008, Cuba became a full member of the Rio Group, an informal association of twenty-three regional countries that formalized itself in 2011 as the Community of Latin American and Caribbean States (CELAC in the Spanish acronym) and seemed to offer a potential challenge to the OAS as the main forum for handling hemispheric issues.

President Obama seemed aware of the changing landscape as he announced just prior to an April 2009 Summit of the Americas that he had abolished all restrictions on travel to Cuba by Cuban-Americans and he would permit them to send unlimited funds to families. But the Latin Americans' lackluster response—that his moves were little more than the fulfillment of a campaign promise—reflected Cuba's own disappointment. To be sure, there was a marked change in tone coming from Washington, as the Obama administration restarted semiannual migration talks with Cuba and increased diplomatic contacts at a slightly higher level than before. But the administration advanced no effort to chip away at the US embargo, remove Cuba from the list of state sponsors of terrorism, or close down several programs that harmed or threatened Cuba.

One project, the Cuban Medical Professional Parole (CMPP) program created in 2006, was designed to encourage Cuban doctors serving abroad to give up their citizenship and emigrate to the United States. By the end of 2015, the United States had approved more than seven thousand applications by Cuban medical personnel.[21] The CMPP was one reason a planned US-Cuban cooperative project to help Haiti after the devastating 2010 earthquake failed. Cuba was concerned that the US Agency for International Development (USAID) would use the project to recruit Cuban doctors, and USAID refused to provide assurances it would not do so.[22]

USAID was the lead agency in spending funds on covert programs that Cuba considered to be subversive. In 2009, it spent $45 million on these projects.[23] The one that created the greatest obstacle for improved relations involved Alan P. Gross, a subcontractor for Development Alternatives International. The Cuban government arrested Gross in December 2009 and asserted that his mission was "to establish illegal and covert communications systems . . . intended to destabilize the existing order."[24] The State Department claimed he was in Cuba merely to provide the small Jewish community with telecommunications equipment that would enable its members to access the Internet without Cuban government interference or surveillance. There are about 1,500 Jews in Cuba; none had requested such assistance.

In fact, what Gross provided was sophisticated satellite communications transmitters that included a subscriber identity module (SIM) card usually available only to the US military or intelligence community. The SIM card could prevent the detection of signals from the transmitters for a radius of 250 miles.[25] The communications setup Gross established would allow a Cuban enemy to communicate with its operatives inside Cuba, or allow subversive groups to communicate across the island by tapping into the equipment that Gross had given to Jewish communities in three Cuban cities.

Following Gross's arrest, the State Department ended the renewed migration talks and refused to consider offers by Cuban representatives to discuss a variety of bilateral issues. Judging that the Obama administration was unlikely to make any major move to improve relations, the Cuban government cut back its purchases of US exports to $533 million in 2009.

As US relations languished, Cuba strengthened ties with China and Russia. In 2007, China's $2.3 billion in trade with Cuba made it the island's second largest trading partner after Venezuela. (China's trade with all of Latin America was $100 billion.) During a November 2008 trip to Cuba, Chinese president Hu Jintao cleared the way for the state-owned China National Petroleum Corporation to invest $6 billion in the expansion of a Cienfuegos oil refinery, intended to produce 150,000 barrels per day, and the construction of a liquefied natural gas plant. He also agreed to continue buying Cuban sugar and nickel, and he "extended the second $70 million phase of a $350 million credit package designed to repair and renovate Cuban hospitals."[26]

On the heels of President Hu's visit, Russian president Dmitri Medvedev came to Cuba to celebrate the signing of several trade agreements involving automobiles, nickel, oil, and the sale of wheat to the island. Russia's deputy prime minister Igor Sechin had made three trips to Cuba between August and November 2008.

Brazil, Norway, Venezuela, and Spain also showed an interest in exploring Cuba's oil fields at this time. Preliminary surveys showed that Cuba had significant reserves offshore in the Cuban Mexican Gulf, ranging between 4.6 billion barrels, according to the US Geological Survey, to perhaps as much as 20 billion barrels, according to Cuban estimates.[27] But the possibility that oil would save the Cuban Revolution was, at best, many years in the future. Raúl Castro had to solve Cuba's economic and political problems immediately.

NOTES

1. Raúl Castro Ruz, "Speech at the Celebration of the Attack on Moncada," Camaguey, July 26, 2007, http://www.granma.cu/granmad/2007/07/27/nacional/artic01.html.

2. Yailin Orta Rivera y Norge Martínez Montero, "La vieja gran estafa," *Juventud Rebelde*, October 1, 2006, http://www.juventudrebelde.cu/cuba/2006-10-01/la-vieja -gran-estafa.

3. Yailin Orta Rivera, "Desenmascaran falsificación de productos en redes comerciales del país," *Juventud Rebelde*, February 25, 2007, http://www.juventudrebelde .cu/cuba/2007-02-25/desenmascaran-falsificacion-de-productos-en-redes-comercia les-del-pais.

4. Anita Snow, "Cuba's Raul Castro Signals More Openness to Debate of Divergent Ideas Than Brother Fidel," Associated Press International, December 21, 2006.

5. Raúl Castro Ruz, "Speech," July 26, 2007.

6. Marc Frank, *Cuban Revelations: Between the Scenes in Havana* (Gainesville: University Press of Florida, 2013), 73–74.

7. United Nations Development Programme, *Human Development Report 2009* (New York: 2009), 167–68.

8. Fidel Castro, "Speech Delivered at the Commemoration of the 60th Anniversary of His Admission to University of Havana," November 17, 2005.

9. Oppenheimer, *Castro's Final Hour*, 422.

10. Kapcia, *Cuba in Revolution*, 177.

11. *Constitución de la República de Cuba* (2002), http://www.cuba.cu/gobierno/cuba.htm.

12. Denise Blum, "Cuban Educational Reform during the 'Special Period': Dust, Ashes and Diamonds," in *A Contemporary Cuba Reader*, ed. Philip Brenner et al. (Lanham, MD: Rowman & Littlefield, 2014), 424–27.

13. Raúl Castro Ruz, "Speech," February 24, 2008, http://www.cuba.cu/gobierno/rauldiscursos/2008/esp/r240208e.html.

14. Erikson, *The Cuba Wars*, 319.

15. Fidel Castro Ruz, "Cambios sanos en el Consejo de Ministros," *Granma*, March 3, 2009, http://www.granma.cu/granmad/secciones/ref-fidel/art91.html.

16. Sánchez Egozcue, "Challenges of Economic Restructuring in Cuba," 129.

17. Ricardo Torres Pérez, "Concluding Reflections of the Current Reform Process in Cuba," in *No More Free Lunch: Reflections on the Cuban Economic Reform Process and Challenges for Transformation*, ed. Claes Brundenius and Ricardo Torres Pérez (Heidelberg: Springer, 2014), 225.

18. US Census Bureau, "Foreign Trade: Trade in Goods with Cuba," 2016.

19. Philip Brenner and Soraya M. Castro Mariño, "Untying the Knot: The Possibility of a Respectful Dialogue between Cuba and the United States," in *A Contemporary Cuba Reader*, ed. Philip Brenner et al. (Lanham, MD: Rowman & Littlefield, 2014), 278.

20. Charlene Barshefsky and James T. Hill, chairs, *US-Latin America Relations: A New Direction for a New Reality*, Independent Task Force Report No. 60 (New York: Council on Foreign Relations, May 2008), 72, http://www.cfr.org/mexico/us-latin-america-relations/p16279.

21. Victoria Burnett and Frances Robles, "US and Cuba at Odds Over Exodus of the Island's Doctors," *New York Times*, December 19, 2015, http://nyti.ms/1SOCpLf.

22. H. Michael Erisman, "Brain Drain Politics: The Cuban Medical Professional Parole Programme," *International Journal of Cuban Studies* 4, nos. 3/4 (Autumn/Winter 2012): 277–79, 284–85.

23. Fulton Armstrong, "Time to Clean Up US Regime-Change Programs in Cuba," *Miami Herald*, December 26, 2011.

24. Josefina Vidal Ferreiro, "Press Conference," December 5, 2012, http://www.minrex.gob.cu/en/press-conference-josefina-vidal-ferreiro-head-united-states-division-cuban-chancery-international.

25. Desmond Butler, "USAID Contractor Work in Cuba Detailed," Associated Press, February 12, 2012.

26. "China Signs Trade Deals with Cuba," BBC News, November 19, 2008, http://news.bbc.co.uk/2/hi/americas/7733811.stm.

27. "Cuba Claims Massive Oil Reserves," BBC News, October 17, 2008, http://news.bbc.co.uk/2/hi/americas/7675234.stm.

Chapter 24

Securing Cuba's Independence through Economic Change, 2010–2016

I have to take a day off a week because there is no other way to get my father to and from the specialty medical center he needs to take care of his illness. Meanwhile someone where I work has to back me up. And sometimes I have to back him up. So it is true that we have an extra radiologist under normal circumstances who theoretically we don't need. But because of other inefficiencies in the society, we do need that. I don't know what they'll do to force us to reduce the number, because it looks like we have too many radiologists for the number of patients, but we don't really.

—Radiologist at a Havana hospital, 2011[1]

The impatience for change was conspicuous everywhere after Raúl's first full year as Cuba's president. As he moved cautiously, the new president frustrated widespread initial hopes that he would make significant reforms immediately. He eschewed describing the process as "change" or "reform." Instead, Cuban officials said they were "perfecting" or "updating" the Cuban model.

"UPDATING" THE CUBAN ECONOMIC MODEL

Downsizing and Decentralization

Despite his proclaimed intention to bring about comprehensive adjustments in Cuba's economy in order to secure Cuba's independence, Raúl still had not proposed a plan to rejuvenate economic affairs by the start of 2010. And time was running out. Before he could implement any plan, the Congress of the PCC had to approve it. The Congress met every five years and the next meeting was scheduled for that very year. So he postponed the Congress and doubled down on developing a program that could gain acceptance.

The first major move came as a shock on April 4, 2010. Raúl announced a plan to reduce the size of the state's workforce by one million employees—a cut of nearly 20 percent.[2] Several problems had combined to lead to this one solution. The government was strapped for cash to pay workers. If state workers were laid off, officials reasoned, some might accept the government's offer of up to forty hectares (about one hundred acres) of free land on which they could increase domestic food production. Cuba had spent 20 percent of its hard currency imports in 2010 on food, especially rice, wheat, and animal proteins such as chicken and meat.[3]

Raúl also believed that government workers treated their jobs as sinecures—guaranteed regardless of what they did—which encouraged sloth that led to inefficiency and low productivity. "We know that the budgeted and entrepreneurial sectors have hundreds of thousands of workers in excess," he charged. "Some analysts estimate that the surplus of people in work positions exceeds one million."[4]

As one might readily guess, popular reaction to the speech was negative. Apart from the shock, the president was ignoring the reality of daily life that Cubans endured, an example of which the radiologist at the opening of this chapter described. From the radiologist's perspective, redundancy in person-

The Guarantors of National Sovereignty and Independence*

Without a sound and dynamic economy . . . it will neither be possible to improve the living standard of the population nor to preserve and improve the high levels of education and healthcare ensured to every citizen free of charge. Without an efficient and robust agriculture . . . we can't expect to sustain and raise the amount of food provided to the population, that largely depends on the import of products that can be grown in Cuba. If the people do not feel the need to work for a living because they are covered by extremely paternalistic and irrational state regulations, we will never be able to stimulate love for work or resolve the chronic lack of construction, farming and industrial workers; teachers, police agents and other indispensable trades that have steadily been disappearing. If we do not build a firm and systematic social rejection . . . of corruption, more than a few will continue to make fortunes . . . while disseminating attitudes that crash into the essence of socialism. . . . We are convinced that we need to break away from dogma and assume firmly and confidently the ongoing upgrading of our economic model in order to set the foundations of the irreversibility of Cuban socialism and its development, which we know are the guarantors of our national sovereignty and independence.

* Raúl Castro Ruz, "Speech at the Ninth Congress of the Young Communist League," April 4, 2010, http://www.cuba.cu/gobierno/rauldiscursos/2010/ing/r030410i.html.

nel was essential, because "other inefficiencies" forced everyone to spend time waiting in lines at bus stops, markets, and government offices. As a result, few people whom we encountered believed the government would enforce the announced layoffs. In fact, resistance to the plan emerged as well from within the government.

In August, the president revised his numbers. He said that the reduction would be more moderate—five hundred thousand would be dropped from the state's payroll, and much of the decrease would occur through retirement and attrition. Nevertheless, he was adamant that change had to come. "We must erase forever the notion that Cuba is the only country in the world where one can live without working," he told the National Assembly. Yet at the same time, he said, the state would not abandon people "to their fate" and "will provide the necessary support for a dignified life . . . to those who really are not able to work and are the sole support of their families."[5]

Downsizing state employment actually had been under way since 1992, because of the exigencies of the Special Period. Recall that two-thirds of the military had been retired from service in the early 1990s. In addition, the government had started to redefine the responsibilities of central state institutions in a slow process of decentralization. Some functions were transferred to provincial governments and ministries gained increased autonomy to make decisions.[6] But until 2011, the decentralization process occurred very slowly.

Privatization

The pace began to change in April 2011 when the PCC approved a major new program, "Guidelines for the Economic and Social Policies of the Party and the Revolution," known as *Lineamientos*, or Guidelines.[7] Cuban economist Juan Triana explains that the Lineamientos provided a fundamentally new orientation for the society. The "consensus that without development it will be very hard to sustain Cuban socialism," he wrote, "is a departure from the past in which socialism was the guarantor of achieving development."[8] Notably, Cuba's leaders acknowledged that development might need to place efficiency and growth ahead of values such as egalitarianism, and that this reorientation would require a greater reliance on market considerations in determining wages and even what enterprises produced.[9]

We can appreciate the importance the leaders attached to the Lineamientos in seeing the process they used to finalize them. In December 2010, the government circulated a draft document and encouraged discussions about it in work centers, mass organizations, and schools. As a result, the initial 291 guidelines became 313 when the Sixth Party Congress took up the report in April 2011. Only 32 percent of the original 291 guidelines remained unmodified. Some were combined with others, and thirty-six additional guidelines emerged from the nationwide series of meetings.[10]

The 313 Lineamientos established a process for expanding the number of permissible private (referred to as "non-state") sector enterprises. It created a commission that initially listed 181 types of jobs that could be performed legally. Within two years, the commission added more than fifty other categories. The list includes mostly service jobs, such as barber or beautician, electrician, bricklayer, plumber, photographer, waiter, truck driver, flower seller, entertainer, sports instructor, and so on.[11]

In addition, several regulations were eased. For example, paladares—the private restaurants in homes—were permitted to employ nonfamily members as workers (see a paladar in figure 24.1). The rule limiting the capacity of a paladar to twelve diners was changed at first to allow up to twenty diners. Later, the limits were scrapped completely. Bed-and-breakfast accommodations previously were confined to rooms within a dwelling occupied by the vendor. The modified regulation allows an entrepreneur to rent out a whole apartment or house—which became the most popular option for Airbnb participants when the company entered Cuba in 2015.

Previously, those applying for a license to open a private business had to wait months for approval, which was far from guaranteed. In contrast, as analyst Phil Peters notes, the first visible sign of a change as a result of the

Figure 24.1.   Paladar Liliam in Havana. Photo by Giselle Garcia Castro.

Lineamientos was the opening of a street-front office in central Havana that "posted instructions outside, assigned one staff member to answer questions and direct traffic of applicants lined up outside, and assigned four staff to taking applications. . . . Most licenses were granted within five business days."[12] The half-million mark of registered cuentapropistas was reached midway through 2015, though economist Richard Feinberg has argued that a more accurate estimate of nonstate sector employment is about 40 percent of the workforce—between 1.7 and 2.1 million people.[13]

The Guidelines themselves, and the way they were implemented in the five years after the PCC approved them, roughly indicate the nature and extent of privatization that Cuba's leaders envision for the country. The vision has the following features:

- Between 40 and 50 percent of Cuba's workers would be employed in non-state sector jobs, preferably by worker-owned cooperatives;
- The major resources of the country—nickel mines, oil fields, energy production—would continue to be owned by the state;
- The state would maintain a near exclusive monopoly to provide education, day care, and health care, though provincial and even municipal governments might gain more authority to engage in experimentation;
- Small, nonstate enterprises would provide many of the other services.

Updating Cuba's Agricultural Production

Slightly more than 75 percent of Cuba's population lived in urban areas in 2009.[14] The plan to increase food production by enticing city dwellers to rural areas with the offer of free land began that year, but there were few takers. Aside from the expectation that the work would be difficult, the incentives were low and the hurdles were high.

The program initially proposed to lease forty hectares to a family for ten years, provided it worked on the land (figure 24.2 shows a farmer's market, while figure 24.3 displays a price list). But a family's rights over improvements—such as a barn—remained unclear. Additionally, the government left in place bureaucratic mechanisms that interfered with decentralized decision-making and created obstacles that prevented the quick processing of loans and technical assistance or made it difficult for farmers to obtain essential supplies.[15] Political geographer Garrett Graddy-Lovelace reports that there was a "thirty percent rate of food loss from field to store" in 2015 because farmers often lacked "bags, bushels, crates, and boxes to transport harvested crops."[16]

Figure 24.2. A farmers' market in Havana. Photo by Philip Brenner.

In 2012 and 2013, the government partially responded to the problems by easing and clarifying some regulations, especially for cooperatives. The area of land a cooperative (but not a family or individual) could lease was increased to sixty-seven hectares (about 165 acres), and leases could extend to twenty-five years instead of ten. Cooperatives also were permitted to sell directly to hotels and other tourism entities instead of going through a state entity. Both cooperatives and individual farmers were allowed to retain the right to the structures they had built on the land.[17] Even so, cooperatives accounted for only 10 percent of land under cultivation by mid-2015.[18]

Meanwhile, through its urban and suburban farm programs, Cuba continued to promote agroecology, emphasizing a minimum use of fossil fuels and locating producers close to consumers. Suburban farmers, though, faced obstacles that are uncommon for urban farmers. Plots in the suburbs are larger, which makes maintenance solely with human labor impossible. Transporting produce to cities also is more difficult to sustain without the use of fossil fuels for trucks. To overcome these hurdles, suburban farmers have relied on

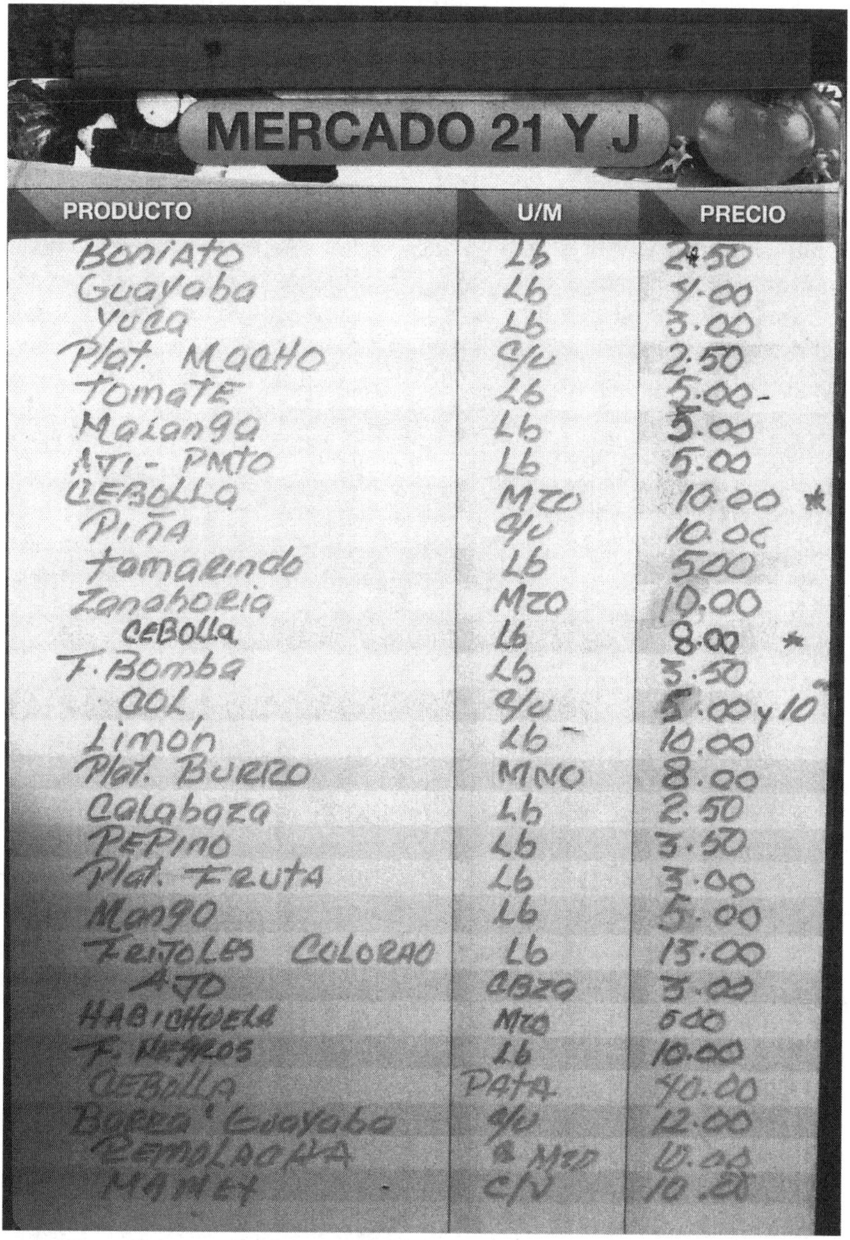

MERCADO 21 Y J		
PRODUCTO	U/M	PRECIO
Boniato	Lb	2.50
Guayaba	Lb	4.00
Yuca	Lb	3.00
Plat. Macho	c/u	2.50
Tomate	Lb	5.00 -
Malanga	Lb	5.00
Aji - Pmto	Lb	5.00
Cebolla	Mzo	10.00 *
Piña	c/u	10.00
Tamarindo	Lb	5.00
Zanahoria	Mzo	10.00
Cebolla	Lb	8.00 *
F. Bomba	Lb	5.50
Col	c/u	5.00 y 10
Limón	Lb	10.00
Plat. Burro	Mno	8.00
Calabaza	Lb	2.50
Pepino	Lb	3.50
Plat. Fruta	Lb	3.00
Mango	Lb	5.00
Frijoles Colorao	Lb	13.00
Ajo	cbza	3.00
Habichuela	Mzo	5.00
F. Negros	Lb	10.00
Cebolla	Pata	40.00
Burro Guayaba	c/u	12.00
Remolacha	Mzo	11.00
Mamey	c/u	10.20

Figure 24.3. The price list at the Mercado 21 y J indicates that staples such as sweet potatoes cost 2.5 Cuban pesos per pound (about US$0.10 per pound); black beans, US$0.40/pound; yucca, US$0.13/pound. The average worker earns about 400 pesos monthly, or about US$17 per month. Photo by Philip Brenner.

animal power—oxen teams—and the Agriculture Ministry set up collection stations to which farmers can travel by carts to deposit their produce.[19]

CONTINUING ECONOMIC PROBLEMS

Halfway through 2016, President Castro told the National Assembly and the country that the Cuban economy was suffering severe problems. Though he dismissed fears that a "collapse of our economy" was imminent, he acknowledged solemnly that it would be "imperative to reduce expenses of all kinds that are not indispensable, to promote a culture of conservation and the efficient use of resources available."[20] In fact, Reuters reported, "Cuban companies are already slashing work hours and limiting the use of air conditioning and cars in order to save energy."[21] Clearly, the reforms approved by the PCC's 2011 Congress had not updated the economy sufficiently. Much still remained to be worked out after five years.

This was essentially the assessment that the Seventh Party Congress made at the conclusion of its April 2016 meeting. It accepted a report that stated only 21 percent of the Lineamientos had been fulfilled completely.[22] Yet the Seventh Congress's principal resolution offered almost no specific plans for dealing with the problems. There had been expectations among analysts prior to the Congress that it would approve some far-reaching innovations because this was the last Congress over which Raúl would preside as the country's president. When the National Assembly reelected him in 2013, he said his current five-year term would the final one. Significantly, the Seventh Congress did reelect him as first secretary of the PCC, and that term will run until 2021.

While critics deride Raúl for making changes too slowly, there is no blueprint Cuba can follow to achieve its goals of development with equity and independence. Vietnam is sometimes cited as a model for Cuba. But the two countries differ in significant ways that make it unwise for Cuba to adopt Vietnam's practices without careful modification. Vietnam's population is nearly nine times that of Cuba's and its land area is three times larger. Even though both states are nominally communist, Vietnam's culture is closer to a collectivist nature, while Cuba's is closer to a Western individualistic one. Two major sources of economic growth for Vietnam have been the production of clothing and coffee. But Vietnam has notoriously terrible factory and farm conditions that Cubans would be unlikely to tolerate. In 2016, Vietnam was one of eight countries (out of seventy-five surveyed) that the US Labor Department cited for using child labor and forced labor in its garment factories and one of sixteen using child labor in coffee production.[23]

The absence of a worthy model to follow is one reason we cannot neatly fit all the opponents of change in Cuba into one box.[24] To be sure, there is a group we would label as *self-serving survivalists*. These are people who found ways to adapt to hardship through informal networks and illegal practices that economic reforms would disturb. Middle-level bureaucrats who try to stifle innovation, merely because "old habits die hard," also would fall into this category.[25]

Yet there are three groups of opponents who seem to be acting from well-intentioned motives. *Resolute nationalists* worry that some foreign investments could make Cuba vulnerable to the demands of another country and vitiate Cuba's sovereignty. In a similar vein, *security-oriented skeptics* view an economic opening as a way for the United States to destroy the Cuban Revolution. Even former US commerce secretary Carlos M. Gutierrez acknowledged the legitimacy of this fear in remarking that some Cubans are "wondering what the US intentions are and whether US policy is designed to help the Cuban people or whether it is something more like a Trojan horse."[26]

This concern is shared by those in a third group. *Resolute socialists* worry that unfettered integration into the global economy will require Cuba to diminish beyond recognition its commitment to equity. They also fear that too great an emphasis on the market will lead Cubans to replace values of social responsibility and communal cooperation with extreme individualism and consumerism, especially given Cuba's proximity to the United States.

The situation of nonagricultural cooperatives illustrates how these motives for opposing change may operate to slow down the process. A municipal agency is able to approve a license for a cuentapropista—individual private business—but only the Council of Ministers can authorize the operation of a nonagricultural cooperative. As of mid-2015, there were a mere 329 functioning nonagricultural cooperatives, most of which were spun off from state enterprises located in Havana.[27] At the same time, few licenses had been issued for most private professional activities—legal representation, architecture, business consulting, accounting—even though post-2011 regulations permit such professionals to form cooperatives.

In a sense, President Castro acknowledged the legitimacy of opponents' concerns by asserting, "We will continue the updating of our economic model at the pace we sovereignly determine, forging consensus and unity among Cubans in the construction of socialism." He added, sternly, that the "speed of changes will continue to be conditioned by our capacity to do things well, since this has not always been the case."[28] Raúl's general remarks about what Cuba must do to solve its economic problems actually contain three specific goals: (1) ending the dual-currency system; (2) acquiring hard currency for development; and (3) meeting energy needs with fewer imports.

Ending the Dual-Currency System

Recall from chapter 18 that the government initiated a dual-currency system during the Special Period as a way to deal with the dollars from remittances circulating in the country. The US dollar was legal tender in Cuba until 2004 when the government established that only Cuban Convertible Units (CUC) could be used as hard currency. It also established two fixed rates of exchange. The official rate used for international transactions is that one US dollar equals one CUC, which in turn equals one CUP, the Cuban peso. But domestically, the exchange rate was set at twenty-four CUP for one CUC.

One can imagine how difficult accounting becomes when an enterprise needs to relate to a foreign firm, or must calculate what to charge for products that include domestic and foreign components. The dual-currency system acts to discourage foreign investors who need to rely on a consistent monetary instrument. This is one reason economist Emily Morris concludes that ending the dual-currency system would be "a greater step towards the transformation of economic decision-making from the state planning system to the market than the much-vaunted opening of the formal non-state sector, which still only accounts for twenty-five percent of national employment."[29]

A move to a unitary system would be quite disruptive for most Cubans. Cuban leaders have been debating and negotiating how such a transition could occur and what value would be assigned to the new currency in relation to the CUC and CUP. The change would likely generate inflation and hurt those on fixed incomes, such as the elderly, and so any change would also require a revamping of Cuba's safety net and set of subsidies. Even before the 2016 economic decline, Cuban economist Pavel Vidal reported that "a high proportion of the population lives under conditions of extreme vulnerability."[30] Thus, it is understandable why Cuban leaders missed the 2016 deadline for creating a single currency—because the resulting shock and likelihood that many would suffer might have been too much for the country to weather in precarious circumstances.

Acquiring Hard Currency for Development

No one disputes that Cuba needs to increase the amount of hard currency it has available for development. But each of the three ways of obtaining hard currency—remittances, foreign direct investment (FDI), and exports—generates its own problems.

Remittances

Estimates of annual remittances to Cuba range from $1.4 to $3.4 billion. In January 2015, the Obama administration eased regulations to allow any US citizen to send an unlimited amount of money to a family member in Cuba, and up to $8,000 yearly to a nonfamily member. Remittances unquestionably help individual recipients to endure hardships. They are also a source of investment for some Cuban entrepreneurs. By one estimate, 80 percent of the recently opened large paladares had expatriate funding behind them.[31] But remittances carry the undesirable side effect of increasing inequality and promoting conspicuous consumption. In addition, the government's efforts to capture the hard currency for development—through taxes, pricing distortions, and fees—has diverted resources, generated antagonism, and produced poor results.

Foreign Direct Investment (FDI)

Foreign investors have tended to see Cuba as providing an unfriendly investment environment, even though regulations revised since 1993 grant an eight-year period with no tax payments on profits, allow a non-Cuban company to own 100 percent of an enterprise, and guarantee full protection against expropriation. But Cuba still "requires all applications for FDI to pass through a complex and nontransparent review process," economist Richard Feinberg observes, "raising obstacles not present in many other Latin American and Caribbean countries."[32] In addition, foreign companies have not been able to pay Cuban workers directly because the government collects the hard currency salaries from a company and pays its workers in Cuban pesos. For example, a Cuban who works for a foreign news bureau in Havana such as China's CCTV might nominally earn 400 CUC each month, the equivalent of about US$400. But the company pays the 400 CUC to the Cuban state, which gives only 400 CUP (Cuban pesos) to the employee—the equivalent of about US$17. Many companies then feel compelled to pay such workers additional funds under the table without notifying the government, which raises their employment costs.

These obstacles begin to explain why the extent of foreign investment has been less—and concentrated in fewer kinds of economic activity—than Cuban leaders projected. By the end of 2011, there were only 258 enterprises in which foreign entities had made investments. (Among the top fifteen countries on the list, Spain had the highest number of companies with forty-seven; Israel was fifteenth, with two.) Forty percent of these investments were in tourism, with far lesser amounts in nickel, agribusiness (mainly citrus), construction, communication, and transportation.

Consider the much-touted Special Economic Opportunity Zone of Mariel, located about twenty-eight miles west of Havana. It consists of a new world-class port that can dock the super-Panamax container ships from the enlarged Panama Canal, the Mariel Special Development Zone (ZEDM), and a new

Figure 24.4. Containers wait to be loaded on cargo ships at the Special Economic Opportunity Zone of Mariel. Photo courtesy of ZED Mariel (Special Economic Development Zone of Mariel), http://www.zedmariel.com/pages/eng/Informacion_General.php.

rail connection to Havana (see containers in the Special Economic Opportunity Zone in figure 24.4). Construction of the port facility, which cost nearly $1 billion, was a joint venture with Odebrecht, the Brazilian engineering conglomerate; the port is managed by PSA International, a Singapore firm.[33]

Cuban officials initiated the project to serve as a regional hub where large ships can transfer containers from Asia to smaller freighters for distribution along the Atlantic coasts of North and South America. Their current expectations for the port are realistically much lower than hoped-for future returns, which will be possible only when the United States lifts its embargo. More troubling is the ZEDM. Covering 180 square miles, the ZEDM's plans include housing for workers and sites on which foreign investors can build factories for goods aimed at the Cuban domestic market, as well as international destinations. The government did ease some restrictions on investments in the ZEDM so that it could almost serve as an export processing zone, an area with no tariffs. But as of mid-2016, there were fewer than ten foreign investors who had signed agreements for the ZEDM. Even Odebrecht held off until February 2016.[34]

Exports

Cuba earned 17.9 billion pesos from the export of goods and services in 2014, which was 18.8 percent of its total gross domestic product. However, goods accounted for only 4.9 billion pesos of the total. Services included the work of doctors, teachers, sports trainers, and other professionals working in other countries. As Venezuela was the largest importer of Cuba's services, the collapse of its economy in 2016 was a major reason Cuba's economy suffered.[35]

The increased number of tourists who flocked to Cuba in 2015 and 2016 partially replaced the benefits of trade with Venezuela and helped prevent a major economic disaster from occurring. More than 3.5 million tourists came to Cuba in 2015, and four million came in 2016. Yet as we have observed in previous chapters, a reliance on tourism can undermine Cuba's long-term development because the jobs do not encourage younger Cubans to advance their education.

Indeed, an important factor in holding down Cuba's export earnings is that officials do not take advantage of Cuba's greatest resource, its educated population.[36] Cubans averaged 10.57 years of education in 2010—the "highest level of any country in Latin America and the Caribbean and one of the highest in the developing world." This level of educational achievement should enable the country to make developmental leaps, Ricardo Torres argues, if it created incentives for young Cubans to gain further education in foreign languages and information technologies. He notes, though, that "Cuba's greatest employment generators are not exactly sectors distinguished by the complexity of skills required in the workforce."[37]

Teenagers see little reason for advanced education in order to obtain farm work and tourist industry service jobs. Yet apart from the pharmaceutical industry, these have been the leading sectors for foreign investment. While services abroad were Cuba's largest source of export earnings and required highly educated professionals, it was a precarious basis for earning hard currency because it depended so heavily on one country, Venezuela.

Strangely, for a country accustomed to central planning Cuba has allowed the structure of its labor force to be determined by the market. In a sharp critique of the "updating" process, Cuban economist Pedro Monreal almost pleads instead for a "comprehensive strategic development plan." The current approach "is based on a relatively limited group of export activities," he astutely observes. However, the high education level "suggests the possibility of a more diversified export profile in terms of the type of activities as well as a greater number of export firms. . . . The country's highly trained workforce is large, but significant segments are not being utilized."[38]

Meeting Energy Needs with Fewer Imports

One of the hopes for Cuban economic development is underwater, literally. As we noted in the previous chapter, Cuban geologists estimate the country has oil reserves of up to twenty billion barrels. Cuba has leased to foreign firms only one-third of the fifty-nine offshore drilling blocks it has mapped.[39] The remaining blocks are those likely to have the most oil. Some analysts surmise, according to an oil industry analyst who wishes to remain anonymous, that Cuba had not leased those blocks in order to entice US firms to lobby for changes in the embargo. But the increased availability of natural gas supplies in the United States makes that scenario unlikely in the near future.

Most of the potential fuel in Cuban territory lies in deepwater trenches off the northwestern coast. Cuba's access to the deposits is contingent on world oil prices—the expense of such deep drilling would be viable only when the price of oil rises above $125 per barrel. Crude prices spiked above that threshold briefly in 2008 and foreign investors did explore the deepwater sites episodically between 2001 and 2013. But given the glut of oil in the world market, Cuba decided in 2014 to shift "its focus away from offshore oil, concentrating on renewable energy and improving output from onshore wells."[40]

Cuba produced domestically nearly 38 percent of the oil it used in 2013.[41] Yet Cubans used 30 percent more energy in 2016 than in 2011.[42] With low

Figure 24.5. The increasing use of automobiles has led to greater gasoline consumption. Photo by Gabriela Veliz.

prices from Venezuelan oil disappearing, the cost of importing the oil that Cuba needs has risen. Hence President Castro's appeal for conservation and reducing fuel consumption.

NOTES

1. Interview with Philip Brenner, December 8, 2011.

2. Raúl Castro Ruz, "Speech at the Ninth Congress of the Young Communist League," April 4, 2010.

3. Armando Nova González, "Cuban Agriculture and the Current Process of Economic Transformation," in *A Contemporary Cuba Reader: Reinventing the Revolution*, ed. Philip Brenner et al. (Lanham, MD: Rowman & Littlefield, 2014), 154; Koont, "Cuba's Recent Embrace of Agroecology," 403.

4. Raúl Castro Ruz, "Speech at the Ninth Congress of the Young Communist League."

5. Raúl Castro Ruz, "Speech at the National Assembly," August 1, 2010, http://www.cuba.cu/gobierno/rauldiscursos/2010/esp/r010810e.html.

6. Antonio F. Romero Gómez, "Economic Transformations and Institutional Changes in Cuba," in *Cuba's Economic Change in Comparative Perspective*, ed. Richard E. Feinberg and Ted Piccone (Washington, DC: Brookings Institution Press, 2014), 32.

7. Sixth Congress of the Communist Party of Cuba, "Resolution on the Guidelines of the Economic and Social Policy of the Party and the Revolution," April 18, 2011, http://www.cuba.cu/gobierno/documentos/2011/ing/l160711i.html.

8. Juan Triana Cordoví, "Moving from Reacting to an External Shock toward Shaping a New Conception of Cuban Socialism," in *No More Free Lunch: Reflections on the Cuban Economic Reform Process and Challenges for Transformation*, ed. Claus Brundenius and Ricardo Torres Pérez (Heidelberg: Springer, 2014), 234.

9. Richard E. Feinberg, *Open for Business: Building the New Cuban Economy* (Washington, DC: Brookings Institution Press, 2016), 28–29; Romero Gómez, "Economic Transformations and Institutional Changes in Cuba," 33–34.

10. Sixth Congress of the Communist Party of Cuba, "Information about the Result of Debate on the Lineamientos," May 5, 2011, http://www.cubadebate.cu/wp-content/uploads/2011/05/tabloide_debate_lineamientos.pdf.

11. Feinberg, *Open for Business*, 140.

12. Philip Peters, "A Viewer's Guide to Cuba's Economic Reform" (Arlington, VA: Lexington Institute, 2012), 12.

13. Feinberg, *Open for Business*, 135–39.

14. Oficina Nacional de Estadística e Informació, *Anuario Estadístico de Cuba 2010*, Edición 2011, table 3.5, http://www.one.cu/aec2010.htm.

15. Nova González, "Cuban Agriculture and the Current Process of Economic Transformation," 155–56.

16. Garrett Graddy-Lovelace, "United States–Cuba Agricultural Relations and Agrarian Questions," *Journal of Agrarian Change* (2017).

17. Romero Gómez, "Economic Transformations and Institutional Changes in Cuba," 34–35.

18. Oficina Nacional de Estadística e Informació, *Anuario Estadístico de Cuba 2015: Agricultura, Ganadería, Silvicultura y Pesca*, Edición 2016, cuadro 9.1, http://www.onei.cu/aec2015/09 Agricultura Ganaderia Silvicultura Pesca.pdf.

19. Koont, "Cuba's Recent Embrace of Agroecology," 405–6.

20. Raúl Castro Ruz, "The Revolutionary Cuban People Will Again Rise to the Occasion," Speech to the Closing Session of the National Assembly, July 8, 2016, http://en.granma.cu/cuba/2016-07-13/the-revolutionary-cuban-people-will-again-rise-to-the-occasion.

21. Marc Frank, "Cuba Rationing Energy as Economy Minister Urges Spending Cuts," Reuters, July 5, 2016.

22. Seventh Congress of the Communist Party of Cuba, "Resolution on the Results of Implementing the Lineamientos," April 18, 2016, http://www.cubadebate.cu/especiales/2016/04/18/resolucion-sobre-resultados-de-la-implementacion-de-los-lineamientos-de-la-politica-economica-y-social-del-partido-y-la-revolucion-aprobados-en-el-vi-congreso-y-su-actualizacion-el-periodo-2016-2021.

23. US Department of Labor, Bureau of International Labor Affairs, Office of Child Labor, Forced Labor and Human Trafficking, *List of Goods Produced by Child Labor or Forced Labor* (September 30, 2016), https://www.dol.gov/sites/default/files/documents/ilab/reports/child-labor/findings/TVPRA_Report2016.pdf.

24. Philip Brenner and Colleen Scribner, "Spoiling the Spoilers: Evading the Legacy of Failed Attempts to Normalize US-Cuban Relations," in *Cuba-US Relations: Normalization and Its Challenges*, ed. Margaret E. Crahan and Soraya M. Castro Mariño (New York: Institute of Latin American Studies, Columbia University, 2017), 406–8.

25. Sánchez Egozcue, "Challenges of Economic Restructuring in Cuba," 134.

26. Quoted in Steven Mufson, "On Cuba, as Politics Advances, Business Leaders Wait for Their Breakthrough," *Washington Post*, February 19, 2016.

27. Feinberg, *Open for Business*, 33.

28. Castro, "The Revolutionary Cuban People Will Again Rise."

29. Emily Morris, "How Will US-Cuban Normalization Affect Economic Policy in Cuba?" in *A New Chapter in US-Cuba Relations: Social, Political, and Economic Implications*, ed. Eric Hershberg and William M. LeoGrande (New York: Palgrave Macmillan, 2016), 123.

30. Pavel Vidal Alejandro, "El shock venezolano y Cuba: Crónica de una crisis anunciada," *Cuba Posible*, July 21, 2016, https://cubaposible.com/shock-venezolano-cuba-cronica-una-crisis-anunciada.

31. Feinberg, *Open for Business*, 96.

32. Feinberg, *Open for Business*, 79.

33. Damien Cave, "Former Exit Port for a Wave of Cubans Hopes to Attract Global Shipping," *New York Times*, January 28, 2014; Eric Hershberg, "Cuban Infrastructure and Brazilian State Capitalism: The Port of Mariel," *AULA Blog*, February 20, 2014, Center for Latin American and Latino Studies, American University, https://aulablog.net/2014/02/20/cuban-infrastructure-and-brazilian-state-capitalism-the-port-of-mariel.

34. Katheryn Felipe, "A Philosophy of 'Surviving, Growing and Persevering,'" *Granma*, February 5, 2016, http://en.granma.cu/cuba/2016-02-04/a-philosophy-of -surviving-growing-and-persevering.

35. Oficina Nacional de Estadística e Informació, *Anuario Estadístico de Cuba 2014*, Edición 2015, tables 5.2, 8.3, 8.4, http://www.one.cu/aec2014.htm; William M. LeoGrande, "Venezuelan Contagion Hits Cuba's Economy, Putting Reforms in Jeopardy," *World Politics Review*, August 1, 2016, http://www.worldpoliticsreview.com/ar ticles/19522/venezuelan-contagion-hits-cuba-s-economy-putting-reforms-in-jeopardy.

36. Romero Gómez, "Economic Transformations and Institutional Changes in Cuba," 33.

37. Ricardo Torres Pérez, "Concluding Reflections of the Current Reform Process in Cuba," in *No More Free Lunch: Reflections on the Cuban Economic Reform Process and Challenges for Transformation*, ed. Claus Brundenius and Ricardo Torres Pérez (Heidelberg: Springer, 2014), 223–24.

38. Pedro Monreal González, "Without Sugarcane There Is No Country: What Should We Do Now?" in *No More Free Lunch: Reflections on the Cuban Economic Reform Process and Challenges for Transformation*, ed. Claus Brundenius and Ricardo Torres Pérez (Heidelberg: Springer, 2014), 238–39.

39. Sarah Stephens, "As Cuba Plans to Drill in the Gulf of Mexico, US Policy Poses Needless Risks to Our National Interest" (Washington, DC: Center for Democracy in the Americas, 2011), 17.

40. Marc Frank, "After Offshore Oil Failure, Cuba Shifts Energy Focus," Reuters, August 11, 2014.

41. *Anuario Estadístico de Cuba 2014*, tables 10.4 and 10.7.

42. Frank, "Cuba Rationing Energy as Economy Minister Urges Spending Cuts."

Chapter 25

Securing Cuba's Independence through Foreign Policy, 2010–2016

The waiting room at Cuba's largest eye hospital, Pando Ferrer, is packed with patients. Many come from across Latin America and the Caribbean, with everything paid for by the Cuban government. Basil Ward is from Barbados and is in Havana to have a cataract removed for free. "I could have had the operation in Barbados but I would have had to wait a year, there's a huge waiting list there," he says. Others do not even have that choice; health facilities are almost non-existent or unaffordable in many of the poorest parts of the region. Mr. Ward is here under a program called Operación Milagro or Operation Miracle. . . . The Cubans have turned mass production eye operations into a fine art. Pando Ferrer Hospital alone can perform three hundred operations a day. Treatments range from cataracts and glaucoma to corneal transplants. . . . There are similar facilities throughout the island as well as dozens of eye surgery centres which the Cubans have opened across the Americas and parts of Africa. Operation Miracle is just one part of an extensive international medical assistance program, which some have dubbed Cuba's "medical diplomacy."

—Michael Voss[1]

As anticipated, once Raúl Castro officially became president Cuba's foreign policy did not depart much from the internationalist path it had taken under Fidel. After all, the new leader had been vice president and minister of the armed forces for more than forty years and was a partner with his brother in establishing the path. Cuba continued to manifest a mix of pragmatic calculations aimed at securing Cuba's independence with altruistic elements intended to assist and strengthen the world's underdogs. Despite this continuity, there were changes occasioned by new opportunities and challenges in the period from 2010 to 2016.

AN OUTSIZED ROLE IN LATIN AMERICA

Even without Fidel as its leader, Cuba continued to play a role in Latin American affairs that was out of proportion to its size. But leadership changes in Brazil, Argentina, and Peru, along with severe economic problems in Venezuela and Brazil, undermined the bases for political and economic relations that Cuba had developed at the start of the period.

Latin America itself had undergone a significant transformation during the two decades prior to 2010. Yet US policy was still rooted in a century-old hegemonic presumption, a belief in a "special relationship" of domination.[2] The United States was the largest trading partner outside the region for most Latin American countries in the early 1990s. But by 2010, their largest trading partners outside the region were China and Japan.

In addition, nearly every Latin American country experienced meaningful economic growth between 1990 and 2010. Brazil's GDP grew by more than forty percent, and it moved from eleventh to seventh place in the world's ranking. Notably, Brazil's growth was inclusive, bringing many more people into the middle class than ever before. Along with Latin America's reduction in inequality and poverty, a growing middle class was a region-wide phenomenon. These changes did not result from the "magic" of the free market or reduced government spending as preached by Washington. Well-planned government programs, such as the Bolsa Familia subsidy in Brazil, brought about the improvements. In short, at a moment when Latin America was feeling stronger and more confident than ever, countries in the hemisphere no longer feared defying the United States by working closely with Cuba.[3]

Recall from chapter 22, that in 2004 Cuba and Venezuela had started an ambitious project—ALBA—to integrate the economies of South America and the Caribbean. With the price of oil still high in 2010, Venezuela was using subsidized sales and loans to purchase influence and goodwill that spilled over to Cuba. ALBA's program also appealed to a new group of leaders in the region who had grown up admiring the Cuban Revolution.

Traditionally, the Organization of American States (OAS) had been Washington's preferred instrument for hemispheric cooperation. But recent US administrations had done little to buttress the OAS's relevance, which created a vacuum that Latin American countries filled themselves with several new regional institutions. The one with the greatest potential is the Community of Latin American and Caribbean Countries (CELAC), whose members include every country in the Western Hemisphere except the United States and Canada.

CELAC was formed in 2010 by the Rio Group, an organization founded in 1985 to provide third-party mediation for the US-sponsored contra war against Nicaragua. In 2008, the Rio Group reached out to make Cuba a full member of the organization. By the next year, the Rio Group had expanded to include all the countries in South America, and it provided a semiformal forum to discuss regional issues. Just prior to the group's 2013 summit, the European Union announced that CELAC, not the OAS, would be its counterpart organization for biregional negotiations, which increased CELAC's importance. The 2013 summit meeting was held in Havana because the members had chosen Cuba to co-chair the organization for that year. Their choice was meant as a not-too-subtle message to Washington, which had prevented Cuba from participating in a 2012 OAS-led hemispheric summit.

Also meeting in Havana were peace negotiators from the Colombian government and the Revolutionary Armed Forces of Colombia (FARC), the main insurgent group in that country. The negotiations began in mid-November 2012. This was not the first time Cuba had tried to help settle a major conflict by serving as a mediator. Donna Rich identified seven instances during the Cold War when Cuba played this role.[4]

The often bitter four years of talks between the Colombian government and FARC concluded with an accord that the Colombian Congress ratified on November 30, 2016. (After Colombians in a national vote rejected the initial agreement signed in June 2016, negotiators returned to Havana and hammered out final changes.) An estimated 260,000 Colombians had been killed during the fifty-year civil war, and seven million were displaced.[5] A non-Cuban observer close to the negotiations told us in April 2016 that the Cuban mediators had been essential in bringing closure to the last difficult rounds of deliberation. "There would have been no agreement had it not been for Cuba's efforts," he said.

Colombia had perhaps the closest relationship to the United States of any country in South America. It was the third largest recipient of US economic and military aid in the world—an average of more than $700 million per year for over two decades. Thus, Colombian president Juan Manuel Santos's stark ultimatum at the end of the 2012 Summit of the Americas shocked US officials. Speaking on behalf of the other heads of state, he declared that none would attend the summit planned for 2015 unless Cuba were permitted to participate.[6]

Shortly afterward, President Obama fired his national security adviser for Latin America. He then agreed to negotiations between Cuba and the United States that led to the restoration of diplomatic relations on December 17, 2014.

A DRAMATIC BREAKTHROUGH WITH THE UNITED STATES

Limited Changes in US Policy

Improved relations with Cuba and Latin America were not high on President Obama's agenda during his first term. He faced a deep recession at home, conflicts in Afghanistan and Iraq that he promised to end, and a health care initiative that he wanted Congress to approve. With respect to Cuba, he had gone beyond his 2008 campaign promise. In 2009, he removed all restrictions on remittances sent by Cuban-Americans in addition to reversing President Bush's restrictive travel policy for Cuban-Americans.

Cuban-Americans Increase Parcel Deliveries after Restrictions End

Brisk charter traffic between the two countries quickly ensued after President Barack Obama ended restrictions on Cuban-American travel and remittances. Nearly every flight leaving for Cuba was accompanied by a second plane just to carry the cargo Cuban-Americans were bringing with them. The Cuban diaspora in the United States was emerging as a new force that favored a pragmatic policy to end the hostile relationship.

Figure 25.1.   Cuban-Americans wait for their parcels at José Martí Airport in Havana. Photo by Philip Brenner.

Even so, in 2011 President Obama increased the level of remittances all US citizens could send to Cuba and he eased some restrictions on educational travel. While he had suspended the semiannual migration talks after the Cuban government arrested USAID subcontractor Alan Gross in December 2009, US and Cuban officials did meet under the radar to discuss several issues. These included monthly meetings to maintain peace and order at the Guantánamo Naval Base fence line and regular cooperation between the Cuban and US coast guards and drug enforcement agencies. In 2011, US and Cuban officials also participated in multilateral talks on responses to oil spills that might result from drilling in the Caribbean, Gulf of Mexico, and Florida Straits.[7] One objective was to establish procedures for the Federal Emergency Management Agency to transfer supplies and technology to Cuba via other countries in the event of a drilling accident. The US embargo forbids a direct transfer, even though much of the oil gushing from Cuba's deep-sea wells would wash up on Florida beaches if there were a malfunction.

But these actions were so limited that they had little chance of developing the trust necessary to overcome the distrust generated by fifty years of hostility. President Obama also tied his own hands by framing Cuba policy in terms of reciprocity, which conditioned US initiatives on changes Cuba made instead of on the basis of US interests, as President Clinton had framed US policy. The Obama administration followed the Bush administration's approach, and like his predecessor, President Obama tended to disparage the significance of Cuba's reforms.[8] In the absence of a determined executive branch policy on Cuba, the US Congress filled the vacuum to thwart any reduction in tension. Ileana Ros-Lehtinen, a Florida Republican who became chair of the House Foreign Affairs Committee in 2011 (and was the ranking minority member of the committee in 2009 and 2010) dominated Cuba policy in the House. Robert Menendez, a New Jersey Democrat who chaired the Western Hemisphere subcommittee, controlled policy in the Senate. Both were Cuban-Americans who had made opposition to improved relations their first priority and both were repeatedly successful in browbeating State Department officials and White House political operatives.

Raúl responded to US policy at the end of 2011 by once again affirming Cuba's determination to maintain its independence. Speaking to the National Assembly, he declared that President Obama "seems not to understand that Cuba made enormous and prolonged sacrifices to win its independence in the nineteenth century and to defend its freedom." He added that US "attempts to convert a handful of mercenaries into a destabilizing opposition . . . does not produce sleepless nights for a revolutionary people like ours."[9]

Alan Gross's continuing imprisonment impeded efforts to improve relations because Obama administration officials said they would not engage in any negotiations until Cuba released him. Yet they also would not acknowledge the seeming subversive purpose of his mission, which we elaborated in chapter 23. This position left them vulnerable to conservative charges that Cuba was holding Gross as a hostage in order to exchange him for the Cuban Five.

A New Resolve in Obama's Second Term

Several events and circumstances in 2013 offered renewed expectations for improved relations. A new Cuban law enabled most citizens to obtain passports, to leave the country for up to two years without an exit permit, and to return without forfeiting their property. The United States had highlighted Cuba's travel restrictions in attacking its human rights record.[10] In May, with the concurrence of the Justice Department, a federal judge permitted René González, one of the Cuban Five, to stay in Cuba permanently after he was allowed to travel there to attend memorial services for his father. He had been released on parole in 2011 after 13 years in prison but forced to serve out his parole in the United States. Then in November, speaking at a Miami fundraiser, President Obama hinted at big changes. "Keep in mind that when Castro came to power, I was just born," he said. "So the notion that the same policies that we put in place in 1961 would somehow still be as effective as they are today . . . doesn't make sense."[11]

On December 17, 2014, Presidents Castro and Obama revealed what had been in the works for the previous eighteen months. Very much behind the scenes, in supersecret negotiations unknown even to Secretary of State John Kerry, two senior National Security Council staff members had been meeting with Cuban representatives.[12] In statements delivered simultaneously from Havana and Washington, the two presidents declared that their countries would resume diplomatic relations.

President Castro also announced Cuba had released Gross on humanitarian grounds and would also release fifty-three political prisoners. President Obama said that he had commuted the sentences of the three remaining members of the Cuban Five still in prison and returned them to Cuba. Cuba did the same for a CIA agent arrested in the 1990s. President Obama also indicated he would consider removing Cuba from the US list of state sponsors of terrorism. (He did so in May 2015.)

In April 2015, Raúl attended the OAS-sponsored Summit of the Americas in Panama, where he had a private meeting with Obama (see the two presidents together in figure 25.2). It was the first time Cuba had participated in this conference, the series of which began in 1994. In July and August, respectively, Cuba and the United States raised their own flags

Figure 25.2. Presidents Raúl Castro and Barack Obama meet at the Summit of the Americas in April 2015. Official White House Photo by Amanda Lucidon.

over their former embassy buildings that had served, formally, as "interests sections" of the Swiss Embassy.

While the restoration of diplomatic relations was a historic step for both countries, it was not the same as restoring normal relations between them. In fact, Cuba and the United States could not restore a normal relationship because one never existed, as we have elaborated throughout this book. Not when Cuba was a Spanish colony; not during the 1898 to 1903 US occupation; not during the 1903 to 1933 period when the Platt Amendment was in force; not during the Good Neighbor period; not during the Batista years; and certainly not during the period of hostility after 1959. Cuba and the United States needed to draw a new map if they were going to travel the road from normal diplomatic relations to normal relations, which is what they began to do in 2015 and 2016.

Making Headway and Building Trust

Headway was made on several matters, such as direct postal service and flights by regularly scheduled airlines, which began in the fall of 2016. Some key issues that were still under discussion at the end of President Obama's second term included migration, the Cuban Adjustment Act, and property claims by citizens of both countries. Issues that Cuba wanted to consider but US negotiators would not discuss were the US occupation of the naval base at Guantánamo Bay, the US embargo, and US activities that Cuba considers subversive, such as so-called democracy promotion programs. The resolution of differences on these issues unquestionably would contribute to the development of a normal relationship. Yet the essential element needed to achieve normalcy is trust.

Policymakers in both countries were discovering that building trust was more difficult than they imagined, because of the long legacy of distrust between Cuba and the United States. Consider that even as many Cubans celebrated the December 17 announcements on diplomatic relations, former president Fidel Castro waited more than five weeks to issue a comment. In a letter to the Cuban Federation of University Students in January 2015 he wrote, "I do not trust the policy of the United States, nor have I exchanged a word with them, but this is not, in any way, a rejection of a peaceful solution to conflicts."[13] Similarly, Fidel was critical of President Obama's lack of empathy about the history of Cuban deaths caused by US actions when the US president visited Cuba in March 2016. He wrote in *Granma*,

> Obama made a speech in which he uses the most sweetened words to express: "It is time, now, to forget the past. . . ." I suppose all of us were at risk of a heart attack upon hearing these words from the President of the United States. After a ruthless blockade that has lasted almost 60 years, and what about those who have died in the mercenary attacks on Cuban ships and ports, an airliner full of passengers blown up in midair, mercenary invasions, multiple acts of violence and coercion?[14]

Both Cuban and US officials have often described their frustrations in dealing with the other country's representatives. In part, this reflects circumstances where the United States is determined to bend Cuba to its will—to make it behave like a small country in the US sphere of influence—and Cuba displays an even greater determination not to bend. This kind of confrontation shaped the relationship during the Cold War and continued to infuse relations after the Cold War, even as the two countries negotiated the opening of embassies in January 2015. For example, when US Assistant Secretary of State for Western Hemisphere Affairs Roberta S. Jacobson said at a press conference that "we pressed the Cuban government for improved human rights conditions," Josefina Vidal Ferreiro, Cuba's lead negotiator, responded sharply, "Cuba has never responded to pressure."[15]

As the United States and Cuba move haltingly toward a normal relationship, their empathetic skills will need finer tuning. Greater empathy will require US policymakers to discard their traditional arrogance, a result of both US invulnerability and the ideology of American exceptionalism. Cuban officials will need to overcome a tendency to be hypervigilant, which in part has been a reaction to Cuba's vulnerability and the result of a national security ideology that its vulnerability engendered.

SOFT POWER

The notion of "soft power" itself is ancient. But it has become associated with political scientist Joseph Nye, who coined the term in 1990 and has since elaborated the concept. "Hard power" involves coercion. "Soft power," Nye explains, is "the ability to affect others through the co-optive means of framing the agenda, persuading, and eliciting positive attraction in order to obtain preferred outcomes."[16] Cuba's medical internationalism is one aspect of what observers describe as its "soft power." By the end of 2016, Cuba still had more than forty thousand health workers spread out over sixty-eight countries. Its commitment in 2011 was greater than the total number of medical personnel from all the G-8 countries combined.[17]

Even President Obama acknowledged that Cuba's soft power might be the kind of influence the United States should deploy in the hemisphere. Addressing the 2009 Summit of the Americas, he noted that when Latin American leaders spoke about Cuba, they "talked very specifically about the thousands of doctors from Cuba . . . upon which many of these countries heavily depend. And it's a reminder for us in the United States that if our only interaction with many of these countries is drug interdiction . . . then we may not be developing the connections that can, over time, increase our influence."[18]

If we look back at Cuba's foreign policy in only this century, we see repeated examples of how Cuba has used the resources Nye identifies. In addition to medical internationalism, it has made itself a center for regional culture events with an arts festival (Havana Biennial) and annual jazz and film festivals. Sandra Levinson notes that the "Havana Biennial has become a major showcase for 'Third World' art, an incredible accomplishment and commitment given Cuba's financial constraints."[19] Latin Americans accord the annual writing prizes from Casa de las Americas the level of prestige that the Pulitzer Prize has in the United States. Cuban music, films, and art—and, of course, Che Guevara T-shirts—are popular throughout the world. The global appreciation for Cuban culture took off during the Special Period when the government permitted artists and musicians to earn money abroad because it could no longer afford to support them. The Internet subsequently gave them the possibility of getting worldwide exposure.

In the regional organizations with which it engages, Cuba focuses on goals it has long advocated, such as the alleviation of poverty, which also provide a basis for countries to work together. As Michael Erisman observes, ALBA and CELAC are rooted in a common framework about development and independence. "Both view integration in more than simply economic terms, seeking also to promote political, social, economic, and cultural unity as well as sustainable development," he explains.[20]

At CELAC's January 2016 summit, the heads of state approved a twenty-eight item "Action Plan." Note how closely the first five subjects correspond to priorities that Fidel and Raúl have articulated as central to the promotion of development with equity: food security and the eradication of hunger and poverty; family farming; prevention and fight against corruption; promoting equity, equality, and the empowerment of women; and elimination of racial and ethnic discrimination against people of African descent.[21] At a time when Venezuela can no longer entice support for such an emphasis with the promise of cheap oil, it does appear that the attractiveness of the ideas and values that Cuba espouses has enabled it to shape CELAC's agenda.

Small states historically have sought to use international organizations as a means of enhancing their power vis-à-vis a large powerful neighbor.[22] "Cuba's diplomatic successes in recent years are almost wholly attributable to the island's soft power," Julia Sweig and Michael Bustamante observe.[23] Certainly Cuba's most notable success vis-à-vis the United States was gaining participation in the 2015 Summit of the Americas. In effect, the political support Latin American countries gave to Cuba was enough to counter the hard power—military strength and financial levers—the United States traditionally used in dominating the hemisphere. It was an instance of what political scientist Tom Long terms "collective foreign policy," where a small country can influence a larger one as a result of its "ability to win international allies and to work with other small and medium states."[24]

Cuba's pursuit of soft power provides an example of the kind of balancing act it has had to perform in recent years. John Kirk points out that the Lineamientos stress "the need to seek financial self-sufficiency while also repeating Cuba's ongoing internationalist solidarity."[25] As a result, while Cuba expanded its medical internationalism program, it raised the cost for countries that could afford to pay for services. It was able to use those earnings, then, to increase the number of personnel in poor countries such as Botswana where it is not compensated.

Raúl has relied on soft power to enhance Cuba's ability to defend its sovereignty. While he has introduced some changes in the financing of international projects, he has not abandoned the genuine humanitarianism that has been an integral component of Cuba's internationalism and that has made Cuba so attractive to other third world countries.

NOTES

1. Michael Voss, "Cuba Pushes Its 'Medical Diplomacy,'" BBC News, May 20, 2009, http://news.bbc.co.uk/go/pr/fr/-/2/hi/americas/8059287.stm.

2. The phrase and concept is from Abraham F. Lowenthal, "The United States and Latin America: Ending the Hegemonic Presumption," *Foreign Affairs* 55, no. 1 (October 1976).

3. Philip Brenner, "The Implications of Political and Socio-Economic Changes in Latin America," in *Political and Socio-Economic Change: Revolutions and Their Implications for the US Military*, ed. John R. Deni (Carlisle, PA: US Army War College Press, 2014), 46–50.

4. Donna Rich, "Cuba's Role as Mediator in International Conflicts: Formal and Informal Initiatives," in *Cuban Foreign Policy Confronts a New International Order*, ed. H. Michael Erisman and John M. Kirk (Boulder, CO: Lynne Rienner, 1991).

5. Virginia Bouvier, "Q&A: Colombia Cease-Fire Accord Marks Historic Turn," United States Institute for Peace, June 24, 2016, http://www.usip.org/publications/2016/06/24/qa-colombia-cease-fire-accord-marks-historic-turn.

6. Brian Ellsworth, "Despite Obama Charm, Americas Summit Boosts US Isolation," Reuters, April 16, 2012, http://www.reuters.com/article/us-americas-summit-obama-idUSBRE83F0UD20120416.

7. LeoGrande and Kornbluh, *Back Channel to Cuba*, 387–94.

8. Pascal Fletcher, "Obama Wants 'Real Change' in Cuba before Normal Ties," Reuters, May 13, 2011, http://www.reuters.com/article/us-usa-cuba-obama-idUSTRE74C3P820110513.

9. Raúl Castro Ruz, "Speech at the National Assembly of People's Power," December 23, 2011, *Granma*, December 26, 2011.

10. US Department of State, Country Reports on Human Rights Practices for 2012, Cuba, April 19, 2013, http://www.state.gov/j/drl/rls/hrrpt/humanrightsreport/index.htm?year=2012&dlid=204441.

11. Barack Obama, "Remarks by the President at a DSCC Fundraising Reception," November 8, 2013, https://www.whitehouse.gov/the-press-office/2013/11/08/remarks-president-dscc-fundraising-reception-0.

12. LeoGrande and Kornbluh, *Back Channel to Cuba*, chapter 10.

13. Fidel Castro Ruz, "Para mis compañeros de la Federación Estudiantil Universitaria," *Granma*, January 26, 2015, authors' translation. The Spanish version reads: "No confío en la política de Estados Unidos," which could be translated as "I do not trust US *politics*."

14. Fidel Castro Ruz, "Brother Obama," *Granma*, March 28, 2016, http://en.granma.cu/cuba/2016-03-28/brother-obama.

15. Bradley Klapper and Michael Weissenstein, "US, Cuba Move toward Embassies, Disagree on Human Rights," Associated Press, January 23, 2015.

16. Joseph S. Nye Jr., "Soft Power," *Foreign Policy*, no. 80 (Autumn 1990); Joseph S. Nye Jr., *The Future of Power: Its Changing Nature and Use in the Twenty-First Century* (New York: PublicAffairs, 2011), 20–21.

17. John M. Kirk, "Cuban Medical Internationalism under Raúl Castro," in *A Contemporary Cuba Reader*, ed. Philip Brenner et al. (Lanham, MD: Rowman & Littlefield 2014), 251.

18. Barack Obama, "Press Conference by the President in Trinidad and Tobago," April 19, 2009, https://www.whitehouse.gov/the-press-office/press-conference-presi dent-trinidad-and-tobago-4192009.

19. Sandra Levinson, "Nationhood and Identity in Contemporary Cuban Art," in *A Contemporary Cuba Reader*, ed. Philip Brenner et al. (Lanham, MD: Rowman & Littlefield, 2014), 340.

20. H. Michael Erisman, "Raúlista Foreign Policy: A Macroperspective," in *A Contemporary Cuba Reader*, ed. Philip Brenner et al. (Lanham, MD: Rowman & Littlefield, 2014).

21. Community of Latin American and Caribbean States, "2016 CELAC AC-TION PLAN," January 27, 2016, http://www.itamaraty.gov.br/images/ed_integracao/ IV_CELAC_SUMMIT_2016ActionPlan_ENG.pdf.

22. Tom Long, *Latin America Confronts the United States: Asymmetry and Influence* (New York: Cambridge University Press, 2015), 12–18; William M. LeoGrande, "The Danger of Dependence: Cuba's Foreign Policy After Chavez," *World Politics Review*, April 2, 2013, http://www.worldpoliticsreview.com/articles/12840/the-dan ger-of-dependence-cubas-foreign-policy-after-chavez.

23. Michael J. Bustamante and Julia E. Sweig, "Cuban Public Diplomacy," in *A Contemporary Cuba Reader*, ed. Philip Brenner et al. (Lanham, MD: Rowman & Littlefield, 2014), 268.

24. Long, *Latin America Confronts the United States*, 224.

25. Kirk, "Cuban Medical Internationalism under Raúl Castro," 257.

Chapter 26

Change, Continuity, and the Future

Apparently, some people used to embrace the illusion that revolutionary Cuba existed almost on another planet, and that in the '60s and '70s Cuba wasn't as homophobic as the rest of the world. It would have been marvelous had that been the case. . . . Prevailing ideas still tend to devalue these [LGBT] individuals and deny them equal opportunities. . . . Homophobia in Cuba and throughout the world is manifested through acts of both physical and psychological violence. Nevertheless, the many years of the Revolution have succeeded in instilling a certain sense of the value of social solidarity and the necessity of a positive reaction when countering injustice. . . . [W]hen inaugurating the National Days Against Homophobia in 2008, Cuba was likewise signaling its desire to re-visit its history. . . . Previously, there was little discussion of these matters and when discussion did occur, it was only to dismiss, indeed, exclude LGBT people. But today Cuban society is engaged in discussing and exposing many points of view, doubts and contradictions. . . . The fact remains that the very experimentation that is Socialism cannot tolerate discrimination of any kind.

—Mariela Castro Espín[1]

A visitor to Cuba in 2016 would have witnessed a historic process unfolding and seen a far different Cuba than when Raúl Castro became president—more open, vibrant, bustling. Some Cubans complained that they were only running in place, that the changes they wanted had not materialized. Still, Cubans are inventive, creative, and entrepreneurial, and these characteristics were flourishing in a myriad of ways that touched their daily lives. Consider the old US Chevrolets, Plymouths, and Lincolns that became a postcard hallmark of the country. Typically, the engine in one of these "American" cars originally propelled a Russian Lada; its brakes were from a Japanese Sentra;

and the transmission relied on gears jerry-rigged from a Czech tractor. Urban farms and organic food producers were teaming up with master chefs at new paladares to create novel restaurant experiences. Scientists at the Centro Ingenieria *Genética y Biotechnología* (Center for Genetic Engineering and Biotechnology) had developed a drug that can prevent diabetes sufferers from losing their limbs (figure 26.1 shows the center). Without access to this medicine because of the embargo, an estimated seventy-three thousand Americans with diabetes have had amputations every year.[2] In 2016, the US Food and Drug began tests to evaluate a vaccine the genetic engineering center had developed to prevent lung cancer.

Figure 26.1.   The Center for Genetic Engineering and Biotechnology has been a source of several life-saving pharmaceuticals. Photo by Peter Eisner.

However, Cubans do not like taking orders or falling in line. Before 1959, Cuban Catholics had the lowest church attendance in the hemisphere—below 5 percent.[3] Communist leaders have been similarly chagrined by the lackadaisical participation of party members. "The Cuban says no, and means it, to all authority; to bosses, kings, generals, presidents, colonels, commanders, doctors," Carlos Franqui, the propaganda chief of the July 26th Movement and editor of *Revolución* who left the country permanently in 1968, observed. "Cuba is an island of immigrants and émigrés," he added. "In constant movement and danger. Coveted by the great powers. Invaded by buccaneers and pirates. Occupied by Spaniards, Britons, North Americans. An island of . . . rebellion itself."[4]

Imagine corralling this whirling dervish of a people onto one boat to travel along a single river. Add to the scenario the social changes that occurred from 2010 to 2016. Then imagine Raúl Castro's frustration in trying to bring an orderly updating to the Revolution.

SOCIAL CHANGE FROM 2010 TO 2016

Greater Open Expression

In 2012, Cuba's Ministry of Culture and the National Book Institute awarded the National Literature Prize to Leonardo Padura for *The Man Who Loved Dogs*. The significance of the decision to give Padura the country's most prestigious award for writing was not lost on anyone: it was an open acceptance of dissent. All of Padura's detective novels had a political edge, exposing some form of corruption beneath the official façade of normalcy. *The Man Who Loved Dogs*, from which we quoted a brief passage in chapter 9, is an epic work that weaves three stories into one. Each challenges an aspect of Cuba's politics, ideological rigidity, or seemingly blind adherence to Soviet dogmas. The central story concerns the assassination of Leon Trotsky, an early Soviet leader. Padura portrays Trotsky as the Soviet leader whose values and goals most closely reflected the ideals of the Cuban revolution. In contrast, his depiction of Ramón Mercader, Trotsky's assassin, reveals Stalin's perniciousness and the callousness of his devotees. Even though Soviet governments after Stalin discredited some of the dictator's actions, they had not resurrected Trotsky from the ignominy Stalin bestowed on him. Cuba had officially followed the Soviet lead in this regard, which made the novel a biting critique of the alleged hypocrisy and opportunism of Cuba's leaders.

Padura's award was just one of many ways Cubans found the heavy hand of the government easing off under Raúl's leadership, giving them a sense that they could express themselves more freely. Peter Eisner, for example, met numerous Cubans willing to speak with him openly about their economic hardships in television interviews for the PBS program *World Focus*. A woman dentist in her twenties whom he stopped while she was strolling one evening on the Avenida de los Presidentes—which was crowded with young people hanging out, listening to music, singing, and dancing spontaneously— said that she saw health as a growing problem. She felt too many Cuban doctors were going overseas, degrading medical care at home. A young man said that he felt his university training had thus far in his life gone to waste. "We shouldn't have spent five years in college in vain," he remarked. "Someday this is going to have to change."[5]

The US media often has presented an exaggerated image of Cuba as a closed society where everyone is afraid to express a critical opinion lest a "Rapid Response Brigade" swarm the critic's home and trash it.[6] To be sure, the government has repressed dissent, imprisoned Cubans for what they have written or produced artistically, and attempted to control information. This behavior can be partly explained by Cuban leaders' tendency to perceive that their context is akin to the kind of extreme threat US leaders perceived after September 11, 2001, which also led to the denial of some civil liberties. After all, the goal of US policy—to overthrow the Cuban government—is explicit in the law governing the embargo. What becomes significant, therefore, is the relaxation of some controls and the reduction in fear we found when someone criticizes the government or PCC, not the continuation of some repression, which will take time to overcome.

Prior to the 2011 PCC Congress, the government itself encouraged active debate about the Lineamientos, and "there were calls for a change of mentality among leaders and administrators . . . to listen to the population," economist Jorge Mario Sánchez noted. Meanwhile, he added, "the press began to publish letters and articles exposing wrong or arbitrary decisions in state enterprises and ministries to public scrutiny."[7]

The shift toward greater freedom of expression actually began before Raúl became president. *Temas* magazine, for example, celebrated its twentieth anniversary in 2015.[8] By publishing articles on topics rarely covered in the official media and with views well outside the mainstream, the magazine has helped to expand the borders of what is acceptable. Its January/March 2002 issue, for example, focused on the sensitive subject of "Identity and Multiculturalism" and as usual included both Cuban and foreign authors. In a similar way, its July/September 2012 issue examined the subject of "Social Development," which included an article about the lack of social mobility and the transmission of poverty from one generation to the next.

Temas was protected initially by Abel Prieto Jiménez, a journalist and novelist who became minister of culture in 1997. By 2012, we were told, when

Prieto stepped down from the post, even usually doctrinaire officials such as Esteban Lazo Hernández, president of the National Assembly and a former Political Bureau member, backed the magazine.

Prieto returned as culture minister in 2016. While his role in championing the free expression of artists and writers had been essential, he was not alone. The Catholic Church also made an important contribution. As early as 1968, when the Cuban bishops' conference issued pastoral letters in support of the Revolution's social justice goals, the Church began efforts to reduce the breach that had occurred with the government. Nearly thirty years later, in 1994, Cardinal Jaime Ortega y Alamino, the archbishop of Havana, asserted that "the Catholic Church had a duty to help preserve the achievements of the revolution."[9]

After 1992, the government permitted the church to disseminate its publications to a larger audience. Cardinal Ortega used this opportunity to create *Palabra Nueva* (New Word), a magazine that became a pioneer in the movement for greater openness.[10] Under Orlando Márquez Hidalgo, the inspiring editor who founded and directed the magazine from 1992 to 2016, *Palabra Nueva* provided both information and challenging ideas that linked church teachings to a range of nonreligious subjects. Márquez told a Washington, DC, audience in 2013 that in his view, "talking about religion is not good enough . . . we must include also other topics which are in the interest of the population." For this reason, he said, "we can write about the economy, we can write about the society, we can write about sports, science, life, the everyday life of the Cubans—the hopes, the expectations, their frustrations."[11] Several of the subjects on which the magazine has focused—the way that the current development strategy has encouraged consumption and increased imports, contributed to underemployment, and weakened Cubans' identification with their country's destiny—were subsequently "recognized by the highest figures in the Cuban government."[12]

In addition to editing *Palabra Nueva*, Márquez served as spokesperson for the cardinal and the Cuban Conference of Catholic Bishops. From this position, he worked with Cardinal Ortega to find common ground between church and government officials, who had previously regarded each other as fundamental antagonists. Their success was evident in the trust Raúl seems to have accorded to the Church as "a valid, internal interlocutor for the first time in almost 50 years."[13] In 2010, the Church was involved in the prison release of fifty-two members of the group of seventy-five dissidents arrested in March 2003. In January 2015, following up on the Cuban-US accord that led to diplomatic relations, the Church again served as an intermediary when the government commuted the sentences of fifty-three people the United States had identified as political prisoners. (Current estimates of the number of political prisoners by various organizations range from nineteen to fifty-one. The government claims all these people were incarcerated for acts other than speech, such as injuring people, damaging property, or espionage.[14])

The Church also spawned *Espacio Laical* [Lay Space] in 2005. While it devoted less attention to Church doctrine than *Palabra Nueva*, it also concentrated critically on economic and political issues and often broached topics that had not been discussed in other Cuban publications. In October 2011, *Espacio Laical* examined how the diaspora community could constructively become involved in developing the Cuban economy. In January 2013, it published a symposium that considered the need for a fundamental restructuring of the media in Cuba to broaden and democratize participation in decision-making.[15] In part, producing that issue stimulated the editors, Roberto Veiga González and Lenier González Mederos, to leave the magazine in 2014 in order to create *Cuba Posible*—an ambitious project that is independent of the Church. *Cuba Posible* organizes public forums, publishes a range of blogs online, and tries to facilitate cooperative research among its growing network of members.[16] It already has acquired an international audience, and the founders' aspiration is that it will become a broad platform for the discussion of Cuba's problems and alternate solutions.[17]

Greater Artistic License

In highlighting some films made during the Revolution's early years (chapters 9 and 10), we suggested that Cuban film directors may have had more creative space for their talents and for criticism than other artists. Considerable credit for that artistic license should go to Alfredo Guevara, the founder of the Cuban Institute of Cinematographic Art and Industry (ICAIC), who died in 2013.[18]

Until the Special Period, ICAIC was the only distributor of Cuban films and provided most of the support for production. But as film making with limited resources grew ever more difficult, the government permitted filmmakers to search for funding outside the country. Coproduction gave them the opportunity to explore subjects previously taboo in Cuba.[19] This was ever more apparent in the 2010 to 2016 period, with films such as *Habanastation* (2011) on inequality, *Revolución* (2010) on underground culture, and *Melaza* (2012) on the necessity to engage in petty corruption in order to survive.

Guevara himself did not shrink from confrontation in defending critical filmmakers. In a memorable 1995 episode, Fidel denounced *Guantanamera* as it began showing in Havana theaters. Directed by Tomás Gutiérrez Alea and Juan Carlos Tabío, the film tells the story of the uncompromising, bureaucratically oriented chief undertaker of Guantánamo Province who must transport a deceased person across the country to be buried. The six-hundred-mile trip reveals to the audience, with humor, the multitude of nonapproved ways that Cubans were engaged in *resolviendo* during the Special Period.

To Fidel, showing the film was like exposing Cuba's dirty underwear to the world. But Guevara shot back publicly, asserting in a television interview, "We Cuban cineastes will be able to prove to the *Comandante en Jefe* that . . . the language of the cinema is either the language of the cinema or it isn't cinema." He added, "we're on the right road, the road of clarity."[20] Fidel responded by backing down, acknowledging that he had not even viewed the film.

Gender Rights

Guevara's efforts had an even greater impact two years earlier. Journalist Jon Lee Anderson assessed that Guevara "helped usher in an era of gradual sexual glasnost" by producing *Fresa y Chocolate* (Strawberry and Chocolate) in 1993.[21] Also directed by Gutiérrez Alea and Tabío, the film examines the developing friendship between a gay artist and a committed young communist who is willing to maintain the nonsexual relationship initially in order to spy on the so-called deviant. It not only portrays a gay Cuban sympathetically; *Fresa y Chocolate* clearly criticizes the ways the government penalized homosexuality in the 1960s and the lame excuses the PCC offered to justify discrimination and repression against homosexuals.

Fresa y Chocolate was the first Cuban film to receive an Academy Award nomination, and its appearance marked a turning point for lesbian, gay, bisexual, and transgender (LGBT) Cubans. Less fearful about acknowledging their orientations, they began to gather openly in clubs, perform as transvestites, and speak out. While subsequent films reinforced their courage, unquestionably the most significant support came from Mariela Castro Espín, a daughter of Raúl Castro and the late Vilma Espín.

From her position as director of the National Center of Sexual Education (CENESEX), Mariela Castro has carried on a crusade for LGBT rights, which has diminished taboos against discussing the issue, engendered a national conversation, educated Cubans, and empowered the LGBT community (see her leading an LGBT rally in figure 26.2).[22] Consider that in 2008 the Ministry of Public Health approved state-funded sex reassignment surgery (which Mariela Castro had first proposed in 2005). Or take the case of Adela Hernández, who was imprisoned "in the 1980s for 'dangerousness' after her own family denounced her sexuality." In 2012, Hernández was the first acknowledged transgender Cuban elected to public office, as a delegate to a city council in Villa Clara Province.[23]

Figure 26.2. Mariela Castro Espín leads an LGBT demonstration in Havana as captured in the 2017 documentary, *Transit Havana*. Photo by Johannes Praus from the film.

In 2007, Mariela Castro took to the streets to lead a parade on the International Day Against Homophobia. This has grown to be a monthlong educational campaign, and she has prominently led the Gay Pride parades in recent years. As an elected member of the National Assembly, she also has openly challenged the government to approve laws that grant the rights to same-sex couples that heterosexual couples have, and to change labor laws to include rights for LGBT Cubans.

Increased Access to Information

The official percentage of Cubans with access to the Internet is one of the lowest in the world. In 2013, less than 4 percent of the population had Internet connections in their homes, and only 25 percent used the Internet.[24] However, the reality belies the data—Cubans have greater access to information from the Internet than the numbers suggest—and even the official numbers are improving.

One reason for the inconsistency between the data and reality is that younger Cubans have tended to use smartphones rather than computers for their connections. A special 2012 report by the *Economist* magazine estimated there were 1.8 million cell phones in circulation in Cuba that year.[25] Cubans also share information readily, passing on news via text messages and email through Cuba's intranet—a system for communication exclusively within the island. Relying on old telephone lines and with painfully slow connections, the intranet is accessible to more Cubans than the Internet.

Recently, *el paquete semanal* has opened the world's media to most Cubans. Ever inventive, they now watch international films and television programs by ordering a custom bundle from a neighbor who has broadband Internet access and has downloaded virtually every popular program from US and Spanish television stations. Once a week, a Cuban visits the supplier with a USB flash drive to obtain his or her bundle of requests. We learned from interviews in 2015 that the Netflix series *House of Cards* was especially popular among university and government specialists who study the United States.

The most recent data does not account for the government's expansion of broadband Wi-Fi access throughout the country, which began in 2015. By mid-2016, it had created more than forty hotspots in Havana at which users could connect to the web at a cost of about $2 per hour. To be sure, for a worker who earns the equivalent of $25 per month, the cost of access made it a rarely used luxury. But with increasing wealth, more Cubans were able to link in.

Both political and logistical reasons account for Cubans' limited Internet access. Some high officials have worried that uncontrolled access would enable enemies to spread lies, foment dissent, and undermine the government's efforts to maintain political support for the system. The United States continued to reinforce these fears with supposed "democracy promotion" programs. One multimillion-dollar program that the Associated Press exposed in 2014 was a Twitter-like campaign that enrolled about forty thousand unsuspecting Cubans. Named ZunZuneo, it had the potential to incite the kind of flash mobs that were prominent during the Arab Spring.[26] Another USAID program attempted to infiltrate "Cuba's underground hip-hop groups scene to spark a youth movement against the government."[27]

Undoubtedly, there are officials for whom the national security rationale of limiting information has served their own interest in avoiding exposure of incompetence or corruption. And for some, old habits of secrecy and control are difficult to abandon. Yet national security concerns cannot be dismissed out of hand given Cuba's vulnerabilities.

Logistical problems emanated from several sources. Technically, the United States would have been the most desirable hub for Cuba's access because of proximity. But until 2015, when President Obama allowed US telecommunications firms to do business in Cuba, the US embargo blocked Cuba's connection. Instead, Cuba turned to Venezuela for help in laying a one-thousand-mile-long fiber optic cable under the Caribbean. But the cable malfunctioned shortly before it was scheduled to go online in 2011. There were unconfirmed allegations that Cuban and Venezuelan corruption led to the purchase of low-quality parts, and in 2012, Raúl fired General Medardo

Díaz Toledo as head of the information and communication ministry, the agency in charge of the project. The cable began operation in 2013, and in 2016, Verizon and AT&T signed agreements that enable their customers to roam with cell phones in Cuba.

CONSEQUENCES OF SOCIAL CHANGE

Cuba's Office of National Statistics and Information (ONEI) has projected that the country's 2015 population of 11.2 million people will rise gradually for another ten years and then begin to decline. By 2050, it is expected to be 10.8 million. Even more problematic, the percentage of the working age (20–64) population will decline from 63 to 52 percent, and the percentage of Cubans of retirement age will rise from 14 to 27 percent.[28] The problem of fewer working adults supporting an increasing number of retirees is not unique to Cuba. Still, it is a demographic change that impacts several other social changes occurring on the island.

Consider the 2013 removal of travel restrictions, a decision that carried with it potentially costly side effects. Families where the parents previously had counted on the state to provide social security, now looked to their children as a source of support. They began to encourage their adult children to work in other countries so that they could send remittances home, some of which would be saved for retirement.

Retirement calculations also shaped decisions about homeownership. Until 2013, the common way to move from one home to another was by barter. When a friend of ours remarried several years ago, he and his new wife traded their two modest-sized apartments for a house. The couple who occupied the house wanted to downsize, and the second apartment went to one of their adult children who had recently married. However, in 2014, as our friend edged closer to retirement, he realized that a monthly government pension of 200 CUP (about $8) meant he would live out his days in hardship. His solution was to sell the house, buy a less expensive apartment, and hope the difference will cover the expenses of his retirement years.

For some Cubans, the new opportunity to buy and sell property—and cars—has been invigorating. They see themselves as entrepreneurs, establishing a bed and breakfast operation or a taxi service that will give them both a good income and some personal independence (figure 26.3 shows one such entrepreneur). Yet thinking about property as a substitute for social security has been jarring for many people. More than 80 percent of the population in 2015 had grown up in a system that was based on the premise that the society, not the individual, had the responsibility to care for the elderly.

Figure 26.3. A self-employed entrepreneur (cuentapropista) on the left provides a service of refilling cigarette lighters on a Havana street. Photo by David LaFevor, www .davidlafevor.com.

Another potential side effect of the 2013 travel decision was a "brain drain." Better educated Cubans were those most likely to obtain good jobs abroad. Their departure could lead to a loss of the country's base for sustained development and its most attractive resource for foreign investors. One reason the government had maintained the travel restrictions for so long was to avoid such a brain drain.

For some, the ability to travel legally offered them a way to emigrate from Cuba. The number of Cuban applications for nonimmigrant visas to the United States jumped from 14,000 in 2011 to 35,000 in 2014. The Florida *Sun-Sentinel* reported that as many as 40 percent may have remained in the United States.[29] Recall that the 1966 Cuban Adjustment Act provides an incentive for Cuban visitors to violate visa stipulations, because the act grants resident alien status to a Cuban émigré one year and a day after being on US territory.

Historian Margaret Crahan astutely observed in 2002 that the inequalities produced by the economic reforms in the 1990s reduced "traditional tendencies towards community solidarity . . . fueling societal decomposition."[30] Yet until 2011, many neighborhoods still retained their hold on residents because of a cumbersome process to move from one house to another and severe restrictions on travel. Even when a Cuban's occupation might have provided the ability to move, such a doctor or engineer continued to live where he or she grew up.[31] The freedom to buy and sell houses and to travel reinforced the other forces that were already diminishing the importance of community in Cuban social life. Similarly, without grandparents nearby to take care of children and with a worker's attention focused on a family's individual benefit, not the general welfare, Cubans experienced a loss of social cohesion in the 2010 to 2016 period.

This depiction of the problems resulting from the social changes in Cuba highlights the major obstacle Raúl faced in trying to upgrade the Cuban model. For many Cubans, the changes that occurred did not produce positive consequences, and they resisted further reform, preferring the devil they knew to the devil they didn't know.

Yet for other Cubans, reform has created a new social structure in which they are comfortable. In her study of the emerging class divisions in Cuba, Hope Bastian Martinez found a new "middle class" in which some people defined their class in terms of their ability to live in "decent" housing and maintain food security while others defined class in terms of access to the Internet and the ability to travel.[32]

Government statistics do not provide the kind of information that would enable researchers to know the size of the new middle class, although scholars at the University of Havana's Center for Psychological and Sociological Research have done path-breaking work in trying to calculate its size. Economist Richard Feinberg took a different route, deriving estimates from official data on occupation, education, the number of workers who were employed by nonstate entities or were self-employed. He concludes that "Cuba looks very much like a middle-class society."[33] He surmises that it is likely this large part of the population will be influential in shaping Cuba's future.

THE FUTURE

Historian Louis Pérez, Jr., opens his masterful study, *The Structure of Cuban History*, with an apt quote from a 2008 documentary: "How does one tell the story of a country whose history is far larger than its size?"[34] Indeed, how does one conclude a history about such a country? We do so by pointing to two constants evident in the Cuban Revolution: adaptation and continuity.

Adaptation

The Cuban Revolution has been an ongoing process, not a singular moment. We examined in parts II and III of this book a society in continual flux as it matched its capabilities to the pursuit of its goals. Even when it seemed to be standing still, there was a dynamism about Cuba, reflected at times in its domestic or foreign policies and at times in its cultural achievements.

A look at Cuba's leadership offers an example of the paradox about Cuban dynamism. As we noted in chapter 24, when Raúl selected Machado Ventura to be first vice president in 2008, there was widespread expectation that meaningful changes would not be forthcoming. Yet beneath the top layers of the PCC and the government, there was a sea change occurring in the leadership. At the provincial levels in 2014, the average age of officials was about twenty-five years less than for officials at the national level. Party chiefs in the fifteen provinces were on average forty-six years old. Half were between thirty-eight and forty-seven and the oldest was fifty-seven. Similarly, 80 percent of the heads of provincial assemblies were under fifty. Rafael Hernández reasonably argued, in presenting this data, that to the extent to which Cuba's institutions mirror the population and provide Cubans with a sense of empowerment, they will create new spaces for political action and impact the nature of the "emerging order."[35]

Dynamism was plainly evident in what Raúl Castro has done as president. Cuban economist Jorge Mario Sánchez well summarized the process of updating the Cuban model as "a change in the basis of government, on a new and irreversible scale, so as to eliminate once and for all the complacency, false triumphalism, and social apathy . . . a negation of the culture and thinking that have been years in the making."[36] Stated in these terms, "revolutionary" is a fitting adjective to describe the fundamental changes that updating has entailed.

Evidently, Raúl saw the reforms this way because in his view they would determine the very survival of the Cuban Revolution. Thus, he asserted that changes had to be carefully planned and implemented, and there had to be a "systematic review and timely rectification of possible missteps."[37] He would not rush the process, but neither would he delay it.

The Death of Fidel Castro

Fidel Castro was the central figure of the Cuban Revolution. His death on November 25, 2016, touched a deep sentiment in all Cubans. He was the father of Cuban independence. Just as most people have conflicted emotions about their own father, Cubans had many feelings about Fidel. But when he died, they shared a common grief. We know critics and devotees who waited together in line for hours to pay their respects at Havana's Revolution Square. As Louis Pérez writes in the accompanying textbox, "the success of his appeal and the source of his authority were very much a function of the degree to which he represented the authenticity of Cuban historical aspirations."

Fidel Castro: A Life—and Death—in Context*

Seemingly implausible outcomes acted to shape much of the history attributed to Fidel Castro: a revolution of uncommon breadth and depth in a country that before January 1959 was thought of as hardly more than a client state, an American playground, a place of license and loose morality; where the United States "was so overwhelmingly influential," Ambassador Earl E. T. Smith later acknowledged, "the American ambassador was the second most important man in Cuba; sometimes even more important than the President."

That the government of Fidel Castro expelled the United States, nationalized U.S. property, and aligned Cuba with the Soviet Union—and also survived decades of U.S. efforts at regime change, including one armed invasion, years of covert operations, scores of assassination attempts, and more than 50 years of withering sanctions. It was precisely this implausibility that so tormented the United States. Fidel Castro cast a dark shadow over the U.S. sense of equanimity, a bad dream that would never go away.

Notions of injured national pride, of humiliation and embarrassment—all attributed directly to the person of Fidel Castro—shaped the mindset with which the U.S. fashioned policy toward Cuba. Fidel had to be punished, and all Cubans would be punished until they did something about Castro. His mere presence served as a reminder of the inability of the United States to will the world in accordance with its own wishes, a condition made all the more insufferable by the fact that Cuba was a country upon which the United States had routinely imposed its will. The Cuban revolution, personified by and personalized in the figure of Fidel Castro, challenged long-cherished notions about national well-being and upset prevailing notions of the rightful order of things.

Cultures cope with the demons that torment them in different ways and the practice of exorcism assumes many forms. Castro occupied a place of almost singular distinction in that nether world to which the Americans banish their demons. Even in death, he was reviled and vilified, denounced as a madman, a megalomaniac, a menace, a wicked man with whom honorable men could not negotiate in good faith. Simply put, he was so irredeemably contemptible as to make even being in his company seem akin to consorting with the devil and the prospects of rapprochement appear an accommodation to evil.

Fidel Castro was in many ways defined through his confrontation with the United States. His uncompromising defense of Cuban claims to self-determination and national sovereignty was a summons to which millions of Cubans could respond unequivocally, without regard to political affinities. What resonated in 1959 and in the years that followed was the very phenomenon of the Cuban revolution, of a people summoned to heroic purpose. Fidel Castro was the most visible representative of that people.

(continued)

---

* Excerpted with permission from Louis A. Pérez Jr., "Fidel Castro: A Life—and Death—in Context," *NACLA*, November 29, 2016, http://nacla.org/news/2016/11/29/fidel-castro-life%E2%80%94-and-death%E2%80%94-context.

Fidel Castro: A Life—and Death—in Context (*continued*)

The Cuban revolution triumphed in a larger context, at a time of decolonization movements in Africa, the Middle East, South East Asia, the Caribbean, and Latin America. To confront the United States in the name of national sovereignty and self-determination catapulted Fidel onto the international stage, as a powerful symbol to sustain Third World intransigence against First World domination. That the Cubans could make good on their aspirations resonated across the globe: Cuba as model, Cuba as example, Cubans defeating the U.S.-organized Bay of Pigs invasion which, they boasted, represented the first defeat of imperialism in the Americas. Cuban bravado reverberated across Latin America. The resolve of the people on a small island in the Caribbean served as a symbol of hope to peoples in distant continents.

It is also necessary to pause in the rush to ascertain Fidel's "legacy." The biography of Castro is not the history of Cuba. The life of Fidel Castro was contingent and contextual. The social forces that crashed upon one another in fateful climax in 1959 were set in motion long before Fidel Castro. This is not to suggest that the Cuban revolution was a matter of inevitable outcome, of course. To acknowledge that the revolution was not inevitable should not be understood to mean that it lacked an internal logic, one derived from the very history from which it emerged.

However large a role Fidel played in shaping the course of Cuban history, it bears emphasizing that the success of his appeal and the source of his authority were very much a function of the degree to which he represented the authenticity of Cuban historical aspirations. Fidel Castro was a historic actor, but he was also acted upon. To explain outcomes of 50 years of Cuban programs and policies as a result of one man's will is facile. Worse, it is to dismiss the efforts of hundreds of thousands of men and women who contributed to the deliberations, decisions, and actions that moved the history of Cuba since the July 26, 1953, attack on the Moncada.

Fidel Castro bestirred the Cuban people to act with sacrifice and selflessness, exhilarated by new possibilities and new promises, but most of all by the prospects of a better future that seemed to be within their reach and through their efforts—in a word, through their own *agency*. He was uncompromising about relocating power over Cuban life from foreign states to Cubans, and making the purpose of power the improvement of things Cuban and the affirmation of the prerogative of the Cuban in Cuba. He framed the exercise of national sovereignty and self-determination as the defining paradigm of the Cuban revolution which gave Cuba's leadership a logic to guide everything else.

In short, the legacy of Fidel Castro? The example of the Cuban people.

One authoritative source told us in December 2016 that Fidel was lucid until the end, detailing arrangements for what should occur after he died. He extracted a promise from Raúl that there would be no statues of him erected, no small statues sold, and no streets or buildings named to memorialize him. The National Assembly honored the request and passed a law a few days later forbidding the production of statues, though many people sought to buy one. The symbolism of the request was clear: the Cuban people, not Fidel, were responsible for the Revolution.

Fidel also requested that his ashes be carried to Santiago along the same route he took in January 1959, when he energized Cubans with a weeklong victory march to Havana. Cubans lined the highway to bid him farewell. They understood that the long funeral march was intended to serve the same purpose, a renewal of vows to continue the revolution.

Continuity

Amid all the changes taking place in Cuba, there was a remarkable pattern of continuity. Cubans did not set the island ablaze, as some American pundits expected, when Fidel relinquished his authority to Raúl in 2006. Historian Julia Sweig was spot on in characterizing the calm transfer of leadership as "Fidel's Final Victory."[38] When Raúl steps down as president in 2018 and then as first secretary of the PCC in 2021, the transition is likely to be equally smooth. No one expects the new leaders to abandon the three mainstays of the Revolution: Cuba's socialist system at home, its commitment to international solidarity, and its determination to be independent.

To be sure, there has been considerable debate and little consensus about how Cuba's model of socialism will evolve, and whether it will include political changes that bring it closer to US ideals of democracy. But Raúl was direct in declaring to the Seventh Party Congress, in April 2016, that Cuba will continue with "a single Party . . . which represents and guarantees the unity of the Cuban nation." Unity, he acknowledged, will be more difficult to achieve in the future, because the new economic model will lead to an "increasing heterogeneity of sectors and groups in our society, originating from differences in their income." This is a situation Cuba's enemies will want to use to their advantage "to weaken us," he warned, which is why they demand that Cuba divide itself "into several parties in the name of sacrosanct bourgeois democracy."[39]

Similarly, there was no indication that Cuba will depart from its global commitment to the poor. International solidarity is likely to continue being a feature of its foreign policy. Yet the fundamental element of Cuba's foreign policy, former ambassador Carlos Alzugaray explained, is "the maintenance of the sovereignty, the independence, the self-determination, and the security of Cuba."[40] This has been a Cuban quest for five hundred years, not merely a posture adopted since 1959. The revolutionaries who gained victory in 1959, and those who sought to continue the Cuban Revolution in the twenty-first century, looked back not only to José Martí but to Hatuey, the Taino chief who refused to bow to the Spanish. Independence and sovereignty are the sine qua non of Cuba libre, the essential ingredients of a free Cuba.

NOTES

1. Mariela Castro Espín, "Socialism Cannot Be Homophobic," *La Jiribilla*, no. 628 (May 18–24, 2013), Wallace Sillanpoa, trans., http://www.walterlippmann.com/docs3816.html.

2. Andrew Schneider, "Cuban Drug Could Help Diabetes Patients Avoid Amputations," *Houston Chronicle*, December 19, 2014, http://www.houstonchronicle.com/news/health/article/Cuban-drug-could-help-diabetes-patients-avoid-5969300.php.

3. Margaret Crahan, "The Pope in Cuba: What Does It Mean?" Wilson Center Latin American Program, September 21, 2015, https://www.wilsoncenter.org/article/the-pope-cuba-what-does-it-mean.

4. Carlos Franqui, *Diary of the Cuban Revolution*, trans. Georgette Felix, Elaine Kerrigan, Phyllis Freeman, and Hardie St. Martin (New York: Viking, 1980), ix.

5. Peter Eisner and Ara Ayer, "Social, Economic Change Is in the Wind in Cuba," *PBS World Focus*, March 9, 2009, https://www.youtube.com/watch?v=-Kr6r1njkYM. We appreciate a note from Dr. Margaret Crahan informing us that in 2016 the Ministry of Higher Education announced it would be creating new degrees aimed at preparing students for the workforce.

6. González Echevarria, "Exiled by Ike, Saved by America," *New York Times*, January 7, 2011, http://www.nytimes.com/2011/01/07/opinion/07echevarria.html.

7. Sánchez Egozcue, "Challenges of Economic Restructuring in Cuba," 125.

8. *Revista Temas*, http://temas.cult.cu.

9. Margaret E. Crahan, "Civil Society and Religion in Cuba: Past, Present and Future," in *A Contemporary Cuba Reader: Reinventing the Revolution*, ed. Philip Brenner et al. (Lanham, MD: Rowman & Littlefield, 2007), 331.

10. Maximiliano F. Trujillo Lemes, "La Iglesia católica, la condición política cubana y Palabra Nueva," *Temas*, no. 76 (October–December 2013): 58.

11. Orlando Márquez Hidalgo, "The Role of the Catholic Church in Cuba Today," Brookings Institution, July 29, 2013, unedited transcript, https://www.brookings.edu/events/the-role-of-the-catholic-church-in-cuba-today, 6.

12. Trujillo Lemes, "La Iglesia católica, la condición política cubana y Palabra Nueva," 59.

13. Márquez Hidalgo, "The Role of the Catholic Church in Cuba Today," 12.

14. Linda Qiu, "Are There Political Prisoners in Cuba?" *PolitiFact Global News Service*, March 22, 2016, http://www.politifact.com/global-news/statements/2016/mar/22/raul-castro/are-there-political-prisoners-cuba.

15. "Cuba y su Diáspora: Partes Inseparables de una Misma Nacíon," *Espacio Laical*, no. 28 (October–December 2011), http://www.espaciolaical.org/contens/28/3247 .pdf; "Propuestas para una refundación de las prensa cubana," *Espacio Laical*, no. 33 (January–March 2013), http://www.espaciolaical.org/contens/33/3651.pdf.

16. *Cuba Posible*, http://cubaposible.net.

17. Interview with Roberto Veiga González by Philip Brenner, December 16, 2015, Havana.

18. Jon Lee Anderson, "Cuba's Film Godfather," *New Yorker*, April 24, 2013.

19. Ann Marie Stock, "Zooming In: Making and Marketing Films in Twenty-First-Century Cuba," in *A Contemporary Cuba Reader*, ed. Philip Brenner et al. (Lanham, MD: Rowman & Littlefield, 2014), 351–53.

20. As quoted in Michael Chanan, *Cuban Cinema* (Minneapolis: University of Minnesota Press, 2004), 3.

21. Anderson, "Cuba's Film Godfather."

22. Emily J. Kirk, "Setting the Agenda for Cuban Sexuality: The Role of Cuba's Cenesex," *Canadian Journal of Latin American and Caribbean Studies* 36, no. 72 (2011); also see Jon Alpert and Saul Landau, producers, *Mariela Castro's March: Cuba's LGBT Revolution*, released November 28, 2016, HBO, http://www.hbo.com/documentaries/mariela-castros-march-cubas-lgbt-revolution.

23. Associated Press, "Cuban Transsexual Elected to Office," *Guardian* (London), November 18, 2012, https://www.theguardian.com/world/2012/nov/18/cuban-trans-sexual-adela-hernandez-elected.

24. International Telecommunication Union, "Country Profile: Cuba," *ICT-EYE*, August 23, 2016, http://www.itu.int/net4/itu-d/icteye/CountryProfile.aspx?countryID=63.

25. "With No Sign of a Cuban Spring, Change Will Have to Come from within the Party," *Economist*, May 24, 2012, http://www.economist.com/node/21550422.

26. David Sanger, "US Says It Tried to Build a Social Media Site in Cuba, but Failed," *New York Times*, April 4, 2014.

27. Desmond Butler, Michael Weissenstein, Laura Wides-Munoz, and Andrea Rodriguez, "US Co-Opted Cuba's Hip-Hop Scene to Spark Change," Associated Press, December 11, 2014, http://www.huffingtonpost.com/huff-wires/20141211/lt-secret-cuban-hip-hop-abridged/?utm_hp_ref=world&ir=world.

28. ONEI, "Proyecciones de la Población Cubana 2015–2050," tables 10.1 and 10.2, 2013, http://www.one.cu/proyecciones de la poblacion 2015 2050.htm.

29. Sally Kestin and Megan O'Matz, "Cubans Assure US They Are Coming as Tourists, Then Stay On," *Sun-Sentinel*, December 12, 2015, http://www.sun-sentinel .com/local/broward/fl-cuba-tourist-visas-aid-20151211-story.html.

30. Margaret E. Crahan, "Cuba: Politics and Society," in *US Policy toward Cuba*, ed. Dick Clark, Aspen Institute Congressional Program, First Conference (Washington, DC: Aspen Institute, 2002), 26.

31. Hope Bastian Martinez, "'Adjusting to the Adjustment': Difference, Stratification and Social Mobility in Contemporary Havana, Cuba," Ph.D. diss (Washington, DC: American University, 2016), 190–91.

32. Bastian Martinez, "'Adjusting to the Adjustment,'" 217–24.

33. Feinberg, *Open for Business*, 168.

34. Louis A. Pérez, Jr., *The Structure of Cuban History: Meanings and Purpose of the Past* (Chapel Hill: University of North Carolina Press, 2013), epigraph.

35. Rafael Hernández, "Demografía política e institucionalidad. Apuntes sociológicos sobre las estructuras políticas en Cuba," *Espacio Laical*, no. 10 (April–June 2014): 33.

36. Sánchez Egozcue, "Challenges of Economic Restructuring in Cuba," 125.

37. Raúl Castro Ruz, "The Revolutionary Cuban People Will Again Rise to the Occasion," Speech to the Closing Session of the National Assembly, July 8, 2016, http://en.granma.cu/cuba/2016-07-13/the-revolutionary-cuban-people-will-again-rise-to-the-occasion.

38. Sweig, "Fidel's Final Victory."

39. Raúl Castro Ruz, "The Development of the National Economy, along with the Struggle for Peace, and Our Ideological Resolve, Constitute the Party's Principal Missions," April 18, 2016 (*Granma International* translation), http://en.granma.cu/cuba/2016-04-18/the-development-of-the-national-economy-along-with-the-struggle-for-peace-and-our-ideological-resolve-constitute-the-partys-principal-missions.

40. Alzugaray, "Cuban Foreign Policy during the 'Special Period,'" 51.

Appendix

Chronology of Key Events

CA. 100–1492

The Guanahatabey, Ciboney, and Taino native peoples arrive on the island from the Yucatan, south Florida, and northern South America, respectively, between 100 CE and 500 CE. Estimates about the number of native peoples living in Cuba in 1492 vary between 150,000 and 200,000.

1492–1595

October 12, 1492: Christopher Columbus lands in the Bahamas with an expedition of three boats.

October 28: Columbus sights Cuba for the first time. In November, he leads expeditions to the island, convinced it was actually Cipangu (i.e., Japan).

September 1493: Columbus sets off on his second voyage to the New World. It is marked by recurrent episodes of violence between the Spanish and the Native population.

January 1511: Spanish conquistador Diego Velázquez de Cuéllar begins the conquest and colonization of Cuba, creating seven settlements.

1511: Velázquez estimates that Cuba's indigenous population is 112,000. By 1519, it was down to 19,000.

ca. 1512–1515: The Spanish begin to bring the first Africans to Cuba to provide labor for gold extraction, agriculture, village construction, and domestic service.

1553: The Spanish governor designates Havana, instead of Santiago, as the capital of Cuba.

1589: Spain builds the Morro Castle fort at the Havana harbor entrance.

1592: Construction of the Zanja Real aqueduct, the first European-style water supply system in the Americas, is completed.

1595: Havana's first sugar mill is established.

1600–1800

1608: Silvestre de Balboa writes *Espejo de Paciencia* (*Mirror of Patience*), the foundational piece of Cuban literature. The work realistically represents Cuban life at the time.

1620: Havana is the Spanish Empire's fastest growing city

1717: All tobacco production is placed under a government monopoly.

1720s: Tobacco growers carry out several unsuccessful revolts against Spanish mercantilism.

1756–1763: The Seven Years' War in Europe pits a Spanish-French alliance against England.

August 1762: A British expeditionary fleet lays siege to western Cuba, seizes Morro Castle, and controls Havana.

June 1763: The Treaty of Paris ends British occupation.

1773: The Real Colegio Seminario de San Carlos y San Ambrosio is established in Havana.

1774: The census records that Cuba has a population of 172,620 inhabitants: 96,440 whites, 31,847 free blacks, and 44,333 black slaves.

1791: Haitian sugar and coffee estates are destroyed as 500,000 slaves take up arms against their owners. Production shifts to Cuba along with 30,000 fleeing French settlers.

1790–1805: Cuban sugar production grows from 14,000 tons to 34,000 tons as Spain removes mercantile trade restrictions and European countries boycott Haitian sugar in response to its 1804 declaration of independence.

1800–1898

January 1812: A series of independent slave insurrections erupt throughout the island, inspired by the Haitian revolution. In April, the Spanish capture and hang José Antonio Aponte, whom they mistakenly charge with being the ringleader.

September 23, 1817: Spain and Britain sign the Treaty for the Suppression of the Slave Trade, intended to prevent their colonial "subjects from engaging in any illicit traffic in slaves." Despite the treaty, the number of Cuban slaves swells from 286,942 in 1827 to 436,495 in 1841.

1830: With a harvest of more than 100,000 metric tons, Cuba becomes the world's largest producer of sugar. The growth is facilitated by the construction of new railroad lines.

1840s: Coffee prices fall, causing a shift in production toward sugar.

1853: The first telegraph line is established.

1860: Sugar accounts for 80 percent of Cuba's exports.

October 10, 1868: With the *Grito de Yara* (Cry of Yara), Carlos Manuel de Céspedes del Castillo calls for Cuban independence from Spain, marking the start of the Ten-Year War. The rebels concede defeat in 1878 with the Zanjón Pact.

March 15, 1878: Antonio Maceo refuses to accept defeat and leads the Protest of Baraguá against capitulation.

August 24, 1879: The Cuban general Calixto Garcia starts the Guerra Chiquita—the Little War—an attempt to continue the liberation war. It ends after thirteen months.

October 7, 1886: Spain abolishes slavery in Cuba.

April 10, 1892: José Martí, along with other Cuban emigrés in the United States, founds the Cuban Revolutionary Party (PRC).

February 24, 1895: With the *Grito de Baire* (Cry of Baire), the PRC begins the "Necessary War."

May 5, 1895: José Martí, Maximo Gómez, and Antonio Maceo meet at Mejorana in eastern Cuba to plan war strategy. Martí is elected as supreme leader of the revolution on nonmilitary matters.

May 19, 1895: Martí is killed at Dos Ríos in eastern Cuba.

September 13–16, 1895: Delegates from Oriente, Camagüey, and Las Villas meet to organize the Republic of Cuba's government. They elect Salvador Cisneros Betancourt as president; Maximo Gómez as general in chief of the army; and Antonio Maceo as lieutenant general.

December 7, 1896: Maceo is killed at Punta Brava, near Havana.

January 25, 1898: The US battleship *Maine* arrives in Havana harbor, where it explodes on February 15.

April 20, 1898: The US Congress adds the Teller Amendment to a war resolution against Spain.

July 16, 1898: Spain concedes defeat and the US occupation of Cuba begins.

December 10, 1898: Spain and the United States sign the Treaty of Paris.

1899–1933

1899–1902: General Leonard Wood serves as governor-general of Cuba, improving some of Cuba's infrastructure, promulgating laws to facilitate the domination of Cuba's economy by US companies, and restricting Afro-Cubans from participation in politics.

April 25, 1900: The Cuba Company is incorporated in New Jersey for the purpose of constructing a central railroad line traversing the island.

February 7, 1902: General Wood issues Order Number 34, which makes the permits granted to the Cuba Company irrevocable.

May 20, 1902: By a vote of 15 to 14, the Cuban Constitutional Convention accepts the Platt Amendment as part of the new constitution, giving the United States the right to intervene in Cuban affairs, limiting Cuba's sovereign right to conduct foreign policy, and requiring that Cuba lease three naval coaling stations to the United States.

July 1902: The North American Trust Company of New York, which acted as the occupying government's fiscal agent, begins to operate under the name of Banco Nacional de Cuba.

May 22, 1903: Cuba and the United States sign a commercial treaty of reciprocity that gives Cuban sugar exported to the United States a 20 percent tariff preference and similar preferential tariffs for several US products sent to Cuba.

May 20, 1906: Tomás Estrada Palma is inaugurated as president for a second term.

August 16, 1906: Rebellion against the government's corruption breaks out, spreading to every province by the end of the month.

September 1906: Estrada Palma asks for US intervention to repress the rebels. US president Theodore Roosevelt sends Secretary of War William H. Taft and Assistant Secretary of State Bacon to Cuba as special representatives. Estrada Palma and his cabinet resign, and Roosevelt names Taft provisional governor of Cuba.

October 12, 1906: Charles E. Magoon replaces Taft as provisional governor. Backed by US occupation forces, he remains in power until January 26, 1909.

May–June 1912: US troops return to help suppress demonstrations led by members of the Partido Independiente de Color demanding an end to racist laws.

1913: Mario García Menocal, an engineer and wealthy businessman, becomes Cuba's third president. He serves two terms until 1921.

February–March 1917: Demonstrations erupt throughout the country against the Menocal administration. The US government sells Cuba ten thousand rifles and two million cartridges and declares its support for Menocal.

March 5, 1917: Menocal requests a suspension of constitutional guarantees. Three days later, five hundred US marines enter Santiago de Cuba to help repress the brewing rebellion.

May 1917: Following Cuba's entry into World War I, the United States sends more than twenty thousand troops to the island. After the war, Menocal requests that the troops stay in Cuba, and they remain there until 1923.

November 1, 1920: In an election plagued by numerous charges of fraud, Menocal's candidate, Alfredo Zayas, wins the presidency.

1922: Inspired by the 1918 revolt of Argentine university students, Cuban students led by Julio Antonio Mella, secretary of the Federation of University Students, begin demonstrations, demanding autonomy for the university from political pressure and the firing of corrupt teachers.

1924: Gerardo Machado is elected president.

August 1925: Groups of socialists, anarchists, and communists come together to found the Cuban Communist Party. Mella is instrumental in linking the party to the Comintern.

April 1928: Machado relies on a "packed" constitutional convention to abolish the vice presidency and give himself a new six-year term without reelection.

June 21, 1930: Congress suspends constitutional guarantees.

March 1933: A revolutionary junta to oppose Machado organizes in Miami.

August 1933: Machado resigns in the midst of a general strike. Carlos M. Céspedes becomes provisional president.

September 5, 1933: Following the "revolt of the sergeants," Fulgencio Batista takes control of the island.

September 10, 1933: Revolutionaries form a new government with Ramón Grau San Martín as president and Antonio Guiteras as vice president. Never recognized by the US government, it becomes known as the One Hundred Days Government.

1934–1958

January 15, 1934: Backed by US ambassador Jefferson Caffery, Batista pressures Grau San Martín to resign and names Carlos Mendieta as president.

January 20, 1934: The United States recognizes the Mendieta government.

May 29, 1934: Cuba and the United States sign a "Treaty on Relations," which replaces the 1903 treaty, abrogates the Platt Amendment, and gives the United States a lease in perpetuity for the Guantánamo Naval Base.

February 1940: The Cuban constituent assembly begins writing a new constitution, which is approved on July 1. It guarantees free universal education and health care and establishes an elected president who names a prime minister.

October 10, 1940: Fulgencio Batista becomes president under Cuba's new constitution.

1944: The Cuban Communist Party changes its name to the Popular Socialist Party (PSP).

1944: Voters elect Grau San Martín as president.

December 22, 1946: Heads of several US organized crime syndicates convene in Havana and divide up their opportunities in Cuba for gambling, money laundering, and related businesses.

1948: Voters elect Carlos Prío Socarrás as president.

March 10, 1952: Fulgencio Batista overthrows the government of Carlos Prio Socarrás.

July 26, 1953: Led by Fidel Castro, 134 rebels (including Raúl Castro) attack the Moncada Barracks in Santiago, marking the start of the insurrection against Batista. Most were killed or captured.

October 16, 1953: At his trial, Fidel asserts, "Condemn me, it does not matter. History will absolve me." He and his brother Raúl are imprisoned on the Isle of Pines.

May 6, 1955: Batista issues a general amnesty. Fidel and Raúl travel to Mexico after their release, where they meet Ernesto "Che" Guevara, an Argentine doctor, and plan for a guerrilla campaign in Cuba to overthrow the Batista dictatorship.

December 2, 1956: Eighty-two rebels return to Cuba aboard the *Granma*, a small cabin cruiser, landing in the eastern province of Oriente.

July 20, 1958: Representatives of all the anti-Batista groups sign an agreement—the Pact of Caracas—endorsing a common program and naming Fidel Castro as the commander in chief of the new united rebel army.

1959

January 1–2: Batista flees and the Rebel Army troops enter Havana led by Che Guevara.

January 8: Following a cross-country march called the "caravan of liberty," Fidel Castro arrives in Havana.

February 16: President Manuel Urrutia names Fidel to replace José Miró Cardona as prime minister.

April 15–26: Castro travels to the United States at the invitation of the Association of Newspaper Editors and meets with Vice President Richard Nixon.

April 21: The Cuban government abolishes racially discriminatory laws.

May 17: The government promulgates the first Agrarian Reform Law, nationalizing about one-third of the arable land in Cuba.

1960

February 4–13: Soviet deputy premier Anastas Mikoyan visits Cuba and signs trade and aid agreements.

March 17: President Dwight D. Eisenhower authorizes a plan for the Bay of Pigs invasion.

May 8: Cuba and the Soviet Union establish diplomatic relations.

June 7: At the urging of the US State Department, US oil companies refuse to refine Soviet crude oil at their Cuban facilities. Cuba nationalizes the refineries.

July 6: The United States suspends the Cuban sugar quota, effectively cutting off 80 percent of Cuba's exports to the United States.

July 10: The Soviet Union agrees to buy Cuban sugar.

August 6: In retaliation for the US suspension of the sugar quota, Cuba nationalizes US private investments on the island worth approximately $1 billion.

August 29: Fidel announces the plan for the National Literacy Campaign. The effort formally begins on June 1, 1961.

October 14: The government approves the Urban Reform Law, which includes a limitation on rental payments to 10 percent of family's earnings.

1961

January 3: The United States breaks diplomatic relations with Cuba.

April 16: At the funeral for victims of US bombing attacks on April 15, Castro declares that the character of the Cuban Revolution is socialist.

April 17–19: A CIA-sponsored invasion force of 1,200 exiles lands at the Bay of Pigs (Playa Girón and Playa Larga). Cuban armed forces and militia defeat the invaders in 72 hours.

September 2: Cuba is the only Latin American state represented at the founding conference of the Movement of Non-Aligned Nations.

November 30: President John F. Kennedy authorizes Operation Mongoose, a covert plan to overthrow the Cuban government with terrorist raids, economic sanctions, political isolation, and military intimidation.

December 22: At the conclusion of the Literacy Campaign, the country's illiteracy rate drops from 24 to 4 percent.

1962

January 22–31: The Organization of American States (OAS) suspends Cuba's membership.

February 4: Castro responds to the OAS suspension with the Second Declaration of Havana.

February 3: Kennedy signs Executive Order 3447, beginning the formal embargo against Cuba.

March: Fidel removes his opponents in the Integrated Revolutionary Organizations who had been senior officials in the PSP (former Communist Party).

April: Cuba accepts a Soviet offer to place ballistic missiles on Cuban territory. Delivery of the missiles, related equipment, and 42,000 Soviet military personnel begins in July.

October 14–November 20: The October (Cuban Missile) Crisis brings the world to the brink of nuclear destruction as the United States challenges the Soviet Union to remove the ballistic missiles from Cuba and take back IL-28 bombers and Komar patrol boats it had delivered.

1963

April 27–June 3: Castro visits the Soviet Union and returns with a new trade agreement and the promise of aid.

June: Kennedy authorizes support for "autonomous" groups that seek to continue terrorist raids against Cuba.

1964

July 26: The OAS adopts resolutions requiring all members to sever diplomatic and trade relations with Cuba. Only Mexico refuses to comply.

1965

April 1: Che Guevara leaves Cuba to wage armed struggle in Africa and Latin America.

October 3: The Communist Party of Cuba (PCC) is inaugurated.

October 10: The Camarioca boatlift and airlift begin as boats from the United States are permitted to pick up Cubans wanting to leave the country at the port of Camarioca, east of Havana near the city of Matanzas.

1966

January 3–15: The first Tricontinental Congress of the world's radical organizations meets in Havana and forms the Organization of Solidarity with the Peoples of Africa, Asia, and Latin America and the Organization of Latin American Solidarity (OLAS).

November 2: US Congress passes the Cuban Adjustment Act (Public Law 89-732), which provides Cubans who have been on US territory for at least one year and a day with resident alien status, regardless of whether they entered the country legally or illegally. The United States gives this privilege to no other migrant group.

1967

June 26: Soviet premier Alexei Kosygin begins a visit to Cuba, during which he has tense meetings with Cuba's leaders over the issue of supporting third world armed struggle.

July 31–August 10: OLAS holds its first conference in Havana, pointedly without inviting representatives of communist parties.

October 9: US-supported Bolivian rangers execute Che Guevara in Bolivia.

1968

January 2: The Cuban government introduces gasoline rationing due to a cutback in deliveries from the Soviet Union.

January 28–31: The PCC holds the first meeting of the full Central Committee, expelling Aníbal Escalante and eight other leaders of the former PSP, whom Fidel calls a "micro-faction" and charges that they were seeking to take over the PCC.

March 13: Castro launches the "revolutionary offensive," nationalizing 55,000 small businesses and essentially ending private enterprise on the island.

August 23: Castro asserts that the August 21 Warsaw Pact invasion of Czechoslovakia was an illegal action but a "bitter necessity" because it "saved" socialism in Czechoslovakia.

1969

July 26: The effort to produce ten million tons of sugar for the 1970 harvest begins.

1970

May 19: Castro announces the harvest failed to reach the 10-million-ton goal, though the 8.5 million tons harvested was the largest in Cuban history.

September 25: The Soviet Union halts construction of a nuclear submarine base in Cienfuegos, complying with a US demand.

November 12: Cuba and Chile restore diplomatic relations eight days after Salvador Allende is inaugurated as Chile's president.

1971

November 10: Castro arrives in Chile for a three-week visit, his first to a Latin American country since 1959.

1972

July 11: Cuba joins the Council of Mutual Economic Assistance (CMEA), the trading bloc then composed of the Soviet Union, East European socialist countries, and Mongolia.

1973

February 15: The United States and Cuba sign an anti-hijacking agreement.

1974

June 30: Matanzas Province holds elections for the newly established "Organs of People's Power." This was followed by the nationwide establishment of local and provincial elected legislatures.

September: US senators Claiborne Pell (D-RI) and Jacob Javits (R-NY) are the first US elected officials to visit Cuba since the 1961 break in diplomatic relations.

November: US and Cuban officials secretly meet in New York to discuss possible areas for negotiations between the two countries.

1975

February 14: The Council of Ministers enacts the Family Code, a set of laws that provide significant protection for women and children.

July 29: A majority of OAS members, including the United States, vote to lift mandatory diplomatic and economic sanctions against Cuba.

August 15: Cuba introduces a resolution to the UN Special Committee on Decolonization calling for the United Nations to recognize the Puerto Rican Independence Party and affiliated organizations as "representing the legitimate aspirations of the Puerto Rican people."

August 21: The US Treasury Department announces it will permit third country subsidiaries of US companies to trade with Cuba.

November 5: Cuba begins transporting troops to help the Angolan government repel an invasion by South African forces launched in October. By the end of 1976, there are 35,000 Cuban troops in Angola.

December 17–22: Ten years after the PCC was created, it holds its First Congress.

1976

February 15: Cubans vote to approve a new constitution, which institutionalizes the PCC as "the superior force in society."

October 6: A bomb aboard a Cubana Airlines plane explodes, killing all seventy-three people aboard, including the two dozen members of Cuba's Olympic fencing team. Venezuelan police arrest Luis Posada Carriles, a Cuban exile and former CIA employee, for masterminding the terrorist act.

1977

March: President Jimmy Carter lifts the ban on travel to Cuba by US citizens.

March: Fidel Castro unsuccessfully attempts to mediate the conflict between Ethiopia and Somalia over disputed territory in the Ogaden Desert.

April 27: The United States and Cuba sign an accord on fishing rights.

September 1: The United States and Cuba begin to use their own diplomats to staff the sections of the Swiss embassy in Havana and Czech embassy in Washington that represent their respective interests. The diplomats reopen and work from the former embassy buildings.

December: Nearly 20,000 Cuban combat troops begin to arrive in Ethiopia to support the government in its conflict with Somalia.

1978

May 25: President Carter mistakenly charges that Cuban troops in Angola were involved in training Katangese rebels who have invaded Zaire's Shaba Province.

October 21: Cuba releases forty-six prisoners in response to negotiations by the Committee of 75, a group of Cuban-Americans seeking to improve relations between Cuba and the United States.

1979

January 1: Cuba permits Cuban-Americans to visit their families. More than 100,000 go to Cuba in the following twelve months.

April 14: The new government of Grenada establishes diplomatic relations with Cuba and begins to develop economic and political ties.

July 26: Daniel Ortega, the Sandinista leader, attends the annual celebration commemorating the 1953 Moncada attack, which is dedicated to the July 19 triumph of the Nicaragua Revolution.

August 30: The United States charges that the Soviet Union has installed a combat brigade in Cuba. Cuba and the Soviet Union assert that the brigade is a training group that had been stationed in Cuba since 1962.

September 3–9: The sixth summit of the Non-Aligned Movement meets in Havana.

October 1: Carter announces the establishment of a US military headquarters in Key West, Florida, and expanded military maneuvers in the Caribbean, in response to the alleged presence of a Soviet combat brigade in Cuba.

1980

March 12: Cubans begin work on a new international airport in Grenada, which becomes an object of concern for the United States.

March: Private farmers' markets open, where individual producers or cooperatives are able to sell any excess over their contracted production level.

April 21: Cuba announces that anyone wishing to leave the country can be picked up at the port of Mariel. By September 26, when the port is closed, 125,000 had left the country.

1981

January 20: The government creates the Territorial Troop Militia, composed of people who are in neither the regular or reserve forces. By 1985, it will have 1.5 million members.

February 18: US secretary of state Alexander Haig asserts that the United States has "to deal with the immediate source of the problem [in El Salvador], and that is Cuba."

October 31: Cuba mobilizes its reserves and goes on full alert as the US Navy begins four weeks of exercises in the Caribbean.

1982

April 19: The US Treasury Department announces the reimposition of restrictions on travel to Cuba.

1983

October 25: The United States invades Grenada, captures 642 Cubans, kills 24, wounds 57, and establishes a provisional government. Of the 784 Cubans on the island, 636 had been construction workers.

1984

June 29: Presidential candidate Jesse Jackson leaves Cuba after a series of meetings that result in the release of twenty-six prisoners, further openings for the church in Cuba, and Cuba's assent to open talks on immigration issues with the United States.

December 14: The United States and Cuba reached an immigration agreement under which Cuba would repatriate 2,746 Mariel "excludables" and the United States would permit the immigration of up to 20,000 Cubans annually.

1985

January: The government creates an Office of Religious Affairs to improve church-state relations.

March 11: The Soviet Union's Communist Party elects Mikhail Gorbachev as general secretary.

May 20: The United States initiates propaganda broadcasts to Cuba over Radio Martí. In response, Cuba suspends the five-month-old immigration agreement.

1986

February 4: The Cuban Communist Party's Third Congress approves Fidel's proposal to begin the "process of the rectification of errors and negative tendencies."

February 25: Gorbachev proposes limited free-market operations under his plan for "perestroika" (restructuring).

May: The Cuban government closes the private farmers' markets.

1988

March 23: Angolan and Cuban troops secure a major victory against South African forces in the battle of Cuito Cuanavale.

May 3: The United States, South Africa, Angola, and Cuba begin negotiations to end the Angola civil war.

November 15: The four-party talks conclude in Geneva, Switzerland, with South Africa's acquiescence to the independence of Namibia and an agreement that Cuba and South Africa would withdraw their troops from Angola.

1989

July 13: Division General Arnaldo Ochoa Sanchez and Colonel Antonio (Tony) de la Guardia y Font are executed following convictions on drug-trafficking and corruption charges. Interior Minister General José Abrantes is arrested for corruption and receives a thirty-year prison term.

1990

January 28: Castro declares the onset of a "special period in a time of peace."

July 25: Gorbachev announces that beginning on January 1, 1991, trade among members of the CMEA will be on the basis of hard currency exchanges instead of barter arrangements.

1991

March 31: The six remaining countries of the Warsaw Pact formally dissolve their alliance.

June 28: The CMEA formally disbands. More than 85 percent of Cuban trade had been within the CMEA.

September 11: Without informing Cuba, Gorbachev announces he is withdrawing all Soviet troops from Cuba and cutting off military aid.

October 10–14: The Cuban Communist Party's Fourth Congress permits religious believers to join the Communist Party.

December 25: The Soviet Union dissolves, leaving the Russian Republic as the successor state.

1992

July 10–12: The National Assembly of People's Power approves constitutional amendments that protect foreign investment in Cuba, permit foreign ownership of Cuban property, and impose new environmental safety regulations.

October 23: President George H. W. Bush signs the Cuban Democracy Act into law.

1993

July 26: The Cuban government legalizes the free circulation and use of US dollars, which creates a dual, peso/dollar economy.

September 9: Decree-Law 141 goes into effect allowing self-employment (cuentapropistas) in 117 new occupations. By 2005, the government will issue approximately 150,000 licenses.

December 31: Cuba's gross domestic product for the year is 30 percent lower than in 1989. Cuba imported only 1.8 million barrels of oil in 1993, in contrast to 13 million barrels in 1991. The average caloric intake of the working population (ages fourteen to sixty-four) falls to 57 percent of the World Health Organization's recommended level.

1994

June–August: An average of more than fifty Cubans per day attempt to cross the Florida Straits in makeshift rafts and small boats.

July 13: A Cuban coast guard vessel sinks a hijacked tugboat with illegal emigrants aboard, drowning thirty-seven people.

August 5: Between five and ten thousand people stage the largest anti-government demonstration since 1959 on Havana's waterfront roadway, the Malecon, demanding the right to emigrate.

September 9: President Bill Clinton announces that the United States will grant twenty thousand visas annually to Cubans and send any Cubans picked up in international waters to Guantánamo Naval Base.

1995

May 2: US and Cuban officials announce the "wet foot–dry foot" immigration policy: Cuban exiles rescued at sea will be repatriated to Cuba; those at Guantánamo Naval Base will be admitted into the United States; any Cuban setting foot on US territory will be considered a political refugee and be eligible for citizenship under the Cuban Adjustment Act.

September 5: The Cuban government approves new laws allowing foreigners to own 100 percent of a business and some kinds of real estate.

1996

February 22: Several leaders of an umbrella opposition organization, Concilio Cubano, receive prison sentences or are detained for allegedly using US government funds to organize a February 24 conference of 130 Cuban groups seeking to change Cuba's form of government.

February 24: A Cuban air force plane shoots down two Brothers to the Rescue planes in international airspace, killing the four pilots.

March 12: Clinton signs into law the "Cuban Liberty and Solidarity Act," known as the Helms-Burton Act, codifying prior executive orders on the embargo. It potentially gives former Cuban property owners the right to sue foreign corporations in US courts as repayment for their "trafficking" with stolen property, and mandates that officers of these corporations be barred from entering the United States.

December 2: The Council of the European Union adopts a "Common Position" on trade with Cuba intended "to encourage a process of transition to pluralist democracy and respect for human rights and fundamental freedoms."

1997

April 12: A bomb explodes in Havana's Hotel Meliá Cohiba. It is the first in a string of hotel bombings in which several people are wounded and an Italian tourist is killed. Luis Posada Carriles later admits to planning the hotel attacks.

October 11: The Fifth Congress of the Cuban Communist Party installs new, younger members in key leadership posts and reduces the size of the Central Committee from 225 to 150 members.

1998

January 21: Pope John Paul II arrives in Havana, marking the first papal visit to Cuba. During his five-day visit, he conducts several open-air masses, which involve hundreds of thousands of Cubans, speaks out against the US embargo, and calls for improved human rights.

September 12: Five Cuban intelligence agents are arrested and charged with conspiracy to commit espionage against the United States. Known as the Cuban Five, they had been involved in efforts to monitor terrorist activities of anti-Cuban groups in South Florida.

October: Cuba inaugurates the Latin American School of Medicine (ELAM) intended for students mainly from Latin America and the Caribbean who receive full scholarships.

1999

January 5: Clinton issues an executive order allowing any US citizen to send remittances to Cubans, and authorizing the Treasury Department to issue group licenses for the purpose of educational, cultural, humanitarian, religious, journalistic, and athletic exchanges.

March 28: The Baltimore Orioles win a baseball game against Cuba's all-star team at Havana's Estadio Latinoamericano. The Cuban team wins a second game on May 3 at Baltimore's Camden Yards.

November 25: Five-year-old Elián González is found at sea after his raft—which also had carried his mother—capsizes. The Justice Department permits the boy to return to Cuba with his father on June 28, 2000.

2000

October 27: Clinton signs the Trade Sanctions Reform and Export Enhancement Act, relaxing some restrictions on the sale of food and medicine to Cuba.

November 17: Panamanian authorities arrest Luis Posada Carriles and three other men with a carload of C-4 explosives and dynamite near the University of Panama where Fidel Castro was scheduled to speak.

2001

June 8: The Cuban Five are convicted of conspiracy to commit espionage at the end of a trial in Miami. The leader, Gerardo Hernández, receives a sentence of two life terms.

November 4: Hurricane Michelle, the worst storm to hit Cuba in fifty years, causes the evacuation of more than 700,000 people from their homes. It leads President George W. Bush to relax some restrictions on the sale of food to Cuba.

2002

January: Prisoners of war from the US-led action in Afghanistan are housed in US facilities at the Guantánamo Naval Base. Cuba does not protest this use of the base.

May 10: Oswaldo Payá, head of the Varela Project, delivers to the Cuban National Assembly a petition signed by 11,000 Cubans calling on the legislature to hold a national referendum on amending the constitution.

May 12: Former president Jimmy Carter arrives in Havana for a five-day visit, which includes meetings with Fidel Castro and a speech at the University of Havana in which he praises Cuban advances in health and education and criticizes Cuba's lack of political freedom and the US embargo.

June 13: Castro announces that the Cuban government is downsizing the sugar industry, closing 71 of the country's 154 sugar mills.

2003

March 18: Cuban police arrest seventy-five people on charges of treason and accepting financial support from the United States for their activities.

June 5: In response to the March 18 arrests, the European Union announces that it will reduce high-level government contacts with Cuba, discourage member states from participating in Cuban events, and encourage member states to tighten trade sanctions.

2004

May 6: President George W. Bush's Commission for Assistance to a Free Cuba releases a report intended to provide strategies "that will help the Cuban people hasten the dictatorship's end."

June 30: The Bush administration imposes new restrictions on US study abroad programs in Cuba and educational travel and family visits to Cuba.

November 8: US dollars are taken out of circulation in Cuba and replaced by the Cuban Convertible Currency (CUC).

November 22: On a visit to Cuba, China's President Hu Jintao signs a contract for 4,000 tons of nickel sinter annually from 2005 to 2009.

December 14: Venezuelan president Hugo Chávez and Fidel issue a joint declaration calling for the "Bolivarian Alternative for the Americas." The leaders also announce that Venezuela will provide oil to Cuba at drastically reduced prices, and Cuba will send doctors to Venezuela.

2005

August 30–31: The trial of Luis Posada Carriles, on charges of entering the United States illegally, opens in Texas. The judge declares a mistrial, and he is retried and acquitted in 2011.

2006

January: The US Interests Section installs a large ticker tape displaying exhortations for the Cuban people to struggle for their "freedom," news headlines, and quotes from Martin Luther King Jr. In response, the Cuban government erects 150 poles carrying large flags, effectively blocking a view of the ticker tape.

July 10: President Bush's Commission for Assistance to a Free Cuba second report recommends an $80 million fund "to increase support for Cuban civil society."

July 31: As a result of major intestinal surgery, Fidel Castro "temporarily" turns over his responsibilities to six officials. Vice President Raúl Castro becomes acting president of the Council of State.

September 11–16: Cuba hosts the summit of the 118-nation Non-Aligned Movement (NAM) for the second time, and becomes the chair of the NAM for the next three years.

October 31: Cuba reports an economic growth rate in 2005 of 11.8 percent, based on measures that include estimates of the market value of free social services in Cuba and medical services exported to Venezuela and Bolivia. Cuba has deployed more than 30,000 medical personnel to South America.

2007

May 17: Mariela Castro presides over Cuba's first celebration of International Day Against Homophobia.

July 26: Raúl Castro indicates Cuba's willingness to improve relations with the United States.

2008

February 24: Cuba's National Assembly elects Raúl as president and José Ramón Machado Ventura as first vice president of the Council of State.

March: Raúl lifts restrictions on the purchase of mobile phones and computers and the ability of Cubans to stay in tourist hotels and rent cars.

July: The government announces it will lease fallow land to private farmers and reduce restrictions on the free market sales of produce.

August: A new labor law allows greater salary disparities by lifting the salary ceiling on highly skilled jobs.

August–September: Hurricanes Gustav and Ike leave 200,000 Cubans homeless and destroy 25,900 metric tons of agricultural crops, including 50 percent of the sugar crop, 90 percent of the tobacco crop, and 80 percent of the plantain and banana crop.

October: The European Union restores economic aid it curtailed in 2003, including emergency hurricane recovery aid of more than $2.6 million in 2008 and $38.9 million in 2009.

December: A poll by the Institute for Public Opinion Research at Florida International University finds that 55 percent of Cuban-Americans living in Miami want an end to the US embargo.

2009

March: Cabinet Secretary Carlos Lage and Foreign Minister Felipe Pérez-Roque, former close aides to Fidel Castro, resign after admitting "errors." Their departure, along with eight other officials, is the first major change in senior government officials since Raúl Castro's election as president.

April: In advance of the Summit of Americas, US president Barack Obama asserts that he wants a "fresh start" with Cuba, lifting all restrictions on family travel and remittances to Cuba for Cuban-Americans.

June: Despite opposition by the United States, the Organization of American States votes to start a process to restore Cuba's membership, which the organization suspended in 1962. Cuba responds that it has no intention to resume active membership.

August: Raúl Castro announces the creation of an Office of Comptroller General to improve fiscal discipline and fight corruption.

September: Colombian singer and Miami resident Juanes headlines a concert in Havana's Plaza of the Revolution, drawing hundreds of thousands of fans. Approval of the concert by both the US and Cuban governments signals greater receptivity to cultural exchanges.

December: Cuban authorities arrest Alan P. Gross, a USAID subcontractor, charging him with committing "acts against the integrity or territorial independence of the state" by installing sophisticated satellite communications transmitters, which may have included the capability to prevent detection of its signals for a radius of 250 miles.

2010

April: In a speech to the Congress of Young Communists, Raúl Castro asserts that the state payroll may be inflated by as many as one million workers. He declares, "The Revolution will not leave anyone helpless . . . but this does not mean that the State will be responsible for providing a job to everyone."

May: After the intervention of Cardinal Jaime Lucas Ortega y Alamino, Raúl Castro agrees to allow the dissident group "Ladies in White," initially composed of the wives and mothers of political prisoners, to hold regular demonstrations.

July: President Castro agrees to free 166 political prisoners, including all of those still in jail as a result of the 2003 arrest of government critics.

September: The Cuban government announces plans to cut over one million state sector jobs and relaxes restrictions on self-employment and small businesses.

November: Raúl Castro's plans for economic reform on the island are unveiled with the distribution of the "Guidelines for the Economic and Social Policies of the Party and the Revolution," which outline 291 proposals for reform. After widespread public discussions, a revised version is approved at the 2011 Communist Party Congress.

2011

January: US president Barack Obama relaxes restrictions on travel to Cuba for academic, religious, cultural, and educational purposes.

April: The Communist Party of Cuba holds its Sixth Congress, the first in fourteen years, and approves the "Guidelines for the Economic and Social Policies of the Party and the Revolution." The party also endorses term limits for all party and government leadership positions.

August: The National Assembly approves several economic reforms aimed at decreasing the state's role in the retail and service sectors, and promoting private small businesses and cooperatives.

September–November: The Cuba government allows individuals to buy and sell houses and automobiles directly to one another for the first time in fifty years.

December: Ahead of a visit by Pope Benedict XVI, authorities release 2,500 prisoners, including some convicted of political crimes.

2012

January: The Communist Party of Cuba holds its first National Conference, a meeting intended to complete work left unfinished at the end of the Sixth Congress.

March 26: Pope Benedict XVI visits Cuba, where he calls for greater religious and political freedoms and meets with both Fidel and Raúl Castro. The pope condemns the US embargo against Cuba.

April: The sixth Summit of the Americas in Cartagena, Colombia, ends without a final communiqué. Speaking on behalf of the Latin American heads of state, Colombian president Juan Manuel Santos declares that there will not be a seventh summit unless Cuba is invited.

November: The Scarabeo 9 deepwater oil-drilling rig is removed from Cuban waters. Intended to probe for oil deposits as far down as seven miles, the rig's departure places on hold Cuba's hopes of tapping an estimated 20 billion barrels of crude oil reserves.

November 19: The Colombian government and the Revolutionary Armed Forces of Colombia (FARC) begin negotiations in Havana to end a fifty-year civil war.

2013

January: Raúl Castro assumes the presidency of the Community of Latin American and Caribbean States (CELAC).

January: The Cuban government eliminates the "tarjeta blanca," an exit permit required any time a Cuban wished to travel outside the island.

February: Cuba's National Assembly reelects Raúl Castro as president of the Council of State. He declares that the five-year term as president will be his last, and he endorses the election of fifty-one-year-old Miguel Díaz-Canel Bermúdez as first vice president.

February: Leonardo Padura receives the National Prize for Literature. A popular Cuban novelist, his works go to the edge of acceptable criticism in highlighting corruption.

March: President Hugo Chávez of Venezuela dies after a long battle with cancer. His successor Nicolás Maduro pledges to maintain Venezuelan ties to Cuba.

June: The Cuban government opens 118 Internet cafes across the island, promising more in the future.

July: The United States agrees to resume immigration talks with Cuba, frozen for two years because of the imprisonment of Alan Gross.

July: Panama detains a North Korean freighter illegally carrying hidden Cuban military equipment through the Panama Canal.

2014

January 28–29: The Second Summit of the Community of Latin American and Caribbean States takes place in Havana.

March 29: Cuba's National Assembly approves a new Foreign Investment Law as part of the economic reforms to attract hard currency to the country.

May: The Council of Ministers of Cuba approves the general bases for the drawing up of a Social and Economic Development Program for the period of 2016–2030.

October: Cuba sends a medical brigade of 165 people—the largest foreign medical team from a single country—to Sierra Leone to fight the Ebola epidemic.

December 17: Raúl Castro and Barack Obama announce that their two countries will reestablish diplomatic relations. Cuba releases Alan Gross on humanitarian grounds and releases a jailed US spy in exchange for the three remaining members of the Cuban Five still in prison.

2015

January: The Cuban government commutes the sentences of fifty-three people whom the United States had identified as political prisoners.

April 9–11: Cuba participates for the first time in the Summit of the Americas, held in Panama. Castro and Obama have a private bilateral meeting for the first time.

May: The US State Department removes Cuba from its list of state sponsors of terrorism.

July 20: The Cuban Embassy officially reopens in Washington, DC, with Cuba's Foreign Minister Bruno Rodríguez in attendance. The US Embassy officially reopens in Havana with the presence of Secretary of State John Kerry on August 14.

July: The Cuban government begins to expand broadband Wi-Fi access throughout the country by creating "hotspots" at which users can connect for a charge of $2 per hour.

September 11: The United States and Cuba hold the inaugural session of the bilateral commission created to organize and provide continuity to the process of normalizing relations.

September 20–22: Pope Francis visits Cuba, during which time he officiates at three public masses.

2016

March 20–22: President Obama visits Cuba with a bipartisan congressional delegation. Raúl Castro and Obama hold official meetings, give a joint press conference, and attend a baseball game between the Tampa Bay Rays and the Cuban national team.

March 25: The Rolling Stones perform at a free outdoor concert in Havana.

April 16–19: At the Cuban Communist Party's Seventh Congress, delegates approve resolutions affirming Cuba's socialist economic model and the proposed vision for the 2030 National Economic Development Plan, and elect Raúl Castro as first secretary for a five-year term.

July 4–8: Raúl reports to the National Assembly that Cuba's gross domestic product grew by only 1 percent in the previous year, half of what was planned.

August 24: The Colombian government and FARC sign a peace agreement in Cuba. After Colombian voters reject the accord in a referendum on October 2, the parties renegotiate its terms in Havana. The Colombian Congress approves the final agreement on November 30.

October 14: Obama issues PPD-43—which consolidates changed regulations with regard to Cuba—and executive orders that authorize, among other things, transactions related to Cuban-origin products, the sale of Cuban pharmaceuticals, joint medical research, and civil aviation safety-related services.

October 26: For the first time, the United States and Israel abstain in voting on a UN resolution that calls for the lifting of the US embargo. The final vote is 191-0-2, in favor of the resolution.

November 25: Fidel Castro dies at the age of ninety in Havana. Cuba declares nine days of mourning, a period that culminates in his burial on December 4 at Santa Ifigenia Cemetery in Santiago de Cuba.

December 12: Cuba and the European Union (EU) sign a Political Dialogue and Cooperation Agreement, which provides a framework for a relationship based on equality, reciprocity, and mutual respect. The signing comes in the wake of the EU's revocation of its 1996 Common Position restricting trade.

Bibliography

Adams, John Quincy. "Letter to Hugh Nelson, April 28, 1823." In *Writings of John Quincy Adams*, edited by Worthington Chauncey Ford, vol. 7: 373. New York: Macmillan, 1913

Aguilar, Luis E. *Cuba 1933: Prologue to Revolution.* New York: Norton, 1972.

Alhajji, A., and Terry L. Maris. "The Future of Cuba's Energy Sector." In *Cuba Today: Continuity and Change since the "Periodo Expecial,"* edited by Mauricio A. Font. New York: Bildner Center, CUNY, 2004.

Allison, Graham, and Philip Zelikow. *Essence of Decision: Explaining the Cuban Missile Crisis*, second edition. New York: Longman, 1999.

Allyn, Bruce J., James G. Blight, and David A. Welch, eds. *Back to the Brink: Proceedings of the Moscow Conference on the Cuban Missile Crisis, January 27–28, 1989.* CSIA Occasional Paper No. 9. Lanham, MD: University Press of America, 1992.

Alpert, Jon, and Saul Landau. *Mariela Castro's March: Cuba's LGBT Revolution.* HBO. http://www.hbo.com/documentaries/mariela-castros-march-cubas-lgbt-revolution. Released November 28, 2016.

Alzugaray, Carlos, and Anthony C. E. Quainton. "Cuban-U.S. Relations: The Terrorism Dimension." *Pensamiento Propio*, no. 34 (July–December 2011).

Alzugaray Treto, Carlos. "Is Normalization Possible in Cuban-US Relations after 100 Years of History?" Research Report no. 6. Havana: Instituto Superior de Relaciones Internacionales, 2002, http://www.isri.cu/Paginas/Investigaciones/Investigaciones/Investigaciones06.htm#adaptation.

———. "Cuban Foreign Policy during the 'Special Period.'" In *Redefining Cuban Foreign Policy: The Impact of the "Special Period,"* edited by H. Michael Erisman and John M. Kirk. Gainesville: University Press of Florida, 2006.

———. "Continuity and Change in Cuba at 50: The Revolution at a Crossroads." In *A Contemporary Cuba Reader: The Revolution under Raúl Castro*, edited by Philip Brenner, Marguerite Rose Jiménez, John M. Kirk, and William M. LeoGrande. Lanham, MD: Rowman & Littlefield, 2014.

Amaro, Nelson, and Alejandro Portes. "Una Sociologia del Exilio: Situación de los Grupos Cubanos en Estados Unidos." *Aportes* 23 (January 1972).
American Library Association. "Report of Visit to ACURIL XXXI and Its Host Country, Cuba, May 23–May 30, 2001." July 13, 2001, http://www.ala.org/offices/iro/iroactivities/alacubanlibrariesreport.
Anderson, Jon Lee. "Cuba's Film Godfather." *New Yorker*, April 24, 2013.
Arboleya, Jesús. *The Cuban Counterrevolution*. Translated by Rafael Betancourt. Columbus: Ohio University Press, 2000.
Armstrong, Fulton. "Time to Clean Up U.S. Regime-Change Programs in Cuba." *Miami Herald*, December 26, 2011.
———. "U.S.-Cuba: Migration Policy Growing Tortuous, Dangerous." *AULA Blog*, Center for Latin American and Latino Studies, February 4, 2016. https://aulablog.net/2016/02/04/u-s-cuba-migration-policy-growing-tortuous-dangerous.
Asamblea Nacional del Poder Popular de Cuba. "Ley No. 72 Ley Electoral." *La Gaceta Oficial Extraordinaria*, no. 9 (November 1992). https://www.gacetaoficial.gob.cu/codbuscar.php.
Associated Press. "Castro Tells Rally Cubans Are Free to Leave Country." *New York Times*, September 30, 1965, 1, 2.
———. "Castro, Praising Carter, Sees a Prospect of Ties." *New York Times*, February 10, 1977.
———. "Huge March in Havana Protests European Criticism of Castro." *New York Times*, June 13, 2003.
———. "Cuban Transsexual Elected to Office." *Guardian* (London), November 18, 2012. https://www.theguardian.com/world/2012/nov/18/cuban-transsexual-adela-hernandez-elected.
Atkeson, Edward B. "Why Cuba Fired." *Washington Post*, March 13, 1996.
Azicri, Max. "The Cuban Family Code: Some Observations on Its Innovations and Continuities." *Review of Socialist Law* 6 (1980).
———. "Women's Development through Revolutionary Mobilization." In *The Cuba Reader: The Making of a Revolutionary Society*, edited by Philip Brenner, William M. LeoGrande, Donna Rich, and Daniel Siegel. New York: Grove, 1988.
———. *Cuba Today and Tomorrow: Reinventing Socialism*. Gainesville: University Press of Florida, 2000.
———. "The Castro-Chávez Alliance." *Latin American Perspectives* 36, no. 1 (January 2009).
Bachelet, Pablo. "US Policy Gives the Bush Administration Few Options in Cuba, Critics Say." *McClatchy Newspapers*, August 2, 2006.
Bain, Mervyn J. "Cuba-Soviet Relations in the Gorbachev Era." *Journal of Latin American Studies* 37 (2005).
———. *From Lenin to Castro, 1917–1959.* Lanham, MD: Lexington Books, 2013.
Barberia, Lorena. "Remittances to Cuba: An Evaluation of Cuban and U.S. Government Policy Measures." In *The Cuban Economy at the Start of the Twenty-First Century*, edited by Jorge I. Domínguez, Omar Everleny Pérez Villanueva, and Lorena Barberia. Cambridge: Harvard University Press, 2004.

Barcia, Manuel. *Domination and Resistance on Western Cuban Plantations, 1808–1848*. Baton Rouge: Louisiana University Press, 2008.

Bardach, Ann Louise. *Cuba Confidential: Love and Vengeance in Miami and Havana*. New York: Vintage Books, 2002.

———. "Twilight of the Assassins." *Atlantic*, November 2006.

———. *Without Fidel: A Death Foretold in Miami, Havana, and Washington*. New York: Scribner, 2009.

Bardach, Ann Louise, and Larry Rohter. "A Plot on Castro Spotlights a Powerful Group of Exiles." *New York Times*, May 5, 1998.

———. "A Bomber's Tale: A Cuban Exile Details the 'Horrendous Matter' of a Bombing Campaign." *New York Times*, July 12,1998.

———. "Life in the Shadows, Trying to Bring Down Castro." *New York Times*, July 13, 1998.

Barshefsky, Charlene, and James T. Hill. *U.S.-Latin America Relations: A New Direction for a New Reality*, Independent Task Force Report No. 60. New York: Council on Foreign Relations, May 2008. http://www.cfr.org/mexico/us-latin-america-relations/p16279.

Bastian Martinez, Hope. "'Adjusting to the Adjustment': Difference, Stratification and Social Mobility in Contemporary Havana, Cuba." Ph.D. diss., American University, 2016.

BBC. "Cuba Claims Massive Oil Reserves." *BBC News*, October 17, 2008. http://news.bbc.co.uk/go/pr/fr/-/2/hi/americas/7675234.stm.

———. "China Signs Trade Deals with Cuba." *BBC News*, November 19, 2008. http://news.bbc.co.uk/2/hi/americas/7733811.stm.

Bengelsdorf, Carollee. *The Problem of Democracy in Cuba: Between Vision and Reality*. New York: Oxford University Press, 1994.

Benjamin, Jules Robert. *The United States and Cuba: Hegemony and Dependent Development, 1880–1934*. Pittsburgh: University of Pittsburgh Press, 1977.

———. *The United States and the Origins of the Cuban Revolution: An Empire of Liberty in an Age of National Liberation*. Princeton: Princeton University Press, 1990.

Benjamin, Medea, Joseph Collins, and Michael Scott. *No Free Lunch: Food and Revolution in Cuba Today*. San Francisco: Institute for Food and Development Policy, 1984.

Bértola, Luis, and José Antonio Ocampo. *The Economic Development of Latin America since Independence*. Oxford: Oxford University Press, 2012.

Beschloss, Michael R. *The Crisis Years: Kennedy and Khrushchev, 1960–1963*. New York: HarperCollins, 1991.

Betancourt, Estrella Rey, and César Garcia del Pino. "Conquista y colonización de la isla de Cuba (1492–1553)." In *Historia de Cuba: La Colonia*, edited by Maria del Carmen Barcia, Gloria Garcia, and Eduardo Torres-Cuevas. Habana: Instituto de Historia de Cuba, 1994.

Betto, Frei. *Fidel and Religion*. Havana: Publications Office of the Council of State, 1987.

Binder, David. "Carter Says Cubans May Leave Angola, Is Receptive on Ties." *New York Times*, February 17, 1977.

Blackburn, Robin. "Prologue to the Cuban Revolution." *New Left Review*, no. 21 (October 1963).

Blanton, Thomas, ed. "Public Diplomacy and Covert Propaganda: The Declassified Record of Ambassador Otto Juan Reich." National Security Archive Electronic Briefing Book No. 40, March 2, 2001. http://nsarchive.gwu.edu/NSAEBB/NSAEBB40.

Blasier, Cole, and Carmelo Mesa-Lago, eds. *Cuba in the World.* Pittsburgh: University of Pittsburgh Press, 1979.

Blight, James G. *The Shattered Crystal Ball: Fear and Learning in the Cuban Missile Crisis.* Savage, MD: Rowman & Littlefield, 1990.

Blight, James G., and Philip Brenner. *Sad and Luminous Days: Cuba's Struggle with the Superpowers after the Missile Crisis.* Lanham, MD: Rowman & Littlefield, 2002.

Blight, James G., and Peter Kornbluh, eds. *Politics of Illusion: The Bay of Pigs Invasion Reexamined.* Boulder, CO: Lynne Rienner, 1998.

Blight, James G., Bruce J. Allyn, and David A. Welch. *Cuba on the Brink: Castro, the Missile Crisis and the Soviet Collapse.* Lanham, MD: Rowman & Littlefield, 2002.

Blum, Denise. "Cuban Educational Reform during the 'Special Period': Dust, Ashes and Diamonds." In *A Contemporary Cuba Reader: The Revolution under Raúl Castro*, edited by Philip Brenner, Marguerite Rose Jiménez, John M. Kirk, and William M. LeoGrande. Lanham, MD: Rowman & Littlefield, 2014.

Bohning, Don. *The Castro Obsession: U.S. Covert Operations against Cuba, 1959–1965.* Washington, DC: Potomac Books, 2005.

Boorstein, Edward. *The Economic Transformation of Cuba.* New York: Monthly Review Press, 1968.

Bonachea, Rolando E., and Nelson P. Valdés, eds. *Cuba in Revolution.* Garden City, NY: Anchor Doubleday, 1972.

Bonsal, Philip W. *Cuba, Castro, and the United States.* Pittsburgh: University of Pittsburgh Press, 1971.

Bouvier, Virginia. "Q&A: Colombia Cease-Fire Accord Marks Historic Turn." United States Institute for Peace, June 24, 2016. http://www.usip.org/publications/2016/06/24/qa-colombia-cease-fire-accord-marks-historic-turn.

Branch, Taylor, and George Crile III. 1975. "The Kennedy Vendetta: How the CIA Waged a Silent War against Cuba." *Harper's* (August).

Breitman, Richard, and Allan J. Lichtman. *FDR and the Jews.* Cambridge: Belknap Press, 2013.

Brenner, Philip. "Washington Loosens the Knot (a Little Bit)." *NACLA Report on the Americas*, March/April 1999.

———. "Overcoming Asymmetry: Is a Normal US-Cuban Relationship Possible?" In *Redefining Cuban Foreign Policy: The Impact of the "Special Period,"* edited by H. Michael Erisman and John M. Kirk. Gainesville: University Press of Florida, 2006.

———. "The Implications of Political and Socio-Economic Changes in Latin America." In *Political and Socio-Economic Change: Revolutions and Their Implications for the U.S. Military*, edited by John R. Deni. Carlisle, PA: US Army War College Press, 2014.

Brenner, Philip, and Soraya M. Castro Mariño. "Untying the Knot: The Possibility of a Respectful Dialogue between Cuba and the United States." In *A Contemporary*

Cuba Reader: The Revolution under Raúl Castro, edited by Philip Brenner, Marguerite Rose Jiménez, John M. Kirk, and William M. LeoGrande. Lanham, MD: Rowman & Littlefield, 2014.

Brenner, Philip, and Peter Kornbluh. "Clinton's Cuba Calculus." *NACLA Report on the Americas* 29, no. 2 (September/October 1995).

Brenner, Philip, and Saul Landau. "Passive Aggressive." *NACLA Report on the Americas* 24, no. 3 (November 1990).

Brenner, Philip, and Colleen Scribner. "Spoiling the Spoilers: Evading the Legacy of Failed Attempts to Normalize U.S.-Cuban Relations." In *Cuba-US Relations: Normalization and Its Challenges*, edited by Margaret E. Crahan and Soraya M. Castro Mariño. New York: Institute of Latin American Studies, Columbia University, 2017.

Brenner, Philip, Patrick J. Haney, and Walt Vanderbush. "The Confluence of Domestic and International Interests: U.S. Policy Toward Cuba, 1998–2001." *International Studies Perspectives*, no. 3 (2002).

Brenner, Philip, Marguerite Rose Jiménez, John M. Kirk, and William M. LeoGrande, eds. *A Contemporary Cuba Reader: Reinventing the Revolution.* Lanham, MD: Rowman & Littlefield, 2007.

———. eds. *A Contemporary Cuba Reader: The Revolution under Raúl Castro*, second edition. Lanham, MD: Rowman & Littlefield, 2014.

Brenner, Philip, William M. LeoGrande, Donna Rich, and Daniel Siegel, eds. *The Cuba Reader: The Making of a Revolutionary Society.* New York: Grove, 1988.

Brugioni, Dino A. *Eyeball to Eyeball: The Inside Story of the Cuban Missile Crisis.* New York: Random House, 1991.

Brundenius, Claes. *Revolutionary Cuba: The Challenge of Economic Growth with Equity.* Boulder, CO: Westview, 1984.

Brundenius, Claes, and Ricardo Torres Pérez, eds. *No More Free Lunch: Reflections on the Cuban Economic Reform Process and Challenges for Transformation.* Heidelberg: Springer, 2014.

Brzezinski, Zbigniew. *Power and Principle: Memoirs of the National Security Adviser, 1977–1981*, revised edition. New York: Farrar, Straus & Giroux, 1985.

Buncke, Julie Marie. *Fidel Castro and the Quest for a Revolutionary Culture in Cuba.* University Park: Pennsylvania State University Press, 1994.

Burnett, Victoria, and Frances Robles. "U.S. and Cuba at Odds Over Exodus of the Island's Doctors." *New York Times*, December 19, 2015.

Bush, George W. "President Bush Discusses Cuba Policy in Rose Garden Speech." October 10. Washington, DC: Office of the Press Secretary, the White House, 2003.

Bustamante, Michael J., and Julia E. Sweig. "Cuban Public Diplomacy." In *A Contemporary Cuba Reader: The Revolution under Raúl Castro*, edited by Philip Brenner, Marguerite Rose Jiménez, John M. Kirk, and William M. LeoGrande. Lanham, MD: Rowman & Littlefield, 2014.

Butler, Desmond. "USAID Contractor Work in Cuba Detailed." Associated Press, February 12, 2012.

Butler, Desmond, Michael Weissenstein, Laura Wides-Munoz, and Andrea Rodriguez. "US Co-Opted Cuba's Hip-Hop Scene to Spark Change." Associated

Press, December 11, 2014. http://www.huffingtonpost.com/huff-wires/20141211/lt-secret-cuban-hip-hop-abridged/?utmhpref=world&ir=world.

Cardenal, Ernesto. *In Cuba*. Translated by Donald D. Walsh. New York: New Directions, 1974.

Cardoso Eliana A., and Ann Helwege. *Cuba After Communism*. Cambridge: MIT Press, 1992.

Cardoso, Fernando Enrique, and Enzo Faletto. *Dependency and Development in Latin America*. Berkeley: University of California Press, 1979.

Carter, Jimmy. Presidential Directive/NSC-6. "Cuba." Washington, DC: White House. March 15, 1977. http://www.jimmycarterlibrary.gov/documents/pddirectives/pd06.pdf.

———. Presidential Directive-52. Washington, DC: White House, October 29, 1979. http://www.jimmycarterlibrary.gov/documents/pddirectives/pd52.pdf.

———. *Keeping Faith: Memoirs of a President*. New York: Bantam Books, 1982.

Casal, Lourdes. "Race Relations in Contemporary Cuba." In *The Cuba Reader: The Making of a Revolutionary Society*, edited by Philip Brenner, William M. LeoGrande, Donna Rich, and Daniel Siegel. New York: Grove, 1988.

Castañeda, Jorge. *Compañero: The Life and Death of Che Guevara*. New York: Vintage, 1988.

Castro Espín, Mariela. "Socialism Cannot Be Homophobic." *La Jiribilla*, no. 628 (May 18–24, 2013). Translated by Wallace Sillanpoa. http://www.walterlippmann.com/docs3816.html.

Castro Mariño, Soraya M. "U.S.-Cuban Relations During the Clinton Administration." *Latin American Perspectives* 29, no. 4 (July 2002).

———. "Cuba-U.S. Relations, 1989–2002: A View from Havana." In *Redefining Cuban Foreign Policy: The Impact of the "Special Period,"* edited by H. Michael Erisman and John M. Kirk. Gainesville: University Press of Florida, 2006.

———. Like Sisyphus' Stone: U.S.-Cuban Relations in the Aftermath of September 11, 2001." In *A Contemporary Cuba Reader: Reinventing the Revolution*, edited by Philip Brenner, Marguerite Rose Jiménez, John M. Kirk, and William M. LeoGrande. Lanham, MD: Rowman & Littlefield, 2007.

Castro Ruz, Fidel. "Discurso." January 8, 1959. http://www.cuba.cu/gobierno/discursos/1959/esp/f080159e.html.

———. "Discurso." March 6, 1959. http://www.cuba.cu/gobierno/discursos/1959/esp/f060359e.html.

———. "Speech." March 23, 1959. http://www.cuba.cu/gobierno/discursos/1959/esp/f220359e.html.

———. "Discurso." October 26, 1959. http://www.cuba.cu/gobierno/discursos/1959/esp/f261059e.html.

———. "Discurso Como Conclusion de las Reuniones con los Intelectuales Cubanos." June 16, 23, and 30, 1961."http://www.cuba.cu/gobierno/discursos/1961/esp/f300661e.html. Author's translation.

———. "Fidel Castro Denounces Sectarianism." March 26, 1962. Ministry of Foreign Relations, Republic of Cuba, Political Documents. http://collections.mun.ca/cdm/compoundobject/collection/radical/id/40999/show/40921.

————. "Fidel Castro Letter to Nikita Khrushchev, October 26, 1962." National Security Archive, Accession No. CU00754.

————. "Discurso en el Acto Clausura en la Primera Conferencia de Solidaridad de los Pueblos de Asia, Africa y America Latina (Tricontinental)." January 15, 1966. http://www.cuba.cu/gobierno/discursos/1966/esp/f150166e.html.

————. "Discurso al Encontrarse con los Integrantes de la Marcha al Segundo Frente 'Frank Pais.'" September 26, 1966. http://www.cuba.cu/gobierno/discursos/1966/esp/f260966e.html.

————. "Speech at Close of Fifth FMC National Plenum." December 10, 1966. http://lanic.utexas.edu/project/castro/db/1966/19661210.html.

————. "Discurso Pronunciado en Memoria del Comandante Ernesto Che Guevara, en la Plaza de la Revolucion." October 18, 1967. http://www.cuba.cu/gobierno/discursos/1967/esp/f181067e.html. Author's translation.

————. "Discurso Pronunciado al Conmemorarse el IX Aniversario del Triunfo de la Revolucion." January 2, 1968. http://www.cuba.cu/gobierno/discursos/1968/esp/f020168e.html.

————. "Speech to the Central Committee of the Cuban Communist Party." January 25–26, 1968, in Blight and Brenner, *Sad and Luminous Days*, chapter 2.

————. "Speech Commemorating the 11th Anniversary of the March 13, 1957, Action Held at the Steps of the University of Havana." March 13, 1968. http://www.cuba.cu/gobierno/discursos/1968/esp/f130368e.html. Author's translation.

————. "Speech Analyzing Events in Czechoslovakia." August 23, 1968, in Blight and Brenner, *Sad and Luminous Days.*

————. "Speech." July 26, 1970. http://www.cuba.cu/gobierno/discursos/1970/esp/f260770e.html.

————. "Speech at the Tenth Anniversary of the Founding of the Federation of Cuban Women." August 23, 1970. http://www.cuba.cu/gobierno/discursos/1970/esp/f230870e.html.

————. "Speech Commemorating the Tenth Anniversary of the Founding of the Committees for the Defense of the Revolution." September 28, 1970. http://www.cuba.cu/gobierno/discursos/1970/esp/f280970e.html.

————. "Discurso en la Clausura del Primer Congreso Nacional de educacion y Cultura." April 30, 1971. http://www.cuba.cu/gobierno/discursos/1971/esp/f300471e.html.

————. "Discurso En el Acto de Conmemoracion del Centenario de la Protesta de Baraguá, Santiago de Cuba." March 15, 1978. http://www.cuba.cu/gobierno/discursos/1978/esp/f150378e.html. Authors' translation.

————. "Speech at the Closing of the Fourth Congress of the UJC." April 4, 1982. http://www.cuba.cu/gobierno/discursos/1982/esp/f040482e.html. Authors' translation.

————. "Speech Delivered on the 25th Anniversary of the Girón Victory." April 19, 1986. http://www.cuba.cu/gobierno/discursos/1986/esp/f190486e.html.

————. "Discurso en la Clausura de la Sesion Diferida del Tercer Congreso del Partido Comunista de Cuba." December 2, 1986. http://www.cuba.cu/gobierno/discursos/1986/esp/f021286e.html.

———. *My Early Years*, ed. and trans. Deborah Shnookal and Pedro Álvarez Tabío. Melbourne: Ocean Press, 1998.

———. "Speech at the Sixteenth Congress of the CTC." January 28, 1990. http://www.cuba.cu/gobierno/discursos/1990/esp/f280190e.html.

———. "Discurso." Santiago de Cuba, July 26, 1993. http://www.cuba.cu/gobierno/discursos/1993/esp/f260793e.html.

———. "Discurso." Plaza de la Revolucion, Havana, July 26, 1995. http://www.cuba.cu/gobierno/discursos/1995/esp/f260795e.html.

———. "Speech at the Cuban Solidarity Rally." New York, September 8, 2000. http://www.cuba.cu/gobierno/discursos/2000/ing/f080900i.html.

———. "Key Address to a Solemn Session of the National Assembly." Caracas, Venezuela, October 27, 2000. http://www.cuba.cu/gobierno/discursos/2000/ing/f271000i.html.

———. "Speech on the Current World Crisis." Havana, March 6, 2003. http://www.cuba.cu/gobierno/discursos/2003/ing/f060303i.html.

———. "Speech at the Ceremony Commemorating the 50th Anniversary of the Attack on the Moncada." Santiago de Cuba, July 26, 2003. http://www.cuba.cu/Gobierno/Discursos/2003/Ing/F260703i.html.

———. "Speech Delivered at the Commemoration of the 60th Anniversary of His Admission to University of Havana." November 17, 2005. http://www.cuba.cu/gobierno/discursos/2005/ing/f171105i.html.

———. "History Will Absolve Me." In *Fidel Castro Reader*, edited by David Deutschmann and Deborah Schnookal. New York: Ocean Press, 2007.

———. "Cambios sanos en el Consejo de Ministros." *Granma*, March 3, 2009. http://www.granma.cu/granmad/secciones/ref-fidel/art91.html.

———. *La Victoria Estratégica*. Havana: Oficina de Publicaciones del Consejo de Estado, 2010.

———. "Para mis compañeros de la Federación Estudiantil Universitaria." *Granma*, January 26, 2015.

———. "Brother Obama." *Granma*, March 28, 2016. http://en.granma.cu/cuba/2016-03-28/brother-obama.

———. "The Development of the National Economy, along with the Struggle for Peace, and Our Ideological Resolve, Constitute the Party's Principal Missions." April 18, 2016. http://en.granma.cu/cuba/2016-04-18/the-development-of-the-national-economy-along-with-the-struggle-for-peace-and-our-ideological-resolve-constitute-the-partys-principal-missions. *Granma International* translation.

Castro, Fidel, and José Ramón Fernández. *Playa Girón*. New York: Pathfinder Press, 2001.

Castro, Fidel, and Ignacio Ramonet. *Fidel Castro: My Life, A Spoken Autobiography*. Translated by Andrew Hurley. New York: Scribner, 2006.

Castro Ruz, Raúl. "Speech at the Celebration of the Attack on Moncada." Camaguey, July 26, 2007. http://www.granma.cu/granmad/2007/07/27/nacional/artic01.html.

———. "Speech." February 24, 2008. http://www.cuba.cu/gobierno/rauldiscursos/2008/esp/r240208e.html.

———. "Cambios sanos en el Consejo de Ministros." *Granma*, March 3, 2009. http://www.granma.cu/granmad/secciones/ref-fidel/art91.html.

———. "Speech at the Ninth Congress of the Young Communist League." April 4, 2010. http://www.cuba.cu/gobierno/rauldiscursos/2010/ing/r030410i.html.

———. 2010. "Speech at the National Assembly." August 1, 2010. http://www.cuba.cu/gobierno/rauldiscursos/2010/esp/r010810e.html.

———. "Speech at the National Assembly, December 23, 2011." *Granma*, December 26, 2011.

———. "The Development of the National Economy, along with the Struggle for Peace, and Our Ideological Resolve, Constitute the Party's Principal Missions." April 18, 2016. http://en.granma.cu/cuba/2016-04-18/the-development-of-the-national-economy-along-with-the-struggle-for-peace-and-our-ideological-resolve-constitute-the-partys-principal-missions. *Granma International* translation.

———. "The Revolutionary Cuban People Will Again Rise to the Occasion." Speech to the closing session of the National Assembly, July 8, 2016. http://en.granma.cu/cuba/2016-07-13/the-revolutionary-cuban-people-will-again-rise-to-the-occasion.

Cave, Damien. "Former Exit Port for a Wave of Cubans Hopes to Attract Global Shipping." *New York Times*, January 28, 2014.

Center for Cuban Studies. "Fidel Castro on Central America." *Cuba Update* 4, no. 4 (August 1983).

Chanan, Michael. *Cuban Cinema*. Minneapolis: University of Minnesota Press, 2004.

Chang, Laurence, and Peter Kornbluh. *The Cuban Missile Crisis, 1962*. New York: New Press, 1992.

Chávez, Hugo. "Interview." *CNN Larry King Live*, September 24, 2009. http://transcripts.cnn.com/TRANSCRIPTS/0909/24/lkl.01.html.

Chibás, Eduardo R. "Eduardo R. Chibás: Last Speech," translated by Walter Lippmann from a transcript prepared by Raúl Chibás, July 31, 1982. Original Spanish version available at http://www.partidortodoxo.org/Aldabonazo.htm; English translation available at http://www.walterlippmann.com/docs3896.html.

Childs, Matt D. *The 1812 Aponte Rebellion in Cuba and the Struggle against Atlantic Slavery*. Chapel Hill: University of North Carolina Press, 2006.

Cluster, Dick, and Rafael Hernández. *The History of Havana*. New York: Palgrave Macmillan, 2006.

Commission on United States-Latin American Relations. *The Americas in a Changing World*. New York: Quadrangle Books, 1974.

Crahan, Margaret. "Cuba: Politics and Society." In *U.S. Policy toward Cuba*, edited by Dick Clark, Aspen Institute Congressional Program, First Conference. Washington, DC: Aspen Institute, 2002.

———. "The Pope in Cuba: What Does It Mean?" Wilson Center Latin American Program, September 21, 2015. https://www.wilsoncenter.org/article/the-pope-cuba-what-does-it-mean.

Crahan, Margaret E. "Freedom of Worship in Revolutionary Cuba." In *The Cuba Reader: The Making of a Revolutionary Society*, edited by Philip Brenner, William M. LeoGrande, Donna Rich, and Daniel Siegel. New York: Grove, 1988.

———. "Civil Society and Religion in Cuba: Past, Present and Future." In *A Contemporary Cuba Reader: Reinventing the Revolution*, edited by Philip Brenner, Marguerite Rose Jiménez, John M. Kirk, and William M. LeoGrande. Lanham, MD: Rowman & Littlefield, 2007.

Crahan, Margaret E., and Soraya M. Castro Mariño. *Cuba-US Relations: Normalization and Its Challenges*. New York: Institute of Latin American Studies, Columbia University, 2017.

Cuba Posible. http://cubaposible.net.

Cuban Government. *Constitución de la República de Cuba*. http://www.cuba.cu/gobierno/cuba.htm.

Cuban Adjustment Act, Public Law No. 89-732, November 2, 1966.

Davis, Richard Harding. *The Death of Rodriguez, A Year from a Reporter's Note Book*. New York: Harper & Brothers, 1897.

De los Angeles Torres, María. *The Lost Apple: Operation Pedro Pan, Cuban Children in the U.S., and the Promise of a Better Future*. Boston: Beacon Press, 2003.

Deere, Carmen Diana. "Here Come the Yankees! The Rise and Decline of United States Colonies in Cuba, 1898–1930." *Hispanic American Historical Review* 78, no. 4 (November 1998).

Deere, Carmen Diana, Mieke Muers, and Niurka Pérez. 1991. "Toward a Periodization of the Cuban Collectivization Process: Changing Incentives and Peasant Response." *Cuban Studies*, 22.

De la Fuente, Alejandro. "Race and Inequality in Cuba, 1899–1981." *Journal of Contemporary History* 30, no. 1 (1995).

———. *A Nation for All: Race, Inequality, and Politics in Twentieth-Century Cuba*. Chapel Hill: University of North Carolina Press, 2001

———. "Recreating Racism: Race and Discrimination in Cuba's Special Period." *Socialism and Democracy* 15, no. 1 (Spring 2001).

———. *Havana and the Atlantic in the Sixteenth Century*. Chapel Hill: University of North Carolina Press, 2008.

Del Valle Jiménez, Sergio. *Peligros y Principios: La Crisis de Octubre desde Cuba*. Havana: Editora Verde Olivo, 1992.

Desnoes, Edmundo. *Inconsolable Memories*. New Brunswick: Rutgers University Press, 1990.

Deutschmann, David, and Deborah Shnookal, eds. *Fidel Castro Reader*. New York: Ocean Press, 2007.

DeYoung, Karen. "Can Elián Case Alter US-Cuban Dynamic? Custody Fight Renews Debate on Relations." *Washington Post*, May 2, 2000, A4.

DeYoung, Karen, and Eric Pianin. "Congressional Mood Shifts on Cuba Trade Ban." *Washington Post*, May 23, 2000, A1.

Diez Acosta, Tomás. *October 1962: The 'Missile' Crisis as Seen from Cuba*. New York: Pathfinder Press, 2002.

Dinges, John, and Saul Landau. *Assassination on Embassy Row*. New York: Pantheon, 1980.

Diuguid, Lewis H. "Spy Charges Strain U.S.-Cuban Ties; Televised Film Shows U.S. Envoys Allegedly Engaged in Espionage." *Washington Post*, July 25, 1987.

Dobbins, James. Special Assistant to the President and Senior Director for Inter-American Affairs, NSC, "On-the-Record Briefing on Cuba." Released by the Office of the Spokesman, US Department of State, January 5, 1999.

Dobbs, Michael. *One Minute to Midnight: Kennedy, Khrushchev, and Castro on the Brink of Nuclear War*. New York: Alfred A. Knopf, 2008.

Dobrynin, Anatoly. "Dobrynin's Cable to the Soviet Foreign Ministry, 27 October 1962." *Cold War International History Project Bulletin* 5 (Spring 1995): 79–80.

Domínguez, Jorge I. "Cuban Foreign Policy." *Foreign Affairs* 57, no. 1 (Fall 1978).

———. *Cuba: Order and Revolution*. Cambridge: Harvard University Press, 1978.

———. *To Make the World Safe for Democracy: Cuba's Foreign Policy*. Cambridge: Harvard University Press, 1989.

———. "U.S.-Cuban Relations: From the Cold War to the Colder War." *Journal of Interamerican Studies and World Affairs* 39, no. 3 (1997).

———. "Cuba's Economic Transition: Successes, Deficiencies, and Challenges." In *The Cuban Economy at the Start of the Twenty-First Century*, edited by Jorge I. Domínguez, Omar Everleny Pérez Villanueva, and Lorena Barberia. Cambridge: Harvard University Press, 2004.

———. "Dialogues within and between Cuba and Its Diaspora." In *A Contemporary Cuba Reader: The Revolution under Raúl Castro*, edited by Philip Brenner, Marguerite Rose Jiménez, John M. Kirk, and William M. LeoGrande. Lanham, MD: Rowman & Littlefield, 2014.

———. "Re-Imagining Cuba's National Assembly." *Cuban Counterpoints*, July 27, 2015. http://cubacounterpoints.com/archives/1697.

Domínguez, Jorge I., Rafael Hernández, and Lorena G. Barberia, eds. *Debating U.S.-Cuban Relations: Shall We Play Ball?* New York: Routledge, 2011.

Domínguez, Jorge I., Omar Everleny Pérez Villanueva, and Lorena Barberia, eds. *The Cuban Economy at the Start of the Twenty-First Century*. Cambridge: Harvard University Press, 2004.

Downie Jr., Leonard, and Karen DeYoung. "Cuban Leader Sees Positive Signs for Ties in Second Reagan Term." *Washington Post*, February 3, 1985.

Draper, Theodore. *Castro's Revolution: Myths and Realities*. New York: Praeger, 1962.

Duffy, Gloria. "Crisis Mangling and the Cuban Brigade." *International Security* 8, no. 1 (Summer 1983).

Duncan, W. Raymond. *The Soviet Union and Cuba: Interests and Influence*. New York: Praeger, 1985.

Echevarria, González. "Exiled by Ike, Saved by America." *New York Times*, January 7, 2011. http://www.nytimes.com/2011/01/07/opinion/07echevarria.html.

Eckstein, Susan, and Lorena Barberia. "Cuban Americans and Their Transnational Ties." In *A Contemporary Cuba Reader: Reinventing the Revolution*, edited by Philip Brenner, Marguerite Rose Jiménez, John M. Kirk, and William M. LeoGrande. Lanham, MD: Rowman & Littlefield, 2007.

Eckstein, Susan Eva. *Back from the Future: Cuba Under Castro*, second edition. New York: Routledge, 2003.

———. *The Immigrant Divide: How Cuban Americans Changed the U.S. and Their Homeland*. New York: Routledge, 2009.

Economist Special Report. "With No Sign of a Cuban Spring, Change Will Have to Come from within the Party." *Economist*, May 24, 2012. http://www.economist.com/node/21550422.

Eisenhower, Milton S. "United States–Latin American Relations, 1953–1958: Report to the President." December 27, 1958; reprinted in *Department of State Bulletin* XL, no. 1021 (January 19, 1959).

Eisner, Peter, and Ara Ayer. "Social, Economic Change Is in the Wind in Cuba." *PBS World Focus*, March 9, 2009. https://www.youtube.com/watch?v=-Kr6r1njkYM.

Eisner, Peter, and Knut Royce. *The Italian Letter: The Forgery That Started the Iraq War*. Amazon Digital Services, 2014. Kindle edition.

Ellsworth, Brian. "Despite Obama Charm, Americas Summit Boosts US Isolation." Reuters, April 16, 2012. http://www.reuters.com/article/us-americas-summit-obama-idUSBRE83F0UD20120416.

English, T. J. *Havana Nocturne: How the Mob Owned Cuba . . . and Then Lost It to the Revolution*. New York: William Morrow, 2007.

Erikson, Daniel P. *The Cuba Wars: Fidel Castro, the United States, and the Next Revolution*. New York: Bloomsbury, 2010.

Erisman, H. Michael. *Cuba's International Relations: The Anatomy of a Nationalistic Foreign Policy*. Boulder, CO: Westview, 1985.

———. *Cuba's Foreign Relations in a Post-Soviet World*. Gainesville: University Press of Florida, 2000.

———. "Brain Drain Politics: The Cuban Medical Professional Parole Programme." *International Journal of Cuban Studies* 4, no. 3/4 (Autumn/Winter 2012).

———. "Raúlista Foreign Policy: A Macroperspective." In *A Contemporary Cuba Reader: The Revolution under Raúl Castro*, edited by Philip Brenner, Marguerite Rose Jiménez, John M. Kirk, and William M. LeoGrande. Lanham, MD: Rowman & Littlefield, 2014.

Erisman, H. Michael, and John M. Kirk. *Cuban Foreign Policy Confronts a New International Order*. Boulder, CO: Lynne Rienner, 1991.

———. *Redefining Cuban Foreign Policy: The Impact of the "Special Period."* Gainesville: University Press of Florida, 2006.

Escalante Font, Fabián. *The Secret War: CIA Covert Operations against Cuba, 1959–1962*. Translated by Maxine Shaw. Melbourne: Ocean Press, 1995.

———. *Executive Action: 634 Ways to Kill Fidel Castro*. Melbourne: Ocean Press, 2006.

Espacio Laical. "Cuba y su Diáspora: Partes Inseparables de una Misma Nación." *Espacio Laical* 28 (October–December 2011). http://www.espaciolaical.org/contens/28/3247.pdf.

———. "Propuestas para una refundación de las prensa cubana." *Espacio Laical* 33 (January–March 2013). http://www.espaciolaical.org/contens/33/3651.pdf.

Espina Prieto, Mayra Paula. "Social Effects of Economic Adjustment: Equality, Inequality and Trends toward Greater Complexity in Cuban Society." In *The Cuban Economy at the Start of the Twenty-First Century*, edited by Jorge I. Domínguez, Omar Everleny Pérez Villanueva, and Lorena Barberia, 219–25. Cambridge: Harvard University Press, 2004.

Estrada, Alfredo José. *Havana: Autobiography of a City.* New York: Palgrave Macmillan, 2007.

Evenson, Debra. *Revolution in the Balance: Law and Society in Contemporary Cuba* Boulder, CO: Westview, 1994.

Executive Branch of the Council of Ministers. "Cuban Family Code." New York: Center for Cuban Studies, 1975.

Facio, Elisa. "Jineterismo during the Special Period." In *Cuban Transitions at the Millennium,* edited by Eloise Linger and John W. Cotman. Largo, MD: International Development Options, 2000.

Fagen, Patricia Weiss. "Antonio Maceo: Heroes, History, and Historiography." *Latin American Research Review* 11, no. 3 (1976).

Fagen, Richard R. *The Transformation of Political Culture in Cuba.* Palo Alto, CA: Stanford University Press, 1969.

Fainaru, S. "In Cuba, Awe and Exhilaration." *Boston Globe,* January 26, 1998, A1.

Feinberg, Richard E. *Open for Business: Building the New Cuban Economy.* Washington, DC: Brookings Institution Press, 2016.

Feinberg, Richard E., and Ted Piccone, eds. *Cuba's Economic Change in Comparative Perspective.* Washington, DC: Brookings Institution Press, 2014.

Feinsilver, Julie M. *Healing the Masses: Cuban Health Politics at Home and Abroad.* Berkeley: University of California Press, 1993.

Felipe, Katheryn. "A Philosophy of 'Surviving, Growing and Persevering.'" *Granma,* February 5, 2016. http://en.granma.cu/cuba/2016-02-04/a-philosophy-of-surviving -growing-and-persevering.

Fernández, Pablo Armando. *Los niños se despiden.* Havana: Casa de las Americas, 1968.

———. Personal interview. April 18, 1980. Washington, DC.

———. Personal interview. January 8, 1992. Havana.

———. "Suite Para Maruja," in *Learning to Die.* Translated by John Brotherton. Havana: Instituto Cubano del Libro, 1995.

Ferreira R., and R. Fabricio. "Graham y Gore Convencieron al Presidente." *El Nuevo Herald,* January 10, 1999.

Fiedler, Tom. "Clinton Backs Torricelli Bill: 'I Like It,' He Tells Cuban Exiles." *Miami Herald,* April 24, 1992, A1.

Fields, Gary. "Economic Development and Housing Policy in Cuba." *Berkeley Planning Journal* 2, no. 1 (1985).

Filkins, Dexter, and Dana Canedy. "Counting the Vote: Miami-Dade County; Protest Influenced Miami-Dade's Decision to Stop Recount." *New York Times,* November 24, 2000, A41.

Fisk, Daniel W. "Cuba in US Policy: An American Congressional Perspective." In *Canada, the US and Cuba: Helms-Burton and Its Aftermath,* edited by Heather Nicol. Kingston, Ontario: Centre for International Relations, Queen's University, 1999.

Fitzgerald, Desmond. "Memorandum for the Record." *FRUS, 1961–1963,* vol. XI, Document no. 348, June 19, 1963, 837–38.

Fleischer, Ari. "Press Briefing." Office of the Press Secretary, the White House, April 29, 2003, https://georgewbush-whitehouse.archives.gov/news/releases/2003/04/20030429-3.html#2.

Fletcher, Pascal. "Obama Wants 'Real Change' in Cuba before Normal Ties." Reuters, May 13, 2011, http://www.reuters.com/article/us-usa-cuba-obama-idUSTRE74 C3P820110513.

Foner, Philip S. *Antonio Maceo: The 'Bronze Titan' of Cuba's Struggle for Independence.* New York: Monthly Review Press, 1977.

Foreign Relations of the United States. *Foreign Relations of the United States (FRUS), 1958–1960, Cuba, volume VI,* edited by John P. Glennon. Washington, DC: Government Printing Office, 1991.

———. *FRUS, 1961–1963, volume X, Cuba, January 1961–September 1962,* edited by Louis J. Smith. Washington, DC: Government Printing Office, 1996.

———. *FRUS, 1961–1963, volume XI, Cuban Missile Crisis and Aftermath,* edited by Edward C. Keefer, Charles S. Sampson, and Louis J. Smith. Washington, DC: Government Printing Office, 1997.

Foster Dulles, John. "Letter from the Secretary of State to the Vice President." *Foreign Relations of the United States, 1958–1960, volume V, American Republics,* Document 42, Washington, March 6, 1958, https://history.state.gov/historicaldocuments/frus1958-60v05/d42.

Frank, Marc. *Havana Revelations: Between the Scenes in Havana.* Gainesville: University Press of Florida, 2013.

———. "After Offshore Oil Failure, Cuba Shifts Energy Focus." Reuters, August 11, 2014.

———. "Cuba Rationing Energy as Economy Minister Urges Spending Cuts." Reuters, July 5, 2016.

Franqui, Carlos. *Diary of the Cuban Revolution.* Translated by Georgette Felix, Elaine Kerrigan, Phyllis Freeman, and Hardie St. Martin. New York: Viking, 1980.

Friedman, Max Paul. *Rethinking Anti-Americanism: The History of an Exceptional Concept in American Foreign Relations.* New York: Cambridge University Press, 2012.

Friedman, Thomas L. "Soviet Turmoil; Gorbachev Says He's Ready to Pull Troops Out of Cuba and End Castro's Subsidies." *New York Times,* September 12, 1991, A1.

Fuentes, Norberto. *Nos Impusieron la Violencia.* Havana: Editorial Letras Cubanas, 1986.

Furiati, Claudia. *Fidel Castro: Uma biografia consentida,* 3a Edição. Rio de Janeiro: Editora Revan, 2001.

Fursenko, Aleksandr, and Timothy Naftali. *One Hell of a Gamble: Khrushchev, Castro, and Kennedy, 1958–1964.* New York: Norton, 1997.

García Luis, Julio, ed. *Cuban Revolution Reader: A Documentary History of 40 Key Moments of the Cuban Revolution.* Melbourne: Ocean Press, 2001.

Garvin, Glenn. "Panama: Exile Says Aim Was Castro Hit." *Miami Herald,* January 13, 2001.

Gelb, Leslie H. "US Relaxes Ban against Trading with the Cubans." *New York Times,* August 21, 1975, 1.

Gjelten, Tom. *Bacardi and the Long Fight for Cuba.* New York: Viking, 2008.

Gleijeses, Piero. *Conflicting Missions: Havana, Washington, and Africa, 1959–1976.* Chapel Hill: University of North Carolina Press, 2002.

————. *Visions of Freedom: Havana, Washington, Pretoria, and the Struggle for Southern Africa, 1976–1991.* Chapel Hill: University of North Carolina Press, 2013.

Gómez-Ibáñez, José A. *Regulating Infrastructure: Monopoly, Contracts, and Discretion.* Cambridge: Harvard University Press, 2006.

Gonzalez, David. "Carter and Powell Cast Doubt on Bioarms in Cuba." *New York Times*, May 14, 2002.

González Echevarria, Roberto. "Exiled by Ike, Saved by America." *New York Times*, January 7, 2011.

González González, Lázaro J. "Melaza (Molasses) That Tastes Like a Movie." *On Cuba*, January 18, 2013. http://oncubamagazine.com/culture/melaza-molasses -tastes-movie.

Gorry, Conner, and C. William Keck. "The Cuban Health System: In Search of Quality, Efficiency, and Sustainability." In *A Contemporary Cuba Reader: The Revolution under Raúl Castro*, edited by Philip Brenner, Marguerite Rose Jiménez, John M. Kirk, and William M. LeoGrande. Lanham, MD: Rowman & Littlefield, 2014.

Goshko, John M. "US Acts to Tighten Cuban Embargo." *Washington Post*, April 20, 1982.

————. "Cuban Aide Defends Air Attack; Supporting Evidence Not Presented to U.N." *Washington Post*, February 29, 1996, A16.

Gott, Richard. *Cuba: A New History.* New Haven: Yale University Press, 2004.

Graddy-Lovelace, Garrett. "United States–Cuba Agricultural Relations and Agrarian Questions." *Journal of Agrarian Change* (2017).

Graham, Bradley. "US Tried to Restrain Group's Flights." *Washington Post*, February 27, 1996, A5.

Gribkov, Anatoli I., and William Y. Smith. *Operation ANADYR: U.S. and Soviet Generals Recount the Cuban Missile Crisis.* Chicago: edition q, 1994.

Guerra, Lillian. *The Myth of José Martí: Conflicting Nationalisms in Early-Twentieth-Century Cuba.* Chapel Hill: University of North Carolina Press, 2006.

————. *Visions of Power in Cuba: Revolution, Redemption, and Resistance, 1959–1971.* Chapel Hill: University of North Carolina Press, 2012.

Guerra Vilaboy, Sergio, and Oscar Loyola Vega. *Cuba: A History.* New York: Ocean Press, 2010.

Guevara, Ernesto Che. "Letter to Fidel." Read by Fidel Castro Ruz in a speech delivered to the Central Committee of the Cuban Communist Party on October 3, 1965. http://www.cuba.cu/gobierno/discursos/1965/esp/f031065e.html.

————. "Speech in Algiers to the Second Seminar of the Organization of Afro-Asian Solidarity, February 25, 1965." In *Che Guevara Speaks*, edited by George Lavan. New York: Pathfinder, 1967.

————. "Vietnam and the World Struggle for Freedom." In *Che Guevara Speaks*, edited by George Lavan. New York: Pathfinder, 1967.

————. "Man and Socialism in Cuba." In *Man and Socialism in Cuba: The Great Debate*, edited by Bertram Silverman. New York: Atheneum, 1973.

Guiteras, Antonio. "Septembrismo." Reprinted in *La Jiribilla: Revista Digital de Cultura Cubana*, no. 290, 25 de noviembre al primero de diciembre, 2006. http:// www.lajiribilla.cu/2006/n290_11/290_07.html. Author's translation.

Gwertzman, Bernard. "Rogers Says Us Is Firm on Cuba." *New York Times*, February 16, 1973, 77.

Haig, Alexander M. "Excerpts from Haig's Briefing about El Salvador." *New York Times*, February 21, 1981.

Hall, Arthur D. *Cuba: Its Past, Present, and Future.* New York: Street and Smith, 1898.

Haney, Patrick J., and Walt Vanderbush. "The Role of Ethnic Interest Groups in US Foreign Policy: The Case of the Cuban American National Foundation." *International Studies Quarterly* 43 (June 1999).

———. *The Cuban Embargo: The Domestic Politics of an American Foreign Policy.* Pittsburgh: University of Pittsburgh Press, 2005.

Hay, John. Letter from John Hay to Theodore Roosevelt, July 27, 1898; reprinted in *Scribner's Magazine* 66 (July–December 1919): 533. https://play.google.com/books/reader?id=peU-AQAAMAAJ&printsec=frontcover&output=reader&hl=en&pg=GBS.PA533.

Hearn, Adrian H. "China and the Future of Cuba." In *A Contemporary Cuba Reader: The Revolution under Raúl Castro*, edited by Philip Brenner, Marguerite Rose Jiménez, John M. Kirk, and William M. LeoGrande. Lanham, MD: Rowman & Littlefield, 2014.

Helms, Jesse. "Remarks." *Congressional Record*, February 9, 1995, S2411; 141 Cong. Rec. S 2399.

Henken, Ted. "Vale Todo: In Cuba's Paladares, Everything Is Prohibited but Anything Goes." In *A Contemporary Cuba Reader: Reinventing the Revolution*, edited by Philip Brenner, Marguerite Rose Jiménez, John M. Kirk, and William M. LeoGrande. Lanham, MD: Rowman & Littlefield, 2007.

Heredia, José María. *Poesias de Don José Maria Heredia*, vol. II. New York: Roe Lockwood, 1853. https://ia802700.us.archive.org/4/items/poesiasdedonjos00websgoog/poesiasdedonjos00websgoog.pdf.

Hernández, Rafael. "Demografía política e institucionalidad. Apuntes sociológicos sobre las estructuras políticas en Cuba." *Espacio Laical*, no. 10 (April–June 2014).

———. "Intimate Enemies: Paradoxes in the Conflict Between the United States and Cuba." in Domínguez et al., *Debating U.S.-Cuban Relations.* New York: Routledge, 2011.

Hershberg, Eric. "Cuban Infrastructure and Brazilian State Capitalism: The Port of Mariel." *AULA Blog*, February 20, 2014. Center for Latin American and Latino Studies, American University, https://aulablog.net/2014/02/20/cuban-infrastructure-and-brazilian-state-capitalism-the-port-of-mariel.

Hershberg, Eric, and William M. LeoGrande. *A New Chapter in US-Cuba Relations: Social, Political, and Economic Implications.* New York: Palgrave Macmillan, 2016.

Hershberg, James G., ed. "Conference of Deputy Chairman of the State Council of the Republic of Cuba Carlos Rafael Rodriguez with U.S. Secretary of State Alexander Haig, in Mexico, 23 November 1981." *Cold War International History Project Bulletin* 8–9 (Winter 1996).

Herter, Christian A. "Memorandum from the Acting Secretary of State to the President." December 23, 1958, in US Department of State, Office of the Historian,

Foreign Relations of the United States, 1958–1960, volume VI, Cuba, Document 189, 305.

Hickling-Hudson, Anne, Jorge Corona Gonzalez, and Rosemary Preston, eds. *The Capacity to Share: A Study of Cuba's International Cooperation in Educational Development.* New York: Palgrave Macmillan, 2012.

Hofstadter, Richard. "Cuba, the Philippines and Manifest Destiny." In *The Paranoid Style in American Politics and Other Essays*, edited by Richard Hofstadter, 147–48. Chicago: University of Chicago Press, 1965.

Holbrook, Joseph. "The Catholic Church in Cuba, 1959–62: The Clash of Ideologies." *International Journal of Cuban Studies* 2, no. 3/4 (2010).

Holmes, Steven A. "Miami Melting Pot Proves Explosive." *New York Times*, December 9, 1990, E4.

Howe, Marvine. "Earl Smith, 87, Ambassador to Cuba in the 1950s." *New York Times*, February 17, 1991.

Huberman, Leo, and Paul M. Sweezy. *Cuba: Anatomy of a Revolution*, published as a special edition of *Monthly Review* (July–August 1960).

———. *Socialism in Cuba.* London: Monthly Review Press, 1969.

Ibarra, Jorge. *Prologue to Revolution: Cuba, 1898–1958.* Boulder, CO: Lynne Rienner, 1998.

Immerman, Richard H. *Empire for Liberty: A History of American Imperialism from Benjamin Franklin to Paul Wolfowitz.* Princeton: Princeton University Press, 2010.

International Telecommunication Union. "Country Profile: Cuba." *ICT-EYE.* August 23, 2016. http://www.itu.int/net4/itu-d/icteye/CountryProfile.aspx?countryID=63.

Jefferson, Thomas. "Letter to James Monroe, October 24, 1824." In *The Writings of Thomas Jefferson*, edited by Andrew A. Lipscomb. Washington, DC: Thomas Jefferson Memorial Association, 1904.

Jenks, Leland Hamilton. *Our Cuban Colony: A Study in Sugar.* New York: Vanguard Press, 1928.

Jiménez, Marguerite Rose. "The Political Economy of Leisure." In *A Contemporary Cuba Reader: The Revolution under Raúl Castro*, edited by Philip Brenner, Marguerite Rose Jiménez, John M. Kirk, and William M. LeoGrande. Lanham, MD: Rowman & Littlefield, 2014.

———. "Polio and the Politics of Policy Diffusion in Latin America." Ph.D. diss., American University, 2013.

Johnson, Haynes, with Manuel Artime. *The Bay of Pigs: The Leaders' Story of Brigade 2506.* New York: Norton, 1964.

Johnson, Leland. "U.S. Business Interests in Cuba and the Rise of Castro." *World Politics* 17, no. 3 (1965).

Jones, Howard. *The Bay of Pigs.* New York: Oxford University Press, 2008.

Kapcia, Antoni. *Cuba in Revolution: A History Since the 1950s.* London: Reaktion Books, 2008.

Kaplowitz, Donna Rich, ed. *Cuba's Ties to a Changing World.* Boulder, CO: Lynne Rienner, 1993.

Kaplowitz, Donna Rich, and Michael Kaplowitz. *New Opportunities for U.S.-Cuban Trade.* Washington, DC: Johns Hopkins University, 1992.

Kennedy, John F. "Address on the First Anniversary of the Alliance for Progress." March 13, 1962. American Presidency Project, University of California, Santa Barbara. http://www.presidency.ucsb.edu/ws/?pid=9100.

Kenworthy, E. W. "Regime Is Scored; People Suffer Under 'Yoke of Dictator,' President Says." *New York Times*, January 4, 1961, 1.

Kestin, Sally, and Megan O'Matz. "Cubans Assure US They Are Coming as Tourists, Then Stay On." *Sun-Sentinel*, December 12, 2015. http://www.sun-sentinel.com/local/broward/fl-cuba-tourist-visas-aid-20151211-story.html.

Khrushchev, Nikita. *Memoirs of Nikita Khrushchev*, edited by Sergei Khrushchev. Translated by George Shriver. University Park: Pennsylvania State University Press, 2007.

Kirk, Emily J. "Setting the Agenda for Cuban Sexuality: The Role of Cuba's CENESEX." *Canadian Journal of Latin American and Caribbean Studies* 36, no. 72 (2011).

Kirk, John M. "Cuban Medical Internationalism under Raúl Castro." In *A Contemporary Cuba Reader: The Revolution under Raúl Castro*, edited by Philip Brenner, Marguerite Rose Jiménez, John M. Kirk, and William M. LeoGrande. Lanham, MD: Rowman & Littlefield, 2014.

Kissinger, Henry. *Years of Renewal*. New York: Simon & Schuster, 1999.

Klapper, Bradley, and Michael Weissenstein. "US, Cuba Move toward Embassies, Disagree on Human Rights." Associated Press, January 23, 2015.

Klein, Herbert S. *Slavery in the Americas: A Comparative Study of Virginia and Cuba.* Chicago: University of Chicago Press, 1967.

Klepak, Hal. "Cuba's Revolutionary Armed Forces: Last Bulwark of the State! Last Bulwark of the Revolution?" In *A Contemporary Cuba Reader: Reinventing the Revolution*, edited by Philip Brenner, Marguerite Rose Jiménez, John M. Kirk, and William M. LeoGrande. Lanham, MD: Rowman & Littlefield, 2007.

———. *Raúl Castro and Cuba: A Military Story.* New York: Palgrave Macmillan, 2012.

———. "The Revolutionary Armed Forces: Loyalty and Efficiency in the Face of Old and New Challenges." In *A Contemporary Cuba Reader: The Revolution under Raúl Castro*, edited by Philip Brenner, Marguerite Rose Jiménez, John M. Kirk, and William M. LeoGrande. Lanham, MD: Rowman & Littlefield, 2014.

Knight, Franklin W. "Jamaican Migrants and the Cuban Sugar Industry, 1900–1934." In *Between Slavery and Free Labor: The Spanish-Speaking Caribbean in the Nineteenth Century*, edited by Manuel Moreno Fraginals, Frank Moya Pons, and Stanley L. Engerman. Baltimore: Johns Hopkins University Press, 1985.

Koont, Sinan. "Cuba's Recent Embrace of Agroecology: Urban and Suburban Agriculture." In *A Contemporary Cuba Reader: The Revolution under Raúl Castro*, edited by Philip Brenner, Marguerite Rose Jiménez, John M. Kirk, and William M. LeoGrande. Lanham, MD: Rowman & Littlefield, 2014.

Kornbluh, Peter. "A 'Moment of Rapprochement': The Haig-Rodriguez Secret Talks." *Cold War International History Project Bulletin* 8–9 (Winter 1996).

———, ed. *Bay of Pigs Declassified: The Secret CIA Report on the Invasion of Cuba.* New York: New Press, 1998.

————. "A Safe Harbor for Luis Posada Carriles." *NACLA Report on the Americas* 39, no. 4 (January/February 2006).

Kornbluh, Peter, and James G. Blight. "Dialogue with Castro: A Hidden History." *New York Review of Books*, October 6, 1994.

Kornbluh, Peter, and William M. LeoGrande. "Talking with Castro." *Cigar Aficionado*, January 2009.

Kosygin, Alexei. "Kosygin's Report on Trip to Cuba to Meeting of Communist Party First Secretaries, Budapest, Hungary, 12 July 1967." Cold War International History Project (CWIHP), Washington, DC. KC PZPRXIA/13, AAN, Warsaw. Obtained by James Hershberg. Translated by Jan Chowaniec. http://digitalarchive.wilsoncenter.org/document/115803.

Kozol, Jonathan. *Children of the Revolution: A Yankee Teacher in the Cuban Schools.* New York: Delacorte Press, 1978.

Kramer, Mark. "The Prague Spring and the Soviet Invasion of Czechoslovakia: New Interpretations (Second of Two Parts)." *Cold War International History Project Bulletin* 3 (Fall 1993).

————. "Ukraine and the Soviet-Czechoslovak Crisis of 1968 (Part 1): New Evidence from the Diary of Petro Shelest." *Cold War International History Project Bulletin* 10 (March 1998).

Krogstad, Jens Manuel. "After Decades of GOP Support, Cubans Shifting toward the Democratic Party." *FacTank*, Pew Research Center, June 24, 2014. http://www.pewresearch.org/fact-tank/2014/06/24/after-decades-of-gop-support-cubans-shifting-toward-the-democratic-party.

————. "Surge in Cuban Immigration to US Continues into 2016." *FacTank*, Pew Research Center, August 5, 2016. http://www.pewresearch.org/fact-tank/2016/08/05/cuban-immigration-to-u-s-surges-as-relations-warm.

Kuck, Peter H. "Nickel." In U.S. Department of the Interior, U.S. Geological Survey, 2003, *Minerals Yearbook—2003*, http://minerals.usgs.gov/minerals/pubs/commodity/nickel/nickemyb03.pdf.

Kuethe, Allan J. *Cuba, 1753–1815: Crown, Military, and Society.* Knoxville: University of Tennessee Press, 1986.

Kushner, Rachel. *Telex from Cuba: A Novel.* New York: Scribner, 2009.

LaFeber, Walter. *The New Empire: An Interpretation of American Expansion, 1860–1898.* Ithaca: Cornell University Press, 1963.

————. *The American Age: United States Foreign Policy at Home and Abroad Since 1750.* New York: Norton, 1989.

Lakoff, George. *Thinking Points: Communicating Our American Values and Vision.* New York: Farrar, Straus & Giroux, 2006.

Landau, Saul. "Asking the Right Questions about Cuba." In *The Cuba Reader: The Making of a Revolutionary Society*, edited by Philip Brenner, William M. LeoGrande, Donna Rich, and Daniel Siegel. New York: Grove, 1988.

————. "Filming Fidel: A Cuban Diary, 1968." *Monthly Review* 59, no. 3 (July–August 2007).

————. "The Confessions of Antonio Veciana." *Counterpunch*, March 12, 2010. http://www.counterpunch.org/2010/03/12/the-confessions-of-antonio-veciana.

———. "The Cuban Five and the U.S. War against Terror." In *A Contemporary Cuba Reader: The Revolution under Raúl Castro*, edited by Philip Brenner, Marguerite Rose Jiménez, John M. Kirk, and William M. LeoGrande. Lanham, MD: Rowman & Littlefield, 2014.

Landers, Jane G. *Atlantic Creoles in the Age of Revolutions.* Cambridge: Harvard University Press, 2010.

Latell, Brian. *After Fidel: The Inside Story of Castro's Regime and Cuba's Next Leader.* New York: Palgrave Macmillan, 2005.

Lavan, George, ed. *Che Guevara Speaks.* New York: Pathfinder, 1967.

Lechuga, Carlos. *In the Eye of the Storm: Castro, Khrushchev, Kennedy and the Missile Crisis.* Translated by Mary Todd. Melbourne: Ocean Press, 1995.

Leiner, Marvin. "Two Decades of Educational Change in Cuba." *Journal of Reading* 25, no. 3 (December 1981).

LeoGrande, William M. "Cuba." In *Confronting Revolution: Security through Diplomacy in Central America*, edited by Morris Blachman, William M. LeoGrande, and Kenneth Sharpe. New York: Pantheon, 1986.

———. "Mass Political Participation." In *The Cuba Reader: The Making of a Revolutionary Society*, edited by Philip Brenner, William M. LeoGrande, Donna Rich, and Daniel Siegel. New York: Grove, 1988.

———. *Our Own Backyard: The United States in Central America, 1977–1992.* Chapel Hill: University of North Carolina Press, 1998.

———. "The Danger of Dependence: Cuba's Foreign Policy After Chavez." *World Politics Review*, April 2, 2013. http://www.worldpoliticsreview.com/articles/12840/the-danger-of-dependence-cubas-foreign-policy-after-chavez.

———. "The Cuban Nation's Single Party: The Communist Party of Cuba Faces the Future." In *A Contemporary Cuba Reader: The Revolution under Raúl Castro*, edited by Philip Brenner, Marguerite Rose Jiménez, John M. Kirk, and William M. LeoGrande. Lanham, MD: Rowman & Littlefield, 2014.

———. "Venezuelan Contagion Hits Cuba's Economy, Putting Reforms in Jeopardy." *World Politics Review*, August 1, 2016. http://www.worldpoliticsreview.com/articles/19522/venezuelan-contagion-hits-cuba-s-economy-putting-reforms-in-jeopardy.

LeoGrande, William M., and Peter Kornbluh. *Back Channel to Cuba: The Hidden History of Negotiations Between Washington and Havana*, updated edition. Chapel Hill: University of North Carolina Press, 2015.

LeoGrande, William M., and Julie M. Thomas. "Cuba's Quest for Economic Independence." *Journal of Latin American Studies* 34, no. 2 (May 2002).

Le Riverend, Julio. *Economic History of Cuba.* Havana: Ensayo Book Institute, 1967.

Lévesque, Jacques. *The USSR and the Cuban Revolution: Soviet Ideological and Strategical Perspectives, 1959–77.* Translated by Deanna Drendel Leboeuf. New York: Praeger, 1978.

Levine, Robert M. *Secret Missions to Cuba: Fidel Castro, Bernardo Benes, and Cuban Miami.* New York: Palgrave, 2001.

Levinson, Sandra. "Nationhood and Identity in Contemporary Cuban Art." In *A Contemporary Cuba Reader: The Revolution under Raúl Castro*, edited by Philip

Brenner, Marguerite Rose Jiménez, John M. Kirk, and William M. LeoGrande. Lanham, MD: Rowman & Littlefield, 2014.

Lipka, Sara. "65 Cuban Scholars Are Denied U.S. Visas." *Chronicle of Higher Education*, October 15, 2004, A40.

Lippman, Thomas W., and Guy Gugliotta. "U.S. Data Forced Cuba to Retreat on Shooting; Basulto Bragged of Buzzing Havana Previously." *Washington Post*, March 16, 1996.

Long, Tom. *Latin America Confronts the United States: Asymmetry and Influence*. New York: Cambridge University Press, 2015.

López, Gustavo N. "Hispanics of Cuban Origin in the United States, 2013." Washington, DC: Pew Research Center, 2015. http://www.pewhispanic.org/2015/09/15/hispanics-of-cuban-origin-in-the-united-states-2013.

López Segrera, Francisco. "Cuba: Dependence, Plantation Economy, and Social Classes, 1762–1902." In *Between Slavery and Free Labor: The Spanish-Speaking Caribbean in the Nineteenth Century*, edited by Manuel Moreno Fraginals, Frank Moya Pons, and Stanley L. Engerman. Baltimore: Johns Hopkins University Press, 1985.

Lowenthal, Abraham F. "The United States and Latin America: Ending the Hegemonic Presumption." *Foreign Affairs* 55, no. 1 (October 1976).

Luis, William. "Exhuming *Lunes de Revolución*." *CR: The New Centennial Review* 2, no. 2 (Summer 2002).

Mandela, Nelson. "Speech at the Rally in Cuba." July 26. In *How Far We Slaves Have Come!* by Nelson Mandela and Fidel Castro. Atlanta: Pathfinder Press, 1991.

Manley, Michael. *The Politics of Change: A Jamaican Testament.* London: André Deutsch, 1974

Manzano, Juan Francisco. *The Autobiography of a Slave.* Translated by Evelyn Picon Garfield. Detroit: Wayne State University Press, 1996.

Márquez, Gabriel García. "Operation Carlota." Translated by Patrick Camiller. *New Left Review*, nos. 101–102 (January–April 1977).

Márquez Hidalgo, Orlando. "The Role of the Catholic Church in Cuba Today." Brookings Institution, July 29, 2013. Unedited transcript. https://www.brookings.edu/events/the-role-of-the-catholic-church-in-cuba-today.

Martí, José. *Obras Completas*. La Habana: Editorial Nacional de Cuba, 1963–1973.

———. "To Manuel Mercado." Translated by Eliana Loveluck. In *The Cuba Reader: The Making of a Revolutionary Society*, edited by Philip Brenner, William M. LeoGrande, Donna Rich, and Daniel Siegel. New York: Grove, 1988.

———. "The Monetary Conference of the American Republics (1891)." In *José Martí: Selected Writings*, edited and translated by Esther Allen. New York: Penguin, 2002.

Martínez, Milagros. "Academic Exchange between Cuba and the United States: A Brief Overview." *Latin American Perspectives* 33, no. 5 (2006).

Mas Canosa, Jorge. "Statement." In US Congress, House, 104th Cong., 1st Sess., "Cuba and US Policy." Hearing Before the Subcommittee on the Western Hemisphere, Committee on International Relations, February 23, 1995.

Masud-Piloto, Felix. *From Welcomed Exiles to Illegal Immigrants: Cuban Migration to the US, 1959–1995*. Lanham, MD: Rowman & Littlefield, 1996.

Matthews, Herbert L. "Cuban Rebel Is Visited in Hideouts." *New York Times*, February 24, 1957.

———. *Fidel Castro*. New York: Simon & Schuster, 1969.

———. *Revolution in Cuba: An Essay in Understanding*. New York: Scribner, 1975.

McFadden, Robert D. "Cuban Attaché at U.N. Is Slain from Ambush on Queens Road." *New York Times*, September 12, 1980.

McKibben, Bill. "The Cuba Diet: What Will You Be Eating When the Revolution Comes?" *Harper's Magazine* 310, no. 1859 (April 2005).

Memmi, Albert. *The Colonizer and the Colonized*. Boston: Beacon Press, 1965.

Mesa-Lago, Carmelo. *Cuba in the 1970s: Pragmatism and Institutionalization*, revised edition. Albuquerque: University of New Mexico Press, 1978.

———. *The Economy of Socialist Cuba: A Two Decade Appraisal*. Albuquerque: University of New Mexico Press, 1981.

———. "Economic and Social Balance of 50 Years of Cuban Revolution." In *Cuba in Transition: Papers and Proceedings of the Nineteenth Annual Meeting of the Association for the Study of the Cuban Economy (ASCE)*, vol. 19 (2009). http://www.ascecuba.org/c/wp-content/uploads/2014/09/v19-mesolago.pdf.

Mikoyan, Anastas, and Fidel Castro. "Mikoyan's Mission to Havana: Cuban-Soviet Negotiations, November 1962." *Cold War International History Project Bulletin* 5 (Spring 1995).

Mikoyan, Sergo, and Svetlana Savranskaya. *The Soviet Cuban Missile Crisis: Castro, Mikoyan, Kennedy, Khrushchev, and the Missiles of November*. Palo Alto, CA: Stanford University Press, 2012.

Miller, Ivor L. "Religious Symbolism in Cuban Political Performance." *TDR: The Drama Review* 44, no. 2 (Summer 2000).

Monreal, Pedro. "Development as an Unfinished Affair: Cuba after the 'Great Adjustment' of the 1990s." In *A Contemporary Cuba Reader: Reinventing the Revolution*, edited by Philip Brenner, Marguerite Rose Jiménez, John M. Kirk, and William M. LeoGrande. Lanham, MD: Rowman & Littlefield, 2007.

———. "Without Sugarcane There Is No Country. What Should We Do Now?" In *No More Free Lunch: Reflections on the Cuban Economic Reform Process and Challenges for Transformation*, edited by Claus Brundenius and Ricardo Torres Pérez. Heidelberg: Springer, 2014.

Morales, Esteban. "Notas Sobre el Tema Racial en la Realidad Cubana de Hoy." *Esteban Morales Domínguez Blog*, September 2011. http://estebanmoralesdominguez.blogspot.ca/2011/09/notas-sobre-el-tema-racial-en-la.html.

Morley, Jefferson. "Shootdown." *Washington Post Magazine*, May 25, 1997.

Morley, Morris H. *Imperial State and Revolution: The United States and Cuba, 1952–1986*. Cambridge: Cambridge University Press, 1987.

Morley, Morris H., and Chris McGillion. *Unfinished Business: America and Cuba after the Cold War, 1989–2001*. New York: Cambridge University Press, 2002.

Morris, Emily. "How Will US-Cuban Normalization Affect Economic Policy in Cuba?" In *A New Chapter in US-Cuba Relations: Social, Political, and Economic Implications*, edited by Eric Hershberg and William M. LeoGrande. New York: Palgrave Macmillan, 2016.

Morris, Emily, and Andrew Hutchings. "Cuba's Dual Currency System." *Latin American White Paper*, September 2013. http://latinnews.com/media/k2/pdf/CDC SWP201309.pdf.

Mufson, Steven. "On Cuba, as Politics Advances, Business Leaders Wait for Their Breakthrough." *Washington Post*, February 19, 2016.

Muñoz, Heraldo, ed. *From Dependency to Development.* Boulder, CO: Westview, 1981.

Murphy, Catherine. *Maestra.* 2012. http://www.maestrathefilm.org.

Murray, D. R. "Statistics of the Slave Trade to Cuba, 1790–1867." *Journal of Latin American Studies* 3, no. 2 (1971): 134. http://latinamericanstudies.org/slavery/Cuba -slave-trade.pdf.

Nagin, Carl. "Backfire." *New Yorker*, January 26, 1998.

Navarro, Mireya. "Nonviolence of Castro's Foes Still Wears a Very Tough Face." *New York Times*, February 28, 1996.

New York Times. "Tobacco Trust in Cuba." *New York Times*, May 29, 1902.

———. "President Sends Crowder to Cuba to Study Crisis." *New York Times*, January 4, 1921.

———. "Céspedes Served Country as Envoy." *New York Times*, August 13, 1933.

———. "Cuban Aid Pledged to US if War Comes." *New York Times*, May 23, 1940.

———. "Travel to Cuba Rises." *New York Times*, January 3, 1951.

———. "Unsettled Labor Frustrates Cuba." *New York Times*, January 4, 1952.

———. "Batista Says Cuba Cleaned Out Reds." *New York Times*, March 11, 1954.

———. "Text of O.A.S. Declaration of San Jose." *New York Times*, August 29, 1960, 3.

———. "Text of Statement by Kennedy on Dealing with Castro Regime." *New York Times*, October 21, 1960, 18.

Newsom, David D. *The Soviet Brigade in Cuba: A Study in Political Diplomacy.* Bloomington: Indiana University Press, 1987.

Nixon, Richard M. "Rough Draft of Summary of Conversation between the Vice-President and Fidel Castro." 25 April. Reprinted in Jeffrey J. Safford. 1980. "The Nixon-Castro Meeting of 19 April 1959." *Diplomatic History* 4, no. 4 (Fall 1959).

Noriega, Manuel Antonio, and Peter Eisner. *America's Prisoner: The Memoirs of Manuel Noriega.* New York: Random House, 1994.

Nova González, Armando. "Cuban Agriculture and the Current Process of Economic Transformation." In *A Contemporary Cuba Reader: The Revolution under Raúl Castro*, edited by Philip Brenner, Marguerite Rose Jiménez, John M. Kirk, and William M. LeoGrande. Lanham, MD: Rowman & Littlefield, 2014.

Nuñez Jiménez, Antonio. *En Marcha Con Fidel—1959.* Havana: Editoria Letras Cubanas, 1998.

———. *En Marcha Con Fidel—1961.* Havana: Fundacion de la Naturaleza y el Hombre, 1998.

Nye, Joseph S., Jr. "Soft Power." *Foreign Policy* 80 (Autumn 1990).

———. *The Future of Power: Its Changing Nature and Use in the Twenty-First Century.* New York: PublicAffairs, 2011.

Obama, Barack. "Press Conference by the President in Trinidad and Tobago." April 19, 2009. https://www.whitehouse.gov/the-press-office/press-conference-president -trinidad-and-tobago-4192009.

———. "Remarks by the President at a DSCC Fundraising Reception." November 8, 2013. https://www.whitehouse.gov/the-press-office/2013/11/08/remarks-president -dscc-fundraising-reception-0.

Oberg, Larry. "The Status of Gays in Cuba: Myth and Reality." In *A Contemporary Cuba Reader: Reinventing the Revolution*, edited by Philip Brenner, Marguerite Rose Jiménez, John M. Kirk, and William M. LeoGrande. Lanham, MD: Rowman & Littlefield, 2007.

Office of the Historian, US State Department. "MILESTONES: 1899–1913: The United States, Cuba, and the Platt Amendment, 1901." https://history.state.gov/mile stones/1899-1913/platt.

Oficina Nacional de Estadística e Informació. "Panorama Económica y social, Cuba 1996." Havana, 1997.

———. *Anuario Estadístico de Cuba 2010*. 2011. http://www.one.cu/aec2010.htm.

———. "Proyecciones de la Población Cubana, 2015–2050," tables 10.1 and 10.2. 2013. http://www.one.cu/proyecciones de la poblacion 2015 2050.htm.

———. *Anuario Estadístico de Cuba 2013*. 2014. http://www.one.cu/aec2013.htm.

———. *Anuario Estadístico de Cuba 2014*. 2015. http://www.one.cu/aec2014.htm.

———. *Anuario Estadístico de Cuba 2015: Agricultura, Ganadería, Silvicultura y Pesca*, Capítulo 9, 2016. http://www.onei.cu/aec2015.htm.

Olavarria, Margot. "Rap and Revolution: Hip-Hop Comes to Cuba." In *A Contemporary Cuba Reader: Reinventing the Revolution*, edited by Philip Brenner, Marguerite Rose Jiménez, John M. Kirk, and William M. LeoGrande. Lanham, MD: Rowman & Littlefield, 2007.

Oppenheimer, Andres. *Castro's Final Hour: The Secret Story Behind the Coming Downfall of Communist Cuba.* New York: Simon & Schuster, 1992.

Padgett, Tim. "Cuba's Catholic Dissident: The Saga of Oswaldo Payá." In *A Contemporary Cuba Reader: Reinventing the Revolution*, edited by Philip Brenner, Marguerite Rose Jiménez, John M. Kirk, and William M. LeoGrande. Lanham, MD: Rowman & Littlefield, 2007.

Padura, Leonardo. *The Man Who Loved Dogs*. Translated by Anna Kushner. New York: Farrar, Straus & Giroux, 2014.

Padura Fuentes, Leonardo. "Living and Creating in Cuba: Risks and Challenges." In *A Contemporary Cuba Reader: Reinventing the Revolution*, edited by Philip Brenner, Marguerite Rose Jiménez, John M. Kirk, and William M. LeoGrande. Lanham, MD: Rowman & Littlefield, 2007.

Pagés, Raisa. "The Status of Women: From Economically Dependent to Independent." In *A Contemporary Cuba Reader: Reinventing the Revolution*, edited by Philip Brenner, Marguerite Rose Jiménez, John M. Kirk, and William M. LeoGrande. Lanham, MD: Rowman & Littlefield, 2007.

Palmer, Elizabeth A. "Exiles Talk of PACs and Power, Not Another Bay of Pigs." *CQ Weekly* (June 23, 1990). http://library.cqpress.com/cqweekly/WR101409626.

Park, Rebecca C. "Brief History of the US Residence and Eagle, Havana, Cuba." June, pamphlet. Havana, Cuba: US Interests Section, 2005.

Parry, Robert, and Peter Kornbluh. "Iran-Contra's Untold Story." *Foreign Policy* 72 (Fall 1988).

Partido Comunista de Cuba. *Informe Central Tercer Congreso.* 1986. http://con
gresopcc.cip.cu/wp-content/uploads/2011/01/Informe-Central.pdf.
Paterson, Thomas G. *Contesting Castro: The United States and the Triumph of the
Cuban Revolution.* New York: Oxford University Press, 1994.
Pavlov, Yuri. *Soviet-Cuban Alliance, 1959–1991.* New Brunswick: Transaction, 1994.
Pedraza, Silvia. *Political Disaffection in Cuba's Revolution and Exodus.* New York:
Cambridge University Press, 2007.
Pérez, Lisandro. "Immigrant Economic Adjustment and Family Organization: The
Cuban Success Story Reexamined." *International Migration Review* 20, no. 1
(Spring 1986).
Pérez, Louis A., Jr. *Cuba between Empires, 1878–1902.* Pittsburgh: University of
Pittsburgh Press, 1983.
———. *Cuba and the United States: Ties of Singular Intimacy.* Athens: University of
Georgia Press, 1990.
———. *The War of 1898: The United States and Cuba in History and Historiography.*
Chapel Hill: University of North Carolina Press, 1998.
———. *On Becoming Cuban: Identity, Nationality, and Culture.* Chapel Hill: Univer-
sity of North Carolina Press, 1999.
———. *To Die in Cuba: Suicide and Society.* Chapel Hill: University of North Caro-
lina Press. 2005.
———. *Cuba in the American Imagination.* Chapel Hill: University of North Carolina
Press, 2008.
———. *Cuba: Between Reform and Revolution,* fourth edition. Oxford: Oxford Uni-
versity Press, 2011.
———. *The Structure of Cuban History: Meanings and Purpose of the Past.* Chapel
Hill: University of North Carolina Press, 2013.
———. "Fidel Castro: A Life—and Death—in Context." *NACLA,* November
29, 2016. http://nacla.org/news/2016/11/29/fidel-castro-life%E2%80%94-and
-death%E2%80%94-context.
Pérez-Stable, Marifeli. *The Cuban Revolution: Origins, Course, and Legacy,* second
edition. New York: Oxford University Press, 1999.
Pérez Villanueva, Omar Everleny. "The Role of Foreign Direct Investment in Eco-
nomic Development: The Cuban Experience." In *The Cuban Economy at the Start
of the Twenty-First Century,* edited by Jorge I. Domínguez, Omar Everleny Pérez
Villanueva, and Lorena Barberia. Cambridge: Harvard University Press, 2004.
———. "The Cuban Economy Today and Its Future Challenges." In *The Cuban
Economy at the Start of the Twenty-First Century,* edited by Jorge I. Domínguez,
Omar Everleny Pérez Villanueva, and Lorena Barberia. Cambridge: Harvard Uni-
versity Press, 2004.
———. "Foreign Direct Investment in Vietnam and Cuba: Lessons Learned." In *No
More Free Lunch: Reflections on the Cuban Economic Reform Process and Chal-
lenges for Transformation,* edited by Claus Brundenius and Ricardo Torres Pérez.
Heidelberg: Springer, 2014.
Peters, Philip. "International Tourism: The New Engine of the Cuban Economy."
Arlington, VA: Lexington Institute, 2002.

———. "Cuba's Small Entrepreneurs: Down but Not Out." Arlington, VA: Lexington Institute (September 2006).

———. "A Viewer's Guide to Cuba's Economic Reform." Arlington, VA: Lexington Institute. 2012.

Peters, Philip, and Joseph L. Scarpaci. "Cuba's New Entrepreneurs: Five Years of Small-Scale Capitalism." Arlington, VA: Alexis de Tocqueville Institution (August 1998).

Pettavino, Paula, and Philip Brenner. "More Than Just a Game: The Dual Developmental Aspects of Cuban Sports." *Peace Review* 11, no. 4 (December 1999).

Pew Hispanic Center. "Cubans in the United States." *Fact Sheet*, August 25, 2006. http://www.pewhispanic.org/2006/08/25/cubans-in-the-united-states.

Phillips, J. D. "Machado 'Leave' Sought by Welles as Cuban Solution: Ambassador Suggests Naming a New State Secretary Who Would Succeed President. Executive Bars Quitting . . . Toll of Rioting Now 30." *New York Times*, August 9, 1933.

Phillips, R. Hart. "Cuba Is Betting on Her New Gambling Casinos." *New York Times*, November 6, 1955.

———. "Batista Major Condemned in Havana Stadium Trial." *New York Times*, January 24, 1959, 1.

———. "Castro Links U.S. to Ship 'Sabotage'; Denial Is Swift." *New York Times*, March 6, 1960, 1.

Platt, Orville H. "The Pacification of Cuba." *Independent*, June 27, 1901.

Playboy. "*Playboy* Interview: Fidel Castro." January 1967.

Portilla, Miguel León, and Nicolás Sánchez-Albornoz. *América Latina en la* época *colonial.* Barcelona: Critica España, 2002.

Prados-Torreira, Teresa. *Mambisas: Rebel Women in Nineteenth-Century Cuba.* Gainesville: University Press of Florida, 2005.

Preston, Julia. "The Trial That Shook Cuba." *New York Review of Books*, December 7, 1989.

Prieto, Abel. "Cuba's National Literacy Campaign." *Journal of Reading* 25, no. 3 (December 1981).

Qiu, Linda. "Are There Political Prisoners in Cuba?" *PolitiFact Global News Service*, March 22, 2016. http://www.politifact.com/global-news/statements/2016/mar/22/raul-castro/are-there-political-prisoners-cuba.

Quirk, Robert E. *Fidel Castro.* New York: Norton, 1993.

Raña, Mario Vázquez. "Interview with Raúl Castro, *El Sol de Mexico*, April 21, 1993." Excerpted in García Luis, *Cuban Revolution Reader: A Documentary History of 40 Key Moments of the Cuban Revolution.* Melbourne: Ocean Press, 2001.

Rasenberger, Jim. *The Brilliant Disaster: JFK, Castro, and America's Doomed Invasion of Cuba's Bay of Pigs.* New York: Scribner, 2011.

Revista Temas. http://temas.cult.cu.

Revolucion. "Fija Fidel Las Cinco Garantias Contra La Agresion a Cuba." October 29, 1962.

Rich, Donna. "Cuban Internationalism: A Humanitarian Foreign Policy." In *The Cuba Reader: The Making of a Revolutionary Society*, edited by Philip Brenner, William M. LeoGrande, Donna Rich, and Daniel Siegel. New York: Grove, 1988.

———. "Cuba's Role as Mediator in International Conflicts: Formal and Informal Initiatives." In *Cuban Foreign Policy Confronts a New International Order*, edited by H. Michael Erisman and John M. Kirk. Boulder, CO: Lynne Rienner, 1991.

Rickover, Hyman George. *How the Battleship Maine Was Destroyed.* Washington, DC: Department of the Navy, 1976. http://babel.hathitrust.org/cgi/pt?id=mdp.3901 5004705649;view=1up;seq.

Ritter, Archibald R. M. "Cuba's Economic Reorientation." In *Cuba: In Transition? Pathways to Renewal, Long-Term Development and Global Reintegration*, edited by Mauricio Font. New York: Bildner Center, CUNY, 2006.

Rivera, Yailin Orta. "Desenmascaran falsificación de productos en redes comerciales del país." *Juventud Rebelde*, February 25, 2007. http://www.juventudrebelde.cu/cuba/2007-02-25/desenmascaran-falsificacion-de-productos-en-redes-comerci ales-del-pais.

Rivera, Yailin Orta, and Norge Martínez Montero. "La vieja gran estafa." *Juventud Rebelde*, October 1, 2006. http://www.juventudrebelde.cu/cuba/2006-10-01/la-vie ja-gran-estafa.

Rodriguez, Felix I., and John Weisman. *Shadow Warrior*. New York: Simon & Schuster, 1989.

Rodríguez, Juan Carlos. *The Bay of Pigs and the CIA*. Translated by Mary Todd. Melbourne: Ocean Press, 1999.

Rodríguez Chávez, Ernesto. "La crisis migratoria . . ." as quoted in Masud-Piloto, *From Welcomed Exiles to Illegal Immigrants: Cuban Migration to the US, 1959– 1995.* Lanham, MD: Rowman & Littlefield, 1996.

Rodríguez Ramos, Reniel. "From the Guanahatabey to the Archaic of Puerto Rico: The Nonevident Evidence." *Ethnohistory* 55, no. 3 (2008).

Rohter, Larry. "Pope Asks Cubans to Seek New Path toward Freedom." *New York Times*, January 26, 1998.

Romer, Christina. "Spurious Volatility in Historical Unemployment Data." *Journal of Political Economy* 94, no. 1 (February 1986): 31.

Romero, Carlos A. "South-South Cooperation between Venezuela and Cuba." *Special Report on South-South Cooperation, South-South Cooperation: A Challenge to the Aid System?* (Reality of Aid Network), 2010. http://www.realityofaid.org/wp -content/uploads/2013/02/ROA-SSDC-Special-ReportEnglish.pdf.

Romero Gómez, Antonio F. "Economic Transformations and Institutional Changes in Cuba." In *Cuba's Economic Change in Comparative Perspective*, edited by Richard E. Feinberg and Ted Piccone. Washington, DC: Brookings Institution Press, 2014.

Roosevelt, Franklin D. "First Inaugural Address." March 4, 1933. http://avalon.law .yale.edu/20th_century/froos1.asp.

Roosevelt, Theodore. *The Rough Riders.* New York: G. P. Putnam's Sons, 1900.

Rouse, Irving. *The Tainos: Rise and Decline of the People Who Greeted Columbus.* New Haven: Yale University Press, 1992.

Roy, Joaquín. "The European Union's Perception of Cuba: From Frustration to Irritation." In *A Contemporary Cuba Reader: Reinventing the Revolution*, edited by Philip Brenner, Marguerite Rose Jiménez, John M. Kirk, and William M. Leo-Grande. Lanham, MD: Rowman & Littlefield, 2007.

Royce, Frederick S. "Agricultural Production Cooperatives: The Future of Cuban Agriculture." *Transnational Law and Contemporary Problems* 14, no. 1 (Spring 2004).

Rucker, Patrick Michael. "European Nations May Downgrade Cuba Ties after Castro Crackdown." *Financial Times*, April 22, 2003.

Sams, Stanhope. "Cubans Not Fit to Govern; This Is the Opinion of an Observer Who Accompanied Shafter's Army to Santiago." *New York Times*, July 29, 1898.

Sánchez Egozcue, Jorge Mario. "Challenges of Economic Restructuring in Cuba." In *A Contemporary Cuba Reader: The Revolution under Raúl Castro*, edited by Philip Brenner, Marguerite Rose Jiménez, John M. Kirk, and William M. LeoGrande. Lanham, MD: Rowman & Littlefield, 2014.

Sánchez-Parodi, Ramón. *CUBA-USA: Diez Tiempos de una Relación*. Havana: Editorial de Ciencias Sociales, 2012.

Sanger, David. "U.S. Says It Tried to Build a Social Media Site in Cuba, but Failed." *New York Times*, April 4, 2014.

Santamarina, Juan C. "The Cuba Company and the Expansion of American Business in Cuba, 1898–1915." *Business History Review* 74, no. 1 (Spring 2000).

Schneider, Andrew. "Cuban Drug Could Help Diabetes Patients Avoid Amputations." *Houston Chronicle*, December 19, 2014. http://www.houstonchronicle.com/news/health/article/Cuban-drug-could-help-diabetes-patients-avoid-5969300.php.

Schoultz, Lars. *Beneath the United States: A History of U.S. Policy toward Latin America.* Cambridge: Harvard University Press, 1998.

———. *That Infernal Little Cuban Republic: The United States and the Cuban Revolution.* Chapel Hill: University of North Carolina Press, 2009.

Schwab, Stephen Irving Max. *Guantánamo, USA: The Untold History of America's Cuban Outpost.* Lawrence: University of Kansas Press, 2009.

Schwartz, Rosalie. *Pleasure Island: Tourism and Temptation in Cuba.* Lincoln: University of Nebraska Press, 1997.

Scott, Rebecca J. *Slave Emancipation in Cuba: The Transition to Free Labor, 1860–1899.* Princeton: Princeton University Press, 1985.

SED CC Department of International Relations. "Information on the Third Plenum of the Central Committee of the Cuban Communist Party and on the Attacks of the Cuban Communist Party against the Socialist Unity Party of Germany." January 31, 1968, History and Public Policy Program Digital Archive, Woodrow Wilson International Center for Scholars, Washington, DC, http://digitalarchive.wilsoncenter.org/document/115812.

Serra, Ana. *The "New Man" in Cuba: Culture and Identity in the Revolution.* Gainesville: University Press of Florida, 2007.

Seventh Congress of the Communist Party of Cuba. "Resolution on the Results of Implementing the Lineamientos." April 18, 2016. http://www.cubadebate.cu/especiales/2016/04/18/resolucion-sobre-resultados-de-la-implementacion-de-los-lineamientos-de-la-politica-economica-y-social-del-partido-y-la-revolucion-aprobados-en-el-vi-congreso-y-su-actualizacion-el-periodo-2016-2021.

Shambaugh, David. "China's New Foray into Latin America." *YaleGlobal Online Magazine*, November 17, 2008.

Silverman, Bertram. "Introduction: The Great Debate in Retrospect: Economic Rationality and the Ethics of Revolution." In *Man and Socialism in Cuba: The Great Debate*, edited by Bertram Silverman. New York: Atheneum, 1973.

Simons, Geoff. *From Conquistador to Castro.* New York: Macmillan, 1996.

Sinclair, Minor, and Martha Thompson. *Cuba, Going Against the Grain: Agricultural Crisis and Transformation.* Boston: Oxfam America, 2001.

———. "Going Against the Grain: Agricultural Crisis and Transformation." In *A Contemporary Cuba Reader: Reinventing the Revolution*, edited by Philip Brenner, Marguerite Rose Jiménez, John M. Kirk, and William M. LeoGrande. Lanham, MD: Rowman & Littlefield, 2007.

Sixth Congress of the Communist Party of Cuba. "Resolution on the Guidelines of the Economic and Social Policy of the Party and the Revolution." April 18, 2011. http://www.cuba.cu/gobierno/documentos/2011/ing/l160711i.html.

———. "Information about the Result of Debate on the Lineamientos." May 5, 2011. http://www.cubadebate.cu/wp-content/uploads/2011/05/tabloidedebatelineamientos.pdf.

Sixto, Felipe Eduardo. "An Evaluation of Four Decades of Cuban Healthcare." *Cuba in Transition*, vol. 12. McLean, VA: Association for the Study of the Cuban Economy, 2002.

Sklar, Barry. "Cuban Exodus 1980: The Context." In *The Cuba Reader: The Making of a Revolutionary Society*, edited by Philip Brenner, William M. LeoGrande, Donna Rich, and Daniel Siegel. New York: Grove, 1988.

Smith, Hedrick. "US Says Castro Has Transferred 60s Policy of Intervention to Africa." *New York Times*, November 17, 1977, 1.

Smith, Robert F. *The United States and Cuba: Business and Diplomacy, 1917–1960.* New York: Bookman Associates, 1961.

Smith, Wayne S. *The Closest of Enemies: A Personal and Diplomatic Account of U.S.-Cuban Relations since 1957.* New York: Norton, 1987.

———. "The U.S.-Cuba Imbroglio: Anatomy of a Crisis." *International Policy Report*, May. Washington, DC: Center for International Policy, 1996.

———. "Provocation, War Spawned Cuba Crackdown." *Baltimore Sun*, April 15, 2003.

Smith, Wayne S., and Anya K. Landau. "Cuba and Bioweapons: Groundless Allegations Squander U.S. Credibility on Terrorism." *CIP Special Report*, July 12. Washington, DC: Center for International Policy, 2002.

Snow, Anita. "Cuba's Raul Castro Signals More Openness to Debate of Divergent Ideas Than Brother Fidel." Associated Press International, December 21, 2006.

Sorhegui D'Mares, Arturo, and Alejandro de la Fuente. "El surgimiento de la sociedad criolla de Cuba (1553–1608)." In *Historia de Cuba 1492–1898*, third edition, edited by Eduardo Torres-Cuevas and Oscar Loyola Vega. Havana: Editorial Pueblo y Educación, 2006.

Spadoni, Paolo. *Failed Sanctions: Why the U.S. Embargo against Cuba Could Never Work.* Gainesville: University Press of Florida, 2010.

Stephens, Sarah. "As Cuba Plans to Drill in the Gulf of Mexico, U.S. Policy Poses Needless Risks to Our National Interest." Washington, DC: Center for Democracy in the Americas, 2011.

———. "Women's Work: Gender Equality in Cuba and the Role of Women in Building Cuba's Future." Washington, DC: Center for Democracy in the Americas, 2013.

Stern, Sheldon M. *Averting 'The Final Failure': John F. Kennedy and the Secret Cuban Missile Crisis Meetings.* Palo Alto, CA: Stanford University Press, 2003.

Sternberg, Bill. "US Works for Regime Change in Cuba, Too." *USA Today*, October 23, 2002.

Stock, Ann Marie. "Zooming In: Making and Marketing Films in Twenty-First-Century Cuba." In *A Contemporary Cuba Reader: The Revolution under Raúl Castro*, edited by Philip Brenner, Marguerite Rose Jiménez, John M. Kirk, and William M. LeoGrande. Lanham, MD: Rowman & Littlefield, 2014.

Stoner, K. Lynn. "Militant Heroines and the Consecration of the Patriarchal State: The Glorification of Loyalty, Combat, and National Suicide in the Making of Cuban National Identity." *Cuban Studies* 34 (2003).

Suchliki, Jaime. "Why Cuba Will Still Be Anti-American After Castro." *Atlantic*, March 4, 2013.

Sweig, Julia E. *Inside the Cuban Revolution: Fidel Castro and the Urban Underground.* Cambridge: Harvard University Press, 2002.

———. "Fidel's Final Victory." *Foreign Affairs* (January/February 2007).

Szulc, Tad. *Fidel: A Critical Portrait.* New York: William Morrow, 1986.

Tamayo, Juan. "Exiles Directed Blasts That Rocked Island's Tourism, Investigation Reveals." *Miami Herald*, November 17, 1997.

Tambs, Lewis, ed. "A New Inter-American Policy for the Eighties." Washington: Council for Inter-American Security, 1980.

Taubman. William. *Khrushchev: The Man and His Era.* New York: Norton, 2003.

Teltsch, Kathleen. "Young, Taking Over U.N. Duties, Prepares to Leave for Africa Today." *New York Times*, February 1, 1977.

Thomas, Evan, and Mark Hosenball. "Cubans at the Wheel." *Newsweek*, December 11, 2000.

Thomas, Hugh. *Cuba: The Pursuit of Freedom.* New York: Harper & Row, 1971.

Thomas, Jo. "Crowd at Havana Embassy Grows." *New York Times*, April 7, 1980, A1.

Tone, John Lawrence. *War and Genocide in Cuba, 1895–1898.* Chapel Hill: University of North Carolina Press, 2006.

Torres Pérez, Ricardo. "Concluding Reflections of the Current Reform Process in Cuba." In *No More Free Lunch: Reflections on the Cuban Economic Reform Process and Challenges for Transformation*, edited by Claus Brundenius and Ricardo Torres Pérez. Heidelberg: Springer, 2014.

Torres-Cuevas, Eduardo, and Oscar Loyola Vega. *Historia de Cuba 1492–1898*, third edition. Havana: Editorial Pueblo y Educación, 2006.

Triana Cordoví, Juan. "Moving from Reacting to an External Shock toward Shaping a New Conception of Cuban Socialism." In *No More Free Lunch: Reflections on the Cuban Economic Reform Process and Challenges for Transformation*, edited by Claus Brundenius and Ricardo Torres Pérez. Heidelberg: Springer, 2014.

Trujillo Lemes, Maximiliano F. "La Iglesia católica, la condición política cubana y Palabra Nueva." *Temas*, no. 76 (October–December 2013).

Tucker, Katherine, and Thomas R. Hedges. "Food Shortages and an Epidemic of Optic and Peripheral Neuropathy in Cuba." *Nutrition Reviews* 51, no. 12 (1993).

United Nations Development Programme. *Human Development Report 2009.* New York: United Nations, 2009.

United States, Atlantic Command. *CINCLANT Historical Account of Cuban Crisis.* Serial: 000119/J09H, April 29, 1963; National Security Archive, Accession No. CC03087, 39–40.

US Central Intelligence Agency. "Taylor Commission Report on Cuban Operations." Memorandum No. 1, June 13, 1961, 10; available at the National Security Archive, Washington, DC, Accession No. CU00181.

———. "Inspector General Report on Plots to Assassinate Fidel Castro." May 23, 1967. National Archives and Records Administration, JFK Record Series; Record Number: 104-10213-10101; File Number: JFK64-48 :F52 1998 .06 .23 .11 :39 :07 :420082.

———. "The Sino-Soviet Struggle in the World Communist Movement Since Khrushchev's Fall." Part 1, September 1967. http://www.foia.cia.gov/document/ intelligence-report-sino-soviet-struggle-world-communist-movement-kruschevs -fall-part-1.

———. Cable IN-73140, October 17, 1967; Subjects: "Background of Soviet Premier Aleksey Kosygin's Visit to Havana; Content of Discussions Between Kosygin and Cuban Premier Fidel Castro," 2–3. Available through Declassified Documents Reference System (DDRS), Gale Cengage Learning.

———. National Archives and Records Administration, JFK Assassination System, Record Series: JFK; Record Number: 104-10213-10101; Agency File Number: 80TO1357A; Releasd, June 23, 1998.

———, Directorate of Operations. "Activities of Cuban Exile Leader Orlando Bosch during His Stay in Venezuela." Digital National Security Archive, Accession number: CL01549; Document number: IN 069101; ProQuest document ID: 1679043549, October 14, 1976.

US Congress, House Committee on Foreign Affairs, Subcommittee on Inter-American Affairs. "Hijacking Accord Between the United States and Cuba." Hearing, February 20, 1973.

———, 94th Cong., 1st Sess. "U.S. Trade Embargo of Cuba." Hearings before the Subcommittees on International Trade and Commerce and International Organizations, Committee on International Relations, on H.R. 6382, May 8 to September 23, 1975.

———, Select Committee on Assassination. "Investigation of the Assassination of President John F. Kennedy," vol. X: Appendix to Hearings, March 1979.

———. "Cuban Democracy Act of 1992." Report from the Committee on Foreign Affairs on H.R. 5253, 102nd Cong., 2nd Sess., House Report 102 615, Part 1, June 25, 1992.

US Congress, Senate Committee on the Judiciary. "The Tricontinental Conference of African, Asian and Latin American Peoples, A Staff Study." 89th Cong., 2nd Sess., June 7, 1966.

US Department of Commerce, Census Bureau. "Foreign Trade: Trade in Goods with Cuba." May 16, 2016. https://www.census.gov/foreign-trade/balance/c2390.html.

US Department of the Interior, U.S. Geological Survey. "Assessment of Undiscovered Oil and Gas Resources of the North Cuba Basin, Cuba, 2004." February 2005. http://pubs.usgs.gov/fs/2005/3009/pdf/fs20053009.pdf.

———. "Mineral Commodity Summaries 2015." January 2015. http://minerals.usgs .gov/minerals/pubs/mcs/2015/mcs2015.pdf.

US Department of Justice, Office of the Associate Attorney General. "Exclusion Proceeding for Orlando Bosch Avila." File: A28 851 622, A11 861 810, January 23, 1989.

US Department of Labor, Bureau of International Labor Affairs. *List of Goods Produced by Child Labor or Forced Labor*, September 30, 2016. https://www.dol.gov/sites/ default/files/documents/ilab/reports/child-labor/findings/TVPRAReport2016.pdf.

US Department of State. "Report of the National Bipartisan Commission on Central America." Washington, DC, January 1984.

———. Country Reports on Human Rights Practices for 2012, Cuba. April 19, 2013. http://www.state.gov/j/drl/rls/hrrpt/humanrightsreport/index.htm?year= 2012&dlid=204441.

US Departments of State and Defense. "The Soviet-Cuban Connection in Central America and the Caribbean" (March 1985).

US Government Accountability Office. "Foreign Assistance: US Democracy Assistance for Cuba Needs Better Management and Oversight." Report #GAO-07-147. November 2006, http://www.gao.gov/products/GAO-07-147.

———. "Broadcasting to Cuba: Actions Are Needed to Improve Strategy and Operations." Report #GAO-09-127. January 2009. http://www.gao.gov/products/GAO -09-127.

US Senate, 93rd Cong., 1st Sess. "US Policy Toward Cuba." Hearings before the Subcommittee on Western Hemisphere Affairs, March 26 and April 18, 1973.

US Senate Select Committee. *Alleged Assassinations Plots Involving Foreign Leaders.* Washington, DC: US Government Printing Office, 1975.

USSR International Affairs. "Text of Joint Statement, Tass in Russian to Europe 2255 GMT 24 May 1963." In "Material on Castro Visit in Soviet Union," *Foreign Broadcast Information Service (FBIS)*, USSR International Affairs, May 27, 1963.

Universidad de Holguín. "¿Quiénes Somos?" http://www.uho.edu.cu/?page_id=526.

Uriarte, Mirén. "Social Impact of the Economic Measures." In *A Contemporary Cuba Reader: Reinventing the Revolution*, edited by Philip Brenner, Marguerite Rose Jiménez, John M. Kirk, and William M. LeoGrande. Lanham, MD: Rowman & Littlefield, 2007.

Valdés, Nelson P. "The Revolutionary and Political Content of Fidel Castro's Charismatic Authority." In *A Contemporary Cuba Reader: Reinventing the Revolution*, edited by Philip Brenner, Marguerite Rose Jiménez, John M. Kirk, and William M. LeoGrande. Lanham, MD: Rowman & Littlefield, 2007.

———. "What Was Forbidden Then Is Promoted Now: Cuba, the Beatles and Historical Context." *Counterpunch*, March 29/30, 2008.

Valdés-Dapena, Jacinto. *Operación Mangosta: Preludio de la invasion directa a Cuba.* Havana: Editorial Capitán San Luis, 2002.

Vanderbush, Walt, and Patrick J. Haney. "Policy toward Cuba in the Clinton Administration." *Political Science Quarterly* 114, no. 3 (Fall 1999).

Vidal Alejandro, Pavel. "El shock venezolano y Cuba: Crónica de una crisis anunciada." *Cuba Posible*, July 21, 2016. https://cubaposible.com/shock-venezolano -cuba-cronica-una-crisis-anunciada.

Vidal Ferreiro, Josefina. "Press Conference." December 5, 2012. http://www.minrex .gob.cu/en/press-conference-josefina-vidal-ferreiro-head-united-states-division -cuban-chancery-international.

Voss, Michael. "Cuba Pushes Its 'Medical Diplomacy.'" *BBC News*, May 20, 2009. http://news.bbc.co.uk/go/pr/fr/-/2/hi/americas/8059287.stm.

Walker, Phyllis Greene. "National Security." In *Cuba: A Country Study*, edited James D. Rudolph. Washington, DC: US Government Printing Office, 1985.

Warner, Michael. "Lessons Unlearned: The CIA's Internal Probe of the Bay of Pigs Affair." *Studies in Intelligence* (Winter 1998–1999). https://www.cia.gov/library/ center-for-the-study-of-intelligence/csi-publications/csi-studies/studies/winter 98_99/art08.html.

Washington, George. "The Farewell Address." Transcript of the Final Manuscript, September 19, 1796; available at the Papers of George Washington, University of Virginia, 5 and 6, http://gwpapers.virginia.edu/documents/farewell/transcript.html.

Weber, Max. *The Theory of Social and Economic Organization*. Translated by A. M. Henderson and Talcott Parsons. New York: Free Press, 1964.

Weinmann, Lissa. Washington's Irrational Cuba Policy." *World Policy Journal* (Spring 2004).

Westad, Odd Arne. "Moscow and the Angolan Crisis, 1974–1976: A New Pattern of Intervention." *Cold War International History Project Bulletin* 8–9 (Winter 1996/1997).

Whalen, Charles W., et al. "A Détente with Cuba." *Congressional Record*, January 29, 1973.

Wieland, William A. "Memorandum from the Director of the Office of Middle American Affairs (Wieland) to the Assistant Secretary of State for Inter-American Affairs (Rubottom)." *Foreign Relations of the United States, 1958–1960*, Volume VI, Cuba. Washington, DC: US Department of State, Office of the Historian. Document 5, January 17, 1958.

Wilhelm, Silvia. "New Cuba Policy Is Cruel, Ineffective." *Progressive*, June 23, 2004.

Williams, Robin C. "In the Shadow of Plenty, Cuba Copes with a Crippled Health Care System." In *A Contemporary Cuba Reader: Reinventing the Revolution*, edited by Philip Brenner, Marguerite Rose Jiménez, John M. Kirk, and William M. LeoGrande. Lanham, MD: Rowman & Littlefield, 2007.

Williamson, John. "What Should the World Bank Think about the Washington Consensus?" *World Bank Research Observer* 15, no. 2 (2000).

Wright, Ilene Ahoha. *The Early History of Cuba, 1492–1586.* New York: Macmillan, 1916.

Wyden, Peter. *Bay of Pigs: The Untold Story*. New York: Simon & Schuster, 1979.

Xinhua. "China's Policy Paper on Latin America and the Caribbean." November 5, 2008. http://news.xinhuanet.com/english/2008-11/05/content_10308117.htm.

Zabala Argüelles, María del Carmen. "Poverty and Vulnerability in Cuba Today." In *A Contemporary Cuba Reader: The Revolution under Raúl Castro*, edited by Philip Brenner, Marguerite Rose Jiménez, John M. Kirk, and William M. LeoGrande, 191–93. Lanham, MD: Rowman & Littlefield, 2014.

Zanetti Leucuna, Oscar. *Historia Mínima de Cuba.* Mexico City: El Colegio de México, 2013.

Zanetti Leucuna, Oscar, and Alejandro García. *Sugar and Railroads: A Cuban History, 1837–1959.* Chapel Hill: University of North Carolina Press, 1998.

Zeitlin, Maurice. *Revolutionary Politics and the Cuban Working Class.* New York: Harper & Row, 1970.

Ziegler, Melanie M. *U.S.-Cuban Cooperation: Past, Present and Future.* Gainesville: University Press of Florida, 2007.

Zimbalist, Andrew, and Susan Eckstein. "Patterns of Cuban Development: The First Twenty-Five Years." In *Cuba's Socialist Economy: Toward the 1990s*, edited by Andrew Zimbalist. Boulder, CO: Lynne Rienner, 1987.

Zimbalist Andrew, and Howard J. Sherman. *Comparing Economic Systems: A Political-Economic Approach.* Orlando: Academic Press, 1984.

Index

People's Movement for the
Liberation of Angola (MPLA),
190, 192–193, 219
anti-imperialism, 53, 132
apartheid, 193, 217, 284–285
Aponte, José Antonio, 19–20, 356
Arab Spring, 344
Arafat, Yasser, 197
Aragonés, Emilio, 125, 150
Arbenz, Jacobo, 70, 88, 131
architecture, 87, 315
Argentina, 21, 49, 99, 176, 196, 278,
284, 296, 325
Armstrong, Scott, 220, 267
army. *See* Revolutionary Armed Forces
Arteaga y Betancourt, Cardinal Manuel,
69
Artime Buesa, Manuel, 107
artists, 201, 235, 332, 340
government repression of, 102, 185
role within the Revolution, 100
See also Cuban Institute of
Cinematographic Art and
Industry; Havana Biennial; protest
music
Ashcroft, John, 270
Asia, 3, 4, 7, 33–34, 36, 161, 287, 293,
318, 350, 362
Association of Veterans of the Cuban
Revolution, 297
Attwood, William, 158
Auténtico Party, 59–60
Autonomist Party, 30
Azicri, Max, 284
Aznar, José María, 283

B
B-26 bombers, 135
Bacardí Ltd., 258
Bachelet, Michelle, 284
Bain, Mervyn, 76
Baker, James, 233
Balboa, Silvestre de, 356
ballet, 96
Balseros Crisis. *See* rafters crisis

bandidos, 106, 208
Barberia, Lorena, 244
Barrio Adentro Deportivo (Sports in the
Neighborhood), 286
baseball, 43, 267, 371, 378
Basic Units of Cooperative Production,
237
Basulto, José, 255, 256–257
Batista, Fulgencio, vi, 52–53, 56, 59,
61–62, 63–64, 68–69, 70, 72–73,
74, 75, 77, 81, 83, 85, 90, 289,
359–360
Battle of Ideas, 275
Bayamo, 6, 8, 19, 26, 242
Bayamo Barracks, 69
Bay of Pigs, 103, 105, 107, 128–139,
145, 147, 153, 157, 158, 188, 213,
255, 256, 350, 361
Beatles, 165
Benes, Bernardo, 203
Bengelsdorf, Carollee, 182
Berger, Sandy, 268
Berle, Adolf A., 137
Berlusconi, Silvio, 283
Betancourt, Ana, 25
biotechnology, 280, 337
Biran, Holguín, 85, 298
Bishop, Maurice, 196, 212
Bissell, Richard, 132
black market, 196, 205, 210, 229, 230,
237, 276
blockade. *See* embargo
blogs, 341
Bolaños, Jorge, viii
Bolivarian Alternative for the Peoples of
Our America/Bolivarian Alliance
for the Peoples of Our America
(ALBA), 286, 287, 289, 333, 325
Bolívar, Simón, 21
Bolivia, 99, 129, 157, 162, 174, 284,
287, 363, 373
Bolshevik Revolution, 150
Bolton, John R., 280
Borges, Jorge Luis, 101
Bosch, Orlando, 259

Sandinista, 196, 215, 217–218, 233, 366
Santa Ifigenia Cemetery, 379
Santamaría, Haydee, 71, 90
santería, 97
Santiago de Cuba, 8, 13, 14, 69, 77,
  86–87, 120, 173, 298, 358, 379
Santos, Juan Manuel, 326, 376
Sartre, Jean-Paul, 101, 185
Scarabeo 9, 376
Schlesinger, Arthur, Jr., 137
Sechin, Igor, 305
Second Declaration of Havana, 150,
  160, 361
security-oriented skeptics, 315
Sékou Touré, Ahmed, 193
Selassie, Haile, 195
self-serving survivalists, 315
Senate Foreign Relations Committee,
  254
Sergeants' Revolt, 52
Seven Years' War, 16, 356
Seward, William Henry, 34
Sherritt International, 236, 273
Shops for the Recovery of Hard
  Currency, 229
Sierra Maestra, 8, 62, 71, 72, 73, 74,
  75, 77
Sino-Soviet relations, 159
Smith, Earl E. T., 77, 84, 129, 349
Smith, Wayne S., 130, 195, 203, 214
socialism
  Cuban, 159, 182, 211, 231, 296, 308,
    309, 315, 336, 351
  European, 164, 165, 166, 363
  Fidel Castro, 70
soft power, 219, 332, 333
Solás, Humberto, 91
Soles y Rayos de Bolívar, 20
Somoza, Anastasio, 196
South African Defense Force (SADF),
  216
South West African Peoples
  Organization (SWAPO), 193,
  219–220

Soviet Union. 76, 122, 129, 160, 171,
  197, 367
  collapse, 232, 233, 236, 272, 288, 369
  Cuba's role in Africa, 191, 193, 194,
    195
  invasion of Afghanistan, 198
  invasion of Czechoslovakia, 164,
    165, 166
  Missile Crisis, 142, 143, 144, 145,
    147, 148, 150, 151, 152, 153, 154
  relations with Cuba, vi, 62, 104, 106,
    126, 130, 131, 159, 161, 162, 163,
    175, 176, 177, 188, 189, 211, 214,
    217, 218, 226, 286, 287, 349, 361,
    362, 363, 364
  relations with the United States, 152,
    215, 366
Spain, 42, 45, 85, 104, 120, 196, 242,
  244, 302
  colonization, 2, 3, 5, 6, 7, 8, 12, 13,
    14, 15, 16, 17, 19, 27, 30, 153,
    355, 356
  Cuban independence war, 23, 24,
    25, 26, 29, 32, 34, 35, 36, 37, 38,
    281, 357
  foreign investment, 232, 236, 283,
    305, 317
Special Period, 225–241, 247, 248, 274,
  276, 282, 288, 294, 296, 298, 299,
  309, 316, 332, 341, 342, 368
sports, 82, 125, 178, 310, 340
  cooperation, 286, 319
Stalin, Joseph, 76, 338
Standard Oil, 131
sugar, 18, 23, 24, 27, 28, 36, 41, 43, 48,
  50, 57, 69, 76, 84, 88, 92, 93, 112,
  159, 162, 171, 175, 176, 177, 202,
  212, 227, 232, 236, 237, 242, 273,
  297, 305, 356, 357, 358, 372, 374
sugar beets, 27, 36, 47, 48
sugar economy, 15–17, 23, 26–27,
  47–48, 60, 93, 112, 114, 120, 121,
  131, 175, 226, 273–274
sugar quota, 47, 48, 57, 131–132, 361